SAINT DOMINIC AND HIS TIMES

SAINT DOMINIC
AND HIS TIMES

by

M.-H. VICAIRE, O.P.

Translated by Kathleen Pond

McGRAW-HILL BOOK COMPANY

NEW YORK   TORONTO   LONDON

First published by Les Editions du Cerf under the title
Histoire de Saint Dominique

This translation © 1964   Darton, Longman & Todd Ltd

Library of Congress Catalog Card Number : 62-8965

Printed in Great Britain by William Clowes and Sons Limited, London and Beccles. Nihil obstat Carolus Davis, S.T.L., Censor deputatus. Imprimatur E. Morrogh Bernard, Vic. Gen. West-monasterii, die 9a Octobris, 1961. The Nihil obstat and Imprimatur are a declaration that a book or pamphlet is considered to be free from doctrinal or moral error. It is not implied that those who have granted the Nihil obstat and Imprimatur agree with the contents, opinions or statements expressed.

CONTENTS

LIST OF ILLUSTRATIONS

We are indebted to the Archbishop of Westminster and Burns & Oates Ltd for permission to quote from the Bible
translated by Mgr R.A. Knox.

INTRODUCTION

THERE has been no lack of lives of St Dominic. In France alone a new one is published on an average every ten years. Only a small proportion has something new to offer—most of them are satisfied merely to reproduce the same series of phrases and incidents, occasionally throwing some new light on them. Some of them display certain literary qualities; others are remarkable for the sureness of their historical intuition, if they happen to be the work of men such as Lacordaire or Bede Jarrett, who were deeply imbued with the spirit of St Dominic and what he came to achieve. Yet it is scarcely an exaggeration to say that no single one of these has been basically built up from the actual documents, nor is there any which makes full use of contemporary critical scholarship and history.

The first two-thirds of the thirteenth century witnessed the appearance of a series of texts which may be considered as the sources of this history, a series consisting of some hundred and fifty documents contemporary with Dominic and his foundation: a few letters; the *Libellus* of Jordan of Saxony, a remarkable account of the beginnings of the order that later liturgical legends have distorted and disfigured but can hardly be said to have enriched; the documents of the canonization process with the two reports from Bologna and Prouille-Pamiers; a few chronicles; edifying incidents relating to St Dominic, preserved in the collections of stories suitable for the use of preachers. At the close of the thirteenth century, the preacher Thierry of Apolda made a life out of all these documents. He had some talent as a compiler, which is not to say that he was satisfactory as a critic. At the beginning of the fourteenth century the Dominican bishop Bernard Gui got together valuable collections of documents, the first constitutions of the order, the acts of the general and provincial chapters, notices about particular houses or individuals, etc. His work brought the series of sources to a close. The oral tradition relating to St Dominic did not attain the extent or the variety of inspiration of that of St Francis. On several occasions during the thirteenth century it achieved permanent form through written expression. Almost all the publications of this type whose existence has ever been known are still extant. There is no likelihood that texts later than the beginning of the fourteenth century will contain as yet undiscovered data resulting from this tradition.

On the contrary, the fourteenth century provides us, in the person of the Milanese friar, Galvagno della Fiamma, with the characteristic type of the corruptor of Dominican historiography. Others, such as Thomas of Siena, Alain de la Roche, Bzovius, followed. The most formidable was Alain de la Roche, who at the close of the fifteenth century propagated, simultaneously and with equal effectiveness, his Rosary confraternities and so-called facts of Dominican history hitherto unknown—learnt, he said, by revelation.

The sixteenth and seventeenth centuries increased the accumulation of authentic documents extracted from the archives and the heavy mass of errors and confusions. The megalomania of the official historiographies as much as the increasing difficulty experienced in the interpretation of the medieval documents were contributing factors in this situation. The latter, from the *Historia general* of Fernando del Castillo, which was in certain other respects intelligent and well informed, to the vast *Annals* edited in the eighteenth century by the first historical college of the Friars Preachers under the aegis of Master-General Antoine Bremond, considerably falsified the already distorted history of St Dominic and his foundation.

Since the end of the previous century, however, one conscientious scholar after another had been insisting on a return to the sources, which they published, and on submitting all the elements of the life of St Dominic in turn to criticism. This was principally the work of Echard, who brought the two fundamental sources of the life—the *Libellus* and the canonization process—into prominence again, at the same time enriching them with accurate commentaries; Cuyper, the Bollandist, continued this work in the Acts of St Dominic. Members of the first historical college, such as Mamachi and Christianopoulo, in turn continued it in the notes of their *Annals* or of the *Bullarium* of the order.

The revolution of 1789, which very nearly brought complete catastrophe to the Order of Preachers, necessarily brought this work of scholarship to a standstill. This situation lasted until the time of the restoration of the French provinces by Lacordaire, a restoration which brought new and vigorous vitality to the order. The lives of St Dominic which began to appear once more were for the most part better than those of the previous age because they were beginning to get out of the rut of prejudices arising from *esprit de corps* and because they were able to utilize as their basis the concise and well-informed notes of Echard. Moreover, an important work of research and criticism of the sources was carried out in the French provinces of the order, and afterwards in Rome and Germany, stimulated by the necessity of re-discovering the primitive Dominican ideal in the face of the divergencies of interpretation which had arisen.

If the research work of Danzas was still somewhat lacking in critical accuracy, the editions produced under the auspices of Master-General Frühwirth and under the stimulus of men as different as Berthier, Denifle and Mandonnet soon provided historians with the best texts of the sources in the collections of the *Analecta* and the *Monumenta*. It was at this time that Balme and Lelaidier, in their *Cartulaire de saint Dominique*, almost succeeded in doubling the number of documents in the archives that had been available to previous historians. If the commentaries with which they accompanied the texts they edited were lacking in historical perspective and in soundness, they none the less frequently provided valuable aids to scholarship. Guiraud, too, procured numerous hitherto unpublished documents for his *Cartulaire de Prouille*. In 1922 Berthold Altaner produced a general criticism of the sources of the life of St Dominic. From 1931 onwards the second historical college of the order has continued to place at the disposal of historians in the annual *Archivum* and in its collections of sources or special studies first-class instruments of research. Lastly, a series of monographs, in particular biographies or histories of the first Dominican provinces, provides a supplementary number of details for the history of the foundation of the Preachers.

This long critical investigation which has now almost reached completion has not so far produced the general history of St Dominic and his work which constitutes its *raison d'être*. Mandonnet, who never ceased to keep this in mind, only produced partial although fundamental studies, of which the complete collection, published in 1938, was not sufficient to constitute a history of the saint. A synthesis of them was attempted by Héribert Christian Scheeben in 1927, but by him alone. His book, carefully based on authentic documents, and written in a most attractive style, is scarcely known outside Germany; it has not been translated, nor has a subsequent edition been published. The reason for this must doubtless be sought in certain historical interpretations not accepted by historians, which are particularly cherished by the author. Unforeseen circumstances, moreover, have rendered the majority of the critical arguments of this book pointless.

The present biography has endeavoured to give these arguments in detail, from motives of sincerity and for the sake of usefulness. Moreover, it is an attempt to replace in their geographical and chronological setting, and within the currents of development which throw light upon them in the course of events, the elements of the life of St Dominic and of the foundation of the Preachers as they are made known to us by the best sources. The combination of political circumstances in Castile, in the territory of the Albigenses and in Lombardy is clearly not the only principle of explanation of events. Mandonnet has already indicated several of the historical perspectives which give to the figure of the founder its exact proportions and its special light in the future of the Church and of medieval Europe—the movement towards association and common life and the rise of lay piety, the scholastic crisis, the transformation of the institution of regular life, the evolution of the pastoral ministry in the Church. Grundmann has recently drawn attention to the important rôle of a movement of 'apostolic life' among the heterodox. (It was to win over the heterodox that Dominic instituted his Preachers). It was shown in 1938 that the appeal of the *vita apostolica* reached Dominic and his work through many other influences than that of the heretics, for this ideal of a return to the Gospel and to the primitive Church was the clerical basis of the Gregorian reform and since that time had spread in the most divergent milieux, giving rise in particular to a movement for canonical life and a revival of the rule of St Augustine. Throughout the ensuing chapters other and different viewpoints will be brought forward, especially that of the *negotium fidei et pacis*, the combined effort of popes, bishops and princes to unite Europe in the faith and in peace, in which Dominic found himself engaged through his preaching.

In the formidable backwaters of these interconnected currents, Dominic opened a unique channel, deep and straight as he was himself. His contemporaries found the term he used—*vir evangelicus*—a man of the Gospel—apt for describing the type of man he succeeded in creating among his Preachers. This type he first produced in his own life. *Vir evangelicus* is the title of the first part of this biography. Because, however, it was in the very heart of the Church and her hierarchy that the founder implanted this form of clerical life, it seemed fitting to give as a title for the second part of the work the opening words which, since his canonization, have been sung in the Mass of the saint: *In medio Ecclesiae*. We hope we may be pardoned for these Latin expressions: *vita apostolica, negotium fidei et pacis, vir evangelicus.* . . . They preserve the flavour and dignity they possessed in the lifetime of the founder better than the colourless words which translate them. A great number of things are included these days in the term 'apostolic'. At that time it characterized exclusively a gift peculiar to the twelve apostles, or to their successors the popes, and aroused in people's feelings a depth of response it is difficult for us to imagine. It is then in the full sense of their meaning that we have deliberately used terms of this kind. Similarly, we have endeavoured not to use expressions which are convenient but anachronistic, avoiding, for instance, the term 'Languedoc' to designate the region north of the Pyrenees, which the people of that time called Provence, the province of Narbonne, or the county of Toulouse. By using the words and expressions proper to the men of the thirteenth century, we penetrate a little further into their world and acquire a more living contact with them.

In bringing this introduction to a close, it remains to thank all those who by their advice, information, or the documents they have procured for us, have collaborated in this work: our confrères of the Istituto Istorico de Sta Sabina, our colleagues, Professors Meersseman and Aebischer, Señor Luis Sánchez-Belda, director of the National Historical Archives in Madrid, Professor J. San Martín of Palencia, Canon A. Peñalba Gayubo, archivist of

Osma, the Very Reverend Father V. Beltrán de Heredia O.P., Monsieur le chanoine Louis de Lacger of Albi, the Swiss national fund for scientific research, a grant from which has made our work possible; finally, our collaborator, Herr Leonard von Matt, some of whose attractive pictures, the choice of which was a labour of love, have already decorated these pages before going to form, with many others, a magnificent album in which they will shed their light on the history of St Dominic.

Fribourg, M.-H.V.

4th October, 1956.

PART I

VIR EVANGELICUS

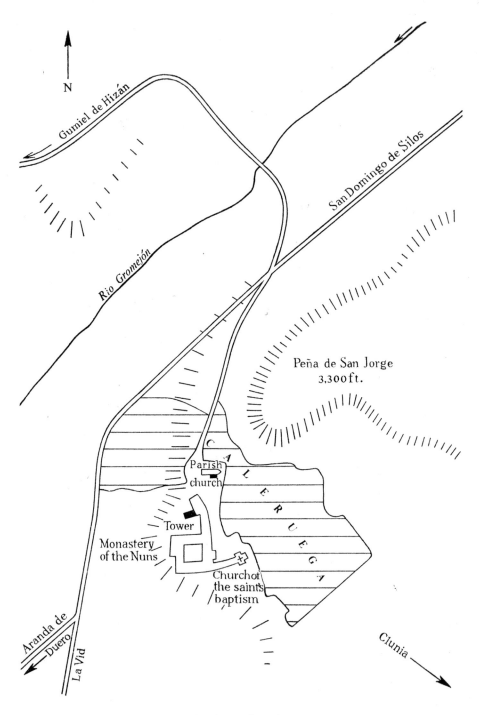

N

Gumiel de Hizán

Río Gromejón

San Domingo de Silos

Peña de San Jorge
3,300 ft.

C
A
L
E
R
U
E
G
A

Parish
church

Tower

Monastery
of the Nuns

Church of
the saint's
baptism

Aranda de
Duero

La Vid

Clunia

Ground Plan of Caleruega

CHAPTER I

CALERUEGA

O speak of St Francis without calling to mind Assisi, its hills planted with olives and vines, the simple piety of the people there, is inconceivable. Similarly, before we begin to study the life of St Dominic, it is only right that we should visit his native village, set on the plateau of Old Castile. To the south-west of the Iberian mountains, on the edge of the high plateau which is crossed by the Douro* as it flows from east to west, geography and history combined to form a region with so marked a character that the passing pilgrim cannot but be deeply influenced by it. Clearly this is true to a much greater degree of the child who is born on this soil and receives from its geographical setting as much as from the peasant community there, the most fundamental of his human impressions. This place is the village of Caleruega.

It is up-hill the whole way to Caleruega. The road from Valladolid follows the green track marked out by the Douro in the midst of the arid landscape, where the whiteness of the barren hills on the horizon reflects the intense heat of the sun. The whole way there is a gradual ascent following the slow rise of the plateau of Old Castile: 2,475 feet at Penafiel, 2,640 feet at Aranda, 3,135 feet at Caleruega, 3,300 at the foot of the mass of white rock of San Jorge which dominates the large village.

Caleruega is no longer at the world's end as it was as recently as thirty years ago. Twice a week a bus starts from Aranda de Duero, where one leaves the train; this bus goes up to Caleruega and then on to Santo Domingo de Silos before going down again towards Burgos and rejoining the main road. As one leaves the Douro, however, and moves closer to the frontier of mountains which, to the north, east and south dominates the plateau with its rugged sierras 7,000 and 8,000 feet high, the impression of leaving behind one a life of comparative ease is unmistakable. The green landscape disappears. The poplars which line the route as long as we continue to follow the course of the Bañuelos, a small tributary of the Douro, disappear after six or seven miles, leaving us with the white ribbon-like road surface in all its bareness. Here and there thick woods of black pine trees still remain, their sap oozing slowly into the resin-containers. The very vines disappear. In places the fields continue

---

* In Spanish, Duero — hence Aranda de Duero — Tr.

but everywhere else there are barren moors. Two or three miles beyond Caleruega, the landscape becomes treeless. As far as the eye can stretch, we can no longer see anything but the soil—glorious soil, red, purple, dark ochre, with white furrows. It has the appearance of a garden that has been tidily raked over the day before a fête. This is because at this time, the beginning of spring, it is in actual fact worked over from one end to the other. It is not always sown with seed, but the whole surface of the soil is tilled, perhaps as a long-term preparation, perhaps to preserve it from premature aridity, perhaps to open it more fully to the rain which it is hoped will come.

The road crosses a slight rise in the ground and Caleruega lies before us. To right and left there is now a wide view. Immediately in front of us a new tier of the plateau outlines against a cloudless sky for more than seven miles or so the unbroken contours of the crest of the ridge. Further away is a line of lofty peaks: Peña de Cervera, Picón de las Navas. Still further in the background are the black, rounded crests of the Iberian Mountains. On the edge of the first terrace are patches of land alternately brick-red and whitish in colour, completely horizontal, intersected here and there by the incursion of small, transverse valleys. The broadest of these valleys is hollowed out by the river Gromejón. To the right of it, on a spur facing the edge of the plateau, are two strong towers, a large building, a fortress-like construction with buttresses, a basilica in the form of a Greek cross, a rocky peak: such is Caleruega, the *torreón*, the church and the nuns' convent; Caleruega, wholly bathed in the transparent light of April at the close of the afternoon.

It is not easy to convey the impression of poverty, proud, yet at the same time humble, that is evoked by such a scene. The village is of the same colour as the soil and is only distinguishable from the landscape, which is likewise formed of the soil, by the light and shadows from the *torreón*, the royal convent or the basilica. There is poverty in the sun-drenched streets which climb up through the village but there is noble dignity in the little romanesque church which St. Dominic knew, and also, and more especially so, in the peasant stock among whom he grew up, a race supple, wiry, full of life, brave and immensely hospitable.

It does not take long to see over the village, with its uneven streets, the old stones of the monastery, the great fountain in the centre of the square, from which the water flows abundantly like an image of grace. Without allowing ourselves to linger over the buildings which we shall have to examine later with closer attention, we are driven by a strong urge along the paths which climb up to the highest point of the village, towards the hill and the rocky heights of San Jorge. In order to rediscover St Dominic, it is not so much the detail that counts, the rare stone touched by him or the romanesque portal through which he passed—it is the general setting, the atmosphere, the background of this vast landscape over which the sun spreads. I cannot indeed imagine that anyone could remain for some time attentive and silent on the heights of San Jorge without being almost immediately struck by the impression of heroism that emanates from the landscape.

Behind is the plateau, now completely exposed to view and entirely barren, rising towards the dark heights over to the north. On the right is the broad valley of the Gromejón, where a few trees, hardly yet in bud, blurred and, as it were, submerged in the shadows which rise up, indicate the presence of running water. The road becomes indistinct and quickly seems to disappear from sight; it divides and, swerving widely, scales the promontories until it appears to vanish once more towards an unknown horizon. To the south, east and west, the Castilian plateau is left to develop unrestricted. It is nothing but patches of land, hard and arid—not a village, not a tumble-down cottage, not a clump of trees to be seen over this expanse which stretches perhaps as far as seventy miles or so from the Sierra de Guadarrama. The life of the place is hidden away in the invisible valleys hollowed out by the rivers. Only the dusty roads which cross the dark soil introduce a note of light which springs up towards the horizon: towards Aranda, Nuestra Señora de la Vid, Gumiel de Izán. It is a challenge to man and a vista of unspoken possibilities.

All is tranquillity and bright sunlight. It is one of those rare moments when winter has just ceased to be and summer has not yet imposed her implacable presence. During the interminable months of winter—nine months of winter, three months of hell, they told us at Valladolid—the wind from the plateau moans and hisses over the heights of San Jorge, lifting the snow until it forms a chill cloud over the vast icy surface. The west winds with their mighty rains then quickly transform this soil into mire. The summer's sun next beats down fiercely on these far-spreading fields, on the roads that no tree shades and whose dread monotony is broken by no oasis. The distant horizons speak to us of majesty, of a humanity vast in its extent, of infinity. Earth and sky, disturbing in their beauty, tell of duty ineluctable, perhaps almost inhuman. The roads call to us to rejoin invisible brethren, hidden away over there in the light or in the dark depths of the sierras, towards the four points of the compass. We are reminded of the harsh masculine vigour and of an existence subjected to the extreme contrasts of the elements and of events, and of the necessity for relentless effort sometimes even without visible hope—such as the ploughing of this seedless land, ploughing which in this month of April has turned over the greater part of the soil spread out before our eyes. There is also the human joy, Christian joy, intense and almost fanatical, of a life which, in spite of everything, makes a place for itself and expands with incomparable generosity in this austere setting. Here are to be found the inspirations of nobility of soul, courage, heroism, which are whispered to anyone who seeks for them with earnest attention by the stones and the fields and the horizon and the mountains and the sun and the sounds which rise up from the village until they reach this glittering limestone promontory where St. Dominic came to play and to cast his eyes over the land, as the boys of Caleruega still do today.

Evening begins to fall, and the shadows over the promontories creep higher. Gradually we become aware of a kind of invasion. From every direction the great flocks of sheep, which for so many centuries now have provided Caleruega with one of its means of livelihood, have begun their trek back towards the village. The imperceptible white dots which a few moments ago were scattered over the surface of the distant fields gather together and begin to move accompanied by a great cloud of dust which the sun turns into a haze of light. Already the herd of black cows has returned to the village—the mules too, and the donkeys with their grey feet, and the herd of white goats. The sheep move forward slowly. A louder bleating and a barking of dogs penetrate as far as San Jorge. The running of the dogs and the shepherds, the movements of the flocks of lambs which dart about in their panic, the slow advance of the main body of the sheep, come fully into view. A blanket on his shoulder, a young shepherd, leaving his sheep for a few seconds, leaps up on the near-by cliffs, calling out a name which re-echoes loudly. The bleating now becomes more intense, rising like a tide. From all sides new flocks appear. The sun goes down. Against the romanesque belfry of the church the gold is changed into red, into flushed pink, into light purple. The storks which lodge in the corner of the torreón flap their wings and fly round and round above the church a few times. The smoke from the houses rises vertically in the peace of the setting sun. Some of the sheep have come back into the folds. Others, in groups, wait before the closed door. Others again, protected from the effects of occasional panic by the energetic efforts of a youthful shepherd, continue to crop the grass right on the side of the hill. The continual sound of their bleating grows persistent and penetrating. It is difficult to say whether it is a lament, an expression of hope or a call for help. Perhaps it is the call of the souls coming from the furthermost horizon that the child Dominic heard of old penetrating right up to the rocky cliffs of Caleruega.

For at that time this land was weighed down under a greater burden of human suffering and human hope or, rather of spiritual drama, than anywhere else. It was here that men by the thousand had fought for their beliefs in centuries gone by. If indeed Caleruega was not yet many years old at the time of St Dominic's birth, it occupied land that had nothing of a new territory about it. There the populations had succeeded each other without interruption for thousands and thousands of years, with arrivals and departures the tragic character of which had become accentuated since Christian times.

A few miles away from Caleruega the remains of a Roman city can still be seen. Its destiny in itself symbolizes the history of the whole territory since the Byzantine Empire. Clunia[2] had her hour of fame during the months of the reign of the Emperor Galba. A colony and a municipium, * the walls of which could easily have contained 60,000 or 80,000 inhabitants, with its theatre and its great aqueducts, it constituted one of the seven centres of jurisdiction of the Roman province of Tarraconensis. It was, moreover, a place where important highroads met. The road cutting directly across Spain from Tarragona to Corunna passed through it, coming from Saragossa by way of Numantia, Olbega (Augustobriga), Osma. At Clunia it forked. Through Roa (Rondu) and Simancas (Septimanca) near Valladolid, it continued to Zamora. Through Palencia the other fork led to Astorga and the sea.[3] Now this fork passed close by Caleruega, slightly to the south of its present site. Its paved, now broken, blocks can still be seen in places.[4] In the thirteenth century it was still intact and fully usable.[5] It was, moreover, the most tangible vestige of what still remained of the great city whose very name was beginning to fade.[6]

Originally destroyed by the Goths in barbarian times, so it is said, Clunia must obviously have recovered sufficiently for history to have thought fit to preserve the memory of its conquest by the Moors. In the first half of the eighth century, however, Alfonso the Catholic drove them away. They came back. In 912, the Count of Castile and Lara, Gonzalo Fernández, retook and repopulated the town. In 918, however, the inhabitants took flight on learning of the approach of Abd-er-Rahman III, and his soldiers pillaged the city with appalling havoc. During the second half of the tenth century, Al Mansour dominated the whole of the upper valley of the Douro and even on one occasion thrust forward as far as Santiago de Compostela which he conquered and destroyed. After his death, Count Sancho of Castile recovered Clunia in 1010. The town, however, was so thoroughly devastated that it practically disappeared from history. Four villages sprang up on its boundaries.[7] Only a hermitage and the chapel of Nuestra Señora de Castro, where the parish of Caleruega goes to make a pilgrimage[8] each year, are left to remind us of the former fortified Roman town.

The history of the other cities of the neighbourhood, Roa, Aza, Aranda, Osma, Górmaz, was similar.[9] After reaching the line of the Arlanzón, to the south of Burgos, about the year 880, the Christian reconquest seemed to slacken. The vast valley of the Douro remained unpopulated like a ramp against the Moslem. Liberating themselves from this static condition, at the beginning of the tenth, and again in the eleventh centuries, the colonizers, the Counts of Castile and other nobles, were able to reconquer the sites, found or re-establish towns and villages and throw them open to the

* A borough town, subject to Rome but governed by its own laws — Tr.

Christian immigrants. The success of this repopulation, however, was insecure. The region had remained a no man's land among belligerents far too long. There was a dearth of men. Men from the Cantabrian mountains, from the Asturias or Galicia, Basques and Mozarabs driven out from the south, were slow in arriving and allowed themselves to be discouraged by the insecurity. Moorish strongholds such as La Aguilera, near Gumiel de Izán, held out until the middle of the eleventh century.[10] It was not until the end of that century that the capture of Toledo, in 1805, finally covered the line of the Douro by securing the line of the Tagus to the Christians and guaranteed by military force the possible rehabilitation of the intermediate region. This was not indeed fully possible until the first quarter of the twelfth century, with the end of the strife between Castile and Aragon and of the deep domestic disturbances in the stormy times of Queen Urraca, and with the coming to the throne of Alfonso VII, the Emperor (1126). At last the plateau of Old Castile, firmly established in peace, was able to repopulate itself and prosper to any extent.[11] By then the birth of St Dominic was not half a century away.

The religious development had followed a parallel rhythm.[12] Up to the time of the dread Al Mansour (939–1001), dioceses and monasteries had declined. In the whole neighbourhood only the community of Silos, given new life by its abbot, Santo Domingo de Silos († 1073), considered itself sufficiently well defended by the deep gorges of its mountains some twenty-five or thirty miles to the north of Caleruega to build, right at the beginning of the eleventh century, its great romanesque cloister, the glory of monastic Spain. A few of the old monasteries were revived. After 1085 the bishops and the secular clergy, simultaneously encouraged by the spirit of Cluny and by the inspiration of the Gregorian reform, actively took their stand. The monk Bernard de Sédirac, of Agen, the first Cluniac abbot of Sahagún to become Archbishop of Toledo, endeavoured to restore the primatial dignity of Spain to its position of authority. Relying on Pope Urban II, who had conferred the pallium on him, and on his capacity as legate, he devoted himself to re-establishing the diocese of Osma, whose see remained vacant, along the upper Douro. Before providing the see with a bishop, he fixed its provisional boundaries with the diocese of Burgos at the council of Husillo (Palencia) in 1088. Urban gave his confirmation of these boundaries in 1094–1095.[13] It was not until 1101 that a bishop was appointed. In 1108 and 1109 several bulls issued by Pascal II again defined the boundaries. Was Caleruega and its surrounding territory included in the diocese thus reconstituted? It is impossible to say, for it was found convenient to attach to the diocese all that had come under the authority of Clunia, that is to say, under the criminal jurisdiction of that former locality—a pleasant way of defining the ecclesiastical boundaries.[14] At last, in 1136, a final charter of division between the two dioceses permanently restored to the diocese of Osma the region comprised between the rivers Esgueva and Arandilla which this time certainly included the territory of Caleruega.[15] From this time onwards the diocese had its cathedral chapter at Osma. It was then that the houses of canons, monasteries or convents that Dominic was to be familiar with were founded one after the other—Augustinian canons of Roa and Soria (1152), Premonstratensians of Nuestra Señora de la Vid (1152), Cistercian nuns of Fuencaliente (1175) and of Aza (1182).[16] Barely a decade or so separated these foundations from the saint's birth; some of them, indeed, came after it.

He was a young man of about twenty when the Cistercian monks established themselves in the former Benedictine house of San Pedro de Gumiel, only a few miles away from Caleruega (1199). This foundation must have made a particular impression on him. For they were curious people, these former monks of the abbey of Fitero in Navarre, and had followed their abbot when the latter, with more courage than the military displayed, had accepted from King Sancho III the outpost fortress of Calatrava, along the road to Córdoba, the defence of which the Templars had abandoned. Though censured by the chapter of Cîteaux, and fought against by their own knights, they had long claimed for themselves, and for themselves alone, the inheritance of the military order. Eventually, through negotiations, they were installed at Gumiel de Izán in an abbey of regular observance independent of the Spanish Cistercians and directly attached to the French abbey of Morimont. The first Master of Calatrava, Diego Velásquez († 1197), went into retirement among them and the knights continued to frequent the monastery as if they were part of the brethren there; they had the right of going to choir with the monks, receiving from them a grounding in regular discipline and coming to them with their faults to do penance.[17] Thus the Cistercians of San Pedro de Gumiel, with the other recently formed communities, contributed in their way to the manifestation of the Church's dynamism, and to the establishment of the atmosphere of new life and of generosity on the religious plane. This atmosphere still vibrated with that enthusiasm over the victories of arms against Islam which was to be found everywhere in the neighbourhood of the Douro in the second half of the twelfth century. Even in his own village Dominic would meet with this atmosphere of youthful enthusiasm.

The site seems to have been colonized only in the recent past. In the records only two mentions of Caleruega appear before the thirteenth century.[18] The chronicles of King Alfonso VII, those of Compostela or Silos, do not refer to it, nor does the valuable collections of charters of the abbey of Silos—all documents which refer to many places in the immediate vicinity.[19] There existed certain lists of these localities in the twelfth century,[20] but Caleruega is not mentioned in them. The silence of the charter of division of 1136 between the dioceses of Osma and Burgos is impressive. This charter in fact enumerates nineteen localities contained within the 600 or so square miles restored to the diocese of Osma by Burgos—Caleruega is not mentioned in it, but Valdeande, about two and a half miles away, a hamlet the territory of which in the following century certainly formed part of that of Caleruega, is.[21] If as far back as this the village of Saint Dominic had formed an agglomeration really worthy of note, would not mention have been made of Caleruega rather than of the hamlet?

The name of the village, so far as we have been able to discover, appears for the first time in 1062, then in 1117 in the Cartulary of San Pedro de Arlanza;[22] in 1202 in that of Silos, [23] then in 1234 in the *Libellus* of Jordan of Saxony, who afterwards transmitted it to Dominican historiography.[24] Except in the first case when it is written Kalerueca,[25] it occurs in the authentic Castilian form, invariable down to the present day, of Caleruega.[26] Jordan is careful to stipulate *que dicitur Caleruega*, as is usual for names in the vulgar tongue for which no Latin transcription exists. It is true that certain manuscripts of the *Libellus* give *Calaroga, Caleroga*; this was the usual spelling of Latin documents whether regional or Roman.[27] It cannot be said that it is a Latinization, scarcely even a simplification. We have, then, the certainty that in the thirteenth century no Latin name or ancient name of the locality was known. If a few souls had formerly fixed their abode on the site of Caleruega, they had left no trace in the memory of man, and their tracks had been buried by the Moorish invasion.

Confirmation of this is found in the name Caleruega itself. It is slightly mysterious and forms a sharp contrast with the names of the neighbouring villages, Villanueva, Baños, Val-de-Ande, Espinosa, which are clear, originating in geographical features or in the circumstances of their colonization. It can, however, be connected with *calera*,[28] chalk oven. Traces of the exploitation of the great calcareous mass which forms the hill of San Jorge above the village are indeed to be noted. Caleruega, the little chalk oven, indicates a name rather than a locality. The word thus preserves no memory of human occupation prior to the Reconquest.[29]

The peopling of the place must have been spontaneous: the village was not founded by a charter of colonization. The foundation of the parish, however, is an indication of the period by which the population had become sufficiently numerous. The parish, as can be seen from a charter of 1270,[30] was never appropriated to a feudal family; it belonged to the bishop and the canons, a proof that it had been founded by them. That could not have been done before the restoration of the see, the creation of the chapter, and the definitive assignment of the territory to the diocese of Osma. We thus find ourselves taken back at the earliest to after 1136, to the time of Bishop Bertrand (1125–1140), the third since the restoration of the see, or of Bishop Stephen (1146–1147), his successor.[31]

An examination of the ancient buildings in the village or of their remains, enables us to circumscribe the problem more closely.[32] These are the *torreón* or fortified tower, now belonging to the nuns; the parish church with its tower; in the nuns' convent three groups of buildings where the construction work carried out from 1952 to 1955 has revealed the existence of large gothic halls; finally, on the brow of the hill against which the village nestles, the trace in the rock of a small quadrangular building, according to tradition a chapel dedicated to St George. In fact, it is the name of this saint that the rocky cliff still preserves today, *Peña de san Jorge.*

So far as this tiny chapel is concerned, it is possible to imagine anything; no trace of it has come down to us in the documents, nor does even a stone remain. It is possible that it is the last vestige of some Christian site dating back earlier than the Moorish invasion, perhaps a hermitage or a votive chapel built by some knight or soldier—St George, after all, is their patron—in the course of the wars of the Reconquest. One thing alone is certain. This tiny sanctuary was never that of the parish in the earliest days of the resettlement. From the earliest documents the parish appears under the patronage of St Sebastian, not under that of St George.[33] In the twelfth and thirteenth centuries substitution of patrons was not customary.

The gothic halls, which are indeed remarkable, are not of earlier date than the thirteenth century. Linked with the former nuns' chapel, as they are to one another, by certain details of style,[34] they formed to all appearances part of one and the same block. They were built by Alfonso the Wise after 1266, to install the Dominican nuns at Caleruega.[35]

The original apse of the parish church, which has been subjected to numerous reconstructions, is still preserved.[36] It is a clearly defined romanesque apse. The nave which formed its extension with its slightly horse-shoe arches, the door with its concentric arches in full semi-circle, its slender columns, its capitals with their plant decoration, the three pillars with Roman capitals discovered in the process of one of the several reconstructions and set above the door, the cornice decorated with chess-boards in relief forming the inner curve of the apse, the corbels with dogs' heads supporting the roof on the outside—all go to prove that this church was constructed in the course of the twelfth century, almost certainly by some of the workmen in the service of the bishop who had then just finished his romanesque cathedral with its cloister (*ca.* 1140).[37] It was in a church newly constructed and still gleaming white that St Dominic received the waters of baptism.

The church tower was built at two different periods. At about 20 feet from the ground is a cornice set above a line of figured corbels continuing those of the apse. The second storey of the tower 30 to 35 feet high and built on this cornice, is of the same workmanship as the apse; semi-circular twin windows inscribed in a further great semi-circle look out on the north side and on both the east and west faces triangular-arched windows are very roughly hewn out. All this might date from the middle of the twelfth century. The lower part of the tower, however, is of a different workmanship. The pieces of stone used are smaller. Its construction, independent of that of the apse which is contiguous with it, does not interpenetrate it. Finally, and most important of all, it is not hollow, but completely solid. To enable it to fulfil its function as the basis of the belfry, a small perpendicular stairway must have been cut out, which provided a complicated means of communication with the first storey.[38] Clearly, this first part of the tower is earlier than the church.

A further fact is no less striking: the different sides of this tower are parallel to those of the *torreón* and the plan of both is similar: a rectangle in a double square. It would thus appear that tower and *torreón*, which are about 160 feet or so distant from each other, formed part of a single whole.[39] There is some indication that would lead one to suspect the existence of still a third tower near the *torreón* in the direction of the church.[40] There was thus a whole system of fortifications, the date of which is a matter for investigation.

The *torreón*,[41] a stout rectangular tower about 55 feet high, with walls 2 yards thick, presents, in fact, no element that might be called characteristic except a very rough triangular-arched door and two double windows with horse-shoe arch, separated by a slender column with fluted capitals. The embrasure of the window and the passage-way of the door, hewn out of the thickness of the walls, are arched in a full semi-circle. Projecting blocks of stone, immediately behind the façade, provided cavities for the hinges of the leaves of the door which closed the two openings. The semi-circularly arched corridors, and the romanesque window somewhat *mudéjar* in style, take us back to the twelfth century at least,[42] the door to the second half of that century. The door, however, is not the original one. It has been clumsily cut so as to fit into the wall.[43] Where, then, formerly was the entrance into this tower the lower courses of which clearly indicate that it was occupied? There is no trace of any other opening but the double window.[44] On looking more closely, it can be seen that the latter was also inserted later, with this difference, however, that an opening lower down has been enlarged to make room for it. The rectangular pieces of stone which block the lower part of the opening beneath the window ledge can be seen clearly. This was the original door. There is nothing surprising in this. A tower for defence and, above all, a keep, had no use for a large window or for an opening level with the ground which would have made it too vulnerable. The door was set at a considerable height to protect it from the danger of an attack. Entry into the tower was by means of a ladder which was withdrawn from inside. The bottom part of the tower served as both cellar and dungeon.[45] In these circumstances there is considerable difficulty in dating this large military construction, of which all that remains today is the massive base of the belfry of the church and the *torreón*. No trace of a moat is to be seen; this is a sign of antiquity. The rectangular towers for their part represent the oldest elements of feudal architecture in Spain. It is possible that the original construction was built by one of the conquerors of 910–912 who fortified the valley of the Douro by a chain of strong castles.[46] We are reminded of that Count of Castile, Gonzalo Fernández who, sallying forth from the fortress of Lara which he had just conquered, relieved Clunia, seven miles or so away from Caleruega, and set up on either side over the Douro, the barriers of Aza and of San Esteban de Górmaz. The small fortress of Caleruega would at that time have protected the traditional route which led to the heart of Castile through the valley of the Esgueva, via Santo Domingo de Silos. It was by this road, which the Romans in former times had used as the military route from Clunia to Astorga, that Count Fernández had come to reconquer the region, and Silos remained in contact with its property in the vicinity of Caleruega.[47] It is possible, too, that the massive portion of the belfry, whose inconsiderable appearance forms a striking contrast with that of the *torreón*, represents an even older element, such as for instance a watch-tower situated on the frontier of the original route to Silos which passed right by the hill.

The important point here is that the tower became a belfry in the middle of the twelfth century, while the parish church was being built, and that the *torreón*, losing something of its military importance through the cutting of a door at ground level and the insertion of a pleasant window through which one looked out towards the south, was adapted to more peaceful uses. Everything points to the same conclusion. In the middle of the twelfth century, the population of Caleruega was rapidly increasing, and it was becoming a parish. The life of rural toil and religious life were now able to develop at their ease. St Dominic was soon to come.

The country around must then have been at the height of its development. There is nothing to indicate that from those distant days to our own, the nature of the economic resources and the manner of using them to the best advantage have undergone any violent change. Certain documents of the future convent of the 'Sisters Preacheresses' even affirm the contrary.[48] The crops of cereals and of citrus fruits were centred along the floor of the valleys of the Gromejón, the Mobrejón and the Bañuelos, where there was water. The vines on the slopes of the hills supplied a red wine which was stored in the cellars of the few houses built of stone and especially in the *bodegas*, deep, cool cellars hewn out of the flank of the hills in the strata of white limestone which outcrops half-way up the slope. Everywhere else, the breeding of horses, cows, sheep and pigs utilized to the utmost the vast expanses of the plateau as pasture-land. A hundred years after the death of

St Dominic a document assigned to the convent of the nuns alone 10,000 sheep, 2,000 cows, 500 mares and 500 pigs.[49] This document granted the nuns grazing rights for cattle and right of way over royal lands. The animals must, of course, have moved to the hills in the summer. Since, however, no property of any extent belonging to the nuns is known of outside the territory of Caleruega, the cattle must at least have wintered there. This enables us to visualize the importance of cattle-breeding in the life of the neighbourhood.

The appearance of the landscape must have been greener than at the present day. A local tradition asserts that in former times the hills were covered with bushes. This is still the natural condition of the hill-slopes in this neighbourhood, as can be seen towards Valdeande and along the road to Silos. It is possible that the breeding of goats—those born destroyers of woods and forests—was in some measure responsible for the deforestation here as in many other places along the littoral of the Mediterranean. Or again it may have been the imprudent destruction of the thick woods by the inhabitants with a view to clearing the ground and procuring the fuel which was indispensable for winter. It was the deforestation, in any case, that was the cause of the aridity and of the cracking of the earth which strikes the traveller so forcefully. A charter of boundary limits in 1272 demonstrates the presence of relatively abundant water, as, for instance, a pond (*laguna*), a pool (*lagunilla*) on the outskirts of Espinosa, and the rich spring known as *Fuente del Rey*.[50] The names of *Baños* and *Bañuelos* (the latter following the course of the ancient Roman road) also implied the presence of abundant and pure water. In the thirteenth century the nuns had springs, water-courses, mills, woods, certain rights in forests whence they could draw three loads of wood each day with which to warm themselves in the winter.[51] In a territory that was less dry, more sparsely populated, the life of Caleruega in its early days met with conditions more favourable in certain respects than today. It was, however, no less hard at this initial period of its beginnings and development. The uncomfortable castle of the lord of the place is a further proof of this.

What was the lord's position? It is not difficult to ascertain what was the condition of the village before the middle third of the thirteenth century, thanks to the numerous documents which King Alfonso the Wise caused to be drawn up between 1266 and 1272, when he resolved to found the monastery of Dominican nuns. He decided to make over to the new institution all the feudal rights of Caleruega and succeeded, though not without difficulty, in persuading their possessors to abandon them.[52] Caleruega was neither a royal domain nor the territorial manor of some great feudal house, but a domain *de behetria*, or, more precisely, *behetria inter parientes*. The villagers, freed men by origin, thus had the privilege of choosing their lord

(Photo: Leonard von Matt)

Tower and apse of Caleruega parish church.

among the members of certain families, whose right, known as *naturaleza*, gave occasion for the levying of a due known as *divisa*, equal to one-half or one-third of the revenues.[53] Actually, in the thirteenth century, the *behetria* of Castile often merged in fact into hereditary estates, the origin of which was no longer referred to except for the rights of *divisa*.[54] This was so in the case of Caleruega.[55] The situation of the overlordship confirms what the position of the parish already indicated: the spontaneous, natural character of the locality, constituted independently of the action of the king or of the great feudal lords.[56]

In 1266, the *diviseros* of Caleruega were fairly numerous. The charters still preserved at the convent list twenty-two of them. Other charters have disappeared.[57] The royal summary names only a few families.[58] They were families belonging to the highest nobility of the realm, of the class of the *ricos hombres*, a nobility of blood, whose members placed their signature preceded by the title of *don* in a column parallel to that for the signatures of bishops at the foot of the great royal charters known as wheel charters; in the case in point, they were the Lara, the Guzmán, the Aza de Villamayor, the Roa, the Sarmiento, as well as the Order of Ucles, that is, of Santiago. At this time several of these great lords played a predominant rôle in the kingdom, sometimes governing vast provinces conquered from the Moors, as was the case with don Alfonso García de Villamayor, *Adelantado mayor* of Andalusia, or his brother, don Juan García, *Adelantado mayor de la mar*, and majordomo to Alfonso X, or don Pedro de Guzmán, *Adelantado mayor* in Castile. There is no reason to be surprised at the presence of such nobles at Caleruega, they were members of the highest-born families in the neighbour-hood. Aza is about twenty miles or so from Caleruega, Roa about twenty-seven, Guzmán about thirty-five. Moreover, such families were inter-related. On closer examination we find that this multiplicity of 'natural' lords could finally be reduced to a single lineage, that of the Aza de Villamayor, who had in fact become hereditary lords.[59] It was the Aza of Villamayor who gave to the nuns' convent the majority of its property, doña Urraca García who in 1248 surrendered one of her hereditary lands at Caleruega to the Bishop of Osma for the maintenance of the first hospice founded near the chapel of St Dominic,[60] or again, don Fernán García, who in 1258 sold all his estates to the north of the Duero, including, it seems, the overlordship of Caleruega,[61] to the Order of Santiago, who reinvested him with the property the following year.[62] It was through his marriage with doña Urraca García, that don Pedro Nuñez de Guzmán with all his descendants had obtained rights of *divisa* at Caleruega.[63] Similarly, don Diego Pérez Sarmiento, don Garciá Fernández Sarmiento, don Gil Gómez de Roa, don Garcí Guttiérrez were husbands, sons, grandsons, sons-in-law of some Aza de Villamayor.[64] Finally, the lords of Lara, independently of the privilege which granted them a *divisa* in each of the *behetria* of Castile,[65] belonged to the stock of the

Aza family. Thus the great majority of the *diviseros* mentioned by the charters of 1266–1272 are found to be among the descendants of the Aza of Villamayor.[66] If it is recalled that the common ancestor, Gonzalo Fernández, Count of Lara, had in 912 'repopulated' the region of Caleruega and built the fortresses of the district, perhaps even the *torreón*, it will not be a matter for surprise that at its inception the village was placed under the protection of his line by *behetria*. Moreover, if we reflect on the complexity which a right extended by descent, marriage or purchase might present—'a matter of *behetria*' the Castilians would say of a case that was proving insoluble[67]—we are surprised to find the situation still so clear round about the year 1270. The conclusion will be reached that two centuries earlier, at the time when Caleruega is first mentioned in the documents, precisely when a *divisa* right in the locality is mentioned,[68] the origins of this overlordship were not far distant. This fits in well with what has been discovered from other sources.

An old tower, a former keep summarily transformed in the middle of the twelfth century to house the lord or his representative, a population slowly and spontaneously gathering there since the beginning of that century, a parish set up by the bishop after 1136 with its completely new church, a relatively recent *behetria* of which the Aza, *ricos hombres* of Castile, were 'natural' lords: such was the village in which the child, St Dominic, came into this world.

'His father was called Felix, his mother Jane.'[69] 'He had good and pious parents.'[70] 'His father was a man looked up to by the villagers and wealthy. His mother, who was virtuous, chaste, prudent, full of compassion for those who were unfortunate and in distress, was outstanding among all the women in the neighbourhood for the excellence of her reputation.'[71] That is all the Dominican legends of Pedro Ferrando, Gérard de Frachet, Rodríguez de Cerrato, the sole sources of the story outside the charters of the convent of the nuns, tell us about the parents of the saint.[72] Pedro Ferrando and Rodríguez de Cerrato are valuable as authorities. The former, who was a Spaniard, filled out between 1235 and 1239 the more than succinct information on this point given by the first biographer, Jordan of Saxony.[73] Rodríguez, a Castilian, native of a valley no great distance from Caleruega, was himself in the village at least in 1272.[74] He is the only one to give information that is in any way extensive on the origins of St Dominic.

According to custom, the hagiographical texts give only the baptismal name of St Dominic's parents, not their complete civil status.[75] They might have done more than this; the charter of the nuns' convent gave more details of the most humble of the village folk. Dominic's father was a person of distinction. 'Vir venerabilis et dives in populo suo', said Rodríguez. Ought we to translate the latter expression by 'the rich man of his village (pueblo)' or perhaps 'the *rico hombre* of his village'?[76] If the second translation is possible,[77] the first, which is probable, does not exclude the information which the other would have conveyed. The unaccustomed expression *in populo* clearly appears to be a superlative. The term *venerabilis* in fact adds to this indication the authority of a social position. It does not indeed characterize the moral value of Felix for in that case Rodríguez would have equally extended it to the mother whose virtue he is eager to praise.[78] In fact, in a lengthy anecdote, Rodríguez shows us Felix in the midst of the village folk whom he calls *vicini sui*,[79] that is, in the Castilian sense of the word, his villagers. It is clearly in this condition that they appear: they gather round him, watch over his property in his absence, march before him in a body when he returns from a journey, make reports to him. Mention is made of a large cask,[80] famous throughout the neighbourhood, from which St Dominic's father slaked the thirst of his retainers.

In those times wealth lay in the land and there was not more than a single step between holding land and being the lord of it. Now the families among which the lords of Caleruega were recruited are known. One cannot, therefore, avoid facing the problem of the connection of the parents of St Dominic with the *ricos hombres* of Caleruega. Actually, a tradition worthy of respect has affirmed in Spain ever since the Middle Ages that the mother of St Dominic was a d'Aza and his father a Guzmán.

Historians outside Spain have either passed quickly over this point or neglected it entirely.[81] They have doubtless considered that nobility of origin would add nothing to the glory of St Dominic and have striven to react against the all too prevalent mentality which multiplied books and *libelli* from the sixteenth to the nineteenth century in an attempt at controversy which was more or less pointless. It is not a question of glorifying St Dominic but of getting to know and understand him. It is difficult to believe that the family from which a great man is descended is not of considerable importance in explaining certain aspects of his temperament, particularly at this period when lineage exerted such a pressure on individuals, when education was primarily achieved by example and training in a society already deeply divided into classes. Nor can we say that there is no interest in ascertaining whether Dominic came from a family of shepherds and farm workers of Caleruega, or from the line of the colonizers of the upper Douro, of the conquerors of Toledo and Cuenca who followed their kings in their daring raids into Moslem territory and saw Christian provinces as vast as kingdoms rising up again under their feet.

The careful investigation, indeed, of the Spanish tradition and of the information provided by a series of documents from the archives, dating from about forty years after the saint's death, enables us to get on the track of what the characteristics given by Cerrato led one to presuppose. This somewhat arid analysis can be read elsewhere.[82] It crowns the tradition with real

probability. Moreover, it defines it in more detail. It would be through his
mother, Jane of Aza, that the family of St Dominic belonged to Caleruega, his
father, Felix de Guzmán, being connected with it only by his marriage. Many
traits of St Dominic's personality seem to find their proper explanation if
viewed in this light.

The Guzmán and the Aza were in possession of the highest degree of
nobility, the *ricahombría* or nobleness of blood.[83] The particular characteristic of the d'Aza family was service of the Church by military activity.
During Dominic's youth several of its members had joined the very recently
established military orders of Santiago and Calatrava, of which they occupied
the highest office, the Grand Mastership, even during his lifetime.[84] It was
probably to the examples of his feudal relatives that the saint owed the spirit
of Christian conquest, his attraction for open spaces, the breadth of vision,
sense of personal engagement and joyous courage that were his, and also the
realism and perspicacity of vision which in each and every situation made
him discover the essential element and the simple fundamental remedy, and
his inflexible constancy when it was a matter of maintaining a decision once
taken. To the relations of his ancestors with the king he owed, perhaps, too,
his great ease in his dealings with the higher authorities, whether counts or
kings, bishops or Sovereign Pontiffs, his habit of consulting the fountain-
head, his way of envisaging problems from above in a general view, his skill
in using the official charters and the texts of the Law.

Shut away in Caleruega and perhaps dying early, as we shall see, it may be
questioned whether Felix had the opportunity of practising the traditional
virtues of his family. Scarcely anything is known of him. The only indication
we have—it comes on good authority, since it is from Pedro Ferrando—
bears on his piety and the care he took that his children should be given a
first-class religious education. Moreover, he administered his property with
firmness and decision. The only anecdote in which he figures depicts him as
behaving somewhat astutely when confronted with his wife's deeds of charity
and seeking to embarrass her.

Jane is somewhat better known. The characteristics which the tradition of
Caleruega attributed to her have been noted: 'virtuous, chaste, prudent, full
of compassion towards the unfortunate and those in distress; outstanding
among all the women of the neighbourhood for the excellence of her
reputation'.[85] That is how she appears to us in the episode of the barrel
which Rodríguez de Cerrato heard related a century after the event. 'Jane
was very compassionate. When she saw the wretched condition of the unfortunate villagers, to whom she had already given many of her things, she
distributed among the poor a certain barrel of wine, which everyone knew
about in the locality.' It was then that her husband, returning from a journey
and hearing what had happened, asked her to serve up some of this wine.

Jane was filled with confusion. In answer to her prayers, however, the barrel was once more found full.[86]

When she died, she was buried first of all at Caleruega, outside the church, against the end wall. It seems that the body was transferred to San Pedro de Gumiel, then, between 1334 and 1340 to Peñafiel by the Infanta don Juan Manuel, there to be solemnly interred in the monastery of the Friars Preachers which the Infanta had just had built. It is still there at the present day. A chapel, however, was erected about the sixteenth century over the former tomb at Caleruega incorporated from this time on in the parish church, the nave of which was enlarged. On the façade of the tiny chapel an inscription can still be read: 'This chapel was erected in honour of the burial place of Saint Jane, mother of Saint Dominic.' A religious cultus was thus preserved and renewed around these different tombs.[87] In 1828 Pope Leo XII recognized this cultus by officially according to Jane the title of blessed.

Rodríguez thinks that the keen sensitivity to the sufferings of others which St Dominic displayed from childhood onwards was inherited from his mother.[88] Such an opinion is easily acceptable. Jane undoubtedly had a very strong influence over the child whom she received from God in a deeply religious spirit and herself directed towards the clerical state. Rodríguez even claims that right from the beginning she consecrated him to the service of God—which would be in no way unusual.[89]

It was in 1170 that she married Felix. The date is confirmed by Thierry of Apolda in the vast compilation which he made in Germany at the end of the thirteenth century.[90] Thierry added that three sons were born of this union. The third would have been St Dominic who, if the compiler is to be believed, would thus be born in 1172 at the earliest. The number of the brothers seems an assured fact.[91] What are we to think of their order of succession? The *Libellus* of Jordan of Saxony, the oldest and one of the best sources, informs us with regard to one of St Dominic's two brothers that he was his half-brother.[92] The term deserves to be remembered.[93] According to this hypothesis Jane would thus have been married twice and Dominic, the son of Felix, would not have been of the same marriage-bed as one of his two brothers at any rate. All the statements made by Thierry could thus not be true at the same time; either the order of succession he assigns to the children or the place he assigns to the marriage in relationship to the births, or perhaps both indications must be called in question, for Thierry's work is late and lacks authority. If Dominic was older than his half-brother, which is plausible since he died much earlier,[94] the explanation is that Felix soon departed this life. The silence of the documents in the archives about him would thus be explained. Jane would not have been long in remarrying. If Dominic was younger it is because Felix was Jane's second husband. Dominic could already have been born in 1171.

What, then, may be asked, is the value of the date of 1170? This item of information has no greater and no less weight than that of the data usually associated with Thierry, that is, very little, as we have just seen in detail.[95] The date, however, is a probability; curiously enough it agrees with the approximate data which we shall gather later as to the age of St Dominic.[96]

Of Jane's two marriages at least three sons were born. Gérard de Frachet presents the first in these terms: 'Dominic had also two brothers of great perfection. One of them, a priest in a hospice, devoted himself unreservedly to works of mercy in the service of the poor. It is said that miracles made him famous both before and after his death'.[97] The Dominican historiographers of the sixteenth century call this brother Antony, without its being known on whose authority.[98] There was no lack of hospices at this time in Castile. They were not hospitals, but houses of hospitality for poor folk, especially for tramps, pilgrims and scholars. They were kept by lay folk who did not even in every case belong to an organized order. The situation was quite different in the houses of the great orders of the Knights Hospitallers which, in point of fact, had just arisen in Spain in the middle of the twelfth century, the military orders of Calatrava (1158), Alcántara (1166) and Santiago de la Espada (1160).[99] Although dependent on the Order of Citeaux, the first two had their own chaplains,[100] just as the independent Order of Santiago had. These priests exercised their ministry in the Comanderías and hospices of their order. It was probably in a hospice of the Order of Calatrava, which seems so closely linked through the abbey of San Pedro de Gumiel with the family of St Dominic,[101] that his priest-brother performed his works of mercy.

The other brother, the one whom Jordan calls his half-brother, is better known to us. He bore the name of Mames.[102] It was the name of a famous Eastern martyr, Mames of Caesarea, whose cultus, introduced into Gaul by St Radegunde, had spread to Spain, where even today at least fifteen localities in the region of León and of Old Castile bear his name, notably San Mames of Burgos and San Mames of Campos (province of Palencia).[103]

'Contemplative and holy,' said Gérard de Frachet, Mames 'for long served God in the order'.[104] Leaving his quiet contemplation, indeed, he placed himself under the guidance of his brother, at least from the foundation of the order,[105] perhaps even much earlier. He was still living just after St Dominic's canonization (1234).[106] Some forty years later, Rodríguez wrote of him: 'This brother Mames was a fervent preacher, virtuous in his habits, meek, humble, gay and kindly. He died at the monastery of San Pedro de Gumiel; he was buried there with honour.'[107] A Spanish friar who had visited Mames's tomb was later to make this statement to Bernard Gui: 'He made himself known there by miracles and prodigies. He is held as a saint in that place and his body is preserved with honour in a tomb venerated at the side of the altar.'[108] Gregory XVI recognized his cultus in 1833 and gave him the title of blessed under the mutilated name of Mannes.

Were there yet other children of Felix and of Jane? Perhaps another son
or daughter. Gérard de Frachet in fact mentions that two nephews of the
saint led a holy and praiseworthy life in the order.[109] One of them was
perhaps the Brother Juan of Caleruega mentioned by one of the witnesses of
the canonization process at Toulouse.[110] It seems certain that both entered
the Order of Preachers after their uncle's death since the latter's biographers
make no mention of them at all. If indeed one had to accept the extravagances
of Galvagno Fiamma in his lengthy chronicle, a third nephew, who was a
hermit, took part in the jubilee of 1300, aged 115, after having already taken
part in that of 1200. He was received in the priory of Genoa where he was
allowed to talk his fill. He wore his hair long in plaits.[111]

The first hagiographers, to mention only those, have collected together
several edifying episodes about the birth of St Dominic, the sole difficulty
about which is that they have already served for other saints; the little dog
which the mother saw in a dream before her son's conception and which she
was to bear in her womb whence it would issue forth holding in its jaws a
flaming torch seeming to set the world on fire;[112] the bees which supposedly
alighted on the lips of the new-born babe,[113] the moon which his mother
saw on the boy's forehead.[114] It was the kind of image which pleased the
people of that time. They liked to perceive grace visibly surrounding the
first hours and first years of the predestined. What people specially liked to
discover, as if it were a presage, was the symbolical résumé of their future
destiny. The dog bearing the flaming torch signified, according to the
Libellus, 'the distinguished preacher who would awaken sleeping souls and
spread over the universe the fire that the Lord Jesus had come to cast upon
earth'.[115] Thus the Preachers of more modern times were to display a
certain ingenuity in inscribing this dog carrying the torch in the armorial
bearings of the order, unfortunately destroying the dignity and simplicity of
the primitive coat of arms.[116] The image of the light on the child's brow,
which clearly signified that he would one day be given as a light to the
nations to enlighten those who sit in darkness and in the shadow of death,[117]
was to become the special sign of St Dominic in iconography. At least it
corresponds to a statement confirmed by history. 'From his brow and his
eyelashes there emerged a kind of radiance which attracted the reverence
and affection of all.'[118] That was how good Sister Cecilia, who had known
him so well in former times, visualized him again in her memories at the
end of her long life; she had been seventeen when he was about fifty. The
transparency and radiance of the look of Dominic as a small child can be
imagined.

It is so easy for us to picture him carried by his noble godmother[119] into
the white romanesque church of the parish of San Sebastián at Caleruega, to
receive baptism there. In the recess at the left side of the nave the

foundations of the font in which he received the holy ablution can still be seen. The font itself is no longer there. Sanctified by this very ceremony it was soon taken away to the convent of the nuns, then transported to Valladolid and finally to Madrid, there to be used for the baptism of the Infantas of Spain, descendants of the Guzmán.[120] But the richness of the silver casket which encloses it today is not to be compared with the light which surrounded it when the child of Felix and Jane received through the water of the sacrament the grace he was to radiate over others.

In baptism he was named Dominic. The name was a common one in Castile, as it was in the village. It was just a century since the name of the reformer, St Dominic of Silos (1073), was spreading over the whole country-side along with the fame of his numerous miracles. 'Dominic' meant 'the man of the Lord'—his servitor.[121] To belong wholly and entirely to the Lord Jesus, a magnificent objective for the child.

It may or may not be true that 'while he was still under the care of his nurse', he was frequently caught by surprise at night, lying on the ground, undressed, having left his bed, as if he 'refused to give way to sleep in the abandonment of a couch that was too soft'.[122] It is a fact that he early acquired the habit of treating his body with hardness, particularly at the time which others devote to sleep, and that at the end of his life, when cares, apostolic labours and the attacks of sickness should have modified his austerities, in his monastery not a cell or even a bed was known as his, scarcely even a hurdle of rope in a corner.[123] Perhaps the small child had heard people talk of the austerities of some hermit, or those of the soldiers in the Moorish wars. The harsh, austere lesson of Caleruega, of Castile, of the times in which he lived, imposed this initial form upon the child's generosity.

A further austere sacrifice was soon to be asked of him—to leave his mother, his brothers and his village forthwith.

CHAPTER II

PALENCIA

WHEN the child Dominic was old enough to learn to read, being then about six or seven, or perhaps even younger,[1] his parents handed him over to the Church for his education.[2] If a strong perfume is poured into a vessel of new clay, it permeates it in such a way that afterwards nothing can obliterate the fragrance. Similarly, from his earliest moments the young boy's soul was impregnated with clerical sanctity.

According to custom, it was an ecclesiastical uncle who took his education in hand.[3] At that time the family was both larger and more closely knit than is usual at the present day and it was frequently the uncle, not the father, who watched over the upbringing of his young nephews, even in its military and feudal aspects. *A fortiori* was this so in the case of the education and upbringing of a churchman. The fatherly care which existed in the hearts of the clergy and to which celibacy was no obstacle was given with predilection to the child of a brother or a sister. Very strong ties were formed from which tenderness was not excluded. Like a big elder brother the priest-uncle made every effort to pass on his spiritual heritage to the nephew they had been good enough to entrust to his care. He endeavoured to provide a background that would be helpful, and trained and educated the young cleric by his advice, often, too, using his own money.[4]

In this case the uncle was a dean.[5] Since the sixteenth century, it has even been asserted that he was parish priest of Gumiel de Izán,[6] one of the parishes nearest to Caleruega. The house in which the child is supposed to have lived at that time has been pointed out.[7] Nothing, however, supports this relatively modern tradition which a single fact is sufficient to disprove— Gumiel de Izán did not possess a deanery prior to the nineteenth century. Deaneries constituted the sub-divisions of the diocese of Osma as in the case of the majority of the Spanish dioceses and their original division must go back at least to the beginning of the twelfth century when the diocese was reconstituted.[8] The deaneries nearest to Caleruega were to be found in Aranda, Roa, Aza,[9] precisely the places of which the families of Guzmán and Aza held overlordships. Perhaps the dean-uncle had been appointed to one of these places. We are certainly not told, however, that he lived in the neighbourhood or even in the diocese.

It may be wondered whether he kept the child with him. Jordan of

Saxony merely asserts 'that he took special care of his upbringing and had
him educated in accordance with ecclesiastical custom from the beginning.'[10]
For a secular education a tutor at home would have been sufficient.[11]
To train a young cleric, it was desirable that he should be sent to a church of
some size and importance, a collegiate church or a monastery. In modern times
the great monasteries of the neighbourhood have simultaneously claimed
the honour of having brought up Dominic as a small boy—the Benedictines
of Silos,[12] the Premonstratensians of Nuestra Señora de la Vid,[13] even the
knights of Santiago de la Espada.[14] The argument of the latter, set out in two
books, is so much empty air.[15] That of the monks of Silos is rather better
established. The presence at Santo Domingo de Silos of a few children, an
indication of the existence of a school within the monastery enclosure, is
attested.[16] In the twelfth century, however, Benedictine monasteries restricted
attendance at such schools to their own oblates.[17] In the case of the
Premonstratensians of La Vid, who declined to receive anyone but adults,
there is no question of a school for young boys.[18] Taking all the factors into
consideration, it must have been in the church of his dean-uncle that the
child was educated by one of the clergy attached to the church.

The expression 'in the church' is correct, for the ecclesiastical building
played an important rôle right from the beginning of clerical education. The
child learnt to read with the help of a primer, and was immediately set to
spelling out the psalms.[19] He learnt Latin at the same time as he learned to
read and the intention was for him to be able to recite this Latin in the
sanctuary in a loud, clear voice and in such a way that he knew how to put
the stress on the essential words and 'comfort the hearts of the listeners'.[20]
The order of *lector*, the lowest rank in the clerical status, would very soon
come to crown this knowledge which was wholly ordained to the worship
of God in church. Thus he learnt to read the psalms, hymns and canticles,
which he had to know by heart, the lectionary and the gradual. During this
time the music of the sacred chant became familiar to him. He was made to
chant responsories and hymns. With a few other boys of his age he formed a
choir which had its place in the chanting of the offices, while waiting until
his admittance to further minor orders should allow him to serve at the
altar. At an age when the tenderness and freshness of impressions is as yet
unspoilt, it was worship in common and the sacred chant which fed his mind
and laid its mark on him. It was a great privilege to have sung for God
during his early childhood. Throughout his life, Dominic was to preserve
this sensitive feeling for the ceremonies of the Church, the divine office and
the Mass which he could not celebrate without tears coming to his eyes in
such abundance 'that one tear would not wait for the next'.[21]

The boy also learned to write on the wax tablets which he held in place
on his right knee.[22] He learnt to count and was initiated into the com-
plexities of ecclesiastical computations. Finally he acquired the first

rudiments of the art of grammar. After five or six years of elementary studies he would be eleven or twelve. Under his schoolmaster, discipline was severe. Things had changed but little since Augustine begged God to spare him whippings at school and declared: 'Who would not feel full of horror and would prefer to die if he were offered the choice between suffering death and beginning his childhood again?'[23] 'From this moment the rod never ceases to threaten them' is what is foreseen from daybreak onwards in the rule for scholars in Ulrich's description of the customs of Cluny.[24] Young Dominic, however, would doubtless have made the same reply as the youthful Guibert de Nogent did to his mother who was beside herself when she discovered the blood-stained trace of the blows on her small boy's back: 'No, you shall not be a cleric, you shall no longer suffer like this to learn your letters . . .'—'Even if it meant dying I would not give up learning or the clerical state.'[25] Dominic, who was later to scourge his flesh to the point of cruelty in the course of his nocturnal prayers, had no fear of the blows.[26] He doubtless discovered in the harshness of the scholastic methods of the time a further occasion for satisfying his precocious appetite for mortification.

Dominic reached the age of fourteen,[27] and the time had come to leave the church of his uncle the dean and to go to the schools.[28] In Castile, at this time, there was scarcely any choice. Whereas Catalonia, the area of which extended on both sides of the Pyrenees, readily sent its clerics to the schools in France and Lombardy then in the full flower of development, Castile, enclosed within its frontiers and, in addition, taken up with the battles of the Reconquest, had to be satisfied with her own slender resources.[29]

There was, of course, the church of Compostela, constantly invigorated by the ever-changing ebb and flow of the pilgrimage to Santiago along the camino francés, also Toledo, where under the protection of the archbishop from Aquitaine, Raymond de Sauvetat, a group of keen and hard-working translators made available to the schools of the north the ancient Arabic and Jewish writings preserved by the Moslems of Spain,[30] and a few primary schools set up in the cathedral chapters, as in Toledo, Salamanca and Osma;[31] but apart from these there existed only one really flourishing centre of learning in Castile: the schools of Palencia.[32] It was in this church that, in a few years' time one would see the first Spanish university come into being (1208–1214) and, what is more, the first university of royal foundation in Europe, a clear sign of the maturity of the earlier schools and of the interest which King Alfonso VIII took in this centre of ecclesiastical learning.[33]

This was because the see of Palencia, restored towards 1030, long before Toledo and all its suffragan sees, partially exercised the function during the thirteenth century of provincial metropolitan see, a title which it actually assumed at one point.[34] Situated in the centre of the land, in the midst of a prosperous agricultural region, close by the royal city of Carrión where the kings liked to stay, it was better placed than Toledo to form the spiritual centre of Castile. Thus the national councils which reorganized the institutions and life of the dioceses in these decisive years met in the cathedral there or in the neighbouring abbeys of San Zöile or Husillo.[35] It is understandable that the school attached to the chapter should soon come to be regarded as the metropolitan school. On 13th February, 1148, it acquired even more widespread fame, when the judgement against Gilbert de la Porrée which was being prepared in Rheims was in the first place pronounced there, by the verdict of Raymond of Toledo, Juan Avendauth of Segovia and Iñigo de Coria.[36] Thus Toledo and Palencia sat in judgement on the master of Chartres and Poitiers.

In the last decades of the century at least one master taught theology in Palencia, and his name can perhaps be found in one or other of the lists of canons which have come down to us from the chapter.[37] Before all else, however, the schools were famous for the teaching of the liberal arts.[38] It was for these that the youthful Dominic primarily went there. The programme of studies which was still referred to under the traditional name of the liberal arts had been considerably enlarged in the course of the twelfth century.[39] It would be interesting to be able to list all that the archdeacon of Segovia, Domingo Gondisalvi, included in this first cycle of studies as far back as about the year 1150.[40] This indefatigable translator of the Arabic writers, one of the most celebrated of the Toledo group, had tried to bring up to date the programme of studies in the West, taking his inspiration from the wealth of learning which he drew with full hands from the words of Alfarabi, Avicenna and Isaac Israeli, as much as from Boethius or Isidore of Seville. His *De divisione philosophiae* thus regrouped the whole of the liberal branches of learning, which he called human sciences, under philosophy. Two preliminary branches of study opened the programme: the science of letters, or grammar, and the civil sciences, i.e. poetry, history, rhetoric. The student went on to logic, a necessary instrument of philosophy and at the same time a science in its own right. Lastly came what were termed the sciences of wisdom—in the first place physics, with medicine, navigation, alchemy; mathematics, with arithmetic, geometry and optics, music and astrology; finally metaphysics, the crown of human wisdom. A long road had been traversed since the time when only the seven arts of the *trivium* and the *quadrivium* were known—grammar, dialectics and rhetoric on the one hand, arithmetic and music, geometry and astronomy, on the other. It is, alas, to be feared that in Palencia the old programme was more closely adhered to than that of the translator of Toledo, whose plan was too novel to be put into practice so quickly in the official schools, since its influence, even in Paris, would scarcely be perceptible before the thirteenth century.

Thus Dominic as a boy, after having spent some time on the subjects of the *trivium* course, in particular grammar and dialectics which could provide a training in logic and literature, devoted himself for some time to philosophy[41] and passed quickly through the rest. Jordan of Saxony who drew his information from former fellow-pupils of the saint in Spain, is quite definite: 'When he judged that he had sufficient knowledge of them, he abandoned these studies as if he feared to waste upon them with too little fruit the brevity of life here on earth.'[42]

We must thus conclude that he did not devote to them the seven years which certain people then assigned as good measure; five or six years (six if one credits a statement by Pedro Ferrando) must have seemed to him sufficient.[43] He certainly did not study through curiosity or through a mere appetite for learning. Nor had he any inclination to linger over the pagan books which served as a basis for these branches of study.[44] Still less was it his intention to utilize his profane knowledge by devoting himself to teaching it, or to prolong his course by studies in jurisprudence which led to the highest offices in the Church.[45] 'He was anxious to pass on to the study of theology and began to feed eagerly on the sacred Scriptures.'[46] If he did not prolong his studies until he became a teacher in his turn, which would have given him the right to be called master,[47] he was at least a *divinus* as it was then called, a well-formed theologian.

He devoted four years to sacred studies. Such was his perseverance and his eagerness to draw upon the waters of the sacred Scriptures that, indefatigable as he was when study was in question, he spent the nights almost without sleep, while in the depths of his mind his tenacious memory retained the truth received by the ear. What he learnt with facility, thanks to his gifts, he watered with his devotion and caused to spring from it works of salvation. In this way he obtained the entry to happiness, in the judgement of Truth itself, who, in the Gospel, proclaims blessed those who hear the word and keep it.[48]

The biographer points out to us that there are two ways of keeping the word of God: one by retaining it, the other by practising it. The second is surely the more important. For the grain is better preserved when it is multiplied by being left to germinate in the ground than when it is shut away in a storing-bin. Dominic, however, used both methods in turn.[49]

His memory, which his training as a young cleric had already developed, now worked on the *Divina Pagina*, the sacred text commented on by the Fathers of the Church. He became so impregnated with it that later he knew whole portions of it almost by heart.[50] His master analysed the text in the pulpit according to the procedure of the time with the help of the traditional commentaries. From time to time he would bring out in his explanation of the text a difficulty in the form of a question which was discussed either in the lesson itself or in a disputation in the regular manner. Dominic showed great intelligence and facility in this exercise[51], which enabled him to deepen his study of the Bible considerably and to acquire a vision of revelation as a connected whole, beyond the word-for-word rendering of the text. At the conclusion of the ordinary lesson, the master condensed his teaching in brief explanatory phrases, the glosses, which he put before his students. Dominic would write them down on his tablets. To ponder more deeply on their meaning, when he got back to his room he would copy them carefully into the parchment notebooks in which he had the text of the Bible copied by a scribe. Thus he had his real treasure in his own home—the books covered with glosses which preserved for him both the word of God and the instrument to penetrate the riches of it.[52]

For he now had a home. During the early days of his stay in Palencia, when he was still too young to live alone, he doubtless lodged with some ecclesiastic, some canon of the chapter of St Antolín, for instance, to whom his uncle had recommended him;[53] such was current practice.[54] Afterwards he had his room, with his books and some personal furniture,[55] living on the allowance made to him by his mother, or perhaps even by the dean.[56] No longer being obliged to conform to the discipline of a presbytery or a collegiate church, he could follow his bent freely and keep vigil as he pleased. It was no longer penance alone, as in the days of his childish fervour at Caleruega, which kept him away from his bed: it was the joy of sacred study, the *lectio divina*. 'Indefatigable when it was a matter of study', he must have passed many a night in meditating in this way, almost without sleep.[57] Clearly the spirit of mortification lost nothing thereby. In addition he imposed on himself for the future abstention from drinking wine, the fine red wine that the peasants of Caleruega carry about with them everywhere in a leather gourd from which, in the heat of the day, they spurt between their half-closed lips a thin stream of sun-drenched sapphire. He continued to practice this abstinence until the day when, having become a canon regular and under obedience to a superior, he had to soften it a little by filling his jug in the refectory with wine so diluted with water that no one, it would seem, was tempted to drink of it.[58]

He lived a rather solitary life. He has been described to us in a hagiographical cliché as a 'puer-senex',[59] a child more like an old man, a little too 'wise and good' for a young boy. Doubtless his early boyhood with his priest-uncle in making him mature before the time, had meant that he was unaccustomed to the contact of other boys and their usual games. This rather harsh fervour must have been equally according to the bent of his ascetic temperament, already preoccupied by the problem of evil and anxious to be hard with itself. As his adolescence advanced, he discovered among certain of his fellow pupils that liberty in behaviour which the moralists of the time never wearied of calling attention to in all the centres of learning, and of stigmatizing relentlessly without, however, any great result—a shameless-ness of manners all the more deplorable since it affected clerics, destined perhaps one day to receive the priesthood.[60] At that time the youthful Dominic came to be somewhat reticent, musing on his own thoughts. He was pure through and through. His chastity—that of a boy who has grown up in the shadow of the sanctuary—preserved, right to the end of his life, not only his utter purity, but the charming delicacy, open and ready to take alarm,[61] of those who have never known any other feminine tenderness but that of their mother.

He did not, however, radically shut himself away from others. On the contrary, in his solitude and his prayer, it was of others that he thought, as events from this time onward were to prove. At this period there was no lack of distress in Spain. The war against the Moslems had broken out again with renewed fierceness since the empire of the Almohades in establishing itself had restored to Spanish Islam that unity, spirit of enterprise and keen-ness which it had partially lost. The struggle among Christian princes had also begun again. Castile, weakened by her separation from León, was threatened by that kingdom's rebirth at the same time as by Navarre. Abandoned by his allies at a most perilous moment, Alfonso VIII finally experienced the terrible defeat of Alarcos in 1195. Innumerable soldiers of Castile were killed or fell into the hands of the Saracens as slaves. The Almohades, however, treated their mozarabic Christian subjects so harshly that the latter fled towards the north. They crossed the frontier in whole groups, in poverty and uprooted from their usual surroundings, to swell the tide of the country's underfed.[62]

For famines, too, reappeared periodically, caused by wars as much as by the elements, aggravated by the difficulty of communications. The memory of a famine more serious than the others, which spread over almost the whole of Spain[63] while Dominic was in Palencia, has been preserved. At Cuenca, the last town which Alfonso VIII reconquered, the bishop, San Julián (1196–1208), whom Dominic would soon hear spoken of if he did not know him already,[64] multiplied his charity which was attended by real miracles.[65] Having spent all his revenues on the relief of the hungry, he worked with his hands to provide his own food, weaving frails, as St Paul had woven tents. He set up a depôt at the entrance gate to his bishop's palace—what was called at the time a 'charity',[66] where the poor came to seek their daily rations. The granary was empty. Nothing remained. The poor, however, continued to come. The bishop sent the servant in charge of the charity[67] to the granary notwithstanding—he found it full.

Dominic, too, in Palencia, saw people perishing of hunger.[68] Hardly any-one among the rich or the authorities came to their help.[69] He could bear it no longer. 'Touched by the distress of the poor and yearning with compassion, he resolved by one single action to obey the evangelical counsels and to relieve the wretchedness of the poor who were perishing, with all his power.' Establishing a 'charity' forthwith, he divided his possessions and gave them to the poor. By this example of generosity, he moved the heart of the other theologians and of the masters to such an extent that the latter, when confronted with the young man's generosity, realizing their slackness and their avarice, from that time onwards[70] began to distribute abundant help.

Let us examine the young theologian's gesture closely. In the Gospel over which he spent his vigils he read: 'If thou wilt be perfect, go, sell all thou hast and give to the poor.'[71] To obtain the premises for the charity centre and establish the daily distribution of food there, even all he possessed was not too much. He then sold all that he had. He became poor. In this way the compassion preached in the Gospel set him along the road to perfection and foreshadowed the future.

One of those present has recorded what he said when he sold even his manuscripts, those manuscripts written on parchment, annotated with his own hand, which we should so much like to hold in ours—'I will not study on dead skins when men are dying of hunger.'[72] The man capable of such words went beyond the limits of simple generosity, for it was not only his goods and what was necessary for his body that he sacrificed, but even a portion of his very being: in a certain sense he sacrificed the life of his mind in the face of his neighbour's urgent distress. Now nothing was left for him to give except his liberty. It would seem that it was at this moment that a woman came in tears to find Dominic. Her brother had fallen into the hands of the Moors, perhaps in the Alarcos disaster (1195). 'Full of the spirit of love, wrung with compassion, Pedro Ferrando tells us, Dominic offered himself for sale, to ransom the prisoner. The Lord, however, did not permit that that should happen.'[73] He offered himself for sale, like a slave.

In the cell at Palencia where no longer a piece of furniture or a book remained, Dominic discovered the meaning of life: to give bread to a whole nation crushed by famine and to give himself for them. Other people and not some of the least important, taken aback by his example, came to join him. They remained faithful to him for the future and later accompanied him in his preaching.[74] He still needed to learn what food it was that the people were so much in need of. God was to send him an ambassador who would take upon himself to teach him—the prior of the chapter of Osma, the venerable Diego of Acebo. Jordan of Saxony shows us this great religious prospecting the countryside to obtain first-class men for his diocese.[75] Dominic's actions and virtues had caused a certain amount of talk in Castile, even persons of the ruling class were talking about them.[76] Diego pointed this out to the bishop, who sent for the young man to be near him and offered him a seat in the chapter of his cathedral. Dominic was ready. He was to be a canon of Osma.[77]

CHAPTER III

OSMA

BURGO D'OSMA is a city of clerics—an episcopal city entirely dominated by its imposing cathedral. The presence of the bishop, the chapter, the seminary, the schools, haunts the length and breadth of its streets, fringed with kindly shade from the wooden porticos. Such was its aspect even in the closing years of the twelfth century when St Dominic arrived there. The cathedral and the romanesque cloister, the recently carved stone of which was still unstained by time for scarcely a third of a century had passed since the building was finished,[1] formed the centre of the place. The population of the *villa* or 'burgo Santa María' had only begun to increase during the past three decades.[2] The place was chiefly inhabited by those who were in the service of the Church and tenants of church land. Accordingly, from 1170 onwards the bishop had obtained the privilege that the town should depend only on himself and on his chapter.[3] This was the beginning of the temporal power which he tried to establish for himself, following the example of his colleagues and the custom of churchmen of those days. Ten years later through his efforts the king renounced his right of spoliation. At the beginning of the thirteenth century the bishop even received the manor and castle of Osma, the somewhat theoretical rights of which holders of the see were to preserve until the close of the eighteenth century.[4] In this way the see consolidated its independence and that of its retainers. Protected against the vexatious interference of the men of the neighbouring *castrum*,[5] the inhabitants of the township shared the tranquillity of the life of the clergy. The bell which rang out the hours in the choir of the cathedral timed their occupations and the prayer of the canons was in harmony with the peace which emanated from the countryside.

When, after having turned up the valley of the Duero and that of its tributary the Ucero, Dominic crossed the deep gorge hollowed out of the rocky edge of the plateau by the latter stream as it rejoined the main river, he would see the small town of Osma directly in front of him. He could not but be struck by the contrast this formed with the harshness of the landscape he had just left. All along the Duero there were nothing but hills of earth and limestone corroded by the elements, bare summits occasionally crowned by some feudal tower. Behind him, on the rocky barrier cutting into the Ucero, one could still see here and there the Roman, Moslem and Christian fortresses superimposed like mighty bolts on this natural gateway through which the diagonal route from Saragossa to Clunia passed. On the right was the *castrum* of ancient Uxama, still inhabited, and dominated by the fortress of the Castilians; to the left a Moorish tower; the Roman bridge over the river was buttressed to the rock, a memory of the passage and of the struggles of the legionaries and of the Saracen knights, and, not so many years earlier, of the Aragonese.[6] Before Dominic's eyes, however, lay the cathedral and *villa* of Osma in the centre of a fertile plain.

Set in a loop formed by the Ucero and its tributary the Avión which on the west and north surrounded it with the flow of their abundant waters and with a belt of fine trees, sheltered from the parching winds of the south by the lofty semi-circle of hills, the town presented the visitor with the restful picture of a centre of prayer.[7] There was indeed a contrast between this clerical city and Caleruega. Over in Caleruega, the broad horizons, the sun, the cold, spreading widely over a landscape which lay exposed to them without defence, expressed the call to heroism that could not be other than tense. Here the city nestling in the hills at the side of the streams, spoke only of recollection.

When Dominic thus looked upon the cloisters of the cathedral to which he was going to dedicate himself by a vow of stability, he must have murmured to himself the familiar psalm: 'Quam dilecta tabernacula tua, Domine. . . .' 'Lord of hosts, how I love thy dwelling-place. . . . How blessed, Lord, are those who dwell in thy house. They will be ever praising thee.'[8] Here and there we can still find tangible traces of the habitations where Dominic lived inserted as relics in the reconstructions of the fourteenth and fifteenth centuries: the chapter room with its graceful columns and carved capitals, the semi-circular arches of its windows supported by a twisted cluster of slender pillars, its three romanesque doors breaking the line of the cloister wall.[9] The black cloak with pointed hood and the white tunic which the young cleric wore[10] under his canon's surplice must have brushed against these pillars. He certainly must have leant against this cornice or the base of that capital the gryphons of which are intertwined so skilfully. He often stayed behind in the cloister to pray, in the deepest recollection. At Caleruega he had discovered the fire of the gospel. At Palencia he discovered its light. At Osma he experienced its inward tenderness. The sacred text which he had meditated upon and scrutinized in every possible way, during his days and nights in the schools, he could from now onwards practice and savour in peace, by collaborating, in his own sphere, in the work of evangelization undertaken for a century past by the bishops of Osma and, more generally, by the bishops of Castile.

This was indeed a noble enterprise, the spiritual counterpart of that undertaken by the kings of Castile to restore the Christian territory. It was, moreover, the joint work of kings and clergy in close collaboration with the popes, which had emanated from the Gregorian reform. When the land had been recovered, the counts and later the kings of Castile turned their attention to repopulating it. As the villages were built the life of the Church there had to be organized. As soon as a minimum of basic institutions had been re-established—the network of ancient or new sees, crowned by the revival of the metropolitan and primatial see of Toledo in 1085—an acute problem arose: to find clerics sufficiently numerous and adequate for the newly created vacancies and, especially, to fill the posts open to the higher clergy. The peasants and soldiers who had been gathered together for the conquest and settlement of the land could not easily be made into churchmen. Three campaigns were made in the province of Toledo, three successive forward movements to provide the pastors of souls and the spiritual guides needed for the reconquered lands.

As far back as the eleventh century, thanks to the generous gifts of kings and lords, the abbeys of the ancient lands had been launching out into new foundations. Thus, even before it was reconstituted, the diocese of Osma witnessed a certain number of foundations of religious houses—San Miguel de Osma (1063),[11] San Pedro de Aza, San Esteban y Santa María—San Martín de Górmaz, San Pedro de Gumiel (1073).[12] Such new communities, perhaps ruined by the civil strife and the raids of the Aragonese at the beginning of the twelfth century, disappeared one after another and their property and wealth were incorporated in more effective institutions.[13] The first forward movement had come.

At the end of the eleventh century a great change was taking place in the Church universal. The revolutionary reform movement which came from the Gregorian popes, from Leo IX to Urban II, ceased to devote its entire effort to the reform of the monks by creating cities of perfection from which the world was excluded: it now turned resolutely towards the world to subdue and guide it towards its Christian destinies. In Castile the monastic movement itself was associated with this impulse which had come from the centre of Christendom; indeed, it took the lead. The Order of Cluny, favoured in every way by King Alfonso VI (1065–1109) (who remembered having worn a monastic habit for a time at the abbey of Sahagún), became the most valuable collaborator of popes[14] and kings in the restoration and regeneration of the Church in Castile.[15] Hugh of Cluny and Peter the Venerable displayed an unceasing solicitude for Castile, which they visited more than once. What was more important, they sent there men who were great religious. After the failure of Abbot Robert, Bernard de Sédirac, who had come from Aquitaine to become Abbot of Sahagún (ca. 1080) and was later Archbishop of Toledo, was to be the dominant figure in the Church in Castile for half a century. Consecrated and invested with the pallium in Rome, soon afterwards legate apostolic, he reorganized the primatial see of Spain and restored almost all of its suffragan sees. Taking advantage of a

short stay in France on his way back from a visit to Rome, he recruited in the
churches and monasteries of the south a vast contingent of monks and clerics
whom he brought with him to make of them bishops, archdeacons and
abbots in his new country. For a generation or two these clergy who had
come from France occupied the principal sees of Castile, indeed, of the
peninsula: Toledo, Segovia, Palencia, Salamanca, Compostela, Cöimbra,
Braga, Valencia, Sagunto, not to mention numerous monasteries.[16] Osma,
at its renaissance, drew its very first pastors from among them: St Pierre de
Bourges (1101–1109)[17] and Raymond de Sauvetat (1110–1128).[18] The
former was a saint, whose tomb and memory still have an influence on the
life of the diocese in our own day; the latter, a scholar who, when he was
transferred to the see of Toledo, presided over the great work of Arabic
and Jewish translations there which we have already mentioned.[19]

This new ecclesiastical movement not only supplied Castile with a series
of prelates who were outstanding for their piety and learning—inspired by
the most recent developments in contemporary Europe, it reorganised the
fundamental institutions of religious life, the network of dioceses under the
primatial see, the system of abbeys in dependence on or at least inspired by
Cluny, the series of Councils at Palencia which were at one and the same
time metropolitan and national.[20] At a time when, in the reign of Alfonso
VII 'the Emperor' (1126–1157), the kingdoms of the peninsula were more
united than would again be the case until the fifteenth century, the links
with Rome and the remainder of the West, still so weak at the beginning of
the eleventh century, were firmly renewed. Through its receptiveness to the
spirituality of Cluny and to the spirit of the Gregorian reform, through the
painful sacrifice of the particularism of the Mozarabic liturgy[21] and even of
the Visigothic script,[22] Spain once more found contact and immense
possibilities of exchange with the Church as a whole and with the Christian
West, contact and exchanges without which St Dominic would not have
achieved the full measure of his stature. That Spain should be open to Europe
and Europe to Spain was essential if the saint who was preparing himself in
Castile was one day to find the stimulus and scope necessary for the world-
wide institution of the Preachers.

In the middle of the twelfth century, however, the tide which flowed
from Cluny ebbed, for its waters had received no new influx. The time had
come for a work that was more strictly national, more Castilian. It was,
of course, true that forces and ideas of considerable import continued
to come across the Pyrenees, especially from the monastic orders. In the
second half of the twelfth century the Cistercians were to find in Castile,
thanks to the support of Alfonso VII and Alfonso VIII (1158–1214), a
welcome comparable to that which Cluny had received in earlier times.[23]
The flourishing foundations, however, whose appearance we have noted, for
instance, in the valley of the Duero,[24] remained, but confined to their own

sphere. Now the centre of the Church's vitality lay elsewhere. A third stream of clergy swept over Castile—the one that brought St Dominic. This stream was purely Spanish. It was diocesan and mixed freely with the world. Foremost in it were the person of the bishop and that of his great officers, the institutions of the cathedral chapter and of the collegiate church with its clergy. It was chiefly represented in Osma by two men—the bishop, Martín Bazán (1189–1201)[25] and the prior of his chapter, Diego de Acebo, who succeeded him in the episcopate (1201–1208).[26] Jordan of Saxony has sufficiently described them both, at the same time confusing them somewhat in his description,[27] (we are not, moreover, in a position exactly to determine their respective share in an activity in which actually they seem to be interlinked),[28] when he thus presents to us the second.

> There was at this time in Spain a man named Diego, bishop of the town of Osma, whose life was worthy of admiration. He was distinguished as much for his knowledge of sacred learning as for the quality of his birth in the eyes of the world, and even more for his behaviour. He had given himself wholly to God through love, to the extent that he sought only the things of Christ, despising himself, and turned the whole effort of his mind and will to render to his Lord with interest the talents he had lent him, by making himself banker for a large number of souls. In this way he endeavoured to attract to himself by all the means at his disposal and in every place he could explore, men recommended for their honourable life and the good reputation of their morals, establishing them by giving them benefices in the church over which he presided. As to those of his subordinates, whose will, neglecting the effort at sanctification, inclined more towards the world, he persuaded them by word and invited them by his example to assume at least a more moral and more religious way of life.[29]

Such prelates, full of zeal for God, had plenty to do. For those of the clergy who lived far from the cathedral in parishes and private chapels, and who were to be known for the future as seculars, the great vices were ignorance[30] and sins against celibacy. At this time Bishop Martín Bazán put very precise questions to Pope Innocent III on what he was to do in the case of clergy whose attitude in regard to a woman (doubtless the woman who looked after their house), was, without being a case of manifest concubinage, clearly open to suspicion. As to concubinage the bishop had no hesitation about taking action. But in doubtful cases, how could one invoke legal action? The Pope advised prudence.[31] Manifestly, instances were not lacking in Osma any more than in the province generally, where a synod convened by the Archbishop of Toledo was to legislate on the same question shortly afterwards.[32] There was so little dearth of such cases that in the middle of the following century all the clergy of a certain rural deanery in the diocese, that of Roa, obtained from King Alfonso X the right to legitimize their children and to transmit the whole of their inheritance to them.[33] With regard to the canons of the cathedral, the central clergy of the diocese,

Martín and Diego did not remain inactive either. Jordan, in fact, adds the following item of information.

> It was at this juncture that [Diego] set himself to persuade his canons, by continually admonishing and encouraging them, to take upon themselves the observance of Canons Regular under the rule of St Augustine. He was so earnest over this that he finally influenced their minds in the direction he desired, although several among them opposed him.[34]

It may be surmised that in such conditions it was not by mere chance that Dominic, the pure and generous-hearted student of Palencia, was attached to the diocese. What awaited him there was not only a haven of contemplation but a college in process of reform, a task in which he was better equipped to collaborate than any other. To be completely convinced of this it is sufficient to sketch in a few words the history of this cathedral chapter of which he was to become a member. In it will be seen clearly reflected religious trends, an institutional movement, and supernatural inspirations which throw a most revealing light on the history of St Dominic.[35]

Bishop (San) Pedro de Osma had established the principles of the life of the diocese, striven to discover afresh the true limits of his territory, reconstituted the patrimony of the Church and begun the construction of the cathedral which Raymond de Sauvetat continued in his turn. It was only their successor, however, Bishop Bertrand (1128–1140)[36] who succeeded in crowning their efforts and setting up a building sufficiently adequate for the installation of a chapter of regular life.[37] Between 1131 and 1136, canons practising common life under the rule of St Augustine made their appearance in the cathedral.[38] They depended closely on the bishop who presided over chapter and office. The prior replaced the bishop in his absence. A provost or sub-prior, a sacristan, a cantor, with the archdeacons of the diocese constituted the dignitaries.[39]

The community certainly did not follow Premonstratensian observance (*arctior consuetudo, ordo novus*), which only won acceptance in the diocese in 1152, at Nuestra Señora de la Vid, a completely isolated religious house situated in the country.[40] Moreover, nothing justifies the assertion[41] that it followed the order of St Rufus (*ordo antiquus*), one of the most widespread forms of the life of the Canons Regular in southern Europe, in Aragon as in Catalonia, but not in Castile.[42] Their customs, however, must have been fairly similar to those of St Rufus, doubtless a moderate observance learnt in the schools of the Canons Regular in Castile and Aragon which were not connected with any specific order.[43]

What is important is not the detail of the customs but the presence of the rule of St Augustine.[44] What was then called by this name was a document composed of two texts, of which only one could be traced back to St Augustine, that is, to Letter 211, very apposite advice on the spirit of common life addressed to a community of religious women which his sister had governed.[45] This letter, then, its feminine genders altered to the masculine, had later been provided with a preface—a brief and somewhat obscure set of regulations (*ordo monasterii*) which legislated for the discipline, the employment of time, the liturgical life and the manual work of a community.[46] In this way a genuine rule was provided, exact in its demands, impressive in its inspiration, authenticated by the name of the greatest of the Latin fathers. Drawn up, perhaps, as early as the sixth century it was yet only at the end of the eleventh that it emerged from obscurity. By that time it had become the standard rule of the reform of the Canons. Its very success had repercussions on the text, which was modified. Around 1130 no more than the opening phrase of the *Ordo monasterii* remained. The popes of the early part of the twelfth century had in effect 'declared' that the sequence of this text had not to be observed and that the usual customs of the Canons Regular must be substituted for the precise regulations, which were thus made to disappear.[47] There remained, however, the second text, the transcription of Letter 211. That indeed was the essential in the eyes of the clergy of that time.[48]

This letter began by proclaiming the absolute individual poverty of the members of the community. 'Since you are gathered together in a single society, see to it that you dwell in your house with one mind. Let no one have anything of his own, let all your goods be common and let your superior distribute food and clothing to each one of you, not in equal measure to all, for your health is not identical, but according to each one's needs'.[49]

The Augustinian text was already sufficiently eloquent in itself since it assigned to the clergy who accepted it as their rule, the very ideal of the life of the apostles and of the primitive Church. The monastic movement had indeed been living according to this inspiration from the very beginning.[50] In the context of the time, however, these words had a supplementary bearing and connotation which it is difficult for us to envisage. They formed in very truth the countersign of a spiritual combat, the formula of a rooting up of less fervent habits, the clarion call of a passionate *sursum corda* in the name of which, for three-quarters of a century past, the demand of the clergy for reform had begun in the city of Rome, afterwards spreading over Italy and the whole of the West. In the face of the all too widespread neglect of the traditional ecclesiastical laws of celibacy and of a certain common life for the diocesan clergy, in the face of the lack of the priestly ideal in that chosen portion of the clergy who lived on Church funds in the centre of the diocese or at the collegiate churches, and who were known as canons, the reformers, of whom Leo IX was the initiator and Gregory VII the fearless and uncompromising instigator, had launched the appeal which could regenerate them—the return to the sources, to the primitive Church, to the example of the apostles.[51]

> We order those clergy who, obeying our predecessor [Pope Leo IX], have pre-
> served chastity, to live within the precincts of the church for which they were
> ordained, as becomes religious-minded clerics, eating and sleeping together and
> possessing in common all that comes to them from the church; we earnestly
> request them to make every effort to attain to apostolic life, that is to say, to the
> common life, in order that, having become perfect, they may deserve to have a
> place in their heavenly fatherland, by the side of those who are now receiving the
> hundredfold promised.[52]

Not all the clergy had obeyed. Not all the canons had given up the old Carolingian rule which allowed them a certain amount of personal owner-ship.[53] Those, however, whose ears were attuned to catch the call of the Spirit to the Church soon found in the rule of St Augustine that 'apostolic' rule which would enable them to live the perfect life in common and so to allow the pattern of life of the apostles and of the primitive Church to exert its influence over the whole of their clerical activity. If they needed a fine example to increase in them the attraction of the ideal to which the rule was forming them, they could read[54] a striking story in the works of Augustine himself.

The incident occurred at Hippo. St Augustine, then a bishop, had long since taken the decision to live with his clergy in a monastery, in order to practise apostolic life in common. The clergy understood and accepted this ideal and the population of Hippo, touched by their example of disinterested-ness and spiritual generosity, derived great benefit from it. We can imagine, then, the reactions of the faithful on learning that one of the priests of the community, on dying, had left a will. He considered himself, then, as having the right to own something. The scandal was great. In the cathedral Augustine assembled his clergy. The faithful stood around. He seated himself on his throne. The deacon Lazarus came to the appointed place and read the Acts of the Apostles. 'There was one heart and one soul in all the company of believers; none of them called any of his possessions his own, everything was shared in common.' Augustine took up the book: 'I, too, will read in my turn; I have greater joy in reading you these words than in addressing my own to you.' He read the text again; then—'That is how we seek to live; pray that we may be able to do so.'[55]

When, some seven centuries later, one of the most zealous preachers of the Gregorian reform, St Peter Damian, in turn took up the text of the Acts to encourage the Italian clergy to discover their ideal anew, he, too, found therein the programme of perfect poverty in common. He gave to this clerical poverty, however, an orientation giving final form to its contempor-ary significance, the interpretation, very characteristic of the Gregorian reform, given to it in Spain—poverty that was triumphant and not only ascetic. Such poverty made the priest a soldier of vigour and zeal in the hands of his bishop, a cleric whose life gave edification in the centre of his Church, a preacher whose life was a sermon at the same time as his words. Such were the apostles, not only in the upper room, but along the roads of Palestine, when Christ sent them on before him to preach, two by two.[56]

'It is important to understand the conduct and the rule of life which the Church observed at the time when the faith was just beginning. "The multitude, says St Luke,[57] had only one heart and one soul, and no one called whatever he might have his own, for all was common among them." Should clerics, then, be given the privilege of possessing what Christ did not allow his apostles? When he sent them to preach, as St Mark says,[58] he gave them instructions to take a staff for their journey and nothing more; no wallet, no bread, no money for their purses . . . The possession of even a little money put by leads the clergy to despise the authority of their prelate . . . it causes them to bow their necks before secular persons under the shameful yoke of a very unseemly dependence. Finally, stimulating in them the love of money, it makes them unworthy to preach the word of God, for those alone are apt for the office of preaching who, possessing nothing as their own, have all things in common. Like lightly-armed soldiers, *expediti*, free from every obstacle, they fight for the Lord against vice and the devil, armed only with their virtues and the sword of the Holy Spirit.[59]'

Such was the ideal of the apostolic life to which (under the stimulus of the Gregorian reformers) the rule of St Augustine won over the communities of canons one after the other: to live like the apostles in the upper room, and on the road during their mission as preachers, in utter and manifest poverty. At the time when the chapter of Osma was established, the rule of St Augustine, under the double action of the King of Aragon and of the Pope's legates, had already won over almost all the chapters of that kingdom.[60] Osma was to be one of the centres whence this rule and the way of apostolic life for the clergy would spread into the kingdom of Castile.

At this time a chapter of canons was far from being merely the ornament of the mother Church and the senate of the clergy of riper years in a diocese. This community of clerics who celebrated the divine offices in the cathedral had seen its administrative rôle increase since the reform of the Church. It was entrusted with the election of the bishop—a circumstance which did not altogether exclude the intervention of the king, for there are many ways of bringing influence to bear on a college of electors, but which nevertheless assured, much more satisfactorily than in the past, the liberty of individual churches. At the same time it constituted the bishop's council and shared in the administration of the patrimony of the diocese which, still undivided,[61] assured both its livelihood and that of the prelate. At this time, men joined a chapter as they entered a monastery. Thus, clergy of all ages would be found there, a body of priests formed in accordance with canon law, of more regular life and better instructed than anywhere else. At a time when seminaries did not yet exist, a chapter was a nursery of future prelates and church dignitaries: archdeacons, chancellors, professors of theology. As far back as the twelfth century the chapter of Osma effectively supplied the churches of Castile with prelates.[62] Above all, it expanded beyond its own confines.

The official populating of Soria, a town near the site of ancient Numancia, on the side nearer to Osma along the great highway from Tarragona to Clunia, had begun in 1113.[63] In 1148 the bishop and chapter of Osma received the church of San Pedro de Soria, with the obligation of setting up a collegiate church of Canons Regular there.[64] Four years later this was an accomplished fact.[65] From the beginning the two chapters appeared to be linked by close ties of brotherhood and to be so similar that certain members in the chapter of Osma one day claimed to subject the collegiate church of Soria to their obedience. The bishop had to intervene in view of the consternation of the Soria chapter, and point out the reciprocal independence of the two bodies. He himself constituted the sole head of two identical colleges, established on a footing of equality.[66] On the occasion of this call to order, he invoked the significant example of the two chapters of Huesca and Jaca in Aragon, which lived on terms of the most complete fraternal charity, although one of them was a cathedral and the other only a collegiate church, under the common direction of the bishop.[67]

In 1143 the repopulating of Roa began.[68] For want of documents it is impossible to determine whether the college of Augustinian canons which was installed there drew its inspiration from the chapter of Osma. It is possible. In any case this inspiration is certain and much more worthy of note in the case of the Cuenca chapter. The town had been reconquered in 1177. In 1183 an episcopal see was set up there and the first bishop, Juan Yanes, was consecrated.[69] He asked the Osma chapter to come to Cuenca and found there a similar institution. A certain number of canons, therefore, went down to Cuenca and were incorporated in the new community. It is clear that they took with them their regular customs with the rule of St Augustine.[70] The close relations maintained right down to our own times between these two chapters provide an indication of their common origin. Now among the canons whom Osma obtained in this way, may be noted a certain Master Lope who became professor of theology there.[71]

In effect, some time earlier the Osma chapter had inaugurated its clerical school. In 1166 and 1168, there is mentioned in the list of the canons a certain Juan, called *preceptor*, that is, master of a primary school.[72] In 1168, in addition to Juan, there were two other masters: Master Bernier

(*Photo: Leonard von Matt*)

A canon of Osma on a journey in the thirteenth century.

and Master Eudes.[73] Thus the chapter was organizing within its precincts an episcopal school similar to that which the ancient dioceses of the West possessed at this time, even before the Third Council of the Lateran legislated on this point.[74] A tradition of learning had to be maintained in the cathedral. The beginning of the thirteenth century was to see a succession of great scholars in the episcopal see of Osma. Diego de Acebo (1201–1208),[75] Rodrigo Jiménez de Rada (1208–1210), one of the most cultured men in Spain at that time, whom the see of Toledo lost no time in claiming for itself, Master Melendo (1210–1225).[76] The clerical milieu of Osma when Dominic came to take his place there was thus not lacking in distinction on the intellectual plane. The catalogue of its library shortly after this period is still extant.[77]

On the other hand, there was one problem that arose, that of regularity. At that time nothing was stable and the most remarkable impulses of heroism sometimes died away surprisingly quickly. It is a fact that the common life which seems to have flourished in almost all the newly founded chapters in Spain in the first part of the twelfth century, was beginning to waver in several communities in the last third of that century.[78] The absolute poverty of the rule of St Augustine was found too difficult. At Palencia, for instance, in 1183 the bishop had to authorize certain canons to make a will, which is an indication of some private ownership.[79] What would the good people of Hippo have said! Osma certainly preserved its strict regularity for a long time. In 1168 the bishop caused a common fund to be established on All Saints day in the chapter refectory.[80] It seems, however, that from this time onwards the spirit of private property was beginning to seep in. This doubtless originated in isolated individuals, a few clerics recommended by persons in high places who endeavoured to get themselves incorporated in the chapter, especially as dignitaries, and to have a portion of the goods of the Church assigned to them, without, however, assuming the obligation of practising the common life and observances.[81] The troubles during the minority of Alfonso VIII (1158–1168), the scandalous pressure then exercised by the nobles and the king's agents on the churches of the kingdom must have multiplied such accretions which were disastrous for the rule of life of the college.[82] In 1160, Bishop Juan had obtained from Pope Lucius III a bull to prohibit the integration into the chapter of anyone who had not made profession and sworn to observe the rule of St Augustine.[83] In 1176 a scandal, however, occurred. The then prior of the chapter, Bertrand, had had himself elected bishop through simony two years earlier. It was a sorry business in which the electors were not innocent, for they had allowed themselves to be bought or manipulated by the king's nobles who had received 5,000 maravedis from Bertrand. Alexander III deposed the simonaical bishop, suspended

the guilty electors and claimed restitution of the sum handed over.
Alfonso VIII made this restitution through his guardians some thirty years
later.[84] Nevertheless, the pressure from candidates eager to obtain a share
of the chapter's wealth and of their powerful patrons must have continued.
In 1182, the bishop, Miguel, a Benedictine, obtained a new bull prohibiting
the incorporation as a canon or dignitary of the chapter of anyone who refused
to accept regular life.[85] Seventeen years later, Bishop Martín Bazán was to
solicit a third bull on this point (1199).[86]

The lack of fidelity had been even more serious. On reading the Pope's
text it would seem that the very principle of common life had been called
in question.[87] The reaction was all the more categorical, and, this time,
completely effective. Before asking for the bull, the bishop had made
certain of the support of his archbishop and of the king's assent;[88] then, by
means of a long work of spiritual preparation, carried out with the collaboration of the prior, Diego de Acebo, had persuaded the canons as a body to
resume the life of total regularity. Some of them resisted.[89] It would be interesting to know if defections, replaced by more genuine vocations procured
by the efforts of the prior, were numerous.[90] The bishop re-established
common life in the strict sense of the word and put into force once more
certain of the former constitutions of the chapter.[91] Then he obtained from
the Pope a *titulus* of confirmation. Now the observance was solidly established in law as well as in the hearts of men. The rule of St Augustine was
once more supreme in the Osma chapter. The ideal of the life of the
apostles in all its purity was the canons' inspiration and was manifested even
in the number of twelve religious which seems to have been regularly
established in the community.[92] Twelve canons, like the twelve apostles,
under the guidance of the bishop, the representative of Jesus Christ. Regular
life was not again to disappear from the cathedral before the end of the
fifteenth century.[93] By that date all the chapters in Castile had become
chapters of secular clergy, in some cases had been so for a long time past.[94]
Osma was to be the last to desire this, so strong had been the renewal of the
canonical spirit of the Gregorian reform in the community in the last years
of the twelfth century. Such was the atmosphere obtaining in the chapter
in 1196 or 1197[95] when St Dominic entered it at the age of twenty-four or
twenty-five.[96]

'Immediately', wrote Jordan of Saxony, 'he began to be outstanding among
the canons, shining like the evening star, the last through his humility of
heart, the first in holiness. He became for the others the fragrance which is
life-producing,[97] scent of olibanum on the summer air.'[98] Each one of them
was astonished at the height of religious life he so swiftly and secretly
attained.[99]

The prayers and mortifications of the child of Caleruega, the clerical life
of the adolescent with the rural dean, the austerities and solitary vigils in

Palencia probably provide a sufficient explanation. Familiarity with solitude prepared him equally for the silence of the cloister and the keeping of his cell. In the programme of imitation of the life of the apostles which the community in its full enthusiasm for reform put before him, Dominic's attachment seemed principally to be to the interior life of the cenacle and to the public prayer of the temple of Jerusalem. The canon's life was traditionally considered as a pure life of prayer. In contrast to the monks who worked with their hands out of asceticism, the canons were exclusively engaged, in the centre of the diocese, in the celebration of the mysteries, in divine praise and intercession. Thus tradition, coming down from Carolingian times, placed their contemplative life in sharp contrast with the active life of the monks—a view which runs somewhat counter to our preconceived ideas.[100] At the turn of the thirteenth century the evidence is clear—the hidden life which Dominic was leading in his religious house was *par excellence* the contemplative life.[101]

It was a community life, certainly, in which friendship and fraternal correction practised each day in the chapter of faults provided elements of moral formation and personal development that Dominic had never experienced; but, it was principally a life of solitude, a life of complete recollection in God. Attention has been drawn to the book always at his bedside whence Dominic derived his initiation into the virtues of his new state as well as into the processes of spirituality—the *Conferences of the Fathers of the Desert* by John Cassian. This Italian monk of the patristic period, trained when he was quite young in a monastery near Bethlehem, for seven years a pilgrim across the holy deserts of Egypt and the Near East before himself going to found two monasteries in Gaul, was the witness and teacher of the solitary life *par excellence*. The discipline of Christ, spiritual struggle, and combat against the demon, silence, contemplation fed by the Holy Scriptures, such were the lessons of the great anchorites. It was obviously to imitate their African austerities that Dominic thought out his discreet abstention from meat.[102] He took other things from them.

'With the help of grace, this book led him to a degree of purity of conscience difficult of attainment, to much light on contemplation and to a high summit of perfection.'[103]

Dominic alternated this interior exercise with the public recitation of the office in the cathedral. This was the obligation and privilege of the cleric, and particularly of the canon, because that had been the task of the apostles.[104] Dominic always found both strength and joy in the recitation of the canonical office, even at the most disturbed moments of his life, even as he travelled along the highroads; on the last day of his life, worn out by fatigue and with the hand of death already upon him, he would still go off to sing Matins in the middle of the night before lying down to rest for ever.[105] Thus he spent little time outside the church and, 'in order to procure time for his contemplation, he was more or less never seen outside the monastery enclosure.'[106]

He had not forgotten his first feelings as a child in the presence of the sufferings of the world or the deeds of heroic mercy which they had inspired in him in Palencia. The evangelical life of the cenacle in no way excluded the service of others and if the apostles instituted deacons to save their time, it was not only to devote themselves the better to prayer, but also to teaching.[107] More than of the miseries of the body, the cleric had to think of the greater misery of the soul which had to be saved. More than the bread for the body, he had to give the living water of prayer and the bread of the word of God. Contemplative prayer then became fervent petition and meditation on the Gospel wholly apostolic.

> God had given him a special grace of prayer for sinners, the poor, those in distress; he made their misfortunes his own in the intimate sanctuary of his compassion and the tears which welled from his eyes were an indication of the fervour which was burning in him. It was a very usual habit with him to spend the night in prayer. With the door closed, he prayed to his Father.[108] In the course of his prayer it was his custom to utter cries and words expressive of his heart's groanings. He could not contain himself and these cries, uttered so impetuously, were distinctly heard from the storey above. One of his frequent and particular requests to God was that he would grant him true and effective charity in such a way that he would devote himself to procuring the salvation of men, for he thought that he would not truly be a member of Christ until the day when he could give himself wholly, with all his force, to winning souls, as the Lord Jesus, Saviour of all men, devoted himself wholly to our salvation.[109]

A great event occurred which gave full meaning to this prayer. A short time after his profession in the chapter, he received the priesthood. He was now twenty-five—the minimum age, it is true, but adequate for this cleric who was over-mature for his years.[110] Moreover, his religious profession, by attaching him to one particular church, provided him with the 'title' without which he could not be ordained.[111] The priesthood. That meant the possibility of frequently adding the sacrifice of the Word, the *Verbum Dei*, to the sacrifice of his lips as they praised the Lord. The possibility, also, of carrying this Word to other men by preaching. He must have begun to preach straight away. A few years later, when his ministry was brought out into the full light of history, Dominic was to appear as a great preacher. He would then no longer be a beginner. Obviously he had already preached the Word of God times without number to the faithful of Osma and to others too. One witness fairly well informed as to his activities at the time relates that he knew how to win for himself the friendship of all, rich and poor, Jews and infidels (who were numerous in Spain), and that all visibly loved him, except the heretics whom he attacked and vanquished in his disputes and sermons. 'Yet he exhorted them and invited them with charity to do penance and return to the faith.'[112] It was not long before certain functions were given him which put him more directly in contact with the spiritual needs of men. A charter of 18th August, 1199 shows that he was sacristan of the chapter, that is, of the cathedral, organizing the whole of the liturgical life.[113] Two years later, on 13th January, 1201, when aged twenty-eight to thirty, he was sub-prior, sometimes called upon to govern his brethren.[114]

From that time onwards Dominic was in charge of souls. He gave Christ to the faithful. He truly became an apostle in every sense of the word. He was led to this gift of himself, to this effective work in the Christian community by the deep instinct of his nature, the inspiration of his bishop and prior, as well as by the general movement of the Church in Castile. From the days of St Peter Damian more than one Canon Regular in the city chapters of the cathedrals and of the reformed collegiate churches also aspired to become apostolic through the sacred ministry. If they led the life of the apostles, it was clearly to make themselves worthy of this work of salvation entrusted to them.[115] Some of them even dared eagerly to maintain that the ministry was the true manner of imitating the apostles.[116] The customs of St Rufus, the influence of which on the Canons Regular of Spain was considerable, did not in any case hesitate to base the primacy of the order of canons on the fact of this apostolate. 'For [the canon] is the successor of Christ and the apostles, substituted for them in the ministry of preaching, of baptism and of the other sacraments of the Church.'[117]

Even in a cathedral, it is true, the number of canons able to devote themselves to the apostolic ministry was very restricted. The chapter of Osma did not even serve its incorporated churches itself. Dominic's preaching was an exception. Necessarily applying himself more closely to pastoral work through his functions as sacristan or as sub-prior, Dominic was already beginning to give himself to men according to the secret desire of his prayer. God, however, was preparing for him, also in secret, an even greater opportunity of giving effect to his prayer.

CHAPTER IV

THE MARCHES

'WHILE the lovely Rachel was warming him in this way with her embraces, Lia lost patience. She insisted that he should compensate her blemish by giving her, through his visit, a numerous posterity.'[1] It was in these terms that the chronicler announced in the language of symbolic theology the great change in the life of St Dominic. Rachel signifies contemplation, Lia action. The contemplative life was to overflow into the life of the apostolate. The cloister of Osma opened its doors and Dominic, in the train of his bishop, was plunged into the great game of the ecclesiastical and temporal politics of Christendom. A tiny pawn, manipulated by a royal hand, he was to move across the whole of the European chessboard which he would one day fill with the activity of his sons.

In the month of May, 1203, Alfonso VIII came with his court to the royal city of San Esteban de Górmaz which was close by Osma.[2] Around the king and his officers could be seen a succession of *ricos hombres* and numerous bishops of Castile: Martín, Archbishop of Toledo and Primate of the Spains, Arderico of Palencia, Rodrigo of Sigüenza, (San) Julián of Cuenca, Juan of Calahorra, Brice of Plasencia, Fernando, Bishop-elect of Burgos and, naturally, Diego, the bishop of the place. At the side of the king stood Queen Leonor, daughter of the all too famous Eleanor of Aquitaine, and a young boy of thirteen and a half, the Infanta don Fernando,[3] sole male heir to the kingdom since the death of his brother, the Infanta Sancho.[4]

On 13th May, these great ecclesiastics, together with the king, the queen and the Infanta Fernando, confirmed the foundation of a convent of nuns of the Holy Spirit which Diego had just established in Soria.[5] Then the court left. Diego followed it. It is known that he was with it in Atienza on the 18th and in Berlanga on the 20th.[6] This was not the first time that the bishop had met the court. Immediately after his consecration, in December 1201,[7] he had rejoined Alfonso VIII at Burgos and he had seen him again quite recently.[8] It was, however, the second time in less than a year that Alfonso VIII had come to San Esteban de Górmaz to hold his court.[9] It is very clear that this was not a case of the royal court coming out of its way for the sole purpose of confirming the foundation of an obscure convent of nuns. Jordan of Saxony informs us explicitly that the king 'came to find' the bishop in order to entrust an important matter to his care. 'He had conceived the project of marrying his son Fernando to a noble girl from the Marches.'[10] The bishop accepted and was soon on the road, taking Dominic with him.

These few laconic words have strangely excited and at the same time embarrassed Dominican historiography down to recent times.[11] Which Marches are in question? Almost a dozen territories were then so called, from the Comté de la Marche in the Limousin, the marches of Ancona and Verona, down to the marches of Misnia, of Lusace and of Brandenburg, and the Danish march. It must at once be pointed out that for Jordan of Saxony, a German from the north-east,[12] the word 'marches' in its absolute meaning could only refer to one of the last four territories.[13] Confirmation of this may be found in the terms he used to describe the length and hardships of the journey;[14] the marches of which he was speaking were those furthest away from Castile, consequently those of the north. This enables us to accept as certain the new detail introduced some thirty years after Jordan by the author of a chronicle—'Marchia Dacie',[15] the Marches of Dacia, that is, Denmark. We may wonder how Denmark came to enter into the projects of the King of Castile.

Actually there is nothing mysterious about the plan and contemporary history gives its significance clearly.[16] In the shifting and entangled interplay of high European politics, Alfonso VIII could not disassociate himself from what was happening even in Scandinavia. The freer contact between Castile and Europe in the time of Alfonso VI and of Bernard of Sédirac had not only brought about fruitful changes in the ecclesiastical order—the sovereigns had begun to turn their eyes towards affairs beyond the Pyrenees. The dynasty itself had ceased to be a closed one and the Burgundian, Toulouse and English marriages had brought such preoccupations even within the range of family interests. At the beginning of the thirteenth century, Alfonso VIII was preparing to recover by arms the inheritance of his mother-in-law, Eleanor of Aquitaine.

He was going to find England against him—its alliance with the Guelph emperor Otto of Brunswick was already in preparation. Accordingly, to counter this, he again approached their adversary the King of France, Philip Augustus. He had given him his own daughter Blanche for daughter-in-law. Earlier, Philip himself had been linked by marriage to the Danish family who possessed rights over England, but feared the Guelph. The bonds between Castile and France against England and the Empire, then, could only be strengthened by a marriage between the two families of Castile and of Denmark. These families, moreover, were already closely connected, some of the alliances being very recent. The late King Cnut VI (d. 1202) had married a niece of Alfonso VIII, whereas Blanche, the daughter of Alfonso VIII, by her French marriage had just become the niece of this same Cnut and of his successor, the reigning King Valdemar II.

The Infanta Fernando was thirteen and a half. It was time to seek a wife for him. Blanche and Louis of France had recently married at the age of twelve. Alfonso himself had been fifteen when he had had his marriage with Leonor of England approved by the Cortes of Burgos.[17] But who was to be the fiancée?

A daughter of Valdemar the Great must be ruled out because of the difference of age.[18] Cnut VI had died without children. Valdemar II was not yet married.[19] Thus Jordan does not speak of marriage with a king's daughter, but with a young girl of noble blood. A Scandinavian historian who has devoted particular attention to the problem[20] considers, after having eliminated the other solutions, that it could only be a daughter of the elder sister of Valdemar II, the wife of Count Siegfried of Orlamund. Connected with the marches of Misnia through his countship, an Ascanian like the other Margraves of Brandenburg, a faithful member of the royal family of Denmark whose leopards his son had incorporated in his coat of arms, Siegfried belonged *par excellence* to the nobility of the Marches.[21] Jordan's expression, 'a noble girl from the Marches', would thus be shown here, as on many other occasions, to be aptly chosen.

The bishop lost no time in getting on the road. It was the end of May. This journey to the north, which according to Jordan must have cost 'many and painful efforts', would be more easily accomplished during the summer months. It was an important affair. A bishop did not move about without his household or a bodyguard. The third Council of the Lateran, a few years earlier, had expressed astonishment at the large number of horsemen which bishops in the course of their pastoral visitations considered it indispensable to take with them and to impose on the parishes which received them. Certain poor churches found themselves constrained to sell even the sacred vessels to pay for their 'procurations', i.e. requirements, and watched the bishop's suite consuming in a few hours a whole year's provisions. Thus the Council fixed as the maximum for the bishop's escort twenty to thirty horses.[22] Sees that were poor were clearly not bound to go to the full limit, and this was the case with Diego's small diocese. A deed of 1270 shows that the Bishop of Osma for his ordinary journeys was accompanied by four horses only, about ten if he was accompanied by an archdeacon and a canon.[23] This time, however, a royal mission was in question. It was necessary to come within reasonable distance of the ceiling fixed by the Council. There were, with the soldiers of the escort, several servants, an interpreter, some merchants from the north who would act as guides,[24] finally a counsellor, as well as a companion in prayer, Dominic, the sub-prior of the church.[25] It is not difficult to imagine Dominic on horseback riding behind his bishop, just like the canon who follows San Pedro de Osma on a bas-relief of the tomb in the cathedral (1258). He would be covered down to the feet in an ample black cloak whose folds protected his hands, whilst he held the reins and manipulated the huge bridle-bit of a somewhat lean horse. A narrow hood, whose point fell behind, entirely enveloped his head. The bishop was dressed in the same way, but he wore on top of his hood a broad-brimmed hat, the emblem of his rank.

The sources tell us little of the journey. The only halting-place along the road which is mentioned is Toulouse.[26] The travellers, following the ancient Roman roads, doubtless went through Soria to Saragossa to rejoin the French road to Santiago at Jaca.[27] Then through the Somport, Oloron, Morlaàs, they reached the capital of the county of Toulouse. This route had the advantage of avoiding Navarre, the enemy of Castile.

As soon as they had crossed the Pyrenees the two men of God were able to confirm a fact which up till then they knew only through public rumour—the countless number of Christians in the lands of the Count of Toulouse who had allowed themselves to be won over to heresy. There were several sorts, grouped together under the geographical name of Albigensians, though the diocese of Albi had not been more contaminated than the neighbouring regions. Some were the late successors of Pierre de Bruys or of Henri de Lausanne;[28] others were Waldenses or poor men of Lyons, disciples of the former merchant Valdes;[29] above all, there were Catharists.[30] This new religion, brought from the east by traders or pilgrims about 1140, perhaps even by oriental missionaries, then disseminated by interchanges which became especially frequent at the time of the second crusade,[31] had taken deep root in the county of Toulouse. In 1173, the religious head of that part of the country, the Archbishop of Narbonne, Pons d'Arsac, could write to the King of France, the supreme overlord: 'The Catholic faith is receiving tremendous attacks in our diocese and the bark of Peter is undergoing such buffetings from the heretics that it is almost on the point of sinking.'[32]

Very early provided with a leader or bishop from the region of Albi, the sect already counted four such in 1167, and would have five in 1229. Historians today know the names of more than twenty of these 'bisbes' of the Catharists of the Midi.[33] The movement, indeed, which had affected Champagne, France, the Rhineland, Flanders, England and even the south of Italy, had likewise taken root in Lombardy. Whereas, however, in the north of Italy Catharism split up after the end of the twelfth century into several hostile churches, in the region of Albi it remained monolithic and radical, under the guidance of its leaders. These leaders, seconded by their 'elder sons', their 'younger sons' and their deacons, had available in each genuine Catharist follower, or 'Perfect', an ardent propagandist. Dressed in black, austere, of an undoubted purity of morals, for they practised absolute continence, sober to the point of abstaining from all food produced by carnal intercourse, such as meat, milk products and eggs, poor indeed, but having at their common disposal very large financial resources,[34] the clergy of the Catharists and the 'Perfect' found among all classes of the population an audience which the Catholic clergy were in the process of losing in a large number of places.

Earlier heresies had paved the way for their success. Sent to preach in the neighbourhood just when this religious sect was beginning to spread, St Bernard had not obtained any permanent result—in one church, even, the failure had been crushing. In 1165 an ecclesiastical assembly which had called upon the chief leaders of the Catharists to appear, at Lombers, had turned into a wrangle from which the sectaries had gone away with more assurance than ever. Shortly afterwards, in 1167, at St Félix de Caraman, the latter held a veritable council, presided over by the oriental 'pope', Nicetas of Constantinople.[35] After that time, neither the repeated sending of apostolic legates, more often than not cardinals or Cistercian abbots, nor certain military expeditions such as the siege of the castle of Lavaur in 1181, nor the application of measures which were a prelude to the birth of the Inquisition, diminished the enthusiasm of the new religion. In the meantime the disaffection of the majority of the lay authorities, and of an important mass of the population, in regard to the Church, eventually produced its fruit—mockery, indifference, sacrilege, churches abandoned or confiscated for profane uses, monasteries despoiled and disorganized, or even contaminated by heresy, grave and violent injustices against the clergy, going even to the point of assassination.

As they advanced on their way, Diego and Dominic learnt to appreciate the extent of the crisis by the sad confidences of the clergy or of the orthodox faithful whom they met by chance along the roads or in the inns. As convinced Christians, their hearts sank. More than for the Church herself, for whom they did not yet quite measure the danger, it was for 'these innumerable souls who were deceived that they felt moved by deep compassion'. They guessed indeed more than they could see. The Christian appearance of the life of the convinced Catharists did not allow them to be easily unmasked. One evening, however, Dominic in Toulouse found himself face to face with one of them—who happened to be his host.[36]

He must have recognized him for what he was through some word of spite against the Church—in their eyes the Babylon of the Apocalypse—through some reticence in regard to baptism or the Eucharist; or perhaps, what would have been particularly painful to him, from an expression of contempt in regard to the sign of the cross. One of his companions who made the sign as he was entering a castle one day heard something of this kind. A knight who saw him cross himself murmured 'may such sign of the cross never assist me.'[37] So people calling themselves Christians were enemies of the cross of Christ.[38] In truth, this was indeed the case. Dominic was going to learn this then and there from personal experience. For he could not but react to the pain of the profound disagreement revealed in this way. He forced his host to justify his belief. Contrary to the great majority of the 'believers' of the Catharists, who held their opinions only superficially, this man was a convinced believer;[39] he may have been one of the Catharist deacons who ran hospices in the towns. All night long, forgetting his condition as a passing stranger, forgetful of the fatigue of the road which he was to resume once more the following morning, Dominic pressed him with his searching questions.[40]

This man's belief must indeed have disconcerted him. At first he saw before him only a Christian gone astray, sincerely impressed by the Gospel. Indeed, as will be seen later, the 'evangelism' of the twelfth century was undoubtedly one of the sources of Catharism. As Dominic, however, gradually constrained his questioner to lay bare the fundamental basis of his attitude, through that art of discussion which is proper to scholasticism, he discovered something quite different. With a hundred years of work on the history of religions behind us, we can today situate Catharism among the dualist tendencies, the manifold springs of which had begun to bubble up long before the time of Christ, not only in the Semitic world but also in Persia and in Greece.[41] More precisely, we have no difficulty in placing it among the forms of Gnosticism, those pre-Christian religions which, as far back as the second century produced a crop of erroneous tendencies even in the infant Church. Catharism, however, despite its assertions,[42] was not directly attached to any form of primitive Gnosticism. At the origin of the Albigenses we can today clearly discern the Bogomils, a movement which began in Bulgaria in the middle of the tenth century.[43] The Bogomils perhaps received some of their dogmas from the Paulicians,[44] who were Gnostics, found in Armenia since the eighth century, several groups of whom were afterwards deported to Thrace. The Messalians are also spoken of . . . . There our knowledge of the earliest influences to which the Catharists were subjected comes to an end. These medieval forms of Gnosticism had developed within the Christian framework and claimed to find their basis in the Gospel rather than in the Bible, the greatest part of which they abhorred. Their common source, however, was not the word of God, nor even a formal doctrine powerfully constructed. It was a spontaneous attitude in the face of life and of evil, an irrational sentiment of the soul's radical opposition to the world. This attitude gave rise to several inter-related doctrines, the elements of which were in a continual state of flux, and to practices equally variable, despite fundamental constants.

Two contradictory principles explained the radical opposition of the world with good. 'Two Gods', said the Albigensian Catharists, won over since 1167 to the absolute dualist doctrine of the 'Dragovitsian' Bogomils, which Nicetas of Constantinople brought to them from the East in that year: the God of good was the God of the Gospel; the other was the God of the Old

Testament. Souls were angels fallen into matter, i.e. under the domination
of the God of evil, those at least whose total chastity and purity revealed
their angelic nature. The extreme austerity of the 'Perfect' was a preparation
for their liberation which was effected by death. The imperfect liberation of
the 'believers' required fresh incarnations upon this earth, a metempsychosis
which might go as far as a return into the body of an animal. Such was the
Albigensian belief stripped of its artificial Gnostic cosmogonies, of its
cultural and ecclesiastical features of recent origin, finally of its Christian
veneer. Its Christianity was nothing more than a garment. Those for whom
evil was either the irresponsible fall of a soul into the world, or the accidental contact with matter and with corporeal life, could have little sense
of sin.[45] Those for whom salvation consisted in delivering oneself from flesh
and from matter could scarcely be said to put all their love and hope in
Christ Jesus. For them Christ was master, not redeemer. His death, Satan's
triumph, had only been an appearance, like his body.[46] His cross was not
the sign of salvation, but a scandal.[47]

Doubtless the poor man who found himself face to face with Dominic on
this night of tense controversy did not see things as clearly as this. The
philosophical weakness of his dualism—for a God who is not unique cannot
be God—escaped him, whereas he found it so convenient to solve the
anguishing problem of evil in a rough and ready way by invoking two
antagonistic Gods. Above all the anti-Christian character of Catharism
remained hidden from his eyes. It is the deep drama of so much hostile
propaganda in lands that have long been Christian, that unconsciously those
who listen to them transpose the words and ideas which are served out to
them into the nearest terms of their atavistic tradition, so much so that they
finally invest doctrines which are in every sense of the word strange with
colours and sentiments properly belonging to Christianity. They then
allow themselves to be seduced by the doctrines so transformed. In the
austerity of the Perfect, inspired by the hatred of matter, the populations of
the Midi of France certainly believed they recognized the spirit of penance
which the Gospel never ceases to urge upon us, in their cold chastity the
purity which reserves everything to God through love, in their poverty,
abandonment to Providence. Dominic was able to disentangle these absurdi-
ties and confusions. Being strong, he was able to argue unfalteringly and
using love, he was able to persuade. The innkeeper could not resist the Spirit
who spoke through lips of such conviction. When day dawned, he surrendered to the light.[48] Dominic went away full of joy at having won over
his brother, slightly taken aback at this close contact with heresy, filled with
encouragement at this first apostolic success outside the frontiers of his own
Castile. Already one of the souls whose vague call he had heard in his childhood, from the high cliffs of Caleruega, had now returned to the fold.
Innumerable others were now calling him across this vast territory of

Europe into which his road was going to take him.

At last the bishop and his escort arrived at the end of their journey. They found the court with which they were going to negotiate and were well received there.[49] There, as in Castile, the bishops held the first place in the Council of the King whose good understanding with the Church was one of the reasons for their success. A section of the higher clergy knew the West, particularly Italy and Paris, where several had done their studies. This was the case with the new head of the Church in Denmark, the Archbishop of Lund, Andrew Sunesen, whom we shall soon meet again. The girl, on her side, granted her 'consent'.[50] The term is in no sense ambiguous. It proves that the procedure for this kind of agreement was by *verba de praesenti* which constituted a genuine marriage though without its forms,[51] except in one case only.[52] Such betrothals were, moreover, current in unions between noble or royal children, in which politics had so large a share. It was, in the circumstances, a marriage by procuration.[53] Afterwards presents were exchanged. The accomplishment of the return to Spain was as laborious as the outward journey had been. The King of Castile, informed of what had been done, thanked and dismissed the bishop, then commissioned him to go out to the Danish March again and this time bring back the girl.[54]

To read Jordan's very concise text, one would imagine that the second expedition was carried out immediately. In actual fact it was only right that the men taking part should be allowed some rest. Moreover it is not easy to see, since the matter had been suggested by Castile and mutual consent had been exchanged in Denmark, why the bishop should have multiplied his journeys in this way at such a short interval of time. It would have been simpler, in that case, to bring the girl back the first time he returned. Doubtless political negotiations which required a certain lapse of time went hand in hand with the marriage proposals. It was perhaps necessary to wait for the age for consummation of the marriage. The Infanta reached the age of fifteen at the end of 1204. The second journey actually took place in the course of the year 1205, according to all appearances in summer.[55]

This time the escort was even more splendid, for it was now a cortège of honour for the purpose of bringing back the distant princess to Castile. They took with them the rich presents which were required in such circumstances, not to mention objects to be sold[56] in the course of the journey so as to provide the finances for it. Dominic again accompanied the bishop, as did also a fair number of clergy.[57] A disappointment awaited the ambassadors. The girl, says Jordan, had died in the meantime.[58]

If, as seems probable, we really are dealing with the daughter of the Count of Orlamund, matters had perhaps been more complicated than was publicly admitted. The learned Scandinavian whom we have already mentioned[59] draws attention in fact to two curious documents. One of them proves that between 1204 and 1206 the Count of Orlamund gave leave to two of his daughters to enter religion and set aside dowries for them at the abbey of Saint Mary and Saint Gothard in Heusdorf (today in Thuringia).[60] It may be asked whether the count had two daughters and whether he was wanting to settle them both at once. Now the other document[61] suggests a hypothesis that cannot be neglected: perhaps one of the two daughters was the bride of the youthful Fernando. The text in fact shows Archbishop Andrew of Lund, the Metropolitan of Denmark, at grips at this time with a difficult marriage case. A noble lady[62] who came under his jurisdiction, had been united by *verba de praesenti*, through the intermediary of an ambassador[63] and the giving of a present or symbolic pledges, to a foreigner of noble birth.[64] Six months later, however, she had gone back upon her engagement because she had heard, she asserted, that the man was a leper. So, to escape from a union which inspired her with horror, she had resolved to enter religion. The abbey had accepted her; however, in view of the fact that she was in some sort pledged to marriage, she was not given the virgins' veil but that of widows.

Her noble fiancé, however, on learning of this religious clothing, had sent a new embassy[65] to his wife to claim her, for he was resolved to consummate the marriage. The archbishop had then intervened, had forbidden any further step until the Church had pronounced judgement, then, having the lady brought before him, had assured himself of the reality of her original consent. He did not, however, wish to decide the question himself. Only the lady was under his jurisdiction.[66] Perhaps also he wanted to avoid too much responsibility. In the course of the autumn of 1205,[67] he sent a report to the Pope and asked for his decision: had the lady to be sent back to her husband or to be kept in the convent ? Such was the matter which had been preoccupying the head of the Church in Denmark since the summer.[68] It is difficult not to imagine that it refers precisely to the bride destined for the Infanta of Castile.

The archbishop was certain that the leprosy was a mere tale. It was manifestly a pretext which enabled the lady to put forward against her union one of the two exceptions which were still in force at this period to dissolve a marriage for which consent had been given but which was not yet consummated.[69] At the same time she had put perself in a position also to invoke the second: the entry into religion.[70] As regards the underlying motive of her action, we can understand only too well the hesitations of the young Danish girl in regard to this marriage which would take her so far away, if we think of the painful memory left in her family by the misfortunes of her aunt Ingeburg, sister of Valdemar II.[71] It was not twelve years since Ingeburg had left for the distant west to marry the King of France. It was the very day after her marriage with Philip Augustus that the unhappy queen, defenceless, and ignorant of the language of her country of exile, had been flouted, treated with contempt, shut up in a convent and repudiated, while an intruder occupied her husband's couch. For twelve years past, neither the authority of Innocent III, nor the threats of the Church, nor even the fulmination of an interdict against the kingdom of France had yet been successful in clearing up satisfactorily the cruel situation in which the queen found herself. It would seem better to shut oneself up at once in a convent in the north of Europe, than to suffer, far away in the south, insults of this type. The girl's father allowed himself to be influenced. In the summer of 1205, however, scruples had arisen in her uncle's court. It may be wondered where these scruples, of which people scarcely seemed aware when she took the veil, came from. It seems probable that they were elicited by the Bishop of Osma at the time when he was returning to Denmark to claim the promised fiancée. It was perhaps he, too, who took upon himself to go and take the request for intervention to the Pope.

Here we can leave the sphere of hypothesis. It is a fact that during the autumn King Valdemar the Victorious and the Archbishop of Lund sent simultaneously, through an ambassador, whose name is not given to us,[72] a series of reports and important requests to Pope Innocent III.[73] The letter relating to the marriage case was among them, which emphazises its gravity. The Pope must have received the packet of letters in December. He replied to them point by point between 12th and 20th January, 1206. It is also a fact, moreover, that on taking the return road to the west, in the middle of this same autumn, the Bishop of Osma, with Dominic still in his train, did not return to Castile. He contented himself with informing the king of the frustration of his embassy through a messenger,[74] a step that would have been very casual if all had been ended. As to himself, crossing the Alps, he went to Rome, to visit the Pope,[75] spending a part of the winter at the papal court,[76] for he was the unpaid ambassador of the King of Denmark. In any case he had several matters to submit in the course of this visit *ad limina*. One of them was personal—he had come to ask the Pope to accept his resignation from the see of Osma. He proposed to devote himself in future to the apostolate of the pagans.[77]

This plan, which is known to us from several simultaneous sources,[78] is an unquestioned fact. It is not what one would expect. Nothing in the bishop's previous activity in Osma or in his attitude in the course of the earlier journey allowed such a decision to be foreseen. It was, then, in the course of his visit to the regions in the north that he conceived it. A proof of this is given to us by the identity of the pagans whom he proposed to evangelize. Jordan of Saxony, who did not know their name directly, was reduced to conjectures about it. The first edition of his *Libellus* speaks of the Saracens, the second corrects this and speaks of the Cumans;[79] in both cases we are dealing with probable suppositions and nothing more.[80] Pierre des Vaux-de-Cernai, a Cistercian monk whose *Histoire albigeoise* is valuable for this part of the history of St Dominic, speaks only of the pagans.[81] In 1217, however, Dominic, who evidently shared in the apostolic projects of his bishop and since then had never despaired of taking them up once more, spoke of them in confidence to a young cleric in the Roman curia. He indicated in clear terms his firm intention, as soon as he had finished organizing his order, of abandoning all position of authority and going to evangelize Prussia and the other nordic countries.[82] It was clearly these pagans who were in question as far back as 1205, for his bishop as for himself. This time again general history throws a very clear light on his intention.

It was more than fifty years since the vast movement of *Drang nach Osten* had begun. This expansion of Christendom towards the east from the central part of the north had not slackened, but had undergone a considerable change at the turn of the thirteenth century.[83] In earlier times it was chiefly the Germans who had been its promoters. At one and the same time military, demographic, religious and civilizing, the expansion found its ecclesiastical roots in the archiepiscopal see of Bremen-Hamburg, and its temporal basis in Saxony (or Brunswick) and Brandenburg. A good part of the remainder of the country, however, collaborated in it by intense emigration. Religious Germany devoted itself to this expansion through the action of its bishops, its regular clergy, particularly the Premonstratensians and Cistercians, and its military orders.

After the death of Albert the Bear and the crushing of Henry the Lion by Barbarossa had broken for a time the force of expansion of Saxony and Brandenburg, Denmark in full phase of development had taken turns with Germany. The independence of the metropolitan see of Lund at the extremity of the Scandinavian peninsula, acquired since the twelfth century, had given the Danes an ecclesiastical centre whose influence soon exceeded that of Bremen-Hamburg, since it finally grouped under its authority as many as fifteen suffragan sees. In 1201 the great archbishop whom we have just met, Andrew Sunesen,[84] was appointed to this see. A man of interior life, zealous, a very good theologian, he enjoyed the confidence of Pope Innocent III who several times appointed him legate of the northern countries. His apostolic energy was later to find itself seconded by the military action of King Valdemar II as well as by the members of his own family, the Sunesønner. Now in this same year 1201, Bishop Albert[85] founded the city of Riga, to which he transferred the episcopal see of Livonia which had been evangelized by the Cistercians for the last twenty years. In 1205, the Archbishop of Lund and the Bishop of Riga prepared in common an extensive missionary campaign in Livonia and Estonia, which was to be protected by Danish and German forces, in particular those of the crusaders of Livonia and the knights known as Sword-bearers recently founded in Riga.[86] The expedition was to be launched the following year and was expected to bear much fruit. All along the Baltic Sea, however, from Pomerania to Finland, from the Isle of Oesel to the Isle of Rügen, the religious orders of the twelfth century and the newly founded sees supported more or less closely by the German feudal lords and the Danish and Polish nobles, devoted themselves to similar missionary enterprises. In such enterprises the considerable progress of the process of Christianization lay either in direct evangelization of the pagans or in their being driven back by Christian emigration from the West.[87]

In this summer of 1205, in the final stages of their journey and during their stay with the King of Denmark and the Archbishop of Lund, Diego and Dominic were thus able to rediscover, in a more intense degree, the atmosphere familiar to Castilians like themselves—projects, negotiations, preparations, recruitment of soldiers and apostles, for whom the horizon of military expeditions was the conquest of souls and of political expansion the planting of the Church. They were amazed to discover towards the East lands with no definite boundary where evangelization could thrust forward in search of pagans without let or hindrance. For they discerned at the same time, what was not the case in Spain, an undeniable effort to pass beyond military enterprises and frontiers and to influence the pagans in their territory by preaching. The mission of the Danes under the direction of Andrew of Lund sought to be more independent of military action than that of the German clerics. Thus, even more than in Spain, workers were lacking for the harvest for which the fields were white. There was a particular need of priests and clerics, and the bishops strove to attract them by all possible means in a recruiting campaign which resembled that of the crusade.[88] Archbishop Andrew liked to take zealous religious from the monasteries to form around himself a fervent community and a team of collaborators ready for any mission in the Church.[89] This was indeed an invitation for apostolic hearts. The quiet diocese of Osma whose reconstruction dated from less than a century earlier, already seemed Christian territory of long standing by the side of these new lands. The savage reactions of the pagans were there, paving the way for opportunities of glorious martyrdom. Missionaries who underwent lengthy tortures and were cut in pieces alive were spoken of. To the end of his life Dominic would preserve heroic regret for such a martyr's death in a very precise image.[90] Henceforward Diego wanted to be a missionary and nothing else, taking his companion, of course, with him. That was what he had come to declare to the head of Christendom, asking him to discharge him from his responsibilities as a bishop. Perhaps the letters in his hands from the Primate of Lund which asked for extraordinary powers from the Sovereign Pontiff for the coming mission in Estonia[91] provided a concrete explanation of this surprising request.

Innocent III refused. Ever since the end of the eleventh century the papacy had been following very closely and seconding energetically the reconquests and evangelization of Spain. Just as Urban II had not accepted the crusader's vow of the Archbishop of Toledo, Bernard de Sédirac, in 1095,[92] so Innocent III would not accept a resignation which proved all too clearly the value of the prelate of which Castile would thus have been deprived. Nor would he agree, despite the entreaties of Diego, to allow the bishop to go off to the missions with a crusader's indulgence, at the same time retaining his episcopal office.[93] On the contrary, he once more enjoined upon him his pastoral mission in the diocese of Osma.[94] As to the matrimonial problem, Innocent's decision was likewise against the conjugal bond.[95] It was thus necessary to start the journey back. In every respect the journey was ending in frustration and the very extensive horizon which had momentarily opened up seemed to be closing in again. On taking once again the road to Castile with their escort, an escort that was now pointless, Diego and Dominic could not help feeling that they were abandoning a providential task. Their immense pity for souls in the world had not ceased to be exercised under the most varied forms: the erring souls of Christians tempted by heresy in the valley of the Garonne and the plains of the Lauragais; the souls of the pagan Slavs—Wends, Prussians, Livonians, Estonians, savage and often even hostile in the far-stretching plains of the north. In the depths of his memory Dominic carried away the image of the sandy coasts of the Baltic sea, of its grey waters and innumerable islands. He hoped one day to return there as a missionary or at least to find genuine apostles for them. Already in his heart this paradox of history was germinating, the paradox that meant that St Dominic, born so to speak next door to the Saracens, was to dream to the end of his life of evangelizing the regions of the north, and was to create among them, during his own lifetime, powerful missionary provinces, whereas St Francis, who did not know the Moslems through the circumstances of his birth, succeeded in bringing the Gospel to them himself and sent them some of his best sons.

What happened then remains rather mysterious. It leads us to think that perhaps the Pope did not totally discourage the missionary goodwill of the two Castilians. Instead of returning to Spain by the route through Provence, the bishop and his companions went back towards the Great St Bernard. Crossing the Jura they passed over into Burgundy to visit Cîteaux.[96] Diego, once more, had just seen the Cistercians at work. The great order which Alfonso VIII was supporting with all his power in Castile had recently appeared to the Bishop of Osma in a less favourable aspect, for his diocese only knew the order under the guise of the fighting monks of Fitero-Calatrava, who had been received at San Pedro de Gumiel.[97] In actual fact the Order of St Bernard was something quite different—an immense reservoir of religious strength, both edifying and generous. Innocent III was continually drawing upon it for the general tasks of the Church. He was going to do so again for the great mission in Livonia-Estonia, for Pomerania, but above all for the Albigensian lands.[98] It would seem probable that he charged the bishop to urge the Cistercians to send into the territories of Toulouse the preachers whom up to that time his letters had reclaimed in vain.[99] Three years later, we learn that, when Milon and Thédise were appointed in Rome legates for the Albigensian territory, they went with all speed to Burgundy to meet the abbot of Cîteaux before going to Provence.[100] Perhaps Diego on his side received some unofficial mission connected with the Cistercians entrusted with the Albigensian territory.[101] An unexpected incident, related by Jordan, might lead us to believe so. When he arrived at Cîteaux, Diego wanted to be clothed in symbolic fashion[102] with the habit of the white monks and did not take the road to the south again until he was accompanied by several of the monks, whom the abbey readily consented to spare.[103]

The clothing in the monastic habit of a secular prelate was not an unheard-of thing; nor was it purposeless. It gave the stranger entry into the fraternity of the order and associated him with its activity. The gesture was particularly charged with meaning in the case of missionary enterprises.[104] When in 1199 Pierre de Castelnau had been provisionally associated with the Cistercian legate of the Narbonensis, he was a Canon Regular and Archdeacon of Maguelonne. Now, a few months before he received this office as his principal function, at the same time as a Cistercian from Fontfroide, in 1203, he was seen asking for the habit of St Bernard in this same abbey.[105] Before this, he had shown no wish at all for it, quite the contrary.[106] We do not know of his motives in detail.[107] One thing, however, is certain—his taking of the habit at Fontfroide ensured unity between the members of the pontifical mission and suppressed many causes of misunderstanding among the collaborators at a period when an over-attention to *esprit de corps* was everywhere multiplying ruinous quarrels.[108] Now Diego, as will be seen, was going to collaborate in the Cistercian mission immediately it left the mother abbey. It would seem that his visit and clothing were a kind of initial contact.

The hypothesis is attractive. It is difficult to decide to abandon it. Other known facts corroborate it.[109] The direct documents, however, do not support it. Jordan of Saxony, the only one to mention the journey to Cîteaux, has given another significance to the clothing—that the bishop was filled with admiration on discovering such a large number of servants of God and a religious life of such a high standard. This would have been the reason for his gesture. If later he met the Cistercian legates of the Narbonensis on the return journey to Spain, it was pure coincidence.[110]

Perhaps Jordan was mistaken or rather did not know the real state of the

matter. If he was right, however, the taking of the habit was an indication of
the place that Diego wanted to make for the Cistercians in his diocese and
even in his own life. It also marked his anxiety to link up the foundations of
the order in his territory with the Burgundian abbey directly and not with
San Pedro de Gumiel, any more than with the network of the abbeys of
Castile.[111] Certain monks were given him for this plan of development.[112] A
most dynamic prelate, he did not linger over projects that were over and
done with, and without delay thought out new fields of fruitful activity.[113]

The matrimonial mission had ended in failure. Providence, however, at its
good pleasure, disposed the ends of this mission in accordance with its
purposes of salvation. Providence thus used the journey as an occasion and a
prelude for a marriage that was of value in a different way, a marriage
between God and the souls which he intended to bring back through the
instrumentality of the whole Church, from many errors and sins, to the
betrothal of eternal salvation. Events would prove this to be so.[114]

CHAPTER V

THE NARBONENSIS

W HEN Innocent III assumed the government of Christendom in
1198, it was a long time since the Catholic Church had been
guided by a hand so mighty, so sure of itself. Certainly to find a
Pontiff equally decided one would have to go back seventeen years earlier,
through a series of short-lived Popes, to the energetic figure of Alexander III.
Innocent, however, was even greater than Alexander. The extent of the
tasks which this Pope of thirty-seven fearlessly devoted himself from the
first moment of his reign, and the effectiveness of the actions he undertook
on all sides at once to carry out his responsibilities, is truly astonishing.
Spiritual and moral encouragement, preaching and supervision of doctrine,
the government of men and of institutions, settlement of an imperial schism
and the correction of kings, the crusade in the East and the reform of the
West; all these he dealt with, together with many other problems, in the
full consciousness of his duty and his powers.

In the vineyards of the Lord that his immediate predecessors had partially
neglected, one matter was to cause him some of his greatest anxieties. He
inscribed it, indeed, in the programme of the Fourth Council of the Lateran
at the end of his life, as Alexander III had done in the Third Council.[1] This
was the peril to the faith in the region that Frenchmen of the time called the
'Albigeois' and the Roman documents, Provence—to speak precisely, in the
territories which found their centre of gravity in the ecclesiastical province
of the Narbonensis and in the lay county of Toulouse.[2] These lands, which
St Dominic was to travel across in all directions during a dozen years,
comprised the archiepiscopal see of Narbonne with its suffragan sees of
Toulouse, Carcassonne, Elne, Béziers, Agde, Lodève, Maguelonne (Substan-
tion),[3] Nîmes and Uzès; to which it was necessary to add a circle of dioceses
—Couserans–Saint–Liziers and St Bertrand de Comminges in the province of
Auch; Agen, in that of Bordeaux; Albi and Rodez, in that of Bourges;
Viviers, in that of Vienne; finally Avignon and Orange in the province of
Arles. To these territories the Pontifical Letters joined, so far as defence of
the faith was concerned, the provinces of Aix and Embrun, which were
partially dependent in temporal matters on the Count of Toulouse.

The activity of St Dominic in the Albigeois was preaching. As such it
formed part of the intensive action against heresies conducted by Innocent in

this territory.[4] This activity in turn appeared inextricably linked, in the documents as in actual fact, with an effort which causes us some surprise, a relentless campaign against bands of mercenaries: 'Almost the whole universe knows how much the Church has struggled through her preachers and her crusaders to eliminate the heretics and the mercenaries from the province of Narbonne, and from the neighbouring regions',[5] was the way the Pope summed up his work in the Albigeois on a solemn occasion. About forty years earlier, the 27th canon of the Council of the Lateran, a result of the Church's experience in this very territory, similarly connected the two together.[6] Finally all this was set within the framework of one general matter, the *negotium fidei et pacis*,[7] the pivot, at the turn of the thirteenth century, of a variety of individual actions of the Church in the south of France, of which the movement of the peace of God had been the source.[8] What was in question was an enterprise of Christian civilization, in which the defence of the faith and of ecclesiastical communities went hand in hand with the safeguarding of peace, the protection of the weak, the freedom of the highways, the prohibition of usury and of new taxes.[9] For this action, in which the bishops and the Pope followed closely the elementary interests of Christian society now confronted with the disorders of the first centuries of feudalism, they had been endowed by that society with means of temporal coercion which would henceforth support the effectiveness of their spiritual sanctions. The background of the actions of St Dominic, 'indefatigable promoter of peace and faith'[10] is thus shown to be singularly complex. The meaning and value of his actions cannot be measured without evoking their context in Christendom.

The attitude of the Christians of that time was relatively simple. The prince, in their view, wielded the sword to ensure the temporal security of the values essential to man. None of them mattered more than peace, the liberty of the Church, orthodoxy. Orthodoxy was more important than all else, since an error in the way of salvation might prove permanently irreparable. It was thus for the Church to watch over orthodoxy and to remind the prince of his duty of defending it at the same time as spiritual liberty and peace. The prince had not the right to constrain the infidel and the Jew to accept the faith, for faith cannot be forced; but he had the duty of obliging the baptized to remain faithful to the promises of their baptism.[11] He protected the people by eliminating heretics, that is to say, those holding perverted opinions who actively propagated their sect from his territory. If, however, the prince did not fulfil his threefold task of peace, of liberty and of fidelity, it was the duty of the hierarchy to constrain him to do so by spiritual sanctions. Equally it could set in motion against him the arm of his overlord or of the king whose vassal he was. Should the suzerain himself be in default the hierarchy was not without a weapon. By releasing subjects from their oath of fidelity, by 'exposing as a prey'[12] the territory of the defaulter, by binding the vassals together in an oath of peace, the hierarchy constituted a half-revolutionary force of coercion in the service of peace and orthodoxy. To defend these essential values it might even summon a real crusade against the unworthy prince. The 27th canon of the Lateran gave the essential rulings for this.[13]

Such were the formulae which governed the *negotium fidei et pacis* in the time of St Dominic. These formulae appeared logical and natural enough. They were to prove as provocative of bloodshed in actual fact as the feudal formulae and were to lead to massacres which inspire us with horror, because they introduced into religious controversies the summary proceedings of political and military operations and the uncontrolled reactions of the instincts of defence and fear of the popular masses. Before judging them, however, it should be remembered that such dramas were the consequence, a consequence which on this point was disastrous, of ideas and sentiments which made Europe and Western civilization—the desire, spontaneous and sincere, despite its compromises with conscience and its blunders, of building a complete human order on a single faith.

Such formulae made the smooth working of Christendom depend on a system of actions which controlled and supported each other in turn. Should one of those responsible for such actions come to default, the reaction of the others should re-establish the equilibrium. A grave crisis could not break out unless such defections extended to almost every sector of the Church. The catastrophe which threatened Christianity in the Albigeois thus had causes which were genuinely complex, and were as much temporal as they were ecclesiastical and spiritual.

They were of relatively recent origin. At the time of the Gregorian reform, nothing had enabled men to foresee this crisis. Careful research[14] has recently shown that the province of the Narbonensis then contained only a very limited number of simoniacal prelates, side by side with good, sometimes very good, pastors. The lower clergy seem to have been less contaminated by incontinence than elsewhere. The abbeys, which were numerous, were still following the influence of the reforming movement which with St Benedict Aniane had gone forth from their midst to renew the spirit of Carolingian monachism. As to the feudal lords of the region, they had supplied the first crusade with its basic contingents and its military leader in the person of the Count of Toulouse, Raymond de St Gilles, most loyal to the mind of the Pope. The reform, coming upon the scene in the midst of these circumstances, had met with good will in the various milieux. Abuses existed, but they were in part unconscious. The laity restored, at least in exchange for repurchase, numerous churches and tithes. The episcopal sees and many abbeys recovered the freedom of their elections.

To defend their independence the bishops could develop their temporal power. The abbeys, moreover, saw assigned to them a sometimes considerable number of parishes which they were to provide with more worthy clergy. Finally Cîteaux, after Cluny, obtained a foothold in the land. After such an inauguration in the twelfth century, this province might have been expected to be particularly brilliant on the Catholic plane. It was the contrary that happened; it may well be wondered why.

As to temporal affairs,[15] one great fact dominated the history of these regions—the powerlessness of the Counts of Toulouse, Counts of Albi, Dukes of Narbonne and Marquises of Provence, to set up a powerful and unified principality, a genuine replica of the kingdom of France which the Capetian dynasty was creating to the north of the Loire. It was true that Raymond V (d. 1194) had extended his suzerainty over vast regions east and west of the Rhône, between the Garonne and the Alps. For the territories to the east, however, he had had to struggle interminably against the house of Aragon. Too weak to continue the struggle, he had finally abandoned the county of Provence to Aragon, and had contented himself with the marquisate, that is to say, with the suzerainty over the fiefs of the north. Around Toulouse, towards the west, his successor Raymond VI had obtained a few victories—Agen, Rodez, Viviers, the Gévaudan; he even finally obtained the homage of the Viscount of Narbonne, a Lara of Castile. He did not, however, bring under his authority either his immediate neighbours to the south, the Counts of Foix and of Comminges, those petty kings of the Pyrenees, or the Lord of Montpellier. Moreover, he possessed only an illusory authority over the chief of his vassals and his adversaries, the powerful Trencavel, Viscount of Béziers, Carcassonne, Razès and Albi, whose domains, solidly grouped to the immediate west of Toulouse, intersected his own territories from north to south and broke his power.

Now the King of England, present in Aquitaine, periodically exerted pressure on the Count of Toulouse to constrain him to do him homage. The King of Aragon, the enemy of Provence, was also master of the Roussillon to the south of the Narbonensis and even, from 1204 onwards, of Montpellier. From there he gave his effective aid to Trencavel's rebellions. Finally, the King of France, the theoretical overlord to whom Count Raymond V had recently launched an anguished appeal for help,[16] paralysed at the turn of the thirteenth century by his own quarrels with England, could not and would not do anything to remedy the disorder of these lands in the south. Add to this the insubordination of the great vassals of Trencavel—the lords of the Lauragais, the Saissageois, the Cabardès, the Minervois, the Termenès, the Razès and of the land Sault; the even more pronounced insubordination of the towns of Toulouse, Carcassonne, Béziers, Nîmes or Avignon; and finally the anarchical spirit of a peasant nobility that was numerous and half-starving—and it will be understood what factors of disruption were at work in the domains of the Count of Toulouse. This land of rebellion was becoming in particular the refuge of heresiarchs expelled in turn from the other principalities of the west. Christian peace and justice were the first to suffer from them.

The life of the Midi of France at the outset of the thirteenth century is all too easily painted in idyllic colours—toleration, easy love, the song of the troubadours.[17] The brilliant splendour of the courts of Carcassonne and of Toulouse in the time of Roger II and of the 'good Count' Raymond V is beyond question. The deep-rooted immorality of these southern princes is likewise beyond question. Far, however, from being an unending source of joy, this lack of moral discipline was one of the causes of the blood-stained dramas of the land. We have only to think of Eleanor of Aquitaine or of Pedro II of Aragón. In any case the drama was real enough. The land was laid waste by continual violence of which the principal cause was the frustration of the effort of unity aimed at by the house of Saint-Gilles. Treaties between Toulouse and Aragon (1176, 1184, 1200)[18] might be multiplied, marriage ties formed between Aragon, Toulouse and Trencavel, the sworn peace renewed in 1191 and 1195[19]—all such remedies were only provisional so long as the political problem of the supreme unity was not solved. Moreover, violence was so deeply rooted everywhere that it continued even within a period of truce—sudden attacks, confiscation, pillage, brigandage by bands of ruffians, continued to increase even in the time of peace.

This was because the vagueness of the link between vassal and lord, by restraining the military power of the feudal leaders, forced them to recruit mercenaries to maintain their enterprises. Thus there arose those bands of mercenaries, Aragonese, men of Navarre, Gascons and even hired soldiers from Brabant, whose brutalities filled the documents of the time.[20] Commanded by the princes who had engaged them or left to their own devices when they were dismissed, the mercenaries recognized no limits. 'They exercised such cruelty in regard to Christians', the Third Council of the Lateran had already declared,[21] 'that they respected neither churches nor monasteries, spared neither widows, orphans, old men, children, age nor sex. Like pagans they destroyed everything and laid waste everything.' With the poor folk whose defence she had undertaken, the Church was thus the first victim of these ruffians who found in sacrilege an additional zest to their cruelties. They were also thought to be linked with the heretics, since they shared their hatred of the clergy. The Church in any case pursued both one and the other with the same movement, in the illusion that by snatching the weapon of mercenary troops from the hands of the feudal lords, she would force them to peace and would then enable them to fulfil their rôle as Christian rulers better by defending the faith.

Her utterances, however, were in vain. At the turn of the thirteenth century the feudal lords, beginning with Raymond VI, kept their mercenaries.

Raymond VI did not content himself with keeping them despite the Church; he was the first to set them against her. When he entered the province of Arles at the head of his Aragonese, ravaging all he found in his way, he was met by the Bishop of Orange who begged him to spare the monasteries and at least to refrain from devastating the land during the times of truce and the great feasts. Raymond, then seizing the bishop's right hand, swore by that hand that he would respect neither times of truce nor Sundays, and would spare neither holy places nor churchmen. Now this oath, or rather this perjury, added Innocent III,[22] 'he observed more scrupulously than any of those he had taken in a just cause'. Pillage and devastation, the usurpation of lands and rights, churches robbed, burned or transformed into fortresses, monks and clerics molested, a bishop despoiled and driven from his see, another imprisoned with his clergy whilst his palace and his chapter were destroyed—such was the violence against the Church to which in 1209 Raymond had to plead guilty. He had committed many other violent actions.[23] Lists equivalent in length or even longer could be established in regard to the other feudal lords of the vicinity[24]—Roger II of Béziers, Raymond-Roger Count of Foix, Bertrand de Saissac, Olivier de Termes, Raymond de Niort and his brothers, etc. Such lists could also be established in connection with certain towns—that of Lodève which robbed and mal-treated its bishop in 1198,[25] that of Carcassonne which in 1207 expelled its bishop;[26] that of Béziers which two years earlier had assassinated the holder of the see.[27] We may wonder what was the cause of such violence.

At this time both the lords and the communes were tempted by the hope of easy gain to assaulting the property of the Church without scruple in many other places of Christendom. The instability and disorder of the Midi, however, lent themselves to this more particularly. The failure of the Count of Toulouse in his efforts at hegemony further exasperated him when con-fronted with the possessions and temporal powers of the Church, to the enlargement of which the restitutions of the Gregorian period had contri-buted in a curious way at the expense of the laity.[28] At the other end of the feudal hierarchy the wretchedness of the country nobles sharpened their instinct for pillage. Egalitarianism of succession, a heritage from Roman law, had brought the feudal patrimonies to nothing, multiplying co-lords in the same locality[29]—thirty-five at Mirepoix, forty-three at Rabasteins, fifty at Lombers, more than fifty at Fanjeaux.[30] The disproportion between the poverty of the knights and the wealth of the monasteries accumulated by mortmain was marked.

The principal cause for the attacks of the laity, however, lay elsewhere. The documents leave no doubt at all as to this. The reason must primarily be sought in the virulent anti-clericalism which the nobility and the townsmen of the Albigensian lands derived from their contacts with the heretics.[31] If the

burghers of Carcassonne had banished their bishop in 1207, it was because
he had dared to speak against the heretics from the pulpit.[32] If the Count of
Foix allowed two monks of Saint-Antonin de Pamiers to be cruelly massacred
by one of his loyal followers, then starved the monks and the abbot by bolting
them into their chapel whilst he defiled, pillaged and destroyed the abbey,
and finally drove these unfortunate men almost naked out into the country,
it was because they dared to close the place whose lords they were against a
certain 'Perfect', his aunt.[33] Bertrand de Saissac, like Guillaume de Minerve,
Pierre-Roger de Cabaret, Pierre-Roger de Mirepoix, Raymond or Olivier
de Termes, was a notorious heretic. Moreover, he was guardian of the young
Raymond-Roger Trencavel, whom he was bringing up in reverence for the
sect.[34] Raymond-Roger, Count of Foix, of whom we have just been speaking
had allowed Phillippa, his wife, to become a 'Perfect' and to go and keep,
in Dun, a house for ladies belonging to the Catharists, at which house he
actually used to go and visit her.[35] He also had two sisters in the sects.
He was personally present at the solemn reception into heresy of his sister
Esclarmonde and of four other ladies, about 1204, in Fanjeaux, in the
presence of the nobility of the district, almost all congregated there.[36] Such
assemblies of nobles were usual in the Albigeois for participation in some
solemn rite of heresy, to listen to a disputation, or to receive the ordinary
teaching of a 'bisbe' or of a deacon of the Catharists; instances at this time
are mentioned by the documents in the majority of places in the Lauragais,
the Razès, and the region of Toulouse. A number of lords had a mother or
a sister living in one or other of the communities of Catharists and they
willingly entrusted their children to them for their upbringing.[37] The
information acquired later by the Inquisition or by the investigators commissioned by St Louis leaves no doubt: at the beginning of the thirteenth
century almost the whole of the feudal class in the County of Toulouse and
the Viscounty of Béziers-Carcassonne was favourable to the heresy, or at
least influenced by its preaching. Whole families of Catharists existed going
back three or four generations. The situation was the same in the majority
of the cities with borough rights. The case of Carcassonne and of Béziers has
already been seen; Toulouse—*Tolosa, Tota dolosa*,[38] said the proverb—had
for long been contaminated to such an extent that the bishop scarcely felt
himself safe there.[39] Finally certain strongholds or castles: Castres, Lombes,
Lavaur, Mirepoix, Fanjeaux, Cabaret, Termes, Montségur, were veritable
bases and strongholds of heresy.[40]

Earlier, however, there had been one exception. On the topmost rung of
the ladder of temporal authority Count Raymond V (d. 1194) sought in all
sincerity to arrest the spread of the heresy. He felt himself, however, crushed
to the extent of appealing in 1177 for help to the kings of France and of
England, while he sent to the General Chapter of Cîteaux the significant
avowal:

I myself, although I am armed with one of the two divine swords and confess that
I am established as the avenger and minister of God precisely for this end, seek
in vain the means of putting a limit or a term to such heterodoxy and I have to
recognize that my strength is not sufficient to overcome so widespread and so
difficult a problem, because the most important nobles of my land are ravaged by
this disease, drawing away after them a very great multitude of men who
apostatise from the faith; so that I neither dare nor can undertake anything.[41]

His son, Raymond VI, no longer suffered this anguish. He refused in fact,
and he sometimes declared this expressly, to disturb any of his subjects for
reasons of heresy.[42] This may be thought indifference or liberalism but such
were not the sentiments of the time. It was rather an anxiety not to weaken
his power in any way by taking measures against a large number of his
followers. It was also beyond question a holding back in his belief. If he gave
no formal sign of apostasy and now and again made gestures in favour of the
Church or of the monks, he made more substantial ones still in favour of
the Catharists. He had also suggested to one of his numerous 'wives'—successive or simultaneous—that she should enter a house of the 'Perfect.'[43] He
was surrounded with familiars who were suspect; it was even said that he
kept two of the 'Perfect' with him wearing ordinary dress.[44]

It was not that any of these feudal lords became a complete Catharist, i.e.
a 'Perfect'. For that it would have been necessary for them to abandon their
occupations and their wealth, practising an austerity and a chastity which
certainly did not enter into their habits of life. There existed, however,
several ways of attaching oneself to the Catharists and many degrees in one's
adherence. A good many contented themselves with appreciating the
preaching and the good example of the Perfect and above all their profession
of absolute poverty. A clergy absolutely poor, living on alms from the
faithful without asking for anything except what people willingly gave, was
attractive. So were communities who were not only poor but very generous. The contrast with the wealthy abbeys of the neighbourhood, and with
the prelates of the Roman Church, was striking. However little one might
be persuaded, as was Raymond of Toulouse, for instance, ' that such and
such a Bishop of the Catharists could easily prove the superiority of his
faith over that of the Catholics',[45] it can be understood that the feudal lords
felt inclined not only to leave the ministers of heresy in peace, but even to
favour them in every possible way.

Many went a step further: they became 'believers' in the heresy. Catharism in the West had largely increased its following by deriving every possible
advantage from the *consolamentum*, a real kind of sacrament bequeathed to it
by the Bogomils. Through an imposition of hands which restored to their
followers his 'holy spirit', a kind of guardian angel of consolation dwelling
near to God,[46] he received the certainty of belonging to the community of
the angels, destined to recover in Heaven, at the moment of death, his

spiritual body in beatitude. Now if the *consolamentum* was usually only conferred after a long and austere penance, it could be granted to the dying without any preparation and by anyone belonging to the Perfect. The 'believer' was in his last hour a candidate for the Perfect. While awaiting this ultimate transformation he could continue his ordinary life. A Perfect linked with him by the contract known as *convenientia* had undertaken to procure the *consolamentum* for him at the right moment. Thus more than one lord kept a Perfect at hand, from whom he expected this service. It was claimed that this was precisely the case of Raymond VI.

It must be recognized that the advantages of this position were considerable, for the feudal lords as well as the burghers. It took them back to those times, before Charlemagne, when the great persuaded themselves that the prayer and penance of the monks whom they maintained by their bequests dispensed them from the obligations of Christian morality. Things were no longer like that in the Western Church, particularly since the time of the Gregorian reform, when popes and bishops had definitely turned towards the world to orientate that too towards the Kingdom of God. They demanded from the ministers of the secular sword, at the same time as the profession and maintenance of orthodoxy, respect for justice, peace and conjugal morals. This was what Innocent III demanded, at the risk of alienating the best political supporters of the Church, even in the Albigeois, an attitude which lacked neither courage nor nobility;[47] whereas the Catharists, so austere in their personal lives, permitted everything to their followers, who were also their protectors.[48] The burghers found them favourable to their policy of unlimited gain, to their commercial transactions and to that loan with interest which the Church then obstinately prohibited. The feudal lords were assured by them of eternal salvation—concerning which they were no more disinterested than their contemporaries—without having to retrench anything from the licentiousness of their morals, or from the violence and injustice of their enterprises. Even more, Catharism, especially relentless against marriage which it accused of multiplying by generation souls which were captives of the demon, preferred the transitory character of debauchery to the stability and fecundity of conjugal relations.[49] At the same time its hatred against the Roman Church—'Synagogue of Satan' 'cavern of thieves', 'great prostitute' of the Apocalypse[50]—fanned the flame of the anti-clericalism of the laity and justified their enterprises against ecclesiastical persons and property.

A firm Catholic conviction would clearly have enabled them to resist temptation. It remained to be seen whether the action of the clergy of the south of France was capable of maintaining or reawakening such a conviction.

One must not be too ready to speak of a corrupt clergy. Clearly, the clergy in the Albigeois had its defects.[51] The commissioners sent by the Pope did not cease complaining of the 'disgraceful conduct of the clergy'.[52] The lawsuits instituted, for instance, against the leader of the Province, Bérenger de Narbonne, provided evidence that the prelate was simoniacal, avaricious and negligent, and did not hesitate to take as his assistant a leader of the mercenaries. In 1198, in 1205 and particularly in 1211–13, the majority of the bishops of the Narbonensis and of the neighbouring dioceses found themselves deposed, or transferred.[53] All things considered, however, the clergy here were perhaps no worse than in former times nor than was the case elsewhere. There is scarcely any talk of immorality nor even of lack of personal piety. It was perhaps secular preoccupations, especially the cares of the temporal power which a good number of them had been developing since the Gregorian reform, that, by absorbing too great a share of their activity, paralysed their pastoral action. This may well have been the case, since it was for his avarice that one or another of them was reproached. Nevertheless, an historian has justly pointed out that the situation of the Church was immeasurably better in dioceses where the prelates enjoyed an extensive temporal power and a considerable revenue.[54] This was the case at Narbonne, with the scandalous Bérenger in particular, and at Montpellier, where the prelates had succeeded in preserving the orthodoxy of their city incorrupt since the twelfth century. On the other hand, it was the two ruined and disarmed dioceses of Carcassonne and of Toulouse that were the most affected. Toulouse, 'the dead diocese',[55] where Bishop Fulcrand had had to live in the style of a humble townsman; where Bishop Fulk, entering upon his office in 1205, found in the episcopal treasury only ninety-six sous of the local currency.[56] It was indeed a diocese so vast, so difficult to govern that in the fourteenth century a whole province could be carved out of it: an archbishopric with seven suffragan sees.[57]

The capital defect revealed by the Pope was, with pastoral negligence, the cowardice of the prelates who dared not tackle the heresy face to face, nor have it proscribed by the lay authorities. 'Dogs, who no longer know how to bark', 'mercenaries who take flight and drive away the wolf neither by their voice nor with their stick', soldiers who 'do not mount upon the breach', who 'forbid their sword to shed blood'. Such were the invectives which Innocent III let fly at the prelates of the Narbonensis.[58] The attitude of one of the best of these bishops, Guillaume Peyre,[59] who governed his diocese of Albi in peace from 1185 to 1227, should be noted. Belonging to the nobility of the land, like the majority of his colleagues, he did not even succeed in preventing the members of his own family from adhering politically to heresy, let alone a number of his subjects. His art of government consisted in lending an ear to everyone, even to the heterodox, in establishing peace and maintaining it among the princes of the region while he strove, with genuine piety, to reform the discipline of his monks and clergy, without moreover being absolutely certain of their orthodoxy. He finally achieved a diplomatic *tour de force*, that of governing his diocese for nearly half a century without it being possible, among the vast collection of his official decrees, to come across any word which might indicate the presence in his territory of a heresy which was nevertheless in the process of ravaging it. He had sometimes preached but in a paternal way, without supporting his words with the weight of authority. His prudence will be understood when the fate is recalled of one of his predecessors at Albi, arrested by Trencavel, and entrusted, through mockery, to the safe-keeping of the heretics,[60] the fate of the Bishops of Agen, Rodez, Carpentras and Vaison, ill-treated by Raymond of Toulouse,[61] that of the Bishops of Lodève, of Béziers[62] or of Carcassonne, imprisoned, assassinated or expelled by the townsmen, and finally, that of the pontifical legate, Peter of Castelnau, massacred in his turn. It may be asked what the one or the other would have gained by setting up opposition and speaking out.

In actual fact, the drama was not on the plane of morality, or of regular procedure or even of courage. At the head of such dioceses not even heroes would have succeeded in breaking the general will of the laity which favoured, or at least tolerated, the activity of the heretics. Saints capable of changing the hearts and convictions of the temporal authorities as well as of their subjects would have been necessary. Holy parish priests would also clearly have been necessary to counter-balance the action of heresy among the masses of the people.

It is here perhaps that we shall best measure the weakness of Catholicism in the face of the preaching of the heterodox. Knowledge about the state of the lower clergy at this time in the Albigeois is inadequate. Neither the reforming legislation of the Councils nor the rare anecdotes which can still be read today in the documents justify us in supposing that it was very different from that of the rest of France.[63] All that is known is that it was under the influence of fear, and sought in its day-to-day life to conceal the signs of its clerical state.[64] This humiliation can scarcely have given it bold-ness in the ministry. If the clergy in the Albigeois conformed to the current type of parish priest of the time, it would have been incapable of measuring itself against the heretical preachers. Chosen by the patron of the parish to suit his own ideas, the 'chaplain' of the Midi was only a minister of the sacraments; no moral or doctrinal formation had prepared him to become an ascetic, a spiritual leader and teacher. Nothing, however, could prevent his being placed side by side and compared with the some two thousand[65] preachers of the Waldenses or of the Catharist Perfect who travelled the country edifying men by their words and their austerity, or presided over the diffusion of the sect in the fixed centres maintained by the houses or communities of heretics.[66]

We are thus brought back to the most important of the causes of the collapse of the Church in the states of Raymond of Toulouse—the spiritual

causes, and, more precisely, the spiritual disproportion between the
ministers of Catholicism and the heretical preachers. Naturally when
doctrine was in question the disproportion was not in favour of the innova-
tors. In the disputations, in which, as we shall see, the Catholics confronted
their adversaries on the plane of ideas, it would seem that the former had no
difficulty in carrying away the victory. This was *a fortiori* the case in their
writings—the literary production of the Catharists was non-existent.[67] What,
however, were such victories worth in the case of simple folk, or even of
their lay lords ? Such men, who knew nothing of Latin or of books, were
more responsive to the example of someone's life than to the value of ideas.

Now it should be made clear at this point that at first sight the life led by
the heretics gave no outward sign of its scandalous character from the
Christian point of view—on the contrary. The Waldenses and even the
Catharists seemed to those of the faithful who were not on their guard,
authentic Christians—one might go further, more authentic Christians than
the others—'good Christians' was, with 'good men', the name given to the
Perfect.[68] They were called—let us admit it—the Christians of the latter
days, those who through the Gregorian reform had been reborn on the
model of the infant Church, the genuine apostles or successors of the early
Christians.

It was not only in collegiate churches and chapters of regular life that the
challenge to imitate the life of the apostles[69] had resounded, the challenge
which the preachers of the Gregorian reform had been addressing to the clergy
since the middle of the twelfth century and to which the canonical movement
had given expression by the revival of the rule of St Augustine. It was the special
characteristic of this reform, which had sprung from the very apex of the
Church, to achieve its aims within the framework of Christendom. Nothing
was done that had not its influence throughout the whole of the Western
world, if needs be by introducing upheaval into it to the extent of civil war.
In their eagerness for reform, indeed, the ecclesiastical leaders following
Gregory VII did not fear to appeal freely to the conviction and elementary
dynamism of the populations, in order to bring pressure to bear, if necessary,
on the ecclesiastical and lay rulers of the Christian provinces.[70] Prohibitions
against the faithful being present at the Mass of married priests, against
receiving the sacraments from them, the order to disobey priests and
prelates who refused to accept the apostolic precepts, the intimation to hold
oneself as not bound by the oath of loyalty in the case of princes who had
rebelled against the new discipline of the reform—it was not long before
these imperative decisions, broadcast by papal letters or by the decrees of
the Councils, caused deep disturbance and sometimes insurrections. The
turbulence of the masses in this century of rising national groups, of social
change, of practical religious fervour, is sufficiently well known. The communal movement, so often in opposition to long-standing institutions,

whether ecclesiastical or feudal, likewise brought its spirit of revolution into the question of the apostolic reform of the clergy. It was not only in the urban *milieux*, however, that this seething fervour was displayed. In all classes of society and even in country districts,[71] both isolated individuals and crowds were to be met with full of enthusiasm for the programme of apostolic life which the popes intended to renew among the monks and canons. This enthusiasm led first to their irritation being allowed to turn into anticlericalism in the case of the clergy who did not accept this programme sufficiently fully, then to turning their backs on them, and finally putting themselves in their places by accepting the reform themselves.

It is indeed clear that the impressive picture, always moving for Christian hearts, of the primitive life in Jerusalem from the book of the Acts, and of the preaching of the apostles from the Gospel, was capable of inspiring something quite different from the monasteries or collegiate churches. Historians today recognize a large number of institutions or of original tendencies, directly issuing from the strictly religious movement which it has been proposed to call the 'apostolic movement'.[72] They have not yet come to the end of discovering the manifestations of such tendencies in the course of the twelfth century.[73] The Midi of France, where the Gregorian influence had brought about reforms of chapters, foundations of Canons Regular, and new monastic foundations, equally witnessed the appearance of the most unexpected manifestations. Such were, for instance, during the first two decades of the twelfth century, itinerant preachers such as Robert d'Arbrissel, whose two religious houses of Ardorel and Candeil in the Albigeois, off-shoots of his foundation at Cadouin,[74] maintained the original spirit for some time. Jesus had sent his apostles, two by two, to preach in the localities he was to pass through himself. Thus the new apostles[75] went off, thin from fasting, with long beards and barefoot, in accordance with the idea they formed to themselves of their model, wearing only one tunic, carrying neither gold nor silver and accepting their food from the populations they evangelized. Austere and impressive in their preaching of penance and of the imminence of the Kingdom of God, they presented a type of wandering or peripatetic clergy, quite different from the traditional clerics, whose canonical status precisely implied attachment to one church.[76] They did however realize much better than even the reformed canons of the diocese the ideal evoked by the mission of the apostles, their detachment and their absolute poverty. This was already the poverty and preaching of mendicants. The crowds were not satisfied with merely listening to them. Certain men left all to follow them. Around these new apostles was set up a circle of believers, *credentes*.[77] It was the primitive Church beginning again, the Church of the poor of Christ.[78] Moreover this Church did not conceal its feelings of opposition to the clergy of the classical type. The latter emphatically reproached the itinerants for their attitude. Their

movement, however anarchical it was, remained in the line of the
Gregorian reform, within the Catholic community, to which the apostle
remained firmly attached. Such an itinerant was not a preacher without a
mandate, the kind of false shepherd dreaded by the Church since her earliest
years, against whom she objected in the words of St Paul, *Quomodo
praedicabunt nisi mittantur*: 'how shall they preach unless they be sent?'[79] As
far as the documents enable us to determine the point, the itinerant preachers
expressly received their preaching mission from the bishop, often from the
Pope himself, like their leaders, as, for instance, Robert d'Arbrissel or
St Norbert.[80]

This was no longer the case with the new itinerant apostles who collected
in the province of Gallia Narbonensis in the second quarter of the century,
after they had been expelled in turn from all parts (the fact is significant for
the process of contamination in the Midi). Pierre de Bruys,[81] a priest from
the Dauphiné who had broken his outlaw's ban, had finally organized his
preaching in the neighbourhood of the Rhône centred around Saint-Gilles,
whence he sometimes extended his operations as far as Gascony. He had
been working unchecked in the province for about twenty years until he was
burnt at the stake by a mob[82] over-excited by his iconoclasm (he had crosses
burnt because they were the sign of the humiliation of our Saviour). Henri,[83]
an apostate monk, was only a deacon. He had nevertheless formerly received
the right to preach in the diocese of Le Mans; but he soon forfeited it and
did without it. It is explicitly stated of him that he practised the life of the
apostles and begged his bread from his flock. As a preacher he must have been
impressive as much for his apostolic aspect as for his eloquence. During
the bishop's absence on one occasion, he caused such an upheaval in the
diocese of Le Mans that the people and even certain of the clergy accepted
him as their true pastor. He was reconciled for a time by the Council of Pisa
(1135), finally welcomed and installed in Toulouse by Count Raymond IV.
It needed nothing less than the sending of a legate and the preaching of St
Bernard (1145) to make him cease his efforts. He had however drawn after
him a section of the people who had doubtless already allowed themselves to
be disturbed by Pierre de Bruys, his predecessor, and by certain imitators
who have not emerged from the silence of time. Despite Bernard's success in
Albi, in Toulouse, though not at Verfeil,[84] many souls remained disturbed.
Pierre, like Henri—those imitators of the apostles—taught a kind of spiritual
Christianity founded, at least for Pierre de Bruys, on the Gospel alone,
without churches, without Mass or Eucharist, prayer for the dead or baptism
for infants. They were separated from the Church of Rome and stirred up their
hearers against the clergy whom they reproached for not practising apostolic
poverty, refusing them any title to respect, any sacramental rôle, the right
to approach the sick and, of course, to receive the tithes and offerings.

When the first Waldenses or poor men of Lyons[85] reached the Narbonensis during the final decades of the twelfth century, there were many who were alarmed by this new type of imitator of the apostles. 'Of no fixed abode,' related Walter Map, 'they go off two by two, barefoot, without baggage, having all things in common, after the example of the apostles. Naked they follow the naked Christ.'[86] Such had their founder, Waldes, the rich merchant of Lyons, resolved to be from the very first day of his conversion.[87] So had he sent his disciples to preach the kingdom of God.[88] Certain priests of the Midi, whether more or less aware of the condemnation of the Waldenses in 1184, received them with all the more facility since these edifying preachers supported the Church against the Catharists whom they attacked with violence. One report mentions their presence in the parish churches of Aigues-Vives and Castelnaudary where they taught and sang their hymns without let or hindrance.[89] Their doctrine does not seem to have been very far removed from orthodoxy.[90] They did not, however, think they were doing any wrong by their violent criticism of the clergy. Above all, they set themselves up in the place of the clergy. They ignored Pope, bishops and priests and claimed that 'only the imitators of the apostles had a right to obedience'.[91] Since they imitated them, they had every right to exercise the 'grace of preaching that God had granted them',[92] without any other mandate. Even women could preach, from the moment they practised this form of life.[93] Moreover, the real imitation of the life of the apostles, symbolized by the wearing of sandals which meant that the foot was bare, conferred on the layman, though he were unlettered, the right 'to give his blessing after the manner of a priest, and even the power of binding and loosing'.[94]

Now it was equally as successors of the apostles and continuators of the primitive Christians that the Catharists represented themselves, in Cologne, in Périgord, in the Narbonensis, in England,[95] from the very beginning of their vigorous development in the West, from 1140 onwards. At the turn of the thirteenth century nothing had changed on this point. The Catholic controversialists, Prévostin, Joachim of Flora, Raoul Ardent, in argument against the Catharists, were aware of their claim to be the only ones to practise apostolic life.[96] This was neither contagion nor imitation on their part. The oriental Bogomils who had transmitted to them the core of their doctrines and practices, joined to the dualist attitude which formed the foundation of their religious position a practice of life which they claimed to derive, with much seriousness and fidelity, from that of apostolic times.[97] They derived this from many traditions of the Eastern Church. The significance of the declaration of the Catharists of Cologne in 1143 will thus be understood—'Their religion had remained hidden from the time of the martyrs and had been preserved in Greece and a few other countries. Thus they were called apostles.'[98]

The historical continuity of the Bogomils and the Catharists with the Gnostic Christians of primitive times is outside the scope of the documents we possess and remains more than doubtful.[99] Despite their dualism, however, their will and determination to continue the life of apostolic times as it is described in the Gospels and the Acts were beyond question. The natural climate of the West, especially of the Albigeois, which had changed the Bogomils into Catharists had only accentuated the apostolic character of the latter. Their poor and penitent Church, community of worldly goods and the begging sermons of the Perfect, the hierarchy restricted to bishops and deacons, prayers reduced to the Pater, their homilies on the Gospel which the Perfect carried about with them in a leather bag, down to the baptism in the Paraclete (*consolamentum*) by imposition of hands, all savoured of the spirit of the New Testament, of the desire to be in all things what the Christians of Jerusalem were, and that alone.[100] Many Protestant controversialists have allowed themselves to be deceived over this since the sixteenth century, and, having been unwilling to consider anything but the practice of life of the Albigensian Catharists to the exclusion of their absolute dualism, have proclaimed them as pure and evangelical Christians.[101] It was not then surprising that at the time of Pope Innocent and St Dominic a great number of simple lay folk should have sincerely accepted them as Christians, Christians perhaps more faithful to the Gospel than the others.

Since the temporal rulers, partly won over by a similar judgement, partly attracted by the advantages of a counter-Church which would have cost them so little for it would have left them so many liberties and possibilities, felt themselves more and more disposed to prefer that to the traditional Church, the situation of the latter had become perilous. It was not, however, desperate.

All this uncertainty of Christians in the Narbonensis did not come so much from decadence as from an overflow of religious vitality and generosity.[102] Before manifesting itself in a burst of pietist fervour in the different classes of society in the Midi, the apostolic evangelism of the Gregorian reformers had borne fruit in the Church.[103] The provinces where the preaching heresies were the most widely implanted were precisely those in which the orthodox apostolic movement had earlier been most developed in the chapters of canons with a rule of life.[104] Until the thirteenth century it continued to inspire in these lands, as it did in the whole of the West, numerous gestures of Catholic fervour. The Church, it is true, had not sought for the majority of the clergy absolute poverty and temporal deprivation—some ownership of private property was doubtless inevitable to protect their independence in the feudal atmosphere of violence and injustice—but she had at least striven to give them the spirit of poverty by multiplying among them the example of the clerks regular and of fervent monks. There have been few periods in which religious foundations have been more numerous in the Narbonensis than the twelfth century. Side by side with the ancient abbeys, many of which continued to live a carefully controlled rule of life, there multiplied the canonical houses of Saint Rufus or of Prémontré, the Commanderies of the military orders, the different houses which provided hospitality. Of the latter the hospital of the Holy Spirit in Montpellier, expanding at the call of Innocent, soon diffused over the whole of Europe the most important of the orders of this type, and was not the least striking.[105] One name, however, sums up better than others this Catholic fecundity—Cîteaux, from which the Narbonensis and the neighbouring dioceses saw emerge a dozen great abbeys, Belleperche, Grandselve, Eaunes, Boulbonne, Callers, Feuillans, in the diocese of Toulouse; Candeil and Ardorel,[106] in the diocese of Albi; Villelongue, near Carcassonne, Font-froide, near Narbonne, Valmagne and Franquevaux in the dioceses of Agde and of Nîmes.

The Cistercian abbeys were not only the centres from which Catholic fervour and asceticism and personal poverty radiated. The result, in part, of the brief appearance of St Bernard in the Albigeois, they supplied the bases and the effective workers for the counter-thrust of the Church, which hence-forward reserved this to them as one of their special missions. Preachers, model bishops, papal commissioners and legates during three-quarters of a century, the Cistercians were called upon without respite for the affairs of the faith in the Midi by the Sovereign Pontiffs.

Similarly, it was a monk of Cîteaux, Master Alain of Lille, who wrote the most remarkable of the first systematic critical studies of heresy at the end of the twelfth century, dedicated to Guillaume de Montpellier (d. 1202).[107] This large work, well arranged, benefiting by the double light of exegesis and of reason, made a brilliant opening to the series of polemical and theological works which developed in the following half-century. Of these it was possible to say that they struck heresy a mortal blow, when the inquisition was barely inaugurated.[108] The fact was that, at the time when apostolic laymen turned in increasing numbers to the Catharist preachers, because they found a means in their theories of satisfying at little cost their taste for explaining everything, the same thirst for knowledge and understanding gave rise among the Catholics to the extraordinary develop-ment of the Schools and paved the way for the inception of the Universities. To bring the religion of the Catharists, which had been born of a sentimental recoil in the face of evil and the world, to be examined on the intellectual plane, was to force it to reveal the philosophical weakness of its dualism, the deep-rooted incoherence of this dualism and of its apostolicity, the gratuitousness of its rejection of the Biblical dogma of creation and of the evangelical dogma of the Cross, the evil-mindedness of its radical condemna-tion of life and matter. There was, however, a dearth of theologians to multiply such attacks. Moreover, it was not the time for arguments when the negligence of the prelates and the favour of the princes towards the heretics seemed on the point of bringing about in the Narbonensis the complete success of the latter.

It was not so much, however, that there were no bishops adequate to the task. Geoffroy of Béziers, Bérenger of Carcassonne, Navarre of Couserans, Garric of Comminges, Hugh of Riez, Raymond of Uzès, were worthy of their mission. Among the princes the Pope had certain loyal followers who seemed reliable—the family of Montpellier and that of Aragon.[109] In 1204, the marriage of Pedro de Aragon with Marie de Montpellier, which meant the introduction of the Catholic dynasty into the heart of the Albigeois, was followed by his coronation in Rome. The king took an oath of obedience to the Pope and of loyalty as his vassal. He had already renewed the measures against heresy decided upon by his father in accordance with the law of the Church.[110] If others joined him, if new prelates, in substitution for the defaulters, backed the zealous bishops, the heresiarchs could be eliminated from the neighbourhood by the joint action of the spiritual and temporal authorities.

Already the 27th canon of the Third Council of the Lateran (1179)[111] and the decisions of Verona (1184)[112] had clearly defined and condemned these heresies of the Midi, detailed the procedure for the seeking out and conviction of the heretics, the penalties incurred by their abettors and protectors, the sanctions and even the crusade that the Church could put into operation to oblige a Catholic prince to fulfil his obligations to defend the faith. Finally a decree of Innocent III himself, in 1199,[113] had set forth the fundamental motive of the combined action of the authorities of Christendom. Heresy fell under the ancient law of *lèse-majesté*, that is to say it attacked God at the same time as the principal foundation of Catholic society, the truth.

The hour for such action was approaching. Linked with it were the campaigns against war and against the mercenaries. As far back as 1198 Innocent had appointed legates[114] to whom he gave the mission of reawakening the conscience of prelates and princes in the struggle against all these disorders. This, however, did not prove sufficient. The heretics could indeed be destroyed or dispersed with the collaboration of the temporal sword; hearts and convictions still had to be won over. Preaching alone could do this. Embodying all the measures against heresy, because it was their principle and their term, preaching remained the chief occupation of all those who had the religious problem of the Narbonensis at heart and viewed it with clear-sightedness. The trail of light of the mission of St Bernard was swiftly fading; as one of his companions had remarked—'a province led astray by such a number of erroneous doctrines would need preaching to for a long time to come'.[115] Others had resumed the doctrinal task from time to time; but their faint trail was in turn fading swiftly. Innocent III had every intention that his legates should be primarily preachers.[116] In 1203, he had it in mind to renew the work of St Bernard, with the help of his Cistercians, through a much more extensive mission. Providence undertook to send him preachers of its own choosing.

Chapter VI

M.ONTPELLIER

ONE June evening in 1206,[1] a small company of horsemen arrived at the gates of Montpellier. Diego of Osma was on his way back from Cîteaux with his religious household—the bishop himself, the sub-prior of his chapter and very dear companion, Dominic, a few of the clergy of the diocese, some Cistercian monks, the serving men. The baggage followed on pack animals. The suite was less magnificent than when the riders had left Castile nearly a year before. Perhaps, however, they were not sorry to have abandoned the most ostentatious part of their baggage on making the journey to the Curia the previous December. Along these roads of the south infested by Aragonese or Basque mercenaries, it was better not to awaken appetites for greed. The riders came down the valleys of the Saône and the Rhône, which they left at Beaucaire, passed through Nîmes, then travelled close to the Mediterranean. At last they entered the city of the Guillem. The mighty ramparts of the town crowned a broad and lofty hill. It was a citadel, a place of respite and peace for Catholicism in the heart of a region which was becoming increasingly less loyal.[2]

A few minutes after passing through the gates, the travellers thought themselves back in the very places they had just left. They ran into another group of churchmen holding session inside the walls.[3] All Cîteaux was there, in the person of its abbot, Arnaud Amaury, monks from Fontfroide, Peter of Castelnau and Maître Raoul, and their suite.[4] Rome was there too. For between the close of 1203 and May 1204,[5] Arnaud, Peter and Raoul had been invested with the office of papal legates to deal with the heretics. Scarcely a month or even a week passed without some series of letters coming to bring them the instructions, counsels, encouragements of Innocent III himself who watched over their legation with most assiduous care.[6]

Events, unfortunately, scarcely corresponded to the Sovereign Pontiff's hopes. Despite their goodwill, their courage and their efforts the legates had no success at all. In the multitude of affairs in which for the past two years they had been obliged progressively to engage, success was rare, disappointment and frustration all too frequent. As their crowning misfortune, they had at times the impression that Rome did not understand them. This was particularly the case in the matter of Archbishop Bérenger of Narbonne which seemed to them of capital importance.[7] God knows the Pope was under no illusion as to the greed for gain, the avarice, simonaical practices and above all the religious laxity and inertia of this prince of the Church who, satisfied with not finding heresy in his archiepiscopal town, dis-associated himself completely from the rest of his province to the extent that he had not even once visited it. From their first contact with the arch-bishop, when they came to present their mandate and ask him to support them in their action against the heretics and to accompany them on their visit to the Count of Toulouse, whose temporal sword was to move hand in hand with their spiritual activities, the legates had sensed that nothing could be done in the Narbonensis so long as this egoist, this useless and scandalous trafficker, was at the head of the province. The Pope was entirely of the same opinion, and on 28th May, 1204 had given them orders to institute a canonical trial with the power to depose the prelate without right of appeal.8 The necessary investigations had thus been made, and the most detailed evidence obtained on oath; the matter seemed on the point of being satisfactorily concluded. Now, a few days earlier, the legates had just received a letter which nullified the efforts of the past two years. Bérenger had gone to Rome. He had caught the Pope off his guard and won his indulgence. He was restored to favour. At the foot of the barren fig-tree, which had previously been pruned, Innocent still wished to hoe out the weeds and fertilize the ground, in a last hope that the tree would yield fruit.9

The heretics whom the legates thought to impress by this sensational justice thus began once more to pour scorn on their preaching and to cast in their teeth with an air of triumph the deplorable example of the clergy. What hope could there be of reforming the heretical members of the Church in the Midi if the head remained corrupt? Moreover, was it the rôle of the legates to plunge into a reform which would never be achieved, in the place of an archbishop who himself did not trouble about it?10 The Pope's ambassadors had already felt their courage weaken. This time the measure was full to the brim. Quite simply they were considering renouncing their mission.

Diego and his companions arrived just at the right moment. Castile was not so very remote a land. The legates, all men from this part of the country, knew the bishop of Osma by repute. They knew him to be a man of holy life, upright and zealous for the faith.11 His recent visit *ad limina* might have given him an insight into some intention or sentiment on the part of the Pope. Perhaps Diego even had some commission for the Abbot of Cîteaux and for his two colleagues. However this might be, they begged him to give his opinion. In those days great importance was attached to these secret councils before action, in which each one must give his opinion in turn and thus take his share of responsibility. Counsel was not only the right but the duty of the vassal to his lord, the baron *vis-à-vis* the king, the canon to his bishop, the monk to his abbot. Similarly, men took counsel of the holy man of the town, of the recluse, of the hermit, of the pilgrim met with along the road. Good counsel delivered by a stranger came directly from God.

Diego and Dominic, made acquainted with the situation as regards heresy, with the precise mission of the legates, with their efforts and reactions in the face of the decisions from Rome, came face to face with a world with which their contact for the past three years had grown continually closer. These two judges of men were able to assess at once the strange opposition between the principal actors in the scene which was described to them— namely, the Pope and the three Cistercians.

Peter of Castelnau[12] was the oldest of the legates. In 1199 he had been associated for some time with the Cistercian, Frère Rainier, for the affair of the Abbot of Saint-Guillem.[13] He was then a Canon Regular and archdeacon of Maguelonne.[14] In the papal letters he is several times given the title of Master, which presupposes theological learning.[15] An experienced canonist, moreover, he had just finished pleading for three years in Rome to defend his office, which the provost of the chapter refused to recognize.[16] He had finally won his case. In Rome his tenacity and his skill in canon law had won admiration and there had followed at once the intention of making use of him for the reform of the Midi. When at the turn of the year 1203 the archdeacon had taken the habit of the order of Cîteaux at Fontfroide,[17] he had become more fitted than ever for the mission in the Narbonensis which the order had made illustrious.[18] He received this office without delay, in October or November of the same year. For five years he was primarily the man of Law, the law of the 27th canon of the Lateran as defined by the decretals. In his fearless hands, these texts were to reveal all their force. It was because he had succeeded in grouping together against the Count of Toulouse, who was recalcitrant in the matter of the heretics, the principal vassals of Provence, in a pact of peace which might one day become a crusade, that Peter of Castelnau was eventually assassinated, on the morning of 14th January, 1208.[19] This intransigent legate, who was effective if he was anything, had several times before this received threats of death.[20]

Maître Raoul,[21] who was also a monk of Fontfroide, appointed legate the same day as his colleague, found himself in opposition to him as the clear light of truth may find itself in opposition to the constraint of a severe law. He was a man of great learning.[22] He had been chosen as theologian, for he had taught in the Schools.[23] His activity in preaching, which unlike the legal action of Peter of Castelnau was not set down in the charters, was none the less very real. We can sense that it was extensive and beneficial in its influence. Raoul and Raoul alone was to remain in close contact with Diego and St Dominic for a whole year, before his death on 9th July, 1207.[24] Across seven centuries of distance this significant contact throws a fleeting light on the features of a countenance which for us are almost effaced.

The legate Arnaud Amaury[25] on the other hand is almost too well known. A former monk and Abbot of Poblet, the monastery of the kings of Aragon, then abbot of Grandselve near Toulouse before becoming Abbot of Cîteaux, he had inspired some six hundred monasteries and tens of thousands of monks who anticipated both the Church and the princes in all the Christian enterprises of the period. Thus Arnaud might seem specially qualified for directing the campaign against the unbelievers of the Midi. He assuredly was so from the day when this campaign was transformed into a crusade of bloodshed. He had the virtues of the leader—the initiative, the uncompromising energy, the sense of organization, skill in drawing up reports and in keeping archives. For the task entrusted to him all that he lacked was perhaps certain aspects of the love of souls. A man of the lineage of the soldier-bishops of the feudal age, he is completely summed up by a phrase of the *Histoire Albigeoise*. The château of Minerva, under siege, was on the point of surrendering to the crusaders. Arnaud was entrusted with deciding the fate of the vanquished. As supreme leader, he could not evade this decision. It was painful to him not to give a free hand to the soldiers of the north whose taste for burnings at the stake he knew. 'For he keenly desired, though as priest and monk he dared not do so, to condemn to death the enemies of Christ.'[26] Regretfully, he had to leave them with their lives safe. Clearly, as when, plunged into the midst of the Albigensian crusade and moving over the whole of Spain, he led over forty thousand men to collaborate with the armies of Aragon, Castile and Navarre in the campaign of Las Navas de Tolosa which for three centuries marked the frontiers of Islam,[27] he was more at home in action than when directing the conversion of the Catharists. Attached after the event on 31st May, 1204[28] to the other two legates that they might have at their disposal the resources and the authority of Cîteaux, it was only after the death of his colleagues that he fully concerned himself with this mission. Then he truly dominated the history of the enterprise and orientated it towards its most radical form. Convinced that any religious action in the Narbonensis would be fruitless so long as men like Bérenger of Narbonne or Raymond of Toulouse were left in peace, he resolved to remove them as quickly as possible. Sometimes he succeeded by legal astuteness savouring of deception towards both the Pope and the victims. Ambitious to extend his powers, whatever the Pope might say, when he became Archbishop of Narbonne, he was seen to take possession of the title of the duchy and, to the general scandal, to embark upon a struggle with the Comte de Montfort whom he had just praised to the skies. To crush heresy, he could not do without using authoritative gestures and the terror provoked by bloodshed.[29] He may or may not have been right on the military plane. This implacable adversary of unbelievers, however, with whom the prosecution of the law was scarcely tempered by mercy, was at the opposite pole from the thoughts of his master the Pope, with whom his disagreements were multiplied almost to the point of rupture.

Innocent was of a different temper.[30] It is true that he was authoritarian and meticulous in applying the canons of the Church. From the very year of his accession, he had indeed strengthened, by invoking the law of *lèse-majesté*, the legal dispositions which enabled him to compel princes as much as the clergy and, through them, the Christian people as a whole, to respect ecclesiastical liberties, peace and orthodoxy.[31] He never forgot, however, that the sole purpose of these powers, which he succeeded in making effective throughout his whole pontificate, was that of saving souls. As soon as this objective seemed to him achieved, he was ready to stay the course of justice and to relax the penalties which he had inflicted upon the culprits in conformity with the law. This was perhaps a political weakness, and the cause of a continual hesitation which baffled his lay and even his ecclesiastical collaborators, but it was a pastoral attitude in every sense of the word. For him, penalties served not so much to punish as to cure.

That was what he demanded of his missionaries.[32] In dealing with the heterodox they were never to forget that they were attacking men capable of conversion, or the weak whom shortcomings or scandals had perhaps led. There were good men among them, whose practices, though not customary in the Church, were nothing but edifying and should bring forth greater fruit in the Catholic order of things. He was told of certain of the faithful in Metz who met in secret groups, were hostile to the Church, and claimed to draw their religion from a direct reading of the Gospel. He did not like this contempt for Christian unity, this taste for secret meetings or this preaching without a mandate. He recognized explicitly, however, that the eagerness to read and understand the Holy Scriptures was worthy of nothing but praise. 'It is not right', he said, 'to weaken the religion of the simple.'[33] It took more than twelve years and innumerable investigations for Innocent to decide to deal severely with schismatics who had avowed themselves to be such.[34] In Lombardy certain weavers, rather similar to the evangelicals of Metz and the poor men of Lyons, were leading a kind of religious life that was unorthodox, but poor, pious and edifying. The Pope laboured so devotedly that despite the prelates of Lombardy who were more than suspicious, despite even his predecessors who had contented themselves with excommunicating these 'Humiliati', he succeeded in bringing back these apostolic communities into the unity of the Church, under a very original form.[35] He would soon be seen, in 1208, and again in 1210, reconciling out and out Waldenses and putting their effective evangelism at the service of orthodoxy against the Catharists.[36]

Thus in the mission that he had entrusted in that part of the world to his two, then to his three legates, the Pope attributed major importance to preaching. This point merits a careful examination for it is sometimes misconstrued. Innocent had defined the original and chief mission of the legates by the stereotyped formula: *ad extirpandam haereticam pravitatem*,[37] 'to extirpate erring heresy'. The words did not specify an administrative and legal mission alone, as we should be inclined to think if we confined ourselves to analysing them in the light of the dispositions of contemporary (canon) Law. The letters and instructions of the Pope, as well as the practice of the legates were proof that the task was infinitely more complex. Here as in many other points, the real depth and quality of the medieval Church can only be discerned in the light of patristic tradition.

St Augustine, in the course of his thirty-four years of pastoral struggle against the Donatists, had progressively adjusted the procedure of the Latin Church for bringing back dissidents, or at least for diminishing the harm they did.[38] Such procedure comprised four terms: argument, warning, excommunication, temporal penalties. For a long time he had thought he could limit himself to the first step, which corresponded so well with that liberty of the faith of which, together with the whole body of tradition, he never ceased to remind men. All he asked of the good will of the prince was to facilitate the colloquies of the Catholics with their adversaries. He was, however, obliged to recognize that the patient explanation of the faith even supported by the heart and genius of a saint, was not adequate. Preaching had to become more insistent: exhortation, reproaches, entreaties, fraternal threats transformed it into a warning, in accordance with the forms envisaged by the Gospel. If the unbelievers remained adamant, it was then necessary to decide to separate them from the flock by pronouncing an anathema, as the apostles had done; for a heretic known to be such is less dangerous for the other faithful than a bad Catholic. After further hesitation, St Augustine had equally accepted the support of the imperial legislation against the heretics, with the exception of the death penalty. With a certain number, fear of temporal sanctions was the final means of making converts of those on whom the word of faith had had no effect.

Preaching, admonition, reconciliation or excommunication, sanctions, such were still the four stages of the operations against heresy which St Bernard recommended to those who wrote to him, or that he distinguished in his sermons;[39] they were the stages that he in turn practised in 1145, against the Albigensians; those he transmitted to his successors and sons, the Cistercian missionaries of the Narbonensis. 'It is certainly not by arms but by arguments that heretics must be won', that is, 'convinced and converted'. 'The faith is transmitted by persuasion and not by constraint.' If the unbelievers, however, would not allow themselves to be converted 'after one, two and even three warnings', they must be separated from the community and 'henceforth avoided'. Finally, if they persisted in their obstinacy and became a danger for the whole flock, it was best to 'put them to flight', expelling them through the secular arm.[40] Between the lines of the

4—S.D.

documents, which unfortunately give few details, we can find traces of the application of this procedure in the later campaign against the Catharists. It was so firmly inscribed in tradition that it can still be found, clearly discernible, in the succession of the acts of the Inquisition from the thirteenth century onwards.[41]

It cannot, however, always be recognized at first glance in the pattern of the Narbonensis mission from 1203 onwards. This is because the special circumstances of the Midi constrained the legates and the Pope to engage in secondary and collateral actions which, in the documents which have come down to us, often occupy the foreground of the picture. Ill-will on the part of the secular arm made the fourth stage of the procedure, namely, the expulsion of hardened heretics, impossible. Thus, to bend the lay princes to the will of the Church, a series of enterprises, of which the crusade constituted the supreme resource, was necessary.[42] From the very beginning, Innocent III had sketched out this collateral action, of which Peter de Castelnau was the principal agent.[43] The grave defection of a section of the prelates of the Midi, who did not of themselves take the initiative of action against the heretics, did not collaborate with the legates' effort, or even frustrated it completely by the bad example of their lives, induced Innocent moreover from 31st May, 1204 onwards, to give the three Cistercians secondary missions which involved them in numerous judicial actions of correction or deposition.[44] Independently of the very extensive powers which he finally granted them on this point,[45] he insisted on renewing these powers for them in a special way in each particular case. Such commissions became multiplied during the course of the year 1205.[46] They formed the theme of the majority of Innocent's letters. To some extent they absorbed the energy of the legates. Such commissions, however, never took priority of place over the primordial mission the legates had received, namely, direct action against the heretics. Finally, among the measures which this main mission had at its disposal—preaching, admonition, reconciliation or excommunication—Innocent, as was natural, though his insistence was remarkable, wished that preaching and conversion should have pride of place in all circumstances.

When in his correspondence the Pope summed up in a brief phrase the ministry of his legates, he spoke of 'going to convey the word of the Lord',[47] of 'consecrating oneself to the ministry of the word and of doctrinal teaching'.[48] If one of the legates was losing courage, he gave him fresh heart by renewing his formal order to him to 'carry out from his heart his own ministry, his office as evangelist, insisting in season and out of season, by his arguments, entreaties, reproaches, in all patience and clearness of doctrine';[49] and in the circumstance this order was all the more significant since it was addressed to Peter of Castelnau, the jurist.

If the Cistercian legates were tempted to overstep the limits of their reforming action *vis-à-vis* the clergy, Innocent brought them firmly back to their essential task, for it was not fitting, he said, to leave aside a task of 'ineluctable necessity', to avoid an obstacle which after all could be borne with.[50] Finally he even took care to indicate the spirit of this action. At the end of an important letter in which he had meticulously set down the duties and powers of his representatives, he added as a *post-scriptum*: 'We will and exhort you to proceed in such a way that the simplicity of your attitude is clear to the eyes of all, closes the mouth of the ignorant as it does that of people without common sense, and that nothing should appear either in your acts or words in which even a heretic could find room for criticism'.[51] Here again was that desire 'not to extinguish the smoking flax' that the Pope had formerly displayed in regard to the evangelicals of Metz.

However, to give this preaching an even wider scope, on 29th January, 1204 the Pope sent a series of letters to the Abbot of Cîteaux, to the Abbot of Valmagne, to Maître Raoul of Narbonne, so that they might put their own preaching or that of certain of their sons at the legates' disposal.[52] At the same time he wrote to all the prelates, abbots, priors and other dignitaries of the Narbonensis to second the action of these preachers.[53] A few years later these letters produced undoubted fruit. The Cistercian mission would then fully merit the name of 'the preaching of the Narbonensis', the legates and their collaborators that of 'preachers against the heretics', which people gave them or which they gave themselves in documents of all kinds.[54]

From the beginning they deserved these names in principle. We know nothing of the detail of the intervention of the legates at Toulouse in December 1203;[55] we know that at Béziers they could not exercise any kind of activity, through the ill will of both the bishops and the consuls.[56] At Carcassonne, however, in February 1204, the good dispositions of the king, Pedro de Aragón, who held the title of Count of Carcassonne, enabled them to introduce action against heresy.[57] By order of the king, one day the Waldenses were invited, another day the Catharists. The bishop, the legates and certain other clerics represented the Catholic Church. The account of the proceedings, drawn up by Pedro de Aragón, laid the emphasis on the legal summing up. He allows us, however, to catch a glimpse of the public dispute which had preceded it. Before a jury composed of Pedro de Aragón, thirteen Catholics and thirteen Catharists, Bernard de Simone, 'bisbe' of Carcassonne, replied by explanations which were at first vague and confused to the doctrinal questions which were put to him. Pressed with questions he ended by replying more definitely in the Catharist sense. The legates took these explanations point by point, and showed the incompatibility of these doctrines with the Catholic faith which they developed with the help of the words of the New Testament. The disputation was prolonged throughout the whole day. The next day the king and his assessors made a formal declaration

of the heresy of the Catharists. There the action against the heretics rested.
It had brought the heresy clearly to light; neither temporal sanction nor
even excommunication was pronounced. The power of the King of Aragon
over Carcassonne was purely nominal.[58] The only one who governed in
actual fact was the Viscount Raymond-Roger.

We have no knowledge as to whether the crowd which, here as elsewhere,
was present at the disputation in which it displayed the liveliest interest,
was impressed by this exposition of Catholic doctrine from New Testament
sources in opposition to the tenets of the Catharists. Given the general
atmosphere, conversions can have been but few. This was frequently the case.

It was in point of fact in their principal mission, namely that of doctrine,
that the legates experienced the deepest of their disappointments. This was
what they confided to Diego and Dominic in the secret meeting at
Montpellier. At the end of their two and a half years' work, 'they had
obtained nothing or almost nothing by their preaching among the heretics'.[59]
And immediately there came once more the excuse, or rather the inevitable
accusation—'through our own fault' or rather 'through the fault of the
clergy', for it is difficult not to look for the explanation of the failure of the
Christians in the lapses of those responsible. The heretics themselves
suggested this explanation. 'Each time the legates wanted to preach to them,
they were greeted with the objection of the bad conduct of the clergy.'
Now 'if they wanted thus to reform the life of the clergy, it was clearly
essential for them to interrupt their preaching'.[60] The situation seemed to
be a deadlock, a genuine case of 'perplexity', to use the word of the
moralists of the time, a situation wherein no matter which alternative he
may choose, man has the certainty of failing in his task.

The depth or shallowness of a man's personality is revealed in situations of
this type. Diego's reply shows the quality of his apostolic mind and the
realism of his understanding of the obstacles. More than ever was it essential
to continue their preaching. For that every other measure must be left
aside.[61] That alone, in fact, was indispensable, and it would be adequate.
When one had used up one's strength in reforming the clergy, even supposing one succeeded, one would not really even have touched the fringe of
the conversion of souls. Moreover, it was perhaps an illusion to attach such
importance to the lapses of the clergy in regard to the canonical ideal.
Diego and his sub-prior were beginning to know the Albigensian heretics.
The legates had once more explained their way of living, of preaching, of
winning souls, but the heretics' demands in regard to the trustees of the
word of God were radical in quite a different sense from those of the most
rigorous Catholic reform. Henricians, Catharists and Waldenses were in
agreement in recognizing as an authentic preacher of the Gospel only him
who lived according to the rules which they discovered in the Gospel.
Whoever practised the manner of life of the apostles was authorized to

convey their message. Whosoever did not do so had no right at all to a hearing. Now, according to their conceptions, to live like the apostles was to go on foot, two by two, in great humility, without carrying on one's person gold, silver, or money, without possessing anything in the world, or expecting one's daily bread from any source but the charity of the populations: it was, in a word, to become a beggar. Naturally, these demands were inacceptable on a universal plane. They were not compatible with the long-standing experience of Christendom and distorted the distinction between precept and counsel. But, once this had been said, everything had not been said. Something remained to be done that was perfectly possible. Men were free to take these demands upon themselves, free to adopt that particular manner of preaching.

This fervent canon, this bishop and former canon, had for long been meditating on the ideal of the apostolic life and had even been living it in many respects. It was sufficient for them to develop it on an itinerant plane. Why should the dissidents have the monopoly of such a way of life ? There was one point on which the Catholics were closer to the apostolic pattern than the heretics: the mission of the Church. To preach because of their mission, to preach in a unique way and with more intensity than ever, joining the example to the word after the pattern of the good Master, on foot, without gold or silver, in perfect imitation of the method of the apostles,[62] such was Diego's advice.

The legates were disconcerted. 'They did not want of their own accord to adopt a method of action which savoured too much of novelty.' This word, indeed, from their lips was pejorative. They might have remembered the apostolic life of the papal legate whom St Bernard had held up as an example.[63] We must not, however, under-estimate the lawfulness of their doubts. Clearly they had never imagined the possibility of preaching in this way. As the Pope's legates, representing the supreme authority of Christian Europe, they had up to the present endeavoured to emphasize the fact by their attitude, their equipment, their escort, indispensable in these parts and moreover a moderate one for the circumstances, and even by their authoritative word. The letters of the Pope showed clearly enough the Church's sorrow over the contempt in which the spiritual sword was held in these parts because it was unsupported by the temporal sword.[64] Was it necessary to increase this contempt by mendicancy? That a priest, even more that a prelate, should beg his bread from door to door would be an occasion of shame for the clergy and for Christian society.[65] Moreover, it was a thing particularly repugnant to Cistercians.[66] Lastly and most important of all, if they agreed to link their preaching with such behaviour, this might be tantamount to countenancing and thereby spreading the principal error of the heretics—namely, the absolute interdependence they maintained between pastoral activity in general and mendicant apostolic life.

They thus received Diego's advice with consternation. In the deadlock which they had just admitted, however, it unexpectedly opened a door. In the inmost heart of the monks of Fontfroide it stirred a courageous response and a hope which could not fail to be impressive to anyone who realized their situation. Stoop to beg ? Why not! With a touch of irony they turned to the Bishop of Osma, and gave their answer: 'If some person of real moral authority was willing first to show them the example by preaching in this way, they would very willingly follow him.'[67]

Diego, being impetuous, was always ready. He offered himself. Full of divine inspiration, he immediately organized the return of the rest of his household to Osma and disposed of all his means of travel—horses, baggage and other objects of equipment. He also dismissed his clergy and kept with him only a single companion, Dominic.[68]

Naturally Dominic was ready. He listened. The entire initiative was his bishop's. With all his heart, however, he approved and made it his own. No document has preserved the direct echo of his reactions for us. Facts, however, are more eloquent than words. In the course of ten years of close companionship, at Osma as in Toulouse, in Denmark as in Rome, he had shared the bishop's daily life, his prayer, his labours and his apostolic projects. When his own trail had separated itself for a time from the deep furrow carved out by the bishop, as in the incident of the innkeeper of Toulouse, the profound identity of inspiration had only appeared more clearly. Then the two trails had again become indistinguishable. They were to continue thus, interlinked, almost inseparable, until Diego's death. Then Dominic was to press more heavily on the handles of the plough, yet without modifying the course of the furrow. It was no longer the time for the somewhat disorderly outburst of generous enterprises, or even for the resumption of the common plans of former days. The mission in the north-east of Europe would remain in the saint's heart as a hope loved, cherished, but never fulfilled. One single purpose would henceforth count in his activity upon earth—to be a preacher of apostolic life, to provide the Church in the Narbonensis, to provide the Church as a whole, with good labourers for the word of God, imitators of those whom Christ had sent two by two before his face, capable of corresponding by their words and example to what was expected of them, or rather, to the true needs of the soul of their neighbours.[69] When at the moment of his death, Dominic was to leave in the Church an army of preachers already superior in numbers to those of the heretical preachers whom he had formerly met on the lands of the Count of Toulouse, he would but have realized, in a measure of fulness at that time scarcely conceivable, the idea glimpsed in embryo when he was with Diego at Montpellier. His contemporaries were not mistaken. Dominic had discovered the idea of the Order of Preachers by sharing from the depths of his being in the decision of his bishop at this memorable encounter. 'And this was the seed that produced the institution of the Preachers. I have heard it affirmed by the first brethren who were with the blessed Dominic in these parts.'[70] Stephen of Bourbon was not the only one to speak in this way.[71] Seven centuries later there is nothing different that can be said. Yet what a long way there was still to travel in order to arrive at this institution or even to imagine it in its full reality.

Each one then reacted according to his temperament and his possibilities. The organizer, Arnaud Amaury, was preparing to preside over the general chapter of his order, which was to assemble from 13th September onwards. He would thus be separated from his companions. Earlier the Pope had asked him to provide the first two legates with Cistercian preachers. He had reminded him of the request when he appointed him third legate.[72] Arnaud had it in mind to comply with this request and to bring back with him after the chapter some of the abbots whom he had met at that world-wide gathering. He would take them as his collaborators in the preaching mission which had been enjoined upon him.[73]

Peter and Raoul, on the other hand, were ready to leave at once. They, too, sent back their escort, their horses, their baggage. They kept only the books necessary for the chanting of the liturgical hours, for theological study and for the immediate preparation of the disputes that they were planning to counter.[74] The little band was formed. It began by giving itself a leader—the Bishop of Osma himself, who for the future directed the affair.[75] They set off on foot, bare-foot even, claims one chronicler,[76] who if somewhat later in date is usually well informed. No charges or expenses; they had taken no money with them. Thus these important legates, this bishop, this sub-prior, and doubtless a few monks or clerics in addition, were now begging their bread from door to door.[77] Today we should find the scene an unusual one. At that time, in those parts, people were even more astonished. This was indeed the voluntary poverty, the humility of the preaching of the Gospel. Jordan notes that from then onwards Dominic no longer bore the title of sub-prior but was called simply Brother Dominic.[78]

It is understandable that several historians, in order to explain such a great change in the psychology of the legates, and especially in that of the Abbot of Cîteaux, should have suspected the intervention of some higher authority supporting the Bishop of Osma—that of Innocent III himself.[79] Certainly if the Pope had asked the bishop on his return to Spain to convey verbally to his legates in the Narbonensis certain counsels requiring too much tact to be entrusted to writing, many mysterious details to which attention has been called in passing would at once become clear.[80] The journey to Cîteaux, the symbolical taking of the habit,. the meeting at Montpellier, the bishop's participation in the council of the legates would be explained; and the harmony between Diego's inspiration and that of the Pope himself, the eagerness to preach before all else, with intensity and without allowing themselves to be turned aside by anything else, the carefulness not to be deceived, not to allow anything of the authentic values the heretics possessed to be lost, the anxiety to respond with tact to requests, requests unbalanced but legitimate in principle—all this would be understandable.

In this case only one gesture would have been unexpected—Diego's decision, at the instigation of the legates, to suspend his return to Castile for a time and to share in the enterprise of apostolic preaching, a spontaneous gesture, quite after the manner of the bishop. In the outburst of his charity, at the challenge of circumstances, Diego was prompt to give expression to the living impulses of the Spirit.[81]

This indeed caused a curious legal imbroglio. A bishop neglecting his diocese, was preaching without a mandate, in a foreign land, unbeknown to his archbishop, and was allowing himself to be constituted the 'guide and leader' of two pontifical legates in the very sphere of their mission. Finally, to crown the anomaly, he was making them adopt a way of life notably under suspicion in the Church at this time and in this province.

Obviously the legates could take as a guide anyone they thought right; but had they, on the other hand, the power to confer a mandate upon preachers whom they had met casually? Perhaps it might be legitimate as a provisional measure.[82] This was sufficient for the initial stages, and at the beginning the bishop doubtless did not know himself that his collaboration in the apostolic work would be relatively long. As the experiment continued, Maître Raoul preferred to refer to the Pope. It is, moreover, possible that at this date the chapter of Cîteaux expressly requested him to obtain Innocent's confirmation of the apostolic method thought out by Diego.[83] The reply left Rome on 17th November.[84] In somewhat over-stylized Biblical language, it covered both the method and the preaching of the Castilians and their Cistercian collaborators whom Arnaud had gone to seek.

We are informed, said the Pope, that the number of apostates in the Narbonensis province has multiplied to such an extent that, through the defection of the temporal sword, the spiritual sword has become an object of contempt . . . and that, to reclaim in the measure possible those who are already lying in the prison of their blindness, no one is rising up as a rampart to protect the house of the Lord, no one has the courage to mount the breaches (Ez. XIII, 5). It is true that this news . . . coming to the ears of a few religious, has stirred their courage, and has urged them to turn against the heretics the streams of their learning and to distribute their waters in public places (Prov. V, 16) in the fervour of the Spirit. But, having received no mandate from anyone soever (Rom. X, 15), they have not dared to assume the office of preacher on their own authority, in order not to share the lot of Dathan and Abiram whom the earth swallowed up alive (Num. XVI, 32 and Deut. XI, 6). So much so that finally there is found no one to maintain the cause of God before the people who wander adrift. . . .

We therefore ordain and prescribe by this apostolic letter that in your discretion you take proved men, apt to fulfil the office which we reserve to them, and determined, in imitating the poverty of Christ who was himself a poor man, to approach the humble in lowly garb, but with the fervour of the Spirit, and that you enjoin upon them in remission of their sins to go among the heretics without delay, so that through the example of their action and the doctrine they preach, they recall them so completely from error, if the Lord deigns to grant this . . . that they may have the joy of one day possessing that which the Gospel saying justifies them in hoping for—'Do not be afraid you, my little flock, your Father is determined to give you his Kingdom. (Luke XII, 32). . . .'

Innocent was far away. He was perhaps under a certain illusion about Diego's scruples. At this time the bishop had already been preaching against the Albigenses for nearly six months with Maître Raoul and Brother Dominic.

Hardly indeed had he taken his decision and sent back his baggage to Osma than he left Montpellier accompanied by the two legates and his companion. The Guillem territory had no need of their services, nor had the diocese of Maguelonne. They moved quickly towards Béziers, travelling along the ancient Domitian Way. After half a day's march they passed into the diocese of Agde; at the day's close they were already entering that of Béziers. From now onwards they were in the midst of completely heretical territory. The extensive overlordship into which they entered belonged to Etienne de Servian, one of the principal vassals of the viscounty of Béziers-Carcassonne.[85] Etienne was a convinced 'believer' and a great protector of the Catharists.[86] He had thrown his lands open to all the heresiarchs who wished to come there and received them in his castles, where he defended and maintained them, allowing them to preach and argue in public and even to keep schools. He thus harboured a whole series of famous preachers, in particular Bernard de Simone, 'bisbe' of Carcassonne,[87] Baudouin and above all Thierry de Nevers.[88] The latter was assuredly one of the most dangerous propagandists of the sect. Originating from France and of noble origin he had for long, under his real name of William, been a canon of Nevers and, according to all appearances, also archdeacon of that diocese. Implicated at the same time as several of his friends, members of the upper clergy, in the heresy trials at Charité-sur-Loire from 1198 onwards, he had seen his uncle, the Chevalier Evrard de Châteauneuf, the trusted friend of the Counts of Auxerre and Nevers, condemned and burned in Paris in 1201. He had then thrown off the mask, changed his name and taken flight. Like so many others, it was in the Narbonensis that he sought refuge. There he was held in special honour, because he was more brilliant than the others and because they were proud of having as their coreligionist and apologist a former cleric from that country of France from which a stream of learning was flowing at that particular time.[89]

Scarcely had they arrived in the township of Servian, at the end of June or the beginning of July,[90] than the preachers of the faith succeeded in organizing a public debate under the presidency of the lord of the place. An exposition by the Catholic preachers, with a counter-exposition by the heresiarchs Baudouin and Thierry and the succeeding controversial dispute, followed its course of development during the week[91] amid a plentiful supply of texts from the New Testament. The population attended, in some excitement. Feeling soon ran high. The bishop seemed to have things all his own way. When he had forced Thierry de Nevers to follow him to his final conclusion, the atmosphere was tense almost to the point of hurling insults. The same Thierry who one day when at the end of his arguments was heard to repeat in a rage: 'The prostitute'—he meant the Church—'has held me for a long time, she shall have me no longer,'[92] now hurled brusquely in Diego's face the insult 'I know not of what spirit thou art. It is in the spirit of Elias that thou art come.' To which the bishop retorted: 'Perhaps in the spirit of Elias; but thou in the spirit of Antichrist.'[93] Thierry wanted to startle his Catharist believers by denouncing in Diego a reincarnation of John the Baptist, in their eyes one of the worst henchmen of the god of evil, the god of the Old Testament.[94] The hour had come for interjections, warnings, threats and entreaties. The people were visibly impressed. They were ready, we are told, to return to the way of salvation in a body, and were already beginning to detest the heresiarchs who had led them astray, and were desirous of expelling them. On similar occasions the crowd had lighted the fires despite the opposition of the clergy.[95] All now depended on the attitude of the lord of the place, Etienne de Servian. He made no move. The heresiarchs were living in his house and had his friendship, for he shared their belief. Despite the success of the preaching, the Catholic cause was again compromised. It seemed certain that, following the departure of the preachers, the heresiarchs, protected by the temporal authority, would soon have won back all their influence over this fickle population. Nevertheless, when the small band of legates went on their way again, the crowd went with them in procession. It accompanied them for nearly a league, that is, almost to the gates of Béziers. For a long time already the disquieting city had been in sight, its towers and belfries standing high up on its rocky promontory, in the loop of the Orb.

In view of their intentions the missionaries needed a certain courage to enter the city. Béziers, the most revolutionary of the communes of the Midi, the one most devoted to heresy, was also the one most given to bloodshed. On 15th October, 1167, the townsmen had assaulted their own lord, Viscount Raymond Trencavel in the church of the Madeleine; there they had killed him, with the same blow breaking the jaw of the bishop who was struggling to defend him.[96] Ever since, the town had remained in a state of ferment and as far removed as possible from orthodoxy. A rough list drawn up by the bishop in 1209, before the advent of the crusade, enumerated more than two hundred notable families who were heretics.[97] Some pushed their hatred of the Church as far as aggression and sacrilege.[98] The viscount and his guardian, Bernard de Saissac, despite formal and recent promises, did nothing to stop them.[99] Thus, when at the beginning of their office as legates, Peter and Raoul had presented themselves before the bishop of the place, Guillaume de Roquessel, to beg him to go and find the consuls and summon them to abjure heresy and for the future to support the Church, he had refused, and had even prevented the legates from taking such action themselves.[100] This had not saved him. A year later, suspended by the Pope, he was assassinated 'by the treachery of his own people'.[101]

The preachings and disputations began again at Béziers in the same way as at Servian. The contest must have been even sharper. It lasted for a fortnight. The heretics were more numerous, the population was more genuinely favourable to them, and in view of the importance of the city, the Catholics, too, were more relentless. People were soon afraid of some untoward happening. The violence and harshness in legal procedure of Peter of Castelnau particularly roused the hatred of his adversaries. Diego and Raoul feared he would be assassinated. They advised him to separate from them for a time.[102] Peter accordingly did so. In the middle of that month of July he had just received a fresh mission from the Pope.[103] It was not until five or six months later that he rejoined the group of preachers. The apostolic character of the preaching undoubtedly gained from this.

It did not however obtain the same success as in Servian. Put to confusion, the unbelievers remained none the less convinced. Only the Catholics of the town, not very numerous, we are told, were strengthened in their faith.[104] Diego, Raoul and Dominic then left Béziers and resumed their journey following the Domitian Way.

All along their route both villages and castles were deeply affected by heresy. A few years later, at the announcement of the arrival of the crusaders and of the taking of Béziers, all the inhabitants of the region left.[105] The preachers, however, did not want to stop on the way. They went direct to the principal centre, Carcassonne. The city stood out then, just as we see it today, on the crown of its high hill, not far away from the Aude. Its principal wall, liberally adorned with towers, the strong castle of the viscount, the two concentric outer bastions each girded with its walls and moat,[106] gave it a formidable aspect. It was a true stronghold of heresy, for its townsmen were known as 'the worst heretics and sinners before God'.[107] The traces of the apostolate of Peter and Raoul had quickly been obliterated. Bishop Bérenger, however,[108] continued to expend all his energies against the unbelievers and his fruitless preachings became increasingly violent. Beside themselves but not converted, his fellow-townsmen soon drove him from the city (mid

1207) by herald's proclamation forbidding the people to have any dealing with him in future, or to buy from or sell anything to him or those of his household.

> 'You will not listen to me' (the bishop thundered). 'Believe me, I shall raise such a clamour against you that men will come from the farthest confines of the world to destroy this shameful town. You can be certain that the walls of this city, were they of iron and raised as high as heaven, will not be able to protect you against the deserved vengeance that the most just Judge will visit upon your incredulity and your malice'.[109]

The band of legates had nothing of this threatening aspect, especially since Peter of Castelnau had left them. They devoted themselves for a week to preaching and disputations. Then they went on their way again.

The chronicler, Pierre des Vaux-de-Cernai, whose account is an invaluable source because he was in direct contact with the majority of the actors in this story and had access to reports and archives of the Narbonensis mission which the legate Arnaud Amaury[110] kept with great care, has not thought it worth continuing to follow the journey, which was prolonged, step by step.[111] We know, however, from another chronicle that one of the first halts after Carcassonne was made quite near Toulouse.[112] The intention of this first part of the expedition was clear—to reach the capital of the county as quickly as possible. Béziers, Carcassonne, Toulouse, in this way the chief centres of heresy which significantly coincided with the political centres of the land, the capital cities of the Saint-Gilles and the Trencavels, would have been dealt with. They would then turn back and by a zig-zag march make the round of the villages and fortified townships to sow the truth of the Gospel everywhere, while disputing with the heterodox.[113]

Each one of the localities in the Toulouse region, in the Lauragais or the Razès had its own history in the sect, often a long-standing one inscribed within the situation of their beliefs as much as in the memory of men. Lavaur, for instance, which the missionaries must have visited about this time,[114] had been the subject of a siege in 1181 by a holy army recently levied by Cardinal Pietro d'Albano, former Abbot of Clairvaux and pontifical legate.[115] This was the first application of the 27th canon of the Lateran. The effect of it had not been lasting. Neither was the effect of the preaching of Diego and his companion decisive. In 1211, a second siege was to end in a massacre of Catharist knights.[116] At Verfeil, the last stage before Toulouse, the insulting reception given to St Bernard was still in men's minds a century after the event.[117] When, in the church, he had tried to speak of the heresy and of the responsibilities of the lay authorities, the lord of the place had risen and all had left the church after him. There were then more than one hundred knights in the town. Bernard had moved out to the public square so as to speak at least to the humble folk; but his adversaries began to cry out and slam their doors with such violence that Bernard, shaking the dust off his feet, had departed, cursing the town—'Green leaf (*Ver(te) feuille*) may God wither you.' Many thought in the years to come that the later misfortunes of this brilliant company of knights were due in part to a saint's curse. They listened with more readiness to Diego who defended the reality of the divinity and humanity of Christ.[118] Once more he revealed the theological naïvety of his adversaries Pons Jourdain, Arré Arrufat and other heresiarchs.[119]

Such was the drama of the Albigeois—the doctrinal poverty of the Catharists and the strength of the influence of their personal attitude, which was austere and apostolic. This would be clearly seen in the single disputation that the documents make known to us in some detail, the one in which for the first time, the figure of Dominic comes into view, the dispute of Montréal.

CHAPTER VII

THE PREACHING OF JESUS CHRIST

B ETWEEN the Mediterranean and the wide valley drained by the
Garonne as far as the Atlantic, the plain of the Lauragais offers easy
passage. The highest point, two or three miles beyond Castelnaudary,
is less than 600 feet high. To the west, a long and shallow river[1] flows
down in the direction of Toulouse. On the east two other rivers[2] flow
towards Carcassonne, where, joining the Aude, they move slowly down until
they disappear in the blue waters of the sea by Narbonne On both sides of
the fringe of the Lauragais, however, the hills soon begin to mass together
and rise into clumps. To the north there is the Montagne Noire, with its
4,000 feet, on the edge of the Cevennes. The torrents hollow out in it deep
ravines, the edges of which are crowned with castles like eagles' nests. To
the south are the successive tiers of the first plateaux, of the Petites Pyrénées
and the Corbières, which form a step-ladder to the high peaks which sometimes rise to 10,000 feet.

This route has been a highway for men to travel along since prehistoric
times, when the final retreat of the sea first opened the corridor of the river
valley to the flow of the streams of humanity. There the Romans established
a lateral branch of the Domitian Way. Later the waterway of the Canal du
Midi and the track of the railway would pass that way. From the beginning
Toulouse at one end, Carcassonne at the other, formed as it were the bolts
of this indispensable corridor. The political axis of the region was thus set in
a determined pattern, at the same time as the economic axis. In the twelfth
century the intensive travelling to and fro of reformers, merchants, pilgrims,
crusaders or preachers, promoters in their different ways of spiritual innovations, made this route equally a religious axis. At the beginning of the
thirteenth century the Toulouse-Carcassonne axis was one of heresy. Since
1206 the Catholic missionaries had been able to do nothing more than travel
slowly through this section of the country, multiplying their deep incursions
into the secondary valleys.

A series of strong castles and fortified townships on the southern edge of
the corridor commanded the plain or controlled the ways of access to a
difficult hinterland at the foot of the Pyrenees—Razès, the Pays de Sault, the
County of Foix. Three of these townships formed a group—Laurac-le-Grand,
Fanjeaux and Montréal. At the beginning of 1207, the missionaries seemed

to become more centred on these townships and not to move far from their neighbourhood. This was because they were now in the very heart of the Catharist heresy.

The castle of Laurac,[3] the former capital of the Lauragais, was the outpost fortress of the Trencavel and the centre of their power in the direction of Toulouse. The powerful family which held it had been completely Catharist for three generations. The grandmother, Blanche, was still living. A series of documents describe her activities between 1200 and 1210. She was then formally garbed as a heretic and directed a community of Perfect women in the place. She had founded similar communities in different localities. She had likewise founded a house of hospitality for the Perfect, kept by Isarn de Castres, a Catharist deacon. The nobility of Laurac and the surrounding district met together with Blanche's community to hear the sermons of another deacon, Raymond Bernard. On certain days Bernard de Saissac could be seen making his appearance there, and even Raymond-Roger de Foix. In 1225, Isarn de Castres would return from Montségur to preach to this loyal aristocracy in the great hall of the castle.

Blanche's[4] five children were likewise known as declared heretics. One of her daughters, Mabilia, directed a community of Perfect women as she did. Another daughter, Giraude, Dame de Lavaur, was to be thrown to the bottom of a well by the crusaders after the taking of the town. A third, married to one of the Niort family, had transmitted her belief to her three sons, Raymond, Guillaume and Bernard-Othon, who would one day inherit Laurac. Lastly, we shall soon meet again Aimery de Montréal, the eldest of the family.

Five miles or so to the west of Laurac, Fanjeaux[5] constituted the most important centre of communications of the region. From the high hill on which it was perched, the town in fact dominated a network of valleys which opened in turn towards the Aude, the Ariège and the Garonne. Set like a gateway at the point where the road from Carcassonne to Pamiers climbed before crossing the plateau, it controlled the route which led to the upper valley of the Ariège, looking from behind as it were on to the counties of Comminges and of Foix. Thus the Romans had established themselves at this crossroad, erecting a temple to Jupiter there as is recalled in the name of the place—*Fanum Jovis*. The feudal lords in their turn had made of Fanjeaux a fortified place with walls and moats, the vestiges of which can still be seen despite numerous sieges, fires and later destruction. More than fifty noble families had their dwellings there. The seignorial rights were divided to the last degree. There were, however, two rulers[6] who predominated over the rest—the *Domina miles*, Dame Cavaers, and Count Raymond-Roger de Foix, who thus secured the gateways of his own territory.

As at Laurac, the noble families of Fanjeaux had been devoted to the Catharists since the twelfth century, several of them for two, three and even four generations. This was the case with the Tonneins, the Assalit, the Mazeroles, the Durfort, the Feste, the Mortier, the Saint-Michel, the Isarn.[7] Dame Cavaers was already a Catharist in 1193. She had had her daughter brought up by the 'Perfect', and the girl for long remained loyal to them.[8] Finally the Count of Foix, though he did not participate in the heretical rites himself, did not hesitate to be present at them, as in 1205 at the sensational entry into heresy of his sister Esclarmonde.[9]

Guilabert de Castres[10] had been directing a community of 'Perfect' at Fanjeaux since 1193. It was still in existence in 1204 and even in 1209, and served as a centre for his preaching. This indefatigable propagandist had been *bisbe* of the Toulouse region[11] since 1208 at least, residing, it seems, at Lavaur. He frequently returned, however, to Fanjeaux. Already in 1195, Guilhelme de Tonneins directed a house of Perfect women there; her daughter Aude succeeded her. Other Catharist communities, male and female, were still to be met with in the locality.[12] Finally a number of women converts to Catharism threw open their houses for sermons, ceremonies or religious discussions, which the nobility of the district were not slow to frequent.

Fanjeaux possessed even more exceptional phenomena. At least two Catharist doctors of medicine were to be found there, Maître Arnaud and Bernard d'Ayros,[13] who practised throughout the Lauragais. With their devoted services they combined religious propaganda and direct invitations to receive the *consolamentum*. Finally there were workshops for craftsmen[14] recalling the connection with weaving of the original heterodox groups of the neighbourhood half a century earlier. Thus equipped, the Fanjeaux centre could reach all classes of the population. It presented the characteristics and had the effectiveness of a headquarters of the dualist religion.

About five miles from Fanjeaux on the road to Carcassonne, Montréal[15] was just such another similar centre. Situated on the crest of a group of hills which served as an outpost, the fortified town cut off the road and looked out over the whole plain. The view from it also took in the boundary of the viscounty and diocese of Carcassonne with the diocese and county of Toulouse. Its lord, Aimery de Montréal et Laurac,[16] was Blanche's eldest son. He was the most powerful lord in the Lauragais and one of the principal advisers of Raymond of Toulouse and of Raymond-Roger of Béziers-Carcassonne. A Catharist believer, like all his family, he was to flee from the crusaders in 1209, submit to them twice to preserve his fief, and twice betray them. It was this that led to his execution at the termination of the siege of Lavaur, together with his sister Giraude. He was the patron of the Perfect. Two deacons were permanently stationed in his township, as well as several communities of both sexes. The principal nobles and townsmen received and entertained the preachers in their houses. They were present in large numbers at their solemn rites, their prayers and their sermons. With Aimery de Laurac at their head, all rendered to their Perfect, at the conclusion of the ceremonies, those signs of veneration which the Catholics classed as 'adoration'.

Such was the stronghold of Montréal where the pontifical preachers were summoned to meet in the spring of 1207. It was about March or the beginning of April.[17] The hills, on the edge of the plain, were covered with almond-trees in blossom. The moist ochre of the soil, still apparent among the vines, formed a sharp contrast with the green of the growing corn. The faint rose colour of the Roman tiles on the flat roofs of the houses was hardly visible in the midst of the clumps of pine trees and cypresses. Neither Diego, Raoul nor Dominic, however, paid attention to the beauty of the countryside in this southern spring. They were on their way to combat. A disputation of importance[18] awaited them in the stronghold of the Catharists. Their hearts were stirred by mixed feelings in which were mingled the joy of the pugilist,[19] the sense of responsibility as champions of the Church, and primarily the charity and hope of the apostle.[20] They thought of the souls they would snatch from the devil and damnation—of mounting the breaches and forming of their persons a rampart for the Church.[21] In any event, they were desirous of bearing witness to their faith and of proclaiming it higher than the roof-tops[22] of Montréal and were determined to give in the presence of these stray sheep the reasons for the faith and hope they bore in their hearts.[23]

It was perhaps the Catharists who had taken the initiative in the matter of the meeting.[24] Momentarily disconcerted by the action of Diego and Raoul, they were no longer satisfied with defending themselves from day to day, as opportunity offered. The closeness of their hierarchical organization in the Narbonensis was considerable. For forty years now they had held what amounted to veritable councils there, imitating the Catholic councils.[25] In 1206, it seems, nearly six hundred of them had met at Mirepoix.[26] Perhaps they had there discussed their counter-thrust against the legates. In any case their resistance quickly stiffened and became organized.[27] It is possible that they themselves conceived the idea of a general meeting in their fief of Montréal.

The famous Guilabert de Castres came down from Fanjeaux for the contest, perhaps even from his bishop's residence in Toulouse. Pons Jourdain, whom the legates had already met at Verfeil, came with him.[28] From the south came Benoît de Termes,[29] future Bishop of the Razès, and from the north the deacon Arnaud Othon,[30] who had been preaching in the Cabardès under the protection of the Sire de Cabaret. Peter of Castelnau, however, joined his colleagues again on the occasion of this disputation.[31]

A large number of secondary collaborators were also present.[32] Thus the leaders, surrounded by their followers, were four against four, bishops against bishops, Church against Church. This was indeed the general disputation[33] spoken of by a contemporary. After ten months of local and partial encounters, the Catholics and the Catharists were going to come to grips in their full strength and on every ground.

The meeting could not have taken place without the intervention of the lord, Aimery de Montréal. It was doubtless he who presided over it. As was customary in this kind of contest, four judges were to be arbitrators of the disputation and to declare which side was victorious.[34] They were chosen among the nobles and the townsmen—Bernard de Villeneuve and Bernard d'Arzens, on the one side, Raymond Got and Arnaud Rivière on the other. The astonishing fact and one which spoke volumes for the religious position of the neighbourhood was that although elected by both parties, the four judges were Catharist believers or supporters. The *Histoire Albigeoise* says so expressly and it is confirmed by the documents. The knights had been declared 'faidits' at the time of the crusade and were dispossessed on that account; the townsmen had frequented heretical ceremonies and sent help to the Catharist preachers.[35]

Fifty years after the disputation, Guillaume de Puylaurens was astonished at the nature and circumstances of this debate. When the theses forming the subject of the disputation were enumerated, he exclaimed: 'How heart-rending. Has the position of the Church and the Catholic faith fallen so low in this Christian land that one is obliged to abandon to laymen the responsibility of pronouncing judgement on doctrines that are so critical?'[36] It was surely to the bishops meeting in council that it appertained to settle questions touching revelation so closely. Shortly afterwards the inquisitor Bernard Gui, in the name of long-standing experience, formally discouraged the debating of questions of faith with certain heresiarchs in the presence of the laity. The simple, he said, might be disturbed by this—'for they are convinced that we have at hand reasons for the faith which are so clear and obvious that no one can put forward any objection without our being able to convince him there and then and in such a way that the illiterate themselves can clearly understand these reasons'.[37] Truth is often less specious than error. Such is the feeling of the Church of our own times, above all since the disappointments of the meetings of the sixteenth century.

This was not the position adopted by the preachers. They were relying on a tradition much older than the Albigensian missions since it went right back to St Augustine. The Bishop of Hippo had not ceased his efforts until he had obtained from the imperial authorities the organization of discussions with the leaders of the Donatists. For a long time the latter made excuses. When, however, the emperor had forced their bishops to discussions with the

Catholics, the collapse of their church, until then solidly unshakable, was precipitated.[38]

In the twelfth century, the mission against the heretics included such discussions together with the sermons, in the very midst of the legal trials.[39] What differentiated one from the other was sometimes difficult to discern.[40] At Lombers,[41] at Toulouse,[42] at Narbonne,[43] at Carcassonne,[44] highly controversial meetings took place. Bernard himself had agreed to participate in them.[45]

Discussion indeed obliged the sectaries to renounce what Christianity most abominated in them by tradition—the clandestine or, at the very least, private character of their 'conventicles', the indoctrination of lay people by preachers without mandate or control;[46] for the future the heresiarch would have to defend his beliefs publicly against theologians and in the presence of bishops. And because the disputation took place before the very people who had heard the heterodox preaching through the evidence of those present, such discussions enabled the identity between the public confession of the heretics and their ordinary teaching to be checked.[47] This was particularly necessary in the case of the Catharists, who excelled in dissimulating their true position, and in turn, according to the circumstances, emphasized their practice which was genuinely evangelical, or their dualist teaching which was in truth so little Christian.[48] Put to confusion, the heresiarch was not converted, but he lost his authority. The laity again heard the authentic word of God in circumstances that were clearly impressive. Finally, the temporal authorities who presided over the disputation were clearly once more set face to face with their responsibilities.

It is true that the heresiarchs often needed courage to present themselves for the public controversy, more dangerous for them than a private interrogation. Henri de Lausanne in Toulouse had not been willing to face up to St Bernard's challenge.[49] This had been the signal for his downfall, since the people did not forgive him for this evasion. The men of that time indeed did not lack the quality of courage. 'To give an account of the hope they cherished.' This phrase of the epistle of St Peter,[50] often met with in the documents, expressed their attitude clearly.[51] In 1207, in the Narbonensis and especially at Montréal, in view of the disposition of the public and of the authorities, such courage was particularly necessary for the Catholic missionaries.

The controversy lasted a fortnight. Arnaud Othon, the deacon, attacked. He set forth the basis[52] of the dispute from the side of the Catharists.

> The Roman Church [he said] is not holy; she is not the bride of Christ. She is, on the contrary, the church of the devil and her doctrine is demoniacal; she is that Babylon which John, in the Apocalypse, calls the mother of fornications and abominations, drunk with the blood of the saints and martyrs of Jesus Christ.

Her discipline is neither holy, good nor instituted by the Lord Jesus Christ; never did Christ or the apostles impose or dispose the rite of the Mass as it exists at present.[53]

The classic themes of the attacks against the early Church will be recognized, themes which the Protestant controversies were so eager to take up again in the sixteenth century. The choice of themes was lacking not in cleverness but in novelty. It was not easy in the simplifications and passions of a controversial meeting to make the necessary distinctions between the divine and human elements of the Church. It was difficult to make the crowds, who were completely lacking in any sense of history, grasp the legitimacy of a homogeneous development of rites.

The Bishop of Osma led the debates on the Catholic side. He was only able to use the New Testament, since the Catharists rejected the rest of the Bible. One can imagine that the missionaries did not remain on the defensive. The question was not concerning the authority of the Roman Church or of the Catharist church, but of the errors for which the Roman Church rejected the Catharists, in regard to the oneness of God, the rôle of Christ and of the cross in the redemption, the nature of sin, of the soul, of salvation. Everyone eagerly bustled around Diego. That it might be more effective, it was resolved to conduct the controversy in writing.[54] That is, the texts and arguments intended for use in the public discussions were set down in writing[55] after which the plan of the arguments and replies was drawn up anew. These texts were then transmitted to the judges to enable them to give their verdict.[56] The drawing up of these different documents before and after the session demanded a great deal of work. If we are correct in relating to this controversy an incident of which all that is known is that it happened in the course of an incident at Montréal,[57] Dominic had been put in charge of certain parts of the debate. One evening he wrote down on a sheet of paper the 'authorities', that is, the texts of the Bible and of the Fathers of the Church, which he had used in the discussion, and transmitted them to his opponent so that he might reflect upon them. The following is what was reported of him later, as it was related to Pierre des Vaux-Cernai:

In the course of the night, the heretics were sitting round the fire. The particular one among them to whom the man of God had handed the sheet of paper passed it to those around him. His companions then suggested that he should throw it into the midst of the fire; if the paper was burnt, it was their belief, that is to say their misbelief, that was true; if, on the contrary, it did not burn, they would acknowledge the truth of the belief of our preachers. In short, all were in agreement. The paper was thrown into the fire, but although it remained for some time in the very midst of the flames, it dropped out of them again without being burnt in any way at all. All were amazed. One of them, harder than the others, said: 'Let it be thrown into the fire again, we shall thus see more fully what the truth is.' It was forthwith thrown into the fire and forthwith it dropped out again unburnt. On seeing this the man who was hard and slow to believe said: 'Let it be thrown in a third time, we shall then know the truth without any more uncertainty.' It was thrown in for the third time and not only did it again not burn, but dropped out of the fire perfectly whole and intact. Nevertheless even at the sight of so many marvels, the heretics were not willing to be converted to the true faith. They persisted in their ill-will and stubbornness and rigorously forbade each other to allow news of the miracle to reach us by talking of it. A knight who was with them, however, and already somewhat inclined to our faith, had no wish to hide what he had just seen and told it to several persons.

The anecdote is typical. The dissidents were not intellectuals and the truth of the parchment seemed to them easier to prove through the intermediary of a miracle than by the reading or study of the texts. They then tried an 'ordeal' by fire, that type of God's judgement of which the feudal and even the ecclesiastical courts made considerable use, despite the reprobation of the Popes.[58] As a rule it was men who were made to pass through this cruel test.[59] The ordeal of a book, however, is not unknown. In former times Alfonso VI of Castile, urged to choose between the Mozarabic and the Roman rite had, so it was said, thrown the books of both liturgies into the fire. The book of the Mozarabic rite did not burn. The king however decided in the sense contrary to the miracle.[60] The men of Montréal did likewise. To touch hearts something more than miracles was necessary.

Dominic's intervention is a proof that in the discussions the procedure of the theological disputations of the time was followed. The themes were divided into series of questions and the process began by allowing secondary theologians to dispute. Then the masters took up one by one the questions which had been unravelled, to arrive at the conclusions or determinations. When the whole of the questions had thus been debated, each of the opposing groups met separately and drew up the scheme of the disputation with arguments for and against, and the conclusions. If credence may be given to a report by Jordan, several preachers summed up the disputation; Dominic's memorandum was judged the best and chosen to represent the Catholic thesis.[61]

As to the lay judges, impressed, we are assured, by the patent defeat of their champions, they refrained from giving their verdict and even from deliberating. They further refused to give the Catholics back their memorandum, lest it should come under the public eye, and gave it to their adversaries. It was lost—either destroyed by the Catharists, or perhaps disappearing a few years later in the upheavals of the crusade.[62] The fact did not prevent imagination from setting to work feverishly on the subject of the memorandum drawn up by St Dominic and the report of the disputation. Between the thirteenth century and the sixteenth century several people claimed to have rediscovered the text.[63]

More lasting and more valuable traces, however, remained in men's hearts. If the Perfect came out of the contest more eager than ever to contradict the pontifical missionaries, if Aimery de Montréal and the secular authorities had no intention of changing their attitude in the slightest degree, one hundred and fifty persons abandoned their heresy. Bernard de Villeneuve later revealed this to Guillaume de Puylaurens. Villeneuve is worthy of credence, for at this time he favoured the Catharists.

After the end of the disputation, Peter of Castelnau left for Provence,[64] for the purpose of binding together the greatest possible number of the vassals of Toulouse in a league for peace. The temporal force thus assembled would enable them to drive out the Catharists. It might even impress the count to the extent that he would be brought to swear peace in his turn and to drive out his heretics. If necessary, he would be constrained to this by the revolt and war of the vassals of the league at the same time as by the excommunication.[65]

Diego, Raoul and Dominic, however, followed quite a different procedure. They did not leave Montréal.[66] They followed up the initial success obtained and journeyed through the neighbourhood, visiting villages and castles, and sowing the seed of the word of God. Vagrants of Christ, conforming to the pattern put before them by Diego, they lived like the apostles and begged their bread from door to door. The Bishop of Osma in particular made an impression. The humility and moral beauty which emanated from the person of this man of God 'won him the affection even of the infidels and penetrated to the very hearts of all those among whom he lived; thus the heretics asserted in regard to him that it was impossible that such a man was not predestined to eternal life. Perhaps he had only been sent to these parts to learn from them the rules of the true faith.'[67]

On 17th April, Dominic obtained from Bérenger de Navarre an important donation for an establishment of converted women which had just been founded between Montréal and Fanjeaux, to which we shall again refer later.[68] The deed is dated from the see of Carcassonne. The Archbishop of Narbonne had doubtless followed the recent important disputation, at the side of the local bishop. The promises he had been forced to make to the Pope in the previous year obliged him to manifest this minimum of goodwill.

At the end of April fresh and impressive support reached the missionaries:[69] Arnaud Amaury arrived in Montréal accompanied by twelve abbots of his order. 'Twelve, in accordance with the most sacred number of the apostles',[70] under the guidance of their leader; each one had with him a companion, for Jesus had sent forth his preachers two by two. The band, to the number of thirty or less, had concentrated at Cîteaux in the course of the month of March, faithful to the rendezvous fixed by the chapter in the previous September. It had reached the banks of the Saône and embarked. Letting themselves drift down the Saône and the Rhône, the company had landed at Arles or Beaucaire.[71] 'Without money for the journey, without horses', to show that in all things they were 'men of the Gospel', the Cistercians came to make contact with heresy, 'armed with the prestige of learning and eloquence, ready to give satisfaction to anyone who should ask them to justify their belief, ready even to risk their lives boldly for the faith.'[72] The promise made by Arnaud a little less than a year earlier, the request made by the Pope to the order as a whole three years before, were now realized.[73]

The mission of preaching decided upon by Innocent III at the beginning of 1204 was at last bearing fruit. For the future the documents would make frequent mention of the preachers, 'the holy preachers', 'our preachers',[74] 'the preachers of the word of God, ministers of His Holiness';[75] they speak moreover of the 'abbots to whom the lord Pope had given mandate to preach against the heretics'.[76] The enterprise as a whole was called 'the Preaching',[77] 'the Holy Preaching'[78]. In view of the field of operations of the delegation, one might call it 'the Preaching of the Narbonensis'. The missionaries' seal, however, displayed a more definite and quasi-official title: 'Preaching of Jesus Christ'.[79]

The name of Jesus Christ had in fact been set up since the twelfth century as the fitting insignia of the enterprises against the infidel, especially against the Catharists. The vocabulary of the Albigensian crusade was to make great use of this. The armed crusade was the *militia Jhesu Christi*; its activity the *servitium Jhesu Christi*; its leader the *comes Jhesu Christi*;[80] it was in the name of Jesus Christ that the challenge against the supporters of the Catharists[81] was launched; a military order against the heretics was soon to be founded in the Albigeois: the *militia fidei Jhesu Christi*.[82] The name, however, was not confined to military activities, a bishop who did not preach against the heretics was an 'enemy of Christ';[83] the *negotium Jhesu Christi*, mentioned by the *Histoire Albigeoise*,[84] covered all matters of faith in the Narbonensis; the 'Preaching of Jesus Christ' was an essential part of it.

Of the forty or so religious who had composed it since April 1207, only certain names are known to us—primarily those of the three Cistercian legates and the two Castilians. Among the twelve abbots were Gui, Abbot of Vaux-de-Cernai[85] (near Paris); he had not yet with him his secretary and nephew Peter, the author of the *Histoire Albigeoise*, who arrived only in 1212.[86] Henri, Abbot of Mont-Sainte-Marie[87] (diocese of Besançon) was there too. Perhaps, but it is pure conjecture, the Abbot of Bonnevaux[88] (near Vienne) and the Abbot of Preuilly[89] (diocese of Meaux), were also there, and it is possible that the Abbot of Valmagne (diocese of Agde) whom the Pope had requested to furnish preachers, had joined the legates. We know nothing of Canon Raoul de Narbonne, likewise placed by the Pope at the disposal of his representative. On the other hand the Abbot of

Villelongue[90] (near Limoux) was on several occasions seen working with Dominic for conversions. The name of another Cistercian, the future Cardinal Rainier Capocci, then Abbot of Trois-Fontaines, was also mentioned.[91]

The group, as will be seen, was composed only of religious, the Bishop of Osma forming no exception. All were Cistercians with the exception of Dominic, the Canon Regular. This type of recruitment clearly had a purpose. It corresponded to the intentions of the Sovereign Pontiff when he decided upon the great mission at the beginning of 1204: a preaching by word and example of which the Cistercians were to be the heart and soul.[92] The inspiration of the Pope in regard to apologetics: 'to say nothing, to do nothing which might provoke criticism even from a heretic',[93] had developed in a positive way by the integral practice of the imitation of the apostles. The general confirmation of this as well as all its details, can be gathered from the documents.[94]

The missionaries properly so-called all had the title of prelate—the Bishop of Osma, the thirteen Cistercian abbots—or the title of master—Peter de Castelnau, Raoul de Fontfroide and Raoul de Narbonne. There still existed at this time a close link between the prelacy and teaching on the one hand, and preaching on the other.[95] It will be noted, however, that no bishop from the neighbourhood joined the group directly; as if, in this phase of the mission against the Albigenses, there had been a desire to make a distinct cleavage between the acts of evangelization and the pressure of authority.[96] In the same order of ideas the thrusting aside of Peter de Castelnau, who was wholly concerned with the manoeuvring of his instruments of spiritual and temporal coercion, was charged with meaning.

Up to this time the missionaries had acted in concert. The company moved from town to town, or spread out in all directions from a centre. After the arrival of the preachers from Cîteaux, it became too numerous to continue to move in a body. Arnaud immediately distributed the abbots over the whole of the Narbonensis.[97] He provided each of them with one or two auxiliaries,[98] assigning to him his own sphere of action or *termini*,[99] within the limits of which he was to move about the district, devoting himself with zeal to disputations and preaching.

Abbot Guy de Cernai left for Carcassonne, of which place he eventually became bishop. He arrived there on 24th June.[100] Abbot Henri de St Marie established himself at Pamiers, where he had arrived by 11th June.[101] Master Raoul must have reserved for himself the Saint-Gilles neighbourhood: he was there at the beginning of July.[102] Dominic remained where he was, between Montréal and Fanjeaux.[103] At the foot of the latter township, at the point at which the Sésoine which flows down the hill along the ravines crosses the route to Montréal, there were a chapel and a few houses. This was Prouille, scarcely a hamlet, which for a few months past now had come into the life of the Canon of Osma. He returned there as to his headquarters. A charter of 17th April, another of 8th August, showed him to be strongly linked to this corner of the earth. A priest who was a native of Pamiers, of the name of William Claret,[104] was with him from this time onwards.

This centre of the apostolate, more permanent than the others, enables us to surmise what this kind of home base of the apostolic preachers must have been like. Prouille formed a *pied-à-terre*, a place with a permanent personnel, the women converts earlier mentioned.[105] It was a place of rest and recollection; also a centre of supplies, the economic basis of which will be more clearly defined later. It was doubtless similar to the hospices where the passing Catharist preachers were received. The freedom of movement of the apostolic life had its own needs and everywhere gave rise to similar institutions. The differences, however, were notable. The feminine group at Prouille was of its nature more stable than the hospices kept by the ladies of the Perfect. It would shortly be made into a regular institution in accordance with the traditions of monastic life. The centre equally constituted the primitive curia where Dominic, in his office as pontifical preacher, delivered the letters of reconciliation.[106] As an official personage, by delegation of the legates of the Holy See, he possessed in effect the seal of the mission. In this way he could stamp with an authentic wax seal the charters he delivered to the converted to certify their return to the faith and to remind them of the conditions of their penance.

The name of Preaching applied to the general enterprise was now transferred to the centre of Prouille. It is in this way that we have precise details of the seal of the mission, which was still found at the foot of certain letters of penance at the beginning of the fourteenth century.[107] Unlike personal ecclesiastical seals, which were in the shape of a shuttle, this was round, in white wax—the shape characteristic of the ecclesiastical tribunals.[108] It corresponded to the powers of jurisdiction of the missionaries against the heretics. An *Agnus Dei*, such as one sees in the hands of St John Baptist, was represented in the centre—the symbol of Christ, crucified and risen again. It equally served as a sign on the standards of the next crusade against the Albigensians.[109] The inscription, somewhat obliterated, can nevertheless be read with certainty: *S[igillum] predicationis Jhesu Christi*.[110] On 8th August, 1207 Sans Gasc and his wife Ermengarde Godoline, both of servile condition, gave themselves and their property to the 'Holy preaching and to the Lord Dominic of Osma'.[111] This formula has given rise to some confusion among historians. Since the group of women converts later became the famous monastery of Sainte Marie de Prouille, it was thought that the name of 'Holy preaching' was the original name of the house of sisters as such. This was not so at all; it was the name of Dominic's centre of operations of which the group of convert ladies still formed part. Moreover this name disappeared

from the documents after the year 1208, when the Preaching of Jesus Christ
was almost completely overshadowed by the crusade.

It was, however, to reappear eight years later with the Preaching of
Toulouse, the first house of the order of Preachers. At that moment Dominic
would bear the title of *predicationis humilis minister*.[112] In 1217 the house in
Toulouse would be called: 'the Preaching of the church of St Romain'.[113]
In 1221, Fulk, the bishop of the diocese, remembering the origins of the
order of St Dominic would once more give to its leader the anachronistic
title of 'master of the Preaching'.[114] Moreover it was for long to remain the
custom to name the Dominican houses in the south of France 'the Preaching
of the house of Prouille, of the convent of Toulouse, of Limoges'[115] and in
the early days the order itself was sometimes to bear the name of 'Order of
the Preaching'.[116]

Despite the dispersion of its centre and of the division of the 'territories',
the Preaching of Jesus Christ preserved its unity. This was clearly due to the
government of its leaders. Mention has already been made of the rôle of
Innocent III. The Pope had conceived, decided on the enterprise, brought it
together and continued to direct it closely. Arnaud's rôle was important too.
He had obtained fresh recruits from his general chapter and brought them to
the site of their labours. Gifted organizer as he was, he divided the region
up so that it was distributed among his apostolic workers.

Arnaud could not, however, remain there permanently. His exalted office
too frequently called him elsewhere. A stable authority, that of the other
legates for instance, was necessary. Peter de Castelnau had other cares and
other gifts than that of preaching. Thus, from the beginning, Diego of Osma
replaced him at the head of the mission, at the side of Raoul de Fontfroide.
If it was not to a decision on the part of the Pope that he owed this position,
he at least held it by the will of the legates. The documents are categorical.
To Diego as well as to Raoul, Cernai assigns the title of *predicationis princeps
et magister*.[117] The title of *magister* should be noted.[118] The term is primarily
of scholastic origin and indicates an intellectual and moral rather than a legal
authority.[119] After the beginning of the twelfth century it was traditionally
used to designate the leader of a company of itinerant preachers holding a
mandate from the Church. Robert d'Arbrissel, St Norbert, Bernard de
Thiron had already been designated in this way.[120] The leaders of heterodox
preachers, Catharists or Waldenses, also used it.[121] It was later given to St
Francis, at the head of his first brethren when he preached in the Sudan.[122]
The reason for the use in this teaching is clearly the doctoral[123] character
of the preacher's sense (*predicator et doctor*) when he has received an official
mission (*officium predicationis, insistens doctrine*). Dominic revived the
title at Toulouse in 1216: *fr. Dominicus, prior et magister predicatorum*.[124] In
1221 the bishop would still call him *magister predicationis*, although this

(Photo: Leonard von Matt)

Servian, first stop on the journey of the itinerant preachers.

original title had at that very moment been replaced by the definitive appellation *magister ordinis fratrum predicatorum*.[125]

The rôle of the Bishop of Osma in the Preaching was considerable. Not only had he introduced the new apostolic method adopted, but he had given the spiritual stimulus which had led to its acceptance and its being put into practice. He was the inspirer and restorer of the papal preaching. He contributed to its organization, directed it and, finally, kept it in being by securing its economic basis.

During its initial years the Preaching of the Narbonensis lived in accordance with the pattern of life of any ordinary legation. The maintenance and expenses of the legates were assured by the 'procurations' which the churches among whom they carried out their ministry provided.[126] In view of the avarice of the Archbishop of Narbonne and the ruinous condition of the sees of Toulouse and Carcassonne, the financial position of Peter and Raoul was far from brilliant. Bérenger sometimes refused them necessities.[127] The nomination as legate of Arnaud, who had the revenues of Cîteaux at his disposal, improved things considerably.

In any case, after the Montpellier disputation, the Preaching's economy was suddenly simplified. The baggage and unnecessary servants were sent away, they travelled on foot and begged. Bérenger naturally found nothing to complain of in this. This life of 'the poor of Christ', which now became the rule of all the missionaries, gave them a remarkable freedom of movement and facility of adaptation.

After the arrival of the twelve abbots, however, some degree of organization was introduced. The interior fervour of men like Diego or Dominic could doubtless easily adapt itself to a continual effort of heroism; it was not possible to ask this of a body of forty or so religious. It was necessary to be able to breathe in between these evangelical rounds of preaching; to gather one's forces together again in some friendly house of hospitality without being solely at the mercy of the very restricted charity of hostile territory. The more systematized taking possession of the region, first given shape by the distribution of April 1207, enabled a minimum of economic organization to be carried out. The Bishop of Osma had the advantage of personal revenues. The proximity of Spain enabled him to have recourse to his funds there fairly rapidly. He made use of them for the upkeep of the missionaries.

From his revenues, relates the chronicler Robert of Auxerre,[128] he provided supplies of food which he deposited in various centres, for the use of the preachers. This was the economic basis of the centres or local Preachings. In August 1207, he decided to consolidate the system and to return for the time being to Castile. He wanted to put his domestic affairs in order and to bring back sufficient resources to provide for the needs of the preachers of the Narbonensis.[129] Dominic's centre at Prouille was clearly to be the first to benefit from this generosity.[130] Already the donations obtained from Bérenger of Narbonne, from Sans Gasc, from Ermengarde Godoline and from a few other persons,[131] were consolidating the material life of this centre. For the future, the 'brothers and sisters' of Dominic in Prouille would enjoy common revenues.

This was in no way a departure from the pattern of itinerant imitation of the apostles. It was the custom of the Catharist and Waldensian apostolic preachers in these parts, who received their food and lodging in solidly endowed hospices in the course of their rounds.[132] The analogy of the Preaching of Jesus Christ with that of the Albigensians was once more accentuated. The analogy, however, was perhaps even closer to the ideal of episcopal apostolic life that Diego had been meditating upon at Cîteaux. St Bernard, as has been said, had formerly drawn attention to the example of this in the person of his friend, St Malachy.[133] The great Irish bishop imitated the apostles by travelling on foot, in strict poverty, the parishes of the diocese which he evangelized unremittingly. He rested now and again for a short while, humbly effaced in the midst of the community, in the holy places he had himself multiplied in Ireland. When he was on the road, however, he sometimes lived by the Gospel, that is to say, on alms, and at other times, with even less demand on charity, on the provisions he had with him, the fruit of his brethren's labour.

The complex system which was thus that of the Preaching of Jesus Christ, in which the itinerant mendicant apostolate depended on a centre which was economically more stable, was in turn to be reproduced at the inception of the Preaching of Toulouse, that is, of the order of St Dominic. From this fact, as from other initial attempts which have been emphasized in the course of the narrative, the influence of the pontifical mission in the life, heart, intentions and experience of the father of Preachers, will be surmised.

At the beginning of the summer of 1207, however, Dominic had very little idea what the future held in store for him. As assistant to the Bishop of Osma, he contented himself with devoting all his energies to his work as evangelist. This was not easy. The Pope had destined his legates to a work that was particularly unrewarding. Guillaume d'Auxerre at this time recalled the memory of Maître Prévostin 'who had for long lived among the Manicheans (i.e. the Catharists) but had only been able to bring back a small number of them to the way of truth'.[134] All the Catholic labourers in the Albigeois were in this position. Peter and Raoul at the beginning had not effected less than their predecessors. In May 1204, the Pope was pleased to emphasize that already 'their labour had not been in vain'.[135] Nevertheless the harvest was too disproportionate to the efforts made for one or other of the legates not to feel discouraged. In May 1206, it will be remembered, they wanted to resign their office, 'because their preaching had had no result, or scarcely any, among the heretics'.[136]

The arrival of the Castilians had given them fresh hope. The first disputation at Servian had been a real success; the later ones achieved less. Soon the ardour of the heretics, aroused by contradiction, was unleashed with more zeal than ever.[137] The arrival of the twelve abbots had no effect on it. Formerly the problem had been the disproportion of the apostolic potential among Catholics and heterodox. The enormous difference of numbers remained. After three months of hard and tiring labours, when they had visited castles, townships and towns, the work of the missionaries could be summed up in two phrases: 'they bring back a small number, they instruct more thoroughly and confirm in the faith the small number of faithful whom they find';[138] they saw the others, infinite in number, imitating the asp of the psalm and stopping its ears with its tail so as not to hear the charmer.

At the beginning of July, Maître Raoul, exhausted, had withdrawn to the abbey of Franquevaux, near Saint-Gilles. He died there on the 7th or 8th of that month.[139] Certain of the abbots, discouraged, were beginning to leave the battlefield.[140] At this moment, the result of the Preaching would still be characterized, according to the *Histoire Albigeoise*, by the melancholy note of the previous year: 'by their sermons, by their disputations, they have only been able to achieve very little, or even nothing at all'.[141] The words of the preachers did not reach men's hearts, they were mocked at: 'It must be said,' exclaimed Guillermo de Tudela, 'bless my soul, these people take no more notice of sermons than of a rotten apple. For a whole five years or thereabouts, they have continued to behave in this way. These erring people will not be converted.'[142]

A few words suffice to sum up the later history of the Preaching. In September or October, almost all the abbots returned to their monasteries.[143] No more than the crusaders did they conceive of their mobilization by the Pope as an indefinite service.[144] The feudal lord judged that he had done enough when he had given his forty days, just the duration of a Lent of penance; he returned having gained his indulgence. The abbots had served four or five months. Other ministries called them elsewhere. The withdrawal of Raoul, that of Diego which would soon be in question, finally the assassination of Peter de Castelnau on 14th January, 1208 and the tidal wave of the crusade of the barons, practically ended the Cistercian Preaching.

Not totally, however. Guy des Vaux-de-Cernai in turn was named 'prior and master' of the Preaching.[145] He preached unremittingly. It must be admitted, however, if the accounts of the *Histoire Albigeoise* are to be relied upon, that his fashion of exhorting the heretics under the threat of the stake was more calculated to send them there than to cast them into the bosom of the Catholic faith.[146] Arnaud, who was to become Archbishop of Narbonne in 1212, and Fulk, Bishop of Toulouse, did not fail to address

similar words to their flocks when the war permitted them to approach
them. 'There is the bee buzzing about', the Catharists would say mock-
ingly.[147] Eventually a certain number of 'preachers of the faith' at the
disposal of the Church were again found for the Albigeois. In 1213 they
would be sufficiently numerous for Maître Robert de Courson, pontifical
legate, in difficulty over finding preachers for the Holy Land, to judge it
profitable to round them up and only to release some of them the following
year. These, however, were preachers of the crusade and the majority of
them preached in France.[148]

There remained, indeed, the humble centre of Prouille. Diego, who saw
the Cistercian mission collapsing, now placed all his hope in the apostolate
of Dominic and his small group. When in September 1207 he decided to
return to Castile to bring back subsidies, he also contemplated bringing back
subjects capable of preaching.[149] If Jordan of Saxony is right, Diego's
intention was to ask the Pope's consent to set up a permanent organization
with the mandate to 'attack unceasingly the errors of the heterodox and
maintain the truth of the faith'.[150] The centre of Prouille, clearly, was to
have been its model and basis.

CHAPTER VIII

PROUILLE

IT is impossible to state with certainty when St Dominic came to Prouille and Fanjeaux for the first time, perhaps as early as 1206 if the preachers preferred to reach Toulouse through these heresy-infected regions rather than by the direct route from Castelnaudary—at any rate not later than the winter following.

It was an important moment in the life of the father of Preachers. Unlike Diego de Acebo, whose overflowing generosity never ceased to imagine new apostolic tasks and to plunge into them impetuously, Dominic was a man of a small number of plans which ripened for a long time in silence and were then carried out with tenacity. It is true he was no less responsive than his bishop to the call of human beings and of events, that is, of Providence. Primarily, however, his encounters with God produced secret heart-stirrings rather than gestures of immediate action. Everything seems to confirm that he received some shattering experience of this kind at Fanjeaux.

The ancient route he followed to climb up to the fortified township can be seen, steep and straight, parallel with the modern road with its twists and turns.[1] At the top of the mountain it passes between two hummocks. The town is on the western summit; its gate opens towards the south. Dominic plunged into the by-ways. Near the rough road of the knights[2] which was bordered by the manorial dwellings of the noble families of the town, he reached the church and the castle, situated at the culminating point of the locality. He had but to take a few more steps northwards to come out right against the walls, at the steepest place, on to a limestone rock. There he saw a sight which moved him deeply. The whole of the Lauragais was spread out before his eyes—this land which must be won back for Christ crucified.

At the foot of the long rise which he had just climbed, there stretched out over the plain five roads which diverged to lead to Laurac-le-Grand, Villasavary and Castelnaudary, Bram and Villepinte, Montréal and Carcas-sonne, Limoux. Behind him the route he had followed continued its course towards Mirepoix, Pamiers and the county of Foix. Twenty-five miles or so to the north-east stood the dark silhouette of the Montagne Noir. Behind him, fifty miles or more away, were the sparkling snows of the Pyrenees.

A promontory, a white rock, a widely extending landscape, roads which

seemed to move swiftly in quest of men, mountains equally forbidding in
their sombre colour or in their inaccessible whiteness—Dominic had seen
all this once before. Earlier he had grasped its message with a perspicacity
so keen as to be almost shattering. A flood of memories invaded and overwhelmed him. The small boy from Caleruega who used to look out over the
land from the heights of San Jorge suddenly came to life in him again.[4] Now
the meaning of the call which he had formerly heard was clear. It was, then,
for this that he had become a cleric, priest, religious, missionary after the
manner of the apostles. God was showing him his flock.

Here the landscape was less barren than on the plateau of Castile. On the
contrary, the land was covered with houses, villages and towns. It was rich
and cultivated everywhere. The Catholic heart of the young preacher,
however, experienced, as he looked at it, an anguish which the boy had
never known. The winter wind which swept over it at this year's close was
more icy than that of the Duero and of the Iberian Mountains. In the
inhabited places hostile towers were more frequent than were friendly
belfries. An endemic war had ravaged the countryside. Countless ruins were
visible on every side even to the crumbling chapels that could be seen along
the road. But this was nothing to the dramas in the consciences of the
people of this land. Many sincere Christians had lapsed, dangerously led
astray by sects far from the ways of salvation, and had set themselves up
against the Church of the Cross and the Eucharist. The indifference and
immorality of the great mass were increased by the discord in belief. The
vices of violence, of love of gain, of lasciviousness, pullulated in the midst
of civil and religious anarchy. Was there anyone to restore true peace and
the true faith to this people? 'Lord, have compassion on your people. What
will become of sinners?'[5] Some such groan doubtless escaped Dominic, as
it did so often on his nights of prayer in the church.

From the foot of his observation post, Dominic now looked out over the
great cross-roads where the routes diverged to all points on the horizon.
There he could see the remains of an inhabited place, with a chapel near.
This was Prouille.[6] He probably understood from that moment that it was
at this crossing of the ways that the base and centre of his missionary
operations should be established. He may even have had a supernatural
intuition which interiorly stimulated his choice. One tradition, the sources
of which cannot be verified and are somewhat doubtful,[7] asserts that a
miraculous event determined this choice. Three evenings running, while
Dominic was looking over the plain from the promontory of Fanjeaux, a
globe of fire came to a standstill over Prouille.[8] The name of *Seignadou*
(*Signatorium*) given to the place at least since the fifteenth century[9] and the
presence there of a cross and a chapel[10] recall this tradition. Whatever its
value and origin may be, it does commemorate a profound reality—the
certainty acquired by St Dominic as he stood on this promontory that it was

in these parts that he had to respond to the call he had heard as a child at San Jorge in Caleruega and that Prouille was to be the centre of his supernatural mission.

Prouille had had a certain importance in the earliest feudal age. In the eleventh and twelfth century the documents sometimes mentioned its noble lineage as, for instance, an Isarn (1125), a Guillaume de Prouille (1139, 1141, 1145), vassals of the Viscount of Carcassonne.[11] From the eleventh century a fortified 'mound'[12] was erected between the river Sesoine[13] and the acute angle of the cross-roads, clearly to control the traffic which was beginning to be considerable. A square tower, similar to the *torreón* of Caleruega, crowned the summit of an artificial hummock, moats and a palisade completing the defence. A few houses had grouped themselves beneath the hummock for protection. Finally a wall, enclosing the whole, had made it into a fortified township, which still figured in the documents at the beginning of the thirteenth century[14]. There was found there a communal oven,[15] a fountain[16] and finally a church dedicated to Our Lady.[17] The church ranked as a parish and had its own cemetery.[18] It also had its tithe-area (*decimarium*),[19] a clearly delimited portion of the surrounding countryside, within the boundaries of which the tenants of the land owed their tithe to the parish priest of Ste Marie. Another sanctuary, the chapel of St Martin, existed nearby, likewise provided with its tithe-area.[20] There was a whole series of others to be found in the hinterland of the place, on the slopes which climbed up towards Fanjeaux—St Pierre de la Terre-Caplade, St Sernin de la Ilhe, St Etienne de Tonneins, St Pierre de Rebenti, each one provided with its *decimarium*.[21]

At the time when Diego, Raoul and Dominic inaugurated their apostolate round about Prouille, the turret on the mound was dismantled and had perhaps disappeared; a windmill stood in its place.[22] The wall had partially collapsed.[23] The surface of the ancient borough and the slopes of the mound itself, having lost their military significance, were parcelled out into a mosaic of fields, gardens and dwellings.[24] The church, in bad enough repair, was no longer a parish;[25] with its tithes, if they were still collected,[26] it was attached to the parish of Fanjeaux.[27] The chapel of St Martin was falling to pieces.[28] The war had passed that way. During the course of the twelfth century, the countryside of the Lauragais had served as a field of operations for the permanent hostilities of the houses of Toulouse and of Béziers-Carcassonne. In the face of the redoubled assaults and the progress of military art, the mound offered only an absurdly inadequate defence. After the dispersal of the people living in the area, to which the numerous chapels round Prouille bore witness, the place had proved untenable. The rural population, like the nobility, had sought refuge in a body in the fortified town of Fanjeaux.

5—S.D.

The Catholic missionaries soon collected a few faithful at Prouille. The ancient seignorial family, now dispossessed, was then represented by the brothers Isarn,[29] and Guillaume Peyre[30] of Prouille. The second was an irreproachable Catholic.[31] The former, who in 1204 might have been seen at a Catharist ceremony,[32] seemed strengthened in his orthodoxy, perhaps thanks to the preachers. The latter further attracted a few good Catholics among the poor folk.

The chapel was open to them for the recitation of their office and for sacred worship. The parish priest of Fanjeaux clearly did not refuse them the use of it. It was dedicated to the Most Blessed Virgin and for a long time, it was said, had been the centre of a popular devotion.[33] Their ministry began and soon harvested its first-fruits, some of which were valuable but at the same time created difficulties.

The pictures it has been found possible to form of the life of the Catharists sufficiently demonstrate the rôle of women in the sect,[34] an echo of the important part they played in the religious life of the time.[35] Since the eleventh century, the movement towards mysticism in Europe had developed particularly in their ranks. Never had they felt such a nostalgia for the 'angelic life'. To such nostalgia the Catharism of the Midi supplied a particularly attractive response. More generous than their menfolk, above all more easily withdrawn from contacts with matter than their warrior husbands, a fair number of noble girls or women had received the consolamentum and were leading the life of the Perfect. Like Blanche at Laurac[36] or Fabrissa de Mazeroles at Montréal,[37] Guillelme de Tonneins[38] at Fanjeaux figured as a matriarch. Their wealth and their labours which they did not spare, their castles, their hospices, without mentioning their personal proselytism, constituted invaluable assets for the activity of the Perfect. In accordance with the custom of the Catholic convents moreover, they received adolescent girls, and sometimes even quite young children of seven, five and two and a half,[39] in their communities to form them according to their own way of life. The customs of the Catholic nobility were repeated among the Catharists. The reasons for which small girls were entrusted to the dualist convents were not only those of education or religious perfection. The frequent poverty of the noble families of the south found itself thereby relieved,[40] and the loyalty of these poor girls to the Perfect was strengthened by the needs of their material life.

Thus the return of these ladies or noble girls to Catholicism set not a few problems. Conversion was only the beginning. After their return to the Church it was essential to find for these women a form of life no less exacting than that of the women of the Perfect, for a conversion should never signify a diminution of generosity. It was also necessary to find them a centre and often even means of subsistence. As to returning to their families, some could doubtless do so, but for others the hostility of a Catharist family made any return impossible. The influence of their lineage was far stronger than that of the actual family tie, but also very much more oppressive. Instances were not lacking at this time in which some member of a family was treated atrociously, sometimes kept in prison for a long time, for matrimonial or religious motives. Even if there were no hostility the poverty of the family caused the convert to be treated as a piece of flotsam and jetsam.

Diego was never at a loss. He decided to set up a convent[41] for these various lady converts. They were thus assured of a refuge at the same time as a milieu of prayer and sanctification. It was thus possible to retrieve the girls whom the women of the Perfect were educating. Moreover, this feminine community, thanks to its stability and to the services rendered by its members would be the support of the daily life of the small group of preachers, as the hospices of the Catharists were for the itinerant Perfect, and would help on their apostolate by prayer and sacrifices. Thus was begun in embryo in the enclosure of Notre Dame de Prouille, at the turn of the years 1206–1207, a Catholic missionary centre which served as a model, a few months later, for the preaching centres of the Cistercian abbots.

It was first of all necessary to obtain the bishop's authorization in conformity with Canon Law. It was likewise from him that the grant of the church of Ste Marie must come.[42] Prouille depended on the see of Toulouse. The bishop, Fulk,[43] had just entered upon his functions at the beginning of 1205, succeeding a bishop who had been deposed. The electing canons, guided by the legates, had chosen for this post of primary importance a remarkable man. A native of Marseilles, a friend of the kings of England and of Aragon, a collaborator of Guillaume de Montpellier, Fulk in his time had been a famous troubadour. In 1196, however, he had entered the Order of Cîteaux, with his wife and his two sons. Soon afterwards, he had become Abbot of Thoronet. It was there that they went to seek him to give him the charge of this 'dead diocese'. As a Cistercian bishop, he was well placed for collaborating with the legates and missionaries of his order. He made no difficulty about authorizing the foundation and assigned to it the church. As to the concession of the tithes and first fruits, which could scarcely be separated from the gift of the chapel, to make this concession would indeed have been meritorious, in such straits were the episcopal finances.[44] Doubtless, however, there was hardly anything to give. It would not seem that a charter of concession was drawn up.[45]

The members of the seignorial family of Prouille, Isarn and Guillaume Peyre, were not in a position to grant anything. They were ruined, like so many of the knights of the region and no longer even had rights over the

feudal mound other than those shared by a family of rich peasants and
Dame Cavaers, the mistress of Fanjeaux.[46] The latter enjoyed seignorial
rights at Prouille. No indication justifies the assertion that she intervened in
the new foundation.[47] Her daughter, heir to her rights as she was to her
name, would not leave the sisters her portion of the mound until February
1244,[48] barely a few days after the departure of the French conquerors from
the neighbourhood and her return to the overlordship of Fanjeaux. More
than twenty years later, she was to give herself to the convent, living and
dying there as a good Catholic,[49] at the term of a long adventure in the ranks
of the Catharist church.[50] The other lords of Fanjeaux who possessed
property within or near the ancient township of Prouille, Isarn Bola,[51]
God, Maurin, Pierre-Roger and Guillaume-Arnaud Picarella,[52] Guillaume
de Durfort,[53] gave nothing either. Their names only appeared in the
charters of the convent later, in respect of exchanges, sales or confiscations
of lands. The big landowners of the place, those peasants enriched to the
detriment of the family of Prouille who were known as the 'Babons'
(Babones),[54] Arnaud, Rouge and his son Pierre, waited until 1215 to give
their portion of the mound;[55] Guillaume and his sister Alazaïce sold only in
1229 a dwelling they had near the cemetery,[56] an irritating enclave in the
sisters' lands.

Fortunately there were people more generous than these families who had
more or less acquired their nobility from the Catharists, or than the
enriched peasants. A cleric and his sister, natives of Pamiers, offered their
property and their persons for the work that was beginning.[57] They were
the first to do so and thus may be said to have started the foundation. They
were William and Raymonde Claret. William was to remain St Dominic's
companion and his second in the administration of the convent.[58] He would
become a Friar Preacher, Prior of Prouille.[59] Later, however, at the end of
1224, on the occasion of the deep upheaval that was so profoundly to
disturb the neighbourhood and its institutions after the departure of the
French conquerors and the return of the 'faidits',[60] he was to pass through
a very serious crisis. He tried, it is said, to cause the monastery under his
charge to pass over to the obedience of Cîteaux.[61] Possibly he thought this
action necessary to save the house which was itself going through a
severe crisis.[62] He himself left the order and joined the Cistercians of
Boulbonne.[63] At the time of the canonization process of St Dominic he was
nevertheless interrogated, in a manner most unsatisfactory from our point of
view,[64] for his deposition, which might have told us so much, was
completely lacking in detail.

A few months later, two serfs of Villasavary, Raymond Gasc and
Ermengarde Godoline, in their turn gave themselves to the 'Lord God,
blessed Mary, all the saints of God and the Holy Preaching and to all the
brethren and the sisters. They likewise gave their house in Villasavary,

their garden and all their fixed and movable goods. Their lord freed them to allow them to make this offering. He also freed men of Villepinte for certain gifts to the Holy Preaching, reserving however his own taxes.[65]

Perhaps it was again at this time that another household 'entered the monastery' by abandoning its property to it—Arnaud Ortiguers and his wife Alazaïce.[66] They would have liked their young son, Guillaume, to do likewise. He must, however, have been more than the age of fourteen.* He refused, but at the same time remained a friend to the community.[67] He became a cleric[68] and, upon reaching an advanced age, carried out his parents' wish by giving himself to the monastery in 1256, long after they had done so.[69]

Already, however, on 17th April, 1207, Dominic had obtained for the monastery a much more important gift—the church of St Martin of Limoux which was granted to him by the lord of the province, Bérenger of Narbonne.[70] Certain circumstances of this donation on the morrow of the great disputation at Montréal have already been mentioned.[71] The number of lady converts to be helped had increased in the course of the disputation; Dominic thus possessed an additional argument to persuade the prelate to support his infant work. The gift was considerable: tithes, first fruits, oblations and other revenues of a large parish, to which were added the revenues of Taich, a neighbouring place. There was only one counter-obligation—the responsibility of presenting and maintaining a parish priest. For the future the sisters considered their property of Limoux one of the best parts of their patrimony. It was necessary, however, to defend it energetically. In 1207, had Bérenger really the right to dispose of it? The actual taking possession was only carried out two years later.[72] Things were even worse afterwards. The powerful abbey of St Hilaire tenaciously claimed this church as its own possession. Long-drawn-out lawsuits in Rome were necessary in order finally to persuade the abbey to desist from its claims.[73]

Prepared for in this way by the gifts of the people of the place who were attached to the Church, as much as by those of the bishop and archbishop, it was thus possible to make the foundation. Whilst Dominic and his companions were tramping the countryside begging their way as they preached, the brethren and sisters of Prouille would have their subsistence practically assured.

In the course of our narrative, we have already met one or other of the first sisters—Sister Raymonde Claret, Sister Alazaïce. The first known list of the community contains a dozen names.[74] The origin of three other sisters is definitely known—Richarde, dame of Barbaira (Aude),[75] Guillelmine de Belpech (Aude), Guillelmine de Fanjeaux (Aude). The others are no

* And so been free to refuse. Tr.

longer anything but names to us—Raimonde-Passerine,[76] Bérengère,
Jourdaine, Curtolane, Gentiane, Ermessende.[77] The details it has been
possible to gather show that several of the nuns belonged to the nobility—
if not all of them, as Jordan of Saxony asserts.[78] Their places of origin
were not a little varied but were nevertheless spread along the Béziers-
Carcassonne-Pamiers route, the scene of the labour of the Catholic
missionaries since the end of 1206. Despite the general indication of
Bérenger's charter—'nuns recently converted by the examples and exhortations of Brother Dominic of Osma and his companions',[79] all were not
necessarily converts from heresy.

Among the converts properly so-called, several were from Fanjeaux. A
certain Bérengère would give evidence at St Dominic's canonization process
that, about the time of the foundation, she had witnessed with her own
eyes and heard with her ears a horrifying scene in the church of this township. Nine noble ladies (*matronae*) had just abandoned their errors. Dominic
then commanded them to look at him who had possessed them until that
time. The devil immediately appeared in the shape of a cat 'whose eyes, as
large as those of an ox, seemed to be burning flames; its tongue, protruding
to the length of half a foot, seemed to be of fire; it had a tail of half an arm's
length and was easily the size of a dog. At the command of blessed Dominic,
it escaped through the hole in the belfry.'[80] The terrifying figure exactly
corresponded to what these poor ladies were prepared to see appear.
The Catholics indeed claimed that the Catharist masters adored Lucifer who
appeared to them under the figure of a cat. They adored him in an ignoble
manner. Thus it was revealed in the great *summa* against heresies that Master
Alain de Lille had recently published at Montpellier. It was from this 'cat'
it was said, that the name of Catharists had been formed.[81]

About the middle of the century the alarming anecdote became considerably embellished in the official legend of the saint by Constantino of
Orvieto[82]. It was then asserted that among the nine converted ladies several
had entered at Prouille.[83] The thing is possible. It is certain, however,
that Bérengère herself was not among them, whatever may have been said,
nor the whole of the group that was converted. Neither, moreover, did
those who were able to enter constitute the initial nucleus of the monastery,
which was in existence before their adventure.[84]

The convent was founded at latest in March 1207.[85] At that date there
was only the group of nuns established with their prioress. The house,
moreover, had not yet its full observance. There could be no possibility of
enclosure or even of completely common life. The smallness of the provisional lodging of the sisters, a mere abandoned hovel near the church of
Ste Marie, did not enable them all to be grouped together. On 17th April,
several of them were still living in Fanjeaux.[86] This was so in the case of the

prioress, Guillelmine. They must have built a convent in the course of the summer. A tradition which cannot now be verified claims that the sisters were all together by 22nd November.[87] It is practically certain that enclosure was established on 27th December,[88] perhaps in 1207, or even in 1212. An attempt will be made later to define the date more accurately.

In any case the enclosure was still elastic. Farmers in the place for many years retained certain fields on the sisters' land.[89] Not until 1294 was a continuous stone wall erected and water brought inside the boundary.[90] Certainly none of the numerous documents of the Prouille cartulary mentions the presence of a nun outside the monastery, not even of the prioress. If it were a question of a gift to be received or of legal action, the affairs of Prouille were exclusively treated by male representatives. At this time, however, cases of abbesses leaving their enclosures to appear in lawsuits were not infrequent.[91] The Prouille enclosure was thus strict. It is possible it was made stricter in 1218 and 1221 as will be related in due course,[92] and perhaps again in the time of Innocent IV. In 1246 the Fathers of the monastery busied themselves with obtaining from the Bishop of Toulouse the chapel of St Martin, which had fallen into ruins and was unsuitable for sacred worship.[93] They reconstructed it inside the house, for celebrating the office and providing for the worship of the lay-brethren and *donati*. They were thus able to make over to the sisters (the church of Ste Marie) more completely and to isolate the two communities entirely. Shortly after this, the pontifical bulls began to give the sisters the title of *sorores inclusae* 'cloistered sisters', a title which they retained for the future.[94]

This time one would be wrong in seeing in the application of this epithet, for the future fairly common, an accentuation of enclosure. It merely signified the entry of Prouille into the general group of feminine monasteries which since 1204 the Pope had been definitively incorporating into the Order of Preachers, giving them this epithet among others.[95] The rule of enclosure, if not its practical realization or rather its provisions in Prouille, cannot have changed since the death of Dominic. In any case it must be admitted that during the initial years, in buildings which were still very inconvenient, the sisters of Prouille kept a sufficiently strict if not completely literal enclosure. It must have resembled that of the Cistercian nuns, the most strictly cloistered of the nuns of the time,[96] a century before a decretal of Boniface VIII defined the classic rule of solemn enclosure.[97]

There were some men forming part of the household. At the beginning Dominic and William Claret took charge of the government of it jointly.[98] As early as the summer of 1207 Diego had assigned to each his rôle. Dominic was to have the spiritual direction and chief authority, William charge of the temporal affairs.[99] Later, Friar Noel replaced Dominic.[100] Then William was made prior.[101] The prior, or procurator, had other priests around him. Dominic decided, doubtless in 1218, that there would be four of these.[102] It was not only with the sisters that this group of priests was occupied. In 1207 it constituted the Holy Preaching. After the institution of the Preachers, we come across the 'Preaching of the house of Prouille'.[103] A few lay-brothers,[104] who could not move to any other religious house,[105] helped with the material side of life. Finally a series of *donati* of different types,[106] clerics, individual freedmen, whole families of freedmen or of serfs,[107] had attached themselves to the convent. The majority administered or cultivated the lands adjoining the monastery or its distant domains. More often than not they had given their property to the house, at least in return for a life interest, and in exchange shared in its life and its spiritual advantages. Some of them had even made a vow of chastity, of obedience or of loyalty.[108] The gesture marking their engagement was that of feudal homage made into the hands of the superior.[109]

This personnel was varied both from the human and from the religious point of view.[110] The economic and social circumstances were such as to elicit donations, as in the case of the sisters. In the face of the difficulties of life or the uncertainty of the times, many people preferred to give themselves to a powerful lord or to some community, both being better equipped to defend them if need arose.[111] Some indeed had given themselves to the dualists for similar reasons, as, for instance, the poor man whom Dominic had converted, who could not leave his Catharist protectors for fear of dying of hunger.[112]

Thus, with its two communities, the monastery and the Preaching, the convent of Prouille fell into the category of double convents, frequent in the twelfth century but in the process of disappearance in the thirteenth.[113] The male section followed the evolution of the Preaching of Jesus Christ, then of the Preachers. The feminine community experienced the painful vicissitudes of the Dominican nuns.[114] Certain particular uncertainties were added to these vicissitudes.

In the initial years, the life of the community depended too closely on its economic system not to follow its fluctuations. The gifts originally given to the sisters by the people of the neighbourhood or by Bérenger of Narbonne doubtless assured their daily subsistence, but did not allow of the construction of a wide range of regular buildings. It was not even possible to think of setting up an enclosure of any size around the chapel. As far back as the middle of 1207 Diego concerned himself with bringing them other resources from Osma. He did not succeed.[115] History is absolutely silent on the life of the convent in 1208, 1209, 1210. It was the time of the great dramas of the Albigensian crusade. For the future war revolved around this very neighbourhood. The flight of the lords of long-standing who were compromised with the Catharists, and the upheaval of the region by cease-lessly renewed military operations, clearly increased the community's distress. The town of Limoux, whence came the best part of its revenues, was to be demolished and twice forced to abandon its site and reconstruct itself in the plain. The convent's material future was thus seriously compromised.

It would seem, indeed, that in the year 1210 Dominic himself was absent. At the side of Bishop Fulk he was devoting himself to an intensive preaching ministry in the city of Toulouse.[116] In February 1211 a visitation of the sisters enabled him to realize the difficulties of their situation.[117] A few weeks later, at the conclusion of the siege of Lavaur, he rejoined Bishop Fulk, who had been forced to abandon Toulouse where Count Raymond had just turned against the church, and Simon de Montfort, the military leader of the crusade.[118]

Dominic made the bishop understand 'that it would be an act of devotion and mercy'[119] to make over permanently the sanctuary of Prouille, with its revenues and other rights of the church there, to the lady converts who were living there. It would seem that Fulk agreed to restore to them the tithes, which were beginning to come in once more.[120] One nevertheless gets the distinct impression that he hesitated.[121] The economic situation of his see had not improved at all.

Simon de Montfort, however, whose friendship for St Dominic will be seen later, gave the example. On 15th May, the Frenchman granted Prouille a vineyard situated quite close to the monastery, on the verge of the Sésoine, which came from the confiscated property of the 'faidit' Bertrand de Saissac. In particular he gave to the prioress, the brethren and the sisters all he had just acquired in the territory of Sauzenc, between Bram and Villepinte, to the north of Prouille.[122] This time Fulk was persuaded. That same day he granted the parish of Bram with its revenues 'to the converted ladies, living the religious life by the church of Sainte Marie of Prouille'.[123] The form in which the deed was drawn up at the same time revealed the reason for the bishop's hesitations. He did not grant this property to the institution as such but to the sisters considered individually, whose names he enumerated, beginning by Guillelmine, the prioress. He gave them this property for the duration of their existence, showing that he had doubts as to the permanence of the community. It will be seen that the monastery's poverty and the uncertainty of the times were responsible for this. Everything, however, was to change.

The great successes of Simon de Montfort in the course of the year 1210 had decided a good number of knights of the region to make their submission to him. These now made their appearance at Prouille and at Fanjeaux.[124] Those who were Catholics by conviction, or even certain lords suspected of having protected heresy who wished to rectify or destroy such suspicions,

began to multiply their generous gifts. In December of that year, a certain
Raymond de Villar gave the monastery all the property he possessed in his
native place[125] before himself becoming a canon of St Antonin at Pamiers.
About twenty years later when he was sacristan of that same chapter
Raymond would find himself entrusted with the inquiry preparatory to St
Dominic's canonization.[126] Then Hugues de Rieux, Isarn Bola, Bernard
Hugues, Amiel Cerdana, others again, made a number of generous gifts.[127]
On 9th February, 1212, the brothers Usalger and Raynès granted to
Prouille their ownership and rights over the land of Fenouillet, that is, over
their patrimony, for they were descended from a younger branch of the
Viscounts of Fenouillèdes.[128] Simon de Montfort repeated his gestures of
generosity several times.[129]

The French crusaders, abundantly provided with confiscated lands from
the viscounty of Béziers-Carcassonne, then made similar gestures. A leader of
the mercenaries, Pedro the Aragonese, who had been reconciled, had given
the initial example.[130] Between February 1212 and June 1214, Frémis le
Français, Robert Mauvoisin, Guillaume de l'Essart, Enguerrand de Boves,
Hugues de Lascy, Lambert de Thury, Alain de Rouey,[131] to whom should
be added Pierre de Vic, Hugues de Nantes and Guy de Levis,[132] all loyal
companions of Simon de Montfort and settled by him in places bordering on
Fanjeaux, gave the monastery some of their new lands. After 1212 the
'Institutions de Pamiers' authorized them to give in alms up to the fifth part
of them.[133] Finally in 1214 the Bishop of Toulouse granted the sisters certain
tithes from Fanjeaux.[134] In some three years Prouille in this way became
solidly endowed, through Limoux, Fenouillet, Villasavary, Villesiscle, Bram,
Villenouette and Sauzenc, apart from the place of Prouille itself and
Fanjeaux.

Without delay Dominic busied himself in getting the principal donations
confirmed. The origin of a good number among them made them extremely
precarious. The intervention of Simon de Montfort would cover them with
the protection of the real head of the country. He did not refuse it.[135]
Soon, as we shall see, Dominic was to succeed in obtaining other, much
more valuable protection, that of the Pope.

These lands, however, which had been acquired at random and piece by
piece from the donations, remained scattered to the four cardinal points.
Dominic endeavoured to establish an unbroken domain, at least around the
centre, Prouille; his successors would do the same with the lands on the
periphery. He sold, bought, exchanged parcels of land, not without a
certain ability for business. He thus succeeded in liberating the greater part
of the ancient township and enclosure of the sisters, rounding off the
neighbouring lands, acquiring a mill and its appurtenances.[136]

After the spring of 1212, indeed, he had at his disposal sufficient lands to
undertake another task—that of building a monastic cloister with its

dependencies at the side of the church. The building began at the beginning of March or April. It was soon completed. After this a series of charters made mention of the 'monastery' and even of the 'newly constructed abbey'.[137] Whether or not this latter designation is to be taken in its technical sense, it was certainly not adopted definitively, for there are found substituted for it at the same moment the more modest titles of domus,[138] locus,[139] ecclesia,[140] or, quite simply, the names of Ste Marie de Prouille and even of Prouille alone. Moreover, neither prior nor prioress ever bore the title of abbot or abbess. Finally, after 1213, the word disappeared. Primarily, we can see in this somewhat grandiloquent title the reflection of the impression made on contemporaries by the relatively ample proportions of the new buildings. The Prior of Prouille probably himself abandoned this name which was valueless from the point of view of apologetics in the territory of the Albigenses. It is probable, however, that the appearance and disappearance of the word abbey possessed a deeper significance, linked with the spiritual orientation of the house.

From the beginning the feminine community had appeared as a 'monastery', the sisters as 'nuns' with a 'prioress' at their head.[141] They had established themselves 'for ever'[142] in their poor lodging. A challenge, in some sense, to the communities of women of the Perfect, Prouille was essentially distinguished from them by the manner in which it conceived the interior life of the community. Their installation in a church alone was charged with meaning. No word or expression in the documents gives the slightest hint that their ordo [or rule of life], which at this point was scarcely beyond the embryo stage, was intended to differ from the types that had become classic in the West. On one essential point, it can even be stated that the contact of the monastery with contemporary Catholic ideas limited the design which had given rise to the foundation—Prouille set itself against any transformation, like certain of our modern convents, into an institution for small girls. Mention is never in fact found in the numerous charters of the convent of any other element than the sisters, or nuns. This allows the following prescription, drawn from a later rule closely associated with the monastery, to be attributed to Prouille[143]:

> It is by no means our custom to receive girls of less than eleven [the precociousness of children in that century and that part of the world must be remembered]. If one or other is received before that age, to prevent a grave occasion of falling or to procure some spiritual benefit, let them be educated apart and be carefully formed until the age of fourteen.[144]

The first part of this prescription, the equivalent of which is found in contemporary rules,[145] has as its context the reaction of the religious congregations against the disorders that the presence of too great a number of small children had brought into the cloisters. The second part, on the

other side, made provision for the intention which had brought the foundation into being, that of preserving souls from danger.

By 1211–1212 the ideal had not changed. The community had remained
stable despite trials. The names of the eleven initial sisters are in fact, found
in the list of sisters given in Fulk's charter on the occasion of the concession
of the church of Bram.[146] Seven new sisters had joined the others. Among
them was Sister Blanche, a rich lady of Toulouse, who had recently given
herself to the religious life at the same time as her husband and whose
fortune was to allow one half of the sisters' dormitory to be erected in fine
dressed stone.[147] The house remained solidly established under the government of the same prioress. What, it may be asked, was the regular orientation of the community ?

The reply can be made with assurance—the orientation was Cistercian.
This is already marked in regard to the enclosure and an ancient tradition
asserts it in respect of the costume.[148] All the circumstances suggest the
same reply. Prouille was born and had grown up among the Cistercians,
who were the principal educators of nuns at the time.[149] At the time of
the foundation Diego's sympathies were markedly Cistercian and Dominic
was in close touch with the order.[150] It is true, indeed, that when Dominic
had first come to the Narbonensis he was neither prepared nor resolved to
become the founder of an order, much less of an order of nuns, for until that
time he had never directed any. On the other hand he could easily procure
from Arnaud, or from one of his numerous confrères, the rules of Cîteaux.[151]
There is some justification for thinking that he did so from the beginning and
that from that time, like Diego, he thought of having his religious house
incorporated in the order of St Bernard as an abbey of women.

It was necessary, however, to wait for it to be sufficiently established. By
1212–1213 the time seemed to have come. It is possible that he took
certain steps to this end. Moreover, it is proved that in this year 1213 the
Order of Cîteaux displayed indeed for the first time a resistance which
became increasingly stiffer against incorporations of feminine abbeys.[152] It
was perhaps owing to this circumstance that Prouille was not officially
recognized as a Cistercian abbey or handed over to the administration of
monks of St Bernard.

It was perhaps now that the enclosure was set up. It would be natural
to await the completion of the regular buildings, that is, the end of 1212,
before doing so. It is possible that Dominic then also drew up a rule for the
sisters. The care and efficiency with which he had just laid down the basis of
the temporal affairs of the monastery led him to concern himself also with
the spiritual affairs. It is possible, however, that on this point he contented
himself with maintaining at Prouille the customs of Cîteaux. The situation
only becomes a little clearer after 1216. At that time there was drawn up,
either written out in full or adapted from a corrected version of an earlier

text a rule of observance which took as its basis the customs of St Dominic's order for men.[153] In 1221 Dominic was to summon to Rome eight sisters from Prouille in order to form for regular observance a new community which he would gather together at the convent of St Sixtus.[154] Now the rule of St Sixtus, as it existed around the year 1232, is still extant.[155] The observances taught by the sisters from Prouille, and consequently the rule of Prouille itself, cannot but be there in part.[156] Otherwise, how could the Prouille sisters declare to the Sovereign Pontiff in 1236 that at the 'moment of their conversion', i.e. at the beginnings of regular life in their monastery, they had commonly adopted as rule 'the rule of the nuns of St Sixtus in Rome'?[157] This declaration, anachronistic but comprehensible, which indicated to the Pope a particular legislation by designating it under the form which would be most familiar to him, cannot signify anything else but textual continuity of the rule of Prouille previous to 1216, with the rule of St Sixtus. It is, however, impossible, in view of the modifications which the documents have undergone, to rediscover with any certainty in the text of 1232, the only one we still possess, the rule of Prouille as it was in 1216,[158] *a fortiori* a possible rule of 1212.[159]

However it was regulated, the life of the sisters of Prouille was devoted to liturgical prayer, asceticism and manual work. A document of the fourteenth century recording a visitation mentions the tradition of the monastery in this connection.

> Each year [it was said] fifteen quintals of wool, very clean and carefully chosen, are distributed to the sisters. They spin and weave it at the hours when they are not engaged at the Divine Office, and they do so according to ancient custom and the formal order of our father St Dominic, who willed this so as to drive away idleness, the mother of all vices.[160]

Independently of the general tradition of Western monachism, the primitive Cistercian orientation of the house would have been sufficient to lay the emphasis on the manual work of the contemplative sisters, the habit of which has become less strong in the modern age of the Church.

The juridical position of the house was strengthened on 8th October, 1215 by the short bull which Dominic obtained from the Pope that day; it extended the protection of the Holy See especially to the various properties which the sisters had acquired from the crusaders.[161] On 30th March, 1218, a consistorial privilege finally brought the supreme Roman sanction.[162] The document was really an extension to the use of the brethren of Prouille of the privilege of confirmation of the Order of Preachers. It primarily concerned the men's community, or Preaching, of the convent. It was, however, drawn up in the name of the monastery whose property it finally confirmed. The sisters were thus officially attached to the Preachers, through their male community. It is possible that they received the rule modified or arranged in accordance with the customs of the Preachers.

In 1236, after a period of acute difficulty when the monastery seemed on the point of being abandoned by the Fathers, it was officially assigned to the direction of the Preachers by a decision of Pope Gregory IX.[163] About this time Prouille merited the praise of Jordan of Saxony in these words: 'The house . . . still exists; the servants of God continue to offer an agreeable worship to their Creator there and lead, in zealous sanctity and the pure light of their innocence, a life which is salutary to themselves, exemplary to other men, pleasing to the angels and agreeable to God.'[164]

In 1248 Innocent IV reiterated this Dominican privilege.[165] He did so again in 1252, by an almost unique exception, the Preachers being allowed by the Pope, in order not to be distracted 'in their studies and their doctrinal teaching', to be free from the care of all nuns.[166] After 1248 the sisters were officially styled 'Cloistered Sisters of the Order of St Augustine, of the diocese of Toulouse'.[167] In 1258 this detail was added to the title: 'according to the institutions of the Order of Preachers'.[168] At this date, Humbert de Romans, fifth General of the order, had just definitively saved the Dominican nuns and edited for them a common rule.[169] The second order was founded and Prouille formed part of it, occupying the place of honour.

At the end of this historical survey which has been extended throughout the thirteenth century in order to show the development of Prouille, it is possible to discern more clearly the part played in the monastery by the different founders. Jordan of Saxony assigned this function to the Bishop of Osma.[170] Later, the Dominican legends reserved it for St Dominic.[171] In 1230 Fulk in a document attributed it to himself.[172]

Diego was the first to decide upon the foundation. As usual, his resolution was prompt. He continued to bear the responsibility for it. When he left the neighbourhood shortly afterwards, it was with the explicit intention of going to seek help for the monastery.[173] Fulk had necessarily to intervene in the foundation since he had to authorize it. This was his right and his duty as bishop of the diocese. In the beginning his rôle stopped there. It took a considerable time for him to realize the importance of the house and not until 1211 did he show himself really generous in regard to it.

Dominic was in quite a different case. He was the father, the nurse, the legislator. The most ancient documents in the archives, contemporary with the origins of the foundation, attribute to him the principal rôle in the recruiting of the 'converted ladies'. They also attribute to him the measure which procured the best part of their patrimony for the sisters. Dominic continued to serve them. It was he who set flowing the stream of endowments of 1211–1212. He then constructed and organized the abbey. He organized the system of direction, the number of fathers, the interior traditions, the sisters' manual work. Between 1212 and 1215 he refused a bishopric which was offered to him, as was the case with several of the collaborators of the Holy Preaching, in order not to neglect, he said, 'the tender plantation of Prouille of which he had the charge'.[174] From that time onwards he watched over it with even more attentive care. In the year 1214 he was to be seen established in Fanjeaux, depriving himself of all he could to maintain the sisters.[175] He was, however, even more preoccupied with feeding their souls with his spiritual instructions. Tradition has carefully preserved the track of the winding path by which he went to and fro between his lodging in Fanjeaux and the monastery down on the plain.[176] Up in Fanjeaux again, while he worked at the labour of converting a town that was relentless in its hostility or while he continued his long prayers in the church, he could hear, ringing in the distance, day and night, the bells of the nuns of Prouille calling to prayer, and the sound gave him courage.

Dominic undoubtedly enjoyed a special grace for the ministry to women. Prouille alone would give proof of this. History has preserved other documents during the Albigensian mission which testify to the same thing, reminiscences of his apostolate among noble ladies who were 'believers' of that sect, whom he brought back to the bosom of the Church by asking them for hospitality.[177] There was the evidence of several women in the investigation of Toulouse. They did not mind showing their tenderness mingled with admiration and maternal compassion, still vivid after thirty years, aroused by the extreme austerity, the fervour in prayer and the generosity of the preacher.[178] Anecdotes emphasize his heroic charity at the appeal of the grief of some mother or sister.[179] Scarcely had Dominic arrived in Toulouse, in 1215, than he opened a house for poor converted girls.[180] He moved on to Madrid and it was the new convent there which has preserved the only letter of his which has been kept. He went to Bologna; there again there was a convent of sisters. In Florence, in Rome, his ministry among women bore new fruit. It was there finally that the papacy entrusted him with an exemplary creation—St Sixtus, which was to serve as a model, not only in the eternal city but in one half of Christendom, for its influence, under the stimulus of Gregory IX, would exceed the sphere of action of the Preachers themselves.

Dominic had not sought this ministry. Neither his childhood with the rural dean nor his studies in Palencia had placed him in contact with women. He rather tried to avoid them, fearing the danger of their company to one who sought to shun the world.[181] It was precisely this reserve which made for his success among them. They sensed that in his evangelization he was wholly disinterested. Moreover this nature of his chastity gave a naturalness and freshness to his spiritual outpourings which added to their value. The confidence at the end of his life that despite his efforts he had not been able to avoid the imperfection of finding more attraction in the conversation of girls than in that of old ladies, is delightful.[182] Dominic was essentially an apostle. He knew how to make himself all things to all men. Because, however, he gave himself very generously to those who sought him, he discovered, without seeking it, the joy of the communication of spiritual things. As exacting for others as he was in the first instance for himself, he was none the less deeply loved, and this affection, the echo of his friendship which flowed back upon himself, gradually opened to him a joy he had not so far experienced. Now the solitary of Palencia, or of the cloister of Osma, was no longer alone with God. He had found his family, a home, where without having to give up anything of his austerity of life or losing anything of his reserve, he could restore his strength, find support for his prayer and finally, to some extent open his heart.

The noonday of life had not yet come nor the hour of maturity in his work. He was, however, at the age when a man leaves the father of his youth to enter upon his definitive task. This time had now come for Dominic. God was giving him Prouille as a strong support just when he was asking a further sacrifice of him. He was to lose Diego.

The Bishop of Osma, who could see the work of conversion to which he had devoted himself for more than a year past taking deep root at Prouille, whereas in the course of this summer of 1207 the Cistercian mission was beginning to show signs of weariness, wanted to leave the neighbourhood for the space of some weeks. He wanted to go to Castile, so that he would not be accused of wholly neglecting his diocese, and to put his domestic affairs and those of his see in order.[183] As ever, he was overflowing with projects of generosity. There he would collect men and resources. The assent of the Pope would be asked, he would then set up in the province of Narbonne a truly permanent Preaching.[184] He allocated the various tasks at Prouille and set off on his journey.[185]

For the first stages, the journey was naturally made in common. Every occasion of travel in these parts provided an opportunity of meeting the heterodox. The bishop thought of crossing the Pyrenees by the upper valley of the Ariège.[186] He would thus take the route through the county of Foix which Fanjeaux in fact controlled: Mirepoix, Pamiers, Foix. Coming into the Cerdagne again, he would then reach Aragon and, through Saragossa, eventually arrived at Osma.

A disputation at Pamiers was foreseen. It was not the first time that an encounter with the heterodox had taken place there.[187] The preachers were joined by Bishop Fulk of Toulouse and Navarre of Couserans,[188] who travelled to the meeting-place along the valley of the Ariège. Several abbots were likewise present,[189] among whom were doubtless Vital of St Antonin[190] and Henri of Mont-Sainte-Marie.[191]

The fortified township of Pamiers, on the banks of the Ariège, belonged to the Canons Regular of St Antonin de Frédelas, whose monastery had been erected outside the walls, half a mile or so from the town.[192] The canons, however, had not been able to avoid enfeoffing their town to Raymond-Roger, Count of Foix.[193] The latter occupied the castle, the terrace of which can still be seen at the side of the cathedral. The count had sworn everything that could be desired for the protection of the faith and the liberty of the canons. He attached, however, too high a value to the possession of the city and he clutched at any means of driving the principal lords from it. One such means was assuredly the diffusion of heresy. He disseminated it through his own family, among them his wife and two of his sisters, one of whom was the famous Esclarmonde. All three were devoted to the sects, two of them to the Catharists, the third to the Waldenses.[194] For a time even, the count had succeeded in establishing in the town his aunt Faïs de Durfort,[195] of Fanjeaux, a major heresiarch of the type of Blanche de Laurac, whose penetrating prosyletism was not without its effect on the population. This was too much for the noble canons. They had reacted and driven Faïs from their city. The count's wrath was unleashed. A canon was attacked while he was in the act of celebrating Mass, and cut to pieces. For several years the blood could be seen upon the altar. Another had his eyes torn out. The count entered the monastery by force, locked up the abbot and religious while he destroyed part of their buildings, then drove them half-naked into the open country.

Raymond-Roger knew how to control his violence when it suited him. Towards the missionaries he was all consideration.[196] He welcomed the participants in the disputation at his own expense, one day entertaining the Catholics and the next their opponents. These were principally Waldenses, but there were also some Catharists.[197] The disputation was held in the castle.[198] The Dames of Foix were not so aloof as their husband and brother and intervened in the course of the debate. One of the sisters was rebuked by a Catholic religious, Fray Etienne de Miséricorde: 'Madam,' he said, 'get back to your distaff. It is not your business to speak in such meetings.'[199] This was truly the tradition of the New Testament: *Mulieres in ecclesiis taceant*.[200] It was not an argument.

The Catholic champions had better reasons at their disposal. By common consent there was chosen as arbitrator a remarkable man, Master Arnaud de Crampagna, then a secular priest well known in the town. He had been attached to the Waldenses.[201] He was convinced and gave his verdict in favour of the Catholics, against both the Waldenses and the Catharists. He then abjured his sect and, in an impressive gesture, gave himself to the Bishop of Osma, both as to his person and his property, by an oath of dependence in feudal form.[202] From that moment he never ceased bravely to attack the sectaries whom the count's family were protecting.[203] Having become a canon and sacristan of St Antonin, greatly attached to St Dominic, he sought him out again for the last time in 1221 in Rome where the affairs

of the county of Toulouse had brought him.[204] He was later to give evidence
at his friend's canonization process.[205]

Many others were shaken. Here, as at Servian, Montréal or Fanjeaux, the
poor and the friends of poverty were easily influenced.[206] An important
group of Waldenses who had for long been attacking Catharist dualism in
terms fairly close to those of the Catholics, returned to the bosom of mother
Church.[207] At their head was Master Durando de Huesca. They went off to
Rome to ask for absolution from their error and for canonical penance. They
wanted something more that no prelate of the Narbonensis could have given
them—the right to continue, as Catholics, their apostolic life and their
work of evangelization, in particular against the Catharists. Innocent III was
sympathetic to their desires. He had been strengthened in his attitude of open-
heartedness towards the *Humiliati* of Lombardy and the Waldenses of Metz
by the success of the apostolic preaching in the Narbonensis.[208] He accepted
the offer of Durando and his companions who were recommended by Diego.
Having asked them for an immediate oath of loyalty, and at the same time a
profession of orthodoxy, he granted them a certain form of regular life and
the right to preach. Thus were established in 1208 the Poor Catholics,[209]
who spread particularly in Catalonia and the Narbonensis. The first mendicant group of the Roman Church, they worked at their evangelical mission
with courage, and knew how to remain faithful. They nevertheless came up
against the instinctive hostility of the populations and of the local clergy,
who could not succeed in distinguishing them from the anticlerical
Waldenses. Despite the definite support of a series of popes, their movement
scarcely developed at all. It was eventually submerged, in 1256, like a
stream in a river, in the fourth mendicant order then organized, the
Hermits of St Augustine. In 1210 another group of the Waldenses of the
Albigeois, led by Bernard Prim, had obtained from the Pope a rule of life
identical with that of Durando de Huesca.[210] They likewise disputed against
the dualists.[211]

Certain Catharists, moreover, had also felt themselves shaken by the
Pamiers disputation.[212] Nothing shows more clearly the deep root taken by
the dualist church in the territories of the Midi than the dialogue engaged
between Bishop Fulk and Pons Adhémar de Roudeille, a knight of
Saverdun,[213] a dispute which did not lack finesse. 'We should never have
been able to imagine', he said, 'that Rome had such telling reasons against
these people.' 'Do you not recognize', said the bishop, 'that they have
nothing left to say against our objections?' 'We recognize it', he said.
'Why', said the bishop, 'do you not expel them from your lands, driving
them away from this place?' 'We cannot. We have been brought up in
their midst, we have certain of our close relatives among them and we see
them living lives of perfection.'[214]

More than anywhere else, the example of a perfect life was needed for the men of these parts, if the truth was to touch their hearts. The Bishop of Osma had sensed with more perspicacity than anyone the need of joining the one to the other in preaching, doubtless because he felt this himself as a need of his personal life. *Facere et docere* the Gospel said of Jesus. 'To put one's teaching into practice.' The insistence of the charters of Prouille, speaking of the ladies converted 'by the examples and exhortations of Brother Dominic' is worthy of note.[215] *Verbo et exemplo*, the formula was an old one.[216] Diego had been able to give it a new freshness by his inspired generosity. On his lips the words the others were using acquired fresh value. A new evangelization was springing to life from imitation of the apostles.

And now Diego was leaving. It was the first time that Dominic had been parted from him for ten years or more. The separation must have been painful to him. His emotion would have been infinitely deeper had he guessed that this farewell was final. It was September, 1207.[217] Diego reached Osma in a few weeks. The crossing of the mountains, the journey on foot at the end of three years of travelling, preaching and controversy in an atmosphere of very great austerity, used up his strength. He had already entered upon his declining years.[218] The work in Osma left him no respite. He made a further effort, put everything in order and was already preparing to start back again,[219] when sickness overtook him and he died. It was 30th December, 1207.[220]

Three weeks later, one blow falling after another, Dominic learnt of his decease and of the assassination of Peter of Castelnau.[221] A member of the household of the Count of Toulouse had killed the Cistercian, in the Trinquetaille quarter of Arles. This last loss must have disturbed Dominic beyond all measure. The whole of Christendom, struck in the person of a representative of the Pope, was shaken and would react in a dramatic fashion. Anything might happen. The announcement of the death of the Bishop of Osma, however, caused in Dominic's whole being an upheaval of a very different nature, the feeling of a crumbling away of his life.

Diego was not only the most prominent personality, whose highmindedness, divine inspiration, knowledge, moral purity, zeal full of effectiveness, all the documents emphasize.[222] For Dominic he was his father and master. After all, they had had all things in common for more than ten years. More than that, each completed the other. Diego, imaginative, excitable and generous, who could not see a supernatural task without devoting himself to it, not superficial or unstable, however, but of incomparable activity; Dominic, calm and thoughtful, however much moved by emotion his sensitive nature might be, of inconceivable continuity in thought and effort, because all in him emerged from a steadily flowing interior life. Less gifted than Diego on the side of the imagination, he was no less dynamic and capable of achievement, because he was the man of a single and great idea.

The idea came from Diego, with the impulse. Dominic could not imagine himself without his father. His humility liked to remain under the shadow of his leader. And now, all that was over.

Raoul de Fontfroide was dead, his colleague, Peter of Castelnau, assassinated, Arnaud Amaury, the third legate, was absent. The Cistercian preachers had left for their abbeys. Diego had just died in Castile. To assume the immense apostolic task, Dominic was alone.

CHAPTER IX

FANJEAUX

URING the year 1208 and the first part of 1209, lowering skies pressed heavily over the Midi of France in unceasing preparation for a storm.[1] On 10th March letters that made sad reading had left Rome. They announced simultaneously to the king, the great churchmen, the chief barons and the populations of the north as of the Midi of France, the tidings of the murder of Peter of Castelnau and the strong suspicions which rested upon Raymond of Toulouse. The crime had occurred the morning after a scene of violence, in which the count, brought to bay, had uttered threats of death against the legate. The Cistercian was preparing to cross the Rhône. Some feudal vassal, approaching from behind, had run him through with his lance. The count, however, far from disavowing the criminal, received him on terms of friendship. Raymond had not yet accomplished any of his promises in the matter of peace and faith and the Pope accordingly pronounced a fresh excommunication against him, released his vassals from their oaths of fidelity and 'exposed his land as a prey'. In strong terms he called upon faithful Catholics to lend their assistance to the Church and conferred on those who did the recognized indulgence of the crusades. One single right remained in reserve, that of King Philip Augustus, the overlord. The Pope once more addressed to the latter a pressing invitation to assume direction of the punitive operations, and to reduce his Toulouse vassal to Christian obedience.

The king, paralysed by the simultaneous threats from England and the Empire, had plausible excuse for not putting himself at the head of the crusade; he could no longer, however, stand out against the deep feeling of his barons. Outdone in generosity by his subordinates, he finally allowed them to respond to the call of the Church as individuals. The enterprise had immense success. Two new series of pontifical letters, in October 1208 and February 1209, completed its organization. Navarre of Couserans and Fulk of Toulouse, in the name of the prelates of the Midi, had gone to Rome and advised the Pope.[2] Arnaud de Cîteaux and Guy de Carcassonne tried to influence Philip Augustus and his barons in France.[3]

In June 1209 the storm broke. The elements of the crusade were concentrated in Lyons from the 25th onwards. It was a strange army, the contingents of which moved forward staff in hand, like pilgrims going to gain an indulgence.[4] Their clergy, who were in their midst, encouraged them by their ceremonies and their preaching; they then assembled them to the cry of 'The indulgence'.[5] But with the baggage, the trappings of war accompanied the pilgrims.[6] When the call 'To arms' should ring out, only a few minutes would be necessary to transform this huge mass of men into a fanatical army. At the beginning of July, the legates joined it. On the 12th, it passed through Montélimar. On the 22nd it camped before Béziers, where for the first time it met with resistance. At the instigation of the young viscount Raymond-Roger, the stubborn town defied the Church and refused to disassociate itself from the heretics. Tents had scarcely been erected when, without the knowledge of the knights, the rougher elements of the camp, armed with clubs and stones, assaulted the town and took it at a single stroke.[7] They then began to pillage and to massacre all they met at random. They even set fire to the city but at this point the knights intervened and tried to control the pillage. It was an appalling slaughter. The official account mentions twenty thousand dead; there were seven thousand alone in the church of the Madeleine where part of the population had taken refuge. The dome of the cathedral collapsed and crashed down in the flames. Terror spread throughout the neighbourhood. A good hundred townships and castles were emptied of their defenders; no time was lost in occupying them. On 1st August the crusaders arrived before Carcassonne where the viscount had entrenched himself. Two weeks later the unconquerable city had to capitulate. The inhabitants only saved their lives by leaving all their wealth and goods and fleeing naked into the open fields. Young Trencavel, falling into the hands of the crusaders, was not long in meeting death in the tower where he was held prisoner. At the end of the month the crusade was in possession of the whole of the viscounty of Béziers-Carcassonne.

Had the King of France put himself at the head of the expedition, it would doubtless have taken the form of a military crusade, like the Albigensian 'pilgrimage' of his son, the future Louis VIII, in 1215.[8] The king's suzerainty in the south of France assured him a right of intervention less disputed among the barons of the neighbourhood than the right of holy war in Christendom formulated by the Church in the course of the twelfth century. The operation would certainly not have been effected without countless cruelties. The king, strong through the submission of Raymond of Toulouse, Raymond-Roger of Carcassonne and their vassals, would clearly have exacted effective measures against the mercenaries and the heretics. Whereas in the case of the latter the pontifical prescriptions only demanded their expulsion and the confiscation of their property,[9] the customs of the north of France and of the Empire had long demanded the stake.[10] The crusaders would not have failed to burn 'with great joy' in town and borough hundreds of Catharist Perfect, as they did at Minerva, Lavaur and Cassès.[11] They would have hanged the mercenaries.[12] Eviction of the local dynasties would at least have been avoided, as would the almost general spoliation of the feudal lords of those parts, a source of ceaselessly renewed acts of treason and of a continuous state of revolt of the population of the Midi, eliciting a ferment of hatred against the north which, for thirty-five years, was to continue to multiply in this unhappy land the anarchy and dramas of earlier times.

If the barons of the Midi had succeeded in coming to an understanding, they might perhaps have been able to resist the invasion of the crusaders. The deep nature of their dissensions, however, did not permit of this.[13] As far back as 1208 Raymond had made up his mind. Incapable of effecting unity around his person he had decided, unlike the young Viscount of Béziers, to bow before the storm. At the beginning of June he met Milon, the new legate whom the Pope was sending him at his request. On 18th June, at Saint-Gilles, in front of the magnificent romanesque basilica which his ancestors had built, a humiliating penance re-established him in the Church in exchange for weighty promises—he would give way to the wishes of the Church, especially in the matter of the heretics, would re-establish liberty and restore ecclesiastical property, would suppress unjust taxes and finally would take then and there and would cause to be taken by every one of the rulers and men of his lands, aged fourteen and upwards, the solemn oath of peace.[14] Finally, on the 22nd he took the cross and, for the future, would ally himself with the cruel operations of war. Matters thus ended in this anomaly that the person chiefly responsible for the disorders in the south, against whom the crusade had been explicitly convened, not only escaped its clutches, but collaborated in its work. By so doing, Raymond VI re-established his compromised authority and kept his territory outside the operations of the crusaders.

No one was more conscious of this paradox than the leader of the crusade, the legate Arnaud de Cîteaux. He was not the man to allow himself to be deceived by vain promises. Raymond VI was obliged to carry out the programme he had sworn at Saint-Gilles and in particular genuinely to engage himself in the struggle against heresy; otherwise, he would be excommunicated again, and his land, laid under an interdict, would be abandoned to the conquering efforts of the crusaders. It is, moreover, clear that Arnaud's history of events was already written. He had known the count too long and no longer had any confidence in him. The affairs of peace and faith in Provence would only be settled by his disinheritance. To replace him the legate soon had his man: Simon de Montfort, Count of Leicester.[15]

Simon was a lord of the Ile de France only modestly endowed. Because of the King of England, he had not been able to take possession of the county of Leicester which he had inherited from his mother. He thus formed part of that body of knights of average position not closely attached to their land who remained available for any great feudal enterprise. A convinced

Catholic, pure in his married life, he had the sense of the service of God
through arms and of loyalty to the Church. Engaged in the fourth crusade,
in 1204 he had separated from it before Zara when he had realized that it
was being deflected from its Christian purpose. A number of companions
had then accompanied him in his deeds of prowess in Palestine. Now he had
found them again in another crusade, in which his neighbour and friend,
Guy des Vaux-Cernai, was involving him. He was a man immediately outstanding among his equals. A soldier of amazing activity, continually in the
saddle and always at the breach, intrepid, loyal to his companions, brutal,
if not cruel,[16] towards his enemies, never discouraged by setbacks or
treason, he possessed the qualities of the tactician as well as those of the
strategist. He had a taste for the offensive and for crushing attacks, the
genius for tackling his adversary at his strongest point, the art of manipu-
lating the drags and mangonels. Thus when Raymond-Roger of Béziers, for
his resistance to the Church, had been declared 'faidit'[17] and his lands
vacant, it was Simon de Montfort who, by common consent of the crusaders,
had acquired the succession. After the Assumption 1209, Carcassonne with
all its booty, belonged to him. In a few days he succeeded in occupying a
large number of places in the flat countryside around. Gradually he established his loyal companions of France on the lands of the other 'faidits'. On
12th November the Pope sanctioned the transfer of the fief. Simon received
the feudal confirmation which was most important to him at the beginning
of 1214, when the king, Pedro de Aragon, suzerain of the greater part of the
land, agreed to admit him to homage. Simon de Montfort, leader of the
crusade, would hold in future, with the consent of the chief of the southern
princes, the Bittérois, the Carcassès, the Lauragais, the Razès and the
Albigeois. At this juncture the lack of willingness or of power on the part
of Raymond VI to fulfil the engagements he had undertaken at Saint-Gilles
gave the legates the opportunity of finally excluding him from the Church.
Excommunicated, a 'faidit', he lost his land. Simon de Montfort, aided by
Arnaud de Cîteaux and all the churchmen round about, prepared to take
possession likewise of the inheritance of the Count of Toulouse. The
operation, begun as early as 1211, reached its peak at the victory of Muret
on 12th September, 1213, when the death of Pedro II of Aragon, who had
turned against the crusaders, meant the supreme collapse of the resistance
of the southerners. Two years later, succeeding at the same time both
the Saint-Gilles and the Trencavel, Montfort obtained, east and west of the
Rhône, a territory that was equivalent to a kingdom.

This boundless appetite for feudal power was the unpleasant side of Simon
de Montfort and his weakness. Others, seeing a dishonour in accepting,
even by right of crusade, patrimonial territory which belonged to another,
had found strength to refuse.[18] Pedro II, realizing that Simon wanted the
whole of the Midi, had made a complete change of front, despite the links

which attached him to the Roman Church. Innocent III, who had confirmed the possession of Carcassonne to de Montfort, was alarmed to see him attack Toulouse. At the end of 1210, he had put a certain restraint upon him by demanding that Raymond VI be allowed to defend himself against the charges of murder and heresy; in 1213 he tried to stop de Montfort and the legates completely and reversed his policy; in 1214 he suspended operations and reserved the final decision to himself; in 1215, despite the almost unanimous pressure of the churchmen, he for long refrained from confirming and, eventually, would not agree to accept without restrictions the substitution of the de Montforts for the Saint-Gilles in the county of Toulouse.[19] The legates, however, like the churchmen of the Midi, were convinced that there was no better way of accomplishing the work of God in those parts. They continually arranged matters so as to prevent Raymond from freeing himself by clearing himself through a liberating oath of the crimes of which he was accused, from the excommunication which threatened to deprive him of his domains. Coming from him, this oath seemed to them completely unworthy of credence. Like the promoters of the Gregorian reform, they considered that the prince was merely the functionary of the Christian people and that he lost his land by right the moment he ceased to fulfil his mission in the Church. Simon had still less difficulty in persuading himself of this. The populations of the south, however, reasoned in a different way. When they understood that the French barons were going to entrench themselves in the land, the struggle became implacable.

The religious inspiration of the holy war, which, in the intention of Innocent, was to facilitate the establishment of order and peace, on the contrary over-excited men's passions in the struggle, making it more dramatic. The eternal salvation of a multitude of people and the community of minds and hearts in the bosom of Western christendom surely depended, in the eyes of the combatants of the north at least, on the outcome of the battles. If the Perfect among the Catharists, if not their feudal friends, were absolutely convinced in their faith, the crusaders were none the less so. The confessions and pardons exchanged on the morning of combat, which the documents mention,[20] were not mere formal rites; as for instance, the offering to God 'of body and soul' pronounced by Simon at the offertory of the Mass said before the battle;[21] the chant, so much dreaded, of the *Veni Creator* by all the clergy at dawn, while the knights attacked Lavaur, St Antonin, Moissac, Casseneuil;[22] or the fervent prayers, shouted to deafening point by legates, bishops and monks, in the basilica of St Sernin at Muret, whilst the decisive battle was being fought.[23] It even seemed to them that God continually intervened in the contest by veritable miracles.[24] On both sides the engagement was until death and men held their own lives cheap as they did those of others.

Simon had in his favour his military valour, which went hand in hand with

the vigour and loyalty of an heroic family—the countess, his brother, his
brother-in-law, his cousins and his sons[25]—and companions truly worthy of
him; interior strength coming from his religious conviction, the purity of
his morals and from a position that was *simpliste* but coherent; the collaboration of the Pope, the bishops and the preachers of France and Germany who
procured for him armies that were sometimes of considerable strength.
Against him he had the precariousness, irregularity and lack of discipline of
these contingents, too often dispersed in the course of the battle because
the crusaders had finished the forty days service required by the indulgence,
while their recruitment dried up almost totally in winter-time. Above all
he had against him the hatred of all those who were attached to the Catharists
or other heretics, to the lords who were 'faidits', to the townships in ruins,
to the dynasties of Saint-Gilles and the Trencavels. Not all the men of the
Midi detested the crusade. The convinced Catholics hoped for a great deal
from it and it was in their thousands that the members of the 'white confraternity' of Toulouse collaborated in its operations.[26] The local churchmen
wanted Simon de Montfort and many of the clergy received him with
gratitude. Certain lords, like Raymond of Toulouse' own brother, Count
Baldwin, were sincerely loyal to him and a number of Frenchmen, like
Guy de Lévis, founded families in the neighbourhood.[27] Nevertheless, the
general mentality was frankly hostile to the crusaders, even in the Catholic
cities of Narbonne and Montpellier, which had not had to suffer from
them.[28]

Such interlocking factors of strength and weakness explain the vicissitudes
of the sentiments and events which, after the murder of Peter of Castelnau,
dominated the life of the Narbonensis, where Dominic was pursuing his
work of salvation.

Between August 1207 and May 1211, no dated account of an event, no
document in the archives, has preserved for us the detailed narrative of the
saint's activity. The preparation and launching of the crusade, precisely in
these very years, meant an upheaval in the Lauragais from end to end. It was
not until 1212 that the war, moving away from the ancient domain of the
Trencavel, would be carried over into the county of Toulouse. It is not
surprising that in the bustle and confusion of the movements of cavalry,
sieges, massacres and councils, it should be difficult to catch the modest
echo of the activity of the Castilian. Jordan of Saxony, however, is our
authority for the continuity of his presence and action in the neighbourhood.
After the withdrawal of the Bishop of Osma and the departure of the
Cistercian missionaries, he tells us, 'Brother Dominic remained where he
was and, alone, unremittingly continued his preaching'.[29] Several documents
confirm and throw light on this general evidence.

The first is a living document—the permanence and development of the house of Prouille. At a time when the population was fleeing before the military, when the enemy forces did not cease to scour the country by turns, the recent and not very strongly rooted foundation would have been unable to survive without the presence and effort of the two men to whom Diego had entrusted it at his departure—[30]William Claret and Dominic. On 19th March, 1209, the former was given actual possession of the property of the church of Limoux[31] which the Archbishop of Narbonne had given Prouille two years earlier by then simply handing them a charter.[32] Doubtless Bérenger had profited by the dispersions and upheavals of 1208 to postpone the fulfilment of his promises. In March 1209 the announcement of the early return of Arnaud de Cîteaux and of the coming of a new pontifical legate,[33] probably roused the archbishop's zeal. Dominic and William hastened to profit by this. Then came the crusade.

In the last week but one of July, the terrifying news of the Béziers massacre reached the monastery. From that moment, the knights and the Dame de Fanjeaux[34] left the township with the whole of the inhabitants, to take refuge in the fortresses on the periphery of the lands of the viscounts of Trencavel, or of the county of Foix. As they fled,[35] they dismantled their fortifications, at least in part. A few days later, a leader of the mercenaries who had rallied to Simon, Pedro the Aragonese, passed through Prouille to occupy Fanjeaux, the fortifications of which he once more put in a state of defence.[36] He must doubtless have guaranteed then and there the security of the religious house. In any event he showed it positive favour and a short time afterwards made over to it a small property at Alzonne.[37]

As soon as the first days of September arrived, de Montfort came in person to secure Fanjeaux and its important junction of routes.[38] There he replaced Pedro the Aragonese, endowing him with lands recently conquered.[39] Prouille must have been relieved at this. The close company of mercenaries was scarcely reassuring for a religious house. Whereas Carcassonne, thanks to its military strength and to the renewal of its population was to constitute the centre and stronghold of de Montfort's power, Fanjeaux would for the future be his headquarters if one can attribute any centre of operations to this warrior who was always on the move. He reserved to himself the direct overlordship,[40] and occupied the castle, by the side of the present church, near the viewpoint over the plain of the Lauragais, which has been named the Seignadou. It was there he liked to station himself between two campaigns, in his observation post as it were, ready to set off again immediately in the direction of Carcassonne, the Razès, the county of Foix, Toulouse or Albi. He must have made prolonged stays there in winter, when the gradual disappearance of his effective forces would oblige him to cease operations and hold himself on the defensive. This began as early as September 1209 with a series of raids spreading out in all directions like the points of a star,[41] which enabled him to install his followers in the country round.[42]

On the 29th of that month, however, when de Montfort had ridden away on a distant expedition, Raymond Roger de Foix tried to take the city of Fanjeaux by scaling the walls.[43] A few soldiers mounted by means of ladders and ran through the streets. Caught by surprise and repulsed, they had to leap from the walls, and every one of them was killed. Nevertheless the resistance of the Midi was stiffening. Montréal, with some forty other places, fell away.[44] At the year's end, besides Carcassonne and Fanjeaux, de Montfort only retained Saissac, Limoux (gravely threatened), Pamiers, Servian and Albi.[45] We can imagine the atmosphere which then obtained around Prouille until at the end of the winter de Montfort gave Fanjeaux a little breathing space by seizing Bram[46] and Bellegarde,[47] a mile or two away from the convent. In September 1221 there was the same dramatic atmosphere once more. After the brilliant campaigns of the summer which had driven Raymond VI back to Toulouse and Montauban, de Montfort again found himself alone. Toulouse and the allies of Foix and Comminges resumed the offensive and laid siege to Castelnaudaury, the gateway to the Lauragais, where de Montfort rushed to sustain the courage of his handful of loyal followers.[48] During this time his wife, the countess, was isolated at Lavaur. His youngest daughter, an infant, was put out to nurse at Montréal, his eldest son, Amaury, lay ill at Fanjeaux.[49] The plain was controlled by the forays of the enemy. From the heights of the Seignadou the varying fortunes of the encounters could be followed. Treason penetrated even into the town; Guillaume Cat, a native of those parts whom de Montfort had knighted, godfather of his little girl and nurse of his son Amaury, had come to Fanjeaux to plot his own defection and the capture by treachery of Guy de Lévis, marshal of the crusade.[50] A column of reinforcements was attacked a short distance away from the walls. The Bishop of Cahors and the clergy of the escort made their way to the city for refuge, while the decisive combat was being fought.[51] A little later two knights fell into an ambush at the gate of the town. One of them was killed; an anniversary was instituted in his memory at Prouille.[52] Finally after 1212, peace was established in the neighbourhood of Prouille; at each season, however, the passage of crusaders in large bodies continued to be an indication of the presence of the war and its tumults. In May and June 1213, de Montfort was living by turns in Carcassonne and in Fanjeaux.[53] It was from the latter that one September morning he set out in haste to deliver Muret, which was being besieged by Pedro de Aragón.[54] The victory that he won there secured peace for the future throughout the Lauragais, as in the rest of the viscounty, until his death.

Thus the superior of Prouille from the very beginning found himself in contact with the man whom the crusade had just chosen as leader. Loyal Catholics were not numerous enough in Fanjeaux for the count to take no

(*Photo: Leonard von Matt*)

Fanjeaux overlooking the plain; just visible on the right: the tower of Seignadou
church.

interest in the monastery. In reality there was no priest or religious in the neighbourhood more important than Dominic, whatever his humility. Close links were established between the two men. Jordan of Saxony speaks of the 'peculiar and warm devotion' which the count[55] showed towards Dominic. One chronicle, very well informed on this point, calls attention to the close friendship which bound St Dominic to the count and his family, particularly to his eldest daughter, Amicie de Joigny, and to the youngest, Petronille, a nun of Saint Antoine.[56] In fact the documents in the archives, from 1211 onwards, show the generosity of Simon, of his brother Guy, and of his eldest son Amaury, in regard to the house of Prouille and its superior— domains or lands at Sauzenc, Fanjeaux, Villarzens, Montbajou, Casseneuil, revenues, exemptions, confirmations, permits.[57] Moreover, certain significant gestures, the memory of which has been handed down to us, throw light on their reciprocal relationship. The countess having given birth to a little girl in February 1211, probably at Montréal, Dominic baptized the child.[58] At the beginning of June 1214, a much more solemn ceremony took place at Carcassonne. Amaury de Montfort was married to Beatrice, the daughter of the Dauphin. To bless this wedding which was to increase the power of the de Montforts in eastern Provence, the count, now arrived at the height of his glory and surrounded by the highest prelates of the Church, would have no difficulty in finding clergy. The fact that for this office he preferred Dominic, then deputy for the bishop of the place, speaks sufficiently for his sentiments.[59] That same year he helped Dominic to set up a fresh 'Preaching' at Fanjeaux. After 1215 the institution of the Preachers in Toulouse naturally increased the reputation of their founder. One can understand de Montfort's consternation when he learnt in the middle of 1217 that Dominic had in mind the dispersal of the first brethren, and he made efforts to cause him to reverse his decision.[60] Dominic, on his side, followed the vicissitudes of Simon's fortunes with great concern.[61] A year before the count's death, he saw in a dream 'a wide-spreading tree of lovely appearance, which was harbouring a great number of birds in its branches. The tree fell to the ground. The birds which were nesting in it flew away in all directions.'[62] In this he saw the announcement in prophecy of the crusader's early death. This decided him to take momentous steps.[63]

History, and even more so literature, have given impassioned and contradictory judgements on Simon de Montfort. It is understandable that he should have been detested. It is likewise understandable that many have been sparing neither of admiration nor of devotion to his memory. His gifts were not limited to the military qualities we have mentioned. He possessed the ability of an organizer and his 'Institutions de Pamiers', by their provisions, suppressed many of the causes of the anarchy of the Midi.[64] He knew how to acquire and keep his friends. An adversary like Raymond VII could recognize his chivalrous qualities.[65] Finally, as has been said, he was simple and pure in his morals and sincerely wished to serve God and the Church. None the less, even assessing at their true value the accusations of unbridled ambition[66] and of brutality which have been levelled against him, it must be said that he was primarily a warrior whose figure stands out for us against a background of battlefields, embellished with too large a number of gallows, stakes and even of massacres. We should have preferred St Dominic not to have been seen at all against this background, by the side of the count and his friends.

Dominic was of his time; he could not always choose his horizons. The pillage and brutalities around him had not begun with the crusade. Moreover, it is probable that he considered the latter legitimate. The almost universal view of the men of Europe on the role of the temporal sword in defence of the Kingdom of God has already been recalled. The service of orthodoxy, of peace, of the liberty of the Christian people was not only the duty of temporal authority, but its very basis. Dominic had known this ideal since his childhood in the Castile of Alfonso VIII, in the full vigour of the reconquest. In 1216, after eight years of the crusade, it would seem that he still retained it if one is to believe two anecdotes, neither of which, it is true, is very well authenticated.[67] The first associates him with one of the repressive actions of Simon de Montfort against the heretics.[68] This was not the Inquisition, the hour of which had not yet come.[69] Apparently he was called on to judge the belief of suspects whom de Montfort's officers had arrested, and to try to convert them in extremis.[70] It is alleged that he snatched one of the condemned men from the stake, although the unfortunate man was convinced but in no wise repentant, and that Dominic knew through a private revelation that this Catharist follower would be converted twenty years later and would become a member of the faithful, full of sanctity.[71] A little earlier, before a crowd of people whom the cultus of Notre Dame de Prouille had gathered around the monastery on the feast of the Assumption, he is said to have pronounced these significant words:

I have sung words of sweetness to you for many years now, preaching, imploring, weeping. But as the people of my country say, where blessing is of no avail, the stick will prevail (on no val senhagols, val bagols). Now we shall call forth against you leaders and prelates who, alas, will gather together against this country the power of the nations and will cause many people to die by the sword, will ruin your towers, overthrow and destroy your walls and reduce you all to servitude— oh what sorrow! Thus the bagols, that is, the force of the stick, will prevail where sweetness and blessing have been able to accomplish nothing.[72]

The curiously similar speech of Bérenger of Carcassonne[73] has already been noted. Diego of Osma had been even sharper. 'Lord,' he had exclaimed, after the manner of St Bernard,[74] in the presence of the hardened nobles, 'stretch forth your hand and smite them.'[75] Sacred invective doubtless formed part of the exhortation, the final stage of the preaching against the

heretics.[76] Such threats, however, were only verbal. The speech attributed
to Dominic, if it really came from him and not from Bérenger, though less
violent than that of Diego, would have a weightier effect. It would make its
author one with the bishops and the Pope who had summoned the crusaders
to action.

It is essential to remember, however, that a cleric had many ways of
identifying himself with the crusade. One could visualize and bring it into
being like Pope Innocent III. One could direct it like Arnaud, the legate,
who, with his council of churchmen of the Midi, was really responsible for
the military and political operation of the enterprise. One could collaborate
directly, after the fashion of the numerous archbishops and bishops of France
and Germany, who in turn brought their troops and their money to the help
of Simon de Montfort and induced the great barons of their neighbourhood
to accompany them. Certain of these crusading clerics, like the archdeacon
Guillaume de Paris, depicted in such vivid colours by Pierre des Vaux-
Cernai,[77] really did go as far as the extreme limit of that boundary between
combatant and non-combatant which they had not the right to cross,
recruiting men and money, collecting siege material, stimulating carpenters,
servants and soldiers to action at the supreme hour of the assault. Others,
finally, more spiritual, put their preaching at the service of the holy war,
whether they preached to the crusaders in the camps and on the field of
battle, or whether in vast circuits in the north, they strove to procure new
contingents for the crusade.[78]

Not a single document justifies us in thinking that Dominic collaborated
in the crusade in any of these ways. Many of them, on the other hand, clearly
establish that if he felt himself to be linked closely with the crusaders, he
was not prepared to be their collaborator but kept himself apart.[79] Among
the many tasks of the 'affair of faith and peace'[80] in which the Church was
engaged in the Albigensian lands, Dominic had chosen his part—the one he
had discerned with Diego one day in May 1206, in Montpellier, and since
then had never abandoned—'to preach, with a mission from the Church,
according to the way of the apostles, in humility not in authority'.

This task was no less urgent than in former times, and was no less
demanded by the Church. In the bull, even, in which he launched the
crusade, Innocent had again imposed on all the Church authorities in the
Midi, by virtue of obedience and in the power of the Holy Spirit, the further
development of the preaching which had been inaugurated and 'to devote
themselves unswervingly, with all their effort and all their care, to counter-
acting the heretical aberrations and confirming the Catholic faith, to uproot-
ing vices and implanting virtues'. At the very beginning of the crusade, the
Council of Avignon had reiterated this order of Innocent in its first canon,
developed the positive and negative doctrinal and moral programme of the

preaching in precise terms, and imposed on the bishops the obligation of obtaining the help of preachers 'full of discernment and moral value'.[81]

It was truly this function, a silent but a fruitful one, that Dominic fulfilled in nurturing and expanding the centre of spiritual life of the brethren and sisters of Prouille. We have just read how, in preaching at Prouille, he summed up his action as a ministry 'of gentleness', 'preaching, imploring and weeping'. He had not, in fact, confined this ministry to Prouille and Fanjeaux. Often taking the road, as at the time of the preaching in the Narbonensis, he would go off on extensive itineraries. No report, no chronicle has related for us day by day these apostolic campaigns, as was done for the crusade. We are reduced to gleaning with difficulty chance echoes of them in the form of some edifying anecdote, an account of a miracle, certain depositions from the canonization process, or belated confessions before the Inquisition. When, however, these scattered items of information are pieced together, the extent of the territory to which they relate is surprising. From east to west—Servian, Béziers, Carcassonne, Montréal, Fanjeaux,[82] Castelnaudary, Tréville, Villeneuve-la-Comtal,[83] Lavaur,[84] Verfeil,[85] Toulouse,[86] along the principal axis of the country, that is of the valley of the Aude and the plain of the Lauragais; towards the south-west—Pamiers,[87] Boulbonne,[88] and the valley of the Ariège going back towards Toulouse;[89] further to the west, in Couserans and its neighbourhood;[90] towards the north-east—Saissac;[91] finally, northwards to Castres,[92] into the Albigeois properly so-called. These data, fragmentary as they are, outline sufficiently clearly the map of the places penetrated by heresy in the dioceses of Toulouse and Carcassonne, or rather in the domains of the Saint-Gilles, the Trencavels and their allies of Foix and Comminges.

Let us evoke in passing the profiles of some of those whom St Dominic reconciled. They emerge from the shadows only for the space of a lightning flash—a chance phrase in a document—to fall back again into shadow almost immediately. It is a gallery of the young, of children even—Guillelmine Martine, who took *canels*[93] to the heretical weavers, from whom she received presents of nuts and bread; P. de Martel, who, after his conversion, attached himself to the saint and for the future lived near him; several little girls confided to Catharist communities by their close relatives, taking the habit of the Perfect and remaining there several years—Na Segura, given to them at the age of ten, Saura at seven, P. Covinens handed over to them at twelve by her brother, little Arnaude de Fremiac, given to them by her guardian, Isarn Bola of Fanjeaux. . . . There were adults, too—the 'Perfect' ladies Raymonde, the wife of Gasc, Ermengarde, the wife of Boër; and men of the Perfect—P. Jaule of Saissac, Raymond d'Autier of Villepinte and Pons Roger of Tréville whose austere letter of reconciliation is still extant. Certain of these penitents came from a great distance. Arnaud Baudriga de Las-Bordes, a Perfect, had taken refuge in the fortress of Monségur; the mother of Marquise, wife of Bertrand of Prouille, had fled, concealing her life as a Perfect in the Catharist centre of Lavelanet, also near Montségur, whence her daughter brought her back; both were eventually reconciled by Dominic at Fanjeaux or Prouille.[94] Side by side with these silhouettes, with the names that are definite and yet, for us, veiled, there must also be set those of the first nuns of Prouille; those of the noble ladies who saw the devil appear after their conversion; the hostesses who were amazed at and became converted by St Dominic's austerities one Lent, several of the witnesses at the canonization process in Toulouse, of course, without indeed forgetting the Toulouse inn-keeper in 1203. These blurred figures, however, can tell us little as to what Dominic really did to convert souls during ten years of ceaseless journeying.

A few chronological indications can be noted. Several of the dates we have indicate a ministry in the Lauragais and in Carcassonne before the crusade, that is, in the middle of 1209.[95] In 1210 should be placed a lengthy ministry in Toulouse and its neighbourhood mentioned by several documents.[96] The interdict on the city had been lifted on 28th March.[97] Fulk had returned to Toulouse, of which he occupied the fortress, the castle of Narbonne.[98] Taking advantage of the agreement between Raymond VI and the crusade, which respected his territory, Fulk devoted himself actively to the reform of his flock. Loyal to the programme of evangelization reiterated by the Pope,[99] in his daily preachings he did not content himself with attacking heresy; he attacked vice, especially usury, which there was no doubt had developed among this people of traders.[100] He relied much on a Catholic organization known as the white confraternity which he had founded for this purpose and solidly implanted in the city; whereas on the outskirts a black confraternity was not long in springing up to thwart his action.[101] Several documents link the name of Dominic with that of the bishop in this apostolic work. Fulk imposed canonical penances on people whom the saint had previously reconciled.[102] Bécède, a nun of Ste Croix, was later to declare at the canonization enquiry in Toulouse that she provided them both with hair-cloths firmly strengthened with the tails of oxen.[103] They had doubtless given each other her valuable address. Two other women, moreover, were equally occupied in supplying Dominic with penitential garments, woven of goats' hair.[104]

The situation in Toulouse, however, was worsening. Excommunication had again been fulminated against Raymond VI on 6th February, 1211.[105] When the March Ember days came Fulk, who wanted to hold the ordinations in his cathedral, innocently asked the excommunicated count to allow him the opportunity to do so by going outside the town for a few hours.[106] This was the count's opportunity to give vent to a terrible outburst of anger. In reality Raymond VI was already preparing to break with the crusade and attack it. At the end of May the city, which had followed him in his revolt, was placed under an interdict. All the clergy and religious, in liturgical vestments, barefoot, left Toulouse, carrying away with them the Blessed Sacrament.[107]

Dominic must have left the town a considerable time before this, for it was in the neighbourhood of Fanjeaux that he had baptized de Montfort's daughter in the month of February.[108] He was, however, again to be found by the side of his bishop and the count on 15th May before Lavaur, and then on 20th June at the siege of Toulouse.[109] Perhaps he had hoped for the rapid fall of the city, which would enable him to resume his apostolate at once, though he doubtless continued it in the country around the besieged town.

One day as he was praying in the chapel of St Antoine near the ramparts and the Garonne, he heard cries.[110] About forty English travellers who were making their way as pilgrims to Santiago de Compostela, learning of the interdict which hung over Toulouse, had crossed the river to avoid the town. Their boat, which was overloaded, had just capsized. Dominic, hastening to the spot, saw that they were drowning. Through his prayer he brought it about that the shipwrecked men floated to the surface and could thus be brought back to the bank safe and sound, with the help of lances and boat-hooks.

The siege, however, failed. Dominic had just obtained from the count and the bishop two generous donations for Prouille, whose economic condition must have worsened during his absence.[111] He went back there and Prouille again became his centre for almost two years. From that time he busied himself actively in establishing a patrimony for it. Donations accumulated. From this time numerous documents give proof of the habitual, if not continuous, presence of Dominic in and around the monastery.[112]

During the Lent of 1213, however, he was living in Carcassonne.[113] The Bishop, Guy des Vaux-Cernai, who had gone to France to seek reinforcements,[114] had appointed him vicar-general *in spiritualibus*.[115] This office, of recent institution, meant that he replaced the bishop temporarily, without, however, having his legal or administrative powers. Dominic conceived the office primarily as a mission to preach without intermission. He spoke frequently, especially during Lent, in the incomparable nave of the cathedral of St Nazaire, at the foot of the stout pillars with their Romanesque capitals. At that time he lodged in the bishop's palace, situated to the north-west of the cathedral.

The following year he was again in Fanjeaux. On 25th May a charter from his bishop gave him the title of *capellanus*, that is, of parish priest of the town.[116] Jordan informs us, indeed, that Fulk had granted him this church with its responsibilities and revenues.[117] He assigned the place to him not so much that he might pursue his ministry among the people of the neighbourhood, as to give him a position in the diocese. Dominic intensified his preaching even more, taking advantage of the peace. 'He gave himself up to it with all his energies.' An increasing number of collaborators helped him in this activity of salvation. A group thus appeared to be in the process of organization.

A tradition dating back before the sixteenth century[118] points even today to the house in Fanjeaux behind the parish church where Dominic then lived with his companions. It was not far from Seignadou and his companions called the place the 'bourguet Sant-Domenge'. This tradition is very probably true. The place was a dependency of the castle, traces of which have now disappeared. It was natural that St Dominic should have been lodged under this protection in a town where Catholicism still had to reckon with many enemies.

The house is not ancient throughout, but a thick wall in which there is a small oven, exactly similar to the ovens discovered in the ancient houses of the neighbourhood, and two stout beams with their pillars may possibly be authentic. Above all, the bare simplicity of this small house which has been preserved with intelligent piety—an altar has been set up there—irresistibly evokes the presence of the poor preacher, the man of mortification and prayer who, in these days of waiting in 1214, busied himself with regrouping preachers to evangelize the region of Toulouse and, without yet knowing it, through his brethren, the world. The following year Dominic established himself in the capital of the county, to remain there until the end of 1217.

Such was the external framework of the ten years of St Dominic's apostolate in the Midi, with its military and political events, such the chronology of his activity, his moves, his social position, his relationships. We must now approach the source of it all—the pattern and inspiration of his apostolate. Nothing shows more clearly the extent to which he held himself apart from the crusade, that he might remain faithful to his ideal and his discovery of 1206 in Montpellier—to be a preacher of apostolic life.

On his arrival in the Narbonensis, he was 'the lord Dominic, sub-prior of the church of Osma',[119] but as Jordan of Saxony informs us, 'from that time onwards he no longer had himself called anything but Brother Dominic, and ceased to be called sub-prior'.[120] The fact is duly confirmed. If the charters drawn up by the scriveners often bore the official title of 'Lord Dominic, canon of Osma',[121] for such he was still, the depositions of the witnesses who related what they remembered used the term of 'Brother Dominic' which they had formerly used.[122] The episcopal curias of Narbonne and Toulouse did likewise.[123] He himself, moreover, when he allowed himself to be inscribed as a witness at the foot of a solemn charter in 1211, wrote on it these simple words: 'Brother Dominic, preacher'.[124] This signified primarily that his canonical mission of preaching, conferred on him by a papal legate, took priority from the legal point of view over his affiliation to the chapter of Osma and gave him the right to reside at a distance from it. It also signified his love of humility.

It was perhaps due to this love of humility that he systematically refused at this time the episcopal office offered to him. The fact is authenticated. It happened on one occasion and probably two.[125] In 1215, Garsic de L'Orte had just been transferred from the see of Comminges to the archiepiscopal see of Auch.[126] As pontifical legate, he knew Dominic well. Backed by the unanimous choice of the canons, he offered him the bishopric of Couserans, his suffragan see. A similar election must have taken place in Béziers after July 1212, or perhaps in 1215.[127] Dominic refused both one and the other. Guillaume Peyre, abbot of St Paul of Narbonne, mentions in this connection the friar's extreme contempt for the honours of the world and earthly glory,[128] as do several of the witnesses who relate the incident. St Dominic, however, had justified his refusal to the authorities by instancing the care he had to take of the recent foundation of the Preachers and of Prouille.[129] But to simple folk he had uttered a phrase which came straight from the heart, which tells us something more: 'He was resolved to flee by night, carrying nothing but his staff, rather than to accept the episcopate or any other ecclesiastical dignity.'[130] There was no longer any question of Prouille or of the brethren. Something, then, was more important to him—the liberty to be a preacher and nothing more.

If there is one point, in fact, which is clearly inscribed in his behaviour, his decisions and even in the texts of his legislation, it is the necessity of radically separating the activity of preaching from all responsibility of administration, spiritual as much as temporal. With his own ears he had heard the legates declare at the Montpellier disputation, after three years of experience that 'if they had to continue thus to correct the clergy, they would have to cease their preaching'.[131] To correct the clergy, an obstacle—yet this was the essential duty of the bishop. What then was to be said of his judiciary functions, so highly developed at that time, of the temporal administration of his diocese and of his episcopal residence, of his feudal obligations, of his service as leader of an armed force and of all that went with it? Such was the state of things by which at that time a bishop was prevented from preaching by a thousand obligations; a canon of the general council was to give official confirmation of this in that same year of 1215.[132] For Dominic, the facts were particularly clear. Guy des Vaux-de-Cernai, his companion in the Narbonensis preaching, had done nothing else but work for the holy war since 1208 and was continually present with the army, when he was not in France for the purpose of recruiting troops; he could not then have preached in his Parisian abbey, and later in the diocese of Carcassonne of which he received charge.[133] Fulk of Toulouse, at war with his diocesans as with the count, caught between the hostilities of the black

and white confraternities, the latter his own creation, before being exiled
by the revolt of his flock, was no less paralysed in his apostolate. Arnaud de
Cîteaux, continually overwhelmed since 1204 by the highest political and
military negotiations, had had no more freedom to preach when, having
become Archbishop of Narbonne and religious leader of the country, he
engaged in a scandalous quarrel with the new political leader, Simon de
Montfort, over the duchy of Narbonne which he claimed for his see. To
such a pitch was the quarrel raised that the count was accused of penetrating
by force into the archiepiscopal city and having Mass celebrated there
despite the prelate who excommunicated him, but to no purpose.[134] All
these examples and innumerable others had only strengthened Dominic's
fully determined will 'to give himself more earnestly than ever to preaching,
leaving aside every other care', in accordance with the advice formulated in
earlier days by Diego,[135] in consequence of the great need of souls:

> He forbade the brethren to concern themselves with temporal things, [we learn
> from an eye-witness of the years which followed][136] with the exception of those
> of them who had charge of such matters. As to the others, he wished them to
> apply themselves unremittingly to study, prayer or preaching. And if he knew
> that one particular friar preached with success, he forebade any other office
> whatsoever to be given to him.

This in fact is what one would shortly be able to read in his constitutions.
The text would specify the reason for it—'so that, in greater liberty, they
may be in a better position to carry out the spiritual ministry which has been
entrusted to them'.[137] And he was to add: 'They shall not take part in pleas
and lawsuits unless it is for some matter of the faith.'[138] The preacher then,
must not be distracted from his office by any responsibility or administration,
temporal, judicial or even ecclesiastical, such as that of bishop or prelate.
Truth which is spiritual must be preached by a spiritual man and by spiritual
means, the same indeed that were used at the time of the Gospel, and to the
heretics as to the faithful. That was Dominic's ideal, the novelty he quietly
introduced into the system of medieval evangelization. Hitherto the preacher
had been a bishop, a prelate, a parish priest, having authority and power of
spiritual and, at least indirectly, temporal coercion. Moreover, this temporal
power and authority were daily becoming weightier in the complex
structure of Western Christendom. Now the preacher was to be a spiritual
man, with no other authority than that which would come to him from the
mission he had received from the Church, from his knowledge of the Gospel
and from his manifest practice of imitating the apostles. Obviously in the
long run this silent revolution proved more effective in spiritualizing the
diffusion of the Church's message than a protest, sterile and moreover
psychologically unthinkable at the beginning of the thirteenth century,
against the contemporary system of a holy war and civil coercion in the
matter of belief.

Before promoting this revolution in the West through his tens of thousands of mendicant religious, despite the fact that a small number of them exercised the functions of bishop or inquisitor, Dominic first carried it out himself. All those who knew anything of his ministry to souls, in particular the many eye-witnesses who describe his relentless activity against the heretics, instance the same means of action and those alone: controversy, preaching and the example of his personal life.[139] On this latter point Dominic even dared, in the case of certain people who could be moved by this argument alone, to let his mortification, his poverty, his apostle's detachment be seen in all simplicity, judging that the time had come to put into practice the precept of Christ: 'Your light must shine so brightly before men that they can see your good works and glorify your Father who is in heaven.'[140] We are fortunate in being able to picture him without difficulty in this continuous apostolate in the Narbonensis. The documents extant for these ten years or so of his life happen to consist of convincing anecdotes told by eye-witnesses.

Here he is, then, on the road from early morning. A companion, often a Cistercian,[141] accompanies him—to go two by two is part of the imitation of the apostles and a tradition in the Church.[142] He grasps in his hand the staff authorized by St Mark, the top of which is barred with a short cross-piece.[143] He carries a knife in his belt.[144] Into the fold of his tunic above the belt he has slipped a copy of the Gospel of St Matthew and the epistles of St Paul.[145] He has only one tunic, coarse and patched,[146] and a cloak poor in quality.[147] No money at all, no purse, no wallet. He has not even the small coin which would enable him to pay his passage across the river.[148] As he goes through the villages he keeps his eyes lowered.[149]

He walks barefoot.[150] This also forms part of his imitation of the apostles, as everyone knows.[151] After 1215, however, to satisfy the Council of Montpellier and distinguish himself from the heretics who, in their literalism, went so far as to make the right to preach dependent upon this bareness of the apostolic feet,[152] he takes care to put the shoes he has been carrying over his shoulder on again when he enters an inhabited place.[153] Thus he only keeps the austerity of walking bare-foot for the bad country roads. If he hurts himself on a sharp stone, it is with joy that he says, 'It's a penance.'[154] He is sad when rain makes the road so slippery that he is obliged to put on his shoes again.[155] His enemies reserve for him an additional mortification. One day he is on his way to a general disputation in company with the bishop of the place. On his advice the bishop has sent away his mounts. They walk on bare-foot. The road is long and difficult. A guide offers his services gratuitously; a secret heretic, he maliciously leads them through so much brushwood and thorns that soon their legs and feet are bleeding. Dominic bears it all with patience. He even sings and joyfully exclaims: 'We can hope for victory, for already our sins are washed in blood.' In fact, they converted many people, beginning with their guide.[156]

There were innumerable other occasions of doing penance along the road, as, for instance, the rivers, so cold when they had to plunge into them to ford across, so dangerous in autumn when they were transformed into seething torrents. Friar Noel, the second prior of Prouille, was to be drowned in the flooded Blau in 1218.[157] Dominic would approach the swirling waters singing the *Ave maris stella*; making a sweeping sign of the cross, he plunged boldly in.[158] One day, half-way across the Ariège, he had to tuck his tunic into his belt higher than usual. His books slipped from the fold of the tunic in which he was carrying them and were swept away.[159] A serious loss. Then there were the wolves, who attacked many people in the forests, especially those travelling alone,[160] or the dog days of summer which burnt like fire and made one parched with thirst.[161] Dominic was careful to drink from a spring before entering an inhabited place in order not to cause trouble to those giving him hospitality.[162] Near Montréal a small monument over the spring he used is still preserved.[163] Finally, the deluge of the southern storms, which transformed the streams into rivers, the paths into ruts, made coarse woollen garments appallingly heavy. On certain days Dominic would arrive at the halting place chilled to the bone. While his companions, however, pressed around the fire using many complicated devices for drying their cloaks and tunics, he would go to the church and give himself up to prayer.[164]

It was night-time. His hostess had prepared a bed. He did not use it.

In the morning [she related] I found the bed just as I had made it the night before. Moreover I often found the blessed man lying on the ground, without any covering over him. I used to cover him up and if I came back afterwards, I found him at prayer, either standing or prostrate. I was full of concern for him.[165] Very often he was taken with great pain. His companions would then put him on a bed, but I saw him pick himself up quickly and lie on the ground, for it was not his custom to rest on a bed.[166]

His austerity was expressed, indeed, in many other ways: the hair-cloth, that is the shirt woven of rough horse-hair which he wore next to the skin;[167] the iron chain which he had bound about his loins and which would be removed only after his death;[168] the discipline, a bundle of small iron chains, with which he scourged himself at night in the course of his prayers;[169] finally, his privations in the matter of food. 'Never', related the hostess again, 'did I see him eat at one meal as much as the quarter of a fish or two egg-yolks, or drink more than one glass of wine three parts filled up with water; or eat more than one slice of bread.'[170] In Lent,[171] he passed the entire forty days on bread and water. He slept on a bare board. He multiplied his vigils further. Finally he reached such a degree of mortification as exceeded human strength. Only supernatural help, those who saw him considered, could enable him to persevere.

It may be wondered what reason he had for such violence towards a body that was so pure. Was he trying to rival the Catharist Perfect, to challenge their prestige in the eyes of simple folk by outdoing their prowess in austerity? There is some trace of such intention in this wrestler engaged in a disproportionate struggle.[172] He was alone against several thousand. Emulation, however, in this case, only stimulated him to a deeper decision. Love of Christ's cross can inspire a more determined austerity than the hatred of the Catharist Perfect for diabolical matter. Dominic knew that the cross was the weapon of victory. Whereas Simon de Montfort massacred the adversaries of the cross, risking his own life with imprudent daring, the preacher, abstaining from the act of killing, could also offer his life through penance, with equivalent heroism. The blood he shed along the road as he went on his way to preach was the pledge of his success.[173]

Thus he never shunned mockery, humiliation, contradiction or violence. They were not lacking in this country, whose hostility against the Catholic clergy had increased since the war had broken out. One enemy spat upon him. Others threw mud at him.[174] 'He received insults as if they were a gift and a great reward.'[175] Thus he preferred to stay on in Carcassonne and that diocese, rather than in the diocese and city of Toulouse, 'because', he said, 'I find in Toulouse many people who honour me, whereas on the contrary in Carcassonne everyone is against me'.[176] It was not always merely insults or dried grass hooked behind his back in mockery that he received.[177] The feudal lords had few scruples about molesting a cleric. One day he was threatened with death. He answered: 'I am not worthy of the glory of martyrdom; I have not yet deserved this end.'[178] Later, men were waiting for him in an ambush to seize him—perhaps half-way along the road from Prouille to Fanjeaux behind the hummock where the traditional cross is erected.[179] Dominic suspected the fact, but he walked on with joyous mien and singing, probably the *Ave maris stella* or the *Veni Creator* which he liked to recite at the dangerous moments of the journey. This joyful calm,[180] this intrepidity, disarmed the soldiers. They let him go past and admitted the fact to their heretical masters, who were possibly knights of Fanjeaux. The latter, through cynicism, or rather through one of those psychological quirks so frequent among feudal knights, discussed it with Dominic. Was he not, then, afraid of death? What would he have done had he fallen into the hands of his enemies?

I should have asked them [he replied] not to wound me mortally at once, but to prolong my martyrdom by mutilating all my limbs one by one. Then to display the pieces of these hacked limbs before my eyes and next to pluck out my eyes, finally to let the trunk steep in its own blood or finish it off completely. Thus by a more lingering death I should earn the crown of a more glorious martyrdom.[181]

These words should be weighed in the light of Dominic's daily experience. As an habitual companion of the Cistercians, and under the protection of the crusaders, he ran every risk. Guillaume de Roquefort had just brutally assassinated the Abbot of Eaunes and one of his monks whom a chance encounter had placed in his way, simply because they were from Cîteaux.[182] The Count of Foix and his son daily provided themselves in their castle with the amusement of atrocious and long meditated tortures upon the persons of crusading pilgrims whom they had caught unarmed along the road, particularly of priests whom they tortured in their private parts.[183] Dominic, however, had offered the sacrifice of his life as Peter of Castelnau,[184] Fulk of Toulouse,[185] and so many others around him had done earlier. The sacrifice of the preacher, indeed, is purer than that of the others, for he has brandished against his adversaries no other weapon than that of speech. Thus to suffer persecution for the name of Jesus was surely one more way of imitating the apostles.[186]

His offering went hand in hand with his prayer. To pray in Osma or even in Prouille was no problem. Here, however, he had to contend with a life of uninterrupted preaching and harassing journeys. From morning onwards he kept silence along the road and 'thought of his Saviour'.[187] His downcast eyes scarcely left the ground.[188] He drew inspiration from the silence of the forests; he lingered behind; when they sought him, his companions would find him on his knees, regardless of the hungry wolves.[189] When he arrived at an abbey at the hour of the liturgy, he immediately went to recite the office with the monks;[190] otherwise he recited it along the road at the canonical times. He especially loved to visit the basilicas where the relics of the saints were kept. In Castres, where the remains of the martyr St Vincent were particularly dear to his Spaniard's heart, it was his custom to remain a long time at prayer after Mass. One day, he experienced there a kind of ecstasy, so impressive that it was this which later decided the prior of the chapter to become one of his sons.[191] But it was especially the nights that he devoted to prayer. No sooner had he arrived than, without even relaxing or drying his clothes, he would go to pray.[192] If he fell asleep for a moment, he quickly recovered himself and prolonged the liturgical vigils by his deep prayer.[193] He prayed in order to come face to face with God. He also interceded for sinners. 'The thought of the sins of others gave him such excruciating pain, the Abbot of Boulbonne said later, that one might apply to him that saying of the apostle, "Who is weak and I am not weak?" '[194] The Abbot of St Antonin of Pamiers heard him 'uttering deep groans in his prayers'.[195] And the Abbot of St Paul of Narbonne heard him cry out 'so loudly that what he said could be heard all around'. It was the phrase already recorded: 'Lord, have pity on your people. What will become of sinners.' He spent whole nights in this way, weeping and groaning over the sins of others.[196]

Strong in the confidence won in prayer and set free by his poverty, mortification and the joyful dismissal of every anxiety and fear, Dominic had no difficulty in approaching men. Discreet with those who lived with him to the extent that a woman who gave him a meal more than two hundred times was to claim that she had never heard an idle word from his lips,[197] he was always ready to 'announce the word of God, by day and by night, in the churches and in men's houses, in the fields and along the roads, in short, everywhere'.[198] Sometimes it was to a travelling companion that he addressed himself, at other times to Catholics gathered together in church, or again and primarily, to the heterodox, 'whom he opposed by preaching, controversy and every means in his power'.[199] What he had done in Béziers, Carcassonne or Montréal, he began again unweariedly throughout the country.

He was a gifted orator. 'When he preaches,' declared one of his listeners, 'he uses tones so shattering that very often he moves even himself to tears and makes those who listen to him weep. I have never heard anyone whose words elicited tears of repentance so effectively'.[200] Two sentiments coming from his own personality and stimulated by his prayer, in fact dominated his apostolate—'the thirst to save souls, and compassion'.[201] He had the art of finding words which soothed and gave comfort and then uplifted those in trouble.[202] His gentleness and understanding endeared him to all, 'rich and poor, Jews and unbelievers'. His charity was equally able to find the necessary reasons and approach to arouse men to repentance and for the conversion of the Christian apostates who at first detested him because he pursued them and convinced them of their error.[203] Yet it was difficult to resist one who, over and above the reasons which convinced and the friendship which touched the heart, was ready even to give his own life to snatch his neighbour away from the bonds of sin or heresy. For he did not merely offer his life by despising each day's perils. One day, learning that it was extreme poverty alone which bound a certain believer to the Catharists who provided for his sustenance, he again proposed, as he had done formerly, he who owned nothing, to reduce himself to slavery to buy back the man's freedom. Providence happily made provision in another manner.[204] Jordan was indeed justified in writing: 'He devoted himself with all the strength of burning zeal to winning for Christ as many souls as possible. In his heart there was an amazing and almost incredible ambition for the salvation of all men.'[205]

In this inspiration of zeal, he converted people and brought them back to the Church. The rites and penalties for absolution were fixed. The reconciliation of heretics, or rather of apostates, for that is how they were regarded at that time, formed part of the major or public cases in law; such people were thus assigned the public penances that the Carolingian church had formerly resuscitated.[206] The administration of such penances belonged to the bishop, the legate, or their delegate, alone.[207] A letter of reconciliation informed the parish priest of the fact and from then onwards he was commissioned to keep an eye on the penitent who for the future must not leave the boundaries of the parish.[208] The rite first of all comprised a ceremony of declaration in which the convert, with bare feet and bare chest, was beaten with rods along the road that led to the church one Sunday or feast-day;[209] then followed a certain time of fasting and abstinence in the matter of food; finally prayers, and the wearing of the distinctive penitent's dress.

Doubtless, as a contemporary has remarked, there was no question of imposing on physical constitutions which no longer had the health or resistance of those of former times[210] the twelve years of penance prescribed by Pope Julius which the canonical collections[211] continued to recall. The year on bread and water and the three 'Lents' or quarantines before Christmas, Easter and St John's day in summer must be understood in the restricted sense indicated by the penitentials.[212] The reconciler had to proportion the penalty to the fault and to the penitent's possibilities.[213] Thus Dominic acted, in the letter of reconciliation he gave to Pons Roger, the converted Perfect.[214] Its elements are well known—the rods, the total abstinence, the three Lents, the fast three days weekly, stability within the bounds of the parish, under the surveillance of the parish priest, the wearing of the religious habit. Certain details, however, are special or new. The wearing of two small crosses each side of the breast appears in this document for the first time in history;[215] it was to become the standard practice in the Albigeois. Particularly painful for the convert because it publicly recalled his former apostasy,[216] it was effective in manifesting the genuineness of the conversion and the penitent's perseverance, for a Catharist follower, even were he one secretly, would not agree to wear upon his person the hated sign of the cross.[217] Moreover, Dominic did not fix the duration of the penance. He left this to the judgement of the Abbot of Cîteaux, from whom he held his office as reconciler,[218] manifesting in this way his hierarchical position and his subordination. Finally he added to the penalty abstinence from any kind of meat, the practice of continence, and prayers seven times a day as well as in the middle of the night. Whatever may have been the alleviations introduced by the text into certain of these provisions,[219] looked at as a whole they are severe. It may be asked what has become of the sweetness and the charity with which Dominic touched the hearts of erring men and converted them.

It is not difficult to understand the reasons for this sternness. One of them is the very reason that inspired the penitential discipline of the time. It was by proportioning the external penance to the gravity of the fault that the Church formed the conscience, wholly objective and unskilful at moral reflection, of the men of the time; there was no fault more dangerous than apostasy. Dominic was, however, moved by another consideration. The fasts, the abstinences from certain food, continency, the prayers he added, were the very things that the Perfect had practised in his sect.[220] It would not do for an austere Catharist follower to have an impression of a lower standard of perfection on returning to Christianity. If the former Perfect lived as a true religious his fervent intention of earlier days would not be lost. Compassion which converts, and demands which uplift—the whole of Dominic is there in these two complementary traits, the product of a single sentiment which governed his neighbour's salvation. Such a love reached its objective, despite the difficulty of the task, for he added to the persuasive strength of eloquence and knowledge, the communicative force of personal heroism.

Austerity, the gift of self, unceasing prayer, the saint's charity, surrounded him with a veritable supernatural halo. If he was jeered at and detested by some he was proportionately loved and admired by others.[221] Not only did the leaders of the crusade, the prelates or religious, the good hostesses who were impressed as they watched him pray and mortify himself, hold him in honour and attach themselves to him; the most humble Catholics surrounded him with affection and considered him as a saint. 'Public opinion, the nun Bécède was to declare, fully confirms all that has been said on this subject, throughout the whole extent of the dioceses of Toulouse and Couserans, as indeed everywhere where the blessed man stayed during his journeys among religious, clergy and lay folk of both sexes.'[222] The inhabitants of Fanjeaux, summoned for the canonization process 'were to proclaim with unanimous voice that they had never seen on earth a man of such great worth and holiness'.[223]

Miracles in turn seemed to add the divine sanction to this approbation of the crowds. Bérengère had seen him discover and drive out the demon from nine poor converted ladies.[224] The parish priest of Villar saw a possessed woman cured by his prayer.[225] A cleric of Fanjeaux, a canon of Pamiers, were cured of the fever by the imposition of his hands.[226] A Premonstratensian saw him put his hand on the eyes of a blind man who instantly recovered his sight.[227] A girl was restored to health through his intercession.[228] The prior and one of the canons of Castres, in amazement saw him raised in ecstasy a good foot above the floor of the church.[229] The rain which was falling in torrents stopped all around him and his companion and this clear space moved with them as they advanced.[230] His books, lost in the Ariège, were found mysteriously hooked to the line of a fisherman who pulled them up absolutely undamaged.[231] A coin was found at his feet by chance, just when the boatmen were roughly clamouring for his fare.[232] On two occasions he was found with his companion on the other side of a fast-locked door.[233] And everyone knew that it happened to him to predict the future, for God, in the intimacy of prayer, revealed to him many things.[234]

Dominic's companions could see another halo on his face, a human one this time, but one which made a deep impression, that imprinted upon his features which were ever changing by the continual succession of his feelings. Habitually calm and serene, his face would suddenly contract when confronted with the suffering of others.[235] He was moved to the extent of tears at Mass, at the Pater, at the recitation of the psalms.[236] Then prayer would establish peace in him once more. Dominic was open and frank when addressing men.[237] All of a sudden a flame of joy would pass into his eyes, his brow would become radiant. His companions knew what that meant— he had met with some suffering, a humiliation, some threat or adversity.[238] He rejoiced in trials and contradictions and they were not lacking. The most painful he experienced in his ministry—the fewness and poor quality of the conversions, which were sometimes the outcome of fear. His joy, however, did not come from the easiness of the task or its success. It was the joy of a supernatural heart which had learnt how to see in the cross both purification and the promise of the grace to come and even now the sign of the presence of Jesus, the joy of the combatant in the full fire of battle who has no time to think of himself and remains convinced that, when God wills, the tide will turn.

The years he spent in this way were full of fervour and enthusiasm. Stripped of all responsibility except that of the direction of his not very numerous daughters whose temporal affairs were administered by William Claret, he was free to go off wherever the Spirit and the need of souls called him. Poor, he was freed by his very poverty from all dependence and painful anxiety as to his daily bread, for the perspective of lacking absolute necessities aroused in his heart a gladness of hope for men's salvation. He was consecrated to an urgent task of spiritual apostolate, of which no-one sought to deprive him, fearless in the midst of brutal enemies and traitors from whom he would perhaps receive the martyrdom desired. He was without any thought of self in the privations and bodily sufferings of cold, hunger, journeying or vigils. And he possessed, as a superabundance of joy, the certainty that by living in this way, he was imitating down to their daily life, with their bare feet and their single tunic, their belt always empty of gold, silver or coin, the apostles as they preached the kingdom of God along the lake of Gennesareth, or crossed hostile Samaria on their way to Jerusalem. To live the Gospel thus, in this way to put one's feet in the imprints of the Saviour, along the road to speak to him alone in order to speak only of him, with the very words of a man of the Gospel, there was no more impressive way of loving Jesus Christ and of bearing him within oneself,[239] nor was there a better way of taking him to others. He must save souls by identifying himself with the divine Preacher.

And he must do this within the context of the Church.[240] The remote preparations of Caleruega and Palencia, the apostolic meditations in the cloister at Osma, the harsh discipline of the journeys to the north and the ministry in the Midi, gradually formed Dominic to this evangelical life. Now he dominated his own ideal by an austerity, a gift of self, a heroism which astounded both clergy and laity, corresponding on a higher plane to the feudal heroism which was shown in the army of the crusaders. But no more than the mighty deeds of the 'Strong count',[241] were his feats of holiness performed for the beauty of the gesture. The joy he derived from them did not only come from the fact that he was thus imitating his Master. He rejoiced in the thought of working by the methods of Christ in the work of Christ himself, that which was being effected by his Church—*negotium fidei et pacis*. For him the phrase was true in a different way from the use for the crusade. Under the orders of the Pope and the bishops, in continuous relation with the legates from whom he received his powers and solicited their confirmation, he himself was the Church who proposed, enlightened, corrected and reconciled. What others attempted to do by the sword of spiritual sanction or by the temporal sword, he effected *verbo et exemplo*. What Catharists and Waldenses undertook by a preaching which was not enlightened by God because it was without mandate, he achieved in the Church. *In medio Ecclesiae*. That was his programme. The poverty of the apostle which freed him from so many frustrating obstacles made of him the *expeditus*, the swiftly moving soldier of the Church, always ready to betake himself where souls were being lost, to pass through each door he found even slightly open.

Despite the tragic times in which he lived these years truly saw the finest and most fruitful flowering of his genius. He still possessed his full strength. His mortifications, his apostolic labours, and his unending vigils of prayer had not yet worn him out. He came out of the austerities of Lent more vigorous than when he embarked upon them.[242] He was still independent. The time, however, was approaching when he would no longer be completely alone. Already a few companions accompanied him regularly. These were no longer only lay-brethren or Cistercian abbots, or William Claret, his companion at Prouille from the earliest days. There was, perhaps also from the earliest days, a Friar Dominic, whose native country was Spain.[243] There was the future Friar Stephen of Metz who lived with him in 1213 at the bishop's palace in Carcassonne.[244] There was Friar Noël who was soon to be his successor at Prouille.[245] There was a certain Friar Vitalis, a priest who is mentioned in the documents covering these years.[246]

In 1214 these men were living with Dominic supported by the tithes of Fanjeaux.[247] In September, Simon de Montfort assigned to them, and to all those who should participate in their ministry of salvation, the revenues of his latest conquest, the fortified township of Casseneuil whose walls he had just razed.[248] A new group of preachers was being formed. They even spoke of becoming a permanent community.[249] Certain traits of accentuated poverty were defined; they distributed their resources to those who were poorer than they, keeping only what they must for themselves.[250] At the frontier of the dioceses of Carcassonne and Toulouse, in that centre of Prouille and Fanjeaux where Dominic now had much more than a mere base, it was clear that the Preaching of Jesus Christ was in the process of a renewal in a wholly original form.

And then, everything changed. Dominic was transferred to Toulouse. It was there that the new institution was to come into being.

CHAPTER X

TOULOUSE

FTER 12th September, 1213, the fate of Toulouse was sealed. The crushing defeat of the men of the south at Muret had finally broken their power. No other resource was left to them but to appeal to the arbitration of the Sovereign Pontiff. For the past eighteen months the Holy See had been uneasy over de Montfort's excessive ambition, and now it intervened. The Cardinal of Santa Maria in Acquiro, Pietro di Beneventi, legate *a latere* of Pope Innocent III, came to take affairs in hand and primarily to bring about peace. He arranged for the son of Pedro II, the young Jaime de Aragón whom Simon de Montfort was bringing up at his court, to be handed over to him. He negotiated the absolution of the Counts of Foix and Comminges and of Raymond VI of Toulouse.[1] One hundred and twenty hostages were furnished by the town and sent to Arles. On 25th April, 1214, Toulouse was reconciled and its clergy came back within its walls after three years' absence.[2] The church and cloisters where thousands of refugees had crowded with their poultry and their animals were once more opened to worship.[3]

Toulouse, however, remained restless. The count had gone off to his brother-in-law, King John of England, to see whether he could not obtain some help from him. His son and his family were still occupying the fortress of Toulouse. The legate, after his brief intervention, stayed on in Aragon, where he had gone to install the boy king and to organize the regency. People were waiting for the hour of decisions and of the general reorganization. It struck on 8th January, 1215, at the Council of Montpellier. Five archbishops, twenty-eight bishops, a host of abbots, prelates and clergy took part in the assembly, which was a veritable assizes of the Church in the Midi under the presidency of the cardinal legate.[4] Earlier, after the initial successes of the crusade, the Council of Avignon had promulgated a remarkable series of measures in regard to preaching, the repression of heresy, public and private morality, peace, the life of the clergy and of monks.[5] The Council of Montpellier completed this legislation, particularly as to the two latter points, in concert with that laid down the previous year by another legate at the Councils of Paris, Rouen and elsewhere, to pave the way for the decrees of the Fourth Council of the Lateran.[6] It now remained to put this into practice. The cardinal formed special commissions and delegated powers to a whole series of persons.[7] Unanimously, we are told, the clergy demanded that the county of Toulouse, whose governorship had fallen vacant by the revolt of Raymond VI, should be assigned to Simon de Montfort, 'as lord and king'. The legate had not the power to do this of his own authority. He transmitted the request to Rome. Meanwhile he once more had handed over to him as hostages twelve of the consuls of Toulouse, with possession of the castle of Narbonne, the fortress of Toulouse, from which the Saint Gilles were expelled.[8] Bishop Fulk took possession of the castle in the name of the legate at the end of January or beginning of February, and installed a garrison.[9] Provisionally, the political problem of the capital was settled. As to the pastoral problem, it is clear that at the same time, the legate persuaded Fulk and Dominic to transfer to Toulouse the Preaching they had just reorganized at Fanjeaux with the support of the Count de Montfort.

It is true that the presence of the Preacher in the city is not attested by charter earlier than 25th April [1215].[10] This charter, however, makes it clear that he had already been there for a fairly considerable time. He could have been in Toulouse as early as the second half of 1214,[11] though it does not seem that this was the case. The only direct document as to his activity which is extant shows that he was acting in Toulouse under the authority of the cardinal legate.[12] Now he could not have met the legate and received his delegated powers earlier than January 1215, at the Montpellier assembly.[13] As superior of Prouille, friend and counsellor of the bishops of Carcassonne and Toulouse, it is not surprising that he should have taken part in this council,[14] neither is it astonishing that he should have received from the cardinal a mission for Toulouse—the very mission he had received in 1206 through delegation of the legate, Arnaud de Cîteaux, and still retained in 1211;[15] that which he held from Bishop Guy of Carcassonne in 1213–1214, as vicar-general *in spiritualibus*;[16] that which he had been exercising in short 'uninterruptedly and with all his strength'[17] for nearly ten years now—the office of preacher of the faith. In 1210–1211 he had helped Bishop Fulk to fulfil his pastoral obligations by preaching at his side in Toulouse.[18] The interdict and the war had prevented the exercise of this ministry in the capital for three years. At the beginning of 1215, the time had come for Dominic to take up once more the task willed by the Pope, demanded by the Councils and delegated by the legate, at the bishop's side. He went back to Toulouse.

The Lauragais route, the general direction of which was towards the west, veered brusquely northwards just as it reached Toulouse. Following the slight rises in the ground which prevented the river Hero from dashing straight into the Garonne, it approached the city from the south. At the precise point where the great river, till then flowing in a north-easterly direction, radically changed its course and set off again towards the Atlantic, Toulouse had been mounting guard over the gateway to Aquitaine for two thousand years. The capital of Western art, a rose-coloured town under the blue of a Tuscan sky, the city of the Raymonds displayed to advantage its churches and its Romanesque cloisters—La Daurade, St Sernin, with its incomparable belfry, the cathedral of St Etienne and the white Dalbade. What chiefly caught Dominic's eye when he arrived, however, were the dark walls encircling the city and its outlying fortifications. In front of him there stood the mighty silhouette of the castle of Narbonne. The rectangular fortress, Roman in origin, flanked by broad towers with a platform to them, defended the Narbonne gate.[19] Now occupied by the Church it was no longer formidable. One day Dominic would install himself under this mighty shadow.

His ministry to souls began at once. The habitual pattern of it is already familiar to us. A preacher by delegation, his activity of reconciliation of heretics meant that he drew up for them official letters certifying their conversion and reminding them of their penance. To these unfortunate men such letters were of primary importance for they restored them to normal relations with the Catholics. An orthodox Christian, in fact, ran the risk of incurring the sanctions against the heterodox if he knowingly gave hospitality in his house to one of them.[20] For a repentant heretic the case was different. One day a master furrier, Raymond Guillaume d'Hauterive, who already had a converted Perfect among his companions, wanted Dominic expressly to authorize him to keep him with him and to confirm in an official document that he would incur neither penalties nor obloquy on this head. In the fourteenth century this testimonial letter, of which we now have the copy, was still extant.[21] Formerly a seal had been appended to it, the one that Dominic had used earlier for the preaching in Prouille.[22] He himself, in the text, taking care to reserve the authority of the cardinal legate, gave himself the title *Predicationis humilis minister*. The former Preaching of Jesus Christ was to flower again in Toulouse under his direction and under the guidance of Innocent III's legate.

Dominic's action produced its usual fruit. This time again it had a deep influence among women. At the beginning of the summer[23] Fulk granted Dominic a hospice which was dependent on the chapter of St Etienne and on the abbey of St Sernin.[24] He gave it with its dependencies, for the work of the converted ladies and for the brethren who governed them in spiritual as in temporal matters. There was no indication in the text as to where these converted ladies originated from. It has been thought that what was projected was the provision of a counterpart and daughter house of Prouille. A year and a half later, however, a letter of Pope Honorius III gave important details.[25] The house had become a true convent, with sisters and a prioress at the head. It was suffering from very great poverty. Dominic had taken advantage of a visit to the Curia to obtain from the Pope a pressing appeal to the charity of the people of Toulouse and of their *capitouls*. To stimulate their generosity the Pope hinted at what a disturbing eventuality it would be, if the distress were to increase still further, when these poor girls, 'regretting the delights of Egypt', would become 'for others as much as for themselves, a snare and a danger of moral collapse'. It is easy enough to see why the Pope spoke in this way. He was referring to a house of penitent girls who had become nuns.[26]

Prostitution, which had made its reappearance in the West with the renaissance and prosperity of the towns, particularly worried all prelates worthy of the name.[27] Conscious of the fact that origins of this evil were primarily economic and social, they did not hesitate to propose the boldest solutions. Innocent III had tackled this problem from the beginning of his pontificate by daring to advise certain charitable Christian men to seek a bride among these poor girls.[28] In Paris, Fulk of Neuilly, a great reformer and preacher of the crusade whom Fulk of Toulouse had certainly known, in 1206 had organized communities of repentant girls, which soon developed into the great monastery of St Antoine.[29] In Toulouse the problem had long been acute. In the middle of the twelfth century the heresiarch Henri de Lausanne, then at peace with the Church, had already initiated a measure for getting prostitute girls married.[30] At the turn of the thirteenth and fourteenth centuries, the sermons of a famous Franciscan were so thoroughly to convert some of these women of pleasure that the abbey of St Sernin gave them a near-by hospice which afterwards became the monastery of the Sisters of St Sernin.[31] This was perhaps the hospice that, less than a century earlier and for the same purpose, the abbey had given St Dominic at the bishop's request. In any case history was repeating itself. The monastery of St Sernin took over and brought to completion the institution formerly initiated by the Arnaud Bernard hospice. Dominic's work had not lasted very long. Doubtless the upheavals of the Toulouse revolt in 1217 had swept it away soon after its inception.

Thus it was not only to the heretics that Dominic preached. He did not only instruct—as a true apostle he also attacked the vices contrary to salvation. When he had touched heart and mind, he stretched out a helping hand to his penitents, paid with his own person and did not hesitate to create yet another convent to eliminate as far as possible the material causes of a moral fall. By so doing, it was not only women he succeeded in gaining. His zeal for souls was so ardent that he collected around him men who were convinced believers. There was no lack of such in Toulouse. Dominic had always had devoted friends and admirers in the town. Some of them wished to go further than admiration. They wanted to follow and imitate him. They were not satisfied, however, with becoming part of the Preaching; they wanted to become his religious, his brethren.

Then there took place the chief revolution in the life of St Dominic, the one which would finally give him his place in history and carry the echo of his personality across the centuries. In the course of his ministry at Toulouse, at last accomplishing a long-standing design, the preacher became a founder, the apostle a patriarch. The order of St Dominic was born into the world.

In April 1215, two important townsmen of Toulouse offered themselves to him.[32] The term—*obtulerunt se*—which the sources use to designate this act, has only one possible interpretation.[33] They bound themselves to him by a religious profession, to form a community. The *Libellus* of Jordan of Saxony emphasizes the solemn nature of this gesture:

> When the date on which the Lateran Council was to open drew near, at the time when the bishops were preparing to leave for Rome, two distinguished and capable men of Toulouse made their oblation to Brother Dominic. One of them was Friar Peter Seila, the future prior of Limoges; the other, Friar Thomas, who was gifted with much charm and eloquence. The former, Friar Peter, was the owner of some tall and imposing houses near the castle of Narbonne. He made them over to Brother Dominic and his companions who, for the future, would make their first home in Toulouse in these houses. From then onwards, all those who were with Brother Dominic began to descend the steps of humility and to conform to the behaviour of the religious.[34]

The historian is not limited to this summary account presented by Jordan under the significant title: *Of the first two brethren who made their oblation to Brother Dominic*. Two documents of primary importance and a few secondary texts enable us to test its accuracy and to comment upon it.

On 7th April, 1214, two brothers, Peter and Bernard Seila, discharged themselves in common of a debt which burdened their undivided property, recently inherited from their father.[35] The late Bernard Seila was a person of high position; as Provost of Toulouse, he had administered the rights of the Count in the city and rendered justice in his name.[36] The inheritance was fairly considerable. On 25th April of the following year, the two brothers divided it between them.[37] The remarkable fact about it was that whereas the elder, Bernard Seila, received his share direct, Peter did not receive his himself; another person by the advice and will of whom the division was made, was substituted for him, Brother Dominic. In 1214 Peter Seila was acting in his own name. It may be wondered what event had since intervened to deprive him of the legal right to dispose of his fortune and accept his inheritance, and to necessitate his making over this right to Dominic. The answer is a public act which in our contemporary societies as a rule no longer deprives a man of such civic rights, but which did however produce such a state of affairs in the Middle Ages and down to modern times—religious profession to a superior. The charter of division is explicit on this point. It even sets down that Brother Dominic did not receive the inheritance from his religious in his personal capacity, but in the name of a community, a 'house of regular life', which he had established.

Jordan of Saxony was thus expressing himself with accuracy in speaking of Peter Seila's oblation to St Dominic. It is from his account, too, that we know the name of a second townsman of Toulouse, Friar Thomas, who off-ered himself at the same time. Finally he stated that these two professions were the community's first. It was thus between mid-January and 25th April, 1215, probably very close to the latter date, that St Dominic set up his religious house in Toulouse, that is, as will soon be clear, his Order of Preachers.[38]

The charter of division instances a few further details on the installation of the community. Of the property of the late Bernard Seila, Dominic and his brethren received only some houses with what was necessary to live in them—half the plate, linen and furniture. The invested monies, the shares in the drapers' mills—one of the riches of the artisans of Toulouse—the fiefs and other sources of revenue were abandoned to Bernard, the younger brother. The poverty of the foundation, without endowment or lands, or property of any kind apart from the ownership of the houses, will be noted.

These houses, to the number of three, were situated near the Narbonne gate. The principal one was joined on the right to the Gallo-Roman wall which still served as the city boundary; on the left it adjoined the house of Pons Estève; in front of it was the public track or highway, behind it the house of Guillaume de la Plaine. The second house was situated at the back of that of Guillaume. The third was on the other side of the highroad and outside the walls, adjoining the castle of Narbonne and the entrance of the count's palace. Providence had served Dominic and his brethren well. Doubtless he had not expressly sought the protection of the castle of Narbonne and the following year he would move with his community right into the heart of the city. The proximity of the bishop's men and his soldiers, however, must have established in this neighbourhood a calm favourable to regular life. And, after all, the Narbonne gate was that which led to the Lauragais, Fanjeaux and Prouille.

The Seilas' principal house is still standing at the side of the main street—almost unchanged outwardly,[39] although its Dominican relics have recently been profaned. Jordan has described it for us in two neat terms: *sublimis et nobilis domus*;[40] that means that it was of stone and provided with an upper storey or upper room. That is still the condition of it today. One can touch the Gallo-Roman wall, particularly an old tower in it which has been named St Dominic's tower. Left by the community the very next year, the house nevertheless remained in the order. After 1233 it was used by the Inquisition.[41] Abandoned in the eighteenth century, it then belonged to religious communities who respected the commemorative chapel which had been installed on the upper floor. This was the actual room of St Dominic, that is, the original dormitory of the brethren where Dominic, when he consented to do so, could lie down during the night. At the beginning of the twentieth century people still venerated there a stone seat about three feet from the floor along the south wall; it was known as St Dominic's bench. It was probably the top of the Gallo-Roman wall, the superfluous[42] width of which on the inside had been left by the medieval masons when they erected the upper room. In this way the friars had enlarged the room in this way by more than a yard and gained a stone bench such as they liked to have among them. After the expulsions of the twentieth century the residence of the Archbishop of Toulouse was installed in the premises. About 1930 a new occupier did away with the altar and the Dominican pictures and levelled the venerable wall. The house was made into apartment premises which it still is today.[43] Will the order of St Dominic find no-one to buy back its true cradle, to clean up the walls by stripping them of their flowered paper, remove the partitions and restore the simplicity of the thirteenth century upper room, as has been so well carried out at Fanjeaux in the case of a maisonnette which does not offer the guarantees of absolute authenticity of the house of Peter Seila?

On the kind of life lived in this house and the activity to which the community devoted itself, a further document, two months later than the charter which made the division, throws considerable light. The time referred to must have been about the middle of June and important events had just occurred.[44] At the beginning of April the Pope, refusing to assign to Simon de Montfort the domains of Raymond VI, with independence *vis-à-vis* the King of France, had contented himself with entrusting to him the guardianship of the conquered territories until the decision of the Fourth Council of the Lateran convened for the coming November had been made. In the same month Philip Augustus at last allowed his son Louis to accomplish his crusader's vow; he was accompanied by Guy des Vaux-Cernai and by numerous barons. Simon de Montfort, Pietro di Beneventum, Arnaud de Cîteaux hastened to meet him. Everything went off splendidly. Louis' forty days amounted to nothing more than a military procession across the Midi which was already subjugated. At the beginning of June, the entire body of these high authorities, both religious and political, entered the capital. Simon had just taken possession of the castle of Narbonne. Before Louis' departure important political and military measures were taken, beginning with the lengthy work of demolishing the walls of the town. The necessary religious measures were likewise taken. Before the middle of June, Pietro di Beneventum left Toulouse to return to Rome. It was necessary to regulate the situation of the Preaching before his departure. Legate, count, the bishop and his advisers turned their attention to this together.[45] Up to that time Dominic had held his powers from the legate. It was now for the

1631 town plan of Toulouse; the street plan is still that of the thirteenth
century. On the right, Porte St Michel on the site of the Narbonne castle.
Slightly to the left of this, Peter Seila's house (No. 38). On the left, at the
end of the Grand Rue, St Romain (No. 43).

bishop to delegate them to him. In accordance with the law of the times, it was likewise for the bishop to approve the religious house which had just been established.[46] He did both things and his intervention was set down in a charter by his chancellery.

The bishop did not assign the function of preaching to Dominic alone—he gave it to all his companions both present and future, that is, to all the members of the community as such. In addition, in conformity with the normal procedure for approval, he inscribed in the charter the 'religious intent' or brief summary of the rule of these brethren. Lastly by means of this document he conferred on the brethren an alms in accordance with certain definite conditions. Such was the charter of Fulk, an authentic charter of approval and mandate for the order of St Dominic. It will be well to quote the text in full.

In the name of our Lord Jesus Christ. We bring to the knowledge of all men, both present and to come, that we, Fulk, by the grace of God humble minister of the see of Toulouse, in order to root out the corruption of heresy, to drive out vice, to teach the creed and inculcate in men sound morals, institute as preachers in our diocese Brother Dominic and his companions, whose regular purpose is to comport themselves as religious,[47] travelling on foot, and to preach the Gospel word of truth in evangelical poverty.

Yet, because the labourer has a right to his maintenance[48] and one should not muzzle the ox that treads out the corn,[49] and because a fortiori the Lord has bidden the heralds of the Gospel live by preaching the Gospel,[50] we will that these men, when they go to preach, receive their food and all that is necessary from the bishop. With the consent of the chapter of the church of Bl. Etienne, and of the diocesan clergy of Toulouse, we assign in perpetuity to the aforesaid preachers and to those whom the zeal of the Lord and love of the salvation of souls may raise up to accomplish the same office of preaching in the same manner, one half of the third part of the tithe which is set aside for the furnishing and fabric of all the parish churches which depend on us. Thus they will be able to clothe themselves, to provide themselves with what they need in sickness, and to take rest when they wish to do so. If something is left over at the end of the year, we will and decree that it revert to us for the embellishment of the same parish churches or for the use of the poor, as the bishop shall judge fit. Since Canon Law envisages that a considerable part of the tithes be assigned and distributed to the poor, it is clear that we are bound to assign by preference a part of the tithes to those who, for Christ, have chosen, with great labour, to enrich all and everyone with the gifts of heaven as much by their example as their teaching. In this way the faithful, whose temporal riches we reap, will provide us with the opportunity of sowing spiritual wealth through ourselves and others,[51] in all appropriateness and opportuneness.

Given in the year of the Incarnation 1215, in the reign of Philip, King of the French, the Count de Montfort holding the principality of Toulouse and the same Fulk being bishop thereof.

At first sight it is not clear whether the religious intent of the preachers referred to in the charter was not an individual purpose rather than a community programme. It is, however, known that St Dominic and his companions had already been formed into a community for more than two months. Furthermore it will be noted that the bishop's alms were given to the group as a whole, without specifying any system of distribution. This confirms the fact of the group's organization.

The preaching programme was expressed in striking terms: 'To root out the corruption of heresy, to drive away vice, to teach the creed, to inculcate in men sound morals.' This was, word for word with its four clauses, the complete programme of pastoral preaching of which Pope Innocent had reminded the bishops of the Midi in his letter of 8th March, 1208.[52] The first Canon of the Council of Avignon, which the legates Hugues de Riez and Maître Milon presided over, on 6th September, 1209, had given the contents of it in detail,[53] 'to set themselves like a wall' against heretical errors and 'to preach the orthodox faith'; 'so vigorously to detest in word and deed adultery, fornication, perjury, usury, hatred, aggression with violence and other mortal sins that one would at the same time instil the virtues of perfection, peace, patience and justice'. The canon gave the bishops a brisk reminder of their pastoral duty of preaching more frequently than ever and with greater care. It required that for this they should have recourse to the help of virtuous and wise preachers. Fulk's charter referred to this provision in its final phase, 'through ourselves or through others'. It might be wondered whether the charter, indeed, was anything other than a putting into execution of the Avignon canon.

The community in Peter Seila's house really constituted a Preaching. We have seen that at this time the saint gave himself the title of *predicationis minister humilis* and continued to use the seal of the Preaching of Jesus Christ. There was thus definite continuity between the old Preaching of the Narbonensis and that of 1215. Neither had other territorial limits than those of the province or diocese in which they were instituted. The object of the new Preaching, however, was wider in extent than that of the Preaching of the Narbonensis. The perspective of the Avignon canon had transformed it. Although the Preaching of the Narbonensis had not neglected to evangelize Catholics, to confirm them in the faith,[54] it only specifically assumed in the preaching of the bishops, action 'against the heretics'. That of Dominic now addressed itself to both the faithful and the heterodox; it was concerned with the morals of the Gospel as much as with the doctrines of the faith. Dominic and his brethren would be actual substitutes for the bishop in the matter of preaching.

The great novelty of this Preaching mission, however, was not primarily the nature and extent of its purpose, but the fact that it was conferred in a permanent way and conferred on a community. Delegation of the *officium predicationis* by a bishop to a preacher was not an uncommon thing.[55] At this time there existed even, despite the reprobation of the Councils, 'hired preachers' and a veritable 'farming' of the preaching of a parish and even of a diocese.[56] Preaching delegated to an entire body, however, was something entirely new, particularly its delegation to the *future*[57] members of a community *in perpetuity*.[58] The provision was so new from the legal point of view that in the drawing up of Fulk's charter, the most elementary details as to the system of attribution of this charge to each of the members of the community and as to the check on the knowledge and morals of the candidates for preaching, were neglected. For this Fulk relied on Dominic, a sign of his complete confidence, and equally a sign of his haste to find collaborators. Consequently it must be said that the taking over of the bishop's preaching, such as it was contained in the charter of approval of the Preaching of Toulouse, constituted an important innovation and signified a decisive step in the development of the pastoral system of the Church. Its consequences would soon be clear.

The proposed way of life of the preachers of Toulouse was equally unheard of for religious. There was doubtless continuity with that of the Preaching of the Narbonensis. The will of Dominic and his companions to pursue 'the imitation of the apostles', of which Diego had been given both the rule and the example: 'to go and preach on foot the word of evangelical truth' and to practise the 'evangelical' type of poverty—can be clearly seen. If we should hesitate as to the interpretation of this latter expression, Dominic's constant practice in his preaching since 1206 would serve as a commentary. The evangelical poverty of the charter of 1215 clearly comprised the command not to ride a horse, the refusal to carry money on one's person, the chance shelter and food of those seeking hospitality, begging from door to door and all the other points of the *regula apostolica*. *A fortiori* it comprised the absence of productive property instanced in connection with the charter of the Seila brothers. Jordan in fact confirms this, assigning to it this motive: 'so that concern for temporal affairs might not be an obstacle to the ministry of preaching'.[59] The mind of Dominic will be recognized here. To live on alms was not only an imitation of the Saviour and his apostles, but a spiritual liberation. He had experienced this ever since the days of the mission in the Narbonensis.

The members of the Preaching of the Narbonensis, however, had not formed a community. Dominic and his future companions in the Preaching of Prouille had been living in a community which was not their own and which they had not to feed. Peter Seila's house, on the contrary, was to be a permanent centre where the preachers were to live,[60] prepare themselves for their task, recuperate after their ministry, be cared for during sickness, find clothes and other indispensable supplies.[61] The continued existence of a house with so many requirements was a problem. Were they to do as the

Catharists did and endow the hospice which was to shelter them? It would be better to give effect to Diego's ultimate intention at the time of his departure by asking some bishop for the necessary resources for maintaining the life of this centre.[62] To be certain of food and shelter through an endowment, however, would seem to run counter to the preachers' evangelical poverty.

One has the impression that those who drew up the charter went to enormous trouble to resolve a quasi-contradictory situation. In any case their solution proved imperfect and unstable. They did not even envisage the principal data of the problem, those which seemed calculated to remove evangelical poverty as far away as possible from the community—the direct preparation of their preaching by intellectual work and the moral and scholastic formation of the recruits, two charges that were equally expensive and unproductive. The bishop assigned part of the tithes in perpetuity for the upkeep of the house. We have called this endowment an alms. Jordan of Saxony, not unreasonably, gave it the name of revenue.[63] It was genuinely a revenue since it was assured each year. Jordan, however, hesitated in his turn—the second edition of his *Libellus* marked a restriction. This was because, indeed, the donor had endeavoured to give to his act the precarious and limited character of an alms.[64]

It was limited in those to whom it was destined. Only the sick and those who were tired and had to rest between two missionary expeditions were to be entitled to it. It was limited, too, in its scope—the purchase of clothes, indispensable medicines and food for those who were resting. Finally it was limited in the time and the extent to which it was permissible to use it. Whatever remained at the end of the year was to be returned to the bishop who would dispose of it as he pleased in favour of the poor and of parish buildings. There had been a similar idea in Fanjeaux, the previous year, of making over to the sisters of Prouille all that could be saved from the tithes of the parish and the revenues granted by de Montfort.[65] Thus the great majority of the community, on the road far from the priory, would not profit by this gift. This majority would continue with the ministry of souls and would be called upon to practise the mendicant life of the apostle.

The nature of the alms, moreover, clearly showed its evangelical character. What was to be given was half the third part of the tithes of the diocese, of those at least which were at the bishop's disposal. Canon law recognized, indeed, in Gaul and in Spain, a division of tithes into three parts. The first two parts were destined for the bishop and the clergy. The third, simultaneously, for the fabric of churches and the poor.[66] It so happened that certain religious were considered as 'the poor of Christ'.[67] Even more was this the case of preachers and masters in sacred learning whose spiritual ministry could have no direct remuneration. In 1220 Bishop Tello of Palencia granted one-quarter of the third part of the tithes of the diocese for the upkeep of clergy assigned to teaching and for the construction of buildings for the Palencia Schools.[68]

The four Scripture quotations cited by Fulk's charter were traditionally used to justify the system of tithes; here they emphasized that this concession did not affect the apostolic character of the preachers' poverty.[69] To recognize this it is sufficient to replace them in their context: Do not provide gold or silver, or copper to fill your purses, nor a wallet for the journey; no second coat, no spare shoes or staff; the labourer has a right to his maintenance.'[70] Thus Matthew wrote in the first text quoted. Similarly, St Paul in the other three, claiming the apostles' 'right not to have to devote themselves to material work', wrote: 'Here are we, who have sown in you a spiritual harvest; is it much to ask that we should reap from you a temporal harvest in return? For the Lord has bidden the heralds of the Gospel live by preaching the Gospel.'[71] By granting them a portion of the tithes provisionally and in a limited way, St Paul's rule was applied. Thus there was no departure from the usual norms of imitation of the apostles.

It must be admitted that the solution was not so clear as the charter intended it to be, even if it be noted that Dominic had at this time abandoned to the sisters all the property received earlier, with the Fanjeaux tithes, and that the Casseneuil donation had provisionally disappeared.[72] Bishop Thierry of Livonia, for instance, the 'new apostle' whose poverty Innocent III recommended to the faithful of Saxony in November 1213, considered it necessary to go further in his poverty than the system of tithes authorized by the words of St Paul:

Although it was allowable to him [wrote the Sovereign Pontiff][73] to reap material goods from the people among whom he was sowing spiritual goods (since one must not muzzle the ox which treads out the corn and the Lord has commanded those who preach the Gospel to live by the Gospel), he none the less refused to allow himself to use this power, in order not to create an obstacle against the Gospel of Christ among those to whom he was ministering who were neophytes. Thus he carried the Gospel without staff or wallet. . . .[74]

Durando de Huesca and the Poor Catholics in their formal proposals of 1208, 1210 and 1212, took upon themselves an even more radical poverty. 'We have renounced the world', they wrote, 'and have given to the poor what we possessed, according to the counsel of the Lord; and we have decided to be poor in such a way that we may have no kind of anxiety about the morrow and not receive from anyone at all either gold, silver, or any such thing, only our clothing and our daily food.'[75]

Comparing the system of the Preaching of Toulouse, with its security as to necessities through a regular alms, with the conventual mendicancy practised some years later by the Order of St Dominic, certain historians are surprised. They think that the ideal of poverty laid down by the founder has undergone an evolution in the course of those years, in the direction of mendancy.[76] They are mistaken. Dominic's ideal from as far back as 1206, as has been seen, was 'the rule of the apostles'. It included mendicancy as an essential. Dominic practised it as the Poor Catholics did. Before 1215, however, no more than the Poor Catholics or the Bishop of Livonia, did he need to inscribe it in conventual life. There lay precisely the difficulty. It is understandable that he should have felt his way before finding the definitive solution. The only evolution that it is possible to discover is not in the ideal but in the legal and practical dispositions which permitted him, between 1215 and 1220, to establish mendicancy even in the conventual life of the Preachers.[77]

Even such as it was, the itinerant mendicancy of St Dominic's companions in 1215 was already a great innovation. This was remarked in connection with the disputation of Montpellier.[78] To return to the subject would serve no useful purpose. It must, however, be added that in 1213–1214 the Councils of Paris and Rouen, convened by the legate, Robert de Courson, had just given expression once again to the traditional opinion on this point. They enjoined upon the superiors of monks and canons a formal precept, each time they authorized one of their religious to go out, 'to take care to supply him in sufficient quantity with the horses and provisions for the journey which were indispensable both for him and his acolytes; for it would be a disgrace both for the Lord and for the position in society of this religious, that he should be constrained to beg'.[79] In 1215, however, nothing of this kind appeared in the canons of the Council of Montpellier, the reforming legislation of which was nevertheless parallel with that of the French Councils. Fulk and the other prelates had had time to gain some knowledge of the experiences of the Narbonensis mission and to appreciate Dominic's ministry. They knew that between 1206 and 1212 a fair number of letters[80] from the Pope had approved mendicant preaching both in this instance and in several others which we shall mention. Perhaps even Fulk the Cistercian recalled the example of St Malachy related by his friend St Bernard.

> He travelled on foot, with other men likewise on foot, when he went to preach in accordance with the apostolic way of life, bishop and legate though he was. . . . In serving the Gospel he lived by the Gospel,[81] as the Lord had laid down in saying that the labourer had a right to his maintenance[82]. . . and when in between times he had to rest, he did so in sacred places.[83]

Thus Fulk had dared to defend the itinerant preaching and the mendicancy of the first Dominicans.

There the information given by the principal documents comes to an end. There is unfortunately no charter extant to inform us about the interior life of the community, their prayer, their observance, as the charters of the Seilas and of Fulk do for the house, the poverty and the preaching.[84] The brethren, says Jordan of Saxony, 'lived in conformity with the customs of religious'.[85] And his commentary on this phrase is an explicit allusion to monastic spirituality from a well-known chapter of the rule of St Benedict.[86] Indications which confirm and detail Jordan's general information can be gleaned from isolated texts.

Dominic's companions were clerics. No one contests this. They would not otherwise have been able to accept the office of preaching. Their prayer was that of the clergy, that is to say, the canonical office.[87] This much can be said at once; this was the universal prerogative of the clergy at this time, both as to their rights and in fact. No indication contradicts this. St Dominic's attachment to this office right until the hour of his death,[88] his perseverance and his extraordinary assiduity at prayer,[89] to say nothing of his fidelity in imitating the apostles,[90] are manifest proofs of it. The community may perhaps have chanted the hours in the house of Peter Seila. On the other hand, since the brethren had not the privilege of a portable altar—this they did not obtain until 1221—'it was quite impossible for them to have Mass in their house'.[91] They were thus obliged to 'run into the town'.[92] One text justifies us in thinking that to celebrate the conventual Mass they went ten minutes' walk away, to the chapel of St Romain, possession of which was granted to them the following year.[93] It was in this chapel indeed that Dominic, in the middle of year 1215, gave the habit to and received the profession of a new religious, Fray Juan de Navarra.[94] The very gesture of the profession is noted—he received it 'into his hands', that is to say, in accordance with the forms of feudal homage that Cluny had adapted to the religious engagement,[95] he took between his hands the joined hands of the brother which were already laid on the Gospel, while the vow of obedience was pronounced.

It will be noted that both ceremonies took place on the same day. Dominic was, then, receiving recruits who were sufficiently reliable for it to be unnecessary to envisage a time of trial or novitiate. It was one problem less to solve in this period of beginnings. Furthermore it was an advantage for the poverty of the house and for the immediate effectiveness of the Preaching.

Since there was a clothing ceremony there was necessarily a habit.[96] One can be sure of this beforehand. The ancient tradition which practically identified the clothing with the profession was still too strong for matters to be otherwise. Even the Catharists and Waldenses had their special habit. Dominic's brethren clearly wore the white tunic of their father.[97] They also wore the clerical tonsure. The Council of Montpellier had just given a reminder about the rule for this and its dimensions for different categories of ecclesiastics.[98] Midway between the upper and lower tonsures it was a circle of hair narrower than that of secular priests, but wider than that of the monks. Finally, they wore high boots.[99]

This was doubtless the costume that was represented on Dominic's seal. The seal was still in existence in Prouille in the seventeenth century at the foot of a charter of 1221. Jean de Réchac there read the customary inscription

'S (igillum) D (ominici) ministri predicationis'. Quétif made a drawing of it which Echard had engraved. This engraving in its turn served as a basis for later reproductions. It was shuttle-shaped and in the space that surrounded the inscription there was represented a religious in a cloak, a staff in his right hand.[100] The title 'minister predicationis' had been used a few months earlier in the letter to Guillaume-Raymond d'Hauterive.[101] It went to prove the real continuity of the Order of St Dominic with the Preaching of Toulouse and the Preaching of Jesus Christ, the seal of which, it will be remembered, had also been used at the foot of this letter. The existence of a new seal, on the other hand, signified legal discontinuity: the transfer from preaching authorized by legates against heretics to diocesan preaching for the instruction of all, faithful and infidels, in the teaching and morals of the Gospel. Dominic retained this personal seal to the end of his life.[102] The contrast between the symbols used by each of these two seals was charged with meaning—the risen Lamb for the Preaching of Jesus Christ, the itinerant preacher for the Preaching of St Dominic.

It would seem that the visit paid one fine morning to the theology professor of the chapter of St Etienne, Alexander Stavensby, the Englishman, should be assigned to some time during the summer of 1215.[103] The master was giving his course. He saw the preacher come in with six (?)[104] companions, all wearing the same habit. They assured him that they wanted to enrol in his school and greatly desired to attend his lessons. They were not all equally in need of them. After this, for a long time to come, the master enjoyed their familiar friendship and instructed them as his pupils. Some ten years later, he evoked the memory of this meeting which had impressed him all the more in that, that very morning, suffering from drowsiness as he was preparing his course, he had dreamt of seven bright stars which soon increased in size so that they filled the world with light. The anecdote is attractive and if its trimmings are not very original,[105] its historical foundation is beyond question.[106] It goes to show the fundamental importance attributed by the saint right from the beginnings of his community to theological studies, the source of preaching. He had been trained in this way himself in Palencia. The ministry at Toulouse was urgent. Fulk was in most pressing need of his preachers. Dominic none the less found the time to take his brethren to school. From this one may judge how important it was to him. Among the indispensable equipment which the tithes were to finance, Jordan of Saxony gives pride of place to books.[107] It is hardly necessary to point out that no trace is found, either at this period or in the following one, of any manual work by the brethren, despite the monastic tradition which was equally current among the Clerks Regular.[108] Its place was taken by study and the ministry of souls. On this point again, the Order of St Dominic in Toulouse showed itself to be original and daring. Many years later this would also be made a subject of reproach,

The number of the brethren increased rapidly. In April 1215, a few days after the professions of Peter Seila and Brother Thomas, another brother entered. He must have been older and more mature than the others, as is evident from the charter of 25th April, for Dominic at once gave him a privileged place in the community, a kind of sub-priorship.[109] His name was Guillaume Raymond. There is no further trace of him and it is possible that he did not persevere or that he died soon afterwards. Whereas Brother William Claret, Brother Noël and Brother Vital had remained at Prouille,[110] it is very probable that Dominic the Spaniard later joined Dominic in Toulouse if he had not accompanied him there straight away. On 28th August Juan de España took the habit, as has been said. From the middle of the summer, then, the Preaching of Toulouse numbered at least six religious—probably many more, for Jordan of Saxony states clearly that the main house was not large enough to lodge everybody. They had to occupy the remaining[111] houses and the following year they moved.[112]

A foundation the development of which was so rapid was clearly not the fruit of chance or merely of circumstances, nor was it solely the work of the founder. In the history leading up to his order we have seen other figures appear in the course of events—Simon de Montfort, the bishops of Osma, Carcassonne and Toulouse, several legates and finally Pope Innocent himself. Now that we have come to the end of the account of the foundation, it is profitable to cast a glance backwards, to determine, so far as it is possible to do so, the help that Dominic received from men and events. The traits of his personality, his own merits and his inspirations will stand out so much the more clearly.

The Preaching of the houses of Peter Seila was certainly not an improvisation. What we know of the firm and reflective character of its creator would suffice to convince us of the contrary. As has been seen, the foundation made at Toulouse was prepared in Fanjeaux the year before.[113] It is doubtless there that it would have come into being if a perfectly legitimate intervention had not happened, deciding Dominic preferably to give effect to his work in the capital of the county.

If we go even further back, we come upon the projects and realizations of Diego of Osma eight years earlier—the plan he made of a group of competent preachers who would be established with the Pope's consent for the spread of the truth of the faith and its defence against heresies;[114] the inauguration, in which he had taken a decisive part, of the Preaching of Jesus Christ. It was precisely from this Preaching against heresies, re-established in Toulouse in the first months of 1215, that the community of the houses of Peter Seila emerged. Dominic had never ceased to be loyal to the inspirations and institutions of his bishop, Diego. The work of 1215 was the fruit of lasting thought, ripened in the light of an exceptional experience. It was only circumstances which had so long delayed its execution. As soon as the time was ripe, however, through the reconciliation in Toulouse, the foundation was made.

As he accepted the convent of Prouille from the hands of his bishop, multiplied its recruits, laid down the lines of its spiritual life, set up its patrimony and erected the buildings, so Dominic accepted the project of a body of preachers who, to defend the Gospel, would use as their weapons imitation of the apostles. The idea, which first arose during the plans of 1207, of applying to the Pope to obtain permission to preach, will be noted. This was quite natural in the case of the members of a pontifical mission. It gave to the project, moreover, a very vast, broad and, so to speak, universal horizon. Eight years after his death, Diego remained St Dominic's principal inspirer, at the very root of his order.

Fulk, moreover, occupied an important place at the side of the Bishop of Osma. If he had been the perfidious, cruel and oppressive prelate presented by too many historical works, it would be difficult to understand the share he took in the foundation or the feelings which united him to Dominic.

> Bishop Fulk of Toulouse, indeed of happy memory [relates Jordan], who felt a tender affection for Brother Dominic, beloved of God and of men, when he saw the regular life of the brethren, their grace and fervour in preaching, was transported with joy at this dawn of new light. With the consent of his whole chapter he granted them the sixth of all the tithes of the diocese, so that with this revenue they might procure themselves what was necessary in the matter of books and of food.[115]

This text is not a bad summary of the bishop's charter. That the foundation was prior to the gesture of Fulk is noted with precision. It is thus unlikely that the evocation of the sentiments that prompted the gesture would be erroneous. In actual fact the factor which led sincere historians astray and disfigured Fulk in their eyes has recently been discovered—the use of a document, now known to be completely without authenticity and, indeed, contradicted by almost all the sources.[116] The sources leave of Folquet of Marseille, now Fulk of Toulouse, the picture of an austere, brave and disinterested prelate, firmly determined to save the faith of his flock but full of pastoral zeal and in no sense unmerciful to men's bodies and souls.[117] He had known Dominic since 1207. Desirous of applying the prescriptions of the Pope and of the Avignon Council, in 1210–1211 he associated Dominic with his preaching. It was natural that he should again want him as his associate in 1215 in Toulouse, together with the methods he valued.

Of himself, however, he would have kept him in Fanjeaux, in that centre of operations so particularly well placed whence his ministry had been expanding in all directions for over ten years. After all he had just endowed his new group there and provided it with the stable foundation of a church. Pietro di Beneventum, however, the legate, had intervened at the Council of Montpellier. He had his own ideas and, perhaps, precise instructions. He who had assembled the Council fairly close to Toulouse, 'because this city, as is known, is the head and sink of all the malice of the perversions of the heretics',[118] wanted Dominic and his companions likewise to be installed in the capital. The Preaching against the heretics was thus re-established in Toulouse under the legate's authority. Some months later it would become the community of regular life which Fulk was to endow. It then expanded into the diocesan Preaching.

The intervention of Pietro di Beneventum continued that of the previous legates, beginning by Arnaud de Cîteaux.[119] The many and continuous links between Dominic and the Pope's representatives in the Albigeois[120] finally set the problem of the share, at least the indirect share, to be attributed to Innocent III in the Toulouse foundation.

Innocent III bears the chief responsibility for the events in the Midi of France in the course of which the Order of St Dominic was born. No one was more fully aware of the crisis in preaching in this region as throughout the Church. With great perseverance, through his letters or through his legates, even after the launching of the crusade, he endeavoured to maintain and intensify the bishops' preaching to the full extent of their pastoral programme. The first canon of the Council of Avignon (1209), an earnest of the 10th canon of the coming Council of the Lateran (November 1215), of which Innocent was the chief author, must be attributed to the Pope's insistence. The charter of approval of the Preaching of Toulouse referred back to this legislation. Dominic owed it to the action of Innocent III that he discerned so clearly both the mission of the Church in defining his order, and the place which this order was to occupy at the bishop's side, as collaborator and ' vicar ' of his pastoral mission.

Should one go further and attribute to the Pope the idea of a group of mendicant preachers? It is certain that from 1203 onwards Innocent was concerned with launching, wherever the ordinary preaching was proving itself dangerously insufficient, missions of exemplary preachers, contingents of whom were principally asked for from the Cistercians. The Preaching of the Narbonensis was not the only one of this type.[121] The Pope endeavoured to inculcate his own spirit in these missionaries—to convert rather than to destroy, to avoid what might shock the heretic himself, to understand and respect in the dissidents all that might be considered as authentically Christian.[122]

In November 1206 he approved the method of apostolic mendicancy among his preachers. Moreover, when in December 1208, as has been related,[123] Durando de Huesca, leader of the group of preachers without a mandate, closely linked with the Waldenses, whom Diego had brought back to the Church on the occasion of the dispute at Pamiers, presented himself before him, the Pope welcomed him with hope and joy.[124] He approved the purpose of regular life of his company of preachers, their habit, their mendicant poverty and, for Durando's lay companions, the right to refuse to take part in wars against Christians.[125] For the next five years, he officially supported by his letters the mission of the Poor Catholics against the heretics and the dissidents in the provinces of Tarragona and the Narbonensis, upholding them with all the weight of his authority and endeavouring to dissipate the tenacious prejudices of the prelates there, who continued to find them too much like the Waldenses. He acted in this way from 1210 with the similar group of Bernard Prim, of Milan, who for several years had been bravely struggling against the Catharists of the Albigeois using the weapon of a mendicant apostolic life.[126] With their houses of converted penitents, their schools, their kind of life and their method of apostolate, these companies of missionaries commissioned by the Pope were an earnest[127] of the order of St Dominic. If after 1213, in the face of the resistance of the local hierarchy and doubtless the blunders of the Poor Catholics, Innocent finally gave up placing his hope for the defence of orthodoxy in these converts of too recent date, he turned immediately towards the ranks of the strictly Catholic clergy in order to elicit or maintain forces of this kind among them. We can understand that a careful historian should have suspected that the legate, Pietro di Beneventum, was only fulfilling an intention of Innocent when he gave Dominic at the beginning of 1215 the powers necessary to re-establish the Preaching of Jesus Christ in Toulouse.[128] For lack of documents this remains a sheer hypothesis, but a hypothesis that is plausible.

However, to show that Dominic, by giving effect to long-tested projects, was responding to invitations coming from his bishops, from legates of the Holy See and perhaps from the Pope himself, and was deriving his inspiration from the experiences which for the past ten years he had watched developing under his eyes, both in the Church and among the heretics, is not perhaps sufficient to explain the work of the founder and might seem to lessen his merits. These facts merely prove his loyalty and responsiveness to the promptings of the hierarchy, his keen sense of the needs of the Church, his farsightedness in the presence of men and events, all very characteristic of him. Moreover, they strangely enhance his genius in that, replying to calls coming from all sides and too often contradictory, and collecting together elements of right conduct, activity, and spirituality so little compatible among themselves that the many attempts to combine them during the previous century and a half had only given rise to unstable, ephemeral or revolutionary combinations, he succeeded in creating an order which would transcend time and would be no less alive in the twentieth century than in the thirteenth. The order of St. Dominic was in some sense a cross-roads. The avenues leading from it opened on very varied perspectives. There was the evangelical work of the canons apostolic, the itinerant preachers, the Poor Catholics; then again the work among the Catharists and the Waldenses. There was the development of the doctrinal mission of the bishops, of monastic poverty, of scholastic studies. Yet the order itself was something quite different from each of its elements and from each of its initial endeavours, just as in geometry the final point is clearly to be distinguished from the lines which converge towards it.

Because, however, it came in point of fact at the end of a mass of research and of efforts, it retained their richness and inspiration. If it achieved great success very rapidly, it was because it gathered together many ideas and forces scattered about the world and responded to the aspirations of a large number of people, to the aspirations primarily of those Christians and true prelates anxious to satisfy such longings—above all, to the aspirations of the Head of the Church, Pope Innocent III, whose concern for faith and peace in the southern part of Gaul was one of his greatest cares.

Dominic in the beginning of the month of September linked himself with the authorities of the region when by a unanimous movement and urged by the whole of Christendom they responded to the appeal of this great Pope for the holding of a general council. The Fourth Council of the Lateran, held in November 1215 in the eternal city, was the most impressive assembly of the Middle Ages. Thus when the founder came to speak to the Pope about his communities of Toulouse and Prouille, he might legitimately hope to obtain all he desired without difficulty.

He came, Jordan of Saxony tells us, to ask for 'confirmation of an order which would be called and would be in fact the order of Preachers'.[129]

PART II

IN MEDIO ECCLESIAE

CHAPTER XI

THE LATERAN COUNCIL

W HEN in the midst of a century undergoing every possible upheaval the Order of Preachers spread widely over the earth with its twelve provinces, its hundreds of convents, its thousands of religious, the friars were amazed. They could not but think that its universal preaching of the Gospel and its effective struggle against vice and error, despite the contradictions which grew in proportion as its activity increased, were the result of a very miraculous intervention on the part of God. It thus seemed inconceivable that an institution so visibly called into being by Providence[1] should have made its entry into the world unheralded. It was sufficient indeed to listen, to interrogate spiritual men favoured with divine visitations, to read the inspired books and the lives of the saints—to find on every side clear[2] premonitions, intuitions, prophecies about the imminent coming of the order of Preachers.[3]

In 1207 a devout monk, unconscious for three days in ecstasy, had seen the Blessed Virgin, kneeling and with clasped hands, begging her Son Jesus not to abandon men, and so obtaining the institution of the Preachers from him. A dead man, who rose again after three days, had told one of the twelve Cistercian abbots during the mission in the Albigeois of an identical scene—which he had witnessed during his unexpected journey. Further, Dominic himself in 1215 had seen this heavenly contest, in a vision he had had in Rome.

Moreover, Blessed Stephen of the Chartreuse of Portes and Guillaume Hélie, the Cistercian bishop of Orange (d. 1221), Ste. Marie d'Oignies, the visionary of Liège (d. 1213), Bl. Bona of Pisa (d. 1207), and the Cistercian abbot Joachim of Flora in Calabria (d. 1202), as earlier still St Hildegarde herself (d. 1179)—had foreseen, predicted, described, sometimes even to their very dress, the apostolic Preachers who were to come.

The young Dominican friars who scrutinized the texts of the Bible in the studium of Paris or Bologna were surprised on many an occasion to discover in the books they were studying, the very name of the 'Order of Preachers' and the description of its prerogatives and qualities. One friar picked out about fifteen such explicit passages in the marginal and interlinear gloss alone, that compilation of the beginning of the twelfth century which made a brief paraphrase of the Bible, following the text word by word. The basis of the gloss was innumerable extracts from the Fathers of the Church. Indeed Augustine, Jerome, Gregory the Great, Alcuin, Rabanus Maurus, Peter Damian, Anselm of Canterbury,[4] and many others, had similarly foreseen the appearance of the Preachers, and even pronounced the particular name of their order long beforehand. At the dawn of the thirteenth century references of this kind were particularly noticed in commentaries on the Apocalypse which were read with renewed interest in those dramatic times. In certain expressions of the seer of Patmos, Anselm of Laon (d. 1117), Richard of St Victor (d. 1173), Martin de León (d. 1203) and in particular Joachim of Flora (d. 1202)[5], discerned the prophetic announcement of the 'Order of Preachers'. Joachim of Flora considered that the world was at its second age, the age of God the Son, who was communicating himself to it through the clergy and preachers. The last twenty years of the twelfth century in which he wrote constituted the passage from the fifth to the sixth periods of this age. A new type of religious was to appear in the Church. With his disciples an indomitable champion of the faith would form the *ordo praedicatorum*, who would imitate the life of Jesus and the apostles and, though attacked by all the false prophets, would preach the Gospel to their contemporaries.[6]

We are not concerned to judge the supernatural inspiration of these visions and prophecies, nor the value of the confidences that the sons of St Dominic with touching simplicity, accepted from all men's lips in the middle of the thirteenth century. The texts, on the other hand, were authentic. The name of 'order of Preachers' found in them was not merely the result of pious interpolation. It had not on the other hand the meaning given to it in more recent times by the institution of the Order of St Dominic. When St Gregory—who was, it would seem, the first to do so—had begun to pronounce the phrase with insistence, by *ordo praedicatorum* he intended to designate the hierarchical class of Catholic preachers, which, according to tradition, was for him identified with that of the pastors or doctors of the Church. The majority of the texts cited were thus only prophetic by a play on words. It would be strange, however, if history had nothing further to say in this connection.

The commentaries of St Gregory, the gloss in particular, were in the hands of all the clergy. Abbot Joachim of Flora had drawn up his commentary on the Apocalypse at the request of Pope Lucius III, and with the approval of his successors, and in the thirteenth century his writings were to meet with remarkable success.[7] The holiness of his personal life and that of his monastery had given him such a privileged position in the eyes of Innocent III that, when in 1215 at the Council of the Lateran the Pope had to reject certain doctrinal interpretations of the Calabrian abbot, he concluded the particular canon of the Council which corrected the Cistercian by an eulogium of his spirit of orthodoxy and his religious work.[8] It is thus of no slight importance from our point of view that at the beginning of the thirteenth century impressive texts should have set out under the name of *ordo praedicatorum*, traditional or even new-fangled conceptions as to the condition and quality of the preachers. They were indicative of the ideas which were coming into existence as to the status of preaching in the Church at the time when Dominic established his order.

The tradition of the Fathers of the Church was formal.[9] For them the preacher was the bishop. To teach the doctrine of Christ by homilies and commentaries on the Holy Scripture constituted his chief function, his essential work as a pastor—a function that was equally represented by the terms which were continually being employed as interchangeable, of 'doctor' and 'preacher'. These two formal functions were to be distinguished by their audiences. The subject-matter, the Holy Scriptures, was the same, but the doctor taught the clergy and the preacher the general flock. The bishop exercised both functions; so that according to a unanimous tradition[10] the *ordo praedicatorum* was identical with the *ordo doctorum* and the *ordo episcoporum*. Ordinary priests were doubtless associated with this order, as they were with the bishop's pastoral work, but through the bishop's delegation and in solidarity with him.

In the twelfth century the traditional conceptions which subsisted as of legal right had remarkably developed, whereas the expressions designating them remained the same. The enormous increase in the number of parishes and their reorganization in the course of the last century had increased the importance of the clergy who formed the second rank in the order of preachers. The clerical order in turn was largely moving out of its earlier framework, the monks having, generally speaking, taken up the clerical state. Thus, right from the beginning of the century, a good number of them claimed the right to be preachers.[11] The new life infused into the clerical milieu by the Gregorian reform, however, thanks to its return to the apostolic ideal, strongly emphasized the connection which should exist between the practice of preaching and the practice of the life of the apostles. This was indeed the fundamental idea of the Italian reformers, of St Peter Damian, for instance. In the face of this movement the bishops of the time, burdened by so many legal and administrative tasks, weighed down by such numerous temporal rights and duties, were far from taking a firm line. These reformed monks and canons seemed more directly faithful to the heritage of the apostles. The heretical apostolic preachers were not the only ones to call in question the monopoly of the bishops and of their clergy. The patristic tradition itself offered the inducement of a distinction within the circle of the classic *ordo praedicatorum*. Among its elements Gregory the Great had discerned a privileged category, the 'sancti praedicatores' who,[12] because they were detached from the world to the extent of having renounced all possessions, were able to preach 'by word and example'.

Such men, it might be thought, were the precursors of the orthodox apostolic preachers much more than twelfth-century prelates.

Thus from this time onwards people began to discover in the order of preachers several different types, not all equally adapted to their task. The idea of evolution, suggested by the theme of the ages of the world, differentiated the class as a whole according to different epochs. The commentators of the Apocalypse attached themselves particularly to the idea that each age was to have its own type of order of preachers raised up by God to deal with new situations; such was, for instance, the idea of Richard of St Victor.[13] Joachim of Flora indeed prophesied that, in the age of the Son of God, the sixth period which had just been inaugurated would be characterized by a new type of preachers of truth. In his visions of the future, visions inspiring, indeed, but blurred and indistinct as is usual in the case of prophecy, he hopefully envisaged this order of preachers no longer as a class, but as a society, if not a religious order, whose exemplary life would be especially devoted to the imitation of the earthly life of Christ and his apostles.[14]

It matters little for our purpose that these apocalyptic views could scarcely be said to be coherent; that they in some degree falsified the patristic or even Scriptural texts on which they were based; that, to the Abbot of Flora, this type of preachers to come at times very strongly resembled that of the religious of Flora . . . .[15] For us the essential is the effort of these spiritually minded men to place their time in the line of historical evolution, and to orientate the Church's investigations accordingly. This work which in the thirteenth as in the twentieth century, was accompanied by so many illusions—for God alone knows the significance of earthly history and he has not revealed it, even in the Apocalypse—was not, however, illusory. It forced these men to look at their own time, its crises, its needs, its mentality. In short, it revealed, better than the documents of canon law, or the theological theories of the moment, the anxieties and longings of the fervent Christians of the time. Even if these prophetic or apocalyptic texts remained unknown to the public and without any influence upon it, which was not always the case, they would still retain for us their value as evidence. At the beginning of the thirteenth century, preaching in the Church was no longer strictly confined in the common view to the bishop and his delegates. The possibility was conceived of a series of *ordines praedicatorum* better adapted to the traditional task and to the needs of the new times than the episcopate itself, orders of preachers which would be religious orders of apostolic life.

At the time when Joachim of Flora died, Innocent III partially gave effect to these visions of the spiritual by multiplying the groups of preachers drawn from the Order of Cîteaux, despite the latter's opposition. Later, he did the same by supporting in the Albigeois and in Aragon the companies of Poor Catholics. When in 1216 Jacques de Vitry, one of the most lucid observers

Eleventh century bas-relief of Christ and the Apostles; this was the first representation of the Apostles seen by the boy Dominic in the cloisters of Silos.

of the Church in his time, journeyed across Italy, he discovered in the province of Milan another foundation of which the Pope was patron, some hundred and fifty houses of Humiliati who were edifying their brethren and defending the Church against the heretics by their preaching.[16] Coming down from the direction of Rome, the bishop met another preaching community which he described with some feeling, the Brethren of St Francis. 'It is', he said in one of his writings,'an order of preachers which we call the order of Minors.'[17] A few years later he saw another, even more characteristic, in Bologna. It was not content with uniting the 'order of preachers' to the order of canons;[18] with the consent of the Pope it appropriated to itself as a particular title which it alone was to bear, the ancient and glorious name. This was, in fact, the Order of Preachers, the Order of St Dominic. By what astonishing ways had it obtained the title which but recently designated a whole hierarchical class?

At the beginning of September 1215, Dominic had set out for Rome, accompanying his bishop.[19] It was the end of summer and the route over the Alps was open. Most probably it was this route they took.[20] The Council of the Lateran had been convened for November. From Esthonia to Portugal, from England to the commercial ports of the Levant, the prelates had set out to meet together and form the solemn assembly. No one was dispensed from attendance, at least by delegation. Only one bishop in each province was authorized to remain at home. At the Council one could count three patriarchs, four hundred and twelve bishops, more than eight hundred abbots and priors, the representatives of those prevented from appearing in person, finally the ambassadors of the majority of the Christian sovereigns. It was one of those rare moments in the history of the world towards which all previous movements appear to converge. The problems that Innocent had vigorously tackled from the beginning of his reign with varying results were approaching their solution. The foundation of the Latin empire of the East and the succession of the Germanic empire, the quarrels of France and England, the crusades of Spain and of the Albigeois, the reform of the clergy and the monks and the constitution of the university of Paris, the government of doctrine and of institutions, each and every one of these problems of the Pope was in the process of settlement, of pacification, of solution, precisely in the sense he had willed. Through him the Church had experienced an appearance of triumph. How much more dramatic would this hour have appeared to the participants in the mighty assembly had they known that its inspirer and leader was to disappear barely a few months after its conclusion.

The Pope had reserved to the Council the final decision in the affair of the faith and peace in the Midi of France. None of the great personages involved in the debate had failed either to be present or to be represented there.

Almost all the bishops of the Narbonensis and the majority of those of the adjacent provinces were present around Archbishop Arnaud.[21] Raymond VII and his son, Gaston de Foix, Arnaud de Comminges and numerous lords of the Midi came to demand the return of their patrimony. Guy de Montfort represented his brother.[22]

As the participants arrived the various committees were formed. At the end of the summer, the first among them held session in the gardens and palace of the Lateran:[23] there was the dispute as to the primacy of Toledo, the suspension of the Archbishop of Canterbury, the choice of the German emperor, the elaboration of the doctrinal and reforming canons, the preparation for the crusade in the East. The business of the Albigenses was then treated at length, in heated debates.[24] The way was thus paved for the supreme decisions which the Pope was to promulgate in the Lateran basilica in the three full sessions of the 11th, 20th and 30th November. In the interval of the meetings, moreover, Innocent continually received groups or individuals for matters of lesser importance.

As early as the first days of October,[25] he received Dominic with Fulk. They spoke of the Preaching that had just been inaugurated in Toulouse and in mutual agreement presented their request to him: 'that the Pope would deign to confirm, to the benefit of Dominic and of his brethren, an order which would be called and would be the Order of Preachers; that he would equally confirm the revenues assigned to the brethren both by the Court and by the bishop.'[26]

The significance of these words, which Jordan of Saxony did not use lightly, must be weighed. To confirm is not the same as to approve.[27] It means, precisely, to make stronger. He who confirms at this stage neither innovates nor gives: he merely indicates the existence of an institution or of an earlier gift to which through his intervention he accords a greater solidity. In this way an already valid election, a statute already obligatory or validly constituted, is confirmed. In particular, to have something confirmed by a higher authority is to remove beyond any chance of repeal or modification on the part of subordinate authority, that which has been established by institution or approbation. In 1215, it had long been customary to solicit such confirmations and Dominic's action in itself had nothing unusual about it.

The confirmation of the Holy See had at first been concerned with material wealth, the possessions of a monastery for instance. It prevented the donor from changing his mind about his generosity and threatened an unjust aggressor with the major fulminations of the Church. After the twelfth century, such confirmation extended to all sorts of statutes. Legal prescriptions already in force were submitted for the Pope's confirmation; in this way they became inviolable without the Sovereign Pontiff's specific consent. Thus the Preachers in 1228 considered asking for the confirmation of the Holy See on three fundamental points of their legislation in order to make them inviolate.[28] They did not do so, however. The only Dominican constitution that was ever invested with the supreme sanction of Rome was the clause whereby the superior-general of the order, unlike the heads of other mendicant orders, had no need to obtain the confirmation of the Holy See.[29] This last objective, indeed, might require certain steps in Rome. Innocent III used this power of authentication and control in a special way, in respect of inventors of new forms of religious life.[30]

Independently of the reasons usual in the case of religious superiors, Dominic had his own reasons for having the revenues of the Preaching of Toulouse and the possessions of the monastery of Prouille, with which he was concerned at the same time, confirmed. A good part of this property had been acquired by right of war in the course of the crusade.[31] The revenues of Casseneuil, moreover, did not even belong to the donor, Simon de Montfort, who had only obtained the custody of them; the donation was very debatable. The tithes granted by the bishop were certainly more solidly established, but what one bishop had done, another could undo; confirmation from the Pope would give the community in Toulouse security from an eventual change of mind on the part of Fulk's successors.

It has been supposed that Dominic also asked for confirmation of a rule.[32] Neither Jordan, nor any of the documents, say anything of the kind. It can, on the other hand, be affirmed with certainty that the founder had no intention at all of having constitutions inscribed in a consistorial bull according to the usual procedure for the confirmation of a rule. This had been done under Alexander III in 1175 for the rule of the Knights of Santiago; again, under Innocent III for that of the Trinitarians, of the Humiliati, of the Order of the Holy Spirit, for the *propositium* of the Poor Catholics, and of the Brethren of Bernard Prim; this would be the case shortly, under Honorius III, for the second rule of St Francis, which for this reason would bear the name of *Regula bullata*.[33] St Dominic, however, would never have anything of his legislative work confirmed, in particular anything of the great legislation of 1220–1221, to which reference will be made in due course. The brethren were not to have their statutes confirmed at any future time either. The constitutions of the Order of St Dominic have never been confirmed. Still less in 1215, could there be any question for the father of Preachers seeking from the Holy See legal sanction for prescriptions which time and the life of the order had not put to the test. The constant attitude of St Dominic, an attitude so prudent and so loyal to the lessons of experience, excludes such an hypothesis.

On the contrary, according to Jordan of Saxony,[34] St Dominic expressly asked for confirmation of a thing to which he clung above everything, because it was the raison d'être and very essence of his order—the title and function of preacher, of Preaching friars.

It was indeed a confirmation that was in question here. The community of Toulouse already possessed this title and function legally granted to them by the official decree of the proper authority, the local bishop. Once more, however, what a bishop had done a bishop could undo. The earlier associations of preachers, for half a century past, had indeed come to naught in the face of the bishops' mistrust, in these very provinces of Tarraconensis and Narbonensis where Dominic's ministry was exercised. It was not possible to found an order in the face of this uncertainty. Moreover, if a bishop had the right and duty to entrust the office of preaching to certain clergy of his diocese, even for their whole lives, had he the power to grant it to a permanent community, so that a man had only to enter this community to obtain the name, and, according to the internal rules of the association, the office of preacher? The Bishop of Toulouse had done so. This was a bold step.[35] It was fitting that it should receive confirmation by the Pope, just when the Lateran Council was clearly disposed to make definitions in such matters.

It may be asked whether we should add to these matters offered for the Pope's confirmation a further point not stated in the text of the *Libellus*: poverty. It is clear that Fulk had already recognized and authorized in his charter of 1215 certain traits of the mendicant poverty of the future Preachers, at any rate, the mendicity of the preacher on his round, in default of that of the convent. Such poverty, however, in some sort individual, had been confirmed by Innocent III in the case of Dominic and his early collaborators, by letter of 17th November, 1206.[36] As to the poverty, if not collective mendicity, of the Preachers of Toulouse, it was real and could claim special confirmation. The practice of renouncing landed property and accepting only revenues, without being entirely unheard of,[37] set the first Dominican community apart from almost all existing communities. The concession of the diocesan tithes, as has been said, was made in such a way as to maintain Dominic's sons in the category of the poor and even of the poor according to the mode of the Gospel.

There is no evidence, however, that Dominic asked for confirmation of this kind of collective poverty. It would not, moreover, be confirmed, and Dominic would have his hands free to modify it in 1220, when he would finish establishing conventual mendicity in his order.

Innocent was no longer solely the spiritual leader who was urging the Bishop of Metz 'not to weaken the religious feeling of the simple', and who was struggling against the bishops of the Midi to maintain in the service of orthodoxy apostolic preachers all too recently converted. The hour of audacious and ephemeral measures was past. Innocent III was sitting in the midst of these very bishops to form the General Council. With them he was about to proclaim the authentic tradition of the Church. He was preparing to define a legislation which would rule Christendom for a long time to come. This necessitated prudence and reflection. But he knew Fulk and Dominic. Without our being able to measure exactly his share in the institution of the Preaching of Jesus Christ and the preaching of Toulouse, we know that it had been considerable. What would his reply be now?

The confirmation of possessions was an easy matter. Innocent accorded this immediately for all the possessions of Prouille. A few days later, on October 8th, his chancellery regularized the favour in the form of a short bull, or *titulus*, which was sufficient for so limited a matter.[38] The confirmation of the revenues of Casseneuil could only be regulated after the decision of the Council as to the inheritance of Raymond VI. That of the donation of the tithes would go with the confirmation of the Preaching of Toulouse.

There lay the crux of the matter. The Pope neither could nor would give an immediate and definite reply. The Council was going to concern itself in a special manner with preaching and with the new religious orders. The Toulouse foundation would be discussed again in the sessions preparatory to the canons relating to these two matters. Meanwhile, Innocent turned over Dominic and his request to a cardinal, for examination. Such was his constant practice in the case of religious who asked for confirmation.[39] The person of the cardinal whom he chose this time may be surmised. It was probably his own relative, Ugolino, Cardinal-bishop of Ostia. The following year a young cleric who was living with the cardinal there frequently met Dominic who had just concluded the business of the confirmation.[40] These visits had doubtless begun from the autumn of 1215.[41]

The preaching commission met during the first days of November. Fulk and Dominic there occupied the front of the stage. The canon was promulgated on 11th November,[42] at the first full session. Like the majority of the canons of the Council, it directly expressed the ideas and decisions of the Sovereign Pontiff. He condensed, in a text remarkably worded, the findings and conclusions of the Curia in this field, those of the popes and their legates since the Third Council of the Lateran; more especially since the seventeen years of Innocent's pontificate. In this case the experience had principally been acquired in the Albigeois. The practical solution had been elaborated in the Narbonensis and in Toulouse. The link was so direct that at times the canon of the Council seemed to evoke the Preaching of St Dominic. For the Bishop of Toulouse this was a reason for just pride. Among his fellows he appeared as the far-sighted and loyal prelate who, anticipating the demands of the Church, provided the pattern of what should be done. It was also a good portent for Dominic. Not everything, however, was equally favourable. The canon emphasized with asperity the insufficiencies and failings of the bishops. Nevertheless, it reasserted the tradition unmistakably. The bishop was, and was to remain, the preacher *par excellence*.

Certainly he was to get himself assistance, but nothing more. Certain prelates would probably find in this the opportunity to react more strongly against all originality in the matter of preaching. The following text is of paramount importance and must be cited.

> Among everything that touches the salvation of the Christian people, the regular dissemination of the word of God is, as we know, supremely necessary to them, since the soul is nourished with spiritual food as the body with material. *Man cannot live by bread only, there is life for him in all the words that proceed from the mouth of God.*[43] Now it frequently happens that the bishops alone do not suffice to distribute the word of God to their people, because of their many occupations, their infirmity of body, the attacks of their enemies, or other circumstances (not to mention their lack of knowledge, which we must reprove in the most absolute manner and which will not be tolerated in the future). The extent of the dioceses aggravates this inadequacy still more. We therefore lay it down, by this general constitution, that the bishops must recruit persons mighty in word and work, capable of fulfilling to useful purpose the duty of holy preaching, who will carry out carefully in the place and stead of the bishop the visitation of the populations entrusted to him when he himself cannot do so, and will edify them by word and example. The bishop will provide them with what is necessary, should the circumstances demand it, in a suitable manner, to avoid their being constrained to interrupt their enterprise for lack of such necessities. We thus prescribe that there shall be established in cathedrals and also other conventual churches, a category of competent men whom the bishop can use as co-adjutors and co-operators, not only for the office of preaching, but also for the ministry of confessions, the assigning of penances and other activities relating to the salvation of souls. Anyone who should neglect to put these prescriptions into practice would be liable to a severe sanction.[44]

In the 11th canon which followed this, the Council promulgated further dispositions with regard to teaching. The existence of two distinct canons clearly showed the distance which henceforward separated the bishop's pastoral ministry from that of his preaching. Certainly he was always the doctor of his Church as he was its preacher. Since Carolingian times, however, the institution of a professor of theology in the cathedral chapter had enabled him to be free from his mission of teaching the clergy. In the twelfth century the multiplication of episcopal schools and their internal development gave such consistence to this decentralization that the bishop no longer even concerned himself with nominating the professor of theology or conferring the licence to teach. He left this matter to the chancellor of his chapter. Things were not all that could be wished for in this domain, however. Many churches did not make provision for the theology professor's subsistence and he sought remuneration from those he taught or, more often than not, deserted his charge. The school then declined and those clergy who were poor were unable to study. The Third Council of the Lateran had thus insisted that every cathedral should maintain a master by means of a prebend, in order that he might, according to Christian traditions, teach without charge.45 The 11th canon of the new Council of the Lateran once more required the institution in every diocese and even in every collegiate church of such masters, duly remunerated, who would at least provide instruction in grammar, that is, would teach secular learning. At the centre of each province, the archbishop was to maintain a school of theology.46

Dominic could recognize in the Council's insistence a weakness he knew only too well. The marvellous flowering of the schools in the course of the twelfth century, which had recently led to the foundation of the university of Paris, had long been prepared for by a concentrated movement. It is unquestionable that the religious schools of Liège, Tournai, Laon, Rheims, Chartres had been alive in the middle of the twelfth century in a way that was very different from their present condition. The attraction of Paris sterilized sacred studies in the other provinces. The result was that matters ended in the painful paradox of a theological learning that continually developed and deepened on the banks of the Seine while it vegetated or receded in the dioceses, leaving the field more open to rising heresies every day. Dominic not only discovered this crisis in the development of the Albigensian errors and of the doctrinal incompetence of the clergy of the Midi; he felt it no less keenly in his responsibilities as founder. Preachers of the Gospel could do little if they were not animated by a constant study of the Holy Scriptures. At Toulouse he was of course well situated in that respect. On this point, too, Fulk was in advance of the Council.

After all, in his simple diocese he maintained a master of theology, as was done in an archbishopric.47 Master Stavensby's small school was none the less a very minor affair for so vast a diocese and for the severe crisis with which the truth was faced. Moreover, when Dominic let his mind dwell on the theological riches of Paris, the dozens of Regent-Masters, the thousands of students who were gathered there, he could not but be haunted by an image. The good grain, piled up, rots. Scattered and sown, it bears fruit a hundredfold.48

The 12th canon embodied an all-important step for the reform of isolated houses of monks or of Clerks Regular. In each kingdom or ecclesiastical province it instituted triennial chapters which were to assemble houses of this kind and secure for them the benefit which the General Chapters of Cîteaux provided for most of the abbeys of the order. The Cistercian customs were given as a model and the religious were asked to have recourse, for the organization of their system of chapters, to the counsels and the assistance of two abbots of that order. The canon also organized the canonical visitation of isolated houses by visitors who would be nominated in such chapters.49

The 13th canon was now promulgated. For Dominic the most discouraging moment had arrived. He who a few months earlier had founded a new religious community and was now in Rome on its behalf, had to hear the formal prohibition of any new foundation proclaimed. The text was not at all long; its very brevity made it all the more trenchant.

> To prevent the excessive variety of religious societies introducing a serious state of confusion into the Church, we formally forbid anyone soever from founding a new religious society in the future. Anyone who wants to enter religion must give himself to one of the approved orders. Similarly, anyone who in the future wants to found a religious house must take the rule and constitutions of some approved religious society.[50]

There were a few explanations of terms. By 'rule' must be understood the fundamental and stable part of the legislation already accepted, a particular or general rule after the fashion of the rule of St Benedict; by 'constitutions', the canonical statutes of a religious society fixed by the prescriptions of the Councils and the confirmations of the Pope.[51] This canon of the Lateran Council thus prohibited the foundation of new communities and even the adoption by an isolated individual of a new form of life. Dominic had reason to be uneasy about the religious status of the Preaching of Toulouse.

In actual fact, he had expected this obstacle. He knew of the difficulties of the Poor Catholics. The increasingly firm resistance of the bishops in the face of the extraordinary expansion, one might almost say fermentation, of institutions of regular life must have formed the subject of his discussions with the Pope or with Cardinal Ugolino. This was both one of the sources and the echo of the movement of association which on all sides, in the cities as in the countryside, in spiritual affairs as in temporal, brought men together at this time through what they had in common to form communities for trade, habitation, for travel, for devotion—as well as for brigandage—without its always being possible to foresee whether they would not one day pass from one particular community to another. The preaching associations of which the silhouette has already so frequently passed through our narrative, only represented an insignificant part of the many foundations, as ephemeral as they were stirring, which were an indication of the desire of the men of that time to group themselves together with a view to practising the Gospel better. The eremitical movement, of which there had been a renewal for more than two centuries now, had multiplied foundations, especially in Italy. It oscillated between the sporadic forms of the solitary and the recluse, and those of the great contemplative orders of the type of the Carthusians. A different inspiration, closely linked with secular life, was penetrating the masses in the towns, and even the married people, whom it grouped in organizations that proved unstable—the penitential movement from which the *béguinages* and the third orders were one day to emerge.[52] The world of the brethren and sisters who were

serving the hospices and the leper-houses, which had undergone a considerable expansion from the High Middle Ages onwards, was now giving place
to religious life.[53] The foundations concerned with the provision of
hospitality had led in their turn to institutions that were not unexpected,
such as the military orders—religious who were warriors and, particularly
in Spain, bound by the ties of conjugal life.[54] Moreover, these currents were
active along the fringe of the traditional movement of the monks, which was
continually working at reform; and of the movement, equally longstanding
but renewed fundamentally, of the canons which, by the variety of its
reforms if not by its stability, came very close to the monastic movement.
Not only this, but these various movements overlapped each other and
sometimes fused to the extent that entire congregations had changed their
rule and a movement inaugurated under apostolic forms of life ended as a
body of monks or canons; the religious associations which had dispersed,
lost or transformed their ideal or which sometimes had turned to
anarchy, schism or heresy, could not even be counted. The anxiety of those
responsible for Christian order in the face of these tendencies charged with
energy, indeed, but capable of almost any metamorphosis—is understandable. Up till this time the Church had tried to control this overflow of
social sap,[55] to stifle what there was in it of extreme anarchy, to orientate
it towards forms that were tried and tested, to forbid transfers from one
association to another, except to some more severe form of religious life,
arctior religio.[56] She now took up a more radical position. In Carolingian
times she had been able to legislate on the movement for the life of perfection as a whole in two series of parallel canons, namely in respect of the
monks and again of the canons. At the close of the eleventh century, this
attitude still found spontaneous expression in the formularies of the Curia.[57]
At the beginning of the thirteenth century, it was still a normal way of
regarding things, although it corresponded less than ever with the facts. The
Lateran Council showed a more realist attitude in its 13th canon. Abandoning the outmoded framework of the two traditional types, it simply
demanded that people should confine themselves to one of the approved
forms of the life of perfection.

The decision, however categorical it might be, was not in itself intended
to stifle the Spirit. Surely the Church had the right to think that she had made
sufficient experiments to provide anyone with the wherewithal to satisfy his
attractions and inspirations. The approved orders offered candidates for the
communal and perfect life an extremely varied range of institutions.

Nevertheless, if among the eremitical, hospitaller and military movements, and naturally, those of the monks and canons, there was
superabundance of choice, the penitential and apostolic movements in
particular were very badly provided for. The apostolic movement, a century
and a half old, had up to the present found no place in the Catholic order of

things except under the form of the Canons Regular. Preaching, however, did not play an essential part in the definition of the canons. No society devoted to preaching as such had succeeded up to that time in stabilizing itself in the Church, less still in obtaining confirmation. Moreover, we can understand the prudence and the anxieties of the hierarchy. In the administration of charity, even in the military defence of Christendom, there is no risk of compromising the truth. Preaching, however, continually implicates doctrine, for which the bishops alone have received responsibility. The Humiliati of Lombardy had the Pope's authorization only for 'moral exhortation', the word of brotherly edification, which had been expressly distinguished from the preaching of the faith.[58] The order, moreover, was much closer to the penitential movement than to the apostolic. The Poor Catholics were not confirmed as an order, only their individual and particular 'intention' had received the sanction of the Sovereign Pontiff.[59] The brothers of St Francis, who likewise might be said to be in a category on the fringe of the penitents and the men of apostolic life, were in their initial stages and so far had only the right to exhort to penance.[60] On the other hand, the preaching movements of the Waldenses and above all the apostolic Catharist churches, so violently anti-Roman, constituted by their very existence a terrible liability for the orthodox followers of apostolic life. It was clear that the 13th canon of the Council had been primarily directed against the collective foundations and even against the individual vocations of the apostolic preachers. It did not leave them, it would seem, any way of access into the Church. It was precisely from this that Dominic was able to derive reassurance. The canon went directly against the Pope's initiatives in this matter since the beginning of his pontificate, especially against the approval he had granted to the proposed way of life of Durando de Huesca, Bernard Prim, St Francis, and their companions;[61] he would know how to defend his own work.

The second full session of the Council came, then the third. At this last session, on the last day but one of November, Innocent promulgated his decision on the Albigeois. Impressed by the general position of the legates of Provence and of the clergy of the Midi—with the exception, it is said, of Arnaud, who was now opposing de Montfort—the Pope definitively renounced the support of Raymond VI. The Count of Toulouse was disinherited without ever having been formally judged on the count of heresy. This was a serious wrong even in respect of contemporary law.[62] Simon received the part of the county of Toulouse which he was already occupying, situated to the west of the Rhône. The rights of Raymond VII over the marquisate of Provence were, however, protected. The decision was dispatched by the chancellery on 14th December.[63]

At this point, the period of business of very grave importance was closed. Lesser affairs could now be dealt with. The Pope had retained the young

Raymond VII for some time, in order to discuss matters with him. He then had to send for Fulk and Dominic to communicate his decision to them. From the legal point of view, this was independent of that of the canons of the Council. Dominic's order had been validly constituted and approved, prior to the great assembly. The Pope was free to treat it as he thought fit. He had, moreover—perhaps it was at this particular time—granted confirmation to the Order of St Francis, which was thus free from the Council's interdiction.[64] But he would not have been either correct or prudent had he taken no account of the 13th canon. If the Pope had thought fit to give way to the reaction of the bishops on the plane of the religious associations as he had done on the political plane of the Albigeois, it was neither through want of courage nor of authority. At this time a Council was such in every sense of the word, and the head of Christendom both respected and listened to it. Moreover Innocent understood the feeling of the Fathers of the Lateran. Without approving the narrowness of view of the majority of the bishops, he had no liking for the anarchy of the 'spirituals' and the 'conventicles' and throughout his reign he worked to bring this back to more normal and more traditional forms. Yet he knew how to discern the spirits and trusted Dominic as he did Francis. On the second he had imposed a direct profession of obedience to his own person, before approving his rule, which was again to be twice modified by the Pope who succeeded Innocent; he only entrusted to him preaching that was limited in its scope.[65] The former he asked to choose, in common with his brethren, an approved rule which would serve as a guarantee for their order so far as the bishops were concerned and would avoid its falling under the grave suspicions which the Poor Catholics had incurred. As soon as Dominic had given his order protection by the choice of a rule, he would only have to present himself to the Curia once more. Innocent promised him then to confirm all he was asking for—possessions, the preaching, and the name of Preacher.[66]

Dominic was able to draw breath. He already had a fairly good idea of what the rule to be chosen would be—clearly the Rule of St Augustine which he had been observing for nearly twenty years. The prescriptions of personal poverty and fraternal charity, and the high standard of morality which it contained, were so fundamental that they could not but go further in the direction he desired, completing the spiritual capital of the brethren without restricting their ministry of the word, so general were their terms. Doubtless the profession of the rule which for more than a century people had become accustomed to consider as the rule of the canons par excellence would involve, directly or indirectly, some obligations or customs which would otherwise not have been assumed. They could not, however, be difficult for a cleric such as Dominic. In his obligations as a canon of Osma, he had found nothing to hamper his preaching and his imitation of the apostles since 1206. No more than the Pope had Dominic a liking for

anarchy or a contempt for clerical tradition. The obligation of the choice of
an approved rule, which for St Francis or Durando de Huesca would have
been heartbreaking, seemed to him a burden easily borne.[67] Moreover in
return, the Pope, for the first time in the history of Christendom, promised
him to confirm in his order the preaching of the faith.

Friar John of Navarre who saw Dominic as he returned from the Curia,
would for twenty years to come retain the memory of the founder's deep
satisfaction. The year 1215, which had been that of Friar John's entry into
religion, would remain in his memory as 'the year in which the Order of
Friars Preachers was confirmed at the Council of Pope Innocent III'.[68] The
expression is not quite correct. The confirmation was only promised. Such
a promise, however, really made it certain. All of them experienced the
same feeling.[69] Confirmation was in fact granted immediately upon the
founder's return to Rome, after choosing the rule—'confirmation of
the order and of all that Dominic had wished, fully and in everything, in
conformity with the plan and organization which he had conceived of
them'.[70]

Addressing himself now to Fulk, the Pope asked him to assign a church to
the infant order.[71] There was no question of binding the brethren to the
parochial ministry. The house of Peter Seila, however, had no consecrated
chapel, as has been said; it was thus not possible, according to the canon law
of the time, to celebrate Mass there. The brethren were to have their own
sanctuary. This would confirm their stability and their fidelity to a very
ancient tradition which required that every cleric should be attached to a
church.[72] It would also emphasize the official and public character of their
preaching. The possession of a church would give them a permanent pulpit
in the cities, independent of the goodwill of the parish priests. Fulk,
however, had no chapel at his disposal in Toulouse. It needed nothing less
than the formal order of the Pope to induce the clergy of the town, through
the intermediary of the bishop, to grant this place of worship.

The departure for Toulouse took place in January 1216.[73] At this period
of the year the passes over the Alps were not open. Dominic and the bishop
doubtless travelled by ship from Genoa to Marseilles[74] in the suite of some
prelate returning in the direction of the Narbonensis. Raymond of Toulouse
had left, en route for Aragon.

In February the travellers passed through Narbonne. Fulk stayed on there,
detained by the quarrel of Archbishop Arnaud and Count Simon on the
matter of the duchy.[75] The quarrel had then reached its sharpest point.
Without waiting for the conclusion of this painful matter, Dominic went on
to Prouille. There there was great rejoicing over the confirmation by the
Holy See of the monastery's possessions. On 2nd March, Dominic, Friar
Noël and William Claret received the donation of Pierre de Castillon,

of Saissac, who was making over certain property to the monastery and made donation of himself with his son, if the latter were willing.[76]

Dominic then left for Toulouse. Simon, Fulk and his supporters also hastened to reach the capital. Whereas the Count was taking possession of the city which the Council had granted him definitively (on 7th March he received the oaths of the capitouls and the population, and pronounced his own on the following day),[77] Dominic was once more in contact with his brethren in an atmosphere of most understandable satisfaction.

The community was increasingly uncomfortable in the houses of the Seila. They had not enough room there. Moreover, the situation in the locality was losing its advantages. With his habitual efficiency de Montfort had begun to fortify the castle of Narbonne.[78] The earth with which the fortress was filled up to the summit was removed. A door was opened on the side leading away from the town to the country, to enable the French to enter and leave unbeknown to the inhabitants. Between the city and the castle, on the site of the gate and walls which had just been razed, a deep trench was dug, and was fortified by strong palisades. The dwelling-place of St Dominic was now separated from the castle by the large trench, the defences of which reared up right in front of the house. Toulouse, moreover, was in a state of upheaval. The destruction of the walls of the borough and of the city, inaugurated ten months earlier by the order of Louis of France, continued relentlessly and with increasing force. Ditches were levelled, the turrets of houses, of which there were many, were knocked down, the chains across the streets done away with. Toulouse acquired the appearance of a city that had been conquered, razed, half ruined—Toulouse which had surrendered peacefully to the Church. On account of this the attitude of the inhabitants underwent a profound change of feeling. The crusaders had never been loved, but how could people have experienced sentiments of anything other than ill-suppressed revolt as they paid their forced homage to Simon de Montfort? Dominic could congratulate himself that he owed his installation in the city to the generosity of a townsman of Toulouse and to that alone. He felt himself more determined than ever to keep his ministry apart from the crusade.

There must be no question of being behind laymen in carrying out the Pope's decisions. The first step was the choice of a rule. In view of the objective and the circumstances, the assembly charged with this choice took on the aspect of a foundation chapter. The Pope had particularly insisted on the necessity of full deliberation and of unanimous consent.[79] Dominic had no need to have this suggested to him. It was his constant line of conduct in his relations with his brethren. It was his intention to do everything in collaboration—better still, to leave the community of the brethren to take the fundamental decisions by provisionally abandoning his powers to them.[80]

The brethren of Prouille, especially Noël and William Claret, took their part in this chapter. They later figured, in fact, as bound by its engagements and members of the community which emerged as a result of its decisions.[81] This fact was perhaps the source of a tradition which locates this chapter at Prouille.[82] The fact is not certain. There is nothing to prove that the chapter did not meet at Toulouse, as was normal. As to the date, it was necessary to wait at least until the week after Easter.[83] The intensive ministry of Lent was particularly all-absorbing in this year of 1216 when, for the first time, the canon *Omnis utriusque sexus* on Easter confession and Communion, came into force. There were many sins to absolve, and spiritual lives to reconstruct in this city of Toulouse, which had been so deeply disturbed in its religion. For this reason it is particularly tempting to suppose that they waited for Pentecost to assemble the Chapter, in order to place it under the light of the Holy Spirit 'by whom the sons of God are given life'.[84] From this would have come the custom, universal from this time onwards right up to the middle of the nineteenth century, of holding the Dominican General Chapters at Pentecost. In 1216 this feast fell on 29th May.

In the Western Church there existed a certain number of rules recently approved—those of St Stephen of Grandmont, of the Templars, of the Holy Spirit, for instance. They had a very limited field of application and were not nearly so well known as the two general rules, of St Benedict—the *regula par excellence*—and St Augustine. The latter had met with so much success since the end of the eleventh century among foundations of canons and hospitallers, that it had completely superseded the earlier rules for the canons. It had even experienced the inevitable penalty of its success. It has already been recounted how the earlier of the two texts which traditionally composed it, the *ordo monasterii*, adopted for some time by the canons of strict observance, had finally disappeared.[85] Its prescriptions, precise but anachronistic, had finally proved impracticable. All that had remained of this part of the text, which had been suppressed by order of the Popes, was the opening phrase, left as a prologue to the moral part of the rule of St Augustine.

For the brethren, as for Dominic, there could be no hesitation. Preachers themselves, with common accord they adopted the rule of the eminent preacher, St Augustine.[86] Humbert de Romans would later explain that the blessed Augustine in formulating his rule had taken as his model the apostolic life. 'The proof of this is found in the antiphons and lessons of his office where it is said that he "*set himself to live according to the rule instituted under the holy apostles*".[87] Did not he himself say in one of his writings—"*We seek in fact to lead the apostolic life*"?'[88] It can be seen how well suited the *regula apostolica*[89] of St Augustine was to the design of the brethren of St Dominic.

Doubtless it only aimed at expressly renewing the communal poverty of the early Christians and had nothing to say either as to mendicacy or preaching. Yet it did not exclude detailed prescriptions of this sort; it even called for them by its reference to the apostles. 'Although it is permitted', Humbert de Romans was to say again, 'when one follows this rule, to have landed property and revenues or not to have them, it is better for the preachers who are living under its authority not to have any, for the preaching of the Gospel is much less suited to the rich than to him who is voluntarily poor'.[90] Moreover, he was to add—

> In instituting the new Order of Preachers, it was necessary to make full and detailed provisions as to the studies, the poverty and other similar points, which had to be added to the rule of the order. It was thus necessary to choose a rule such as would present nothing which would come into conflict with constitutions of this type; a rule such that these constitutions might be added and adapted to it in a suitable manner. Such was in actual fact the rule of the blessed Augustine. It contains only a small number of data, a few prescriptions of spirituality or of common sense, which are not found in the other rules. Thus all the provisions demanded by the statute of preaching can be added to it very conveniently.[91]

In these conditions it may be asked why the Preaching of Toulouse had not placed itself under the rule of the Bishop of Hippo from 1215. For the precise reason that it had no need to do so. The rule had lost its normative value at the beginning of the twelfth century by the disappearance of the *ordo monasterii*, which in itself constituted a detailed code of observance. At that date it nevertheless still preserved its value as a symbol, because of the clearness of its position in the matter of individual poverty. This value, however, no longer existed at a period when religious poverty was moving in the direction of mendicancy. Several indications clearly show that the rule of St Augustine was beginning to lose its high reputation at the beginning of the thirteenth century.[92] Had it not been for the 13th canon of the Lateran, it would perhaps have come to be completely forgotten. On the contrary, after 1215, it once more found its value, at the head of the particular legislation of the new religious orders and their authentication for the future.

The first effect of the rule would be to facilitate the formalities of confirmation. As Augustinian Clerks Regular, the brethren of St Dominic would enter the recognized category of canonical orders. A current procedure was in existence for confirming the property and the constituent elements of these orders, and it was sufficient to have recourse to such procedure. The title of canon, moreover, would cover the new community so far as the local clergy were concerned. Thanks to this, they would avoid arousing the hostility of the traditionalists, at least at a first contact. Experience was to prove that the danger was no chimerical one.[93]

On the other hand, entrance into the canonical category would from the very first confer a certain canonical status. Since the end of the eleventh century, councils and popes had been legislating or taking decisions on the Canons Regular. Preserved in certain collections of official texts, these documents fixed the distinct nature of the Order of Canons in relation to the monastic order, and its clerical character, defended the stability of its profession, determined the obligation of the rule of St Augustine, the poverty of the religious, their right to exercise the ministry of souls.[94] Such provisions clearly could not in any way interfere with the special characteristics of the Toulouse foundation. On the contrary, they brought considerable advantages to a cleric as attached as Dominic was to the tradition of the Church. It was on this canonical status, for instance, that Dominic depended for defining the obligation of chastity of the brethren; their formula of profession was to make no mention of it.

Quite recently the Council of Montpellier had legislated on the Canons Regular of the province of Narbonne.[95] In the majority of its provisions it limited itself to recalling the conditions of individual poverty and moral rectitude of the canons, the prohibitions against acting as lawyers,[96] and passing to another form of religious life unless it should be a higher one,[97] but it added certain regulations of its own which would be found in the practice at least of the brethren of St Dominic. For instance, the precept to collect the remains at the end of the meal so that the whole of them could be given to the poor;[98] the requirement that in the priories which were to serve the churches assigned to them there should be at least three brethren;[99] finally regulations as to clothes by which the Council seemed to set great store, for it imposed them under strict obedience. It was necessary to wear shoes that were close fitting and came high up, long closed tunics, most important of all a surplice, a black cloak of simple material, a wide tonsure in the form of a crown.[100] This may perhaps have been the classic insistence on regular poverty, but it was also the reaction of the authorities against the inferiority complex of the clergy of the Midi to which attention has already been drawn.[101] The Council was forcing clerics, in particular the Clerks Regular, to make known by the tonsure and surplice their priestly character, which they sought to hide so as to avoid insults. The close-fitting shoes, on the other hand, were to distinguish them from the preachers of the Waldenses.

In taking upon themselves these special obligations, the rule of St Augustine and its canonical status, Dominic's brethren were carrying out the will of the Pope. This heterogeneous collection of regulations, however, was in no wise sufficient to direct the life of the community of Toulouse. The foundation chapter pursued its legislative task.

Jordan of Saxony expressly relates that after the choice of the rule of St Augustine, the brethren decided to take upon themselves 'customs of strict observance, relating to the food, the fasts, sleep and the wearing of wool'.[102] To characterize these constitutions he uses the expression *arctiores consuetudines*. These words tell us more than seems possible at first sight.

For a long time past, the orders who were following a traditional rule had added to it under the influence of the various currents of reform. The most ancient type of these additions bore the name of customs, *consuetudines*. It was 'a written law, established by use',[103] which interpreted and developed the observance of the official rule. Since the twelfth century, however, the development of the great centralized orders and of their representative assembly, the general chapter, of which the Order of Cîteaux had provided the model, gave rise to additions which were original in form. Thus there was legislation from a single source, the elements of which were of day-to-day importance, to which was given the name of statutes (*statuta, institutiones*). These statutes had a bearing both on the customary observances, which they corrected or adapted according to the circumstances, and on the organization or constitution of the society formed by a great order—whence the name of *constitutiones* which would be given to them in the course of the thirteenth century. In the case of the rule of St Augustine, so poor in precise juridical dispositions, these customs and constitutions played the principal part. Substituted for the prescriptions of the abolished *ordo monasterii*, they represented the real code of the community.

When the canons had revived the ancient Augustinian rule, to complete it they simultaneously adopted observances that were more or less moderate. This was the *ordo antiquus*,[104] the moderate observance of the canons of the twelfth century, of which the Order of Saint Rufus supplies the classic example; it was this the chapter of Osma followed, as did the majority of the chapters of the south. The institution of Springiersbach, however, then of Prémontré in the second decade of the century, introduced a second type of customs, the *ordo novus*, or *arctior consuetudo*.[105] This was diffused through especially fervent communities or even won the support of communities of longer standing—a thing that did not happen without causing a stir. It was to this *arctior consuetudo* that the community of Toulouse had recourse. Clearly, they would not seek the model of strict observance from the reformed canons of Springiersbach in Germany. They took it from Prémontré.

A few decades later Humbert de Romans would testify to this fact. His commentary deserves to be quoted at length—

The Premonstratensians [he recalled] have reformed and developed the religious life of the blessed Augustine, as the Cistercians have done in the case of blessed Benedict. They outstrip all the members of this family by the austerity of their life, the beauty of their observances, the wisdom of their government of very large numbers of religious, thanks to the general chapters, canonical visitations and other institutions of this kind. Thus, when the blessed Dominic and the brethren of his time could not obtain from the lord Pope a new and severe rule in accordance with the fervour which inspired them, and when, turned aside from their project, they chose the rule of the blessed Augustine, with just reason they adopted, in addition to this rule, all they found that was austere, beautiful, wise and yet adaptable to their purposes in the constitutions of those religious who surpassed the others in the Augustinian family.[106]

During his childhood at Caleruega Dominic had known the Premonstratensians well in the nearby abbey of Nuestra Señora de la Vid, the only one of this type in the diocese. He often heard it spoken of again when he was Canon of Osma, especially when the observance for the reform of the chapter was discussed. During his ministry in the Narbonensis, he saw still more of the Premonstratensians. Navarre d'Acqs, indeed, the Bishop of Couserans, a place where he often preached, was Abbot of the Premonstratensians of Combelongue.[107] Nothing was easier for him, moreover, than to procure their customs. It is possible that he had already used them to provide a rule for the sisters of Prouille.[108]

We still possess the findings of the chapter of 1216. Written on parchment before being inscribed in the daily life of the brethren, who had too rapidly become founders of convents in their turn, this law of observance subsists in the text of the primitive constitutions of the order, where it forms the prologue and the first distinction (or part), to which must be joined the 'rule of the lay-brethren';[109] the second distinction, as will be seen, represents the fruit of later legislation.[110]

The prologue, the division and the first part of these constitutions are for the most part textually borrowed from a version of the customs of Prémontré which goes back to the last quarter of the twelfth century.[111] These texts as a whole have only been very slightly modified since. They constitute a pure law of observance—canonical office, meals, fasts, food, sleep, the sick, novices, silence, clothing, the tonsure, list of faults and of the penances which correspond to them. In the prologue they bear the very apt title of *Liber consuetudinum*. They are also given, however, the significant title of *regula canonicorum*.[112] These names exactly fit the contents.

The comparison of this primitive rule with the customs of Prémontré which served as its substance is very significant. Dominic and his brethren made their choice. What they borrowed was not selected at random. What they left, or replaced by new dispositions, still less so. If they took over into their text words or prescriptions which they might have left aside, it is because they desired them, or at any rate, did not find them repugnant. Now this is the case with terms as typical as 'canons', 'canonical order', 'canonical religion (or discipline)'.[113] Once even, and in an original text, they mentioned the promise of 'stability',[114] which was to close the noviciate. If they had had the least desire not to entangle themselves in the canonical traditions, they would carefully have avoided words of this kind capable of an interpretation disastrous to the special characteristic of the order—its liberty of operation and its independence.

Dominic and his brethren thus adopted the canonical life without hesitation. What they sought from it, through the text of Prémontré, was regularity, that is to say, liturgical life—the morning chapter, Mass, the canonical hours solemnly recited in the church; ascetical life organized down to its very details in accordance with the strictest monastic tradition— fast from 14th September to Easter, and on Fridays, vigils and Rogation days, perpetual abstinence, the hard couch, the poverty and roughness of the woollen garments;[115] the formation of the moral life by the attitude of constant humility and common charity and by the frequent chapter of faults, with penances graded in accordance with a detailed and severe scale;[116] finally, the best part of the classic conventual inheritance, the contemplative life for which the brethren appeared to have an aptitude from the beginning.[117] It will later be seen more clearly how Dominic reconciled these provisions of austerity and contemplation with the ministry of the word, precisely through his idea of the evangelical life.

As early as 1216, it seems,[118] he showed something of his inspiration in the chapter on the master of novices, in a long original text, as fresh and moving as the ideal novice whose portrait he intended to draw.

The master teaches his novices humility of heart and of body and strives to form them to this, according to this saying—*Discite a me quia mitis sum et humilis corde.* He teaches them to go to confession frequently with sincerity and discernment, to live without possessions, to give up their own will, in all things to practise spontaneous obedience in regard to the will of their superior. He teaches them how to behave in every circumstance and in every place; how to remain in the place where they have been put; how to make the inclination to whoever gives them anything or takes anything from them, to whoever speaks to them kindly, or harshly; the reserve to be kept in certain places, keeping one's eyes lowered; the prayer to be recited, and how to say it in silence so that the noise does not disturb the others. To ask pardon whenever they receive a reprimand from the superior; not under any circumstances to argue with anyone at all; finally, to obey their master in all things; to see that they carefully follow the companion who walks at their side in the procession round the cloister; not to speak at forbidden times or in forbidden places; to say *Benedictus Deus* when they are given some garment, making the deep inclination; never to judge anyone deliberately. If they see something done which seems to them evil, let them ask themselves if it is not perhaps good, or at least done with a good intention, for the judgment of man often goes astray. He shall show them how to make the *venia* at chapter or wherever they receive a reprimand, frequently to undergo the discipline, not to speak of the absent except to say good of them, to drink with both hands and seated. He shall teach them with what care they must handle the books and clothing and other property of the monastery; what application they should have in study, so that by day and by night, in the house and on a journey, they are always occupied in reading or meditating on something, striving to retain by heart all they possibly can; and what fervour they will have to have in preaching when the time comes,[119]

The last phrases are especially remarkable. We can go carefully through the earlier canonical customs, those of St Victor, of Marbach, of Ste-Marie-du-Port, of Prémontré, of St Rufus, but we shall find nothing like this.[120] Dominic was giving to regular life a strong impulse and orientation towards preaching, but as an outcome of study and contemplation; no interior disposition seemed to him more important in this sense than humility of heart in poverty.

The same orientation inspired a series of hitherto unknown dispositions. A code of silence, in which the penances became more severe with the number of infractions, helped to maintain the atmosphere of recollection and study even in the refectory.[121] To the faults which formed the subject of *culpae*, collected and classified by the Premonstratensians into five categories, a certain number were added—all of them bore on study, preaching, absences from the monastery required by the ministry.[122]

The most notable, however, of the transformations which Dominic and his brethren imposed on regular tradition to adapt it to the ministry of preaching, was the extensive system of dispensations which they provided for in the life of observance, for reasons of study and no longer only for that of health.[123] No mistake would be made in viewing this as one of the most characteristic innovations of the Dominican order, preoccupied as it was with maintaining the balance between elements of the life that were rich indeed but sometimes in opposition. Dominic introduced this in 1216, in five paragraphs of the customs, in regard to the conventual chapter, recitation of the office, the fasts, meals in common and the sick.[124] Later he was again to make general the rule of dispensation for reasons of study and the ministry, to the extent of making of it a fundamental law of the observance of his order.

Regular austerity and liturgical life, however, did not at first manifest themselves to Dominic's eyes as an eventual obstacle to the ministry of souls. He saw in them much more a direct preparation, the point of departure of the imitation of the apostles and the condition of a ministry *verbo et exemplo;* from which sprang the severity of the observance he chose, more rigorous than the strictest of the canonical observances.

The 'apostolic rule', however, did not as yet influence the customs. It is to be found only in a single disposition, the suppression of the prohibitions in the matter of food, should the friar find himself in the position of a guest.[125] The prohibition against riding a horse without grave necessity, to be found in the manuscript, is an addition later than 1216.[126] The rule of poverty, in particular, was not set down in the text. Jordan of Saxony tells us, however, that it was brought forward by the chapter under the form of an 'institutional proposition'—not to receive landed property, but to accept revenues provisionally.[127] For the brethren of St Romain, however, the 'apostolic rule' was already explicitly contained in a document which still retained its value, the charter of Fulk of 1215.[128] This was sufficient to define the purpose of the order, the preaching, and its fundamental inspiration, evangelical poverty.

On Pentecost evening 1216, the community of the preachers of Toulouse could consider that it had made a satisfactory achievement. It possessed a classic rule against which to judge the sincerity of its life; it had fixed its own status and form of life within the framework of the Augustinian family by its customs and observances. The charter of its bishop gave it its hierarchical mission and sanctioned its own particular spirituality. These documents had both the detailed precision and the elasticity necessary to obtain the confirmations promised by the Pope and to enable the brethren to face the future without fear. If the detailed law of observance could assure fruitfulness and unity in daily life, the constitutional law, on the other hand, reduced now to two or three principles, could be developed almost indefinitely. Times were not ripe to give it more precise shape. It was first necessary for the order to live and develop.

The years which were coming would see the order extended throughout the world. The customs of 1216 would be put into practice by increasing numbers of brethren who had not been present at the foundation. Dominic could now put these detailed regulations into practice among them with rigorous fidelity.[129] It is not, then, surprising that these brethren should have attached to this set of regulations such importance that it eclipsed in their thoughts the rule of St Augustine itself. It is a fact that twenty years later, when the brethren spoke of this legislation, they would use terms which would signify its exact value—'the rule of the order', 'the rule of St Dominic', 'the rule of the Friars Preachers', or simply, 'the rule'.[130] It was, moreover, the name that was given to it.[131]

Dominic's rôle at the centre of the community was not only that of a father, of a counsellor full of experience and inspiration. He was the master and leader to whom all had given themselves by the profession of obedience. It remains for us to consider this point, which will throw considerable light on the sequence of this narrative.

In the customs of 1216, an archaic formula of profession is met with which the present formula shortly afterwards replaced. The novice after his time of probation was to promise 'stability and common life' and to make vow 'of obedience to the superior and his successors'.[132] This formula had emerged out of that of the Canons of Prémontré.[133] The original element, the gift of the religious to the church of the monastery, had been discontinued.[134] Similarly, the qualifying phrase which specified the local character of the stability promised had been dropped.[135] Dominic and his brethren were thus careful not to dedicate themselves to the service of a sanctuary and its patron, as all the canons did. They thus avoided confining themselves within the precincts of a monastery, in accordance with the ancient conception of the monks. The promise of stability which they agreed to make had no meaning apart from that of stability in the order.[136] It was really a duplication of the promise of common life. The latter was finally to be identified with the vow of obedience to the superior, who was the guardian of this common life. Thus the ultimate formula of the Dominican profession would retain only the third promise. Eventually, the construction of the order would thus rest, as it still does today, on a single vow—the immediate profession of obedience to the superior of the order and his successors. This was in fact the case right from the beginning. The first sign of the coming into being of the order was the oblation which Peter Seila and Thomas of Toulouse made of themselves to St Dominic. Such a disposition was indeed unusual.

At that time it did not, however, lack models or precedents, as, for instance, profession of obedience into the hands of a superior pronounced by the vast number of Cluniac monks to the single Abbot of Cluny,[137] or, more precisely, the profession of the Spanish Knights of Santiago de la Espada (1175), reduced to a single vow of obedience into the hands of their master, without any vow of chastity or common life;[138] or again, an even more direct instance, the vow of obedience into the hands of a superior that Diego received from Arnaud de Crampagna after his conversion, in Pamiers,[139] or that which Pope Innocent had exacted of the apostolic preachers, Durando de Huesca, Bernard Prim, St Francis.[140] All these precedents, had indeed one single source despite their deep variety—the general system of ties of dependence which, in every sphere of Western civilization, sought to add to the various hierarchies in order to strengthen the traditional communities by ties from man to man sealed by an oath. Through his homage as a vassal, a man made over his activities to his lord, linked his lot to his and gave him his fidelity. The lord in return became his protector and his guarantor, henceforward bearing the responsibility for his acts. Now such bonds of feudal dependence had for a long time past made their appearance in the framework of the Church. Pope Innocent III had given them a considerable place in the sphere of Christian politics by the system of vassal kings. In the absence of any institutions capable of welcoming and directing the forces of the apostolic movement towards their real goal, it was in an oath of this kind that he placed his confidence. The profession of pure obedience of Dominic's brethren to their 'prior and master',[141] was an echo of these oaths to the Pope, as it was the parallel of the professions of serfs and donated persons which the founder had received at the monastery of Prouille.[142]

Such a position might have turned to absolutism, if not to tyranny. It found its natural counterpoise in the mentality of the times, that of the community. Hence the attitude already noted in the case of Dominic—the continual anxiety to stand aside before the counsel, deliberation, the common decision of his brethren. He knew how to use his authority; he also knew when it was necessary to waive it before the community in the interests of a happy equilibrium. This explains the extreme elasticity of the Dominican foundation during its initial years. Nothing as yet depended on authorities or external documents. Everything rested on the brethren and on the founder. In 1215, when the order had not yet fixed its observance and when its activity was not yet approved by the bishop, it was already solidly constituted in the house of Peter Seila by the profession of obedience. In 1216, when the exigencies and prohibitions of the Council of the Lateran might have endangered the new foundation, the order had adapted itself without difficulty, because the essential of its constitution was the obedience of the brethren to Dominic and the obedience of Dominic to his bishop. In 1217, when the order would experience rapid growth, and a the same time a dispersion far and wide, it was to remain solidly united by grace of the direct bond between the brethren and the founder. Neither the bishop nor the Pope would have need to intervene in the order, to consolidate it. The legislation would remain in the hands of the community of the brethren alone, the brethren in the hands of Dominic who had received their oaths, and of him alone. This legislation, however, elaborated stage by stage in accordance with the lessons of experience, would soon lay down and make plain in a collection of texts the rules of obedience and of common life, eventually permitting the founder to efface himself without danger. Then would be realized, by harmonious exchange between the authority of the master, to whom all are linked by the profession of obedience, the evidence of the text, which each friar can read over for himself, and the unanimity of hearts—the work of perfection and fraternity which had been recalled as far back as 1216 by the prologue borrowed from the customs of the Premonstratensians.

> Since the rule commands us to have only one heart and one soul in the Lord, it is meet that, living under a single rule, bound by the vows of a single profession, we should find ourselves equally unanimous in the observance of our canonical religion, so that the unity which we should conserve in our hearts may be fostered and shown forth to the world outside by the uniformity of our behaviour. Now it is very certain that we shall be able to practise this observance and keep it in mind with more resolution and more completely, if what should be done is set down in writing, if each one can learn from the evidence of a written document the way in which he should live, if no one has permission to change, add, or retrench anything whatsoever of his own will. For if we were to neglect the smallest details, we could not but fear a progressive fall from grace. Thus in order to provide for the unity and peace of the order as a whole, we have carefully drawn up the book which we call the book of customs.[143]

The question of the church and of the new convent now became of first importance. The brethren had, however, to wait a few more weeks for it to be settled. On the morrow of his return to the capital, Fulk had set off again to accompany Simon de Montfort, who was going to France, in an atmosphere of triumph to pay homage to the king, Philip Augustus.[144]

The bishop only returned in June. A few days later,[145] he gathered the canons of his cathedral together in chapter. Strongly urged by Fulk,[146] the provost and community consented to deprive themselves of the chapel of St Romain[147] in favour of Brother Dominic, 'prior and master of the Preachers', and of his companions present and to come. They gave him the sanctuary and the offerings of the faithful, in exchange for a quit rent of three 'sous' yearly, but not the parish rights. The brethren might set up a cemetery for their personal use. The canons, however, would not authorize them to bury any stranger, and there they laid down in minute detail what should happen in the case of some dying person who was desirous of profiting by burial by the brethren and their suffrages and, in order to get round the prohibition, should take the habit *in extremis* and make profession.[148] There was no danger, however, of the Preaching of Toulouse lessening the revenues of the chapter of St Etienne, particularly since the bishop was soon to incorporate in the cathedral community several churches in the diocese.[149]

It is possible that the brethren had been using St Romain since the previous year.[150] They could not, however, do anything more than celebrate the office there. The donation of July 1216 enabled them to lodge in some adjoining premises, then to begin to build. Three months after this donation, they received from a Toulouse couple, Raymond Vital and Bruniquel his wife, a house with dependencies and newly planted vineyards. The house was adjoining the convent, whose domain it increased. The vineyard, whose value was increased by the share of one-eighth in a land mill situated by the weir of the Daurade, permitted them to buy through exchange from Vital Autard and from Grande, his wife, a house adjoining the convent. The share of the mill belonged to Thomas de Tramesaygues, whose widow would later become a nun of Prouille.[151] The Vital belonged to the best burghers of Toulouse. A man of experience and integrity, one of the twenty-four consuls of Toulouse—like his brother Pierre, Raymond Vital had played his part in the administration of the borough and the city. And it was his paternal mansion, it seems, that he was giving to enlarge the convent.[152] The Toulouse foundation of St Dominic, made possible by the donations of the Seila and of Bishop Fulk, maintained by the gifts of the canons of St Etienne, of Raymond Vital and of Pierre Tramesaygues, marked by the religious profession of several members of the town, thus proved itself to be strictly local and independent of the crusade.

Having now sufficient room at their disposal, the brethren were able to carry out the majority of their projects. A cloister was erected beside the church. A storey of cells was installed above the cloister. Jordan gives the detail that these cells enabled them 'sufficiently' to sleep and study.[153] That is to say, they remained poor. The brethren, however, were not lodged in a dormitory after the manner of other religious. The distinctive character of these preachers was emphasized by this fact.

New brethren had entered the order since 1215. Certain of them came from the world, others from religious communities. The Dominican ideal made an evident appeal to generous hearts. On his side Dominic inaugurated from this time onwards the policy of intensive recruitment which he pursued until his death, particularly in the case of young clerics. Finally the choice of the rule and of the statutes of strict observance made it possible for religious or canons of common observance to go over to the *arctior religio* of the preachers of Toulouse. Canon law explicitly reserved the possibility of this, even despite the opposition of superiors or of earlier established communities.[154]

It was at this time, at all events, that Matthew of France left the chapter of Castres, of which he was prior, to join his friend Dominic once more.[155] Having come from France with Simon de Montfort, this great religious would soon be returning there to spread the new order. A group of Castilians or Spaniards entered the community before the summer of 1217. Among them was Mames, Dominic's own brother.[156] Another came from the neighbourhood of Osma—Miguel de Ucero.[157] The others were Miguel de España, Pedro de Madrid, Gómez.[158]

Another of the brethren was a native of England—Lawrence the Englishman;[159] a lay-brother, Friar Odier, was from Normandy.[160] Finally, Toulouse again supplied Dominic with one of his best collaborators, Friar Bertrand of Garrigo,[161] whose family was later to hand over to the order its rights over the site of the future convent of Toulouse, when the cloister of St Romain had clearly proved itself too small.[162]

If we add to these newcomers those who were already in the order in 1215—Friar William Claret, Friar Dominic of Spain, Friar Noël, Friar Vitalis, Friar Peter Seila, Friar Thomas of Toulouse, Friar Guillaume Raymond, Friar John of Navarre, perhaps Friar Stephen of Metz—it will be seen that the number of the brethren at the beginning of 1217 would amount to about twenty, twelve of whom were certainly present in the middle of 1216, doubtless with a few others—Jordan says, about sixteen.[163]

From the completion of the foundation chapter, or for the newcomers from the end of the time of probation that was perhaps assigned to one or the other of them, the brethren had to pronounce their vows according to the new rule and constitutions. It is very probable that Dominic was the first to give them the example of this.[164] A change of observance, naturally in the direction of what was more austere, necessarily involved the change of profession. It was only then that the founder broke the legal ties that bound him to his original chapter and that he ceased to bear the official title of Canon of Osma.[165]

The order was henceforward definitely established in its rule, its convent, its profession, its ministry. Wearing the white tunic and hooded scapular[166] which partially concealed the linen surplice of the canons of the Narbonensis,[167] wrapped in the black cloak and wearing the close-fitting shoes, their heads encircled with the large clerical tonsure,[168] the brethren of the preaching of Toulouse worked at the salvation of souls, in accordance with the mandate received from the Bishop of Toulouse. Their important and increasing number could not but fill the latter with hope.

Fulk was obsessed by the vast extent of the diocese he had to evangelize. At this time he was considering decentralizing it. Taking advantage of the restitutions of churches that Simon de Montfort had just made to the diocese in September[169] in compliance with the statutes of Pamiers,[170] he set aside six of these in October to the profit of the canons of the cathedral of St Etienne. The latter, moreover, undertook to resume regular life to its fullest extent.[171] Thus they secured for these parishes, through a parish priest whom they knew how to choose with care, or even by a subordinate priory which they might found there, a fruitful pastoral ministry.[172] The bishop acted similarly with his other college of canons, the preachers of St Romain. This time, however, the concession of churches arose out of an even more deeply rooted inspiration. With an abnegation rare among prelates, the bishop adopted the heroic means of cutting down his authority for the major part, by dividing his diocese into sections. He was soon to write to the Pope to submit his project of dismemberment.[173] At the same time he agreed with Dominic to divide the sphere of operations of the Preaching of Toulouse in accordance with the same plan. Supplementary centres of ministry would be founded, priories of the order,[174] where three brethren at least would lodge and exercise their influence over the corresponding portion of the diocese.[175] With this end in view, he granted the Preaching two new churches. One at Loubens,[176] about nine miles away from Pamiers, would serve the valley of the Ariège, that is to say the part of the diocese situated in the county of Foix to the south-west of Toulouse. The other, between Puylaurens and Sorèze,[177] would work the north-eastern portion of the diocese, which bordered on that of Albi. Prouille, however, at the frontiers of the diocese of Carcassonne, would continue to serve as a centre for the ministry of the Lauragais. Freed by William Claret from the cares of the administration of the monastery, Friar Noël and, doubtless, some companion with him, there pursued Dominic's ministry.

At the time when he was preparing to travel to Rome to obtain the confirmations promised by the Pope, the founder attached himself more and more systematically to the evangelization of the diocese of Toulouse. Nothing indicated that he was envisaging a wider sphere of action. Everything was, however, to be transformed, in the course of a stay of a few weeks at the centre of the Church.

CHAPTER XII

THE ORDER OF PREACHERS
SPREAD THROUGH THE WORLD

DOMINIC set off about the middle of October.[1] It would be interesting to know who the companion was who made the journey with him, but this time we are left in the dark.[2] Before leaving, the Master had appointed a brother from the neighbourhood of Toulouse, Friar Bertrand of Garrigo, to act on behalf of St Romain.[3] Bertrand received the gifts necessary for the new convent in the name of the founder and of the community.[4] He thus had the mission of superintending the building operations. This was no light responsibility, as Friar Rodolfo, procurator of the convent of Bologna, would later experience to his cost. It did not take Dominic long to criticize the constructions as over-fine or over-spacious.[5] Friar Bertrand would not abuse the saint's trust.[6] He was on intimate terms with him and had received his confidences as he went with him on his apostolic journeys—there were few brethren who were to such an extent impregnated with Dominic's thoughts and example. Bertrand believed himself a great sinner and was so excessively distressed over his faults that he was finally told to pray in future only for the sins of others—this he did from then onwards with much zeal. Moreover, he mortified himself with equal zest. Jordan describes him at this period as a brother 'of great holiness and of inexorable rigour in his own regard, who mortified his flesh very severely'.[7] The cells of the new convent complied with what was expected. They were just sufficient and no more for the installation of a mattress with a desk for study.[8]

The development of the situation since the earlier journey to the Curia had been unexpected. It can even be said that it was reversed. In 1215 everything seemed indicative of peace and of hope. Now everything gave cause for anxiety. Events had been particularly precipitate during the last few months, both in Rome and in the county of Toulouse.

A few weeks before his departure, Dominic had been present at scenes that were extremely painful.[9] The Count de Montfort, returning in July from his triumphant journey to the King of France, had found the marquisate of Provence in open rebellion through the work of the youthful Raymond VII. Only the castle of Beaucaire still held out with a few loyal followers. Despite all his efforts, Simon was unable to deliver it and retake the city. The echo of this first cruel set-back resounded over the whole country for a long time. Now everything was going wrong. The pendulum of fortune, motionless for a short time, was beginning to swing again, but in the reverse direction. Simon learnt that the people of Toulouse were plotting with Raymond VI, who was collecting troops in Aragon in order to win back his capital. Irritated by his set-back, by these intrigues and by certain acts of treachery which cut him to the quick, he violently attacked the turbulent town. Toulouse, three parts dismantled, was as incapable of triumphing totally over the Count as the latter was of mastering the city by street combats. At one particular moment the crusaders, driven back into the cathedral and the houses adjoining the castle of Narbonne, reacted by setting fire to the city at various points. Simon even contemplated destroying it from end to end. He finally contented himself with hostages, seized unawares, and with an enormous fine. Such was his first appearance as the man who was to govern the capital. He had never won the heart of the men of Toulouse and now he had lost his last chances of holding the land peacefully.

Besides this, he had gravely compromised his bishop.[10] On two occasions Fulk, helped by the Abbot of Saint Sernin, had intervened between the Count and his subjects. Misinterpreting the exasperation of the feudal lord, Fulk had probably gone too far. His promises were not kept. He was accused of having drawn his fellow-citizens into a trap, of having plotted for their ruin, of having delivered them up by ruse to their adversary. The bitterness of these townsmen had ample time to become inflamed during the months which followed, when by order of the count his men continued to knock down the walls and feudal towers with which the city was covered, the symbol and instrument of the power of the urban dynasties;[11] on the other hand the exactions, necessitated by the collection of the fine, daily kept alive in their hearts a particularly bitter wound.[12] After this, Fulk had little chance of obtaining a hearing for religion from his flock. The work of reconquest or of strengthening of the Catholic faith would seem to be dangerously threatened by a political conjuncture as unfavourable as this. Such were Dominic's discouraging thoughts as he hastened towards Rome.

What would he find there? That side of the horizon, though not so dark, showed itself uncertain. Five months earlier, when the chapter of St Romain had made choice of the rule of St Augustine and set down the customs of the order in detail, Dominic had thought that all the obstacles in the way of confirmation were lifted. The unexpected death of Pope Innocent III on 16th July, 1216, news of which had reached Toulouse in the middle of the summer, might easily lead to a revised decision. One can imagine the uneasiness of the man of God. For one who during the General Council of the Lateran had lived over again the history of this pontificate, in some sense at its greatest moment, the disappearance of the great Pope in the prime of life could not but be a crushing loss. All the more was this so for the founder of a preaching order which had only pledged itself to go forward boldly because it was well aware of the courageous and uncompromising attitude of the Sovereign Pontiff in the matter. The Pope had for long fought against the misgivings of the bishops; if he had none the less been obliged, and that at the height of his power, to give way in some degree to their opposition, who would keep that opposition within bounds for the future? He had made formal promises to Dominic's order—his successor would have no obligation to keep them. He might not understand the order's vocation and the necessity for its continued existence.

As soon as he arrived in the eternal city, Dominic was reassured. Cardinal Cencio Savelli, whom the Sacred College had elected two days after Innocent's death, had no other programme than that of his predecessor. He was, wrote Jacques de Vitry on the morrow of the election, 'a good old man, full of religion, very simple and kindly, who had distributed to the poor practically all he possessed.'[13] Organizer of the pontifical finance, he had played his part discreetly in the brilliant college of cardinals which Innocent's genius had gathered together, formed and utilized throughout the Church as legates or commissioners. The college of cardinals was fully determined to continue this work. So swift an election of Innocent's successor could be taken as a guarantee of this.

Such was the good news which the founder learnt immediately upon his first visit to the Cardinal of Ostia, Ugolino, perhaps the most prominent member of the whole sacred college. He was able to verify the correctness of this information on the occasion of the first audience the Pope granted him in his palace of the Vatican.[14] The confirmations asked for and promised would be given him. As to the canonical community and their property, the matter would be dealt with without delay. The formula of the great privilege *Religiosam vitam* was precisely framed for that purpose.[15] Dominic was invited to set down in detail the provisions he wished to see incorporated in the bull. The Pope granted him these in a later audience and had the definitive text drawn up by his chancellery. It was necessary to wait some time longer for a meeting of the consistory, that is to say of the college of cardinals met together in the council of the Sovereign Pontiff. The consistory was held a few days before Christmas and at it the bull was accepted. On 22nd December, at St Peter's, Dominic finally received the document so long desired.[16]

The consistorial privilege of 22nd December, 1216 bore from the beginning the name of 'confirmation of the order'.[17] It is indeed the classic document of confirmation, an important bull corroborated by the *rota* of the Pope and the signature of eighteen cardinals, among them Ugolino, Cardinal-bishop of Ostia and Velletri,[18] and Robert de Courson, Cardinal-priest of St Stefano. The original, brought back by Dominic to St Romain and preserved in the convent of Toulouse until its suppression, is today to be found in the archives of Haute-Garonne.

It was not the first time that the Roman chancellery had transcribed the formula *Religiosam vitam*. Innocent III had often made use of it for monks, canons, certain hospitallers. Honorius made use of it even more: in the last three months of 1216, he issued it six times at least.[19] This formula, or rather this collection of stereotyped formulae, some of which had been static since the ninth century, in effect made it possible for the most varied institutions to be confirmed and enriched with privileges. Founders had the choice between about fifty traditional provisions; they took one or rejected the other according to their own intentions; the prologue, equally traditional, was added, as were the final clauses. After this, if the Holy See were in agreement, the text was confirmed as a whole by the Pope and cardinals in the course of a consistory. Thus the great privilege was merely a mosaic of ready-made formulae. The composition of this mosaic, however, remained charged with significance. This was the case with the privilege obtained by Dominic.

After the formula of address and the prologue, the privilege took under the protection of St Peter the church of St Romain and confirmed the observance (*ordo*) instituted in that church. It then confirmed the present and future possessions of the brethren and declared their gardens[20] and the pasture ground of their beasts exempt from all tithes. It secured liberty of recruitment and stability of profession, guaranteed the right to choose the incumbents of the incorporated churches, protected the house against unjustified exactions and censures—finally, granted privileges, in the case of a general interdict, for clerical consecrations and ordinations and for burials.[21] The confirmation of the liberty of the elections and of the legitimate immunities and customs of the church completed the terms of enactment of the privilege, which was rounded off by anathemas and final privileges.

The bull was addressed to Dominic, prior of St Romain of Toulouse, and to his brethren, present and to come. Thus it gave confirmation only for the house of Toulouse, the only part of St Dominic's projects which had so far been carried out. Only that which is in existence can be confirmed. This house, however, like every other foundation, had the right to expand. The confirmation would be extended, with the order, to any new houses or priories. It is in this sense only that the bull confirmed the order, that is to say, the society of Dominic. On 30th March, 1218, for instance, the brethren of Prouille would in their turn receive the same privilege.[22] At the same time, the brethren in Paris, in the process of founding their convent, would again be called brethren of Saint Romain[23] and the confirmation of 22nd December, 1216 would cover them with its authority.

Thus the *ordo* which the first phrase of the terms of enactment confirmed did not refer to the Dominican society but to the observance of the clerics attached to the church of St Romain. Here the society was only given precise form through the rule of St Augustine. Complementary constitutions were not mentioned.

The official formula defined the *ordo* more precisely by an epithet: *ordo canonicus*. The brethren had in fact entered the category of canons and, through it, that of approved religious. This title would be given to them in different documents for more than thirty years.[24] Later history would show, however, the distance which separated them from the canons in the ordinary acceptation of the word. In the privilege *Religiosam vitam*, the word *canonicus* preserved great elasticity. The chancellery of Innocent III, for instance, had applied it equally to Premonstratensians and other Canons Regular, to the clerical portion of the Humiliati of Lombardy,[25] to the religious of the hospital of Caen.[26] Such a formula thus expressed the genus rather than the proper species of the foundation of Toulouse. It was this canonical genus that was solemnly confirmed at the request of St Dominic with its clerical character, conventual organization, novitiate, regular life, office—in short, the *institutio* or Augustinian canonical statutes. If we reflect on Dominic's extreme reserve in his requests for confirmation[27] and on the liberty he enjoyed for the composition of his collection of formulae in the bull *Religiosam vitam*, we shall attach considerable importance to this first series of confirmations.

In the paragraph confirming the property, its enumeration was equally charged with significance. Seven properties are mentioned. There were four churches—St Romain of Toulouse, Prouille, Ste Marie de Lescure, Ste Trinité of Loubens; the hospice Arnaud-Bernard; the town[28] of Casseneuil; the tithes granted by Fulk. Now these churches also housed or were to house communities of brethren. The Arnaud-Bernard hospice, indeed, housed a collateral work entrusted to St Dominic.

It now remained for the Preaching to be confirmed and for the brethren to be given the name which corresponded to the founder's ambitions. There the difficulty really began. Under what form was the Preaching to be confirmed without giving flagrant proof of the novelty of the order and incurring the risk of contravening the Thirteenth Canon of the Lateran? Consultation and search were necessary. Dominic multiplied his visits to Ugolino, who appeared in his rôle of counsellor and patron of religious foundations. Nearly a month had to elapse before a solution could be reached.[29] In the meantime many events had occurred which gave a new turn to the handling of the problem.

After the Christmas festivities during which all audiences were interrupted, the Pope left St Peter of the Vatican and took up his residence at the Lateran basilica[30] where his youth as a cleric had been spent. He was overwhelmed by a multitude of cares. The royal minority in England, where his legate had succeeded in rallying the barons to the boy king whom he had crowned;[31] the reassembling of the crusade for the Holy Land, the date for which was approaching;[32] disorders in Bohemia, instigated under cover of the crusade.[33] The affair of faith and peace of the Midi of France was not the least disturbing of these cares. Now that he had quarrelled irrevocably with the Count de Montfort, Arnault de Narbonne was no longer sending in the triumphant reports which he formerly composed after the victories of Béziers, Carcassonne or Muret—'Gloria in excelsis Deo . . . .'[34] He now denounced the enterprises of Simon. There was no longer a legate actually present to give the Pope information in a less one-sided manner. Instead of this, a most alarming letter had arrived from Fulk of Toulouse.

The situation was not improving. Plots and antagonisms were increasing in number. The exceedingly false situation in which the bishop found himself was paralysing his ministry. After eleven years of futile attempts in all directions, in which his efforts as preacher and pastor had alternated with those as judge and leader in collaboration with the temporal authorities, in the face of the doubtful fortune of the crusade and the uncertainties of peace, the old wrestler was discouraged. What could he do for his unruly city that would not be taken in bad part? He wrote to the Pope to offer his resignation.[35] If the Pope would not accept it, at least he asked to be discharged from the major part of his responsibility by the dismemberment of his all too vast diocese.

Honorius III fortunately had at hand an exceptionally well-informed adviser who could ring the bell to a different tune from that of the prelates of the Midi. Already there was a beginning between the Pope and Dominic of that confident relationship, with authority commanding obedience on the one side, and generous initiative on the other, which would open the way to a daily increasing collaboration, the founder placing at the service of the Church, under the direct impulse of the Sovereign Pontiff, a spiritual army increasingly more numerous and better adapted to its task. The Pope would protect this work with his authority, enriching it with privileges and, more important still, making full use of it in the most varied fields of the ministry of souls. More than sixty bulls, letters and privileges of the Popes to Dominic's order during the five remaining years of the life of the founder would soon provide impressive evidence of this collaboration and were, moreover, its instrument.

Instructed and perhaps guided by the suggestions of the preacher and of his ordinary advisers, Honorius had drawn up for the Albigeois four decisive bulls, on the 19th, 21st and 28th January. The first appointed a legate for the whole of Provence, 'torn by continual wars, wallowing in the errors of perverse heresies'—Bertrand, Cardinal-priest of SS John and Paul.[36]

The second was addressed to the university of the masters and students of Paris.[37] The Pope recalled the religious crisis of the region of Toulouse and the route which had just been thrown open by the servitors of the faith, crusaders or preachers. He endeavoured to persuade some of the university

men to come and devote themselves to the teaching and preaching of the
Christian faith and morals there. 'For long enough', he said, 'you have been
sitting beside the stack of wheat. If you transfer yourselves there, you will in
the future bear more fruit.'[38] Dominic thought precisely the same. If the
bull was to persuade some men of goodwill to offer themselves, the route
he had just traced out for the Lord in Toulouse, the form of life which
he had set up, might suggest itself quite naturally to them. It was precisely
this form of life which was referred to in the third bull:[39]

> Honorius, bishop, servant of the servants of God, to our dear sons, the prior
> and brethren of St Romain, Preachers in the country of Toulouse, health and
> the apostolic blessing.

'Preachers.' The Pope was giving them the name so much desired. As
to how he had arrived at this solution, possible explanation would soon be
provided by an anecdote in the order, the details of which are uncertain.[40]
A dialogue was supposed to have taken place between the Pope and his
notary. After having tried another title, 'brethren who preach in the country
of Toulouse', whose import was merely transitory, the Pope was said to
have finally resolved to assign to Dominic's brethren a term with lasting
significance, that of Friars . . . Preachers. A letter emanating from the
Sovereign Pontiff thus confirmed the title and the function, previously only
assigned by Fulk. Because they were the brethren of Dominic, present and
to come, the bishop had recently considered them en bloc as preachers,
leaving to their community itself the responsibility of determining who
should exercise this function. The Pope did the same in the bull. No more
than this was needed to give Dominic the essential thing he wanted. In fact
when, in a not far distant future the brethren of St Romain were to set off
to propagate the order and to preach throughout the diocese, they would
bear this glorious title of preachers by the will of the Pope and could
exercise its function, in their own churches as elsewhere, without it being
necessary for them to obtain anything else than the investiture of their order.
No appeal to the bishop would be necessary. No trace of the intervention of
anyone among them in this sense was to remain in the documents. When
later in the legislation of the Preachers the position of the brethren in
regard to the bishops would be defined, it was to be written: 'Let no one
preach in the diocese of a bishop who forbids him to do so. . . .'[41] Thus the
bishop would retain only the right of *veto* which the Pope could in point of
fact suspend. The brethren, moreover, would impose upon themselves the
duty of deference and of subordination. 'When our brethren enter some
diocese to preach, they shall first visit the bishop if they can do so, and shall
take inspiration from his counsels to produce among the people the spiritual
fruit which they seek.'[42] Deference and *veto* are something different from
institution. For the first time in the Church, the canonical mission, without
which there is no authentic preacher of the Gospel, would no longer be

conferred by the bishop, but by incorporation in a society, explicitly confirmed in this function by the Pope. The ministry of the Preachers would no
longer totally depend on the arbitrariness and good will of the local clergy.
The obstacle on which all preaching movements since the twelfth century
had come to grief had been removed.

Between 1217 and 1221, Honorius would be occupied with inserting in
the Bulls of Recommendation which he was to multiply in favour of the
Preachers, increasingly explicit formulae as to their delegation to preach the
word of God, by virtue even of their profession as regulars.[43] The most
precise of these formulae, however, were found implicitly contained in the
address of the bull *Gratiarum omnium largitori* of 21st January, 1217.

Thus the text of this bull seemed no longer to have anything new to say.
It contained enthusiastic expressions of satisfaction, a warm exhortation to
pursue the task without discouragement—'for the issue alone, and not the
struggle, confers the crown'. 'You are Preachers', it seemed to declare,
'well, be Preachers!' The mandate, the principal part of the bull, did not
express anything different. Composed of Pauline phrases—'each day, confirmed more deeply in the Lord, you should apply yourselves to announcing
the word of God, insisting in season and out of season and gloriously
fulfilling your function as ministers of the Gospel'[44]—it did not confer on
the brethren of Saint Romain the mission they already possessed; it affirmed
it as their essential and particular business. This was truly the confirmation
of Dominican preaching by the Pope, while the expressions used in the
prologue and the terms of enactment—'inwardly burning with the flame of
charity and spreading outwardly the odour of good renown', 'careful
physicians of the souls whom you make fruitful by your salutary eloquence',
'unconquered athletes of Christ . . . who magnanimously brandish the
sword of the word of God against the enemies of the faith . . .'—surrounded
this concession with a halo of truly exceptional praise.

The terms of enactment, however, granted the brethren two privileges of
value. The burden of their apostolic labour was assigned to them, 'in
remission of their sins';[45] this was to grant them a share in the privileges of
the crusade. This would seem only just, at a time when the first cleric who
came along, if he joined the crusade in the Albigeois and spent forty days
there, could obtain such an indulgence. Finally in its last phrase the bull
conferred on the Preachers the title of *speciales filios*, special sons of the Holy
See. Recently indeed, in the time of Alexander III, this title had signified
exemption from excommunication.[46] If it had lost this meaning, it at least
conferred the assurance that for the future the brethren would no longer be
able to incur excommunication except from the Pope or from a legate
a latere.[47] This was a security for evangelical preachers, so readily an object
of suspicion to the diocesan clergy in those difficult years.

The address of the bull, while it set down the name of the brethren, did not give that of the order. This was still being sought for. In the course of this year a charter of Fulk was to use with some insistence the expression, 'Brethren of the Preaching'.[48] The phrase was an old one; it had served from the beginning to designate the Preachers of the Midi.[49] In another charter of 1217, and frequently afterwards, the expression would be used 'Brethren of the Preaching of St Romain', of the Preaching of Toulouse, of Prouille, of Limoges.[50] The title 'Order of the Preaching' derived directly from this. It would be used in Spain in 1219.[51] Fulk would again use it in 1221.[52] The use of the name of Preachers, however, as early as 1217, in a pontifical bull, orientated the Curia towards quite a different title. At the beginning of the following year, Honorius III himself inscribed in his first letter of general recommendation of the order, the title, definitive at last, of 'Brethren of the Order of Preachers'.[53]

The fourth bull of Honorius (28th January) was addressed to Fulk of Toulouse.[54] The Pope restored his courage. He accepted neither his resignation nor the dismemberment of his diocese. Once more, it was not a mediocre cleric of scandalous life who was proposing to lay down his charge; he represented a force which it was necessary to maintain at the service of the Church. The Pope, however, did not content himself with verbal refusal and encouragement, since he had just taken a number of very wise steps with a view to giving fresh vigour to the evangelization of Toulouse.

Dominic was certainly there whilst he was drawing up the bull. The same day, indeed, the Pope wrote a letter to the capitouls of Toulouse and to their fellow-citizens, to recommend to them the Arnaud-Bernard hospice and its community of penitent women, which was in danger of perishing if help was not forthcoming quickly.[55]

While the Roman chancellery was dispatching these documents, there was considerable excitement in Rome over the arrival of new visitors. The thrust towards the east and the north of Europe had continued with its contrasting aspects of pure mission, migration of peoples and conquests that were sometimes cruel. Innocent had, however, endeavoured, through the sending of missions of Cistercians and Premonstratensians, to make the religious aspect predominate. In Livonia and Esthonia two bishoprics had been formed, whose bishops had been present at the Council of the Lateran.[56] So great, however, was the agitation in these frontier regions in the course of recent years, that whole provinces had not been able to make up their minds to participate in the great assembly. Despite Innocent's severe objurgations,[57] almost all the Churches of Scandinavia had defaulted. One single 'bishop of Dacia' for the provinces of Lund, Uppsala and Nidaros arrived.[58] It was little indeed.

In the middle of the month of January, the Scandinavians arrived in the eternal city, in the person if not of the metropolitan of Denmark and primate of Sweden, Archbishop Andrew Sunesen of Lund,[59] at least in that of an archiepiscopal and royal embassy which must have been fairly impressive.[60] A few days later Polish envoys arrived in their turn.[61] Then some Hungarians.[62] At the same time news flowed in about the preparations for the crusade in the east. On 23rd January, Cardinal Ugolino received from the Pope the mandate to organize the crusade in Tuscany and Lombardy.[63] On 25th, Andrew of Lund, a personal friend of Pope Honorius,[64] obtained his first privileges[65] which were to crown the granting or renewal of the titles of legate and of apostolic visitor of the Churches of Denmark and Sweden.[66] The archbishop was then preparing, at the same time as Scandinavian participation in the crusade in the east, a new campaign in Esthonia. All the discussions in the Curia were now of distant expeditions, missions to the north or in the east, the cruel reactions of the pagans against the newly baptized,[67] who also had to be protected against the enterprises of the Christian adventurers,[68] of convents which were installed or developing in the new lands of Christendom, of the dearth of priests and apostolic workers.[69] The pontificate of Honorius was already marked by this orientation towards the outer lands, with which for the future it would be deeply marked.

If we admit that Dominic, as is possible, had already known and desired to join the Archbishop of Lund in his missionary ministry on the occasion of his two great journeys to the north, we can imagine his emotion when he heard his new expedition spoken of. It is, however, not even necessary to invoke this plausible hypothesis to imagine that the Preacher was deeply moved on meeting the living witnesses of a Christianity in full development. For him their presence evoked unknown lands and distant peoples, still 'sitting in darkness, in the shadow of death'. Less than this was needed to fill him with compassion. He saw himself once more in Rome, eleven years earlier, at the side of Diego of Osma. The bishop was begging the Pope to receive his resignation so that he might be free to go and evangelize the pagans, with his companion. Eleven years—it seemed like a long parenthesis in the life of Brother Dominic. It was in some sense a dream, almost a nightmare. Eleven years of preaching, almost alone and without striking result, in the Albigeois, whereas in the north, where he first thought of going, bishoprics were rising up, nations were accepting baptism.

The latest news from Toulouse came back to his mind. A dull irritation surged up in him against these old Christian lands of the Narbonensis where the sowing of the seeds of the Gospel no longer produced harvests; against the Catharists, unconvertible despite their apostolic garb, obstinate in their poor philosophy and their sectarian spirit, 'enemies of the cross of Christ'; against the debauched and impious feudal lords; against the usurers and worldly townsmen. And to think of the Catholic preaching paralysed by the military and political enterprises with which it appeared to be inextricably linked, to say nothing of the moral laxity and temporal ambitions disguised under the cloak of zeal which in the end were choking it! Whilst he was wearing himself out over there, whilst here he was using up his energies in negotiations with the Curia to organize the apostolate in an ungrateful diocese, soul after soul was being lost on the confines of Christendom when he would have been able to win them to Jesus Christ in a less equivocal and more lasting manner than that of the German crusaders. Without renouncing the work begun, there was perhaps a possibility, as soon as that work was self-sufficient, of going to seek, under other skies, new souls who would not abuse grace.

Dominic certainly did not keep secret these thoughts which were tormenting him. He had entered into contact with many people—clerics, in particular, whom he tried to win over to his apostolic ideal and to his mission of salvation. He had no success with an archdeacon of Mâcon, Barthélemy de la Cluse, who went to confession to him.[70] His efforts with a young cleric of very noble origin who was then lodging with Cardinal Ugolino were differently rewarded. Guillaume de Montferrat was preparing to keep Lent in the city of the Popes.[71] He made the acquaintance of the founder on his frequent visits to Ugolino, was won to him by his attitude and began to love him. A close friendship was established between the two men. They talked about their own salvation and the salvation of others. Never had Guillaume met so spiritual a man among the many religious with whom he had spoken. Above all, he had never seen one consumed to the same extent with zeal for the salvation of the human race. Dominic, for his part, loved the young cleric and opened his heart to him in complete trust. One of the characteristics of his temperament that most drew men to him was this gentle confidence which turned him towards the young with their pure hearts and spontaneous generosity, He attracted them without imposing himself in any way, by sharing with them the very high ideal by which he was living himself. He confided in Guillaume about his longing for the pagan missions and an immediate ministry. Doubtless when he instituted his order, in preparing a generation of true apostles, he was indirectly working for the conversion of souls. Yet, if he could no longer preach the Gospel himself, his misfortune was great indeed. He wanted to begin again, and for all he was worth, to preach—especially to the pagans. Guillaume understood this perfectly. He wanted to do this too. He resolved to follow him. He was, however, fully aware of the insufficiency of his studies. Finally they decided together that Guillaume should go to Paris forthwith and that two years later, when he had studied theology and Dominic had sufficiently organized his order, they would both go off to convert the pagans who lived in Prussia and in the other regions of the north. About this time, it is said, the founder allowed his beard to grow, as was the custom for missionaries.[72]

The mystery of Rome was influencing St Dominic. Already, in Toulouse, he had begun to enlarge his horizon. After having devoted himself to preaching against the heretics for nine whole years, he had assigned to the company of Preachers a programme of preaching in its widest sense, preaching that should be positive rather than defensive, moral as well as doctrinal, and directed alike to the faithful and to the infidel. In 1216, however, he again confined the activity of the order to the field in which he had laboured without respite since 1206, the Narbonensis, the diocese of Toulouse itself, on which henceforward he concentrated his effort. In Rome he came to realize the universality of the Church and of her mission. The barriers were broken down. His vision overran the narrow viewpoint of the Albigeois and of its crises, and, moving to the centre of the Church, became universal. Doubtless in the course of the two journeys in Dacia and on the occasion of his first visit to Rome he had sensed this catholicity. The Council of the Lateran had given him an impressive manifestation of it, the sight of the Churches of East and West gathered in the person of their bishops around the Sovereign Pontiff to decide the universal rules and tasks of the Catholic world and to share experiences and resources in common. The 10th canon of the Council on preaching had expressed one of these universal tasks in terms which moved him at once. Dominic, however, was at that time deeply engaged in the body of the clergy of the Narbonensis, fully occupied by the cares of the affair of faith and peace in which in founding his Preachers he intended to collaborate. Now, at the side of Honorius who had confidence in him, in this centre to which the life of all the Churches, especially the Churches of the Christian Marches, came to derive new vitality and to bear it back again whence they came, he heard the Catholic call. He could not continue to be linked to a single diocese, to a province, to one sole problem. It was difficult to accept a field of action more limited than the field conferred by Jesus on the apostles—'all nations'.

Everything in Dominic's thought was focused around this point—the anxieties which drew his attention away from Toulouse, his missionary aspirations, his sense of universality. He had seen the Pope striving to attract some theologians from Paris to Toulouse to improve the Catholic preaching there. Why not reverse the position and move the brethren from Toulouse to Paris, and indeed all over Christendom? This intention was already half revealed in the advice to Guillaume de Montferrat. In 1216 there had been no question of this at all. A great change had thus come about in the heart of St Dominic.

Clearly in a soul as profound as his no conversation, no emotion produced by a chance meeting would have sufficed to bring about this change. He was a man who methodically pursued a long-term policy and for him to modify seriously the route he had traced out for himself and along which he had progressively travelled during the course of eleven years, he must have become aware by repeated meditations of a clear call from God. In the intervals of his audiences with the Pope and the cardinal, Dominic had full leisure to continue his life of charity and prayer in Rome. Certain documents show him to us visiting the prisoners, who in Rome were incarcerated in the towers of the ancient city wall,[73] and visiting those voluntary women prisoners known as recluses, devout women who had themselves shut up in narrow cells near to some holy place.[74] Wholly concerned with higher realities, they were disinterested and much sought after religious advisers and Dominic loved to consult them, after having conferred on them his priestly ministrations. Above all, he had ample time to continue his untiring prayers in the most moving sanctuaries of Christendom.

All those who approached him in the course of these years, whether strangers or his own brethren, were convinced that in his meditation he received special messages from God, true light as to the future or on the conduct to be followed.[75] Such faithfulness in keeping himself in the presence of his Creator would seem to invite God's intimacy. The religious men of the time, accustomed to set great store by the intuitions and images which they experienced during moments of semi-consciousness, half-way between true sleep and recollection, especially during prayer in the night hours, would have been astonished if the saint had not been favoured with visions of authentic prophecies. They had manifest proof of this when, on leaving his interior colloquies, Dominic announced decisions that were unexpected for all of them but for him unshakable, the success of which soon gave sanction to the inspiration.[76]

Thus in the Dominican thirteenth-century sources we meet with a good number of accounts of supernatural visions with which Dominic is said to have been favoured at the time of the order's confirmation. Not all these accounts are equal in value.[77] One only is solidly attested—the vision of the approaching end of Simon de Montfort, under the figure of a great fallen tree; it was no doubt this that decided Dominic to disperse his brethren.[78] There is one other account equally worthy of record and valuable.

Very little is known about the saint's spiritual history. His confidences were always rare. Up to his last hour a great modesty guarded the secret of his relations with God.[79] The account of this vision, however, entrusted perhaps to some discreet companion, would seem to reveal that, in the early months of 1217, his life saw the occurrence of a certain serious event in the interior life, a kind of mystical experience, an illumination which gave him the certainty of a new mission and opened to him vast horizons on which contemporary events and his later actions provide the commentary.

Constantino d'Orvieto relates this event in his inner life, the date of which he did not learn directly, but which he inserts with confidence in his legend at the only moment at which it could be placed, at the time when Dominic was asking for confirmation of the order from Rome.[80] After the fashion of medieval writers, the chronicler makes the interior

phenomenon objective and describes it under the form of an imaginary
vision.

> Whilst God's vassal, Dominic, was in Rome and was pouring out his prayers in
> the presence of God in the basilica of St Peter for the preservation and extension
> of the order which God's right hand was propagating by his care, the hand of God
> came upon him. He saw Peter and Paul, those princes full of glory, appear. The
> first, Peter, gave him the staff; Paul, the book; and both added—'Go and preach;
> for God hath chosen thee for this ministry'. Then in a flash it seemed to him that
> he saw his sons scattered throughout the world, going off two by two to preach
> to the people the word of God.

It is essential to grasp the symbolism of this vision, of which the second
part is of paramount importance. Peter and Paul symbolize the Roman
Church. The staff is the official insignia of God's messenger;[81] the book,
that of doctrine. Dominic understood that he must make his order coexten-
sive with the world and receive his mission direct from Rome. At the same
time he understood that he must separate preaching, more completely
than was possible in Toulouse, from the defence of the faith. Finally he
understood that the order given by the Council to all the bishops to attach
preachers to themselves was to open to his brethren all dioceses without
exception, and that the determination of the popes to enforce the application
of a canon which they had for so long been preparing would, if necessary,
force open these doors. Everything had prepared him for the understanding
of this. Only one final light was lacking. He obtained it from God in prayer.
And at Rome.[82]

Dominic's task was not ended. In the projects he confided to young
Guillaume de Montferrat, he was still giving himself two years to organize
his order,[83] for the work was not completed by the confirmation. What,
then, was Dominic discussing with the cardinal, who was heir to the
deceased Pope, collaborator of the present Pope and himself future Pope,
and finally special promoter of new religious orders? Clearly the transformation of his society, under the mandate of the Holy See, into a universal
order, as the mystic vision in the basilica of St Peter had required of him.
It was that which he would in point of fact carry out, with an astonishing
decisiveness, on his return to the Narbonensis, choosing Rome as his focal
point for the future, and as the pivots of his society of Preachers, Paris and
Bologna, the two intellectual centres of the Christian universe. Constantino
concluded the account we have just quoted with these words: 'that is why he
returned to Toulouse . . . gathered his brethren together and told them that
he had taken the resolution to disperse them all, despite their small number,
to different parts of the world; for he knew that if the good grain were
scattered it bore fruit, but that stored up, it rotted'.[84] We can recognize the
words of Honorius.[85]

Before leaving Rome to carry out his plans, Dominic obtained a final bull on 7th February.[86] At first glance the text is surprising. It is a short bull, in point of fact a *titulus*. It copies, in a less solemn framework, a paragraph of *Religiosam vitam*, that which protects the order against the instability of its members.[86A] No one can leave the order without the permission of his superior; one can only do so to enter a more austere order; no one can retain a fugitive religious. On comparing the two formulae, however, a new feature can be perceived. The earlier text said, 'after having made profession in your church'. The new text substituted 'monastery' for 'church'. The earlier document ran 'without the permission of the prior'. Now it was worded, 'without your permission as prior, my son, and that of your successors'. A new phrase at the same time puts a new power in the hands of Dominic. To sanction its authority, the order will be able to promulgate a sentence in due form and order against its defaulting sons and the religious of other orders who retain them unduly.

Thus the bull of 7th February provided Dominic with a new copy of an important clause of the great privilege—as if the founder, foreseeing the separation which would deprive him of the original, which was addressed to and was intended to remain at St Romain in Toulouse, wished at least to preserve in documentary form a provision which in his eyes was essential. The substitution of 'monastery' for 'church', which was to be reproduced in the reissue of the great privilege on 30th March, 1218,[87] was equally significant. To make profession in a church had a precise meaning in canonical institutions. It was to bind oneself by a vow of local stability, again insufficiently flexible, to the church building of stone and to its holy patron. Dominic had endeavoured to avoid this bond by eliminating the mention of the saint in the formula of profession; yet so strong was the general custom that the Preachers were to be named for a long time to come, despite the resistance of certain of their superiors, by the name of the patron of their conventual church.[88] People would speak of the brethren of St Romain, of St Nicholas, of St Jacques. The latter name would even become, up to the end of the eighteenth century under the form of 'Jacobin', the usual name of the Preachers of Paris and in France. There was no such inconvenience if one made profession in a monastery. The brethren no longer appeared bound to Dominic by their donation to the church of some particular saint, but by their profession in the community. They were becoming mobile in quite a different way. Above all, the new text, by recalling the personal powers of the founder in regard to his brethren, added still further to these powers. In these conditions the bull *Justis petentium* which the saint obtained from the Pope at the moment of leaving Rome, does not seem wholly insignificant. In its own way it prepared the decisive transformation of the order.

In the absence of any legislation on this point, the social constitution of the Preachers was again reduced to a single element—the direct bond of obedience of each brother to Dominic. That which constituted its flexibility might, however, become its weakness. The bolder Dominic's plans in January 1217 were, the more difficult were the task and sacrifice he sought to impose on each of his brethren-to-be, the more acute the temptations to become discouraged, and the more necessary the strengthening of the links of dependence on which the order hung. The bull *Justis petentium* demanded by the saint at the moment of departure is perhaps more eloquent than any of the documents as to the revolution which had taken place in his soul. Arriving in Rome with the intention of permanently settling his community of Preachers in the Albigeois, Dominic set out again with projects on a world-wide scale and the instruments necessary to carry them out.

He had no longer any reason to linger in Rome and he now returned to Provence. From the beginning of March he was again in Toulouse[89] and gathered his brethren in chapter. The brethren from Prouille whom he collected on the way were also there.[90] In the presence of the assembly, he communicated the letters from Rome—the confirmation, the letter of 21st January, so well adapted to give them courage, the title of 7th February which strengthened the cohesion of the brethren. We can imagine the joy and relief of the community. Did the founder then reveal his projects for the future? Perhaps not yet. There was no particular hurry about sending brethren to Paris; it would be necessary to wait for the summer and the approach of the beginning of the academic year on the feast of St Denis.

One detail, however, preoccupied the chapter. The property of the Prouille community in Limoux had once more been called in question by the monks of Saint Hilaire. A formula of settlement elaborated by Maître Thédise, Bishop of Agde, was adopted. A few days later, on Friday, 31st March,[91] this settlement was signed by Dominic and William Claret for the one part, and by Alboin, Abbot of St Hilaire, and Prior Anselm of the other part; the Abbot of St Michel de la Cluse et de St Salitor, visitor of the abbey of Saint Hilaire, which depended on his own house, subscribed the document.[92]

After his return to Provence, Dominic could see that the political situation, despite its fluctuations, was continually deteriorating.[93] It was no longer a question now of Catharists or Catholics. The Midi was defending its political independence against the north and protecting itself against new compromises with the heretics. As to Simon, he defended his conquered possessions, strong in his title as crusader. The line of the Rhône indeed was intersected by the towns handed to Raymond VII—Marseilles, Arles, Saint Sernin (which would later be Pont Saint Esprit), Beaucaire and Tarascon, Avignon. The bridges were in the hands of de Montfort's adversaries. Bertrand, the legate, was blocked in Orange, to the east of the Rhône. When Simon, who had been fighting all the winter to the south-west of Toulouse, came to join him, the legate had to go back as far as Viviers to find a passage.

De Montfort forced the crossing of the Rhône. For him the whole summer was to pass in re-establishing the situation in eastern Provence. His absence, however, was taken advantage of in the west. Now it was in Toulouse that the storm was gathering. Whilst the de Montfort ladies took refuge in the castle of Narbonne, plots were being hatched in the city. Raymond VI had regrouped his followers in Aragon. The nobles of that country were burning to avenge the death of their king, Pedro II, while the Aragonese and Catalan mercenaries were ready to provide new contingents.

On 13th September, 1217, taking advantage of a 'miraculous' mist,[94] Raymond VI came out from his advance post and, crossing the Garonne at the ford of the Bazacle mill, plunged into an attack upon his capital. From that moment everything was lost. The immediate thrusts of Guy or d'Amaury de Montfort, the lightning return of Simon, the most pressing, the fiercest attacks, could not make the city yield, despite the fact that it was demolished. Soon the moats were dug out, the defences were taken over; the mangonels and the perriers flung their blocks of stone. The tragedy of Toulouse was played out to the bitter end; the citizens stood firm in a struggle in which— Simon and the legate did not disguise the fact—the final destruction of the city was intended. One day a missile, flung by a perrier thrower 'hit the mark'. Struck on his iron helmet, Simon collapsed 'bloodstained and black'.[95] A few weeks later Amaury, the heir, raised the siege. Never again would Toulouse belong to the de Montfort family.

Long before this Dominic and his religious had left the town. Warned by his brethren and friends in Toulouse, Dominic was able to follow the premonitory symptoms of the insurrection in men's minds. He remembered 1211 when the convents, following the clergy carrying the Blessed Sacrament, abandoned the city which remained closed to them afterwards for nearly four years. The same painful situation might easily recur. In any event a long lasting revolt would confine all the brethren to Toulouse and separate them from their diocesan field of action. Why then wait until the last moment? The time had come to carry out the plans conceived in Rome and to extend the order. The decisive scene took place at the end of the spring, perhaps at Pentecost (14th May).[96] All the brethren summoned to St Romain, were met in chapter. Dominic declared to them that he had taken the resolution to send them throughout the world, despite their small number; they would no longer all live together, for the future, in the cloister which was scarcely finished. Each one was astonished at the unexpected decision, which seemed to them to have been taken so rapidly. Dominic, however, appealed to his authority, to which his sanctity gave additional prestige. The majority acquiesced easily enough. Full of hope, they already saw in imagination the happy issue of this decision.[97] All, however, were not in agreement.

Dominic's friends and protectors were even more disconcerted. He had been able to join de Montfort in May.[98] Fulk of Toulouse, Arnaud de Narbonne and other prelates approached in turn, were in agreement with the Count that they would resist with all their power a project which seemed to them fatal to the order itself as well as to its ministry in Toulouse.[99] Dominic asked the brethren that they should put fear aside, telling them that all would succeed. To the prelates, to the Count, as to the brethren, he repeated these words which throw some light on his character: 'Leave me alone; I know what I am doing.'[100]

On 15th August,[101] 1217, the feast of the Assumption, the Preachers met again for the last time. It was perhaps at St Romain of Toulouse,[102] where all those who were going away were gathered, or at Prouille, in accordance with a fairly weighty tradition.[103] We cannot be quite certain. The time to scatter the seed had come. Before the community dispersed, Dominic made them elect a superior. The choice fell on Matthew of France,[104] who would henceforth bear in Paris, up to 1220, the title of Abbot of St Romain.[105] We may wonder what was the reason for this title, which would not be continued in the order, and for this election.

Jordan of Saxony, who knew Matthew under the title of abbot, thought that it already signified the authority of the superior-general who would soon be called master of the order.[106] This is not quite correct. The superior-general was Dominic, to whom all the brethren were linked by their obedience. He would remain superior-general and would be the first to bear the title of master of the order. 'Abbot' had not this significance. In the traditions of the canons of France, it designated the superior of a particular chapter and signified the same thing as prior in the regions of the south.[107] In 1217, Matthew was merely elected Prior of St Romain, in conformity with the provisions of the privilege of confirmation.[108] The step was natural and did not signify that Dominic had abandoned the supreme authority or was preparing to do so.[109] On the contrary he affirmed this authority by setting up between his person and the general body of the brethren, a local superior.[110]

Until further orders, however, the one juridical community of the brethren would remain the convent of St Romain. The dispersion would not dissolve it. Legally, Matthew would thus remain abbot of all the Preachers.[111] If Dominic were to disappear, the brethren, scattered throughout the Church, would nevertheless remain united under the authority of Matthew. Without being in any sense Dominic's vicar, since he had not been invested with the powers for this, he was as it were a provisional heir, a leader in the case of his death. We do not know what to admire most in the founder, the boldness of his decisions or their juridical strength. These two characteristics, however, are really linked.

Dominic looked upon his brethren, met together for the last time. He was moved. He loved his community. It was true he was not losing them for ever. He would soon see them again one after another in the course of his visits to wherever they were dispersed. But they would no longer be quite what they were now, the first loyal and brotherly band. They would be surrounded by new faces. Such and such among them would have become prior, founder, provincial, the mainspring of a whole region. Another would have lost the initial generosity of his religious life. There would perhaps be dramatic gaps in the little flock.

For Dominic's first brethren were not all outstanding men. In general they were simple and for the most part without much learning.[112] There were some who were afraid of sacrifices; others who lost their footing in material difficulties. The special genius of a founder, however, is to bring the best out of all those who come under his influence. Dominic made apostles of mediocre men of good will. This was because he placed his trust in the man each of them might become and above all in the grace with which God would inspire them and in the Providence which was guiding them. He trained them by example. He raised them to the supernatural plane by prayer. Then he launched them into full activity, ready to correct them severely, but not without charity, in their false steps or their discourage-ment. One has the right to be weak, but not faint-hearted when it is a matter of saving souls. 'Full of confidence in God, he sent out even the least skilful to preach', relates John of Navarre. ' "Go with assurance", he said, "because the Lord will give you the gift of the divine word. He will be with you and nothing will be wanting to you." They went away and everything happened as he had told them.'[113]

Later, Peter Seila would often relate to the young religious whom he received into the order, how Dominic sent him to found a convent. 'He put forward the difficulty of his ignorance, his lack of books, for he only possessed a single notebook of the homilies of the blessed Gregory. "Go, son", the Father answered him, "go with confidence; twice a day I will take you with me before God. Do not doubt; you will gain many souls to God and will bear much fruit." '[114]

The most important group was destined for Paris, the university city, capital of theological thought. They were seven, split into two sections.[115] The first comprised, with Matthew of France, Friar Bertrand, Friar John of Navarre and Friar Lawrence the Englishman.[116] Matthew of France[117] was the chief of the entire band. A native of that part of the Ile de France from which the principal crusaders and the monks of Vaux-de-Cernai had come, he had recently come to the Midi with de Montfort, who made him prior of the new chapter of Castres. He was a tested churchman, who would replace Dominic among the group of brethren. He was charged with the responsi-bility of 'making known the order' in France, with founding convents and preaching with his brethren. John of Navarre and Lawrence the Englishman were still young and ill-instructed. They were sent to Paris especially for their studies.[118] Lawrence[119] was a contemplative. In the course of the journey he received light, which the future would confirm, on the installation of the brethren in Paris. John of Navarre,[120] a native of Saint Jean Pied-de-Port, the senior of the brethren who gave evidence at the canonization process, was the *enfant terrible* of the band. Impulsive, capable of gestures of generosity but equally of revolt and discouragement, all things considered, very obstinate, he was to cause the founder many a disappointment. He loved Dominic, however, and admired him. Deeply sincere and a realist, he did not hide either his own faults or the sanctity of his leader. And eventually he learnt to serve as a true Preacher. Bertrand of Garrigo[121] was just the opposite. He pursued his life of apostolic austerity with singlemindedness. A great servant of God and the order, he was to be the first provincial of Provence.

A second group also left for Paris. It was led by Friar Mames,[122] the contemplative, the half-brother of Dominic, whom he had joined, coming from Spain to do so. He was accompanied by Friar Miguel de Cabra,[123] a noble Castilian who, going later to Catalonia, became confessor to King Jaime I, and would share in the expeditions to Majorca and Valencia, where he was to found a convent of Preachers. Learned and a good theologian, he would be, it was said, the first professor of his brethren in Paris. Friar Odier,[124] a lay-brother, accompanied the two Spaniards, whose vitality proved to be greatly superior to that of the first group. Leaving at the same time as the other group of friars, they arrived in Paris on 12th September. The other four only reached the city three weeks later.

Dominic did not forget his own country. He sent four of the brethren to Spain. Friar Pedro de Madrid[125] and Friar Gómez[126] met with good success. They preached with fervour and made the order illustrious. In the following year Dominic's visit to the parts where they had already been working made the foundation of convents of Preachers possible.[127] The other part of the team, Friar Dominic the Spaniard[128] and Friar Miguel d'Ucero,[129] was less brilliant. Theirs was not the temperament of founders. They were not, however, lacking in generosity. Jordan of Saxony and Etienne de Bourbon had edifying things to relate of the first of these two brethren. 'He was a man of exceptional humility, of little knowledge but magnificent virtue.'[130] His naivety suggested to certain unkind persons the idea of drawing him into a trap, with the complicity of a courtesan. His 'magnificent' virtue alone drew him out of this difficult situation, to the benefit of his ministry, moreover, for he converted her. Meeting one day at St Antoine de Paris, doubtless on the occasion of a general chapter, the young Petronilla de Montfort whom the founder had baptized in 1211 near Fanjeaux, he obliged her, not without severity, to adopt a more modest head-dress.[131] He was perhaps tactless. It is a fact that neither he nor his companion would succeed. The pair became discouraged and soon left

Spain, to shelter themselves once more under the shadow of their chief.[132] It is possible that both had been colleagues of Dominic in the chapter of Osma.[133] Their canonical life had given them an insufficient preparation to become Preachers.

St Romain was not abandoned. It was, however, assigned to brethren who were natives of Toulouse. The nationalistic character of the insurrection made this step desirable. The privileges they had received enabled the brethren to remain and continue their religious life even in the case of interdict. Peter Seila, who may be said to have received the order rather than the order receiving him, for it was lodged in his house,[134] was not to leave to make a foundation in Toulouse until two years later. He would come back to Toulouse as prior and inquisitor. Friar Thomas,[135] who had received a special gift of preaching from God, remained with him, and Friar Guillaume also, if he were not dead or had not left the order. Protected by his friends in Toulouse and by the authorities of the town, who were careful no longer to give any religious pretext to the action of their adversaries, St Romain passed safely through the dramatic events in the Midi until the day in 1230 when the Preachers, abandoning their cradle which had now become too small, would let it pass out of the order, without in any way allowing themselves to be moved by so many cherished memories.[136]

Prouille kept its first religious, of whom Friar Noël was superior and Friar William Claret administrator. The house was already too firmly rooted for the war, when it began again, really to put it in danger. The neighbourhood, moreover, remained calm for some time longer.

Such a separation was not effected without suffering or anxiety. The replies Dominic made to the brethren's hesitation,[137] and even certain direct information, enable us to estimate the gravity of this trouble. Several of the brethren were anxious about the order's future. They doubted themselves, if not Dominic. Only the founder's supernatural firmness gave them strength. 'I know what I am doing.' What made the master's strength was that his decisions were never in any sense taken at the level of daily events. They came from a deeper source, were long in forming and were linked with a whole network of facts and intentions which controlled each other. Thus they were irrevocable. John of Navarre, however, resisted almost to the point of rebellion. It was against his will that he was being sent. He was not willing to set off in such conditions. He afterwards related to Etienne de Salagnac, from whom our account of the incident is derived,[138] the painful scene he then made in the presence of his founder.

When our father St Dominic sent him, as has been said, with the Brother Lawrence of whom we have spoken, John demanded something for his expenses, a provision for the journey. The saint did not want to give him this. He exhorted him to go on his journey like the disciples of Jesus Christ, without carrying gold or silver. *It is for you, his chosen servants, to fear the Lord; those who fear Him never go wanting* (Ps. XXXIII, 10). John, however, would not give in; on the contrary, he directly refused his obedience to what the saint had said. When the holy and loving father saw the unhappy man's disobedience, he threw himself at his feet, wept and lamented over this unfortunate friar who would not weep over himself, and finally gave orders that they should give him twelve pence merely as provision for the journey as far as Paris.

Salagnac saw in the revolt of John of Navarre real disobedience. It would be so in the light of later legislation but not in that of the time. The brother's position is much more subtle. John took advantage of a real juridical difficulty to embarrass his leader and marked his opposition in a way that was certainly very cruel for the founder.

The itinerant mendicity of the Preachers was in no sense optional at this date, and formed as essential a part of the programme of the brethren as it did of Dominic himself. The document which imposed this, however, was the charter of the Preaching of Toulouse, the text of 1215. It was an epis-copal charter and was valid only for the diocese. Dominic, as has been seen, had not had this provision confirmed by Rome. He reserved the legislation on poverty for a later stage.

Now in the Paris towards which the first seven Preachers were making their way and indeed in the whole of France, obligatory prescriptions had been in existence for the Canons Regular since 1213. They imposed on the superior of a chapter or religious house, under a formal precept, each time they sent one of their religious on a journey, 'to be careful to see that they provided him in sufficient quantity with the horses and provision for the expenses of the journey which were indispensable for the canon, as for his acolytes; for it would be a disgrace for the Lord and for the category of this religious that he should be constrained to beg'.[139]

The fluidity of the legislation might present advantages in the transition period. It was not without its disadvantages. In the face of the decisions of a provincial council sanctioned by a legate of the Pope, Dominic could not appeal to the authority of the diocesan charter of Toulouse. He could not even appeal to the authority which came to him from the profession of obedience. All that remained to him was his moral authority. He humbled himself, he entreated, he wept. His emotion was all the more intense, since John's action raised the question of the future loyalty of the Preachers of Paris. There was a danger that, enlarging on the example given by John of Navarre, they might make the statutes of the synod of Paris the basis of their legislation as canons and Preachers and leave aside the Gospel pattern of their master inscribed in Fulk's charter.

Dominic, however, had to give way. He had to give John the twelve pence. He felt them burn his fingers like the thirty pence of Judas. He was, however, reassured by the attitude of the other six brethren assigned to

Paris. Their loyalty was sufficient indication of the soundness of the evangelical tradition of the Preachers. In the years that followed, however, Matthew of France would turn to the legislation of the Parisian synod for justification for departing from this tradition in certain particular cases.[140] The idea of dispensation, it has been said, is at the root of Dominic's legislative ideas. Not until the important general chapter of 1228 would it be laid down clearly what could or ought to be dispensed and what, in the programme of the Preachers, could not be abrogated.[141]

The last of the itinerant brethren has disappeared from sight along the high road and Dominic returns to the convent. Small as it is, how large and empty the cloister of St Romain now seems. The warm fraternal atmosphere has gone. So has the motionless presence of the brethren, impressive in its silence, as they worked in their cells; and the return from the ministry each evening of the preachers who asked his blessing; and the liturgical prayer, in which Dominic, going from one choir to the other, encouraged the brethren in their chanting. The founder sometimes wondered if he had not perhaps undermined or destroyed his work by this dispersion.

Dominic drove away these images of discouragement. He took advantage of his last hours in the city to give himself to a more intense apostolate and to finish putting the affairs of St Romain in order. On 11th September, he was to meet Fulk at Castelnaudary to settle a difficulty in the collection of the sixth part of the tithes.[142] Two days later, he learnt of the insurrection of Toulouse. After that time he was cut off from his sons who were unable to leave the city.

He remained in the neighbourhood, however, for two months more. On 13th December, he obtained a guarantee from Simon de Montfort for the property of Prouille, and the revenues of St Romain in Carcassès and the Agenais.[143] It was a farewell. The interview was dramatic for them both. Dominic was plunging his person and his order into the unknown. Simon was at the end of his strength. He was no longer the bold, indefatigable and ever victorious warrior of the early days, nor the ambitious and triumphant leader of 1214; he remained merely the loyal soldier, a noble, in short, who really believed he was putting his sword at the disposal of Christian truth and morals. It seemed to him that God was abandoning him. His troops, like his resources, were dissipated. His most desperate attacks failed one after the other. After nine years of daily battles, each day of which was spent in the saddle, his body was exhausted. The cruel ironies of the legate, who reproached him for being ignorant and cowardly, crushed his pride without succeeding in spurring him on to fresh efforts. It is said that he asked God to give him peace with death.[144] Dominic suffered in his friendship for the Count. He knew that he would not see him again.

In the middle of December 1217, for the fourth time, he went down to Rome.

CHAPTER XIII

FROM ROME TO MADRID

IKE a good husbandman, Dominic had sown the seed of the Preachers. Now it was essential that the harvest should come to fruition and increase. In the meantime the founder did not remain inactive. He journeyed to the centre of the Church to obtain the support of the Pope. He was already gathering together other fruitful seed and was preparing other fields with a view to sowing his grain there.

Nothing is known of his journey. Having set out from the neighbourhood of Toulouse after 13th December,[1] he reached Rome a little before 11th February.[2] Two months—double the time necessary for the journey. It is possible that he made a détour and lingered en route. A chronicler somewhat late in date, and of no great reputation, mentions his passing through Milan, another, a visit to Bologna.[3] The second piece of information would corroborate the first. It is, indeed, very plausible. Bologna was the second intellectual centre of Christendom;[4] the universal centre of canon law, as it was of Roman law. On account of the thousand and more students the town had gathered together,[5] the influence of its masters in the religious and political life of the Catholic nations, the echo of its doctrines in the life of the Church, finally through its geographical position between the Empire and the Pontifical States, turned towards Germany and Central Europe as much as towards France and the remainder of the West, Bologna could not but attract Dominic. He had sent the most important group of his sons to the university of Paris—*the* theological centre—to study and to make the order known. Just when anxiety about recruitment was coming to the forefront of the matters that preoccupied him, he came to Bologna, rather than any other place, to seek for new brethren. There, more than anywhere else, young clerics were in danger of losing their generosity and wrapping themselves round with selfish and sterile self-interest. The study of Law threw open to them the most lucrative careers in the Church and even in the world. To win them over to theology and the apostolate was to give them back to their vocation and to the urgent tasks of the hour.

Adjoining the small church of Santa Maria di Mascarella, on the northern edge of the city, a hospice had been opened for Spanish pilgrims.[6] It was run by men from Navarre, canons of Roncesvalles. If Dominic's companions were shortly afterwards seen to take up residence with them, this was because their master had begun by residing there thus paving the way for their friendly reception among his compatriots. It would even seem that he won over a certain recruit there, who was quickly formed and linked to the order by profession. A certain Richard the elder figures from the outset as superior of the Preachers of Bologna;[7] he does not seem to have come from elsewhere and Dominic must thus have recruited him from Bologna itself, perhaps with a companion. Then, leaving this small nucleus as a touchstone and promising to send reinforcements soon, the founder set off again and reached Rome.

Immediately on arrival he saw the Pope. Fourteen months earlier, when he was still envisaging establishing himself firmly in the neighbourhood of Toulouse, the support he then asked from the head of the Church consisted of a series of confirmations—of his order, of his preaching, of his privileges. Now that his sons were setting forth to preach on the great highroads and were presenting themselves as unknown men—particularly under suspicion at this time, for they had the external appearance of apostolic preachers—a letter of recommendation from the Sovereign Pontiff would be an invaluable help to them in overcoming or surmounting initial mistrust. Honorius was perfectly ready to draw up such a letter. It was issued by the chancellery on 11th February.[8]

This was the first of a series of bulls, the initial drop of moisture of a veritable shower of recommendations which would in future emanate from the Curia and during three years penetrate to every corner of Europe where the Friars Preachers made their appearance.[9] After seven centuries, after the destruction or the falling into oblivion of a large number of texts belonging to the archives, even today more than thirty copies of such recommendations issued by the Pope between 1218 and 1221 can be found in different places.

One fact emphasizes the principal share of Dominic in this shower of recommendations—he was scarcely dead, in the middle of 1221, when it ceased entirely until the end of the pontificate of Honorius. Clearly the initiative came from the founder, not from the Pope. Having elicited this series of recommendations himself, Dominic showed considerable skill in maintaining and directing it. It was not continuous but, during the course of these three years, followed the rhythm of the preacher's action. It was to hand at each period of intense creative activity, on the morrow of the new dispersions which were the seeding-grounds of convents—at the beginning of 1218, the end of 1219, the first part of 1221. On the other hand it ceased almost entirely in 1220, the year devoted by Dominic to the organization and strengthening of what he had just established.

Dominic, however, was not alone. In 1218, as at the end of 1219 and beginning of 1221, he once more found Cardinal Ugolino at the Curia. The part played by the Cardinal at the time of the confirmation is not the only reason which suggests his intervention. One fact enables us to establish it beyond doubt. Scarcely had Ugolino, whose influence seemed to suffer a decline after the death of the founder, succeeded Honorius III under the name of Gregory IX (1227), when he resumed the distribution of bulls of recommendation which had ceased for the last six years. To do this, he utilized the formula obtained by St Dominic a few months before his death. In 1218, he was almost at the summit of his prestige.[10] The former Pope had concentrated his limited energy on the crusade and the missions, but Ugolino, the most conspicuous among Innocent's former cardinals, carried on his shoulders the weight and burden of the important affairs of the previous reign, problems of high politics, problems of faith and peace, the problem of the religious orders. His spiritual sensitiveness, prompt to be moved in the presence of the evangelical simplicity of St Francis, attached itself with a sort of nostalgic regret to the generosity of St Dominic, so very like that of the apostles.[11]

He saw in the order which the founder had built up with a master hand, the providential instrument of that orthodox learned and reforming preaching, the urgency of which he recognized as Innocent III did. He thus again brought the Preacher into touch with the Pontiff and supported him with all his credit. He helped him to prepare the text of the bull by the formulation which he gave to the request.

The bull was addressed under the form of an 'apostolic pastoral letter' to the whole of the prelates of the Church. It described the brethren under the name coveted since 1215, and for the future to be definitive, of 'brethren of the Order of Preachers'. It described in two phrases their useful ministry and their religious life, which, the Pope thought, was pleasing to God. They set the word of God before all men (he said) and did so gratuitously, for they had no other ambition but the profit of souls and followed the Lord alone, proud of the title of poverty. In his name and the name of the apostolic see, the Pope recommended them to all the prelates, to whom he addressed an insistent command to support them in their praiseworthy design and to assist them in their daily needs.

Dominic had the Pope's recommendation registered forthwith in the books of the Curia.[12] He asked for and obtained a certified copy sealed with lead on hempen cord. At the first opportunity he transmitted this to the brethren in Paris. In the following year, the brethren who left Paris to found the convent of Poitiers took this bull with them. It is still in that city, in the archives of the department of Vienne.

The founder could congratulate himself on such a document. A long stretch of road had been traversed since 1215. All they had then desired was now granted and recommended by the Pope. But it would be naïve to think that the bishops would give an immediate welcome to these genuine preachers who gave their services freely, and support these poor volunteers who were offering themselves as their collaborators. It was not long before Dominic received news from Paris, from Toulouse and from Spain, that was not encouraging.

One day, two religious exhausted from their long tramp, had just rejoined Dominic at the hospice where he was lodging.[13] He could not dissimulate his somewhat sorrowful surprise, for indeed he did not expect to see them. They were two Preachers—two Castilians, his old companion, Friar Dominic of Spain, and Friar Miguel de Ucero. He had recently sent them in the hope of reaping rich harvests in Spain. They came to admit their failure and discouragement. Whereas Friar Gómez and Friar Pedro of Madrid were meeting with abundant success, they had reaped nothing in Spain. It was difficult to be a prophet in one's own country! The intellectual mediocrity of Friar Dominic was scarcely compensated for by Friar Miguel. Still insufficiently adapted for this life of heroic initiative, they had not been successful in their preaching and had perhaps experienced insults in their begging. They had soon reached breaking-point and, being humble, had judged that their only resource was to return to the founder.

Dominic understood men too well to waste time pitying or consoling them. It would not do for them to remain in this state of frustration for a single moment. They must set off again and do better in some other place. There was nothing for them to do in Rome, where he had no convent and where he did not intend to stay permanently. He was at the centre of the Church only to promote and direct the first expansion of the order, backed by the Pope's authority, but he was ready to leave his observation post as soon as he had seen the effect of the initial measures. So the founder sent the two brethren to Bologna, to the small nucleus of friars whom he had recently left at Santa Maria di Mascarella. They could remain there; he would not be long in joining them.[14] Somewhat bewildered, Friar Miguel took up his staff again and set out, accompanied by Friar Dominic.

About the month of April, two other brethren arrived from Paris.[15] These Dominic expected, at least the elder one, Friar Bertrand.[16] His companion, John of Navarre, was, according to instructions, to continue studying theology in Paris and not to tramp the roads.[17] Doubtless he had again been creating difficulties, and this had decided Matthew of France to provide him with a little breathing-space by assigning him to Friar Bertrand as *socius*.

The latter came to render account of the arrival and installation of the brethren in Paris. Dominic, it will be remembered, had sent them off in two parties.[18] The group of Spanish friars had moved more quickly than the others. Leaving shortly after 15th August, they had entered the capital on 12th September. The others, headed by the superior, abbot Matthew of France, had followed only after three weeks. The academic year was about to begin once more at the university. Time was pressing. They had dealt with the most urgent problem and rented[19] a poor house by the side of the hospital of Notre Dame, opposite the gates of the archbishop's residence. The brethren were thus now lodged in the heart of the capital, on the Île de la Cité opposite the cloister of Notre Dame where the oldest school of the Faculty of theology held session.

Yet it was a difficult position for the sons of St Dominic—to be forced to rent their lodging and consequently to beg for the rent, since they had nothing of their own. This fact alone indicates the kind of welcome which the city of the King of France gave to them. During the eight months they had actually been there, no one had yet offered these poor religious hospitality. It was clearly thought that the canons of St Romain of Toulouse[20] who had come to study, could not be lacking in resources. It was not for public charity but for their house in Toulouse to supply them with what was necessary, in conformity with the decisions of the recent synod of Paris.[21] It was 'a disgrace for the Lord and for their profession that they should be thus constrained to beg'. God was for all, but each one in the city was for himself. Moreover the scarcity of lodgings in Paris was assuming alarming proportions and in the city the invading flood of partially starving students increased daily.[22]

The group of Preachers, however, was not a haphazard collection of needy men. Their voluntary poverty was the basis of their ministry of the evangelical message. It was this principle that did not meet with universal acceptance. It had about it a flavour of the Waldenses, the Catharists, those heresies of the south . . . like the brethren. Moreover, it is abundantly clear that among those who might be expected to make full use of their help, the ministry of the Preachers had excited no greater interest than had their poverty. The clergy of Paris, strong in their orthodoxy of which the presence of the university was a guarantee, did not in general experience the need of assistance.[23] The friendships which Matthew of France had kept up with several of the clergy, especially with the university men,[24] were not sufficient to awaken an interest of any significance at all in the brethren of St Romain. And then scarcely any of the brethren—Castilians, men of Languedoc, even Englishmen—knew anything of the speech of the île de France. Their influence was limited to those who could be reached by the language of the Church, the scholastic milieu of the Latin quarter.

Yet the bull of recommendation dispatched on 11th February had certainly reached the bishop, Pierre de Nemours. Although he was the one to whom it was chiefly addressed, he seemed scarcely impressed at all by the mandates of the Sovereign Pontiff. He was preoccupied by other cares. He was preparing to leave for the crusade in the East, where, moreover, he was to lose his life in the course of the siege of Damietta.[25] In June 1218, a very few days before his departure, he made his will. The text, which is still extant,[26] bequeathed legacies to numerous convents in Paris and the provinces, to the canons of the Cathedral, to various hotêls-Dieu. Nowhere was there a mention of the Preachers or brethren of St Romain. Yet this was surely the moment to think of the protégés of the Pope. If he forgot them in this way and left Paris, others were not likely to know of their presence. Dominic, in Toulouse, known to everyone, backed by the Count, the bishop and the legate, had had to wait a year and a half to obtain a chapel; Matthew of France and his brethren, almost an unknown quantity if not objects of suspicion to those who thought themselves the models of orthodoxy, found themselves in anything but a comfortable position in Paris.

Other news, more mixed in character, at last arrived from the Midi. If Prouille was pursuing its regular life without difficulties and even saw its patrimony further increased,[27] this was not the case in Toulouse. The siege of the town continued, increasingly relentless. The brethren, unable to leave the city, did not allow themselves to be considered bad citizens and stood firm. Nobody would later reproach them for having abandoned the place, as a good number of townsmen had done from the very beginning of the revolt. St Romain would be neither confiscated nor sold by auction with the property of those who had fled.[28] Their position, however, was becoming difficult. In the besieged city, their preaching carried no weight with a population which was struggling for its very existence against a papal legate and filled with hatred for all the crusaders. Moreover, the brethren's Catholic opposition to Raymond VI could scarcely be disguised. The position of Peter Seila was particularly delicate. Recently bound through his family and his own person to the house of the Count de Montfort, he had now become his adversary.[29] There was reason to fear that someone might wreak vengeance on him.

Dominic's reaction was immediate. He had already on 30th March had the privilege of confirmation of the order drawn up in the name of the prior and the brethren of the monastery of Prouille.[30] The text of the document was identical with that of the privilege granted on 22nd December, 1216 to the prior and brethren of St Romain of Toulouse. There was only one change—the word 'monastery' was substituted for the word 'church'.[31] Dominic had already effected this substitution in the bull of 7th February, 1217.[32] It obviated the necessity of tying down his canon-preachers to a definite sanctuary. The property confirmed was, or very nearly so, that which already appeared in the *titulus* of 8th October, 1216. Thus the masculine section of the house of Prouille was confirmed as a community of Preachers and received its privileges accordingly. The document established its independence in regard to the community of St Romain, of which the brethren of Prouille had legally formed part since 1216.[33] Should St Romain come to disappear before any other convent was founded, in Paris or elsewhere, the flame of the order would not for that reason be extinguished; it would continue burning in a legally constituted community, the Preaching of the monastery of Sainte Marie de Prouille.[34]

On 26th April Dominic had a new issue registered of the bull of recommendation.[35] A phrase of primary importance was added to the earlier letter, at the head of the terms of enactment. The first duty that the Pope imposed on the prelates of the Church in relation to the Preachers was 'with kindness to admit the brethren to exercise the office of preacher, to which they have been assigned'. The Pope understood the position exactly, and this clause would never disappear from the later bulls.[36] The text inscribed in the registers of the Curia mentions three brethren of the Order of Preachers whose initials alone are given—P., T., R.[37] If we take up the list of the brethren at the time of the dispersion, little different from the list in April 1218, one single reading is possible and must be accepted— Peter Seila, Thomas of Toulouse, Raymond de Fauga, the three principal brethren of Toulouse. Dispatched in one single, or in three distinct certified copies, the bull of 26th April paved the way for an eventual dispersion of the house of St Romain. Whatever might happen, the future was safeguarded. Peter Seila, in fact, would not be long before taking the road to Paris, where Dominic would meet him again the following year. Raymond de Fauga, who remained in Toulouse, was to go off in 1220 to found the convent of Montpellier.[38] He would later become Bishop of Toulouse.

A further certified copy of the bull was addressed that very day to the bishops of Spain. Over in Spain Friars Gómez and Pedro of Madrid were in no need for the moment of such a document. 'They are sowing the word of God in this place and that,' said Jordan of Saxony, 'and are gathering abundant fruit.'[39] Thus the clergy of the provinces they passed through had understood their mission and could make use of it. Dominic, moreover, was preparing to join them, as will be seen. This bull was to help the first foundations there, and, in fact, it led to the foundation of the convent of Salamanca, in whose collection of archives it formed the first document.[40]

Something must now be done for the brethren in Paris. Dominic had an audience at the Vatican.[41] Shortly afterwards, an insistent letter was dispatched by Honorius III to the university of Paris.[42] Next to the bishop, indeed, the corporation of the masters and students of Paris constituted a most important and powerful ecclesiastical body. It had, moreover, no reason for refusing anything to the Pope, who had confirmed it, reformed it and protected it in its independence. It had a particular responsibility towards the Preachers, who were students of the university. The Pope thus earnestly begged the university to procure a lodging for these poor religious in one of the hospices which the corporation was beginning to receive from donors in favour of poor students, an earnest of the future colleges.

Finally there was Bologna. Dominic had sent Friars Bertrand and John of Navarre there. It was now the end of April.[43] He doubtless gave them also a copy of the second bull. After the departure of the two Preachers, his ministry brought him fresh recruits. One of them was a lay-brother whose name we do not know. The other was called Christian. It seems indeed that he should be identified with the Cistercian brother who would later be one of the founders of Cologne.[44] After listening to Dominic, he desired to become a Preacher. This was not easy. The Order of Cîteaux in its extreme austerity was not considered an order from which one could easily depart, for at that time the passing from one order to another was only possible if the subject entered a more austere order. Moreover profession in the order was defended by strict privileges. The Preachers themselves had had to inscribe in their first constitutions a prohibition against receiving Cistercians. They had made the reservation, however, of any intervention by the Pope,[45] and it was this that set Friar Christian free from his Cistercian engagement. With the lay-brother, Dominic sent him to enlarge the group in Bologna.[46]

Despite his great longing, Dominic still had to wait to join them for another companion, whom he had just persuaded to leave everything to become a Preacher. This was the most remarkable of all his conquests for the apostolic work and the history of it was clearly providential.

While the founder was concerned with the promotion of his order with the support of the Sovereign Pontiff, he did not in effect remain idle. A few audiences, visits to the chancellery, conversations with Ugolino, were little for his apostle's heart. Lent had begun on 28th February. Dominic preached without intermission in the churches and convents of the town,[47] as he had preached the Lent in Fanjeaux, Carcassonne or Toulouse. It was one of his special characteristics that he was never completely absorbed by his tasks as founder, legislator or superior. His effectiveness in the organization, which sometimes seems to us bewildering, was only an addition to, or rather the overflow of a fulness of earlier generous activity. The direct ministry of souls, through prayer or the spoken word, continued to form the thread of his life and the subject of all his cares. Thus he had a certain detachment in respect of his work, an interior liberty in regard to it, which in no sense diminished his effectiveness—on the contrary. He would not have elicited solid vocations among the young, if he himself, in his ardent love of souls and of Christ, had not been the type of apostle-preacher.

Now at this particular time, a group of clergy from Orleans were keeping Lent in Rome, with Manassé de Seignelay, their bishop.[48] The French prelate was on his way to join the pilgrimage to the Holy Land,[49] with his household. In their number was the dean of the important collegiate church of St Aignan of Orleans. Reginald[50] was an outstanding priest. He was well known, for he had recently been teaching canon law for five years in Paris. As dean, since 1212 he had displayed exceptional qualities of prudence, love of peace, human feeling. Matured by his teaching and his earlier life, he was endowed with keen sensitivity. Formerly he had given himself up too much to the comfortable dignity of a life of culture and 'delicate' living, as was the expression of the time—with its suggestion of something derogatory.[51] His heart, however, had remained generous. He had the gift of revolutionizing men's lives by preaching. Very well informed as to the wretchedness of souls and the needs of the Church, in particular in regard to the Albigensian crisis, for his bishop had gone on crusade there in 1213,[52] and he himself had been there in 1214,[53] he was troubled by the wretched condition of the Catholic preaching which the Council of 1215 had emphasized. In the heart of this mature priest who was almost crushed by administrative cares, a great appeal made itself heard. The well-to-do life of a chapter dean weighed down upon him like remorse. He wanted to liberate himself from this life which was too worldly and produced too little fruit. He dreamed of leaving it all, of living 'like an apostle', going from one township to another preaching, in voluntary poverty.[54] Many a great heart had felt this call during the past hundred and fifty years.

At Rome, it is said, he confided in Ugolino. He had heard him speak about the Preachers.[55] He heard Dominic preach. One day the founder missed him; the reason was that Reginald was ill. He visited him and spoke to him of following the poverty of Christ, of sharing the lot of his brethren. The two men understood one another perfectly. Reginald agreed and then and there bound himself by vow to the order. The following year, in a conversation in Paris, Dominic would relate the sequel to this story. The illness became very dangerous. Death seemed almost inevitable. Reginald was cured, however, but not without a miracle.

> For the Virgin Mary, queen of heaven, mother of mercy, came to him under visible form amid the fire of the fever, and rubbed him with a healing ointment which she brought with her. She anointed his eyes, nostrils, ears, mouth, navel, hands and feet, adding these words: 'I anoint your feet with holy oil, so that they may be ready to announce the Gospel of peace.' Then she presented him with the complete habit of the order. He felt himself cured forthwith and so suddenly made whole throughout his entire body that the doctors who had almost despaired of saving him, were astonished to note the indications of a perfect cure.[56]

On learning of Reginald's vow, Manassé of Orleans was greatly distressed. Perhaps he remembered Dominic, with whom he had been in contact for a few days in Fanjeaux in May 1213.[57] He had no suspicion then of what would be taken from him. He was attached to Reginald whom he called his 'father', doubtless because he asked him for advice and confided his spiritual life to him.[58] The dean of St Aignan had given his word however. Yet Dominic had to agree to allow him at least the time to finish the pilgrimage to the Holy Places with Manassé. It was understood that immediately upon his return, Reginald would make his way to Bologna,

Dominic realized what an influence this former professor of law, whose apostolic soul was so close to his own, would be able to exert over the university. To this recruit who had not yet even the habit, he abandoned himself with such an impulse of joyful confidence that he already gave him the delegation of his authority over the community of the brethren. As soon as Reginald reached Bologna, he would be there as his vicar.[59]

It was in the midst of the Paschal season in the first half of May.[60] This was the time for the pilgrims to reach Genoa if they wanted to take advantage of the 'general passage' towards the East fixed for 24th June next.[61] Perhaps Dominic accompanied them for part of the way. There was nothing to keep him in Rome any longer. Ugolino himself had left.[62] The founder was going to begin the visitation of his groups of brethren throughout Italy, Spain, Provence and France, to encourage, organize, reform and, if possible, stimulate them to go further and higher. Thus he would give the impetus to the unending journeys of the Dominican Masters-General, who for a very long period, would have no permanent seat, but would be always travelling from country to country to keep alive and renew among the Preachers the spirit of their institutions and of their ministry.

Before leaving Rome, however, Dominic obtained one last audience with the Sovereign Pontiff. It was perhaps then that a new project was outlined—the installation of a Dominican house in Rome. It is quite certain that the idea was in the air. In the course of his ministry Dominic had seen the benefit that would accrue from this, as he had seen its possibility. The Papacy too, moreover, had precise and long-standing projects. One thing is certain in any event. On 3rd August, 1218, Honorius III set down in a letter the first of a series of acts which were to secure the convent of St Sixtus for the Preachers as soon as the founder returned to Rome.[63]

For six months, all direct trace of the traveller is lost. It cannot, however, be doubted that he first visited Bologna.[64] It was there that the first of his four groups of brethren were. It was time, moreover, that he should visit them to give them courage. In their hospice of the Mascarella, they were experiencing poverty which bordered on distress, 'angustia' said Jordan of Saxony.[65] The provision of 1216, in Toulouse, which authorized that 'there should still be revenues' seemed rather like irony. Here there was mendicant poverty. Dominic saw in it a sign from Providence. As he would so often do, he invited his brethren joyously to give thanks to God.

Certain measures, moreover, were to reduce these material difficulties. He sent back to Paris the brethren John and Bertrand, certainly before the end of June.[66] The former, at least, was to continue his studies. Bertrand, who had his full confidence, acted as liaison officer between the Master and his communities. The founder would moreover take the two Castilians with him to Spain; the fact is certain at least in the case of one of them, Friar

Dominic the Spaniard, who was later to become prior in his own country.[67] Thus of the recent arrivals, there would only remain in Bologna Friars Christian and his *socius*, the lay brother who had come from Rome. In a swift apostolate, however, Dominic enlarged the contact of the Preachers with the clergy. He once more made known the pontifical recommendations. And then he went away, leaving the brethren reassured. He could not linger, for other tasks claimed him. Moreover, he judged it right to oblige his brethren to be self-sufficient.

Thus after thirteen years of absence, he set off again for his native country. He had not seen it since 1205. It would be interesting to know by what route he travelled, and what were the places he visited on his way. It would seem that a sea crossing, from Genoa to Barcelona, for instance, can be excluded, for the passes over the Cottian Alps are free from snow in summer and open in the direction of Provence. He most probably paid a visit to his brethren in the Narbonensis. He certainly visited Prouille once more. He brought the bull which canonically erected the male section of the community into a convent of Preachers. This implies a certain legislative change. It was perhaps at this time that Dominic also inaugurated among the sisters a revision of the rule of Prouille, redrafted in accordance with the 'customs' of the Preachers.[68] After 25th July, it was possible to enter Toulouse once more. Amaury de Montfort, who for a month past had succeeded his father Simon, then abandoned the siege of the town.[69] It was perhaps at this moment that Dominic sent Peter Seila to Paris[70] and the founders of the convent to Lyons.[71] Despite everything, St Romain had stood firm under the trial and several brethren of note had entered there.

The later stages of the journey are totally unknown to us. Did Dominic pay a visit to his native Castile, Osma for instance, or Caleruega, Burgos[72] or Palencia? Unreliable modern traditions, of insufficient antiquity and unsupported by valid documents, merely express the likelihood of one or other of these visits.[73] Those traditions which, on the other hand, claim to attribute to St Dominic the foundation of other houses than those of Segovia and Madrid, are incorrect, because they contradict the explicit assertion of Jordan of Saxony.[74] The only plausible tion, for it appears to be supported by numerous thirteenth-century documents, concerns the Dominican nuns of San Esteban de Górmaz, who were to transfer their convent to Caleruega in 1266.[75] It is sufficient, however, to examine these documents closely to realize that they in no sense attribute to Dominic, on the occasion of a visit in 1218 or at the beginning of 1219, the creation of their monastery; still less, as Fernando del Castillo who in this respect corrupted the later historiography, claimed in the sixteenth century, do they prove the transformation by the efforts of St Dominic of a so-called Augustinian monastery into a monastery of Preacheresses.[76]

It is thus necessary to accept that we cannot know what the patriarch did between July and November 1218, the date on which one next finds trace of him again. He certainly did not spare himself during this time. Four long months; for the Preacher that meant many a journey, much apostolic sowing and reaping.

About the middle of the autumn, he was in Guadalajara, on the road from Saragossa to Toledo. The ancient Roman and Moorish city stood erect on the banks of the Henares, in the heart of New Castile. Friar Dominic of Spain was no longer with him now. He had perhaps sent him with some *socius* to join Pedro of Madrid. He was however surrounded by a new group of clerics and lay brethren who had been won to the ideal of the Preachers in the previous weeks and were already bound to the order by oath. The devil had been causing the wind of acute discouragement to blow upon the saint's little company. What the tempter suggested to them can be guessed only too easily—the uncertain future of this new order, the fatigue of the road, the begging of one's bread, the hard beds of the mendicants. . . . In spirit Dominic saw the mouth of hell swallowing up these deserters and these perjurers. His despairing words could avail nothing. They fled. Only Friar Adam and two lay brethren remained faithful. What Dominic had not obtained from men, however, he obtained from God. He gave himself to prayer. Soon all, or almost all, came back to him.[77]

Shortly afterwards he received a gift in the Roman city of Brihuega, a few miles away.[78] The priest of the church of San Miguel, Emiliano, granted him and the brethren of the order a house which had come to him from a certain Juan el Calvo. This may have been with a view to a foundation at Brihuega or elsewhere. The gift was only conditional. There was a possibility of its reverting to Emiliano, either the latter reserving the right to take back his gift in the case that the foundation should not succeed, or Dominic himself not wishing to acquire landed property as a permanent possession.

In the course of the month of November, the founder had the opportunity of getting this donation confirmed and completed by the Archbishop of Toledo himself.[79] He found Rodrigo Ximenes de Rada at Talamanca, twenty miles or so to the north of his favourite see of Alcalá. Dominic visited the ecclesiastical head of the province where he intended to sow the word of God. In addition to this general motive, he had a more personal reason. The prince of the Church whom he was going to meet, Primate of Spain and legate of the Sovereign Pontiff, a prelate who was both a great historian, a theologian and a preacher with a scintillating gift of expression, had for some time been his bishop before he was transferred to the primary see of all the Spains.[80] Appointed to Osma, in effect, on the morrow of the death of Diego (1208), this former Cistercian must have regulated Dominic's case, authorized him to remain far from his brethren and to preach in the Narbonensis; he had sent him a *socius* and perhaps even other brethren.

Later he had doubtless noticed him at the Council of the Lateran, while he himself, in five different languages, was defending the rights of his primacy.[81] He was, moreover, most fully aware of the canons of the Council in regard to preaching. Thus we should not find it surprising that every one of the authentic documents in relation to the ministry of Dominic and his brethren in Spain in these years 1218–1219, depicts them as being in some locality of the jurisdiction of the great archbishop.[82] As he had recently welcomed Friar Gómez and Friar Pedro of Madrid, so Rodrigo Ximenes generously welcomed Dominic. He opened his province to the Preacher's ministry. Finally he authorized the gift of the house in Brihuega by the parish priest of San Miguel and granted it as far as it lay in his power. He laid down that if this gift should come to be no longer required after the death of the priest Emiliano, it should revert to the archiepiscopal see. The donation was addressed to 'Brother Dominic, minister of the order of the Preaching, and to other brethren of this same order'.[83]

This welcome was a stimulant. The Guadalajara temptation would not recur. After Talamanca, Dominic went to Madrid. We do not know why he chose that place whose future glories were as yet hidden. Alcalá, Toledo, both seats of an archbishopric, were better suited to a foundation. It would seem likely that Pedro of Madrid had, very naturally, returned to his native town the previous year to carry out his ministry there.[84] The ground was already ploughed, sown, and the harvest was whitening. In fact the founder, Jordan of Saxony tells us, soon 'began'[85] a convent. The word was well chosen. It was as yet only a rough outline, a preaching of humble dimensions. It was not isolated, however. As in Prouille, in Toulouse, later in Bologna and in Rome, the Dominican apostolate had borne fruit in feminine hearts. Dominic himself gave the habit to several women and attached them to the community of the brethren.[86] They were still scattered and, for lack of a suitable installation, could not yet live together. The positions of Prouille were, in short, reversed. There it was the monastery of the sisters which served as a basis for the Preaching. Here it was the house of the brethren which furnished the centre to which the sisters were attached.

The gift of the archbishop and of Emiliano provided the initial endowment. In the following month of May, in Madrid, Jaime Mames and his relatives gave to the 'Order of the Preaching', a rural property situated at San Julián de Val Sadobral.[87] In the month of March 1220, Honorius III thanked the people of Madrid for their generosity towards the brethren 'of the Order of Preachers'.[88] The Madrid house was thus at this date still a male community. In the month of May following, however, in the general chapter at Bologna, Dominic gave the order to transfer to the sisters the building and the entire property. For the future the house was to become a monastery of nuns.[89]

The impossibility of obtaining for the sisters a house capable of holding all of them so that they could live a regular life together, and the necessity of not multiplying communities of his order in a locality that was still rather unimportant, doubtless led Dominic to this solution, but it was due above all to the wish to give immediate effect to the decision of the chapter of 1220, which renounced any kind of property for the houses, as for the individuals of the Order. The brethren would remain in Madrid as directors and confessors to the sisters, a function which would not prevent them from exercising their outside ministry in mendicant poverty. Here we have the position of the preaching of Prouille in regard to the monastery—that of the Catharist Perfect in relation to the communities of women Perfect.

At the same moment Dominic wrote to the nuns, who were taking upon themselves the burden of regular life to its fullest extent, the only one of the letters of his which we still possess.[90] It does not waste time in expressions of feeling, but its virile tone is perhaps the founder's finest gift to the brethren and sisters of his order. Short, vigorous, balanced, it touches the essential points and leaves to the superior of the sisters, whom it endows with the indispensable authority and powers, the care of regulating everything else. It came indeed from the hand of the religious legislator who had just organized his order in a masterly way, from one who was a tense, heroic wrestler, but sensitive to human weakness for which he made provision by dispensations. Here is the document. Although he was addressing sisters it was drawn up in Latin—the current practice at the time.[91]

> Friar Dominic, Master of the Preachers, to the dear prioress and to the whole convent of the nuns of Madrid, health and daily progress.
>
> We greatly rejoice and give thanks to God that He has granted you the favour of such a holy life and has liberated you from the sordidness of this world. Wage war by your fasts, daughters, against our ancient enemy, for only he who has honourably fought will be crowned.
>
> Up to the present you had not a suitable place for carrying out your religious life; now you can no longer plead this excuse for, by the grace of God, you possess buildings sufficiently well adapted for the maintenance of regular life. I therefore wish you for the future to keep silence in all the places where speaking is normally forbidden—refectory, dormitory and oratory; as to all the other places observe your rule. Let no one cross the threshold to go out, let no one come in, unless it is the bishop or some prelate to preach to you or to make a visitation. Spare neither disciplines nor vigils. Obey your prioress. Do not chatter among yourselves and do not lose your time in gossip.
>
> Not being able to help you in economic matters, we do not want to burden you by empowering any of the brethren to receive women into or impose them on the community. Only the prioress has this power, with the council of her convent.
>
> Moreover we prescribe to our most dear brother, who has gone to very great trouble to enable you to embrace this most holy estate, to dispose and ordain all things as it shall seem useful to him so that you may conduct yourselves in a most

holy and religious fashion. Finally, we give him power to visit and correct you, even to depose the prioress in case of necessity, with the consent of the majority of the nuns, and we grant him permission to dispense you in certain points, if it seem good to him.

Fare you well in Christ.

The most dear brother to whom the letter refers, the superior whose name it does not give because he is known to all, is Mames, Dominic's brother. This is confirmed by one of the variants of the text.[92] Mames, however, was not there from the beginning. At the close of this year 1218 when the community in Madrid was beginning to take shape, it was Dominic the Spaniard who was placed at the head of the brethren and the sisters.[93] He, indeed, knew something of the life of the nuns of Prouille at the same time as that of the Preachers. He stayed in Madrid a little under a year. In the middle of 1219, when Dominic had left Spain and arrived in Paris before returning to Italy, he found Friar Mames there. It was then that he sent him to the convent of Madrid to relieve Dominic of Spain, charging him to pave the way for the regular installation of the sisters. The letter alludes to his meritorious work and to his good success. It also indicates that the sisters have already had for some time a rule (ordo) which fixed the details of their daily life. This was clearly the rule of Prouille, in accordance with which Mames had striven to form them before gathering them together in the convent.

Around the feast of Christmas Dominic crossed the Sierra de Guadarrama, which, bordering the plateau of New Castile, marks the limits of the diocese of Toledo, and went to Segovia.[94] The warrior city raised its crenellated walls on the summit of an abrupt rock which separated the dark waters of the Eresma and the Clamores until they met beyond it. The friars may have come there before him. No house, however, was in existence for the Preachers. As in Toulouse, Dominic was lodged with a good lady who gathered up memories of the saint with devotion.[95] It was thus that, deeply moved, she preserved the tunic of coarse sack-cloth which he wore under his clothes in the guise of a hair-shirt and which he abandoned when he found a genuine hair-shirt which pricked as much as he could wish. The tunic was later to work miracles. In the end it found a home among the Cistercian nuns of Las Huelgas in Valladolid.[96]

In Segovia as elsewhere, Dominic was a preacher before all else. Certain anecdotes, for once fortunately preserved, allow us to glimpse his manner of acting.[97] He did not only make Latin sermons for a few initiates. He preached in the vulgar tongue, on every occasion, to the entire population as a whole or category by category. His audience could not be contained in a church, nor even in the city, for at that time, in the towns of the thirteenth century, large public squares were not yet known. The sermon was delivered on some unappropriated ground outside the city wall, it is said on the banks of the

(Photo: Leonard von Matt)

The citadel of Segovia at the confluence of the Clamorès and Eresma.

Eresma.[98] The saint was not abstract in his language, nor were his words remote from the sentiments of his hearers. He felt keenly the hopes and trials of this agricultural population which at the time was suffering from the effects of a persistent drought. For lack of rain, and because it was already the end of December, they had not yet been able to sow the crops. Moved with compassion, he promised in the course of a sermon that the Lord would soon give them rain. Heaven's reply was not long in coming. Before the sermon was ended a terrible downpour occurred. The congregation had difficulty in hastily regaining the town and their houses.

With the important men of the town council, Dominic was more severe. The council had been assembled on a certain feast-day, doubtless immediately after Mass. This time again, the meeting was held in the open air. The nobles were present, proudly seated on their horses. A letter from the King of Castile communicating his edicts was read aloud. Dominic seized the opportunity to present the commandments of the King of eternity. One of the nobles grew angry with this chatterer who was preventing him from getting to his dinner. He turned his horse and went off. This contempt for the word of God drew down upon him a terrible denunciation from the preacher, the announcement of a drama the fulfilment of which would not be long delayed, in which the proud man would unhappily succumb.

This ministry threw Dominic and his Preachers into the full current of the religious life of the city. Recruits offered themselves to him. A house was given to him.[99] The convent of Santa Cruz was founded at the very place where it still stands today, below the gate of San Ciprián which leads towards the bridge. History makes no mention at any time of a change of place. Since the Madrid house soon became a monastery of nuns, the convent of Segovia would in fact be the first convent of the Preachers in Spain.[100] Once more it was a humble house. It did not, indeed, take long to erect. At the close of the Middle Ages the Catholic kings built in Segovia a masterpiece of the architecture of the time.

Below this house, half-way down the slope which drops towards the Eresma, and facing towards the north, a grotto is hollowed deep into the rock. A modern tradition claims that Dominic at the time of his stay, spent long hours in prayer there, bruising his flesh by disciplines that drew blood. In the sixteenth century drops of blood, as fresh and brightly coloured as if the saint had just shed them, could still be seen on the walls.[101] Fernando del Castillo, Colmenares and the later historians even declare that it was by this grotto that the convent began, Dominic having chosen the harshness of this site to withdraw to, to sleep there and give himself over to his macerations.[102] This description is opposed to the primitive data which assert that the gift of a house was the origin of the convent. Above all, it gives a false picture of the founder and depicts him in the perspective of an eremitical life of which there is no trace in the course of his history. Dominic was a community man, a man of the town, he lived in the midst of men and not among rocks and savage beasts. As Jordan said:[103]

> He manifested himself everywhere as a man of the Gospel, in word and in deeds. During the day, no one mixed more than he did in the society of his brethren or his companions along the road, no one was more joyous. But in the night hours, no one was more eager to watch, to pray and make supplication in all possible ways. His tears pervaded the evening and his joy the morning.[104] He gave the day to his neighbour and the night to God, knowing that God assigns His mercy to the day and his song to the night.[105]

If in Segovia Dominic did not live the hermit's life that has been claimed, it is possible on the other hand that, at the same time that he lived with his brethren in the house in which the first Spanish convent was founded, he liked to retire and pray at night in this grotto, which for him did duty as an oratory while the chapel was being constructed and that there, as in all places through which he passed, he accompanied his prayer with his usual mortifications. Thus the *sacra cueva* where so many holy persons—Teresa of Avila for instance[106]—and in particular so many Friars Preachers, have come to derive edification from the memory of the prayers and penances of St Dominic, does nevertheless transmit an authentic message. It is good for men to listen to what it has to tell, in order the better to understand and imitate the saint. For, in truth, it was in the course of these prayers and penances that he learnt love and compassion towards Christ and the men who were his brethren. If he was so indefatigable in seeking out the wretched, sinners and those who had gone astray, so bold in approaching them, so anxious to convert them, it was because during his nights he had wept unceasingly over the tragedy of their lives and desired for them as for himself the salvation and joy that God alone can give. Then prayer became urgent in him, to the point of causing him to cry out; then the discipline with the three iron chains which John of Navarre mentioned at the canonization process,[107] struck his shoulders with greater cruelty. This was one of those weapons which, if united to the Cross, proved the sincerity of his prayer of intercession and prepared the shower of graces of the morrow. If, however, these interminable vigils and these penances frighten our weakness, do not let us forget that they were only one expression of his affectionate love of Christ and his brethren. Thus when the light of day drove away the tears of the night, to speak like Jordan of Saxony, the same affectionate love was transformed into joy and friendship in the life of brotherhood,[108] into mercy ever ready to be moved on meeting the suffering, or sinners.[109] Such was the attitude, austere in the secret of prayer, lovable and compassionate in its relations with men, that Dominic showed in Segovia, as throughout his whole ministry. He was neither a hermit among the rocks nor an ascetic in the desert, but an apostle of Christ, crucified with his master, yet open and joyous after the manner of the Gospel.

For the first four months of 1219 his history again eludes us. Did he return to the diocese of Toledo to preach the Lent there? Did he go to Palencia where not so long ago he had made his sacred studies? Its schools had since become a university, the first in Spain, through the collaboration of King Alfonso VIII and Bishop Tello.[110] After a beginning full of promise, it had been undergoing a crisis since 1214, by reason of the disorders which followed the death of the king.[111] The apostolic constitution of 22nd November, 1219, which renewed with insistence the scholastic decrees of the Lateran and took steps to facilitate their application, would revive the bishop's courage. The latter took steps, confirmed by the Pope in October 1220,[112] which would cause the university to flourish again for a few years. Nothing justifies the assumption, however, that this movement was launched in the spring of 1219, and that it was this that attracted Dominic, still less that it lead him to plan a foundation in Palencia. No glimpse of the convent of Palencia can be derived from the documents before the spring of 1220. This was to be the second house of the province of Spain.[113]

Dominic left the peninsula. He crossed over into the Narbonensis about May.[114] Prouille had been experiencing certain difficulties. Since the death of Simon de Montfort the disorders in the viscounty had increased. Bernard de Rochefort, the Bishop of Carcassonne under grave suspicion who had had to resign in 1211, had returned to his see, and Guy des Vaux-Cernai left for his abbey again.[115] This was a revenge of the clergy of the Midi on the clergy of the crusade. At once the monks of St Hilaire, whose abbey was in the same diocese, became emboldened to the point of force. By force of arms they occupied the church of St Martin of Limoux, which they had never ceased to claim from Prouille, and drove out the brethren who were in charge. William Claret reacted with energy, appealing to Archbishop Arnaud de Narbonne, in whose diocese Limoux was situated. Despite this intervention, however, on 26th November, 1218,[116] and that of Bernard de Rochefort on 13th April, 1219,[117] the sisters were to wait a long time yet before recovering their property.[118]

Another misfortune had occurred. Shortly before November 1218[119] the faithful Friar Noël, prior of Prouille since 1215, was drowned in the Blau, a small tributary of the Hers which was in spate. The brethren of Prouille, in conformity with the privilege of 30th March, elected William Claret as prior, and he effectively bears that title in the two deeds mentioned—he is even called, in the second, 'prior and procurator of the monastery of Ste Marie de Prouille'.

In the midst of these vicissitudes the life of the monastery continued to flourish. At the beginning of this year 1219 several people in the neighbourhood made certain fresh gifts to Prouille,[120] a proof of the deep root the institution had taken in the neighbourhood. Two new brethren, or rather 'two canons-priests' to use the terms of a charter, had entered the men's community, Friars Noël and Guillaume-Pierre de Malras.[121]

In Toulouse, St Romain had likewise been consolidated. The convent would develop in the ensuing years, despite the new and fruitless siege of Louis of France and his crusaders against the city of Raymond from 16th June to 1st August, 1219.[122] It was to give birth to convents of Preachers in the Midi: Lyon, if it had not already been started, Montpellier, Bayonne.[123] Although at this time there was no further indication of the existence of the hospice Arnaud-Bernard, it had not perhaps disappeared. At St Romain, Dominic found Friar Bertrand again; he brought news fresh from Paris.

Both left for France at the end of May or beginning of June.[124] The old pilgrimage route crossed the Quercy and passed through Rocamadour to the north-west of Cahors. Dominating the deep and narrow valley, a mighty precipitous rock bore on its very summit a strange tier of chapels, crowned by a fortress. There lay the crypt where, according to tradition, the mysterious hermit Amadour, who has been identified with Zacheus, paid his homage to the Most Blessed Virgin. How many pilgrims to Santiago, above all since the twelfth century, have lingered in this sanctuary![125] Faithful to his custom, Dominic, and Bertrand who emulated him, spent the whole night in prayer.[126]

> The next day [relates Gérard de Frachet][127] along the road they fell in with some German pilgrims, who joined themselves to them through devotion, when they heard them recite their psalms and litanies. Arrived at the halting-place, the Germans invited them and, according to their custom, shared with them a very abundant meal. They did this for four days. Dominic said one day to his companion, sighing—'Friar Bertrand, truly I have a bad conscience; we are reaping the earthly goods of these pilgrims, without sowing the goods of the spirit among them. Thus, if it please you, let us pray the Lord on our knees, that he grant us both to understand and speak their tongue, so that we may preach the Lord Jesus to them.' Having done this, they spoke German in an intelligible manner, to the stupefaction of all. They marched with them once more for four days and spoke to them of the Lord Jesus. They then arrived at Orléans. The Germans, who wanted to go to Chartres, left them on the road to Paris, recommending themselves to their prayers with humility.

A few days later, Dominic and Bertrand arrived in the capital. At the beginning of the summer the Île de France displays all its attractions.[128] The Seine meanders lazily along its broad valley. In the midst of a curved sweep of the stream, we see the Île de la Cité with Notre Dame and King Philip's palace, we see the bridges and the pointed towers of the churches, and on both sides of the river the battlements of the fortresses crowded together on a mighty wall. In the foreground the hill of St Geneviève and the Porte St Jacques, the direct termination of the road from Orleans. Scarcely had they crossed the gate, towards the left, when Friar Bertrand pointed out to Dominic the former hospice of St Jacques, now the convent of the Preachers.

About thirty[129] young friars, deeply moved, welcomed Dominic and embraced this father to whom they were bound, though they did not know him, by a profession of obedience. Matthew of France and his early companions had worked well. The Preachers had taken their place in the university of Paris.

Chapter XIV

FROM PARIS TO BOLOGNA

THE urgent step taken by Honorius III did not remain without effect. The Pope's letter which was dispatched from Rome about the month of April 1218 was successful in obtaining a lodging for the Preachers in Paris, from the month of July. A master of the Faculty of theology in the university there[1] gave them a hospice with a chapel at the far end of the 'Grand' rue Saint Benoît', near the Porte d'Orléans.[2] The Preachers took possession on 6th August.[3]

The donor, Maître Jean de Barastre, chaplain to Philip Augustus and at the same time dean of the chapter of St Quentin, had been teaching in Paris for more than ten years.[4] He was a generous man. He had founded this house of hospitality in 1209 with the help of his friend Simon de Poissy[5] who was preparing to join the Albigensian crusade,[6] and had entrusted the house to the care of some lay-brothers.[7] The chapel was dedicated to the apostle James the Greater, whose name would soon be that of the nearby gate. One day, moreover, the Grand' rue Saint Benoît would be renamed and become well known to future generations under the name of the rue Saint Jacques. Pilgrims to Compostela, at the moment when they were preparing to pass through the Porte to the Route d'Orléans as they left the city, said a final prayer in the chapel. The hospice was able to receive pilgrims such as these and other necessitous travellers, in the course of their journey. The intervention of the university of Paris at the side of Jean de Barastre in the deed which placed the hospice at the disposal of the Preachers made it abundantly clear that this asylum had not been primarily intended for poor travellers. It had been instituted for students and that was how the corporation of the masters and students came to have supreme control over it.[8] At the request of the Pope, the abbot of St Romain and his Friars Preachers were not only received as poor men or even as religious, but as students of the university of Paris.

As Jordan of Saxony expressly remarks, the donation was only provisional. It would be necessary to wait two years for it to be made absolute and final. In the meantime, the bonds between Maître Jean de Barastre and the Dominican students were to be strengthened in an unusual way. At the formal request of Honorius III,[9] but also through a feeling of attachment to which he would give clear expression in the charters, he would give his lectures in the actual convent of his 'very dear Friars Preachers', 'whose religious life, fruitful and pleasing to God, and indispensable ministry, he would strive to promote',[10] he said, borrowing the Pope's own terms.[11] In giving them full and entire possession of all he owned in front of the church of St Etienne des Grès on 3rd May, 1221, he would only claim the usual privileges of the founder and patron, on a personal title to be valid during his lifetime.[12]

The university on their side, while renouncing their special rights about the same time, demanded privileges which may seem onerous[13]—confraternity and participation in the fruits of the brethren's prayers and good works, two solemn Masses of intercession each year, one for the living and the other for the dead, right of burial and suffrages for the Masters of all Faculties, with the right of burial in the brethren's chapter for the Masters in Theology. The Preachers made no difficulty about these conditions for, beyond all question, they strengthened the bonds between the convent of St Jacques and the university of Paris.

Possessing within its own walls, thanks to the ordinary teaching of Maître Jean de Barastre, one of the schools of the Faculty of Theology, and linked by confraternity and the religious services to the corporation of the university, the convent of Preachers in Paris would figure at the very centre of the order and among the general run of the religious houses of the period as one of the most original of institutions, a university college which was at the same time a convent of regular life. This position was to give it a rôle in the Order of St Dominic that was of primary importance and at the same time irreplaceable.[14] From now onwards it would constitute the *studium generale* towards which students from all the provinces of the order would flock and whence the doctors and preachers, solidly trained, who were to propagate the splendours of the theology of Paris in the cities, townships and even in the missions beyond the Church's periphery, would return to their different convents. This situation would in turn react on the order as a whole—an order which had become by force of circumstances, because it was the Order of Preachers, an order of theological learning, with a life that was closely linked with the university. 'Honeste vivere, discere et docere.' 'To live a godly life, to learn and to teach', such was to be for Jordan of Saxony, St Dominic's successor, the rule of the Preachers.[15] This programme would already be carried out in the order in St Dominic's lifetime, thanks to the links between the convent of St Jacques and the university of Paris.

Since February 1220, Honorius had been stressing the special position of this convent by designating its religious by the title of 'Brethren of the Order of Preachers, studying sacred learning in Paris'.[16] The Pope had himself been working since 1218 to establish this position by asking the university to welcome and lodge the Preachers. Finally, the person ultimately responsible for this orientation was indeed Dominic himself when in 1217, at the moment when he dispersed his brethren, he had chosen the university of Paris as the fulcrum of the mighty lever which his Preachers were to provide to raise the standard of doctrinal preaching in the Church.

In this month of June 1219[17] when Dominic reached Paris, an additional circumstance helped to mark the scholastic character of the convent of St Jacques. Although the brethren had possessed a chapel for nearly a year, up to this time they had not been able to celebrate Mass or the Divine Office publicly, or consequently to exercise the ministry of the Word in public.[18] The chapter of the cathedral had prevented them from so doing by a formal prohibition. A simple glance at the geography of this part of the capital[19] enables us to understand, if not to justify, the interference of the canons of Notre Dame.

The chapel of St Jacques was situated in the territory of the parish of St Benoît, whose sanctuary stood at the bottom of the Grand' rue some two hundred and fifty yards away. Barely a few yards, however, from the convent door, on the other side of the street, began another parish, St Etienne des Grès. Now St Etienne and St Benoît, each of which was endowed with a parish priest and a college of canons, formed part of four 'daughter churches' of Notre Dame, under the jurisdiction of their mother church.[20] Hence the indignation of the cathedral. What had these newcomers come to do in the neighbourhood? To open a new collegiate church at so slight a distance from the other two! And why not a cemetery to receive the dead with their legacies?[21] Especially since within a radius of some three hundred yards several other parishes or conventual churches could be numbered, among them St Cosmas, St Symphorien des Vignes and the ancient abbey church of Ste Geneviève. There was a danger that indiscreet competition might harm everybody and, so to speak, make perquisites that were already too restricted still more meagre.[22] Thus, strong in their rights as to parochial jurisdiction, the canons of the cathedral, to suppress the crisis at its inception, prohibited the practice of public worship in the chapel of the Preachers altogether. What they overlooked, however, was the need of souls and the non-existence of their own preaching. In other towns where the order wanted to make foundations they were not to lack imitators.

What was the solution? Dominic had no means of action against the will of the powerful Paris chapter. The only superior, the bishop, was not there; he had left for the crusade in the East.[23] The provisional administrators of the diocese, archdeacons and chancellor, were members of the chapter; they were at the same time judges and interested parties. Clearly the key to the situation was no longer to be found in Paris. The founder went to seek it at the Curia.

Meanwhile the brethren followed the offices in the parish of St Benoît. As to their preaching, they were able to exercise this in other churches in the capital. Letters from the Pope would one day express warm thanks to the Benedictines of St Magloire and Notre Dame des Champs.[24] Doubtless among the good offices which these monks rendered the Preachers must be reckoned the most valuable of all—the placing at their disposal of a church in which to preach and hear confessions.

In the city as at the convent Dominic multiplied those familiar instructions which were called 'collations'.[25] The chapter of Notre Dame could not prohibit these conferences or private talks which allowed of a tone of confidence and an intimacy which their private nature made all the more persuasive. Dominic, moreover, only addressed people who spoke Latin, fortunately numerous in this university city. One day, in one of these conversations, he related the extraordinary story of Master Reginald's cure and of his vocation to the poverty of the Preachers.[26] It moved almost to tears all those who had known the Master when he was teaching in Paris. Among those who were present, a recently elected Bachelor in Theology listened with the deepest attention. He felt his generosity moved to its very depths. Jordan of Saxony made his confession and opened his inmost heart to St Dominic.[27] The latter was content to wait upon the movement of divine grace. It seemed to him that the hour was not yet come. He did not try to win this theologian of good will for the Preachers and merely asked him to consecrate himself more completely to God by receiving the diaconate. He perhaps foresaw in this cleric the one who, less than three years later, in this same convent of St Jacques, was to succeed him as head of the order.

The impossibility of preaching at St Jacques had not destroyed the convent's sphere of influence. The thirty brethren with whom the master was surrounded were evidence of this, in addition to which Matthew of France at the beginning of the year found himself in a position to send a group of brethren to make a foundation at Orleans. 'Humble seed, which would nevertheless later be the origin of an abundant posterity', declared the *Libellus*,[28] characterizing in two words these 'young, simple' brethren.

The recruitment of St Jacques was indeed that. Young, simple brethren, students recruited by scholastic contacts at the university rather than through the ministry of pulpit or confessional. For, though Mames or Matthew of France might be prevented from preaching in their chapel, it was impossible to shut out the light diffused by this group of poor students, austere, generous, and guileless as their white habits, persecuted by comfortable canons, whose manner of living the Gospel was so infectious. As students, it was on their student companions that their influence was exercised, through the mysterious power of the young over the hearts of those of their own age, in the mutual contact of work or of life in common.[29]

A touching story of conversion, written with a psychological finesse rather rare at the time, enables us to come into direct contact with this mode of conquest among students.[30] A few months from this time, when Jordan of Saxony decided to become a Preacher, he would not rest until he had also won over his friend in heart and spirit, the future prior of Cologne, Friar Henry of Germany. Everything went to show that Henry was destined to become a Friar Preacher—his mortification, his purity, his tender piety, the extraordinary grace for preaching he had received which would enable him before long to influence the hearts of the clergy in Paris. Henry, however, resisted the instances of friendship.

'His reason convinced him that it was necessary to acquiesce, but his rebellious and passive will made him feel the contrary.' He struggled, nevertheless, almost in despair at feeling his heart so hard. Thus one night he came to assist at Matins in the church of Notre Dame.

> He stayed there until the first hours of the morning, begging and entreating the mother of God to bend his will to this vocation. His prayer, however, seemed to bring no progress. . . . Then he began to be sorry for himself and was preparing to leave, saying, 'I see now, blessed Virgin, that you disdain me. I shall not have my share in the college of the poor of Christ.' At the very moment when he was preparing to leave the church, struggling with himself and in deep distress, He who looks on the humble with mercy,[31] completely changed his heart. He surrendered himself wholly to the Lord, a flood of tears came over him and at last his spirit found relief.

Then and there he ran to utter the vow to enter the order and returned to Jordan.

> I noticed the traces of tears on his angelic countenance and asked him where he came from. 'I have made my vow to the Lord[32] [he said] and I shall accomplish it.' We put off the beginning of our novitiate until Lent. That enabled us in the meantime to win Brother Leo, the one of our companions who was later Friar Henry's successor in his office of prior.

We know the names of a certain number of the religious whom Dominic found at St Jacques during the summer of 1219. Together with the early friars of Toulouse—the group of Friar Matthew, that of Friar Mames, finally Friar Peter Seila—there was Friar Henry of Marsburg, the first German to enter the order, and one of the community's first recruits,[33] and Friar Guerric, the future founder of Metz.[34] The presence of other religious who are usually mentioned, Friar Philip,[35] Friar Guillaume,[36] Friar Pierre de Rheims, later Provincial of France,[37] and Friar Etienne de Bourbon, to whom we owe valuable anecdotes on the beginnings of the order,[38] is possible but cannot be proved. Dominic had the joy of giving the habit to a theologian whom he knew particularly well, Guillaume de Montferrat, whom at the beginning of 1217 he had won over to the apostolic ideal at Cardinal Ugolino's. The two years they had agreed upon had passed. Guillaume had profited well from his theological study. The time had come for him to

1552 plan of Paris, after Truchet and Hoyau. Porte St Jacques on the right and immediately to its left the Convent of the Frères Prêcheurs, the 'Jacobins'. Opposite the latter, St Etienne-des-Grès; further to the left, beyond the Sorbonne, the 'Cloistre de St Benoist'. St Geneviève can be seen at the top, near the Porte Bordelle.

join St Dominic's ministry of salvation by becoming one of his brethren and even, for nearly a year, his principal travelling companion.[39]

The motives which brought these novices to St Jacques were varied. Some of them differed in nothing from the usual reasons for entering religion—the acute sense of the passing of time, of the vanity of the world outside the service of God. Guerric heard a voice singing in the street and at first was moved by the sweetness of the song alone; then he was forcibly struck by the words

> The time goes by
> Nought do I
> The time goes by
> And I do nought.[40]

Henry of Cologne had a vision of the same import—'And you', said a terrifying apparition, 'what have you left for the Lord?'[41] Henry of Marsberg returned from the crusade on which he had set out, in order to deliver his feudal lord and uncle from the fire of purgatory; a supernatural intuition led him to the Preachers of Paris to perfect this work by giving himself to a higher service.[42] Beyond these general motives, which were an indication of the sense of the eternal in these young Christian men and of their fundamental generosity, more particular attractions could be discerned. 'I have not read', one of them said, 'that the Lord Jesus Christ was a monk, either black or white, but a preacher in poverty.'[43] By the majority among them, in fact, apostolic poverty was put in the forefront. Friar Guillaume and Friar Jordan thought of the souls to be saved.[44] The two Friars Henry and Friar Jordan laid the emphasis on poverty.[45] To enter among the Preachers was 'to share in the poverty practised by Christ and observed by the apostles in imitation of him, it was to despise the world wholly for love of him'.[46]

The poverty of the community of St Jacques was evident. It was no longer that of the early times, in the hospice near Notre Dame. In the month of February Friar Matthew had received from Jean de Briard and his wife Amicie de Breteuil, a generous family of noble birth from the Ile de France, the tithes at Villers near Corbeil.[47] The gift was important for, the following year, it was to serve as a basis for the foundation of a convent of Cistercian nuns.[48] It put St Jacques in a similar position to that of St Romain. The impression produced on the Paris students by the poverty of the convent showed that Matthew of France, despite certain dispensations, had not been disloyal to the spirit of St Dominic and that he utilized these tithes in accordance with the principles of the fundamental charter of Fulk of Toulouse. That is to say, they enabled the friars to procure the books, clothes and other objects of necessity, to provide for the sick and for the brethren who were in need of rest from thier preaching.[49] Because of the rapid development of the community, these different charges absorbed the revenue of the tithes. The remainder of what was needed was asked for from the charity of Christians.

Dominic was impressed by the generosity of his brethren. He loved them too much, however, and had formed too lofty an idea of the task which he was assigning to them in the Church, to allow them to dally or even to relax. Instead of congratulating them, he called upon them to move forward to a new stage. The experience acquired in Bologna, Madrid, Segovia, as in Toulouse, showed that it was possible to go further and imitate the apostles more closely still. Matthew of France allowed the brethren to travel on horse-back; some, it is said, carried money on them.[50] All this must be given up once and for all. The continual wearing of the surplice which the Council of Montpellier had made obligatory in the Midi could also be abandoned. Dominic even envisaged a measure which was heroic in another way—the making of mendicancy a general practice. He spoke about this with Friar Matthew and the chapter of the convent. On this latter point, however, it was desirable that there should be further reflection. The decision would not be taken until some months later.

In the meantime he busied himself attentively with the correction of the rules for the life of the brethren. All the witnesses for this period of his life stress the strictness, even the 'rigidity' with which he observed the rule of the Preachers, and had it observed by the others,[51] 'as to garments, food and drink, the fasts and all the other provisions'.[52] If he noticed a brother at fault, he likewise punished him 'with rigidity', in accordance with the detailed code of the faults and penances of the text of the rule.[53] This may have been a manifestation of the heroic austerity of his temperament, but in regard to himself, not in regard to his brethren. These same witnesses as to his life insist on the gentleness and kindness with which he imposed the hardest penances. 'If he saw a brother commit some fault, he passed by as if he had seen nothing; afterwards, however, he would go up to the brother calmly and say to him gently, "Brother, you have acted wrongly, admit it." ' The kindliness of his words led them all to confess their faults and do penance. He punished their transgressions severely, but the humility with which he spoke to them caused them to go away consoled.[54] He could also be generous in dispensations with anyone other than himself. He wanted them, however, to reach a higher standard. To be a worthy emulator of the apostles of Christ, to announce the Gospel by example as much as by words, it is necessary to be heroic. Above all, it was essential that the first Preachers should be irreproachable in the practice of their rule.

Here we come up against one of the crucial points of the psychology of St Dominic, at the same time as the explanation of his most astonishing acts of boldness. Dominic could now visualize in its plenitude the work which he had to lead to its successful completion. He saw it as the Pope saw it, *in medio Ecclesiae*, in a vision which embraced and surpassed the narrow confines of Christianity. He realized both the importance and the urgency of it. That was why he hastened to bring it to completion. If he almost short-circuited the various stages, however, it was because he aspired to take up once more, personally and to the fullest extent, the ministry of souls.[55] It was also perhaps because he was beginning to feel his strength betray him. Two years later he had gone from this world, prematurely exhausted. In his boldness, however, he was neither presumptuous nor imprudent, for his actions were the fruit of reflection and preparation. He knew men and knew how to discern the spirits. Above all, for the formation of his Preachers and to cement the community of his order in the fewness of days left to him, he possessed the form of life which he had laid down after twelve years of experience and which the rule had inscribed in a clear and concise text. Hence his strictness in the application of the rule, his demand for complete fidelity as the mainspring of these early beginnings. If the brethren in effect strove to carry out to the last detail the letter and spirit of the rule, he could, without delay, disseminate the communities he had just gathered together and this dispersion would hinder neither the unity nor the unanimity of the order, it would only expand both. He could send brethren across the world only a few months after their taking the habit 'to study, preach and found convents',[56] and these brethren would remain authentic Preachers and be able to produce faithful copies of such preachers from their own prototype.

This was precisely what he had in mind to do for the second time before leaving Paris, a few weeks after his arrival. Among the thirty brethren whom he met there, a few had already pursued their studies to a sufficient degree. There was no reason why they should remain there, crowded together. He was going to send them out to preach. Certain historians have spoken of a dispersion from Paris parallel with that of Toulouse.[57] This is not correct. They have been misled by an error of interpretation which dates back to the fourteenth century, when Bernard Gui thought he could fix in 1209, after St Dominic's visit to Paris, the creation of the convents of Limoges, Rheims, Metz, Poitiers, Orleans.[58] The real facts are rather different. Before going away, Dominic decided with Matthew of France and the chapter of St Jacques to send a few brethren on the mission. Later convents would arise from their activities.[59]

A group had already left for Orleans.[60] Friar Mames was sent to Madrid.[61] Peter Seila found himself assigned to Limoges, for which he set out in January 1220 in order to be there before the beginning of Lent.[62] It is possible that certain brethren went to Rheims.[63] The documents tell us nothing more. St Jacques would certainly find itself weakened by these departures. That did not matter. God would send other novices, for generosity attracts generosity.[64] To accelerate the work of Providence, Dominic, moreover, had his plan.[65] He would carry it out from Bologna where he would stay for the future. In mid-July 1219, Dominic left Paris.[66]

The founder took with him at least two companions, Friar John, a lay-brother whom he had brought from Spain and who was later to die as a missionary in Morocco,[67] and Friar Guillaume de Montfort.[68] The travellers took the ancient road to Italy through the Simplon or the Great St Bernard, travelling slowly up the valley of the Seine to reach the Jura, then the shores of Lake Leman.[69]

Two isolated anecdotes illustrate conditions of life on the road. In crossing Burgundy, at Châtillon-sur-Seine, the travellers were given hospitality by the parish priest—simple hospitality which an accident was to transform into a magnificent reception. The nephew of this priest, a small boy who was playing on the terrace of the presbytery, toppled over into the street and was picked up half dead. The prayer of Dominic, however, restored him alive and well to his mother, whose grief was already beyond bounds. Accordingly the parish priest gave a great banquet, at which, among other things, eels were served.[70]

The crossing of the Alps was particularly trying. In the course of the ascent, Friar John felt his strength fail. In these poor valleys begging could not have brought in much. The unfortunate brother, who had sat down to rest, tried in vain to get up, so much did his legs tremble. To Dominic, who was uneasy about him, he declared that, quite simply, he was hungry. This time again Dominic's prayer brought the remedy in the form of an appetizing loaf which was found, wrapped in a pure white cloth, a stone's throw away. Friar John went there with tottering steps, but a fragment of this loaf was sufficient to give him the strength to go as far as the hospice where they found the necessary refreshment.[71]

A few days later the travellers were in Milan, which the founder had already visited several times. It was perhaps then that he won to the order Friar Amizo, the future prior of Padua, who was to give evidence at the canonization process.[72] This friar could not have known the founder long, for his evidence, as dry as a notary's document, brought nothing new. The route then passed through Piacenza, Parma, Modena, where Dominic was to preach the following year.[73] Then they arrived at Bologna. Their welcome was even more moving than in Paris.

It was no longer a poor, unknown band of men that was waiting for them in Bologna; it was a fine convent erected in the church of St Nicholas of the Vines and a vast community of brethren, gathered together and formed by the care of Master Reginald. There were many students, but also Masters of the university who had put on the white tunic and black mantle of the Preachers. All had heard Dominic spoken of. They already knew him in imagination through Reginald's affectionate admiration. They welcomed him with great joy and received him as their father, with deference and respect.[74]

When Reginald had arrived in Bologna on 21st December 1218, the band of Preachers was still in the Mascarella largely ignored and unknown. In a few days there was a complete metamorphosis.

> He devoted himself wholly and without delay to preaching. His eloquence was like a flaming fire and his discourse, like a burning torch, inflamed the hearts of all his hearers. Very few people were so stony-hearted that they could resist the effects of this fire. The whole of Bologna was in effervescence. Anyone would have thought that a new Elias had just risen up. At that time he received a large number of men of Bologna into the order.[75]

It was not only the Frenchman's natural eloquence which conferred a prophetic inspiration on his words. Two sentiments, equally powerful, contributed to his intense exaltation. The joy of being freed from a life that was too human and of which he had finally conceived a horror, and of having given himself up without reserve to the Gospel, as a fully-fledged priest in voluntary poverty and the ministry of the Preacher;[76] the joy of the communion and fraternal devotion he had just experienced. As he confided a few weeks before his death to Friar Matthew of France: 'When the latter, who had known him in the delicate life he had led in the vain and difficult world, asked him if he did not sometimes experience a certain repugnance in his new life, he replied bowing his head—"I do not think I have any merit in living in this order, for I have always found too much joy there".'[77]

Thus Reginald's voice was not only that of a witness of Jesus Christ which transmitted the appeals and promises of the Master in words which went straight to one's heart, it was at the same time the voice of the humble group of the brethren of Bologna. They had remained in the town for nearly a year, unknown, despised and perhaps under suspicion. They now spoke in the presence of all through the marvellous instrumentality of their elder brother. At the same time that Reginald was kindling the apostolic ideal in the heart of the clergy of Bologna, he was showing them the way to come closer to it by taking the habit of his brethren. The witness of the Preaching Friars added its eloquence to that of the preacher himself, and the latter's words possessed all the more force to stir up souls in that he had himself given the example of leaving all things, in the prime of life and at the height of a brilliant career, to become a poor man among the poor of Jesus Christ. A priest, a master in law, for five years a professor at the university of Paris, he belonged par excellence to the milieu of his audience. It was the spiritual crisis of the university men of his time that he had felt in his heart. The gesture that he had accomplished, others would be called upon to make. The drama of his conscience awakened a similar drama in the conscience of each one of those who were listening to him. An episode which occurred on the feast of the finding of the body of St Stephen[78] among others, must have brought explicit proof of this.

> While he was devoting himself with great fervour to preaching and attracting to the order a good number of clerics and masters, Master Moneta of Cremona,[79]

then famous in the whole of Lombardy for the way in which he taught in the Faculty of Arts, began to be afraid at the sight of so many vocations that if he listened to the words of the religious he would in turn be caught. Thus he avoided Reginald as much as he could and dissuaded all the students, by word and example, from going to his sermons. On the day of the feast of St Stephen, his students tried to get their Master to the sermon. He could not withdraw behind the excuse of lectures he had to give, nor find any reason for refusing. He could only ask them to go first of all to St Proclus to hear Mass. They went, and instead of one Mass they heard three. The students continued their insistence. 'Let us go to the sermon, then' said the Master. When they arrived Reginald was still preaching and the cathedral[80] was so full that they could not get inside. Moneta had to remain at the door. He listened, however, and from the first words was won over. '*Behold*,' said the Preacher, '*I see heaven opening*.[81] Yes, it is clear that today the heavens are open for us to enter in. Anyone who wishes can penetrate those wide opened doors. Let those poor negligent men who shut their hearts, mouths and hands against God think of this and tremble, let them tremble lest God shut the kingdom of heaven against them and they themselves cannot enter in. Why do you delay, beloved ? Behold the heavens are opened.' As soon as the sermon had ended Master Moneta ran to Reginald, his heart pierced with contrition by the word of God, and, setting before him his situation and obligations, he made profession into his hands. He was, however, held back by all sorts of obstacles. He obtained permission to continue to wear his secular clothes for more than a year. This was not without its effect. In compensation for the large number of people whom he had recently turned away from Reginald's preaching, he brought many more, not only to the sermon, but to the order. In taking them to these sermons, he decided first one and then another to ask for entrance into the order, and seemed to be renewing his own profession with each one of them.[82]

One of the immediate effects of Reginald's preaching was to win firm friends for the Preachers. Dominic's vicar to the group in Bologna,[83] the former dean of St Aignan, had taken the community in hand. His first care was to take it away from the hospice of the Mascarella. For this he needed a church.

The brethren had one in view, St Nicholas of the Vines.[84] The priest who served the church there had become their friend and said he was willing to let them have it. For this, however, it was necessary to obtain the authorization of the bishop, and in particular of the lay patron. Henry of Fratta, bishop of Bologna, did not seem to trouble much about the Preachers, despite the Pope's letters. He allowed them to live and that was all. Reginald, however, had a great means of action for cases of this kind, the friendship of Ugolino. The Cardinal of Ostia had been going round northern Italy since 1218, acquitting himself in a masterly manner of his legation of peace and of the crusade. Taking advantage of the passage of the Cardinal Legate through Bologna or in its neighbourhood,[85] Reginald obtained his insistent intervention with the bishop. The latter took the necessary action—he granted the friars the church of St Nicholas.[86]

All was going well. The priest who served the church, Rodolfo de Faenza, was still prepared to give up his claim. He had even decided to ask for the habit of the order;[87] in this way he could hand over his church to the community without completely abandoning it. He did so without delay. Later, indeed, he was to be a loyal and devoted Preacher.[88] Greatly attached to Dominic, whose life he followed closely when the saint was staying in Bologna, he was to supply extremely valuable evidence at the canonization process. Reginald entrusted the material care of the community to him forthwith, in particular the adaptation and reconstruction of the buildings for the brethren's installation. First, however, the consent of the lay patron, Pietro di Lovello, of the powerful family of the Carbonesi di Guiterno, was necessary.[89] This was not an easy matter.

Situated in the neighbourhood of the abbey of St Proclus, in the southern suburb that the city had recently included within its walls, the church stood out prominently on the summit of a slight rise in the ground. A large piece of sloping ground, also belonging to Pietro di Lovello, separated it from the moat of Bologna which passed to the south. It was parcelled out into a series of gardens where some houses were erected. This was the suburban domain known as 'In the vines' which gave its epithet to St Nicholas.[90] Now the dependencies of the sanctuary were insufficient for the installation of a convent in the church. It was thus necessary to obtain from Pietro di Lovello not only renunciation of the patronage, but also the sale of the land. At Master Reginald's first overtures, the landowner refused point-blank. All, however, was not lost.

Andalò, the son of Pietro di Lovello, had a daughter named Diana.[91] Moved, like so many others, by the preachings of Reginald, Diana soon detached herself from the vanities of the world and the luxury in which she was made to live. She had become the familiar friend of the Preachers, with whom she had frequent spiritual conversations. She took the matter of the land in hand and used her skill as a woman to obtain it from her grandfather. In the end the good man yielded. On 14th March, 1219, for the price of three Bolognese pounds per plot, he granted the land and undertook to clear it of all the houses which were built upon it, on condition that the just price was paid. Finally, for the love of God, he renounced his rights as patron, with the exception of those which a layman might preserve over a conventual church. His wife Otta on her part renounced her mortgages.[92] Friar Rodolfo was able to adapt the buildings. The Preachers took possession of their new convent around Easter.[93]

It was time, for the community was increasing rapidly. Before the arrival of Master Reginald, hardly any religious had joined the small group of the early brethren of the Mascarella—Friar Richard, Friar Christian and the

Roman lay-brother—perhaps Friar Tancred, a knight from the imperial court who was soon to become Prior of Rome.[94] After Rodolfo di Faenza, Frogier of Penna, founder of the friary in Siena, had entered on 20th February,[95] Paul of Venice on 3rd March;[96] Friar Walter, future founder and Prior of Brescia,[97] Master Clair, professor in arts and canon law and later Roman provincial, had doubtless preceded them.[98] Roland of Cremona entered about the beginning of May,[99] Buonviso of Piacenza certainly before St Dominic's arrival;[100] Friars Simon of Sweden and Nicholas of Lund took the habit on 15th August.[101] Many other clerics imitated them, among whom must doubtless be reckoned John of Salerno, the first Prior of Florence, Friars Giacomo and Robaldo, the founders of Milan. . . . A student, whose name is not known, came to look for the grotto of Bethlehem at the convent of St Nicholas, 'with the crib of chastity and the fodder of doctrine, the ass of simplicity and the ox of discretion, Mary who gives light, Joseph who makes one grow and Jesus who saves'.[102] The climate of Italy clothed the evangelical themes of the life of the Preachers in brighter colours than in the north.

All vocations were not equally deep-rooted and, when the first enthusiasm was over, nature, habit and the demon, it must be said, strove to recover their rights. More than any other place in the order, the convent of Bologna would serve as lists for the single combats of the religious with the unclean spirit with which the chronicles of medieval cloisters overflow. The collection of anecdotes of Gérard de Frachet contains narratives on this point enough to make one's hair stand on end.[103] It was to one of these episodes that we owe, after Dominic's death, the institution of the impressive custom of the *Salve Regina*, the Preachers' greeting to the Blessed Virgin at the close of the day.[104] Reginald however dominated this wrestling of the spirit as he did the other crises.

A true emulator of Dominic, he drove out the demon by adding hard penances to the austerities of the rule. It was thus that he won back only just in time a novice who was seeking to flee in a moment of aberration, by imposing a cruel discipline on him at chapter, while the community prayed aloud. Conquered at last, and freed from temptation, the brother repented and promised to stand firm.[105] Above all Reginald was pitiless in the matter of poverty. If the devil took upon himself to punish a brother who had brought back the money from a sermon,[106] Reginald had another brother who had accepted a piece of cloth without permission humiliated and punished in chapter, in such a way that those present had tears in their eyes. The cloth was burnt in the cloister.[107] The delinquents, moreover, were not the only ones to receive the discipline. Under Reginald's impulse, the Preachers mortified themselves zealously each evening in the convent of St Nicholas.[108]

Hardness? Not at all. It was rather the manifestation of an heroic zeal for living the Gospel and for saving souls, which raised the tone of the whole community, after having inspired the words and mind of Master Reginald. Thus it showed an ardour of life overflowing on the university and eventually upon the city. Moreover what happened was that the inspiration thus set in motion flowed back from the city on to the brethren themselves and, in certain hours of dangerous depression, such as the medieval Christian, generous and unstable like an adolescent, experienced all too often, came to give them fresh heart in a truly providential fashion.

The community, recently installed at St Nicholas of the Vines, was still fragile.[109]

An uneasiness [relates Gérard de Frachet] was suddenly manifested among the brethren like a temptation, an inferiority complex which depressed them to such an extent that a good number of them began to discuss the order to which they might transfer. They feared in fact that the foundation, so recent and so insecurely established, would soon totally collapse. Two of the most important of the brethren even obtained from the cardinal-legate who was then in the vicinity[110] letters which allowed them to pass to a monastery of the order of Cîteaux. They presented these letters to Friar Reginald. . . . The latter summoned the brethren in chapter, and put the matter before them with great grief. Tears flowed on all sides and the earlier trouble only increased. Reginald raised his eyes to heaven and spoke to God in whom lay all his confidence, in his heart, while Friar Clair, with the great authority of his virtue and his competence . . . began to speak to the brethren and strengthen them by many powerful arguments. He had scarcely finished speaking when Master Roland of Cremona,[111] a Bologna professor then highly reputed, who was held as eminent in the field of philosophy—he was afterwards to be the first to teach theology to the brethren in Paris—arrived all alone, fleeing from the world in a sort of spiritual intoxication or fire which was kindled in him by the spirit of God.[112] Without exordium or explanation, he asked to be received into the order. Overcome with joy, Reginald did not wait for the brethren to go and look for a habit. He took off his own scapular with the hood and clothed Master Roland with it there and then; the sacristan rang the bell;[113] the brethren sang the *Veni Creator* in the measure in which the flood of their tears of joy allowed them to sing. An immense crowd of men, women and students rushed forward. The whole town was beside itself. The recent devotion towards the friars was again renewed and the common temptation vanished completely. The two brethren threw themselves down in the midst of the chapter, avowed that they had done wrong and, renouncing their letters of dismissal, promised to persevere in the order.[114]

We can imagine Dominic's enthusiasm when he discovered the community at the end of August 1219.[115] Three masters in canon law or in philosophy among the brethren, a fourth, still a secular, but already professed in the order, mature and tried clerics, religious full of manly virtue, students full of zeal—what could he not envisage with such an instrument in his hands? The need of northern Italy was precisely to receive in great number new apostles such as these. It was indeed as much contaminated by the Catharists

as the Midi of France.[116] And then, what a reservoir of new strength for the
whole of Christendom was this legion of students of Bologna, whose movement towards the order was initiated in such an outstanding way. Finally,
what an advantage for an order whose legislation was not yet completed,
was the presence of the university of law and the collaboration of its masters,
of whom several had become brethren. Dominic decided to remain for the
future in Bologna,[117] except for indispensable journeys to the Roman Curia
or in the neighbouring dioceses which he could evangelize,[118] while waiting
to go away one day with a few disciples to carry Jesus Christ beyond the
frontiers of Christendom.[119] For the moment he devoted himself to the
upbringing of 'the still tender infancy of his new nursery by his spiritual
instruction as much as by his example'.[120]

The first step he took was indeed of great spiritual import. It was concerned with poverty. In view of the experiences in Spain and France, this
gesture was decisive. When Friar Rodolfo, not without a certain satisfaction,
brought him the news that 'the lord Odoric Galiciani intends to give the
brethren some of his properties which are worth more than five hundred
Bolognese pounds', and that the charter was already signed before the Lord
bishop of Bologna, the founder refused. He gave orders for the charter to be
cancelled.[121] After all, he was only respecting the statute of the community
of the brethren in 1216. *Tantum reditus*—no landed property, nothing but
revenues.[122] Now, however, he was going further. He desired that the
brethren should likewise renounce other possessions, whatever be their type.
'For the future let them live only on alms, and even so let them use them
sparingly.'[123] It was only, indeed, a counsel, a desire. In a matter such as
this, only the community of the whole order could take a decision that was
binding; it was, however, a pressing counsel. In view of the kindness which
the population of Bologna showed in regard to the Preachers, in view of the
courage with which the first brethren bore the wretched poverty in the
hospice of the Mascarella, the convent of Bologna might well make trial
of a more clearly marked mendicancy. One circumstance in particular was
to help them.

A few days after his arrival, Dominic made contact with Diana of
Andalò.[124] His special gift for the ministry of women displayed itself once
more. In him Diana found what she wanted. She soon attached herself to the
founder with all her affection, and discussed with him the salvation of her
soul. Dominic had just been admiring at St Nicholas the work of a generous
man. He was now to discover what a woman could do. Or, rather he sensed
this beforehand. He had realized from the beginning of his preaching
the incomparable rôle of women among the Catharists—a Blanche of Laurac,
a Hélis of Mazerole—and had immediately, by the foundation of Prouille,
answered the legitimate religious appeal which was contained in such
devotion. He laid open to Diana the immense field of the interior life

and apostolic action. A short time later, kneeling before the Preacher, her hands between both of his, she made profession. It was an engagement to religious life without any convent yet being designated, at the same time as a vow of obedience to Dominic. Master Reginald, Friar Walter and Friar Rodolfo were there as witnesses. Indeed a large number of ladies of Bologna was also present. The matter became public. It stirred up a mighty current in Bolognese society. Andalò and his sons filled or would soon fill the most considerable offices in the Italian cities—'praetor of the mountain' for Bologna, podesta of Milan, Piacenza, Genoa, Florence, even senator of Rome.[125] By their riches, their authority, their ancient lineage, this patrician family was one of the first in the city. The current of interest and sympathy for the Preachers was further extended among the ladies of gentle birth and of the nobility. They frequented the brethren on terms of friendship and entrusted the care of their salvation to them in spiritual conversations. Finally, the whole of upper class society, men and women, came to the help of the convent and surrounded it with veneration. Dominic and his brethren lived with the poor through their mendicancy, but linked the rich with their work of evangelization. There is no soul that is not valuable in the eyes of God.

Evangelization in the city became daily more intense. For preference Dominic devoted his attention to students. He did not content himself with waiting for them at St Nicholas but went to pay them friendly visits in their lodgings.[126] He was sometimes unusually outspoken with them when he discerned the call of God.

When I was studying in Bologna [relates Friar Stephen] Master Dominic came there. He preached to the students and I confessed my sins to him. It seemed to me that he loved me. One evening, as I was preparing to have a stolen supper with my comrades, he sent a message to me by two of the brethren: *'Friar Dominic asks that you should come to him immediately.'* 'I will come after supper', I told them. *'No,'* they said, *'come immediately.'* I left all, got up and went to him. I found him with numerous brethren at the convent of St Nicholas. He said to the brethren, *'Show him how to make the venia.'* When I had done this, I gave myself over into his hands by vow. He clothed me with the habit of the Friars Preachers before I went away. *'I want to give you'*, he said to me, *'the weapons with which you must fight all your life against the devil.'* I was greatly astonished and still wonder by what instinct he called me in this way and clothed me with the habit of the Friars Preachers. For never before had I spoken with him of my entering religion. I think it was through an inspiration or revelation from God.[127]

His vision, however, went further than sanctifying a soul or filling a convent. As in Paris, he was concerned with extending this sphere of influence and distributing the energies which were accumulating in Bologna. He sent some brethren to preach in Bergamo, where the second convent in Italy would be founded a few months later.[128] He also sent some to Florence, where the Preachers seem to have been installed since November 1219.[129] About Easter of the following year, two further houses came into being, in Verona[130] and in Milan;[131] these were convents with churches and their installation presupposed an earlier ministry of at least some duration. It is clear that Dominic decided upon these various missions and set them on foot from Bologna. It was also from Bologna that he directed the somewhat simple Friar Buonviso to Piacenza, who came from that city.

> I was still a novice [he would say] without any experience of preaching, for I had not yet studied the divine Scriptures. To be dispensed from going, I alleged my little skill. The blessed father, however, with very gentle words, persuaded me that I ought to go there and said to me: '*Go with assurance, for the Lord will be with you and will put on your lips the words that you should preach.*' I obeyed, went to Piacenza, preached there, and God attached so many graces to my preaching that, after having listened to me, three brethren entered the order of Preachers.[132]

This was only the initial step. Buonviso brought back his three conquests to Bologna and it was not long before he set off with Dominic for about ten months.[133] The convent would only come into existence after his return.[134]

The founder's vision, however, extended far beyond this. He greeted with joy the presence in Bologna of two Swedish brethren. He would soon have the opportunity of sending them off to the Scandinavian lands.

Before leaving for the Curia, where he would be occupied with a Roman foundation, Dominic finally decided upon one last mission which would involve a particularly painful separation for the community in Bologna. The convent was overflowing with vitality. Personalities were not lacking there. They were all too rare in Paris, where the recruitment was almost exclusively among students. The time had come to send Friar Reginald there that he might create among his compatriots and especially his former colleagues and students of the university, a movement comparable to that of Bologna. Moreover, there was the possibility that his authority and his juridical skill might liberate the convent of St Jacques from the obstacles created by the clergy. When the founder announced the news, there was deep grief in the convent and in the city. The bonds were already too long-standing and too deep to be broken without suffering. Each one of those whom this great religious had 'engendered in Jesus Christ by the word of the Gospel' wept to see himself so soon torn away from him who was nurturing him.[135]

> All this, however [concludes Jordan] was accomplished by a divine instinct. It was wonderful to see how the servant of God, when he distributed his brethren hither and thither in the various quarters of the Church of God, did so with certainty, without hesitation or wavering, although others at this very moment were of opinion that it should not have been done in that way. All happened as if he were already certain of the future, or as if the Spirit had given him information by his revelations. Who, then, would dare to call the matter in question ? At the beginning he had only a small number of brethren, simple for the most part

and not well-instructed, and he divided them, scattering them on the mission throughout the churches in such a way that this children of the world in their wisdom thought he seemed to be destroying the embryo work rather than enlarging it. But he helped his missionaries by the intercession of his prayers, and the power of the Lord worked for their multiplication.[136]

At the end of October, Dominic in turn left Bologna and went to the Curia again.[137]

CHAPTER XV

VITERBO AND ROME

A SMALL band of religious travelling on foot climbed slowly across the Romagna Apennines—Dominic, with his brethren Guillaume de Montferrat,[1] Buonviso de Piacenza[2] and Frogier di Penna.[3] They tramped over the passes and came down into Tuscany. In Florence they found once more the brethren who had recently been sent from Bologna. The preachers had not as yet any convent of their own in the city. Each evening, when their preaching was over, the brethren retired to the hospice of St Pancras, an asylum for poor folk.[4]

Dominic stayed there a few days. Doubtless he wanted to visit the authorities, and to assess the tasks to be undertaken and men's goodwill. As usual, he gave himself at the same time to the direct ministry of souls. An obituary list has preserved the memory of a lay-brother of Florence named Guy the Little to whom he gave the habit in the hospice of St Pancras.[5] It may have been then, or at his next visit in the following month of May, that he brought back to penance and fervent life a woman who was given over to the pleasures of the flesh. This Béné, who was one day to become Sister Benedict, would in any case continue to be the subject of his fatherly care. He saw her on each of his visits and whatever his own anxieties might be, gave his attention to solving the problems and calming the fears of his spiritual daughter.[6]

The stop was only of a few days' duration. Before 11th November, Dominic and his companions were at the Pontifical court.[7] They caught up with it at Viterbo. In view of the fact that democratic agitation had been rife in Rome since the death of Innocent III, Honorius had left the hostile city in June.[8] He had been installed in Viterbo since the beginning of October;[9] Ugolino was there too, having returned from his embassy.[10] Losing no time, the founder asked for an audience of the Sovereign Pontiff. Thus in the middle of autumn, after having finished, so to speak, the sowing of the crops, he came to ask for a new shower of apostolic letters which would raise up the harvest.

Indeed the account of his round of visitations across Spain, France and Italy, could not but impress the Pope. When he set out, Dominic had only two houses, one of men and the other of women, with about twenty brethren and sisters scarcely more numerous. Now he had seven or eight houses completely formed, several others in the course of formation, and could count more than a hundred brethren.[11] Above all he had launched among the more learned clerics a great movement which was continually expanding and which, in Paris and Bologna, placed such clergy at the service of the preaching which the Church was asking for.

Dominic presented two requests in particular which would remedy the actual difficulties of the brethren and were the considered result of acquired experience. The first concerned the relations of the Preachers with the secular clergy. If the brethren really fulfilled the expectation of the Church and the papacy in the ministry of souls, if they came to remedy a tragic weakness which the clergy was in general powerless to overcome without other help, through lack of preparation and all too often of good will, the Preachers' ministry of salvation must not remain inextricably linked to the good will or otherwise of these same clergy. The example of Paris on this point was typical. As a result of rights acquired, of perquisites or of funeral dues, the population of Paris was left without sermons, though the urgency of such preaching had been solemnly recognized. Thus it was for the Church to intervene and with her mighty hand constrain the diocesan clergy to receive the brethren, allow them facilities for action, and, even more, to have recourse to their services while supporting them to the utmost.

Moreover, Dominic had seen for himself how the rule of the Preachers and, above all, their special inspiration worked under test. He was able to declare emphatically in the presence of the Pope that the programme of imitation of the life of the apostles was directly responsible for the attraction felt for his order both by young clerics and elderly professors, and for the great fruits of their preaching. They would not have filled the convent of St Jacques and revolutionized the university of Bologna if they had merely offered the intellectual world the ideal of just any chaplain or of a traditional monk. It was only poverty carried to the utmost limits, and intensive work in the service of the salvation of souls that had been successful in winning, in a burst of enthusiasm which had never slackened, Reginald, Roland or Moneta of Cremona—full of joy at this opportunity of becoming wholeheartedly faithful to the Gospel which meant so much to them, and faithful in their capacity as clerics. Thus the time had come to put the finishing touches to the inscribing of the apostolic rule within the rule of the Preachers, by the adoption of a clause which would impose mendicancy on the convents, and by the general organization of the brethren's preaching. Because on these two points a large part of the Church was liable to be scandalized on account of the precedent created by the schismatics and the Catharists, it was necessary that the Pope himself should consent to allow these statutes to be adopted and to cover them with his authority, notwithstanding the 13th canon of the Lateran.

Either at Dominic's side or in some private conversation, Cardinal Ugolino gave similar testimony. The close relations which he had just had with St

Francis and St Clare of Assisi had finally persuaded him of what he had already long suspected.[12] For reanimating Catholicism, there was at the time no energy comparable to apostolic evangelism. It was essential to allow Dominic to effect in his order what he had made trial of in his personal preaching since 1206.

Honorius was also convinced. It is only necessary to read his letters in chronological order for the movement of his feelings towards the Preachers and St Dominic to be understood.

The first bull of all, in December 1216, contained not a single personal word, being merely a formula from the chancellery. A few days later, however, the second bull expressed the Pope's sentiments in regard to the Preachers.[13] The glorious name of 'unconquered athletes of Christ', however, which it conferred upon them did not yet sufficiently characterize their nature; at that time it was likewise used to designate the crusaders who were fighting against the Albigenses.[14] The first general bull of recommendation, of 11th February, 1218, on the other hand, definitely pronounced in favour of the 'useful ministry' of the Preachers and of their religious life 'pleasing to God, as We believe'.[15] It was not long before the restriction of 'We believe' disappeared. The 'useful' ministry soon appears as 'necessary';[16] even 'more than necessary'.[17] Finally, the order, in the eyes of the Pope, was 'raised up by the Lord as a solution to the overflow of iniquity and to the coldness of the charity of the multitude';[18] 'set apart in view of the profit of the universal Church, for the ministry of the Gospel'.[19] The expressions of attachment undergo a parallel *crescendo*. In 1218 the order was merely recommended. At the end of 1219, it was recommended 'with affection',[20] in February 1220, 'with sincere affection'.[21] In the middle of the same year it was recommended with a 'sincere charity which embraces the brethren in the Lord'.[22] At the end of the year the Pope 'embraces the whole order in the arms of a sincere charity, attaching himself with affection to its progress in the Lord'.[23]

These subtle nuances in official formulae may perhaps surprise us. They will seem less astonishing when it is realized that on this last visit to the Curia, perhaps even on one of his previous ones, Dominic became close friends with a high functionary of the pontifical chancellery. William of Piedmont, later Bishop of Modena before becoming Cardinal of Sabina,[24] was won over by Dominic's attitude to the point of asking him to receive him, Carthusian as he was, into the fraternity of the order; this should be understood on the plane of spiritual union. Dominic, attaching himself for his part to this great religious, very close to him in outlook, in the future submitted to him important business affecting the Preachers, as if he were a counsellor of the order.[25] Now between 13th December, 1219 and 24th February, 1220, William of Piedmont became Vice-Chancellor. As such he was the leading official in the pontifical administration. He drew up, revised, or at least checked all the writings of the Holy See. His genius consisted precisely in inscribing in chancellery formulae the subtle nuances of the Pope's intentions.[26]

Such expressions must be viewed in their context. These were no ordinary letters, in which the Pope was allowing himself the expansions of personal feeling; they were official documents charged with august authority and destined to be made use of in all sorts of circumstances. At the time they were read with the same careful attention with which they were drawn up, and preserved with so much care that they have finally come down to our own day. Thus the pontifical letters never contained a single word used without due reflection—a joy for the historian who can give full import to every one of such expressions. Through these dry parchments he can see deepening in the mind of the head of the Church, confidence, attachment, enthusiasm and resolute devotedness in regard to the Friars Preachers and their founder and master.

Dominic knew this and acted accordingly. He established himself in Viterbo where he would remain until half-way through December. At that time he was to leave for Rome on a mission for the Pope. He would stay there for the first weeks of 1220, returning to Viterbo about the middle of February.[27] Thus established at the centre of the Church as in a command post, he took full advantage of the kindness of the Sovereign Pontiff to intervene through this authority, week after week, at every point of Christendom where his order was in process of development. On one occasion he would solve by this powerful aid a difficulty which a letter from the brethren submitted to him. At another, using his initiative, he would make them take a step forward, correct some weak point, or decide upon a new foundation.

Shortly after his arrival, he obtained a new series of recommendations. The prototype of this letter was registered in the month of April 1218.[28] It was thus sufficient to ask for certified copies of it at the Chancellery. The bull contained a description of the order—its ministry, which was the office of preaching, and its religious life under the aspect of poverty. It commanded all the prelates of the Church to treat the brethren as men recommended by the Apostolic See, to encourage them in their own vocation, to make use of them in the office of preaching to which they had been assigned—in short, to assist them in their needs.

On 15th November Dominic had this bull sent to all the prelates of Spain. The document was eventually to lead to the foundation of the convent of Zamora, which was perhaps not fully established until after his death.[29] Before this they were able to use it for several foundations, among which those of Palencia and Santarem should possibly be numbered.

A further copy was dispatched on 28th November to the Midi of France. This led to the foundation of Montpellier.[30] It was clearly this that gave rise to the establishment of this convent, which Bernard Gui, particularly well

informed as to the origins of the Preachers in Provence, places in 1220, after
an unsuccessful attempt at Narbonne.[31]. In sending this bull to the brethren
of the Midi, that is, to the brethren of Toulouse, Dominic gave effect to a
project elaborated among them on the occasion of his visit the previous
spring. Montpellier was to be an important centre for the order. It was the
third university of Christendom, where medical teaching did not exclude
other branches of learning, and also a considerable reservoir of clerics
whence the order could draw recruits. Finally, it was the principal centre of
orthodoxy in western Provence.

A third certified copy of the bull left on 13th December for St Jacques in
Paris, where Reginald had just arrived. This bull did not arrive as a mere
isolated document. With it came a large packet of letters, dated 1st, 11th,
12th and 13th December, which resolutely grasped and sought to solve the
main problems of the Preachers.

The letter of 1st December[32] was only a preamble. In a single phrase it
granted the brethren authorization to celebrate divine worship—by this
should be understood publicly and solemnly, as was then the custom—in the
chapel they had received from the masters of the university. Thus the right
was defined—there now remained its application.

By the bull of 11th December,[33] Honorius appointed a committee of
important people, the priors of the abbeys of St Denis and St Germain des
Prés, and the Chancellor of the Church of Milan who was then in Paris. Up
to that time the chapter of the cathedral had prevented the Preachers from
celebrating the offices in their chapel, although the latter had received
authorization to do so from the Papacy. The chapter ought, on the contrary,
to have helped and favoured them, in view of the disinterestedness of the
brethren and their religious intention, in both of which things the Pope
placed such strong hopes. Honorius was not unaware of the real cause of the
attitude of the canons. Accordingly he instructed the committee to assess a
reasonable indemnity for the adjacent churches, and at the same time to
constrain the chapter (under threat of the censures of the Church), to
allow public worship in the Preachers' chapel.

The principle which governed the solution should be noted. In this very
first conflict between secular clergy and mendicants—a conflict which in
the course of the thirteenth century was at times to assume alarming proportions—the attitude taken by the Church and by the order, by Honorius
and by Dominic, was already that which would finally prevail. To give
freedom to the ministry of the Preachers, there was no necessity to deny the
prior rights of the secular clergy. Nor was it a question of carving out a new
sector for them in the midst of the network of parishes. At that time the
Pope was not in the habit of intervening in matters of parochial boundaries.
Dominic, on his side, did not want to receive the charge of souls; his
attitude on this matter at the time of the preaching in the Midi, when

he shunned and refused the episcopate, has been noted. The order was content to superimpose itself upon the parishes without interfering with them, claiming only the minimum of liberty in which to exercise its spiritual activity—the chanting of God's praises and the sacred mysteries in the course of which it was to preach the word of God. The Preacher is a spiritual man, not one of the authorities.

To these three bulls was added another on 12th December,[34] which it is proposed to call the Bull of Mendicancy. By its composition as by its contents it recalled that of 21st January, 1217, the first confirmation of the title and essence of the Preachers.[35] The Pope expressed his certainty as to the manifold fruits which the brethren would produce; he knew the weight of the fatigues and dangers to which they would be exposing themselves for the salvation of others through the use of the means of preaching to which they had given themselves. He enjoined these sufferings upon them in remission of their sins. Thus the sanctification and remission of sins that monks, traditionally, expected from the exercises of their penitential state, the Preachers were to expect above all from their sacrifices for the salvation of souls; that is to say—for every one of the words of this letter must be weighed with care—the sacrifices comprised in the type of preaching they had chosen the better to save souls. As to what this type was, the letter is explicit—and it is in this that it is distinguished from that of January 1217 and is indicative of a step forward in the realization of the idea of the Preachers—it is preaching in deep-rooted poverty. To 'prepare themselves to give the Gospel' in fullest authenticity, they had thus freed themselves from the 'burden of the goods of this world' and had decided to carry out their role as Preachers 'in the abjection of a voluntary poverty'. What was to save them and procure for them the same advantage as the practices of the cloistered religious was thus not only the labour of the word of God and the fatigues or dangers of their journeys in quest of souls, but also the poverty to which they were exposing themselves because they had chosen as their rule wholehearted imitation of Christ and the apostles.

The expression *in abiectione voluntarie paupertatis*, which appears in the letters from the Pope to the Preachers between the 8th and 13th December, 1219, and would remain as a permanent feature of such letters, should be carefully noted;[36] it was absolutely new. Earlier the Pope had only spoken of the *titulum paupertatis*, i.e. of the general poverty of the religious orders. But if the expression was new for Honorius, it was not so for Dominic. It was an echo of that which Innocent had employed thirteen years earlier in the confirmation of the mendicant poverty of the preachers of the Narbonensis: 'The poverty of Christ in a despised garment', *in despecto habitu*. At a time when the convenient term of mendicant poverty had not yet come into use, it would seem that it should be sought, in the bulls of the Pope or the documents of the period, under the expressions just cited. That is why it is proposed to give to this bull, a replica of that of 17th January, 1217, as well as its completion, the name of 'Bull of Mendicancy'.

These expressions had such importance in Dominic's eyes that four days earlier he had them inscribed in a new type of recommendation (II), intended to replace the original type for the future.[37] The triple mandate of the first bull, encouragement, utilization, assistance, is again almost identical in the new text. The explanation of motives, however, is considerably modified. In the description it gives of the religious attitude by which the brethren prepare and support their preaching, the bull of recommendation presents the essential terms of the Bull of Mendicancy—'repudiation of the riches of this world', 'in the abjection of a voluntary poverty'. In the eyes of the whole of the Church, as in their own eyes, the Preachers would for the future appear as poor men of the Gospel. A copy of the new formula of recommendation dated 13th December was sent with the packet of letters to St Jacques. Dominic clearly further added a letter from himself, with explanations and detailed instructions.

Each of these missives soon produced its effect. The entry into the lists of the committee of three and the personal activity of Master Reginald decided the chapter of Notre Dame of Paris to relent in some degree. Without yet granting the right of burial—at this very moment all too moving evidence of this was to be forthcoming[38]—it provisionally gave permission for the offices at the convent of the Preachers. On Ash Wednesday at latest, thus on 20th February, 1220, the community of St Jacques sang the office publicly.[39] This definitive ruling was put into practice with discretion. It was to come up in the following month of December in a lawsuit by Archdeacon Stephen, assisted by two canons of the cathedral.[40] The document brought the proof that the sole motive for the prohibition was the financial anxieties of the parish of Saint Benoît in the matter of offerings and of funeral perquisites. The conditions for the authorization of worship were rigorous. The brethren must close their doors to the faithful on the occasion of the feasts of Easter, Pentecost, St Benedict, All Saints, Christmas. If on such a day the faithful had to be satisfied with the sermon of the parish priest, at least they would be in no danger of taking their alms to the Preachers. If by chance the latter nevertheless received something on these feasts, they were to be careful to return the whole of it to the parish. They must also pay an annual indemnity to the parish priest and another to the canons, to compensate for the probable diminution in the perquisites. Finally they undertook to have only one bell, the weight of which should not exceed 300 pounds. In compensation they acquired the liberty to celebrate the sacred offices and even a limited right of burial. In the meantime Honorius had been able to receive the representatives of the chapter in Rome, in connection with the entangled problem of the succession of the bishop of Paris.[41] The Pope did not hide from them what he thought of their attitude.[42]

At a time when the canons of the cathedral were meditating levying a tax on the poor, Friar Reginald, Friar Matthew and the community of St Jacques decided to give themselves up to that mendicant poverty which Dominic had just recommended to them by the letters of the Pope as much as by his own. They renounced their claim to the deed of tithes granted by Jean de Briard and Amicie his wife. The motive which urged them to this was even inscribed in a charter. 'We have judged it good,' they said, 'not to preserve any kind of temporal wealth, for we consider that the state of poverty increases merit, inspires better counsels and gives rise to less anxious cares. And we abandon the care of our life for the present and the future to the assistance of divine Providence.'[43] The same act further revealed that the decision, which handed over to public charity a community of some thirty religious, was taken with the assent of the conventual chapter as a whole.

What was to be done with these tithes? Friar Matthew, who had acquired them through his relations with the former crusaders of the Albigeois, approached the Cistercian nuns of St Antoine, so closely linked with the de Montforts.[44] One of the almoners of the abbey, Friar Beuve, was given on 31st March the responsibility of disposing of the tithes and of the corresponding house.[45] Two documents throw further light on this gesture. A confirmation of the archbishop of Sens, dating from May 1220, made public the fact that Friar Beuve had conferred these tithes on the abbey of Cistercian nuns that Dame Amicie de Breteuil, now widow of Jean de Briard, was busy founding at Villiers.[46] Further, in 1225, when the arrival of the nuns effectively brought the community into being, Friar Matthew reiterated that since 1220 it had been the will of the brethren to abandon the tithes altogether.[47]

Thus Dominic's action on the occasion of his visit to St Jacques, in favour of absolute evangelical poverty, had not been in vain. Reginald, Matthew of France and the early brethren who were still with them at the turn of 1220 made the spirit of apostolic life which obtained in the order at the time of its beginnings come to full fruition once more among the young friars of St Jacques. In Paris as in Bologna they were ready to take the decisive step of the general declaration of mendicancy in the order of Preachers, which had been directly prepared for, since 8th December, by a series of pontifical bulls.

At this time, too, Dominic endeavoured to lead the brethren of the Midi to the same point. The Bull of Mendicancy of 12th December[48] and the recommendation of the 13th were dispatched to them also.[49] The circumstances were perhaps not sufficiently favourable or perhaps it was the lack of a Reginald or a Matthew of France in those parts. Dominic's initiative did not produce so prompt an effect in Toulouse as in Bologna or Paris. It was not until 17th April 1221 that he was able to have the charter of tithes, which had formerly been granted by Fulk to his preachers, nullified.[50]

The month of December 1219 was truly one of the vital moments in Dominican history. It was then that Dominic brought to completion three years of experience and investigation. It was then that he paved the way for future developments. We have seen that, at the same time that he obtained the Bull of Mendicancy, he also received a new formula of recommendation. It was not one, however, but three new formulae of this kind which were then issued by the Curia. The fact, surprising at first sight, is explained when the three documents are compared.[51]

Type II, the letter *Dilecti filii* which replaced the original type of 1218, has already been mentioned. This bull, which made declaration of the mendicant poverty of the order, was specially suitable for the foundations of convents. It recommended the Preachers under collective form.

On 11th November, however, i.e. on the occasion of the very first audience in Viterbo, Dominic had already received another recommendation, type III,[1] *Cum qui recipit*. This bull did not yet contain the mendicancy clause. On the other hand, it put the whole emphasis on the ministry of the Preachers. Clear allusions in its prologue or its terms of enactment to the 10th canon of the Lateran on preaching, have as their evident aim the presentation to the bishops in the person of the Preachers of those irreplaceable people who will enable them to satisfy the obligations of the canon of the Council. It mobilized in some sort to the benefit of the Preachers, the full import of the requirements of the Council that Honorius' legates were endeavouring at that moment to have applied in the Christian provinces. To this was added the special weight of the authority of the Sovereign Pontiff. A clause altogether new, however, was designed to protect the poverty of the brethren against temptations and reassure the prelates on the disinterestedness of these new apostles. If it should happen that the self-styled Preacher demanded money, the prelate was to arrest him forthwith and condemn him as a perverter and slanderer of the order. This bull, which summarized the triple mandate of the original bull, was particularly apt as a recommendation of the individual activity of the Preachers. It would in fact serve several times for personal testimonials.

Dominic valued it greatly. In 1221, he often requested its dispatch. The significance of his preference is obvious. The bull clearly expressed the liaison between the Order of Preachers and the 10th canon of the Lateran. It gave as an objective to the brethren a universal, ordinary and positive evangelization—the spiritual nourishment and moral formation of men, without restriction of place or person, such as Christ demanded. On 11th November 1219, Dominic obtained the first copy of this bull. It had finally reached Sweden. The context of this dispatch will soon be clear.

On 13th December following, Dominic received a bull of another, different type (IV[1]), *Quoniam abundavit*. In its terms of enactment this bull merely contained a pressing mandate of recommendation. This time the accent was placed on the reasons which lay behind the movement. The Order of Preachers there appeared in the perspective of the interventions of Providence against the enemies of the Church and the evils from which she suffered. 'The Lord, seeing iniquity overflow and the charity of the people growing cold, has raised up, as we believe, the Order of Friars Preachers who, seeking not their own profit but the profit of Christ, have given themselves to the evangelization of the word of God, as much to put to flight heresies as to uproot other mortal contagions, in the abjection of voluntary poverty.' This description was well calculated to attract to the Preachers the attention of those bishops whose diocese was undergoing a crisis, attacked by heresies or undermined by grave moral deviations. Dominic, however, scarcely made use of this formula at all. It presented only one aspect of the activity of the Preachers, the preaching of controversy, and not the peaceful and joyous setting forth of the truth of the Gospel. On the other hand, Gregory IX, who in 1227 had scarcely ascended the pontifical throne, was to take up this text, which had been forgotten since 1221, once more. He was to enrich it with the greater part of the clauses of the other bulls and would in this way set up the formula of recommendation of the Preachers which would be classic for the future. The activity of the order would be presented in such a sort that it appeared in the perspective of a struggle against evil and error. The fact is significant on the part of the Pontiff who busied himself with organizing the inquisition and with imposing on the Preachers the largest part of its working.

The first copy known of this bull, delivered on 13th December, 1219, found a home in Germany. An attempt will be made to assess how it came to get there.

While Honorius III was contributing with so much effectiveness to the development and solid establishment of the order of St Dominic, he was preparing to entrust to the founder a task which he had very much at heart. One of the cares of Innocent III in Rome had been to install in the city a certain number of model institutes, for instance the hospital of the Holy Spirit, an extension of the famous hospital at Montpellier.[52] He had concerned himself particularly with founding a new monastery of women, where women from Rome itself and nuns coming from convents that were decadent or in part disintegrating would be gathered together under a strict rule.[53] For this purpose he had chosen the ancient church of St Sixtus to the restoration of which he gave his attention. His death had brought all this to a standstill.

Loyal to his predecessor's general programme, Honorius also wanted to pursue this intention of Innocent's. He lacked, however, the indispensable workers. Innocent had entrusted the work of regrouping to those who were specialists in dealing with nuns, the canons of Sempringham.[54] These religious had been founded in England, towards the middle of the twelfth century, to serve as chaplains to a certain number of abbeys of women. They formed small colleges of seven canons, whose house adjoined that of the nuns on the other side of an inviolable enclosure wall, to form a double monastery. Now the religious of Sempringham, who were insular if they were anything at all, had never come to take possession of St Sixtus. The Pope summoned them once more, on 3rd August, 1218,[55] under penalty of losing the church and the house reserved for them, to supply before Christmas of that same year, the religious necessary to establish it in accordance with the prescriptions of their order. The building work was to be done at the expense of the Apostolic See.

The period assigned had elapsed. The Pope nevertheless waited a further year. In November 1219,[56] when two canons presented themselves before him, Honorius still seemed resolved to reserve the mission for them. They brought with them, however, an avowal of their inability to do what was asked. The order was not capable of supplying even the four religious asked for.

On 4th December Honorius withdrew the church of St Sixtus from them[57] and immediately turned to Dominic.[58] It is possible that the Pope expected this refusal and had already foreseen a different solution. The swiftness of his reversal of policy would seem to give proof of this. It is even possible that he had only waited to counter the failure of the English religious until the year 1219 had fully expired, in order to have Dominic near him. It is more difficult to decide whether he already had this in mind when he sent his ultimatum of 1218 to England. It seems, however, that Dominic, when he left Bologna for the Curia in October 1219, knew that a foundation was awaiting him in Rome. Otherwise it is difficult to see why he should have brought with him Friar Buonviso, Friar Guillaume and Friar Frogier.

Thus, thirteen days after the letter to the canons of Sempringham, Honorius was able to write to the brethren and sisters of Prouille, Fanjeaux and Limoux, to announce to them the donation of St Sixtus to St Dominic and the order. At the same time he gave them command to hold themselves at the disposal of their General, ready to come at his request to lead their religious life at St Sixtus, in accordance with their own rule.[59]

It was not, then, a house of brethren that Honorius asked Dominic to set up in Rome, but a house of nuns. The appeal to the sisters of Prouille and to their chaplains is significant. The Pope, however, knew that Dominic had more than once based the ministry of his brethren on houses of women, at least during the early days. There was in Prouille an authentic convent of Friars Preachers annexed to the house of the sisters. What had taken place there could be renewed at Rome. It seems highly probable that we can affirm that the Pope was aiming at the installation in Rome of a house of the brethren at the same time as of a community of sisters on the model of Prouille. For it is not credible that he who urged the prelates of Christendom with so much vigour to install Dominic's sons in their respective dioceses, should not seek first of all to plant them firmly at the centre of the Church. Confirmation of this is found in the somewhat late chronicle of Benedetto de Montefiascone[60] and particularly in a contemporary letter of Conrad de Sharfeneck, Chancellor of the Empire and Bishop of Metz. When this witness as to the main intentions of the Papacy and of the institutions of the eternal city at the close of 1220 proposed to introduce the Friars Preachers into his episcopal city at the beginning of the following year, he did not hesitate to declare that he was acting 'after the example of the Lord Pope, who has granted them a house in Rome, and of many archbishops and bishops'.[61]

The Pope's last letter is not dated from Viterbo, but from Civita Castellana, a halting-place on the way to Rome. The Pope, in fact, had set out with the Curia to spend the feast of Christmas at St Peter's.[62] He took Dominic with him. There was no more than one day's journey to accomplish. On the day following this audience, the founder and his companions installed themselves in the church that had just been given to them.[63]

At the side of the Appian Way, opposite the baths of Caracalla, a stational basilica had since the fifth century kept up the cultus of the Pope and martyr Sixtus II. The site was not an advantageous one. At the foot of the Coelian Hill and of the Lesser Aventine, it consisted of low ground which the breaking down of ancient aqueducts had turned into a swamp. Moreover, the fire, pillage and other destructions which war had multiplied in Rome in the course of the twelfth century had gradually ruined the noble basilica. Like all the ancient buildings in Rome, it had progressively sunk into the ground, whereas the level of the streets had risen by several yards. Innocent III's architects had completed the interment of the building—destroying the aisles and walling up the arches between the pillars; they had built on the top of the central nave a church which measured no more than half of the width of the earlier sanctuary. The new apse rose in its turn upon the walls of the buried one. It was thus somewhat out of proportion, but in a way that lent itself better to the establishment of a choir of religious. Such was the church that Dominic and his brethren received at the close of 1219. It was left for them to construct the convent.

It seems very possible that Dominic may actually have lived in St Sixtus on the occasion of his previous visits to the city. Nothing is known of his lodgings in Rome in 1215, 1216–1217, 1218. The Pope was able to authorize him to make use of this church 'for long deprived of the ministers which it ought to have'[64] through the fault of the canons of Sempringham. No document, however, no indication allows us to establish the fact in a positive manner. It can only be asserted, contrary to the great majority of modern historians,[65] that on his last stay in Rome in 1218, Dominic had still not established a community of Preachers in the city, since he systematically directed to Bologna all the religious he acquired in Rome, whether brethren already of the order who came to rejoin him, or novices who gave themselves to him.

On arrival, then, the community was set up in the unsatisfactory buildings near the church, and the construction of a regular convent at the expense of the Sovereign Pontiff was begun. It would be interesting to catch a glimpse of this third convent built by Dominic. This time a real cloister, doubtless very simple, but devotional, and of regular design, gave superabundant testimony, if it were necessary, of his intelligence and his taste for the life of classic observance. Alas, very little remains of the block of buildings.[66] The church, reconstructed throughout in the eighteenth century, has no longer anything of its thirteenth-century appearance. In the vicissitudes of its history the convent has been entirely changed. Intelligent restorations, however, in 1855 by Fathers Mullooly and Besson, in 1936 by Cardinal Liénart, titulary of St Sixtus, have restored certain thirteenth-century parts of the church —a part of the apse with something of the frescoes, and in particular the chapter-room with its two windows with Roman columns each side of the door. As to the site, made more healthy but rendered characterless by urbanization, it has lost all its power of evocation.

Moreover, scarcely any ancient document shows us the life of Dominic and his brethren in these first months of 1220. None of the reliable sources has a word to say of it. All that is to be found is Constantino di Orvieto's account of two miracles which should be assigned to this period.[67]

The brethren had not yet been long in Rome. Public opinion still regarded them with mistrust. Neither their true life nor the solidity of their religious society were known and people were all too ready to speak evil in their regard. Now whilst they were working on this ancient soil, where the sub-soil conceals enormous masses of old masonry and unsuspected cavities, a serious landslide occurred, and an architect whom the brethren had engaged was buried in a cellar. They could not succeed in freeing him from the rubble which was weighing him down, and when he was finally extricated, he was dead. The brethren were dumbfounded. They were deeply distressed at one of their collaborators dying without the sacraments. They also dreaded lest the superstitious crowd should see in this accident a sign of divine disapproval of the Preachers and should conceive hatred for them. Dominic's prayer assuaged everyone's fear by obtaining the return to life of the unfortunate man.

Once erected, however, the convent began to extend its influence. Of the religious whom Dominic received at this time, a single name has survived—Friar Giacomo de Bella, a Roman born and bred and very well known in the city. Very soon he was made procurator of the community. For mendicant religious still unknown to the public, this choice was too great an advantage not to give rise to comment. What was their distress, then, when the brother fell ill. Never had a procurator been the subject of so much solicitude—all the more so, when the sickness became serious. Giacomo's natural strength declined, and he no longer responded to treatment. In consternation the community gave him extreme unction and gathered around his pallet to defend his soul, now entering upon the last struggle, by their prayers.

Dominic's compassion was moved at this sight of his brethren's distress. Renewing the gesture of Eliseus,[68] he made them all go out and then stretched himself out against the body of the dying man. Through the force of his prayer he held back the spirit which was already leaving the body. After this, recalling his brethren, he again enjoined his office upon the procurator. The latter related the miracle himself to a group of brethren at the provincial chapter of Rome in 1243 or 1244.[69] Constantino di Orvieto who heard it, related it for posterity.

What, after all, does it matter if the number of anecdotes preserved is but slight? We know clearly what the activity of Dominic and his brethren was. They practised a deep-rooted poverty. As has already been seen, the founder inaugurated at St Sixtus from the beginning the conventual mendicancy which he was striving to inculcate in the older convents. If the Pope was financing the building work, he had not to feed the brethren. Divine office and prayer alternated with the ministry. Dominic now added to his sermons in the city churches his preaching to, and conversations with, the nuns. The chief group of nuns aimed at by the reform and for which the new convent was being prepared, the community of Santa Maria in Tempulo, was lodged quite near to St Sixtus, on the other side, near the Capena gate on the Via della Mole.[70] There were other communities also concerned, and individual nuns.

While the new monastery was slowly rising, Dominic was in contact with the nuns, edifying, exhorting, and directing. He held discussions with the superiors. He consulted. The first thing was to see the possibilities as they actually were, and the extent of the nuns' goodwill, before giving Prouille instructions to send a group of foundresses. It was also essential to construct the cloister. This year, moreover, Dominic could not stay sufficiently long in Rome to allow the sisters from the Midi the time to arrive if he sent for them. It was necessary to wait.

At the end of six weeks, in fact, the founder was able to assess the situation sufficiently. The convent of the brethren was solidly established and their ministry sufficiently engaged in the city. Dominic left them to their responsibilities and set off to the Curia again. In the meantime he had received news from the majority of his convents. He was going to prepare a new stage in the organization of his order. Buonviso and Guillaume accompanied him to Viterbo. Frogier de Penna, on the other hand, remained with the new recruits to encourage the ministry of souls and to supervise the building operations.[71]

During the course of this journey to the Curia, Dominic, for the second time, had a serious attack of illness. Guillaume de Montferrat had already seen him sick when they were on the way to Rome.[72] He was ill again at Viterbo. The brother did not quite know what he was suffering from. On the journey, it had been an attack of dysentery. This is not the first or the last time that we hear this disease mentioned, a chronic enteritis with severe crises and bouts of fever which took away all his strength from him.[73] In his ministry at Toulouse, devout women who had had the opportunity of seeing him at close quarters when he was lodging with them, had noted 'that he was very often a prey to great suffering and that his companions had to put him to bed. He did not remain there long, however, and soon lay stretched out on the ground'.[74] He was then in the prime of life. Clearly he was worn out. He was forced to call a halt and take to his bed.

He could scarcely be other than at the end of his strength. After twelve years of unremitting ministry, for two years now he had been travelling almost continually, each day covering stretches of from thirty to thirty-five miles,[75] going along the roads bare-footed, with no regularity about meals, often contenting himself with the bread people gave to beggars.[76] At night he would lodge in hospices crowded with poor tramps. Before going to bed, he would go to pray in a church, at any rate until Matins time, and when he finally yielded to sleep, he would throw himself fully dressed 'on a little straw and never on a bed'.[77] When he arrived at a convent, he did not go to rest, but summoned the brethren 'to make them a sermon, explain the word of God to them and comfort and encourage them'.[78] Then he discussed the business of the community with the superior. Afterwards he prolonged his vigils interminably, sometimes the whole night through. The accounts of eye-witnesses are as definite on this for the later years of his life as for the years spent in Toulouse.[79] He was sometimes so exhausted by these vigils and by fatigue that he would be found asleep on the church floor or sitting down, or he would fall asleep at table.[80] As soon as morning came, he would begin his sermons again, his visits both to those in good health and the sick, confessions, direction, and all with so much intensity that he was unable to occupy himself with his brethren or the sisters until very late in the evening when people had already retired. He none the less had the community assembled. Then he preached and soon went on his way again.[81]

Despite this superhuman activity, Friar Guillaume gave evidence that 'he observed with extreme strictness the rule and observance of the Friars Preachers. If he made little difficulty about granting dispensations to his brethren, he never dispensed himself. In health as in sickness he observed all the fasts prescribed by the rule. During the serious crisis of dysentery from which he suffered while journeying to Rome, he did not break his fast or eat meat. He contented himself sometimes with having a special dish prepared of fruit or of root vegetables. He did this, whatever disease he was suffering from'.[82] In this state it often happened to him 'not to have suitable food or drink, not to be well looked after, to have an uncomfortable bed'.[83] In no convent had he a room for himself or even his own bed.[84]

He could not really recover in such conditions; nor could he continue to last out. It was not long before the crises began again to become increasingly more serious.

On 17th February he obtained a new bull.[85] The Pope conferred upon him the power of dispensing brethren who had been ordained contrary to the canonical rules before entering the order. They would be able to use the powers they had received and proceed to major orders. Doubtless Dominic had just met some case of this kind which he would be glad to be able to arrange then and there, without the delay involved in referring it back to Rome. The bull is interesting not only for the sentiments of the Pope which it expresses—'a full confidence in the discretion' of the Master; it also gives Dominic a new title in the address—*prior ordinis predicatorum*, 'head of the Order of Preachers'.[86]

Dominic had already obtained from the Pope a power over the brethren as a whole—on 22nd December, 1216, in the privilege of confirmation and on 7th February, 1217, in a Bull on Apostates. At that time the founder was prior of a regular convent and the Pope was giving him powers in regard to his community. The links between a prior and his convent were clear in the eyes of the Pontifical Chancellery. Today, however, Dominic was no longer prior of St Romain. It may be asked in the name of what authority, in virtue of what constitution of his religious society, Dominic could possess a power over his brethren as a whole.

Outwardly the society of the Preachers was still inorganic at its higher level. It was materially constituted by a certain number of convents of canons-Preachers. Inside such convents, the classic organization of the monks and canons obtained. The rule of St Augustine, the privilege of foundation and the customs of the Preachers had fixed the rights of the prior. No text, however, no general institution, had yet laid down in detail the relations of such convents among themselves and with Dominic, or the relations of Dominic with each one of his Preachers.

It was true that several important orders of monks and canons possessed a large number of religious houses. They were grouped into vast federations which each year held session in general chapters where decrees of government and laws were passed. Clearly the group of the Dominican convents could not possess a federal constitution on the model of these classic orders, Cistercians or Victorines, for instance. For if one or the other of these orders possessed a kind of general head in the Abbot of Cîteaux or the Abbot of St Victor, such a person was only head of the order because he was primarily the superior of the leading monastery. Moreover, he was *primus inter pares;* he did not command, he merely represented the common authority of the federation of the convents met in chapter.

Now Dominic was prior of no community of his order, nor was there any particular house of Preachers more important than the rest. The link between Dominic and his brethren was of another nature and moreover stronger in a different way. It was the personal and immediate link which he formed with each of the religious of his order on the day of his profession made into his hands or at least in his name. Each conventual prior, when he received the profession, was from this point of view Dominic's vicar, as, for instance, Reginald in Bologna or Paris. At the beginning of this year of 1220, as in the first days of 1215, the whole order was really in the hands of St Dominic. Despite the still inorganic appearance of the convents of Preachers, Dominic held them together by his authority. He was no longer prior of St Romain, he was prior of the order.

The bull of 17th February, in giving him this title for the first time, showed that the Papacy had become aware of his special situation and recognized it. Thus the letter bore evidence of an organization in fact of the whole of the order, radically different from that of the orders of canons. As he had just declared by the bull of mendicancy that the usual norms of poverty in common of the canons had been superseded in favour of the Preachers, Honorius also declared by the new bull that the traditional federal constitution had no application among the Preachers. The text thus manifested Dominic's original position at the head of his religious society. It paved the way for the early definition of this position, the early constitution of the order as such.

We have seen this situation arising as far back as 1215, as much through the wish of St Dominic as through his relations with the Papacy. Because his order was a society which preached, he could not be satisfied with the usual organization of federations of convents. He must have a supreme leader in control, to apply the order to its task in the place where it was needed, as a general commands his troops. The Preaching in the Narbonensis had its 'priors and masters', as had that of Toulouse, masters who were themselves under the command of the legates, i.e. ultimately of the Pope. A head was especially necessary in the case of a preaching order, for preaching presupposed a mission, which in turn presupposed a hierarchy. The fact that this preaching, by becoming the order of Preachers, had become universal did not necessitate changing its constitution—on the contrary. More than ever it must remain governed by its master so that it might be governed by the Church. Moreover, this was what had been taking place since the beginning. The links had not ceased to become stronger. It was now necessary to define them clearly and give them permanent form in a legal document. In this month of February 1220 it is clear that Dominic was paving the way for having the centralized constitution of his order clearly defined.

It is also clear that he was preparing to have the counterpart defined, the constitution of his order as a community. We have already instanced in Dominic's attitude his care constantly to marry the personal responsibility of the chief with the collective legislation of the community. If he did not attach deep importance to the intervention of the whole of the brethren in his decisions, as in the constitution of his order, through his personal temperament as through his medieval formation, he had a very simple means of obviating this, namely, to have full powers granted him by the Pope, to establish legislation in writing and to have it confirmed once more, to send it to all his brethren and impose it upon them in virtue of the obedience promised on the day of profession.

Now he did not do this then and in fact never did so. It is true that a few months later it would be possible to declare that at this time Dominic possessed the plenitude of powers in regard to his order.[87] He had not, however, asked for these powers from the Pope. They came to him from the profession of his brethren. Thus he would make them over, for the whole duration of the chapter, to the community of the Preachers present in its representatives.[88] The decisions of this chapter would become obligatory for him as for the other brethren, independently of any intervention or confirmation by the Holy See.

Thus he was head, but under the control and within the limits of the community. Such was his double position which would become clear forthwith and be defined in a text of the constitutions. This position had already been realized in fact since 1215. The Curia expressly recognized the existence of the first phase of it by giving him the title of *prior ordinis*. He himself was to make manifest the second by a decisive gesture a few days later.

Towards the end of the month of February, he wrote to his convents in Spain, Provence, France and Italy, as well as to the isolated brethren, to instruct them to designate a certain number of representatives—four for Paris—and to send them to Bologna where on 17th May, 1220, the feast of Pentecost, he assembled a Constituent Chapter.[89]

The letters were scarcely written, perhaps not even sent, when he received heart-breaking news from Paris—Master Reginald was dead.

He had died there a few weeks after his arrival.[90] Dominic's sensitive nature experienced a cruel shock. He had so quickly and so completely attached himself to this brother of his own age, to this apostolic soul so like his own, to this loving heart capable of so much energy. He had even worn him out prematurely by treating him as he treated himself; by abusing his generosity without limit; by tearing him away from his valuable work in Bologna when it was beginning to bear great fruit, to turn him out on to the highroad and oblige him to begin all over again in Paris. Reginald, however, had died in complete peace, full of joy at dying poor in the midst of his brethren.[91] As they brought him the last sacraments, he had recalled as a sweet memory that the Blessed Virgin had already in some sort given him extreme unction. He had nevertheless received the ecclesiastical rite and had fallen asleep as one predestined.[92]

Dominic was given one poignant detail, however. The obstinacy of the canons of Notre Dame, by forbidding the brethren to have a cemetery, had not even allowed them to keep the body with them. Fortunately the Benedictines of Notre Dame des Champs had been more than willing to receive his mortal remains.[93] It was there they lay at rest while waiting for eternity.

Dominic then took a step which tells us much, both of his grief and his sensitive nature. What the brethren of Notre Dame des Champs had done for the Preachers of St Jacques in receiving Reginald had been done to himself. He thanked them for it in his name. More than this, since it was a Preacher that was in question, might not the Curia make some gesture? The news had deeply grieved Ugolino and many other people who knew Reginald well. The Pope agreed personally to express his gratitude to the Benedictines of Notre Dame des Champs, and so a bull was issued from the Chancellery on 27th February.[94]

The Pope had just learnt that the prior and convent of Ste Marie des Vignes (Notre Dame des Champs) had by their affectionate care consoled 'the brethren of the Order of Preachers studying holy doctrine in Paris'. 'So that you may know then,' said the Pope, 'the pure affection that we have for these brethren . . . we command you all . . . through reverence for the Apostolic See and for Our Person, to continue to favour them with your benefits as you have so well begun to do.'

At the same time Dominic requested from the Pope an identical letter for the university of Paris.[95] In the following month this letter was, slightly modified, three times addressed to the people of Madrid (20th March), to those of Segovia (23rd March), to the podestà and people of Bologna (24th March).[96] Thus the Papacy showed itself so sensitive to the needs of the Preachers, so convinced of their providential appearance, that it did not confine itself to recommending them—it thanked in its personal name those who showed themselves generous and understanding towards them. With the Pope, the Catholic Church itself appreciated as a service done to herself the services rendered to this order and gave deep and sincere thanks for them. There was however a higher source than the Pope and the Church. Christ himself had expressed his gratitude towards the benefactors of the brethren when he pronounced these words, taken up again by the Sovereign Pontiff: 'He who gives a prophet the welcome due to a prophet shall receive the reward given to prophets',[97] and especially: 'When you did it to one of the least of my brethren here, you did it to me.'[98] There is indeed in the

Pope's action when recommending his Preachers, a particularly devoted care, a specially paternal tone, on account of their humility and their complete poverty. The Church was now no longer afraid of the mendicancy of one of these orders of apostolic life which she had recently regarded with uneasiness. On the contrary, it was because of this lowliness, this 'abjection in poverty' that she engaged herself with Christ and gave thanks for them in a great movement of hope. Dominic was at the root of this profound change.

In the course of the month of March or April, new perspectives opened from the direction of Spain. The university of Palencia was to be re-created. A foundation of the Preaching Friars would certainly be indicated in the scholastic centre of Castile. It would at the same time establish the Preachers in the heart of this kingdom. Whether the brethren in Segovia had taken the initiative of the project, or whether Dominic formed it himself, on 13th April he obtained a copy of the recommendation *Dilecti filii* (II)[99] which he intended for this foundation. In Bologna, with the Spanish brethren who had come for the chapter, the possibilities would be investigated. Dominic's wish was that the order should also take root in Aragon. The Archbishop of Tarragona, Sparago de Barca, a native of Montpellier, was not remaining inactive in the face of the Albigenses who were filtering into his province. Yet he lacked suitable preachers, since he was reduced to getting Carthusians, whose merits he extolled at this time,[100] to preach against them. Yet this was the work of the Preachers. Dominic obtained for him a copy of the bull *Quoniam abundavit* (IV[1]),[101] which was specially adapted to fit the case. It was issued from Viterbo on 6th May. Dominic himself entrusted it to some brethren who were being sent from Bologna to Aragon. They were not successful in their mission. Doubtless the archbishop kept up against the Preachers the ostracism which his predecessor had shown against the Poor Catholics. Mistrustful of all that resembled the apostolic movements, he refused the remedy while admitting the disease. The first foundation in Aragon would be made elsewhere.

Finally, on 12th May, the Pope addressed a very surprising letter to a number of religious in Italy.[102] It was primarily surprising through the heterogeneous collection of those to whom it was destined—five monks and a Canon Regular, belonging respectively to Vallombrosa near Florence, to St Victor near Bologna, and to four abbeys in the south of Italy—Silla, Mensa, Aquila, Flora.[103] Honorius informed all these religious that Friar Dominic, Prior of the Order of Preachers, had declared to him that the special grace of preaching that they had each received from God could bear very great fruit for the salvation of one's neighbour if they consented to place themselves under his direction. The Pope thus gave them the order to set out to join him and preach under his direction; each one of them moreover would retain his own habit.

How had Dominic come to know these religious? What was the mission the Pope had reserved for him? What would be the effect of the summons? We shall try to answer these questions later. In any case it is difficult not to compare this bull of Honorius III with the bull of 29th January, 1204 by which Innocent III placed at the disposal of the Abbot of Cîteaux, and obliged to comply with his summons, a phalanx of religious or priests coming from all parts and among whom, one day, Dominic found himself engaged. The change since then is striking.

But what is more striking in the step which the bull revealed is that it dates from a time when Dominic's devotion for the salvation of souls could most legitimately be submerged in the foundation of his order. So great, nevertheless, was the Preacher's fervour of evangelization that it overflowed on all sides, submerging his activity as a founder. Here we find once more the continual surpassing of the work by the workman which has already been stressed. Like St Paul, the measureless charity of Christ constrained him to such a point that he could not content himself with a limited object. Whatever his effort to assemble brethren, form them, cast them even prematurely into the ministry of salvation, that did not yet sufficiently bring about the general preaching which he had conceived and wanted to undertake with all the forces of the Church. It did not matter if he could not bring to the task under the habit of his order all the collaborators he came across. He was ready to do so under some other habit. The essential was not the habit but that they should announce Christ everywhere, bring light, dissipate error and that the poor should have the Gospel preached to them.

The pagans themselves were the subject of one of his most insistent cares. In the first place, those of the north, whom he had been longing to work amongst ever since 1205. His desire was still keen. At the Curia he had not only confided this to Ugolino or to Guillaume de Montferrat. He had also spoken of it to his friend and counsellor Gulielmo de Piedmont. People, in fact, attribute to Dominic's confidences the attraction which Gulielmo felt for the ministry of the north, of which he would soon receive the charge as pontifical legate.[104] Before Gulielmo, however, was in a position to favour the Preachers destined for Scandinavia in all possible ways, Dominic had found the opportunity of sending them there. In this winter of 1219–1220 he met in fact in Viterbo or in Rome a Swedish prelate, the provost of St Peter of Sigtuna, Gaufred,[105] who had come to defend in the Curia the interests of the crown of Sweden against the King of Denmark.[106] A mission of the Preachers was quickly decided upon. Precisely on the previous 15th August two Scandinavian brethren had been received at Bologna. If the prelate would be good enough to accompany Dominic to Bologna, he would hand over the two brethren.[107] He would provide them with the recommendation he had received on 11th November (III¹).[108]

The brethren, setting out with the provost in May 1220, installed themselves that summer in Sigtuna, the former see of the diocese of Uppsala and the metropolitan see of Sweden. A monastery dedicated to the Blessed Virgin Mary was to be founded, which on 11th January, 1221 Honorius III would recommend to the charity and devotion of the faithful of Sweden.[109] It was, however, to experience many vicissitudes and even disappeared after 1224.[110] The brethren, however, would be received in another foundation which St Dominic had begun preparing in 1221.[111] Thus the founder would have the joy, before leaving this world, of preaching in the northern lands at least through his brethren, to the pagans as much as to the Catholics.

Another group of pagans, moreover, had begun to move his generosity for several years past, the Cumans, in the east of Europe.[112] Coming from the continually turbulent territory of Siberia, these warlike populations carved out between the eleventh and thirteenth centuries an immense territory between the Altai and the Danube. In the winter they attacked the southern regions and in summer transferred their devastating raids towards the west and north. The disaster of Adrianople suffered in 1205 by the Latin Empire in the East revealed their power and their cruelty. With the Wallachian and Bulgar elements which they bound up with their lot, they never ceased attacking the Christians on the frontiers of Hungary. In 1211, King Andrew II for some time summoned the Teutonic Knights against them. The Church, however, equally had recourse to her missionaries. Although it was a question of cruelly hostile pagan populations, the preaching of the Gospel had begun. In 1217 and 1218, the letters of Honorius III already mentioned a bishop of the Cumans.[113] From this time Dominic sometimes envisaged this new field for his activity and, perhaps, martyrdom.[114] In 1221 he sent some brethren on a mission to Hungary, with express instructions to reach the Cumans.[115]

Finally, as has been noted, the first known copy of the bull of recommendation *Quoniam abundavit* (IV[1]), dated 13th December, 1219, eventually found its way to Germany. How it got there is not known. In May 1221 the long-standing existence of a community of preachers is known of at Friesach, in Carinthia, whose prior, and moreover sole priest, had deserted the order.[116] Was it to this apostate brother that Dominic had handed the bull in sending it from Viterbo or Rome? Was it to some brother sent in the direction of Germany in May 1220? One can only form hypotheses. But the facts which give rise to these suppositions are already significant. The preparation of the two foundations, in Germany and in Sweden, in the course of the year 1220 proves that during his visits to the Roman Curia, Dominic seriously contemplated extending the influence of the order to the eastern and northern extremities of Europe until it finally reached the pagan territories.

It was thus with projects and very precise plans for the constitution of his order, with unrestricted support on the part of the Papacy, with a Catholic horizon even wider if it were possible, that at the beginning of May 1220 Dominic prepared to leave the Curia to rejoin in Bologna, before Pentecost, his brethren assembled in chapter by his orders.

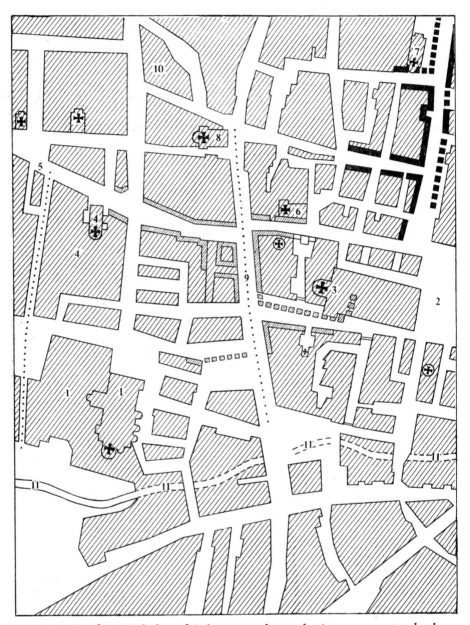

The Church of St Nicholas of Bologna in the 13th century was in the heart
of the university district.   This plan, after F. Cavazza and A. Hessel, is the
present-day street plan of this section of the city.   The Law Schools are shown
edged in denser shading, the Faculties of Art and Medicine edged in black.
1. Church of St Nicholas (now San Domenico).   2. The former main square.
3. Former Church of St Ambrose.   4. Church and Cloister of St Proclus.
5. Former St Proclus Gate and southern boundary of the town after 1208.
6. The Celestines.   7. Church and Cloister of St Saviour's.   8. St Paul's.
9. Former 'University Street', southern town boundary in the 12th century.
10. Spanish College.   11. Course of the River Aposa.

CHAPTER XVI

THE FIRST CHAPTER IN BOLOGNA

DOMINIC hastened on his way. He had only about ten days in which to reach Bologna for the rendezvous he had fixed with the brethren.[1] He took the shortest way through Tuscany. Friar Buonviso accompanied him.[2] They made a brief halt in Florence, where the brethren were no longer lodging at St Pancras but in the collegiate church of St Paul. The Master again saw Dame Bene and freed her from her sins as well as comforting her in her trials.[3] He crossed the Apennines with the delegates from Florence. On the eve of 17th May, the fast of Pentecost, he arrived at St Nicholas of Bologna. A large community was there to welcome him, the numbers of the brethren of the convent being increased by the group of fathers gathered for the chapter.

It is not difficult to imagine what this reunion was like. The convent hummed like a bee-hive after the breaking away of a swarm. About thirty delegates at least arrived—doubtless the majority of the original brethren, chosen by their convents as representatives.[4] If Dominic had met one or other of them during the past year in the course of his travels, the brethren had not seen each other for nearly three years. Their attitude had changed since the dispersal. They had given themselves to the order with generosity, it is true, but not without some apprehension. Moreover anxiety had dominated them more than once in view of the uncertain future. The order now lay before them as a powerful institution, full of conquering energy, already solidly implanted on the soil of Europe, welcomed and thrust to the fore by the Church, whose expectation it fulfilled. The young friars in Bologna pointed out to each other with admiration their brethren Simon of Sweden and Nicholas of Lund, the first-fruits from Scandinavia;[5] the brethren from Madrid and Segovia who had arrived from Castile; brethren from Provence; the four brethren from Paris.[6] Among them was one religious whose clothing had taken place less than three months earlier, but of whom each one knew that he was Master Reginald's finest recruit during the few weeks of his stay in Paris. A master of arts and bachelor in theology, already mature in years, for he was only a few years younger than Master Dominic,[7] Jordan of Saxony was, with Matthew of France, the principal personality of the convent of St Jacques.[8] By the side of the masters of arts and of law who peopled the convent of Bologna, he represented the literature and theology of Paris. Friar Ventura of Verona who was only awaiting Dominic's arrival to take the habit and make profession in his hands, would represent the convent of Bologna at the chapter,[9] doubtless with the new prior, the master in decretals, Paul of Hungary,[10] his colleague Master Clair and also probably Master Roland and Master Moneta of Cremona.

The day of Pentecost was devoted exclusively to the Lord. The choir of the church of St Nicholas of the Vines was too small for such a large number of brethren. With what fervour did they inaugurate the great session 'invoking the Holy Spirit by whom the Sons of God are moved'![11] Dominic sang the Mass with that supernatural inspiration that carried him beyond himself each time he celebrated the Catholic mysteries. And to unite these brethren assembled from the four corners of the horizon whose voices, accents and customs were not used to blending in harmony, in the chanting of the canonical office at which he presided 'he goes from choir to choir to stimulate his brethren to sing true and clearly and to infuse their psalmody with devotion'.[12]

On Whit Monday the founder gathered the community in the chapter-room of the monastery. The Holy Spirit was again invoked and Dominic preached to the brethren the word of God. They again prayed for the dead and every one thought of Master Reginald whose presence was so palpable in this monastery and at this gathering. Those brethren of Bologna who were not members of the chapter then withdrew and the session began.[13]

Dominic's authority, so sure of itself since 1217—'I know what I am doing'—was more firmly established than ever. Events had indeed brought the approbation of supernatural success, that of Providence, to his earlier decisions. No John of Navarre would now dare to pit his obstinacy against him. To do so would be tantamount to obstinacy against the Church, for the Pope had full confidence in Dominic and regularly protected his initiatives by significant bulls. All the brethren were aware of this authority which Ventura of Verona was later to describe in these terms: 'At this time, the blessed Brother Dominic had full power, after the Lord Pope, to organize, order, correct the order of Friars Preachers in its entirety.'[14] Now Dominic at first tried to divest himself of this power.

The emotion must have been considerable when the founder was seen to rise, pronouncing the words reported by Friar Rodolfo—'I deserve to be deposed for I am useless and lax'—and humiliate himself to the utmost.[15] It was all too easy to guess what prompted this—not false modesty or pusillanimity, but his feeling of being completely used up. He had long felt his strength betraying him, especially during the last few months, and feared no longer to be able to lead to heroic virtue an order whose function it was to preach Christian heroism by its life as much as by its words. He would so much like to hand over his government to others and to consecrate his remaining strength to direct preaching.

In the face of the refusal and the very emphatic reaction of his brethren, however, he retracted. He would remain at his post. During this session, nevertheless, he wanted to be only a chairman and to remit the whole of his powers and even his person to the community. The assembly was, moreover, too numerous to assume the legislative charge indiscriminately. 'He was thus pleased to set up *diffinitors* who, for the duration of the chapter, would have authority over him, over each one among them and over the assembly as a whole';[16] they were to have 'full powers to decide, order, legislate and punish, in regard to the order as a whole, under the single reservation of the respect due to the superior of the order'.[17]

How many *diffinitors* were elected? No direct information gives the number, but it may be presumed that the classic figure of four was adhered to.[18] Among them in all probability were the two masters in decretals of the convent of Bologna and, we believe, Jordan of Saxony.[19] The other members of the assembly exercised the function of counsellors and, after deliberation, prepared the provisions that the *diffinitors*, under the presidency of Dominic, elaborated, drew up and imposed. Thus the result of this work in common had not the impersonal character of the former *consuetudines*, of customs for observance. Accordingly the documents were given the new name of *institutiones*,[20] 'institutions of the Friars Preachers', because they were statutes evolved by the Dominicans collectively. They were soon to be called 'constitutions'[21] because they organized the order into a society. That is the name they still bear today.

Before beginning the discussion of the details, the founder had a general decision taken. It concerned the binding force of the 'institutions' themselves. Were they to be absolute to the extent that superiors could not dispense from them? In several clauses of the customs of 1216, Dominic had already inscribed the possibility of dispensation.[22] He now had it put on record as a general rule.[23] This was not, however, the traditional dispensation which makes room for human weakness. What was envisaged was an organic dispensation which was to enable a very complex mode of life, the several elements of which occasionally came into conflict, to attain its objective more effectively. It was a dispensation in the interests of effectiveness. Dominic took this opportunity of reminding them in a preamble of what the end was to which all else must be subordinate. The Preachers were fortunate to have the founder's idea set before them in a definition that was concise, well thought out, vigorous, and rendered the context even more pregnant. For if Dominic recalled this purpose, it was not as the logical principle from which the constitutions of the Preachers had derived, but as the supreme and always living inspiration to which the brethren must continually have recourse in order to measure the right to the dispensation and its mode, so that each of the elements of their life might be set in its right perspective with regard to their mission as a whole. In 1216, this definition could not yet be written down, for the idea of the order had not yet received confirmation and all innovations had just been proscribed. In 1220, the situation was completely changed. A considerable number of pontifical bulls had confirmed the fundamental idea.[24] The founder had given it permanence by inscribing it in the prologue of the institutions of his order. The text had just reminded the brethren:

> that no one has permission to change, add or subtract anything whatsoever of his own will. For if we were to be careless about the smallest details we should have reason to fear a progressive fall from grace.
> On this point, however [he added], let the superior possess, in his own convent, power to dispense the brethren each time that he shall consider it fitting, principally in what might form an obstacle to study, preaching or the profit of souls. For it should be known that our order, from the beginning, has been instituted for preaching and the salvation of souls, and that our very studies should tend in principle, when used with fervour and to the full, to make us able to be of use to our neighbour's soul.[25]

The decision of Dominic and his brethren was not an act of liberalism or of decreased trust in the traditions of regular life. There was at the time nothing to prevent them, if they thought it necessary, from attenuating the rigour of an observance which they had chosen for its exceptional severity and made more severe still. Now they did not do this. Neither did they give each religious the responsibility of himself deciding how much he should assume of the common rule. They maintained the initial severity for all. They did, however, make an act of faith in the capacity of superiors to direct their brethren for the best in their mission as Preachers. The law of dispensation set the authorities of the order above laws of the community, under the single controlling principle of the supreme purpose of the order, the work of the salvation of souls.

We learn from history that a cognate problem was brought up in the course of the discussion, which Dominic solved in a similar manner.[26] Formerly, religious lived under an ancient rule, surrounded with the halo of the distinguished authority of a St Benedict or some other patriarch. Any failure in observance of the precepts of such a rule, to which one had bound oneself by oath, was a grave sin. This was the classic teaching of the monks. St Bernard had reaffirmed this position in the case of the Cistercians. But was a failure in observance of the constitutions elaborated year by year by the community of the Preachers of equal gravity? Certain members of the chapter in Bologna thought so. It is possible that they even desired it to be inscribed at the head of the constitutions that they were binding under pain of sin, according to Bernard's ideas. Others of the brethren, however, who had come from the towns, where numerous common rules for confraternities, trades or cities were imposed without any strictly moral perspective, vigorously protested. Dominic was on their side. The regulations themselves, he affirmed, did not always bind under pain of sin. 'If he knew that some of the brethren thought otherwise, he would go round the convents and, with his own hand, wipe out the regulations by erasing them with his knife.'[27]

Thus it was not to the institutions emanating from the community, which were general, and made no attempt to deal with particular cases, that Dominic gave priority, but to the decisions of the superior. These decisions alone bound under pain of sin. It was these decisions that applied the common laws to the circumstances of the moment and, by placing them in a particular perspective, gave final form to their binding force. Thus such decisions could dispense from these laws. The two conclusions were related to and supported each other. Such was, as far back as 1220, the origin of a provision which would not be inscribed in the Dominican documents until 1236,[28] opening an entirely new channel in the legislation of religious orders—the purely penal obligation of the constitutions.[29] In the Bologna chapter the solution was not formulated but it was foreshadowed. By remitting the legislative power into the hands of the community of Preachers, Dominic in no sense weakened the authority of the superiors of the order. To them he entrusted the executive power. Thus he reserved for them the principal authority which binds and looses consciences. At the same time he set free the pusillanimous from innumerable difficulties and scruples which might arise in the legislation of their brethren in the general chapters.

In convening his brethren, the founder had himself defined the two great objectives of the deliberations—the juridical constitution of the society of the Friars Preachers, and the insertion in full in the documents of the legislation of the *regula apostolica*. This presupposed a series of exceptional rulings on preaching and on mendicant poverty. Thanks to Dominic's efforts since 1216, above all since his great round of visitations in 1218–1219, the brethren were ready to adopt these rulings; they were even to be found in outline in the life of the Preachers. A considerable work of adjustment was nevertheless imperative. There were all-important details which remained to be settled.

Two supreme organs were thus to secure the unity of the order and its existence as a community—the head of the order and the general chapter. As to the former, the Bologna assembly passed no legislation.[30] It was not concerned with defining his power or even with fixing his official title. Documents drawn up at the close of the chapter constantly give him the abstract title of *prelatus maior*;[31] the Pope would continue to call him *prior ordinis*;[32] the brethren and Dominic himself would continue to use the current expression of *magister, magister praedicationis, magister praedicatorum*.[33] The profession of obedience remained the basis of the Master's power and secured his authority. It was the supreme power in the executive order, as we have defined it earlier, which Dominic enjoyed. No order of monks or canons possessed a head endowed with this power. The abbot of Cluny himself, to whom all the monks were bound by profession made into his hands, did not derive from that institution a power similar to that of the Master of the Preachers. This conferred on the order an unparalleled dynamism, that of an army fighting for the Church.[34]

It will be noted that postulants at this time made promises of two quite different types. The first was a promise to enter religion, which after 1216 appeared in the customs of the Preachers under the formula *seculo abrenunciare*.[35] By this promise the novice made a complete renunciation of secular life at the time of his clothing, but did not bind himself to the Preachers. If he were not accepted by the order at the conclusion of his probation, or if he himself did not wish to remain with them, to keep his promise it was sufficient for him to seek another order. Such was for some time the case of Diana of Andalò.[36] The other engagement was the profession properly so-called. The profession, which in the monastic life of ancient times was given expression by the taking of the habit, was in the thirteenth century clearly and distinctly separated from it. In Dominic's dispensation the profession usually took place after a certain time of probation. It could also, however, follow immediately after clothing, as was the case for John of Navarre and many other brethren in the first years of the order. It might even in certain cases precede it—such was the case for Reginald, Moneta of Cremona, Jordan of Saxony and Henry of Cologne.[37]

Dominic thus handed over to the assembly of 1220, in the person of his *diffinitors*, his personal powers. In union as he then was with the brethren constituting the assembly, he decided to assign such powers to the chapters general which would for the future be convened each year for the feast of Pentecost and would be held alternately in Paris and Bologna.[38] The reason for the latter decision was not solely the size of the convents in those cities, the only houses of the order capable, when they were constructed, of receiving so vast a gathering;[39] it was much more their position in the order, near the two universities of Christendom. It was laid down indeed that the next meeting would be in Bologna in 1221—clearly because the intention was to continue the work of the formulation of the constitutions there. It was planned, however, to hold the chapter in Paris the following year; there were certain points in the scholastic and theological programme of the order of Preachers which could only be conveniently argued out in all their implications on the banks of the Seine.

General chapters of orders were no novelty.[40] A tradition more than a century old had elaborated their pattern, the model of which remained the chapter of Cîteaux, governed by the famous 'charter of charity'. The Council of the Lateran had just proposed this as an example to all the regular clergy.[41] Composed of all the Cistercian abbots, it revised and perfected from year to year the legislation of the order, the order which it also corrected, controlled and administered at the highest level. Nevertheless, the ancient abbatial tradition, with the abbot's preponderant authority and the monk's established position, considerably restricted the higher administration of the general chapter of Cîteaux of Prémontré. Such restrictions no longer existed in the case of the general chapter envisaged by the Preachers, whose powers, coming from the tradition of the thirteenth century, were singularly strengthened. In fact, the general chapter of the Preachers, composed of representatives elected by the priories,[42] possessed complete control of government throughout the whole order.

In the first place it possessed the legislative power, and it was alone in possessing this. On this point, the tradition of capitular assemblies was so universal that the chapter of 1220 did not trouble to put the fact on record. It was not until 1228 that the legislative procedure which the order still preserves today was given fixed form:[43] a regulation only becomes a law of the order after the action of three consecutive chapters, by initiation, approval, confirmation. The chapter equally undertook to reply to the questions priories might put in regard to observance and preaching.

United to the superior of the order, the chapter also possessed supreme executive power. One point in particular formed the subject of careful definition in 1220. It was a fundamental point. The Friars Preachers entrusted to their general chapter the recruitment, promotion and canonical mission of the preachers.[44] It was in this way that the unheard-of power that the Pope had entrusted to Dominic and his order, the free conferring on the brethren of the *officium predicationis*, the office of preacher in the Church, was administered. The chapter and the Master exercised their power of administration in common, correcting and punishing, assigning the brethren to studies, sending them forth to preach, giving them missions. The chapter even concerned itself with settling differences relating to material goods. Among the latter, and the fact is significant, only books were explicitly mentioned. The matter was not dealt with in chapter, for it was not sufficiently important, but in a separate session, after the meal.[45]

Finally the general chapter of the Preachers received judiciary powers in the matter of regular observance, according to tradition. The Master himself came under its jurisdiction. This was the founder's express will, manifested by his attitude which was later given permanent form in a document.[46] To secure this control, at the beginning of the sessions the chapter became a chapter of faults. It pronounced immediate judgement on those persons present who accused themselves or allowed themselves to be accused. It judged on verbal report or on written statements those houses and individuals who were absent. A series of visitors nominated by the chapter was charged to make such reports.[47]

Comment has just been made on the first part of the legislative work of 1220. Part of this is directly brought to our attention by history,[48] and the whole by the document which the *diffinitors* then drew up. Curiously enough, this document, which scholars of the eighteenth century had in their hands because a Friar Preacher of the fourteenth century had carefully preserved and transmitted it,[49] almost disappeared under the hands of the historians of the end of the nineteenth century. A fatal error of interpretation prevented the latter from recognizing what was an authentic survival from the work of the fathers of the Chapter of Bologna.[50] During the last twenty years, however, it has become possible to correct this error[51] and to reproduce the original document with accuracy.[52] It is an admirable piece of work, wholly contained in the second 'distinction' of the original constitutions in what is known as the Rodez ms., within a framework of later texts. With its own expressions (*prelatus, prelatus maior, fratres nostri*), its alert and sensitive style, its literary continuity, its spiritual inspiration, it is easily distinguishable from the rest of the 'distinction' as soon as the whole is submitted to a careful analysis. It is introduced in the prologue of the primitive institutions by the title: 'Of the chapter general, of the study and of preaching.'[53]

This text has taken nothing from the customs of Prémontré or from those of any other order. It is original in all its parts, and has avoided the literary form of the legislations of observance which served as a model for the customs of 1216 (first 'distinction' of the ms. of Rodez). If in default of a source a literary precedent must be assigned to it, the charter of charity of Cîteaux should be named, that document at this time exactly a century old which created a new genre in religious legislation, the first constitutions of a religious order in the proper meaning of the term. Thus the document elaborated by the Dominican *diffinitors* at Pentecost 1220, might be called the 'charter of preaching'. It represents in effect the constitutional charter of the Order of Preachers—that which organized it into a society, provided it with its terms of reference, prescribed its end and ruled its spirit—as much as its fundamental activity, mendicant preaching. The following is the first part of it, on the general chapter.[54]

> The General Chapter shall be held one year in Paris and the following year in Bologna. On Pentecost Monday, when the brethren have entered the chapter-room, they shall first begin by devoutly invoking the Holy Spirit who moves the sons of God. The versicle *Emitte spiritum tuum, et creabuntur* shall be said, with the prayer to the Holy Spirit. Then, when the brethren are seated and all have their places, the divine word shall be preached to the community to strengthen them by the word of the God of heaven. All those who wish for spiritual encouragement may assist at the sermon. When it is finished, as it is meet and right to go as quickly as possible to the help of those who are in need, the obit of the brethren who have died during the year shall be recited in common, a general absolution given and the psalm *De profundis* said for them. If there are letters to be presented, let them be given and received; reply will be made to them in due course, after

reflection. Then all those who do not form part of the chapter shall go out. When they have left, the brethren whose function it is to present apologies for the absent may do so. Then begins the hearing of the faults against the rule.

After this the visitors have to render account, by word of mouth if they are present and in writing if they are absent, of the brethren they have visited. Are they living in continual peace, diligent in study, fervent in preaching; what is their reputation, the fruit of their efforts ? Are the observances respected in accordance with the tenor of the Institutions, as to eating and drinking and on other points ? If the visitors have found any slackness anywhere, the one who is concerned must spontaneously rise on hearing himself accused, ask pardon and await the corresponding penance with humility. Those who were to make the visitation in the present year and have not done so as was agreed, shall accuse themselves and submit to a deserved punishment. Then a penance is sent in writing to the absent who ought to be there and to those who have committed some fault and have not made satisfaction.

After this, the brethren who are considered capable of preaching shall be presented to the chapter and those who have not yet received the licence to preach from a major superior or chapter, although they may have licence and mandate for it from their own prior.[55] All the brethren are examined in private by competent persons, appointed for this office and for other questions that may be raised in the chapter. The brethren who live with them shall be carefully interrogated, as to the grace God has given them for preaching, their studies, their religious sentiments, the warmth, resolution and intensity of their charity. If favourable testimony is given on their account, by consent and on the advice of the major superior, the decision considered most fitting is taken whether they are still to be left at their studies, or allowed to try their hand at preaching with more experienced brethren, or are considered capable of profitably exercising the ministry of preaching of themselves.

At this point, the brethren who have questions to submit, whether personal or general, concerning the observance or preaching, shall set them forth in order, one after the other, while a brother notes them down carefully, so that those whose function it is to reply to them may resolve and conclude them definitively in fitting time and place. When one rises to speak, let no other raise his voice. And so that due measure may also be observed in the matter of withdrawals, let no one go out without permission or necessity; when he has gone out, let him not wander about but return as quickly as possible after having attended to what was necessary. If some dissension should arise among the brethren of the order— may God preserve us from this!—over books or other material objects, this shall not be discussed at the chapter; for spiritual affairs must take precedence of temporal ones. Brethren who are expert in such matters will be chosen and they, after the meal, in a suitable place outside the chapter room, will settle the dispute by seeking the truth of the matter and will re-establish peace among the brethren. The major superior, helped by those who are assigned to this purpose, shall likewise concern himself with resolving and concluding questions, with correcting the brethren, with assessing penances, with sending preachers with their *socius* to preach and to study, fixing time, place and duration.

11—S.D.

All that is ordained in this way, by the grace of the Holy Spirit, the chapter shall receive wholeheartedly, unanimously and eagerly. Let no one murmur, no one protest, no one contradict. At the end there shall be a confession and general absolution, the blessing of those who persevere, the malediction of the apostates and deserters branded with anathemas.

After this the assembly concerned itself with inscribing in the legislation the apostolic rule. A brief phrase, but one of great import, serves as prologue to the whole paragraph: 'Neither property nor revenues of any kind shall be accepted.'[56] This is of course the declaration of the preachers' mendicant poverty.

In the conciseness of the phrase the art of the medieval jurist will be recognized. Its words are so well chosen that in 1274, when the second Council of Lyons wanted to legislate on mendicant religious, it could not find a better definition for them than to reproduce these terms exactly—'the orders who are forbidden by their rule or constitutions to have property or revenues'.[57] Nothing else remains in fact to those who have forbidden themselves all regular resources and envisage as the sole form of their work study and preaching, but the daily charity of Christians in the name of Providence.

The practice of conventual mendicity is given more exact definition by contemporary customs which the brethren themselves were doubtless already practising. Since the middle of the twelfth century, for instance, these usages had been included in the legislation of the Order of Grandmont.[58]

> Each time that in one way or another you have the wherewithal to feed yourselves for one day without begging, you will not allow yourselves to go out and beg. . . . But if God tries you, by allowing you to come to such scarcity that you are totally without food . . . , let two brethren long established in religious life go out on the quest with humility. Let them beg alms in kind from mills and houses, from door to door, as other poor men do. When they have received sufficient alms to feed themselves and the other brethren for a complete day, let them return to the monastery and share what they have with each, with giving of thanks.[59]

Dominic and his brethren, in fact, were familiar with the Order and legislation of Grandmont. The practice of conventual mendicity was not the only point which interested them in the system of poverty of the eremitical order founded in the eleventh century by St Etienne de Muret. The brethren of Grandmont, earlier than the Friars Preachers, had renounced property, buildings and lands, flocks and herds, incorporated churches and other revenues—in short, all regular resources; but, also like the Preachers, they accepted the ownership of the monastery, its chapel and its garden.[60] Like them too, they desired that their clerics should be solely applied to spiritual work, which for them was contemplation and divine praise. Thus their founder had made provision that only the lay-brethren of the order should be concerned with temporal affairs and that they should have authority over the clerics themselves in this sphere.[61] Dominic had been deeply impressed by the example of Grandmont, which he had had the opportunity of coming into contact with not long before in Provence,[62] or more recently at the Curia. He wanted to introduce it into his order as it stood and formally proposed this to the chapter.[63] It would be a great advantage if the preachers who were clerics could be delivered from temporal involvements to reserve their whole strength for the ministry of prayer, study and the word.

On this point the brethren resisted him. The rule of St Etienne was not conspicuous for its sense of proportion. Five popes, among whom was Honorius himself barely a year ago, without mentioning the King of France and his barons,[64] had been constrained to intervene to resolve the crises emerging from its prescriptions, particularly from the preponderance accorded to the lay-brethren in the government. The brethren were afraid of undergoing similar crises if they accepted this provision. On this point Dominic gave way to the judgement of the fathers of the chapter. He contented himself with having it defined that no temporal charge or administration would be imposed on those who had been assigned to study or preaching, unless it were perhaps provisionally when there was no one else to assume such functions.[65] After all, it was not a bad thing that a preacher should feel in passing the weight of the monastery's daily cares; it is so easy to exhort others to detachment from material goods, when one is free oneself from all preoccupation through someone else's labour.

The preacher, moreover, would normally escape this danger by himself begging in the course of his rounds. This practice of apostolic life which had been specified in the charter of 1215, but which it had not been possible to inscribe in the customs of 1216, in 1220 formed the subject of precise prescriptions—primarily, the prohibition to carry any kind of money on one's person in the course of the journey; thus the text of the Gospel required it. Dominican mendicity thus excluded any begging for money as such.[66] One could only beg in kind, for food, necessary clothing, books and other indispensable objects. To this was added the prohibition to go on horseback. Finally, it was forbidden to travel alone; they must go to preach two by two, in accordance with the Gospel.[67] The first two prescriptions gave rise to new faults which were added in the corresponding chapter of the rule of St Dominic, the chapter of grave faults.[68]

This was, however, a negative way of putting things. These prohibitions, indeed, corresponded to a spirit, the spirit of the Gospel itself, but they only gave the obverse side of it. Dominic accordingly had these provisions summarized in a positive form in a general document. Thus was created the attractive portrait of the Dominican preacher which will be given shortly—the man of the Gospel who, his eyes fixed on the pattern of Christ and the apostles, sets out in quest of the souls to be saved and finds in the closeness of his life to his model, the ever-flowing source of his contemplation as of his preaching, the source that feeds his generosity.

Back in his priory again, the Preacher should find the tokens of his poverty there. Dominic had a final paragraph drawn up regarding the humble nature of the buildings, which should be such as would not only prevent his brethren from being crushed by expense but also avoid scandalizing secular priests and layfolk by over-costly buildings.[69]

The members of the chapter had already legislated for the recruitment and promotion of the preachers. Designated provisionally by his prior, definitively by the chapter after a careful examination, the preacher needed a careful intellectual and moral training. The question of the studies occupied the Bologna chapter at some length. A new authority in the regular life was created, the master of students, the counterpart of the master of novices.[70] Special premises, time-tables, programmes and exercises were established, of which the tradition of regular life hitherto had known nothing. Discovery was immediately made of new types of virtues or faults, to which the attention of those responsible was drawn. The document which the *diffinitors* drew up[71] was again realistic. It portrayed the student preacher in his own milieu and activity, in the picturesque scene of the rehearsal of a theological 'disputation', such as could be seen in the schools of that time, or again it suggested the picture of the brother who succeeded in his studies and had the enjoyment of a cell to himself with permission to read, write, pray and even watch there during the night. The horizon of these studies was not so much learning as contemplation and the salvation of souls.

The chapter again drew up a series of prescriptions on the exercise of preaching in the Church,[72] in which one can see the experience of St Dominic and his attitude. Mention was made of the respect due to the authority of the bishops; the visit which must be paid to them on arrival in a diocese to ensure the effectiveness of the friars' ministry; the obedience which must be given to them in everything which does not contradict the rule; the humble and fraternal spirit which must be shown to the clergy; the good understanding one must maintain with one's *socius*. The elaboration of the apostolic code of the preacher was thus completed, the second part of the charter of preaching clearly indicated in the title: *Of the studies and the preaching*.[73]

Since it is essential to surround the students with careful foresight, they are to be entrusted to one particular brother, without whose permission they cannot copy the texts,[74] or attend lectures. He shall correct everything in their studies which seems to him to merit correction. If some point exceeds his competence, he shall submit it to the superior. The students ought not to take as the basis of their study the books of the pagans and philosophers, even if they consult them in passing.[75] There shall be no study of secular sciences[76] nor even of the arts known as the liberal arts. The young, like the others, should study only theological books.

The superior shall grant the students such dispensations that their studies cannot lightly be interrupted nor can they be disturbed for matters of service or similar reasons. If the Master of the students esteems it beneficial, special premises shall be reserved for them in which, after the disputation and the lessons of Vespers, or even at other free times, they can meet in his presence to set forth their doubts and their questions. When one of them propounds a question or sets forth an argument, let the others be silent, in order not to embarrass the one who is speaking. And if anyone, in propounding a question, objecting, replying, show himself impolite or unmethodical, or peevish or even abusive, the one who presides must correct him immediately whoever he may be. A cell shall not be given to all the students, but only to those among them who can draw profit from it in the judgement of their master. If someone fails to make progress in his studies, his cell shall be given to another and he shall be employed on other tasks. In the cells those who wish may study, write, pray, sleep and even keep vigil during the night for reason of their studies.

Those who are capable, when they have to leave the monastery to go out preaching, shall receive from the prior the *socius* he considers suitable for their habit of life and their dignity. Having received a blessing, they shall thus go forth and comport themselves everywhere as men who seek their salvation and that of their neighbour in all perfection and in a religious spirit. Like men of the Gospel, following in the footsteps of their Saviour, they shall speak with God or of God, in themselves or with their neighbour, and avoid the frequentation of company that is suspicious. When they thus go forth to exercise the ministry of preaching or travel for other reasons, they shall neither receive nor carry gold, silver, money or any other present, with the exception of food, clothes, other objects of necessity and books. None of those who are assigned to the ministry of preaching and to study shall receive any charge or temporal administration, so that, in greater liberty, he may be the more capable of fulfilling the spiritual ministry which has been entrusted to him—unless it so happen that one can find no other person who can attend to these necessities, for it is not a bad thing that at times one should be checked by having to attend to day-to-day needs.[77] They shall take no part in pleading and law-suits, unless it is for a matter of the faith.[78] When our brethren enter a particular diocese to preach there, they shall first of all visit the bishop if they can do so, and take inspiration from his counsels to bring about in the people the spiritual fruit which is their objective; they shall obey him devotedly in all that is not contrary to the rule so long as they remain under his episcopal jurisdiction. The brethren must beware of scandalising religious or clerics in their preaching by their way of 'speaking against superiors'.[79] They must, on the contrary, strive to correct in them the defects which seem to merit it by exhorting them privately as fathers.

The preachers and itinerant brethren, when they are on the road, shall say their office in the measure in which they know it and as they can.[80] They shall content themselves with the office which is recited in the churches where they stop on the way; they can also celebrate the office or hear it said by bishops, prelates and other persons, according to the customs of those with whom they are living during this time. The itinerant brethren shall also carry with them testimonial letters and in the monasteries where they make a stay, shall submit to correction of the transgressions they have committed. On the road the superior shall be he who is the most senior in the order, unless he has been assigned as *socius* to a preacher or unless the superior at the moment of departure shall have arranged otherwise. The *socius* of a preacher owes him obedience in all things.

Our brethren must have only low, unpretentious houses, so that they are not crushed by expense and so that the secular clergy and other religious are not scandalized by the sumptuousness of our buildings.[81]

Thus ends the remarkable document which we should like to call the charter of preaching. Who was responsible for drawing it up in this particular form? It will be noted that it was not the work of a jurist, though it is true that all the legal niceties are to be found in it. Yet they are not there under the form of a code, which will always be somewhat dry and abstract. They are inserted in a series of lively and evocative pictures, swift-moving and clear. We can see the workings of general chapter under the impulse of the Holy Spirit, the brethren receiving edification, or praying, the 'visitors' getting up to speak, others making the *venia* and asking pardon. One committee sits in private after the meal. We assist at theological exercises where the excitement rises in *crescendo*. We follow the preacher along the road, with his *socius*. Sometimes the narrative shows us his very heart, where he is speaking with the Lord; or again we are taken into the presence of the bishop, where the preacher acquires information and adapts himself to the needs of the situation; or perhaps into the presence of the crowds, where the preacher's contemplation overflows into the word of salvation.

Was this the work of Dominic? The witnesses in Bologna in the process of 1233 in fact attribute to him several of the phrases of this text, which are indeed among the finest, those most charged with spiritual vitality.[82] It is sufficient, however, to look closely at their testimony to realize that all they attribute to Dominic is the inspiration of the phrase and not its exact wording. *Fecit scribi, poni,* 'he had it inscribed in the rule'.[83] He had, in fact, an editor close at hand, an excellent stylist whose letters and the *Libellus* happily preserved enable us to make profitable literary comparisons with the *Institutions* of the capitulary fathers of Bologna—the former professor of literature,[84] Jordan of Saxony. In both these writings there is the same skill in painting pictures full of life, in penetrating into the feelings of the characters,[85] in evoking a spiritual attitude by an accumulation of touches of two or three words each,[86] by raising to the supernatural plane at every moment, by a brief apposition, the most simple actions.[87] Finally, when the text describes the student in theology, carried away by the discussion to the extent that he soon breaks out into insults, or the preacher who carves out for himself in public an easy and scandalous success by declaiming against the clergy, we can recognize in these portraits taken from life and without malice, the art of gently ironical correction of the second Master of the

Preachers. Moreover no one was better placed than this bachelor in theology from Paris to edit a text on the studies of the brethren.

In the course of the foundation chapter in 1216, and of the general chapter of 1220, Dominic and his brethren endowed the order with a complete body of legislation. The prologue and the two distinctions of the institutions of the Preachers present a definition of the order, a law of observance and of liturgy arranged in paragraphs, a constitutional law written at one sitting. The literary sources, considerable in the prologue and the first distinction, non-existent in the second, are limited to the customs of Prémontré. The historical sources, on the other hand, cover the whole tradition of regular monastic life in the Church. Some fifty years later Etienne de Salagnac stressed this fact without ambiguity.

> Augustine and Benedict, those glorious confessors, adapted [Dominic] to his ministry of preaching by arming him in each case with the discipline of regular life. A canon by profession,[88] he was none the less a monk by the austerity of his religious life, in his fasts, abstinences, clothing, sleep, in the discipline of silence and the chapter and in the other observances contained in the rule of blessed Benedict. He has taken over into his constitutions almost the whole of such observances, joining to them more special ones, has followed them out in fact and made his sons follow them, just as we, like him, make profession of the rule of the blessed Augustine.[89] Nevertheless, by a further increase of grace, he drew from the apostolic rule, adding it to this collection of precepts, that we should not travel on horseback, that, going on foot here and there to evangelize and work for the salvation of men, we should carry neither gold nor silver, content to receive our food in accordance with the words of St Luke X—*eating and drinking what they have to give you*. Now even on this point, seeking something more, the saint abstained and ordered his sons to abstain completely from meat, not forgetting that it was said to the innkeeper: . . . *on my way home I will give thee whatever else is owing to thee for thy pains*.[90] Thus whoever passes a judgement free from envy will see that this saint was a canon by profession, a monk by the austerity of his life, an apostle by his preaching.[91]

This the Preachers carried out in their turn. As a religious of the thirteenth century, Etienne de Salagnac judged the order from the concrete details of its observance and marvelled at the accumulation of its austerities. He suggested, however, in one or other of his phrases that this state of things was not the result of a mere race to beat the record in the competition of the religious orders. The accumulation of observances was sought out by Dominic and his brethren to prepare their life for the ministry of preaching and the salvation of souls. Today we are impressed above all by this central inspiration, the principle of unity of a whole so rich that at first sight it seems an almost disorderly pile.

Indeed, the collection of duties which Dominic and the fathers of the chapter imposed on the Order of Preachers for the future was of such an extent that they seem almost mutually exclusive. Contemplation seemed opposed to the intense activity demanded by the ministry of souls. The long liturgical prayer seemed to take up the time that study demanded. The asperity of vigils, abstinence and fasts might weaken the vital forces demanded by study and preaching. It is purposeless to hide these contradictions. The legislator of 1220 was not unaware of them, since he partially solved them by the power of dispensation placed in the hands of the superior. He was, however, at the same time convinced of the necessity of each of the parts, as much as of the whole, because the occasional opposition of the elements to each other was only one of the aspects of reality, a consequence of human weakness. On the other hand, and this was the principal point because it had for him the force of grace, these elements mutually evoke and support each other. The discipline of the observances, to use Salagnac's terms, 'adapts the religious for preaching', because it forms him morally, detaches him spiritually, purifies and enriches him supernaturally with merits and, making him share in the cross of Christ, prepares the 'grace of preaching',[92] the source of the effectiveness of the ministry by 'word and example.' This indeed was the fruit of Dominic's experience in his years of preaching in the Albigeois. Theological study, canonical prayer, private prayer, the successive facets of one and the same contemplative activity, in turn indispensable ('Which is better', Jordan of Saxony was to say, 'always to drink or always to eat?')[93] are the only authentic sources of Christian preaching. What St Thomas would express in the form of a maxim, *Contemplata aliis tradere*: to hand on to others the fruit of one's contemplation',[94] Dominic expressed in a wholly objective fashion, after the manner of the Gospel, by giving a portrait of the true Preacher going forth to men 'speaking only with God or of God, in himself or with his neighbour'. This time again, Dominic had begun by putting into practice what he said.

Three powers, three sources of energy coming from the Church of the thirteenth century, or rather from the whole history of the Church, met in the Order of Preachers thanks to the genius of Dominic—a mission from the Church, a constitution of regular life, a spiritual idea which was also a force. The mission from the Church was the preaching, which Dominic gave as end, definition and title to the Order of Preachers, because the Church had had sufficient confidence to entrust it to him. The form of regular life was the canonical tradition, with its liturgical prayer, its observances, its conventual organization, the milieu of life and moral and religious training in which Dominic had lived before making his brethren live in it. The idea which was at the same time a force, was the *vita apostolica*, the imitation of the apostles. Externally these three currents appear heterogenous and, in fact, for many years, they had moved apart from each other and diverged, even being in opposition in very serious crises, of which the Albigensian crisis was only an outcrop. Dominic and his brethren, however, had discovered the profound unity of these currents and forces. It was entirely bound up with one word—-the Gospel. For it was from the Gospel that the mission of the apostles, the community of Jerusalem, mendicant preaching had derived. As is fitting, it was the third term, the spiritual ideal, which made the unity of the whole. Dominic kept under his eyes the picture of the virile fishermen whom Christ had called upon of old to bear witness to the ends of the earth. In former times he had imitated them in the common life in Osma, when he had with his brethren 'one heart and soul . . . everything was shared in common'.[95] As a canon he had imitated them in the prayer in the temple at the third, sixth and ninth hours, of which they had expressly reserved the office to themselves by instituting deacons.[96] He, an authentic preacher, had imitated them receiving from Christ through the Church the mission to preach.[97] He, the preacher, again imitated them when he went forth with his *socius*, without gold, silver or money, staff in hand and begging his bread, to announce the kingdom of God.[98] It was not mere chance if, in the institutions of 1220, the most moving phrases taken under his dictation directly evoke the sacred image of the apostle going to save souls. In this picture which was for him overwhelming, Dominic inscribed for his brethren the fundamental experience of his life, the evangelical inspiration of his order, the unique source of the very rich life of his brethren, the supernatural mystery of the order of Preachers. 'Like men of the Gospel, following in the footsteps of their Saviour.'

The general chapter finished its task. Paris and Bologna had already brought themselves to accept mendicancy. The case of Madrid would be regulated by the abandonment of the house to the sisters. A letter was sent to them— perhaps Friar Mames was a member of the chapter and brought the letter with him. The case of Toulouse was also regulated in principle; certain property was restored to the diocese,[99] other estates were given to Prouille,[100] other property would form the subject of later negotiations with the diocese.[101]

The discussion on the studies of the Preachers had made clearer than ever the necessity for having the support of the university of Paris. The Preacher was to be an informed and enlightened theologian. It was not sufficient that he should have received his training; it was essential that he should keep up his knowledge and find in his house someone who could provide for this. A conventual theological school was indispensable, not only to form the preachers, who could not all be sent to Paris, but to maintain the studies of those who had been formed there. It was, moreover, the natural complement to their preaching since it influenced the local clergy by its teaching. It then established, at the same time as the programme of preaching of the Council of the Lateran, its scholastic programme.[102] A constitution of the Pope a few months earlier had in point of fact recalled the urgency of this programme.[103] In this way the Preachers collaborated in every aspect of the doctrinal mission of the bishop.[104] The letter of Conradin of Metz already cited several times would soon bring the proof that such ideas had been as familiar to the Curia since 1220 as they clearly were to the Preachers.[105] It was at the chapter of Bologna that they must have been published.

Thus it was essential that the Preachers should have their Masters trained in the one place where the universal licence to teach theology in the Church was granted, in the university of Paris. The chapter considered plans for enlarging the convent of St Jacques,[106] sending students there from all parts of the order,[107] securing for it an internal teaching,[108] in short, strengthening the bond between the convent and the university of Paris. The first thing to be done was to obtain the hospice as a permanent gift. This would be an accomplished fact on 3rd May following. Jean de Barastre and the university, as has already been said, had now definitely abandoned their claims on the house.[109] In return, the order would allocate founder's privileges to the Dean of St Quentin and receive the corporation of the university into its fraternity; and—an even more remarkable fact—Jean de Barastre at this time transferred his chair of theology to the house of the Preachers;[110] the brethren, who had not the right to leave their convent to attend the courses in the faculty,[111] thus had them under their own roof; they were permanently incorporated in the university. Jean de Barastre had acted at the express demand of the Pope. These events were thus not the fruit of steps taken by the Preachers of Paris and their friends alone, but also by Dominic at the Curia. Courses of theology were also instituted at the convent of St Nicholas of Bologna.[112] The university, which had no faculty of theology, would for long let this school of the Preachers, and later, those of other mendicant orders take its place. The university orientation of the Order of St Dominic which was to produce incomparable fruit in the course of the thirteenth century, was thus the result of the decisions and conscious efforts of their founder and his first brethren, particularly in 1220.[113]

Since the confirmation by the Pope of the two houses of Preachers of St Romain (1216) and of Prouille (1218), no official act, to our knowledge, had come to sanction the foundation of a community of Dominicans. Many houses had however come into being since then, beginning with those of Paris and Bologna. It does not seem, however, that, in respect of these houses, they proceeded to that declaration of rights which is known as a canonical erection. The superior of the brethren in Paris, Friar Matthew of France, continued to style himself in 1220 'Abbot of the Friars Preachers dwelling in Paris',[114] which is merely a reduced form of the complete title 'Abbot of the brethren of St Romain of the Order of Preachers',[115] as if all the Preachers of France, Spain and Italy continued to belong to the community of Toulouse. It would seem that from that time the general chapter raised into convents those existing communities which fulfilled certain conditions. In any case, it fixed the title of their superior. Friar Matthew would in future be called 'Prior of the Preachers of St Jacques in Paris',[116] like Friar Paul at St Nicholas of Bologna,[117] Friar Giacomo at Milan[118] and Friar Tancred in Rome.[119]

The chapter decided moreover on the mission to Scandinavia. Friars Simon of Sweden and Nicholas of Lund were sent with Provost St Peter of Sigtuna who was waiting for them. The bull of recommendation of 11th November, 1219 (III)[120] was entrusted to them. How they very quickly constructed a monastery in Sigtuna, which would only last for a few years, has already been told.

The Provost of Sigtuna was not the only one to ask for Preachers, if an ancient document of the convent of Barcelona[121] is to be believed. The bishop of that city, Berenger of Palou, is also said to have met the founder round about that date and to have obtained a few religious from the chapter of Bologna for his city, and to have taken them back with him.[122] The document is not wholly trustworthy. It seems that the bishop did obtain the brethren for the foundation, after the death of Dominic, most probably at the chapter of 1222. In 1220, the only sign of the interest taken by the Preachers in Catalonia was the bull of recommendation of 6th May, to the Archbishop of Tarragona,[123] which has already been mentioned; it does not seem to have produced results. On 7th December, 1221, a more summary bull to the Bishop of Barcelona doubtless led to the step and the success of 1222.[124] The church of the monastery would not appear until 1223.[125]

The expansion and influence of Paris was not as rapid as that of Bologna. The chapter decided to intensify it. Some brethren were sent to Amiens, where from the autumn their activity seemed to be on the point of leading to a foundation.[126] The action of the chapter cannot but have had a hand too in the foundations soon after of Rheims and Poitiers.[127] It is probable too that the foundations which were to arise in the course of that year in Spain, Provence and Lombardy or in Tuscany were the subject of the deliberations of the chapter. We have no direct echo of this.

The chapter was finished. After the prayers, anathemas and final benedictions, all dispersed. Each one, his heart full of beautiful memories, still completely radiant with happiness from the fervour of Dominic and his loyal companions, set out again for his priory, carrying with him the new *Institutions* of the brethren.

Dominic went off to preach in northern Italy. How free his heart was as he gave himself to his ministry—he had organized his order.

CHAPTER XVII

'THE PREACHING' IN LOMBARDY

ON 12th May, 1220, while Dominic was on his way to Bologna, letters left Viterbo for the north and south of Italy bearing orders from Honorius III to five religious to place themselves at the disposal of the Master of the Preachers.[1]

It is not without justification that we have compared this recruitment of preachers from monasteries of different origin—Augustinians, Benedictines, Cistercians—with that made by Pope Innocent III on 29th January, 1204, for the Albigeois. In 1204, the Pope had collected preachers under the direction of the legates and soon of the Abbot of Cîteaux himself. To these preachers the leader in charge was to add others, whom he would recruit from the numerous abbeys of his order.[2] In 1220 the Pope again collected together an army of preachers and placed it under the authority of the head of the Friars Preachers, who was in no need of a special recommendation from the Pope to associate his brethren with his preaching. This is not, indeed, the only analogy that can be noted between the two enterprises. The similarity extended also, as will be seen, to the congregations to which both preaching expeditions were directed.

Dominic took his part in both, but in the interval he had seen his position considerably changed. Originally he had found himself accredited to the mission of the Cistercians in the Albigeois as a humble preacher of whom for long the official documents had taken no account; now he was the head of the new mission which by that very fact became the mission of the Friars Preachers. Moreover, among the religious of other orders whom he attached to his troops was a monk of the abbey of Flora, of the Order 'of Cîteaux and of Flora' (to use the same terms as the Papacy[3]) who not so long before had been in charge. The rôles were thus reversed. It might be said that it was a sign of the times and that since 1220, as would effectively be the case for the future, the first of the mendicant orders found itself replacing, for the great tasks of evangelization, the Order of Cîteaux which since the twelfth century had been ubiquitous. It would, however, be an exaggeration to say this. In 1220 and for several years to come, the immense army of the Cistercians would remain, in the eyes of the popes as in actual fact, the principal source of the missionary forces of the Church which could be drawn on in all circumstances.[4] It was clear, however, that on 12th May,

1220, for a mission of capital importance, the Order of St Dominic occupied a place that a few years earlier had been entrusted to the Order of Cîteaux— a striking testimony to the confidence and wide hopes placed in it by the Pope and the Curia.

The documents which would provide accurate details of this mission are lacking. We no longer possess the Bull of Institution addressed to St Dominic. There remains, however, the letter to the five religious. It contains the essential phrase. The religious were to leave their monastery and set out in the train of the head of the Preachers 'to propound the word of God to any person to whom [Dominic] shall judge it expedient that this shall be done. By manifesting the light of truth to these stray sheep, they will bring them back to the way of truth'. It was thus a question of going to people who had gone astray in error and of bringing them back to the truth and to Christian life. These straying souls were not identified either by name or place. Dominic's mandate was completely general, and he had no rule other than his own decision. History, however, tells us how the Preacher defined it. In 1220, he would journey through the whole of Lombardy from the last days of May until the end of the year;[5] between 1220 and 1221, he would traverse 'almost in its entirety the Marches of Treviso' and 'the territory of Venice'.[6] Lombardy, the Marches and Venetia, in other words the whole of the north of Italy, he was going to comb through with his brethren, who were no longer young acolytes but men in full maturity,[7] and perhaps one or other of the preachers sent to him by the Pope. The wandering sheep to whom he would be addressing himself were at last specified. They were all those who, in northern Italy, were systematically separating themselves from orthodox Christianity, and principally the Waldenses and the Catharists. The mission of 1220–1221 was really comparable with that of 1203. Like the Abbot of Cîteaux earlier in the case of the preaching in the Narbonensis, the Master of the Preachers was charged to organize the preaching in Lombardy.

Until quite recent years nothing was known of the very wide extension of heresies and especially of the Catharist heresy in North Italy. It was known, it is true, that the townsmen of the proud cities of Lombardy which seethed with activity, perhaps the most brilliant civilization of the Europe of the time, were manifesting their vitality and their spirit of independence by a great show of welcome to religious trends and movements coming from every horizon. Milan provided the example of what might be met with in all the cities through which the Pô flowed or which enjoyed the protection of the mighty buttresses of the Alps to the north of the vast plain. Jacques de Vitry in 1216 depicted it as 'a den of heretics'[8] an expression which does not fail to recall the terms in which Pierre des Vaux Cernai stigmatized Toulouse.[9]

The affair dated from far back. The deep stirrings of the Gregorian reform had begun in Milan, where the religious fervour of a mobile population, inflamed by the call to a return to the primitive Church launched by the reformers, had more than once set against the feudal lords and the main body of the clergy the 'patares' who were allied to the Papacy. To these causes of general disorder, the revolutionary ardour of the communal movement and the increasing violence in the course of the twelfth century of the conflict between the Clergy and the Empire, had added their causes of anarchy. Lombardy was indeed the classic battlefield between the two powers, and the Lombard League had been founded to play the decisive part in the war which they were waging against each other. At the heart of the ceaselessly renewed politico-religious agitations of which they were often the deciders, the cities in the plain of the Po had increased each day in importance and in insubordination. Swayed in turn by the Empire or by the Papacy, according to what was most profitable for their interests at the time, moreover opposed to each other by implacable quarrels which were no less violent and whose intentions were no less sordid than the struggles of the feudal lords among themselves, finally rent by internal rivalries between townsmen and feudal lords, and, since the end of the twelfth century, between small and great, populo grasso and populo minuto, the cities of the north of Italy presented a perfect ground for the germination of religious sects. They could preserve with difficulty a sufficiently real sense of the transcendence of the link that bound them to the Apostolic See when they were each in turn induced to combat it on the political plane. The anarchy of their daily life could not but react on their religious life. The tendency was particularly strong in the case of those who presided over the temporal destinies of the city, collective authorities and, increasingly often since the beginning of the thirteenth century, the podestà engaged by the townsmen to govern the city. Should any one of such authorities be sympathetic towards one or other of the anticlerical or heretical sects which had been pullulating in the city since the time of the reform, this was perhaps looked upon as something in his favour. For the political power of the city thereby evaded the loyalties and scruples which limited the action of an orthodox Catholic. Thus can be explained the phenomenon, at first sight surprising, of the presence of heretics among the communal authorities in localities which were in no sense won over to heresy. Innocent III had had experience of this even in the patrimony of the Roman Church. Viterbo and Orvieto, so close to Rome, had presented him with the cruel surprise of electing Catharist magistrates.[10]

Catharism, indeed, had obtained a foothold in Italy in the second part of the twelfth century and bringing to the unorthodox sects and religious currents which were spreading themselves in all directions the benefit of its vigorous organization and of its dogma—unmistakably anti-Roman. Catharism in turn, however, had not been able to avoid suffering the influence of this extremely undisciplined area, especially in Lombardy. Whilst in

Southern France it had developed in great unity, beyond the Alps it had soon broken up into several contrary tendencies, sometimes in violent opposition to each other.[11]

It was at Concorezzo, on the outskirts of Monza, about twelve miles or so to the north of Milan, that the heresy had taken root. In the last third of the twelfth century, a certain Mark, a grave-digger by trade, had been initiated into the sect by a travelling notary from France. Mark had become the first Catharist bishop of the north of the Peninsula. The initial form of Catharism in Lombardy thus drew its inspiration from a moderate dualism as had been the case in France. The visit of Papanicetas, however, the emissary of the Dragovitsian Catharists at the Albigensian Council of Caraman, brought a similar change in dogma on both sides of the Alps. Italian Catharism turned towards the radical dualism which was now firmly established in France. It was not long however before the influence of another moderate form of Catharism, emanating from Slavonia or Bosnia came into conflict with the absolute dualism of the Lombards. Disorder was then rife in the community—various statements, emanating from these different sources, sowed in men's consciences an unbridled trouble that was typical of the religion of the Catharists. This was not indeed dogmatic doubt, but what for them was much more decisive, doubt on the authentic 'angelism' of one of their bishops, or, which amounted to the same thing, of one of their oriental consecrators. They had been caught by surprise, it was asserted, with women. The hierarchy issuing from these false 'angels' at once fell to pieces. The communities split up.

In Dominic's time there existed in Italy six differing Catharist communities, four of which were in Lombardy. The bishops who governed them were not united in some general organization and did not divide up the territory between them as Catholic bishops would do. On the contrary they opposed each other in their independence. The two most important of them mutually excommunicated each other. The churches overlapped and placed their deacons side by side in the same towns. The bishop, moreover, did not have his seat in the important towns which were the centre of his sphere of influence, but in some village of the outskirts, doubtless from motives of security. So important was his rôle in the community that he gave it his name. At the beginning of the thirteenth century, the different branches of Catharism bore the name of one or other of their early bishops.

Such was the case of the *Garatenses* (from their bishop Garatto) or Catharists of Concorezzo (Milan), the most important of these churches. Particularly active around Milan, it was also found in the whole plain of the Pô. In Dominic's time the bishop was a certain Nazarius, recently the 'major' son of the founder Garatto. The church had derived its moderate form of dualism from Bulgaria. It excommunicated the Dragovitsian church of which mention will be made but it made peace with the Lombard churches which had emanated from Slavonia.

The church of the *Albanenses* (from Bishop Albani?) established at Desenzano, on the south bank of Lake Garda, had issued from the reform of Papanicetas; it was then Dragovitsian, i.e. absolute dualist. Less strong numerically than the Garatenses, its radicalism gave it a stronger hold. From time to time it influenced the *credo* of the neighbouring churches. Verona, where the bishop of Desenzano would eventually reside, was its principal centre. The sect, however, was also present in the cities which border the fringe of the Alps and in those of the middle Pô. At the time of St Dominic, the bishop was called Belesmanza.

The church of Bagnolo (near Mantua) was of the Slavonian type, i.e. moderate dualist. Its influence extended to Mantua, Brescia and Bergamo and reached certain individuals in the Milan region and the Romagna. Around 1220, the bishop was called Andréas. The church of Vicenza extended its activity throughout the Marches of Treviso. It, too, was of the Slavonian type and thus moderate, although it was influenced by the increasing contamination of the church of Desenzano. Its bishop in 1220 was Pierre le Gaulois. He was later to be converted to Catholicism.

There was also a Catharist church in Florence, a result of the first reform of the Lombards. It stood for absolute dualism. Its bishop, Philip at the time of St Dominic, ruled over a vast territory stretching from Arezzo as far as Pisa. The Catharist bishop of the Val de Spoleta, the sixth of these churches at the beginning of the thirteenth century, worked throughout Roman Tuscany and in the patrimony of St Peter. Absolute dualist in dogma like the churches of Florence and Desenzano, that of Spoleto had been very active in Viterbo from the time of Innocent III, who in 1205 had the heresiarch Tionisi (? Denis) expelled, and in Orvieto. These last two Catharist groups are less well known than the others.

The six churches appear to have been flourishing in numbers and vitality, especially in Lombardy. Thirty years after Dominic's death, when they had already suffered considerable losses from the fact of the apostolate of the mendicant orders, they still counted, in addition to their bishops with major and minor sons, dozens of deacons and some 2,500 Perfect, 1,500 of whom belonged to the church of Concorezzo and 500 to that of Desenzano. As to the number of believers who accepted their influence, it can be estimated as more than 100,000.[12] At this time the geography of the Catharist heresy in Lombardy could be presented as follows: four large centres with bishops whose *credos* differed, in Milan, Verona, Mantua and Vicenza. The deacons of the different branches, especially those of Concorezzo and Desenzano, were installed at fixed posts in the majority of the large cities, doubtless running hospices and communities of Perfect, as was the custom. Such deacons were to be found in Alexandria, Pavia, Lodi,

Piacenza, Bergamo, Seprio, Brescia, Cremona, Mantua, Verona, and in ten
or more towns of the Marches of Treviso. At the time of St Dominic, the
diffusion of the six churches must have been wider still, especially in Emilia,
where the apostolate of the Preachers of Bologna had not yet penetrated.[13]
From this can be measured the importance of the preaching of Lombardy.

It would be wrong, however, to see only heretics in the stray sheep whom
the Pope was asking Dominic to bring back to the truth. The action of the
Church at this time was a universal tutelary action for good and against the
perils of Christian society. The partiality of our curiosity or our prejudices
of today must not be allowed to falsify the image which we form to ourselves
of them. The abuses of the power of money, which we do not yet know how
to control satisfactorily and which are all included with insufficient discernment under the name of usury, also constituted major obstacles to
Christianity in this society where the *bourgeoisie* of the artisans and traders
was now in full expansion. The Lombards, indeed, were the great financiers
of Europe. Dominic, as will be seen, also busied himself with these practical
deviations.[14]

Primarily, however, he had to concern himself with the most virulent of
the scourges of this land and the times, that abuse of violence in all classes of
society which was manifested by continual brutalities and above all by war.[15]
Lombardy was given over to the most devastating rivalries. The picture of it
is perhaps worse than that which has been drawn of the anarchy of the Midi
of France, because in northern Italy the towns, more prosperous, had
succeeded better than anywhere else in taking their place by the side of the
feudal lords whose ambitious and warlike customs they adopted; because the
communes were grouped in continually changing leagues, ceaselessly renewing themselves, until they culminated in the redoubtable Lombard League,
whose rôle in the highest political affairs of the time, the struggle between
the Clergy and the Empire, has already been recalled. Yet however numerous
might be the occasions of war furnished by the interminable quarrel of the
two leaders of Christendom, it was far from being the case that the Guelf
and Ghibelline cities limited their bloodthirsty encounters to these conflicts.
Each group of cities had its own ambitions. Each city had its covetous desires
and its fierce enmities, the fruits of local ambitions or long and deeply
rooted resentments. Within the towns themselves, the unrest of the *populo
minuto* was combined with the old struggles of parties or clans. Within the
feudal or patrician classes, pitiless feuds decimated families and sometimes
had their repercussions throughout an entire province. Hatreds were
multiplied even in the bosom of families. The passions of domination and
vengeance rent Italy with that fierce fire and those sudden excesses which
characterized the whole of life in this privileged region of the West. In
Bologna itself, Dominic had all too frequently under his eyes 'the sanguinary
effusions of blood which the monstrous fury of long-standing enmities

unleashed among noble families',[16] and which, two years later, a year after the Preacher's death, the devastating words of St Francis on the square before the communal palace would appease only for a few moments.[17] In Lombardy, as in Narbonnaise Provence, Dominic was to show once more by his efforts in preaching, his ardent love 'for the faith and peace'.[18]

Eventually, in Lombardy, as in the Narbonensis, the mission that the Pope gave him was inscribed in a general pontifical enterprise of which Cardinal Ugolino was the principal operator in North Italy. The historical circumstances explain the origin and plan of this enterprise.[19] During the last years of Pope Innocent and the first of Honorius, the war between the Papacy and the Empire flared up once more. Calm was restored after the defeat and death of Otto IV in 1218. The Church's candidate, the youthful King of the Romans, Frederick II, triumphed. He prepared himself to receive the imperial crown in Rome at the end of 1220 and undertook to set off on a crusade to retake Jerusalem. Pope and king concerned themselves in turn with restoring order in Lombardy which the struggle had thrown into confusion. Each of them did so according to his own point of view, his own interests and his own traditions.

In the course of 1217, and then from the spring of 1218 to the spring of 1219, Cardinal Ugolino went into the north of the country as papal legate.[20] The object of his mission was the preparation of the crusade. What was wanted was to obtain the participation of the cities by persuading them to send a contingent on the great expedition which Honorius was launching in the East to carry out the decisions of the Lateran Council. This was the opportunity to restore order in Lombardy in accordance with the standards of the Church. In particular, it was essential to bring about a lasting peace between the urban groups, of which Milan and Cremona were the leaders, and moreover to appease the cities two by two, and finally, to profit by the great revision of rights and positions so as to induce the cities to respect the liberties of the clergy, the property of the Roman Church, especially the heritage of Countess Matilda, and the decrees of the Lateran Council. The problem of the heresies condemned by the Council clearly formed part of this programme, as did the struggle against usury and the abuses of violence. We can judge of the complexity of the affairs among which the cardinal, who achieved more through his skill as a diplomat than through his power to impose an interdict, had to move. He obtained only a limited success, a pacification that was provisional and not even all-embracing.[21] The question of orthodoxy and of anti-Christian practices, remained in 1220 practically untouched.

In Italy as everywhere else,[22] the medieval Church tried to obtain from the Christian temporal rulers a promise that they would recognize the Catholic canons as laws of the land and thus give them executive force. Urban legislation had been established for a century past. It was essential that the cities should remove from their statutes the anti-ecclesiastical provisions which were present in them and should insert in their place the decisions of the Councils and other canonical rulings which concerned them, at the same time undertaking to apply them. Now the authorities of the towns, wilfully anticlerical and moreover indulgent if not positively disposed to heresy, were visibly reluctant to do this. It would be difficult to persuade them to do this. The feudal lords, frequently siding with the Empire, were often ill-disposed and, what was more, powerless; the Lombard cities had settled their relations with the local feudalities in quite a different manner from that of the cities of France. At the conclusion of very bitter struggles, the urban authorities dominated the nobles and often even brought them to a gentler mood. The future emperor might use persuasions. At this time he was disposed to show goodwill towards the Sovereign Pontiff. If the legation in Lombardy of the Chancellor of the Empire, the Bishop of Metz and Spier, Conrad de Scharfeneck, whom Dominic had the opportunity of meeting in the summer of 1220, had as its chief aim the opening of a peaceful passage for the cortège of the King of the Romans on his way to the coronation,[23] the coronation itself would, on the other hand, give the Papacy the means to cause the new emperor to intervene in Imperial Italy side by side with the Church. The canons of the Lateran Council, in particular the provisions against the heretics, at the same time as a series of measures for the protection of the weak, would be declared laws of the Empire.[24] This means of action, however, was to remain limited, as the emperor's effective power in these regions was limited, to say nothing of his goodwill in regard to the Church.

One other means was left, the most effective and most legitimate of all, the action of the Catholic populations on the magistrates they gave themselves. The cities were not always in agreement with their magistrates. The patricians themselves had other adversaries, in addition to the feudal lords. The unrest of the *populari*, without being properly speaking democratic revolts, demonstrated an internal ferment in the city, with which the magistrates had to reckon. In certain cities—this was the case at Milan after 1222—the *populari* would even seize the power. Now the mass of the population was faithful to Christianity and the Church in a different way from the nobles and patricians of the towns. In awakening a Catholic sense in the urban masses, they could thus be brought to act on their magistrates, to constrain them to pledge themselves in favour of the Christian life, ecclesiastical order and orthodoxy. Who could better exert their influence in this sense than the apostolic preachers?

It can be affirmed that these ideas were clearly expressed in Dominic's presence in Viterbo, in the autumn of 1219 or spring of 1220 when Cardinal Ugolino gave an account of the results of his legation in Tuscany and Lombardy and of the data he had been able to collect on the situation of

Catholicism in those territories. Despite the poverty of the sources, this policy can in fact be seen to manifest itself shortly afterwards among the Catholic authorities and missionaries of the region. It made its appearance in Milan immediately upon the seizure of power by the *populari* and from that time continued to develop until it reached its apogee at the time of St Peter Martyr.[25]

It was not a question, it should be noted, of attributing to Dominic a mission of religious policy. Ugolino and the other legates of the Holy See, with the local prelates, were sufficient for that. In confiding to the Preachers and their collaborators, however, the general evangelization of the country, it was indeed hoped to elicit a general renewal of Catholic conviction and practice in the contaminated cities, at the same time as a gradual breaking-up of the heterodox positions. This movement of evangelization would be a long-term one. In proportion as it developed, however, its effectiveness would be doubled by obtaining from the magistrate, through the pressure of public opinion and of the popular party, an action in conformity with the decrees of the Church which would achieve the destruction of errors, wars and abuses. Such was the complete context of the mission entrusted in May 1220 to Dominic and to the assistants who were found for him. It took its place within a general action against the persons and practices forming an obstacle to Christianity in Italy, which was the same as with the *negotium fidei et pacis* of the Albigeois.

As formerly in the Narbonensis, Dominic claimed for himself and his collaborators a clearly defined and limited rôle in the centre of the general enterprise. He did not, of course, want the political rôle of a legate, not even that of the spiritual authority which governs, controls and punishes, after the manner of a bishop. A few months after this time, in the course of the famous meeting with Francis of Assisi at Cardinal Ugolino's, Dominic would once more emphasize his formal will to refuse the episcopal office for himself and his sons.[26] On the other hand, the bull of 1220 clearly expressed the mission that he claimed—that of the preacher of doctrine who carries to all the evangelical 'word of truth', by setting forth 'the light of the truth',[27] by his discourses and even more by the example of his humble life, poor to the point of mendicancy.

It would be pleasant now to follow Dominic in the various stages of this ministry. Detailed documents are unfortunately lacking. The effect of the letter to the five preachers is not known. We do, indeed, know something of the journey. Friar Buonviso, Friar Ventura, Friar Paul of Venice, who accompanied him with others, were to leave vivid descriptions of the behaviour of their master along the road or in the religious houses they visited.[28] These accounts, however, formed part of their evidence at the canonization process. Thus they retained only the features which emphasised the sanctity of the patriarch and did not trouble to indicate the setting, the development and the results of the preaching in North Italy. A few details, however, have survived.

Immediately after the chapter of Bologna, still at the end of May, Dominic went to Milan with Friar Buonviso and Friar Ventura of Verona. There he fell ill once more. This is the third attack of serious illness that has been mentioned in less than a year.[29] As soon as he was better, he continued his ministry. He doubtless also devoted his attention to the permanent installation of the brethren at St Eustorga, which the provost and canons of that church had agreed to hand over to the Preachers. A series of documents gave legal effect to the cession from the month of August.[30]

Dominic went on to Piacenza, then to the neighbouring abbey of Columba, with Ventura of Verona.[31] Columba was a Cistercian abbey,[32] the first one of the order in Italy, near Borgo San Donnino, on the Emilian Way. On this occasion Buonviso is no longer mentioned. It is in fact known that Dominic parted from him at latest in July.[33] Perhaps he remained in Milan or in Piacenza, his native city, able to testify to his first apostolic successes.

It is doubtless after the visit to Piacenza and Columba that a ministry of Dominic in Modena, also on the Emilian Way going towards Bologna, must be placed. A dean from France, on his way to the Curia, heard Dominic preach and confided to him his confusion when faced with certain temptations of the flesh; Dominic restored his hope and courage and promised him the help of his prayer, which was to prove effective.[34]

If credence may be given to an anecdote related by Constantino of Orvieto, the patriarch returned to Bologna for the feast of the Assumption.[35] On the eve of the solemnity he is shown to us in company of one of his Cistercian friends, the Abbot of Casamari near Frosinone to the south-west of Rome, who was later Bishop of Alatri.[36] The abbot took advantage of a mission to Germany where the Pope was sending him, to visit his friend. They spoke of the spiritual life and of the force of prayer. Dominic allowed himself to make a confidence: God, he avowed, up to the present had never refused anything to his prayer. Immediately an idea crossed the monk's mind. He suggested to Dominic, as a challenge of chivalry, to ask God in his prayer for the vocation of Master Conrad the Teuton, a doctor of Bologna whose entrance among the Preachers he knew that the brethren ardently desired. Dominic, taken by surprise, took up the challenge, but he also insisted with humility on the collaboration of the other's prayer. They prayed at night until Matins, then began again, after the office. At the hour when the brethren were singing Prime, as the day broke, it shed its light on Master Conrad, who had come to beg for the habit of the order. Such is the account of Constantino of Orvieto. One could wish it were better authenticated. What is unusual in this story is not the intensity of the prayer of the two religious, still less the grace of God, but this character of prowess. However this may be and whatever is said about it, this Master Conrad the Teuton was not the future provincial of Germany,[37] still less was he Conrad of Marburg, the inquisitor of sinister memory, who was not a Dominican.[38]

After Bologna, it is uncertain whether Dominic returned to Lombardy. It may have been then that with Paul of Venice and a companion he visited Dugliolo, near Budrio and not far from Bologna,[38] and Legnago on the Adige, downstream from Verona.[39] He would then have inaugurated the apostolate of the Marches as early as 1220.[40] It is difficult to be sure. Henceforward and until the end of the year, no further reliable document about Dominic will be found. This was the time when Conrad de Scharfeneck visited the cities of Lombardy in his capacity as legate of the Empire. The impressive cortège of the King of the Romans crossed the plain of the Pô in September. On 3rd October he was in Bologna where he stopped for a few days, then, following the Emilian Way, he came down slowly towards Rome where the coronation took place on 22nd November. Italy was completely taken up by these great external events. In the brilliance of this halo of glory, the deeds of the humble team of preachers of the Gospel and of their master are blurred for a few months to the point of being effaced from our view. Perhaps Dominic also took the Emilian Way in the month of October or November to reach Rome, where he certainly was at the end of December.[42] There is no reason to suppose that he attached himself to the imperial cortège.

The depositions of Buonviso, Stefano, Ventura of Verona and Paul of Venice, who knew him well in the course of this ministry, give us a glimpse of the oratorical zeal and of the eloquence of their master. 'He gave himself assiduously and with the greatest diligence to preaching. When he preached he found tones that were so deeply moving that he moved even himself to tears and made his hearers weep.' So much was this so that Friar Stefano, who gives us information of this kind, 'has never heard a man whose words excited the brethren to compunction and tears so effectively'.[41]

It will be noted that the brother primarily refers to Dominic's sermons to his religious. This was the case of the majority of the other witnesses at the process of Bologna.[44] Dominic, in effect, preached frequently to his brethren, 'almost every day'.[45] Whatever his fatigue might be when he arrived in one of his houses, he immediately called the brethren to chapter and began to preach.[46] He did the same in the case of religious who gave him hospitality.[47] Moreover he did so for the travellers whom he joined along the road.[48] Did he also preach to the crowds in the church? No account comparable to those which describe the sermons in Segovia has come down to us from an Italian witness. The anecdotes which mention such sermons are relatively late.[49] This sets a problem. In the mission in Lombardy, was Dominic content to collect and form his men, to teach the method, to excite their fervour and to lead his brethren and collaborators to the conflict? Did he reserve his eloquence for religious, for clerics, in short for all those whom he could reach by using Latin?

His situation as a foreigner in the country might lead us to think so. As a Castilian, he certainly found many difficulties in adapting himself to the varied dialects of North Italy—Tuscan, Lombard, Emilian—and in making himself understood by the simple folk. It would seem likely, however, that he nevertheless succeeded and that he preached publicly and frequently in Italy as he had done for twelve years in the south of France. At a time when the romance idioms had not yet developed and given permanence to the literary forms of their languages, difficulties would be unlikely to be made over the forms of expression of a foreigner who preached. Dominic, in familiarising himself with the tongues of Languedoc and Provence, had recently made a considerable step towards learning the dialects of North Italy. Finally it is clear that he did not shrink from any effort to learn the language of the people with whom he was in touch. He was too much of a preacher to be satisfied with living in a country without entering into contact with the natives. His companions of that time were unanimous in stressing his persistence in joining in conversation with all those he met on the way, that he might speak to them of God, and the success of his efforts.[50] Had he not succeeded by the grace of God, along the road to Orléans, in speaking even German?[51] Was he not going, in a few months' time in Rome, to devote long hours almost every evening, to forming a community of nuns who certainly did not know Latin and still less Castilian? Thus the references, even if long after the event, to his popular preaching in Modena, Bologna or Rome, should not be rejected a priori.[52] Such sermons, however, in an idiom which was not familiar to him, clearly had not the inspiring eloquence of those which he could make in Latin to his brethren. It will be understood that it was this latter type of sermons that the witnesses of Bologna preferred to recall when they were trying to draw attention to his overwhelming eloquence.

No text, unfortunately, has preserved the content of his sermons for us. It is possible at least to surmise. Quite certainly he endeavoured to carry out in the pulpit the general preaching plan which he had defined as far back as 1215 and had inscribed in the formula of pontifical recommendation which he preferred—the explanation and defence of Christian doctrine and morals, i.e. the general subject of episcopal preaching.[53] This was: 'To speak of God or with God',[54] the formula which he loved to repeat and which he had inscribed, even in the Constitutions, indicating clearly enough that he envisaged a preaching that should be positive, doctrinal, theocentric to use an over-modern term—an exposition of the Christian revelation. The tears he shed as he preached,[55] as he did in celebrating Mass, are proof that he spoke for preference of Christ, of the Cross, of salvation, of the love of one's neighbour. He also spoke with deep feeling of the great tragedy of sinners. His prayer was also dominated by a penetrating compassion for the guilty and those gone astray. The words 'compunction' and 'tears'[56] used by Friar Stefano are significant. At this period they principally described the neart's conversion, repentance in the face of sin and the cross of Christ; more deeply, and in accordance with the best spiritual tradition, the suffering of the Christian soul faced with its sinful condition, hard pressed by concupiscence and error, obliged to live in the midst of evil and widely separated from God. Dominic's sermon was thus a continual call to conversion—the 'Repent and believe the Gospel' of Christ.[57]

In view of his special mission among the heterodox of Lombardy, Dominic clearly had to insist in detail on the errors of the Catharists and Waldenses and on the authentic dogmas and practices of Christianity that were opposed to those errors. The great experience acquired in the Albigeois could not fail to be of use to him and direct his action. He did not fear to tackle burning problems directly, even in hostile circumstances. This was one of the marks of his strong character. If he had not to hold public disputations in Lombardy after the manner of those of the Albigeois—no trace of any has come down to us and the situation of the country would not seem to lend itself to them—he replaced them by the explanations he gave in his preaching.

After having preached, Dominic visited, exhorted, consoled, heard confessions. It was there that he succeeded in influencing and converting souls. We shall speak later of his spiritual direction to religious. His effect on the students has been noted. It is remarkable that several anecdotes depict him at the bedside of usurers.[58] Dominic only granted absolution if the goods unjustly gained were restored. And the better to succeed in detaching souls from avarice, he gave the example, in his own person and in that of his preachers, of a detachment that was heroic.

He was poor in his garments, in his wretched tunic, which was, moreover, the only one he had, and which he wore both winter and summer.[59] He wore a short scapular of very coarse material, and he did not try to hide its poor quality under his cappa.[60] He was poor in his convent, which he wanted small as in the premises assigned to regular life like the cells, and modest as in the church;[61] 'no liturgical vestments of silk or purple', 'no vessel of gold or silver with the exception of the chalices';[62] no desk a little better than the ordinary for the professors.[63] He was poor in the matter of food. 'You are killing the brethren with these supplements' he whispered to good Friar Rodolfo who had had a 'pittance' prepared one feast day.[64]

It sometimes happened that one item of food, the wine, even the bread, was short at the monastery. The procurator would come to find him to let him know of their penury. 'Go and pray,' said Dominic, 'and the Lord will provide.'[65] He often joined the brother in the church. He acted in this way in the face of any distress of which he was informed. 'And', continued Friar

Rodolfo, the hero of these adventures, 'God did so well that the brethren always had the necessary food.'[66] Sometimes he gave Rodolfo the order 'to put the little bread they had on the table, and the Lord will supply what is wanting'.[67] Friar Buonviso, who but lately had seconded Friar Rodolfo in his office, related that 'on a certain fast day the bread failed. Friar Dominic made a sign to put some before the brethren. The brother told him there was none. Then, his face radiant, the Master raised his hands, praised the Lord and gave thanks. At that very moment two men entered, bearing two baskets, the one full of bread, the other of dry figs, so that the brethren were able to eat their fill.'[68] Such is, in its original account, the anecdote that tradition has named the 'repast of the angels'. The deposition of the first-hand and somewhat naïve witness is surely more valuable than the distortions or embellishments of Constantino of Orvieto or of Sister Cecilia.[69]

On the road Dominic ate what was given him, except that always he removed the meat from it. But he was particularly joyful when he was badly fed.[70] 'From time to time', said Paul of Venice, 'he went to beg alms from door to door and to receive his bread like a poor man. One day, in the village of Dugliolo where he was begging, a man gave him a whole loaf. The father received it on his knees, with much humility and devotion.'[71] The practice of mendicancy now led to the multiplication of incidents of this kind in the order. How one would like to be able here to put on the screen at some length the pictures coming from the primitive sources. Here are the two lay-brothers from Viterbo who beg for their convent and bring back flour; their benefactress finds her sack, which they have left after emptying it into theirs, full again.[72] A group of novices was travelling with Jordan of Saxony, who told them in the village to go separately to beg their meal; they found only a little black bread; they said grace nevertheless, and accepted their discomfiture so joyfully that a good lady heard them and, touched, procured for them bread, wine and cheese in abundance.[73] Two brethren were returning to Spain after their studies in Paris; the hour was getting late and they had eaten nothing; they argued about the moment of beginning the quest; the hungrier wanted to beg in a poor hamlet which they were just coming to, for Providence was able to find them abundant alms even among very poor people. 'I know that Providence can do so,' said the other, who wanted to wait for a big village, 'but it is not God's custom'; at this a noblewoman on a journey came up and had them served by her young boy; the brethren gave thanks on their knees and prayed for the handsome boy who would one day become a Friar Preacher.[74] These pictures of youthful generosity attract us by their freshness. But how much more moving is the mature gesture of the founder a few months before his death; the counsellor, the friend of the highest personalities in the Church, the preacher whose voice and life were worn away in the effort to save souls, kneeling with humility on the threshold of a house because an unknown man gave him a whole loaf.

The work of founding and of extending the houses of the Friars Preachers was included in the general plan of campaign in Lombardy. There were now at least four of them—Bologna, Bergamo, Milan, Verona. We have seen the almost unvaried procedure of their foundation—to obtain from the bishop an already consecrated church, suitable for public worship. Thus it was done in Toulouse, Paris, Bologna, Florence, Milan. Sometimes the bishop took the initiative. At other times it was the clergy of the particular church who proposed the translation, some chaplain or canon going away elsewhere, or sometimes, as in Bologna or Florence, becoming a Friar Preacher. The house was truly the fruit of the preaching; the brethren, or Dominic, had elicited the gift by their personal attitude or by the fruits of their ministry. At the same time, however, the Pope, by verbal order (Toulouse), by special letter (Paris, later Amiens, Piacenza, Barcelona), by the action of his legate (Bologna, soon afterwards Brescia, Florence), or at any rate by the bull of recommendation, had intervened to awaken or even to call for the goodwill of the bishop and his clergy.

The convents also were born in, and out of, mendicant poverty. The cession of a church to the Preachers, in fact, presupposed their renouncing its patrimony which reverted to the diocese or to the community who owned it. The act of cession sometimes expressly mentioned this condition. This contributed in no small way to facilitate the contract.[75] The procedure of foundation was thus very different among the Preachers from what it was in the traditional orders; it was even practically the reverse. The monks and canons could not found without the intervention of a powerful donor who conferred on them the original landed property. The Preachers, by taking under their charge a church, and stripping it of its patrimony which they restored to the owners, thus founded their convent rather by giving than by receiving. Mendicant poverty was not only an imitation of Christ and the apostles; it was a liberation.[76]

Thus it made the order more flexible, more mobile, more dynamic. It enabled it to establish itself without difficulty in the cities where it was particularly urgent to develop the ministry of souls. It secured for it the resources which the urban populations could more easily give. The monastic and canonical orders were remarkably adapted to the agricultural system of the closed economies of the High Middle Ages. The mendicant Order of the Preachers on the contrary found itself adapted to the new economic system of Europe founded on the circulation of wealth. Jordan of Saxony grasped this fact and gave it clear expression. One day when the Cistercians put before him the objection of the instability of a religious life which depended on alms and on a charity which must one day grow cold, he merely pointed out to them that if charity grew cold among them, men would become persecutors and it would not be long before they were stealing monastic lands. The monks when dispersed would perish, whereas the Preachers, even more like the apostles through persecution, would see their effectiveness further increase, while they would continue to practise their rule in begging in order to live.[77]

On one of these returns to Bologna, at the time of the Assumption, or perhaps later, Dominic had to concern himself with two construction works at the same time. The contract made the previous year with Pietro di Lovello had permitted the enlargement of the monastery. Thanks to new gifts Friar Rodolfo had been able to buy back on 11th and 22nd July two of the houses installed on the territory 'of the Vines'.[78] Building began at once. On his return from preaching, the founder was greatly upset—Friar Rodolfo had taken advantage of the building work to raise the ceiling of the cells, which the brethren found too low, by a cubit. Dominic was grieved about it even to tears—'Then you already want to renounce poverty and construct great palaces!' He gave orders to stop the work begun. It would in effect remain unfinished until his death.[79] A few months earlier, St Francis, passing through Bologna on his return from the East, had experienced the same despair on seeing the constructions of the convent of his brethren.[80]

A further reason, however, stopped the building work of the Preachers—they were preparing to undertake another foundation.[81] Diana d'Andalò had not forgotten her vow to enter religion. She came to remind Dominic of this. She understood that this vow, made into his hands, bound her to the Preachers and saw no other solution than the foundation of a convent. Dominic assembled his brethren in chapter. What did they think of the construction of a 'house of nuns which would be said to be, and would effectively be, of the order?'[82] Each one gave his opinion and Dominic held up his reply until the next day, wanting first of all to consult the Lord. The reply would be categorical as was his habit. The next day there was a new chapter. They prayed. Dominic seated himself and declared: 'It is essential in every way, brethren, to build a house of sisters, even if for that it were necessary to cease constructing ours.' This was a generous declaration of the close link which, in Dominic's life as in his thought, indissolubly bound the Dominicans to their sisters. It will be readily imagined that the chronicler of St Agnes of Bologna was careful not to forget it.

Dominic was soon to leave Bologna, so he handed over this construction to a committee of four brethren, Master Paul of Hungary, the prior, Friar Guala and Friar Ventura of Verona, two brethren full of maturity, and the procurator, Friar Rodolfo. The latter went ahead with the work and soon found a piece of land which seemed completely suitable. This was not the opinion of the bishop, who thought it too near to Bologna. Doubtless he wanted to avoid accumulating convents, whose maintenance would finally fall on the charity of the city. It was already much to have authorized in the city the mendicant convent of the brethren of St Nicholas. The foundation of the sisters seemed doomed to failure. Diana was in despair. With her accustomed energy, she was not long in finding another solution which would at first take a dramatic turn. Dominic was no longer there to advise or decide. In company with Friar Tancred, he had left again for Rome where he arrived at the end of December.[83]

CHAPTER XVIII

SANTA SABINA AND ST SIXTUS OF ROME

THREE purposes brought Dominic back to Rome: to render an account of his experiences in Lombardy, precisely at the moment when, by the proclamation of the law of the coronation, the importance of the decisions and prescriptions of the Church was to experience a remarkable increase in North Italy; to settle with the help of the Curia a good number of affairs concerning the Preachers in Europe; and to realise the project of the convent of St Sixtus.

The third matter presupposed a long-term work of approach but could only be concluded with the arrival of the nuns from Prouille; they would not be in Rome, it seemed, before the month of April. The second would be dealt with in accordance with the reports received and the circumstances. The first purpose perhaps necessitated Dominic's return before the detailed discussion of the future law, about 10th November.[1] No indication allows us to assume Dominic's presence in Rome between 10th November and the end of December.[2] After that date, however, several of his affairs could be settled, for the pontifical Curia, despite the work involved over the coronation, was pursuing its ordinary activity.[3] It must then be presumed that Dominic only arrived in the eternal city in the last days of 1220. On 27th, 30th and 31st December, in fact, the Chancellery issued a series of letters which go to prove the founder's presence.[4]

In the first place he was concerned with Paris. The decisions of the General Chapter had increased the importance of the convent of St Jacques in the scholastic life of the order and in its ministry in France. On this account it was necessary to enlarge the house, increase its connections with the university, encourage and multiply protectors; finally, it was necessary to obtain the permanent concession of the buildings. In December 1220 the agreement between the canons of the cathedral and the Preachers was finally concluded.[5] At Dominic's request the Holy See intervened in the matter. In three letters of the 27th and 30th December and 2nd January, the Pope thanked the Benedictines of St Magloire of Paris for their good offices towards the Parisian Preachers; doubtless they had helped out their poverty with material gifts and placed a church at their disposal.[6] He likewise thanked the university of Paris for its good offices towards the Preachers and the favourable reception it had always given to the requests of the Pope in regard to these religious.[7] Finally he recommended himself to the prayers of Dominic's brethren 'sitting with Mary at the Lord's feet'.[8] These letters were to be carried to those to whom they were addressed by a young Preacher, Friar Guillaume, a member of the Pope's household, who was not allowed to leave without great regrets, 'so much was the Pope attached to his dear presence'.[9] Thus he recommended him with much affection in these three letters to these different authorities.

Who was this Friar Guillaume whose friendship brought the presence of the order of Preachers under a particularly engaging form even into the personal life of the Pope? It is impossible not to think of Guillaume de Montferrat, the friend and familiar of Cardinal Ugolino with whom in 1217 he was living,[10] and a close relative, if not the son, of Marquis Guillaume de Montferrat whom the Emperor sent on an embassy to the kingdom of Arles. Honorius had just recommended him to the prelates of the same province as well as to the legate of the Albigeois and would soon entrust him with the crusade and the highest missions in the East.[11] Dominic in point of fact had left Friar Guillaume with the Pope at Viterbo in the previous month of May, whereas up to that time he had kept him at his side as his principal *socius*.[12] Neither Friar Guillaume nor Dominic, however, dreamt of exploiting, by prolonging it, a situation which caused the Pope's kindness towards a member of his household to overflow on the order as a whole. Friar Guillaume was aspiring to pursue his theological studies in Paris. Dominic authorized him to go there and leave the Curia, as did the Pope.

The affairs of St Jacques were, moreover, proceeding satisfactorily. In the month of May the Pope would once more intervene in Paris to protect the rights of Jean de Barastre, the professor of the Preachers.[13] Shortly afterwards Dominic was to learn of the successful issue of all questions pending in reference to St Jacques;[14] this has already been referred to.

The spread of the houses of Preachers in France, envisaged and decided upon by the chapter of Bologna, seemed on the point of being realized. A foundation was planned at Amiens, where the clergy had received the brethren with favour. On 31st December, 1220, the Pope thus invited Bishop Evrard and his canons to procure them a church in the city.[15] Unfortunately this letter would not produce the expected result and the Preachers would not establish themselves in Amiens until 1243.

Whether or not he was urged to do so in the course of his recent legation in Italy by Dominic, by Cardinal Ugolino or by the Pope himself, the Chancellor of the Empire and Bishop of Metz and Spire, Conrad de Scharfeneck, agreed to a foundation of the Friars Preachers in Metz. Passing through his episcopal city in April, the bishop made his protection a fact, by drawing up a charter. In very precise terms he described this order 'which the Pope has constituted and confirmed, urged by zeal for souls and under the inspiration and directives of the Holy Spirit'. If the Preachers, he declared, 'had an establishment in the town, their presence would be of great profit to the laity through their preaching and also to the clergy through their courses of sacred science'. There, however, the Chancellor stopped short, and while invoking the example of numerous bishops, arch-bishops and the Pope, 'who had granted them a house in Rome', abstained from doing likewise. He ended by exhorting the laity of the town to show themselves more generous than he was.[16] Frederick II's Chancellor had recently learnt in too good a school the art of appearing to give much without engaging oneself.

In Sweden, the Provost of Sigtuna had obtained a protector in his town for the brethren whom he had taken under his patronage. A monastery, consecrated to the Most Blessed Virgin, was in process of coming into being, not without difficulties. The Pope endeavoured to attract the generosity of the faithful to it by granting on 11th January, by a bull, an indulgence to those who frequented the church on the day of the Assump-tion.[17] The house was to disappear a few years later in the face of the opposition of the Archbishop of Uppsala.[18]

Prelates were decidedly lacking in generosity or in comprehension towards the Friars Preachers. Without the near presence of the Pope and, above all, without the pressing action of his legate, Ugolino, the development of the order in Italy would not have been so rapid. Thus, after 4th February what Dominic frequently asked the Pope to grant almost to the exclusion of other bulls was the bull of recommendation 'Cum qui recipit' (type III), which pre-sented the ministry of the Preachers in the perspective of the 10th canon of the Lateran.[19] This canon imposed on the bishops the pressing obligation to accept the help of preachers. As a consequence they should surely try to attract and lodge among them 'these kind auxiliaries who, without causing them any expense, will co-operate in the salvation of the people which is entrusted to them. Thus the Pope addressed the Bishop of Amiens.[20]

The register of the archives which comprised a copy of this bull provides certain details.[21] Such archives are those of the convents of Toulouse, Montpellier, Magdeburg (three issues of 4th February, 1221) and the State archives in Schwerin (issue of 6th May); two further issues of 5th April and 22nd May, preserved in the general archives of the order, no longer bear any indication of their provenance. Toulouse and Montpellier were already in existence in 1221. The copies of the bulls which have remained in their archives thus did not serve for their foundation; if they were destined for some other foundation, this cannot have been made—otherwise the bulls would have remained in the new convents, whose archives they would have inaugurated. Magdeburg was erected after Dominic's death (1224). It is possible that the bull only reached the archives there after having been used for another convent which Dominic had in mind on 4th February, 1221. This was, perhaps, the convent of Friesach, the first house in Germany, which Friar Solomon launched in the middle of 1221. Only the issue of 6th May preserved at Schwerin possesses clear significance. Its purpose was to render the King of Denmark favourable to a foundation in the metropolis of Lund.[22]

In the meantime Dominic extended the order directly from Rome. Friar Frogier, but recently left at St Sixtus, and a Friar Benedict (Bene) who, moreover, is not known from any other source, went to Siena. It is impossible to say whether they went to preach or were sent by Dominic to give effect to projects which had been planned for some time. All that is certain is that on 16th February they received 'in their name, in the name of the order and of their prior the lord Dominic',[23] the chapel of St Mary Magdalene at Siena. This chapel was that of a hospice set aside for the poor and for pilgrims. A pious foundation of the rich citizen of Siena, Raynier Rustichini, at the beginning of 1212[24] it was kept by a widow, Sister Emilia, and by four other sisters. The son of the founder, also named Raynier, retained the patronage of it. He was present at the signing of the deed and approved it. The sisters gave the church, its dependencies and its access as well as an adjoining vineyard. On the other side of the vineyard, however, they reserved for themselves the hospice which they would continue to administer. They placed themselves, moreover, under the spiritual and moral direction of the Preachers, to whom they gave themselves 'in commendum' as they did the house. The Preachers were thus more than substitutes for the previous incumbents of the hospice chapel—they became the religious and civil superiors of the house of sisters.

The donors, however, imposed a series of conditions, of which the principal ones were—the maintenance of the patronage to Raynier Rustichini, who would control the election of the prior; a prohibition against alienating the property; the obligation to preserve in that place the centre of the priorate and 'school' of the Preachers of Siena; concession to the community of the sisters of a share in the whole of the prayers and spiritual fruits of the convent and of the order (to our knowledge this was the second engagement of the order in regard to the communication of merits; the first concerned the university of Paris). These conditions were onerous. In their desire to begin the ministry of preaching and to implant themselves in Siena as soon as possible, Friars Frogier and Benedict did not hesitate to accept. They had evidently received power of attorney from Dominic, in whose name they engaged themselves.[25] It was, indeed, a fairly constant habit of the founder to intervene at the side of his brethren as a party in private contracts.[26] He thus strengthened the unity of his order. Fairly long negotiations between Siena and Rome must have preceded the conclusion of the act of 14th March.[27]

On 10th May, Dominic obtained a further intervention of the Holy See in favour of the Preachers of Piacenza.[28]

Five days earlier he had received a very important privilege. Everywhere where the brethren had a house, they would for the future have the right to celebrate on a portable altar, i.e. since only stone altars built in as part of the church were capable of consecration, of celebrating in a non-consecrated chapel.[29] Earlier the Preachers did not think themselves authorized to do this—which throws significant light for us on their liturgical ideas. To celebrate the divine offices, when they did not possess a consecrated church they had to borrow one, sometimes a long way from the priory. Lodged often enough outside the towns, beyond the ramparts, they must have lost a good deal of time in getting to and from the church. The new privilege would considerably simplify their life since it would allow them to open a provisional chapel inside their house. Above all, it would greatly facilitate foundations. Up to the present, in order to establish themselves in a town, the Preachers had endeavoured to obtain the concession of an existing church. They often met with many difficulties in this and all too often the foundation failed. It would now be sufficient for them to obtain any kind of house in which they would then erect a provisional chapel. A new technique for foundations was thus taking shape. It must have speeded up the spread of the order, especially in Germany. The bull was dispatched forthwith to Friesach and to the Midi of France.[30]

Dominic procured a certain number of bulls of recommendation for isolated brethren, designated by name, who thus received from the Pope a general preaching mandate. These valuable testimonial letters were probably granted on a wide scale. Of their nature they were intended not to last longer than our modern identity papers. Carried continually by the beneficiaries on their travels, these poor pieces of parchment very soon became battered. Thus only a small number survived, four up to St Dominic's death.[31] A copy of *Cum qui recipit*, of 31st March, 1221, which reached as far as Valladolid, concerned a certain Friar Pedro, doubtless Fr Pedro de Madrid. The other three letters were in the name of Dominic. The fact is significant. It was to this name that they owed their preservation; people looked upon them as testimonials of the saint and preserved them as relics. Out of these three letters one, a copy of *Quoniam abundavit* of 18th January, 1221, was addressed to 'Brother Dominic, canon of the order (of Preachers)'. It was found in the archives of the general headquarters of the order of Rome. The second and third, examples of *Cum qui recipit* of 29th March and 28th May, were addressed to 'Brother Dominic prior of the order of Preachers' and to 'Brother Dominic of the order of Preachers'. They were found in the archives of Fiesole and Bologna.[32]

The habits of the Roman Chancellery do not allow us to think that the omission of the mention of the title of St Dominic in bulls of recommendation which concerned him was an oversight. The first and third bulls were thus addressed to a Brother, or Brothers, Dominic distinct from the founder.

In the case of the first bull, it is difficult to decide who is meant; the original destination of this document eludes us. On the other hand, it is possible to form some idea as to the addresses of the third. A charter of 17th February, 1223 does in fact indicate the appearance in Bologna of a Friar Domingo de Segovia in the capacity of provincial of Lombardy.[33] He is clearly the friar who had been replacing Jordan of Saxony in this office since May 1222. There is every reason to suppose that he was already in Bologna at the end of May of the previous year, either because he had entered the order there, or, which is more probable, because he had just arrived in the city for the general chapter. It was at the close of this chapter that the bull must have reached him.

Perhaps the attribution to the founder of the testimonial letter of 29th March, 1221, addressed to 'Friar Dominic, prior of the order of Preachers' should likewise be called in question. The title of prior was itself ambiguous since the chapter general, and could designate a conventual prior. However 'Prior of the Order of Preachers' was not so at this date, we believe, and could only be fittingly applied to St Dominic. Why did the latter have this testimonial letter given to him on 29th March? It might be for a purely incidental reason, for instance the loss of an earlier letter. It is also possible that he had asked for it with a view to some particularly delicate enterprise, and we are reminded of the imminent foundation of St Sixtus. This does not go beyond the sphere of hypothesis; it would be good to have a clearer view of the matter.

Between 23rd January and 10th February, Dominic dispatched a pontifical letter to a whole series of convents to reiterate the prescriptions of the Holy See against deserters and apostates. Certified copies of this letter have been found in the conventual archives of Santa Sabina in Rome, of Barcelona[34] and of Brescia.[35] It was a general precautionary measure for which it would be idle to presuppose a movement of disaffection among the brethren or any particular untoward happening. The order was in full development and the defeatist psychology of certain people in 1217 or 1218 had no longer any raison d'être. Moreover, these legal protections against the weaknesses and instability of the religious were classic since the twelfth century; they formed part of the canonical status of the orders in question. Dominic had obtained them in December 1216 in the great privilege of confirmation.[36] After 7th February following,[37] he had them renewed under the form of personal bulls. We have commented on these texts which, it is satisfactory to find, emphasize the authority of the master from the very outset.

The issue of 1221, however, included a considerable change, a clear reason for a new edition after the first general chapter. As formerly, the religious were prohibited from leaving the order or living outside it without written leave from the master and community and it was also forbidden to anyone to retain them; i.e. all religious orders were forbidden to accept former Preachers in their ranks. It was not so much a matter, in these documents, of putting an obstacle in the way of apostates as of preventing the Preachers from deserting their order to the profit of some other form of religious life. Now came the point that was new. The privilege of 1216 reserved one traditional exception: 'unless it were a question of entering a more austere religious order', a door open towards the heights.[38] The Church who showed herself extremely severe at this period against de-serters—she saw in this an act of mercy in order to save them—never-theless intended to allow to all the possibility of rising higher. Now in the letters of January and February 1221, the exception of the more austere religious order had disappeared. Clearly the order was henceforward con-sidered by the Curia as a peak from which one no longer had the right to descend.

On the other hand, a provision inscribed in the constitutions shortly afterwards[39] would authorize the superiors of the order to receive into its ranks religious from other orders. The only exception made for some time to come would be the Cistercians. A special authorization from the Pope, however, would enable the Friars Preachers to receive even these religious. This reservation was finally dropped in 1240.[40] By that date the perfection of the life of the Preachers would have received in the estimation of the Papacy and of the order itself the supreme consecration, that which the Order of Cîteaux had obtained in the course of the twelfth century vis-à-vis the whole body of the religious families. One could only fall lower by abandoning the ideal and the life of the Preachers.

Projects, attempts at or success in foundations at Metz, at Amiens, in Sweden, in Siena, in Piacenza, the development and equipment of the houses in Paris and elsewhere, the sending of the brethren to their studies and to preaching, the protection of their profession, the preparations for the mission in the north of Italy, such were the manifold affairs that Dominic was governing from Rome, thanks to the kindness and authority of the Pope and the collaboration of the Pontifical Chancellery. Each of these questions had formed the subject of earlier negotiations, of reports received, of decisions transmitted in writing. A voluminous correspondence was ex-changed between Dominic and his brethren. Several times one comes across a mention of it in the documents, even in the papal bulls.[41] Letters on the studies,[42] a convocation for some general assembly,[43] a note of direction or encouragement addressed to some holy woman,[44] a letter of government written to a convent,[45] a missive to a great personage,[46] these are only exceptional echoes of an exchange that was very extensive indeed. Scarcely anything of all this has come down to us—only the solitary letter to the sisters of Madrid. There is no collection of letters of St Dominic similar to that which the sisters of St Agnes gathered together with so much love in connection with Jordan of Saxony.

Dominic's decision to make Bologna his headquarters takes on striking relief in this perspective. A scholastic centre at the same time as a centre of exchange, linked with the Empire as it was with the Roman Church, geographically in the best position to extend its influence over the various regions of the West, because of its merchants and scholars, Bologna had couriers and mails leaving and arriving daily. This was the case, too, with the Roman Curia where Dominic stayed when he left Bologna for a time. Thus he could remain in close contact with the whole of his brethren, and at the same time that he was conceiving, in contact with the Pope and his Cardinals, projects of evangelization on what was then a world scale, he was able to follow the growth of his *novella plantatio*, his 'seminary' of apostles, down to its last details.

The Pope's confidence in Dominic and his brethren was more whole-hearted than ever. He had first admitted to his friendship one of the Preachers in the person of Guillaume de Montferrat, at whose request he granted the whole order the free gift of the acts of the Chancellery[47]—a thing which was not without importance in view of the extensive use which the founder made of them. Moreover, Dominic then possessed the friendship of the head of the Chancellery, Gulielmo di Modena. He had that of Cardinal Ugolino of Ostia, who was preparing to associate him more closely still with his high mission in Lombardy, and at whose house, according to the tradition of the Friars Minor, he then met St Francis.[48] This was Dominic's most intimate and powerful link with the great personalities in Rome though not his only one. Conrad of Urach, Cardinal of Oporto and former Cistercian abbot of Villers-en-Brabant,[49] had known Dominic's work in the Narbonensis since 1217.[50] He met the founder again at the Curia in 1219–1220. A few months later, appointed legate for the Albigeois,[51] he passed through St Nicholas of Bologna, wanting to judge the tree by its fruit. *Laudare, benedicere et praedicare*, the formula he found in the Missal just as he was preparing to preach to the brethren, filled him with enthusiasm. 'Although I am wearing the habit of another profession, it is your spirit I bear in my heart. Do not doubt it, I am wholly yours; yes, I am of your order'.[52]

Again there was at the Curia the Cardinal of St Theodore, Gregorio de' Crescenti. Appointed legate for Denmark that same year, he contributed upon his arrival to the decision to found the first house of the friars in Denmark (1223) at Lund, and their first house in Poland at Cracow (1223).[53] There was also Cardinal Rainier Capocci de Santa Maria in Cosmedin, another Cistercian, perhaps one of the twelve abbots of the Preaching of the Narbonensis; he would himself found the house of the Friars Preachers in Viterbo (1227).[54] Again mention must be made of the Cardinal of the Twelve Apostles, Stefano de Fossanova, a Cistercian once more, and of Cardinal Nicholas di Tusculum who will soon come into this narrative; also the Cardinal of San Stefano *in monte Coelio*, Robert de Courson, who inter-

vened in the Albigeois in Dominic's time. All had had relations with the
founder, either directly or indirectly, and had once helped him with the
beginnings or in the spreading of his order. During his last stay in Rome,
Dominic enjoyed an incomparable prestige and influence at the Curia which
clearly reflected back on his Preachers. One final undertaking, particularly
successful, came to increase this prestige still more.

The origins of the convent of the sisters of St Sixtus, in the spring of 1221,
are well documented. Besides the collections of charters[55] of the two
principal monasteries which fused to form the new community, we possess
several letters of the Pope on this subject,[56] other notarial acts,[57] a chronicle
of the beginning of the fourteenth century by the superior of St Sixtus,
Benedict of Montefiascone, who had the ancient archives in his hands;[58]
finally, a series of picturesque narratives, sometimes moving, detailed down
to the proper names and most insignificant circumstances: the miracles of
St Dominic recounted by Sister Angelica. It so happens that these miracles
have as their local and temporal setting the vicissitudes of the foundation and
as guarantor one of the foundresses, Sister Cecilia, then aged seventeen.[59]

Sister Cecilia was quite old, aged from seventy to eighty, when these
miracles were set down in writing from what she remembered of her
experiences at the convent of St Agnes of Bologna by Sister Angelica, who
had of course seen none of the events herself. In the texts as a whole there are
accounts which border on indecency or on childishness.[60] Others repeat
anecdotes already reported by direct witnesses, but embellished with
embroideries or exaggerations taken from life.[61] Finally a taste for the
marvellous has distorted proved facts. Thus historians today no longer dare
to take as basis, as was usually done in former times, the good sister's
narrations. On the other hand it would be wrong to ignore them.[62] Certainly
the figures should not be taken as reliable and one should be on one's guard
against false perspectives, the infiltration of the marvellous, perhaps certain
confusions of dates. On the other hand credence can be given to certain of
Sister Cecilia's narratives, provided certain precautions are taken, for a good
number of her indications as to places, persons, events which can be checked
by reliable documents, have been found to be exact.[63] In taking as point of
departure the documents in the archives, a well-established account of
events can be built up, which the narratives of Sister Cecilia can sometimes
implement. Three clearly marked periods in the history of St Sixtus can be
discerned in the sources.

Primarily, and this must have been immediately upon Dominic's arrival in
Rome, there was the Preacher's action in regard to the nuns whom the Pope
desired to reform. The principal community of these religious, the
monastery of Santa Maria in Tempulo, situated, in regard to St Sixtus, on the
other side of the cross-roads of the Appian Way, has already been mentioned.

Dominic also used his influence over the ancient Benedictine community of St Bibiana, on the Esquiline, not far from the St Lawrence gate.[64] Benedict of Montefiascone states that Dominic visited other nuns too and a number of devout Christian women.[65]

The founder's objective was not only to restore order to these communities and to bring them back to their rule. To carry out Pope Innocent's wishes, taken up by his successor, he intended to introduce an institution which the Benedictines of old did not practise—complete enclosure.[66] This discipline,[67] which feminine monachism had experienced in its full rigour under the rule of St Cesarius, was progressively revived between the twelfth and the thirteenth centuries, and at the end of the latter its laws were fixed and disseminated by a famous decretal of Pope Urban VIII. In the time of Innocent III and Honorius III it had already gained a good deal of ground. The Cistercians were anxious to strengthen their own law of enclosure. Ugolino granted the Poor Clares their total 'inclusion'. It was not chance alone if Innocent, earlier, had entrusted to the order of Sempringham the model convent he wanted to found at St Sixtus; the full and detailed rule of St Gilbert had been organizing this uncomprising enclosure in a practical way since the middle of the twelfth century.[68] Dominic was going to accomplish it. As soon as he arrived, he set himself to the task.

It was not easy. Certain nuns included in the Pope's projects decided to resist with all their might.[69] The previous year had shown Dominic that this would be the case. No one can tell the limits of feminine obstinacy, particularly when it can base itself on an undisputed juridical text—the rule on which they had formerly made their vows, which did not include this strict enclosure. Moreover, no one could foresee what help this resistance might find in the Roman entourage. The Pope sent a warning to certain cardinals whose authority and relationships in the city would perhaps be indispensable. We are given the names of Ugolino of Ostia, of Nicholas of Tusculum, of Stefano of Fossanova.[70] The name of the third indeed appears in several of our charters,[71] as that of the benefactor, perhaps of the cardinal-protector of the monastery in Tempulo, in accordance with the recent formula introduced by Pope Innocent. It is possible that Nicholas of Tusculum played a similar part in regard to the sisters of St Bibiana.[72] As to Ugolino, a specialist in nuns[73] as well as in the Roman milieux, his counsels were certainly valuable for Dominic. He was to leave Rome, however, about the middle of March, to rejoin his embassy.[74]

The founder's action in regard to the nuns of Santa Maria in Tempulo was not long in achieving results. His preaching and spiritual direction were received by nuns, and above all by a superior, of goodwill. The ruinous state of the temporal affairs and of the buildings of the abbey,[75] which was too dilapidated to feed and lodge its religious for long, perhaps had some part in this docility. The old Abbess Eugenia[76] had done what she could to defend her sisters' property[77] and consolidate the ancient buildings;[78] she found herself however in the clutches of a creditor, Cencia Gregorio Rampazoli, who little by little gained through mortgages the greater part of the nuns' lands;[79] only the Pope or the Pope's representative could save the community.[80] It was necessary to strike while the iron was hot. On Ash Wednesday, 24th February, 1221, at that liturgical time which invites to penance and inward renewal, Dominic assembled the sisters in the church of St Sixtus, to which he wanted to attach them.[81] All of them, with a single exception, bound themselves by profession into the hands of the friar to enter the enclosure when he should judge fit. The abbess likewise renounced her authority and handed over to the founder the property and rights of the monastery.

The nuns, however, placed a typical condition on their engagement. In their sanctuary they possessed a picture of the Blessed Virgin greatly beloved of the Romans, a focal point of the piety of the community. It was the celebrated miraculous Virgin of St Sixtus.[82] It is said that this picture had always refused to allow itself to be placed elsewhere. Carried off to the Lateran in former times by Pope Sergius III, it had come back to Santa Maria, 'flying through the window like a bird'. The sisters thus specified that if the icon, which should clearly accompany them to St Sixtus, refused to remain there and returned to its original church, they should be released from their vows by this fact. Dominic accepted the condition. Then, in the name of his new authority, he asked the sisters to return to their own monastery, for that of St Sixtus was not yet in a condition to receive them. For the future they would no longer go out to visit their families or do anything at all in the city as they had done hitherto.

When this news was learnt in the city, there was an explosion of anger. Roman families were not in the habit of accepting quietly decisions of the Church or of the Pope which ran directly counter to their customs. The very recent history of the order in Italy was already full of anecdotes in which families could be seen intervening by word and in deed against the monasteries—enclosure violated; novices removed by force and deprived of their religious habit;[83] neighbours taking up arms to defend the convent;[84] a sister dragged away from her cloister with so much brutality that one of her ribs was broken;[85] a brother having to hide to avoid receiving a letter obtained from the Pope by fraud, which would release him from his vows;[86] another brother, hastily sent by Dominic outside the city, being pursued by his family who were only stopped in their chase by a river in spate.[87] This time they were content with subjecting the abbess and her nuns to a siege, reproaching them with wanting to destroy such a noble convent and giving themselves up into the hands of an 'unknown ribald'. Several of the sisters began to waver. Dominic hastened to intervene.[88] On the morning of the

28th,[89] he turned up at Santa Maria, said Mass, preached and completely disarmed the sisters, whose oath to remain in the enclosure he demanded then and there. The whole community, including the wavering sisters, realized what was involved and took the oath. During this time lay-brethren locked the convent doors. Dominic received the keys and entrusted the lay brothers with the supervision of the enclosure night and day and the maintenance of the sisters. The latter would no longer be able even to speak with their relatives.

This energetic reaction dumbfounded the families who for the future remained quiet. Doubtless the intervention of the cardinals, who were Dominic's support, had something to do with the lulling of this local storm In the meantime other nuns were secured for the convent of St Sixtus to join those of St Bibiana.

It was essential not to dally over the foundation, but there was still one obstacle in the way of the transfer. The buildings were scarcely finished and the community of the Preachers was in occupation of the existing premises.[90] In view of the large number of nuns who were preparing to enter there, there could be no question of leaving the majority of the brethren, who were much more numerous than the masculine personnel required for the care of the sisters at St Sixtus. Another monastery was therefore necessary. On the Aventine the Pope possessed a vast fortress, the Rocca Savelli, which he himself had had constructed for his feudal family when he was only Cardinal Cencius; the greater part of the walls and bastions on the crest of the hill have lasted down to our own times. A fifth-century church, the basilica of Santa Sabina, was incorporated in them.[91] Dominic had long wanted this and had already boldly asked the Pope for it. At last he obtained it, not without difficulty.[92] The brethren moved to the Aventine with their books and furniture and installed themselves in the premises arranged for the clergy in the porch of the church and the wing of the ruined four-sided portico which extended on the north-west.[93] The construction of a new monastery, the ownership of which the Pope would give to the order in a bull of 5th June, 1222, would soon be begun.[94]

Shortly after Easter (11th April), between 15th and 25th April,[95] the third and final stage in the foundation was realized. That day Dominic seated himself at the entrance to the church at St Sixtus and received the nuns of Santa Maria in Tempulo, to the number of about forty.[96] He gave them at once the white tunic, white scapular and black veil of the sisters of Prouille and Madrid. Then, going up to the altar again, for the third time he made them make profession. The engagement of obedience towards his person remained the same as on the other two occasions. The formula of the oath, however, had been further enriched, which justified the reiteration. The sisters undertook to live according to the rule and institutions that Dominic gave them. The same day, a few isolated persons, either religious or seculars, also entered the community.[97] Finally, another fairly compact group joined them, the majority of the nuns of the monastery of St Bibiana. At the close of this glorious day, sixty-one nuns of Rome found themselves together in the new monastery.[98]

During the following night a discreet procession led the icon of the Most Blessed Virgin to its new residence.[99] They did not want to do this in the full light of day, fearing a rising of the population who would thus be disturbed at their devotions. Dominic and the two cardinals, Stefano and Nicholas, accompanied by chosen brethren and members of the faithful, carried the image on their shoulders, with bare feet, in the light of torches. The sisters, likewise bare-footed, awaited it in prayer. With great reverence it was placed in the restored basilica. 'It is still there today', declared Sister Cecilia at the end of her life; and we can guess from her satisfaction the fear she felt at the time of the translation, of seeing the statue depart again for its first refuge by supernatural means.

If they had waited so long to effect a migration decided upon from the beginning of Lent, it was to allow the sisters from Prouille to arrive and form the fundamental community into which the others would have to be fused. They came to Rome, in fact, a few days before the translation and occupied and organized the new monastery forthwith.[100] It was the Bishop of Toulouse who brought them, with the help of a few of the clergy of the neighbourhood.[101] Dominic rejoiced to find among them several of his former collaborators. It was a happy reunion of brothers in arms and of spiritual friends. There was Arnaldo di Crampagna, the former friend of the Waldenses whom Diego and Dominic had formerly brought back to the Church which he was now serving with all his power. There was another friend, a direct collaborator of Dominic's preaching, Aimery of Solignac, with two other monks from the Cistercian abbey of Grandselve, near Toulouse. Fulk watched with hope the spirited advance of the order he had seen born and brought into being, and from whom he expected much for the Church in the Midi, where the situation seemed to be getting daily worse. On 17th April, Fulk and Dominic brought to a conclusion by a final act the questions that were pending between the Friars Preachers and the see of Toulouse. The order renounced the tithes of the see. Fulk gave the Preachers the church of Fanjeaux with its tithes,[102] a donation which the Pope would confirm eleven days later.[103] This gift would at first sight appear surprising, since it would seem to run counter to the prohibition to receive revenues. The text, however, proves that the foundation of a monastery of Friars Preachers in the Church was then envisaged.[104] Moreover, these tithes were not intended for the brethren; the sisters of Prouille had been in possession of them practically since 1214; doubtless, an act which has not come down to us would soon regulate their permanent attribution to the nuns. The Dominican monastery of Fanjeaux was not to come into being until the fourteenth century. In the meantime, the sisters would receive the gift of the church in 1227.[105]

We know from the chronicle of Benedict of Montefiascone that eight sisters had come from there.[106] Their superior was Sister Blanche, the native of Toulouse who, entering with the Sisters while her husband became a Friar Preacher, had given her property to the monastery. Dominic appointed her prioress immediately. Keeping to the figures we have quoted, late in date no doubt but apparently drawn from documents in the archives, about the middle of the month of April the community of St Sixtus thus counted sixty-nine religious. No more than six Friars Preachers were left, chaplains or lay-brothers of the convent.[107]

The good offices and gifts of Cardinal Stefano and other benefactors, however, had improved the situation of the patrimony of the nuns of Santa Maria in Tempulo. On 15th April,[108] Dominic handed to Master Cencio Gregorio Rampazoli the sum of ninety 'livres provins' of the Senate, the amount of five different debts of the former abbey. In this way the securities given to Master Cencio on the gardens of the monastery at the *Circus Maximus* and on the former endowment of Cassaferrata, near the Porta Santo Paolo, gift of Pope Sergius in 905, were recovered.[109]

Finally, on 25th April,[110] the Pope gave the crowning touch to the whole of the operations by transferring to the prioress and sisters of St Sixtus the reconstituted property of the abbeys in Tempulo and St Bibiana, of which, however, he reserved the domain of Anguillara for the use of the sisters of the second monastery who had not accepted the reform. He would further grant them on 6th May[111] a revenue of fifty pounds sterling assigned on the church of Bamberg of the chapter of St Oswald, at Nostle in England. On this occasion the Pope specified once more that St Sixtus belonged directly to the Holy See.

At the end of April 1221, the monastery of St Sixtus was thus fully established. Its major superior was Dominic, but he appointed a prior, Friar Eudes, according to Sister Cecilia.[112] The procurator was Friar Roger.[113] There must have been in addition one more priest and three lay brothers. The prioress was Sister Blanche, likewise appointed by Dominic.[114] Again according to Sister Cecilia, the former Benedictine prioress of Santa Maria in Tempulo, Sister Constance, was in charge of the window or grille, and of the tower which, after the office of prioress, was the most responsible charge in the community.[115] Sister Cecilia also mentions the names of Sisters Nubia, Theodora, Thedrana, Nympha, Maximilla, Sabina.[116]

The rule the founder gave to the community was that of St Augustine, completed by certain constitutions.[117] The latter have fortunately come down to us in their entirety.[118] Their basis was the former rule of Prouille, of which they kept the law of observance, the customs relating to silence, in particular, which the sisters of Prouille were specially concerned with

Santa Sabina, Rome.

(*Photo: Leonard von Matt*)

inculcating in their new companions, and the various lists of faults with their penances.[119] To this text, directly inspired by the first customs of the Friars Preachers but making reference to the rule of St Benedict and to the customs of Cîteaux, was added a series of texts which organized the enclosure, the work, prayer and offices of the monastery. They were inspired, it would seem, to sum them up, by the rule of Sempringham, giving effect as far as possible to the wishes of Innocent III on the subject of St Sixtus.

The best rule, however, is inadequate. Either at the beginning of Lent, when he visited the nuns then still in their former convents or after the foundation when he came down the Aventine hill from Santa Sabina to St Sixtus, Dominic devoted himself to forming his daughters in their religious life. Time pressed. His business at the Curia and his apostolate among the people of the city were not the only things to claim his attention. He also had brethren at Santa Sabina, the community of which was increasing under the direction of Friar Tancred, the prior.[120] Sister Cecilia mentions a good number of brethren, some of whom, moreover, are known, such as Friar Tancred, Friar Gaudion,[121] and perhaps Friar Lawrence the Englishman.[122] Friar Gaudion and Friar Henri[123] were won to the order at the very time of the foundation of St Sixtus; others like Friar Giacomo of Rome, had entered recently and were still novices.[124] Dominic lived in close contact with them and took several of them with him on his ministry or on his visits to the sisters. At night he slept at Santa Sabina—which is a manner of speaking, for he kept to his habit of unending vigils in the church interspersed from time to time with a doze leaning against the steps of the altar. Sometimes, however, he retired to the dormitory where his brethren slept, at the end nearest to the basilica. This corner, later rebuilt in the form of a chapel, is today venerated under the name of St Dominic's 'room'.[125] He often came, as soon as it was morning, to St Sixtus to celebrate Mass and to preach.[126] A number of anecdotes, preserved somewhat at random, depict the founder under an aspect that we have so far insufficiently described, in his rôle as spiritual director and educator in the intimacy and attractiveness of the life of fraternity.

In following St Dominic's life step by step, from the austerity of his infancy to the uttermost gift of himself signified in his last years by the extension of his ministry at the same time as the foundation and development of his order, one cannot but be struck by its character of heroism, sternness, tenseness. It was so in very truth. The continuousness of the penance, the silence, the vigils of prayer, the labours of the ministry left him no respite. That is why he was soon to succumb to the task. He was equally severe in regard to his brethren. The continual *sursum corda* he addressed to them by his preachings, his direction and also his example, have something inexorable about them. Accordingly, those of our contemporaries who have formed for themselves a harsh and stern picture of the father of Preachers are numerous. A hero, no doubt, but devoured by an interior fire like a figure of El Greco, a fire which he cast upon the world like the flame issuing from the hound which has been put into his armorial bearings.[127] He is pictured without a smile, without even a moment of relaxation. That picture is not a true one.

To give such a picture is to forget the almost contradictory resources which go to make up any real personality, and even more so the true saint. As Dominic advanced towards maturity, whether because he found it easier to give himself to others, or because his inner life was reflected more clearly by an increasingly large human entourage, one can more easily see these rich qualities. All the witnesses who speak of his rigidity in the application of the rule with its penances are unanimous in noting that he reproved and punished with so much 'gentleness' and 'goodness'[128] that the brethren at fault accepted the penance with patience and went away comforted. 'He was full of poise,' said one of them, 'patient, good and very merciful, very homely in his approach, and just.'[129] Another described him as 'gay, full of joy, patient and merciful, full of kindness to the brethren's consolation.'[130] This was indeed the picture which stood out in their memories.[131] God had given him an extremely tender heart, prompt to rejoice with those who were joyful and to weep with the unhappy.[132] A great simplicity which knew neither calculation nor pretence,[133] made him immediately responsive to the feelings of others and his countenance soon reflected these internal changes.[134] They did not break his flight towards high things, nor the balance of his judgement on men, but made him deeply lovable and at the same time responsive to others.

All men had access to his affection, but especially those who were brought nearer to him by the deeper things they had in common, priests, religious and above all his brethren.[135] He wanted to give to all what he believed to be his best possession, the knowledge and friendship of Christ. It was in this hope that he found the courage to be very demanding, but he was so from the background of a friendship which prevailed over all.

Thus he was especially accessible to the young, to novices, to brethren who were tried or tempted.

> The brethren, and strangers also, [said Friar Stefano] never had a better or greater consoler in temptation. I know this well, for at the beginning of my religious life, when I was a novice, temptations of every sort assailed me en masse. And I was fully comforted by the counsels and preaching of Brother Dominic. And I have heard many novices say that they also had experienced the same comfort.[136]

How are we to understand the word comfort of which the witnesses of his life make such an extensive use in this connection? Words of gentleness which speak to the heart? The expression of a feeling? A light to unravel some difficulty of the mind or in action? Rather, for comfort is often spoken of in connection with the sermons, the evocation of the presence of the great Christian realities; also as the support of his example and of his living charity. When returning to Santa Sabina one evening, Dominic found the young Friar Giacomo utterly crushed and determined to flee from the monastery as soon as the doors should be open after Matins, he tried the direct approach. His words were powerless. The brother had already cast off his habit. Then he was silent, prostrated himself and prayed. The brother, bathed in tears, fell at his feet.[137] To comfort is not to lull to sleep or even to soothe. For Dominic it meant reconstructing the interior strength of those who were stumbling and giving them back all their enthusiasm.

That presupposes too a certain training and teaching. He spoke, in private, or in a group, with his brethren and his sisters. 'He used', said Sister Cecilia, 'the day for winning souls by preaching and hearing confessions, or by devoting himself to other works of mercy. But when it was evening he would go to the sisters and give them an instruction or a sermon in the presence of the brethren and teach them what the order was; for they had no other master to train them in the life of the order.'[138] This was what he did in Rome in 1221. He had done the same earlier in Bologna, Toulouse, Prouille, and in many other places. His 'comforting' conversations are generally instanced in connection with the convents of Preachers and even other religious communities which he came across on his way.[139] The daily chapter, especially the chapter of faults, was particularly suitable for these moral instructions. It was not unintentionally that Dominic took from the Premonstratensians, for his brethren as for his sisters, the numerous paragraphs wherein are enumerated the *culpae*, or light, medium,[140] grave, graver, very grave faults. No other order had this. By their richness and unusual detail, they made provision for fruitful examinations of conscience, at least as to the faults committed in the presence of others, and thereby a moral training from which the Preachers would also profit in their ministry to souls. The best part of this moral education Dominic found, however, in the continual activity of the monastery and of the road, in the observances, prayers and the ministry itself.

In the course of a daily intimacy, nourished by exchanges of every kind, familiar contact grew into friendship without difficulty. This sentiment of friendship was already incipient in Dominic's kindly welcome towards all those whom he met. The sternness of his moral and spiritual effort had somewhat isolated him in his adolescence and first youth. In proportion as he dominated himself and gave himself increasingly, friendship broke into his life like a gradual dawn. After Osma, he was no longer solitary. After Prouille he had his family. After Toulouse he had brethren who were at the same time sons. A halo of friendliness surrounded him. What he had given of his heart to his brethren and sisters now came back to him in filial fervour, enriched and multiplied like the order itself. The friendship vowed to him by Friar Bertrand, Friar Guillaume, Friar Reginald or

Friar Stefano, shows through their acts as it does through their words. It was made up of admiration and respect, of community of ideal and of efforts shared while pursuing the same path; of tenderness too. Dominic responded by his eager concern, always ready to be moved and to act. How touching is the story of the young novice of Apulia, that Friar Thomas whom Dominic loved so much for his innocence and simplicity that he called him 'his son'. One day he had to tear him away, without any other weapon than his prayer, from comrades who had carried him off and already, in the neighbouring vineyards, had deprived him of the Dominican habit.[141] Touching too is the scene of frequent occurrence in which, according to an old canonical custom, Dominic in the course of the night passed through the midst of his sleeping brethren to cover them up and to bless them.[142] One night when, standing still under the little lamp which lighted the dormitory, he was looking at them tenderly, he is said to have seen the Blessed Virgin herself, with St Cecily and St Catherine, carrying out the same office for them.[143] Above all, however, he showed his friendship by leading his sons to combat. 'I give you the weapons with which, your whole life long, you will have to fight the devil',[144] he said to Friar Stefano when he clothed him. Young and awkward as they still were, he sent Buonviso to preach, Peter Seila to make a foundation, John of Navarre to beg, concerned before all else with forcing them to act, to put their principles into practice, and to adapt themselves as quickly as possible to their mission of salvation.

In the evening, however, when there was a halt, when the struggle was over for a time and the family assembled, he relaxed and made them relax too. For the story she has left us we can forgive Sister Cecilia many deficiencies in her account.

He came one evening later than usual; accordingly the sisters, thinking that he would not be coming, had left their prayer and gone to the dormitory. All of a sudden, however, the brethren rang the small bell which served as a signal to call the sisters together when the blessed father came to visit them. At this call, all the sisters came quickly to the church, the grille was opened, they found him already seated with the brethren and waiting for them. . . . He then gave them a long instruction and showed himself full of kindness for them. After this interview he said: 'It would be good, sons, to taste some refreshment.' And calling Friar Roger, the cellarer, he told him to bring wine and a cup. The brother brought what was asked for and the blessed Dominic ordered him to fill the cup to the brim. Then he blessed it, drank of it first himself, and after him all the brethren present. . . . When the brethren had all drunk, the blessed Dominic said: 'I want all my sisters to drink too.' And calling Sister Nubia, he said: 'Go in your turn, take the cup and give it to all the sisters to drink.' She went with a companion and took the cup, full to the brim. And although this cup was full to the brim, not a drop was spilt. Thus all the sisters drank, the prioress first, then the others as much as they wished; and the blessed father often said to them: 'Drink as much as you wish, daughters.'[145]

Towards all he used this direct, refreshing simplicity—with the poor along the road among whom he slept in the hospice, as with important personages of the world or the Church, to whom he knew very well how to speak.[146] Jordan of Saxony truly summed up the sentiment expressed by all the witnesses of his life when he wrote: 'He received all men into the immense heart of his charity, and since he loved everybody, everybody loved him.'[147]..

Thus he could not come across some distress of his neighbour, whether of body or soul, without trying to remedy it. When he could no longer accomplish anything by human strength, there remained his intercession. It seemed that God could refuse him nothing. This was the source of certain supernatural facts, the memory of which, handed down by the legends, bears witness to the extent and effectiveness of his compassion towards all.

Only one fact, solidly attested, will be cited, in accordance with the account that the best accredited witness[148] made to Jordan of Saxony. It actually happened in front of St Sixtus, at the time, it would seem, when the sisters of Santa Maria in Tempulo were preparing to take their first oath.

A young man, a relative of Cardinal Fossonova, was amusing himself foolishly by letting himself be carried away by his horse in a wild race. He had a very serious fall. Weeping they carried him away and he was believed to be nearly, if not quite dead; he undoubtedly remained unconscious. The distress around him increased. Master Dominic arrived. Friar Tancred was with him, that good and fervent friar who was prior of Rome and from whom I have the story. 'Why evade the issue', he said to Dominic ? 'Why do you not beseech the Lord ? Where is now your compassion for your neighbour ? Where is your close confidence in God ?' Deeply moved by the brother's pleadings, and at the same time overcome by a feeling of burning compassion, he had the boy discreetly moved into a room which could be locked, and, by the virtue of his prayers, restored to him the warmth of life and gave him back to all safe and sound.[149]

The generosity of Cardinal Stefano of Fossanova towards Dominic's work takes on a new light from this event. On leaving the brethren of Santa Sabina and the sisters of St Sixtus shortly after 10th May, 1221, St Dominic did not only leave two fervent communities which he had just founded and lovingly instructed, with numerous friendships. He left in the eternal city two important centres for the influence of the Preachers. In particular Santa Sabina, which would one day become the mother house, occupies a symbolic position on the Aventine. It was set in the very heart of the Pope's fortress, as the order in the heart of the Church. Dominic could withdraw. Perhaps he surmised that he would never again see either St Sixtus, the Pope or Rome.

Chapter XIX

THE SECOND BOLOGNA CHAPTER: DOMINIC'S DEATH

FOR the sixth time Dominic was returning from Rome to northern Italy. How different his feelings must have been on these various journeys. This time the travelling was more of an effort to him than formerly. At the main halting places, however, he had the joy of no longer being lodged among strangers. In Siena as in Florence, he was received by the brethren in the convents he had founded. In the hospice of St Mary Magdalene in Siena, the Preachers were in the very midst of the work of installation and full of the attendant joyful enthusiasm. In Florence, on the contrary, where the convent founded by the brethren was entering upon its third year, Friar John of Salerno and his companions were experiencing reverses. Certain of the canons who had left them the church of St Paul because they were more or less constrained by the bishop, or by the parishioners who wanted the Preachers, could not brook this success of theirs, which for them meant the frustration of their own ministry. Resentment of this sort always finds a way of manifesting itself. In a mass as mobile as the population of Florence, no one could tell what ravages a tenacious hatred might provoke by calumnies. Dominic gave his brethren and his friends encouragement. A mendicant has nothing to fear, when he is always ready to give up his rights, to put a stop to wrangles. In the worst eventuality, the brethren would abandon the sanctuary to their detractors. God would see to it that they had a lodging elsewhere. Their adversaries, moreover, were not beyond conversion. The most relentless of them, Dominic affirmed, would himself one day become an edifying Friar Preacher.[1]

A few days before May 30th, Dominic arrived in Bologna. The chapter general had just assembled. The progress of the order in the world could be measured by the number of those taking part in the chapter. At this time about twenty houses of Friars Preachers and four of nuns were established. Three or four others were in progress of formation. This made at least fifty delegates to the chapter. It is not known whether Dominic recruited them in the same way as the previous year, by asking the various houses to choose their own *diffinitors*, or whether on the other hand he sent for the priors, accompanied by one or two brethren nominated by the conventual chapters. The direct history of the chapter is almost non-existent, amounting to barely two phrases from Jordan of Saxony:

In the year of our Lord 1221, at the general chapter in Bologna, it seemed fitting to the members of the chapter to impose upon me the office which they then created of prior of the province of Lombardy; . . . so that I was placed at the head of the others to govern them before I had learnt myself to govern my imperfection. At this chapter a community of the brethren was sent to England, with Friar Gilbert as prior.[2]

These phrases express more than one would think. They reveal that at this chapter—the only one during Jordan's lifetime at which he was not present —the whole order was reorganized the better to spread it further afield. The chapter of 1220 was the chapter of the constitution of the order; that of 1221 was the chapter of its distribution throughout Christendom. The former established the centre and unity of the order on a strong basis. The second created the intermediary organs, moreover without diminishing either the unity or the movement of expansion; on the contrary, it accelerated this.

Dominic's efficiency in the diffusion of his order has something about it that amazes us. An effort is needed to realize that the mendicant who spent his nights in prayer, his days in preaching, always journeyed on foot and slept in any refuge to hand at night, should have been able, in less than four years, to recruit one by one several hundred apostles of all ages, to form them, to disperse them, to create twenty-five communities and to govern them by a legislation so full of prudence and vigour, that all that was needed in the future was an elaboration of the details. The complete mastery of ends and means from the first moment, the absence of any merely tentative efforts, are no less astonishing than the rapidity. The flow of ideas is equally amazing. Christians are never surprised at seeing the extraordinary find a place in the life of a man of God. But it has to be realized that here the extraordinary is on a more imposing and impressive scale than those miracles of prophecy or healing at which St Dominic's contemporaries marvelled. For here the power of God did not show itself by effacing in some way the personality of the wonder-worker; it was expressed on the contrary through an enhancement of his personality, through the actions proper to his genius, through his intuitions and inward generosity. It is permissible to say that the figure of Dominic appears even finer in his deeds and in his works than in his miracles.

In 1221, his vitality, however, seemed to have reached its limits—the limit of his poor strength, the geographical limit of his influence too, for he was increasingly linked to Italy and even to Lombardy. He could not now begin over again his great journey of 1218–1219 in which the seed was sown. Moreover, hampered by the difference of language and of mentality, his action in Paris was always somewhat slight. In Germany it was almost nil. Yet at the general chapter of Bologna, thanks to the counsels and decisions of his brethren, Dominic was to try to surpass this limit and to succeed.

The fathers of the chapter set up in union with the founder a territorial subdivision in the order generally—the future province, which they designated by the term, still insufficiently defined, of *provincia vel regnum*.[3] By this subdivision, they established an intermediate organ of government of the Preachers. They could not conceive such an organ as of a different type from the central organ of government. That is to say that, like the latter, it had a dual aspect, composed as it was of a head and of an assembly representative of the community. The head was charged with recruiting and training the religious, with directing them to their ministry of salvation and with retraining them; the assembly, united to the head, must legislate, govern, supervise. Such was the complex organism which directed the order as a whole. Such would be the organism which, in the territorial subdivisions, would relay the central authority and, more especially, that of Dominic.

The assembly was given the name of 'provincial chapter', the head that of 'prior of the province or kingdom'. On this occasion and to avoid all ambiguity, they were forced to establish other official titles, and primarily that of 'Master of the Order of Preachers' which was substituted for the title of 'prior of the order' which the Curia had been using since 1220 to designate the supreme head. Only the title of Master, suggested by a Dominican tradition already of long standing, appears, in fact, after May 1221 in the legislation[4] and the texts in the archives.[5] Perhaps the title of 'conventual prior' was established at the same time and for the same reasons.[6] Moreover, certain prescriptions were adopted which would be inscribed in the constitutions forthwith. They can still be read in their original context in the manuscript of Rodez, as a prologue to the charter of preaching.[7]

We legislate that the priors of the provinces or kingdoms after a careful examination be confirmed or removed by the Master of the order and the *diffinitors*, in the course of the general chapter.

The prior provincial enjoys the same power in his province or kingdom as the Master of the order and those belonging to the province shall render him the same honours as they do to the Master of the order, unless the Master shall happen to be present.

The prior of a province or kingdom who might have sons suitable for teaching and capable of becoming Regent Masters within a short time, shall take care to send them to a centre of studies.[8] Those to whom he sends them shall not be allowed to employ them for any other purpose or to send them back to their province so long as they are not recalled.

The provincial chapter shall be held on the feast of St Michael at the place agreed upon in the province or kingdom and chosen by the prior of the province or kingdom on the advice of the *diffinitors*.[9]

Once more it was by the most recent canon law of the Church, actually from the 12th canon of the Fourth Council of the Lateran,[10] that the legislators of the second chapter of Bologna were inspired. The notion of territorial subdivision within which they distributed and regrouped their convents in a region, *provincia sive regnum*, in fact, had been elaborated by the Council in 1215.[11] By province was to be understood the ecclesiastical province. By adding province or kingdom, they showed clearly the flexibility with which they intended this distribution and regrouping to be done, sometimes following the great subdivisions of the Catholic Church and sometimes those of the nations, as seemed most convenient.

Now the purpose of this 12th canon was, by deciding on the regional regrouping of a certain number of religious houses according to provinces or kingdoms, to pave the way for an annual assembling in chapter. Thus it also supplied the legislation of the Preachers with the idea and model of the annual provincial chapter.[12] The matter was so clearly expressed in the canon that for some time the Preachers did not even trouble to define the tasks and organization of this chapter. The twelfth canon of the Lateran would take the place of legislation. The history of this canon, however, enables us to grasp more clearly the original characteristics of the institution of the province among the Preachers.

In the continual work of reform which constituted one of the chief tasks of the medieval Church, the papacy also concerned itself with extending its influence on religious by utilizing, or if necessary erecting, intermediate instruments. The progressive centralization of the orders of monks and canons, of which general chapters were both the sign and the instrument, had provided it with an excellent means of doing this; a means, however, that was only valid for federations of religious houses or universal orders. How were the very numerous isolated communities throughout the Church to be effectively covered? The Council of the Lateran then thought of reducing to a general form the more or less spontaneous attempts dating from the twelfth century, and of regrouping the autonomous convents into 'provinces or kingdoms' and causing their representatives to assemble each year in order to procure for them some of the advantages that the general chapter afforded the centralized orders.[13]

Clearly, however, there is a great difference between the general chapter of an universal order and the provincial chapters which the fathers of the Council had in mind. If the former is particularly desirable for matters of legislation, the latter has all the advantages when it comes to reform. Because it is regional, or national, it is much better placed to correct the religious. It sees, in fact, weaknesses and needs from closer quarters and can better adapt its decisions to the regional circumstances. Thus the provincial chapter is something different from a mere replica at a lower stage of the general chapter or a pure reflection of it. In comparison with the general chapter, the organ of legislation par excellence, it constitutes the principal instrument of control and of regular reform. It has kept this character down to our own times. Thus the Preachers, who took over the general chapter from the Cistercians or the Premonstratensians, also adopted the provincial chapter of the Council of the Lateran.

It was not only, however, to permit the holding of provincial chapters that the Dominican capitular fathers decided to regroup their convents into 'provinces or kingdoms'. It was equally, or even more so, their intention to establish a subdivision of the territory occupied by the Preachers, in order to place the new areas under the responsibility of regional heads, the priors of 'provinces or kingdoms'.[14] The phrase of Jordan of Saxony already cited in regard to the second chapter of Bologna, announcing as it does the creation of the office of prior provincial, enables us to know precisely what the institution of the provincial subdivisions was. The most urgent work to be done and that most easily capable of achievement was the simplification of Dominic's task by establishing intermediate authorities. It was essential to relieve Dominic, or rather to enable his own government, through the action of his subordinates, to extend its sphere, to act with more vigour and in a way that was better adapted to the circumstances.

Dominic, at least once, had already provided himself with a lieutenant of this kind. If Matthew of France had been Dominic's eventual successor rather than his vicar, Reginald, on the other hand, really fulfilled that function. In Bologna and then in Paris, he widely extended Dominic's action and influence, making it more effective precisely because his own activity was exercised more directly and in a manner better suited to his compatriots. In proportion as the order extended, the necessity of multiplying such intermediaries became even more and more important. In the winter of 1220–1221, Dominic felt the need of allowing others to act in his place, at the same time attaching them very firmly to himself. This was the reason for his keenness to intervene as a third party in the charters signed by the local priors. It is remarkable that at this very time, in his negotiations with the local authorities of the order, Cardinal Ugolino was carefully insisting that these authorities should act 'in the place and room of Brother Dominic, prior of the order of Preachers'.[15] Doubtless it was in the course of exchanges of views between the founder and the bishop of Ostia that the desirability of setting up a hierarchy of regional vicars was clearly grasped. Such would be the priors provincial, set over vast territories at the head of the Friars Preachers who were there, to multiply the brethren, train them by study and regular life, to direct them to their ministry according to the needs of the country and to correct them according to the circumstances.

It will be remarked that, in the legislative texts of 1220–1221, neither the powers of the provincial nor those of the chapter are defined. It was considered sufficient to state that this power was identical, in its scope, with that of the Master of the order. This definition, however, remained as it were in suspense, for the power of the Master was not defined in the text of 1220, or even in the later legislation. For the moment Dominic's practice was sufficient to determine it. It was, in fact, the fulness of executive power. The first provincial priors, as will be seen, were directly nominated by the general chapter. No law yet determined their appointment, which would be thrown open to election in 1224.[16]

Jordan has only preserved for us the name of one of the provinces erected in 1221, that of Lombardy of which he became prior.[17] With its six houses, Lombardy was clearly ripe for constitution as a province. From other sources we know the names of the priors provincial nominated in 1221 in Provence and in Spain. It can be affirmed that the provincials mentioned before 1224 in France and in the Roman province, if not in Teutonia, were also appointed in 1221. Provence, Spain, France and the Roman province, each one consisting of two or three houses, were equally fitted for receiving the provincial institutions in all their fulness, with prior and chapter. Apart from these regions the order only existed under the form of isolated houses— one in Germany, another in Sweden. Did the chapter of 1221 create provinces of the order in these regions and did it appoint provincials there? This is not in itself impossible. A vicar, or lieutenant, of the General could be effectively appointed for these territories, with the function of diffusing and organizing the order in a region so far scarcely touched by its ministry. This would be the case in Poland in 1225.[18]

Bernard Gui, followed by Dominican historiography in general,[19] was to assert at the beginning of the fourteenth century that in 1221 the Bologna chapter set up eight provinces—'Spain, Provence, France, Lombardy, the Roman province, Hungary, Teutonia and England'.[20] This assertion is true of the first five territories, as has been seen. No document existing today allows of proof in the other three cases. Moreover, as has been said, Teutonia had only a single convent. England had none. It is precisely in the case of England, however, that Bernard Gui is emphatic, giving the name of provincial to the religious whom the chapter sent in 1221.[21]

The information given by Bernard Gui cannot be lightly set aside, coming as it does from a conscientious scholar. He investigated, sought out and collected documents; when occasion demanded, he was prepared to admit his ignorance.[22] Moreover, it will be noted that the order in which he enumerates the eight provinces, which is also the order of precedence among representatives of the provinces in the chapters general at the close of the thirteenth century,[23] is almost the primitive one. It appears, in fact, as early as 1225 in the text of the institutions.[24] Moreover, this order was not founded upon seniority but upon geography alone.[25] This clearly shows that among the eight provinces there is none older than the others. Seniority would not have failed to produce among them, as it did among the various houses, a hierarchy of precedence. Were they then contemporary in their institution, and thus of 1221?

In spite of everything we hesitate to accept without question this some-what late information, for the best sources, when speaking of the missions that the chapter sent to England and Hungary, do not say that their leaders, before departing, received the office of prior provincial,[26] which they would not fail to say in this precise context, if that were so. For Teutonia documents are altogether lacking. Thus only the foundation of the five provinces already instanced can be beyond question attributed to the second chapter of Bologna.

It must, however, be added that the chapter directly paved the way for the foundation of other provinces. It is, in fact, pointed out in the sources that it sent brethren, missions, sometimes communities organized under the guidance of a prior, into a large number of territories. Thus is sketched the geography of the Preachers across Europe in bold outline, the vision that, in a few weeks' time, Dominic would see rising in his thought when, on the point of dying, he prayed for a long time for each of his absent brethren.

In the Spanish group were five kingdoms, Aragón, Castile, Navarra, León and Portugal. Its boundaries were geographical and marked by the two seas and the Pyrenees. At that time there were two houses there—Segovia, and Palencia in Castile; it would not be long before Zamora, also in Castile, came into being, but it did not yet exist.[27] The same was the case with Santarém in Portugal.[28] Finally two monasteries of nuns existed in Castile— Madrid and San Esteban de Górmaz. The prior provincial, who was nomina-ted by the chapter in 1221, was a Friar Suero,[29] whom tradition has tried to identify with the Friar Gómez, founder with Friar Pedro de Madrid of the Dominicans in Spain.

Provence was neither kingdom, ecclesiastical province nor geographical entity. With its three houses of Toulouse, Lyons, Montpellier and its monastery of Prouille, it seemed to be aiming at extending itself to the whole of that country which would later be called the 'langue d'oc', or again, the country of written law; in short, the southern half of Gaul which, despite its heterogeneous character, was in opposition through its original culture with the countries to the north of the Loire. This would be even more marked when in 1224 the province of Provence abandoned the convent of Lyons to France, to receive in exchange Limoges.[30] Before the end of the year 1221, it would be enlarged by the convents of Bayonne[31] and of Puy.[32] Friar Bertrand of Garrigo was provincial of it from 1221, by appointment of the chapter.[33]

The province of France only corresponded very roughly to the kingdom of that name with the important convent of St Jacques in Paris and the house in Rheims. Limoges and Poitiers, indeed, where its second and fourth convents were, depended on the English. Metz, where a house would probably be founded before the end of the year, depended on the Empire. It would seem that Matthew of France was named provincial in 1221.[34]

Lombardy corresponded neither to a kingdom nor to a province of the

Church. It had as its basis a highly characterized and sufficiently homogenous political and social entity. Situated between the Apennines and the Alps, in the rich plain of the Pô, it possessed clearly defined frontiers. There were in May 1221 six houses there—Bologna, Bergamo, Milan, Verona, Piacenza, Brescia. It cannot be proved that Faenza[35] and Parma[36] were yet in existence in 1221. The provincial appointed by the chapter was, as has been said, Master Jordan, who would be succeeded in the following year by Friar Domingo de Segovia.[37]

The Roman province was one of the least homogeneous. It corresponded to Tuscany and to the patrimony of the Church. Florence, Siena and Santa Sabina of Rome were its first three houses of friars, St Sixtus its monastery. It seems that the Bologna chapter appointed as provincial a Friar Giovanni (or Giacomo) of Piacenza, about whom nothing is otherwise known.[38]

Such were the great divisions that the chapter of the Preachers carved out in the Christian West in 1221. It can be seen to what extent the expression 'province or kingdom' was approximate. Geography, sometimes politics, or the relationship of the houses to each other, these in turn directed the legislator in the grouping of them into provinces. In his eyes the essential was not the principle which allowed the formation of groups, but the convenience of the grouping for the administration of the order.

With the enumeration of these five territories the static description that can be made of the geography of the order is in some sort complete. It must be continued under the form of a narrative, for in the rest of Europe the installation of the Preachers was in full development.

Giving effect to one of the wishes dearest to the founder's heart, the chapter general sent to Hungary the prior of Bologna, Master Paul of Hungary.[39] This professor in canon law, who was still exercising his functions, had just compiled, at the request of Dominic and for the use of his brethren, a *Summa de penitentia* which constituted one of the very first manuals of confession in the Church. Its only equivalent was the handbooks that the Preachers of Paris, Barcelona and Germany received from their brethren about the same time, to prepare them for the ministry of penance and of spiritual direction demanded by the Lateran Council in regard to the Easter Confession and Communion.[40] Leaving Bologna, his brethren and his studies, Paul of Hungary set out with four brethren, among whom was Blessed Sadoc, future prior of Zagreb. They stopped at Raab, on the Danube —where their community was increased by three recruits—at Veszprim, where they founded a house, and finally at Albe Royale (Székesfehérvár), where they were received in the convent but recently founded by another Friar Paul.[41] This was to be the basis of a fruitful apostolate among the schismatics and heretics between the Save and the Drave and, further off still, among the Cumans and the pagans. After the death of Paul of Hungary in 1223, the first provincial was to be Friar Theodoric.[42]

The chapter also sent Friar Solomon of Aarhus to Denmark.[43] He carried letters from the Pope to King Waldemar II[44] and to Andrew Sunesen, Archbishop of Lund. To these Dominic added his own letters. Friar Solomon was given for companions several German brothers, among whom must have been Friar Christian,[45] one of the founders of the convent of Bologna. The German brethren remained in Cologne, and Friar Solomon, having no companion left to accompany him to Scandinavia, joined some brethren who were going to Paris. There they gave him as *socius* a lay-brother from Lombardy, with whom he reached Flanders and embarked for his own country. A storm cast him ashore in Norway, in the neighbourhood of Nidaros (Trondhjem). After many perils and sufferings, both on land and sea, he finally reached Copenhagen and met the archbishop of Lund. Andrew Sunesen made up to him for all his troubles by his welcome. He read the letters from the Pope and from Dominic and gave full vent to his satisfaction and his joy. 'You are truly welcome. May heaven grant that in each of the Churches which depend on this court, we possess at least one convent of this order.' In the meantime the legate of Dacia, Gregorio de Crescentio, recently arrived from Rome, took the brother with him and made use of his education and his talents as a preacher. The following year (1223?) at Pentecost, they were back in Lund where the archbishop, encouraged by the legate, made the brother the gift of a piece of land. A convent was soon erected there. Brother Solomon became its prior, and it was not long before the Scandinavian brethren who had entered the order in Paris and Bologna filled it. The brethren of Sigtuna, persecuted by the Archbishop of Uppsala, abandoned their convent about 1224 and took refuge in that of Lund. It would seem that the first provincial of Dacia, Friar Ranold, took possession of his charge in 1226.[46]

The order had made a beginning in Germany about 1220, with the foundation of the convent of Friesach—a difficult beginning if we are to believe a Scandinavian chronicle the initial data of which, it is true, are not well founded.[47] The prior of Friesach, led away by Satan, returned to the world after the foundation, abandoning his brethren as he did his vows. Now he was their only priest. Master Paul, on his way to Hungary, found them discouraged. He saved the convent by leaving a priest there—who was actually Friar Solomon of Aarhus. The latter also shared, after Pentecost 1221, in the foundation of Cologne.[48] A painful episode, the distorted account of which may be read in the homilies of Cesarius of Heisterbach, put the existence of the new foundation in danger.[49] The Cistercians, in fact, demanded back Friar Christian, the founder, who was formerly one of them, and whose profession the Preachers had at the time no right to receive.[50] It is possible that the arrival of Friar Henry of Cologne, the intimate friend of Jordan of Saxony, was providential in saving the convent at the end of 1221. The brother was preaching in Rheims about the same time.[51] He

The hill of Santa Maria dei Monti at Bologna. The round church where Dominic
died is hidden by the classical villa on top of the hill.

became in effect the first prior of Cologne. A certain Friar Bernard would shortly afterwards occupy the office of Provincial of Teutonia.[52] Friar Conrad of Höxter would replace him between 1224 and 1225.

The English brother, Gilbert Ash, was sent by the chapter of 1221, with a community of Preachers, to found the order in England.[53] They landed on English soil at Dover on August 5th of the same year. Conducted by the Bishop of Winchester, they were at Canterbury on the 10th and Oxford on the 15th. They at once made a foundation in the university city and constructed an oratory to the Virgin in the parishes of St Edward and St Aldate. There they met difficulties very similar to those at St Jacques in Paris and had to change the site of their convent. After 1224, the brethren also had a convent in London. It was perhaps at this date that Gilbert Ash received the title of provincial.[54]

It was again the second chapter of Bologna which gave the mission to Friar Jacek of Opola (St Hyancinth) to go and found in Poland with Friar Henry of Moravia.[55] The life of this holy religious by Stanislaus of Cracow, written in the middle of the fourteenth century and the source of later historiography, unfortunately presents so many distortions and glaring errors that it is difficult to give a true account of the entry into religion and mission of the saint and his companion. One thing is certain, however. The two preachers arrived at Cracow in 1222. The bishop, Yves, received them favourably and lodged them in a dependency of his palace. On 12th March, 1223, in the presence of the Cardinal Legate, Gregorio de Crescenti, he consecrated the small church of the Holy Trinity, of which the brethren would take possession on the 25th. In 1225 came the first provincial, Friar Gerard of Breslau, sent by the general chapter of that year.[56] The province then still possessed only the house in Cracow, but Gerard would found others without delay.

An anecdote related by Gerard of Frachet allows us to conclude that in 1221 the fathers of the chapter, under the impetus of Dominic, also sent founders to Greece, that is to say into the Latin empire of the East.[57]

Of this journey across Dominican Europe, throughout the years 1221–1226, a few general features should be mentioned. In 1221, the second chapter of Preachers under Dominic's presidency really constituted five administrative subdivisions or provinces—Spain, Provence, France, Lombardy, the Roman province, each one provided with a chapter and a prior provincial. Moreover it sent missions, with someone in charge and more or less numerous religious, to Hungary, Germany, England, Dacia (Scandinavia), Poland and Greece. In 1223, Hungary and Germany would already have their provincials. In 1226, 1227 at latest, all the other territories would have them in their turn. It can be proved that at this date they had officially become provinces.

In 1225, in fact, the order would adopt a remarkable body of legislation

which, completing and correcting the earlier provisions concerning the
province, would finish the setting up of the constitutional system of the
order. The province would receive its permanent place in the life of the
Preachers. It would participate in elections, in the confirmation, government
and, above all, correction of individuals and communities.[58] Now the document which was drawn up in that year by the sixth chapter general (or fourth
of Bologna) enumerated eight major provinces equipped with full provincial
rights—Spain, Provence, France, Lombardy, the Roman province, Hungary,
Teutonia, England,[59] and perhaps four minor provinces still insufficiently
developed—the provinces of Jerusalem, Greece, Poland and Dacia.[60] The
geographical framework of the order with its twelve provinces, was now
fixed for the future. It would not be modified until the outset of the fourteenth century. With the exception, perhaps, of the province of Jerusalem,
arising out of the collaboration of the Preachers in the efforts of the Church
for the crusade in the Holy Land, these provinces were all instituted or
directly prepared in 1221. One is thus led to the conclusion that at the
second chapter of Bologna, a little more than four years after the confirmation of the Preachers by the Pope, in the presence and by the will of St
Dominic, the order had determined the territorial system in which, for the
present, it would live out its first century. The order was founded, confirmed, endowed with its institutions as with its spirit, equipped with a new
and well-balanced legislation, which was given effect to in a geographical
framework which through its subdivisions extended throughout Europe.

It is, perhaps, useful to emphasize in a few words the greatness of the work
accomplished. The three combined forces of St Dominic's work—the
Church's mission or preaching, the regular clerical institution, the spirituality of apostolic life—have already been mentioned. To these must now be
added legislation as fully adapted to his mission as to the spirit of the Canon
Law of the times. It was not for nothing that this legislation came into being
at Bologna. Its source was the latest findings of the law of the Church. It was
closely inspired by four canons of the Council of the Lateran—canons 10 to
13, on the preaching, the theological teaching, the provincial and general
chapters, attachment to regular tradition. Behind this lay the all important
ideas on moderate government that emanated from the university and
urban centres. The executive was very strong, since, by the immediate
profession of obedience and formal precept, the Master of the Order
possessed unlimited authority over each religious, and the provincial as
well as the conventual priors were his lieutenants; but the legislation and
control which can go to the extent of deposing all authorities, the Masters
included, were outside it; at all stages they were in the hands of the community, under the form of the chapter. The choice of the leaders by election
extended from those of the lowest rank to the Master, but authority came
down from the Master through profession and confirmation, the sources of

strict obedience. The order was universal and had as its focal points the two centres of learning of Western Christendom, Bologna and Paris, not to mention the Roman Curia which was working with enthusiasm for its extension; but in the provinces it possessed intermediate instruments which were at the same time subordinate, in the person of the priors, and de-centralized in the institution of the chapters. Now all this was contained in a concise constitutional document, in which legal precision in no sense excludes its spiritual inspiration.[61]

In the first days of June 1221, it was not only the chapter which was drawing to a close, it was Dominic's work in regard to his order. He had finished. He could now preach in full independence. It still remained, how-ever, for him to devote himself to the affairs of the priory of Bologna. The departure of Master Paul of Hungary made it necessary to replace the prior. Ventura of Verona was placed at the head of the community of St Nicholas, probably by election.[62]

On 13th January previous, Master Paul had finished paying off to Pietro di Lovello the price of the lands around St Nicholas which had been pur-chased.[63] On Monday, 7th June, Dominic made a new purchase from Pietro.[64] The deed was drawn up in the church, near the door, before the altar of Our Lady. The general chapter which was still complete was present, as well as the chapter of the convent. What was in question was the purchase of a fairly considerable piece of land, about one and a half acres, which would extend the garden of the convent in an easterly direction, along the road which bordered the communal ditch. Even further purchases would have to be made—many houses not belonging to the order remained on the lands of St Nicholas. In the month of October one of the first acts of Master Jordan's provincialate would be to buy back one of them.[65] Others were recovered later.[66]

The document drawn up by the notary instanced the generosity of a friend of the convent. Master Ugolino, Doctor in Law of the university of Bologna, had given the Preachers a hundred Bolognese pounds, to help them to pay for this land. This was not the first manifestation of friendship of this Master who enjoyed great authority among the civil lawyers of Bologna.[67]

The end of the document insisted at length on the engagement taken by the elderly Lovello in the name of his son, Andalò. He must take care, it said, that his son accepted the contract and undertook to defend the new property of the brethren in the eight days of appeal which he would receive from them. Pietro di Lovello had already had the deed of the previous January countersigned by Andalò.[68] The brethren took their precautions in regard to the powerful and violent patrician, their neighbour and their creditor, who might as easily help as create great difficulties for them.

Dominic had very special reasons for dreading a scene from this noble family, for he had in fact accepted the vow of religion of Andalò's daughter. By this oath Diana had given effect to a vocation which had been growing slowly for some time and would in the future form the subject of a violent disagreement between her will and that of her father, or rather of the whole family.[69] It was a common enough story in the Middle Ages, but in Italy, however, presented certain special characteristics owing to the scenes of violence, passionate to the point of sacrilege, to which it might give rise. The family and the daughter seem to have won the victory in turn. Diana had been able to reject proposed offers of marriage. The family had been able to conspire against an attempt at monastic life at San Gregorio in Bologna. Who would win the third round? Diana thought she had triumphed by the installation of the convent of sisters decided upon by St Dominic. The prohibition by the bishop, however, perhaps through some intervention by the family, of the plan to build the convent in the place proposed by the brethren, had ruined Diana's projects. Had her father won the final victory? Dressed according to her rank as a patrician lady, covered with priceless jewels, Diana remained at home, but beneath her attire of silk and purple she wore a hair-shirt. She prayed for long periods, observing total silence from the time of rising until Tierce. Moreover she communicated something of her interior life to her large circle of women friends. Dominic, immediately upon his return to Bologna, hastened to visit her. Perhaps he was told the secret of the bold plan she had conceived to give effect to her vow, despite all the opposition.

The founder was not to see the conclusion of the matter. After 7th June, happy over the good work accomplished at the chapter, refusing to take any rest, he left for the Marches with Paul of Venice and a few other brethren.[70] He was going to rejoin the cardinal-legate, Ugolino of Ostia, who was awaiting him in Venice.

Ugolino had left Rome about the middle of March to carry out his mission in the north of Italy.[71] He was accredited to the patriarchs of Aquileia and Grado, the archbishops and bishops of Ravenna, Genoa, Milan and Pisa, finally to all the prelates of Lombardy, the Marches, the Romagna and Tuscany. Invested with the double authority of Pope and emperor, he was to preach and prepare for the crusade, make the rights and liberties of the Church respected, establish peace between and in the cities, act against heresy, arrange the promulgation by the civil authorities of the canons of the Lateran and the law of the coronation, and have these taught by the Masters of Bologna.[72] Siena, Florence, Piacenza, Milan, Brescia, were visited by him in turn between 25th March and 25th May. While the Preachers were holding their chapter, he was at Desenzano on 1st June, in the heart of Catharist territory. Between 2nd and 4th June, he passed through Verona. On the 13th he was at Venice.[73] It was there that he saw Dominic, who would in the future not stay with his entourage, arrive.[74] Ugolini was expecting him. The great business of the crusade of peace and faith that he was pursuing reserved an essential place in its policy for the sermons of the Friars Preachers. The general evangelization that Dominic and his brethren had planned the year before, principally in Lombardy, was to begin again more extensively in the Marches of Treviso and Venice, this time linked with the action of the legate, and having as its base the Dominican convents whose number had further increased.

Two documents indicate the important place the Preachers held in the preoccupations and plans of Ugolino. On 24th May previous, while Dominic was hurrying towards Bologna, the cardinal-legate invested Friar Guala of Bergamo, prior of the Preachers of Brescia, with the church of Saints Faustino and Jovito, martyrs.[75] Separating the church, the adjacent premises and the enclosed land from all the other property and revenues of SS Faustino and Jovito, he gave the former to the brethren and left the other as an annuity to the previous clergy, specifying in detailed terms that after the death of the latter, the bishop should dispose freely of the prebends. The brethren were to remain twelve years in this church.

Twenty days later, this time at Venice, Ugolino appointed a committee of three priests and sent them to Florence.[76] It was to set up an investigation in the city on the temporal and spiritual situation of the church of San Pietro Scherraggio. It was said that it was gravely compromised from both points of view. The commissioners would use the legate's authority and be armed with the counsels of the bishop. Strengthened by the wishes expressed by all the parishioners, they tried to induce the clergy of this church to abandon it to the Preachers. The committee, however, did not attain its objective. Before the end of the year, the cardinal was to change his point of view and again intervene in Florence.[77] He eventually obtained for the Preachers, in conditions similar to those of former times, the sanctuary of Santa Maria Novella which they still possess today.

The authoritative interventions of the cardinal-legate to procure for Dominic's brethren a well-placed establishment, capable of extending the effectiveness of their ministry of souls in Brescia as in Florence, are characteristic. When the first step was taken, Ugolino had not renewed his contact with Dominic. He was thus giving effect to a plan drawn up earlier in Rome, with Dominic, in their conversations in the winter. Moreover, the sending of the commissioners to Florence who would procure precise information as to the feelings of the parishioners of San Pietro Scherraggio in regard to the Preachers and knew the latters' difficulties with the clergy of San Paolo, was an indication of Dominic's arrival in Venice before the drawing up of the charter of 13th June; a small detail confirms this: one of the three commissioners designated by Ugolino six days earlier acted as a witness to Dominic's charter in Bologna.[78] Above all, these two cases of intervention are an eloquent testimony to the unanimity of the two Churchmen in their desire to advance the work of the order.

Clearly this unanimity was primarily manifested in religious action properly so called. Dominic and his brethren preached, while the Cardinal dealt with the authorities of every kind whom he had summoned before him. Alas, once more the activity of the preacher altogether eludes us, for want of documents. Clearly it remained what it had been in the Narbonensis and in Lombardy—a fervent evangelization in which the example of the preacher's prayer and heroic poverty emphasized his love of the Saviour and of souls; a word which was spoken to all, to good Christians to raise them up by the spiritual life and generous action, to heretics whom it confronted directly in order to enlighten them and bring them back to the risen Christ. It is particularly tantalizing not to be able to catch any echo of this preaching, at the time when Dominic was attaining the apogee of his sanctity upon earth, in the last weeks of his preaching. Ugolino was using Venice as his headquarters.[79] He was at Murano on 21st June, on 1st July again in Venice, on the 8th in Padua, the 12th in Treviso, returning to Padua on the 14th. Then, from the 18th to 21st at Mantua, journeying towards Emilia, which he entered at Reggio on the 24th. Dominic had not to follow the impressive cortège of the cardinal in its journeys to and fro. Indeed he did not desire this. He was too faithful to the spirit of Montpellier which was now that of the order. He preserved contact, however, with the legate from a distance and gradually moved closer to Bologna. It was near Reggio that he learnt of the audacious escapade of Diana of Andalò.

For more than a year d'Andalò's daughter had remained at home, apparently paralysed by fear of her relatives.[80] Her energetic soul, however, worthy of her family, did not despair. She reproached herself as for a crime, for not having yet brought about, with the aid of the brethren, the monastery promised to Dominic for the order. On 22nd July, the feast of St Mary Magdalene, she announced her intention of riding to the monastery of the Augustinian nuns of Ronzano, about a mile and a half to the south-west of the town. She set out in great state, surrounded with a numerous escort of patrician ladies of Bologna. On arrival at the monastery, where there was nothing rigid about the enclosure, she entered the sisters' dormitory alone and, without warning, demanded and obtained the habit of the nuns. A violent dispute broke out among her companions. A messenger promptly hurried to Bologna. The whole town was in an uproar. The idlers of the city could not refrain from taking a part in things and relatives, friends, clients, the inquisitive, men and women of all classes, all rushed off to Ronzano. The d'Andalò preceded them, invaded the monastery and dragged Diana away with so much brutality that one of her ribs was broken. She felt the effect of this until her death, and, meanwhile, lay on a sick-bed in her house for a year. Dominic was grieved to learn of this catastrophe. Diana was cut off from the world. Andalò mounted guard and did not allow anyone whatsoever to speak to his daughter in private.

Dominic left Ugolino, or rather preceded him to Bologna, continuing his ministry of the word at each stage of the journey. It was high summer. The heat was stifling. The alternation of harassing marches and uninterrupted preachings was all the more tiring in that in his relations with the cardinal, Dominic had to conform to the rhythm of the legation. Once more he reached and exceeded the limits of his strength. He was utterly worn out, and was longing to rest among his brethren. He reached Bologna shortly before 28th July.[81] Paul of Venice was no longer with him.[82] He had doubtless left him as the convent of Verona.

He would not rest. At the end of a day's march in the stifling and humid atmosphere of the plain of the Pô, when he finally reached St Nicholas it was to shut himself up with the prior and procurator of the convent, Ventura and Rodolfo, and treat with them of the business of the order.[83] The conventual buildings, the current ministry, the mission in Lombardy, the institution of the monastery of the sisters and the future of Diana . . . subjects of conversation were not lacking. The night was advancing and Friar Rodolfo, who wanted indeed to sleep, in vain begged Dominic to go and lie down for a little, and above all to dispense himself from getting up for Matins. The Master would not give way to his invitation and went into the Church. There he prayed on indefinitely. When the brethren arrived for the office, Dominic was there and joined them. Then they came to tell Friar Ventura that Dominic was suffering from a very severe headache. It was the first symptom of the illness which was going to carry him off.

This time again he would not give up. The bouts of fever and colic succeeded each other. Evidently the dysentery from which he had already suffered so much was coming back in a most pernicious form. Dominic put up resistance and mastered himself once more. With the cardinal-legate who had just arrived in Bologna, he visited Diana of Andalò in her father's house.[84] They could not close the door to visitors of this sort; but in the presence of the family who demanded to be present at the whole interview, the visit remained one of pure formality, and Dominic was reduced to the expedient of making use of clandestine letters to comfort his daughter. It was in these last days of July, too, that he went to see some students of Bologna in their room. He loved these impromptu visits. In the familiarity of conversation he opened his heart to these young men. He felt death coming and said so simply, taking the opportunity to raise the mind of his friends towards the life that was true and eternal.[85]

At the beginning of August, he could no longer remain on his feet and finally decided to go to bed. In the corner of the dormitory where Friar Rodolfo at night-time placed a bedstead with rope stretched across it and a blanket so that the Master might rest on occasion—for he would not have a bed—he accepted for the first time that they should give him a wool mattress. The disease gripped him. When the bouts of fever were severe, he remained motionless.[86] Only the lips which moved gently, or certain changes in his expression which were usual in him when he was in contemplation, showed those around him that he was pursuing his prayer without interruption. He never complained. He did not groan. On the contrary, on his thin face there was a sweet, smiling and even joyful expression, in accordance with his habit of showing greater joy in adversity than in prosperity. In the moments of relief from the illness, he spoke of God to the brother who was nursing him, or asked for a book to be read to him.

There was no longer any doubt that he was very seriously ill. Nature was finding it increasingly difficult to defend itself. He was growing weaker. Several times he called the novices to his bedside, comforted them and urged them to the pursuit of goodness with very gentle words and an engaging insistence. This restful conversation, in which he gave his spirit to the young friars, was his best comfort. The brethren, however, did not yet wholly despair of curing him. The atmosphere of Bologna in summer is trying and unhealthy, especially on the St Nicholas side where the waters of the ditch and of the river Aposa, are more or less stagnant. The poisoned miasma of such an atmosphere was an obstacle to his recovery. The brethren moved Dominic to the south of the city, to the small Benedictine priory of Monte-Mario. On the summit of the hill the air circulated more freely and seemed more healthy. It was, alas, too late. His weakness increased from hour to hour.

Dominic was going to die. In the morning of 6th August, he asked the brethren who were watching by his bedside to call Ventura. The prior came with a large group of brethren, about twenty at least, who collected round the founder in their distress. They were there, on their knees, or leaning over his low couch, representing the brethren of St Nicholas, the Preachers then distributed throughout the world, the immense army of Dominic's sons and daughters from the beginnings until our own day. And for all those who would hear him from the far ends of that earth, with which he was already identified, Dominic pronounced in a long monologue words so profoundly moving that Friar Ventura did not remember ever having heard anything more edifying. Only a few details have come down to us.[87] He spoke of the sanctity of his brethren, of the perseverance which must be shown, of the prudence that must be exercised over the people whom one frequented, specially in the case of young women, for a well-purified heart was necessary to avoid the risk of a false step. He had discovered in himself, though God in his mercy had allowed to preserve the virginity of his flesh until the end, the imperfection of finding more attraction in the conversation of girls than in that of old ladies. He spoke above all of the fervour with which it was necessary to love the order and promote it; of loving souls; of poverty.[88]

Already the solemn liturgy of the agony and death, in accordance with the moving rite of the canons or of the university of Bologna, was beginning to enwrap and fraternally to sustain Dominic.[89] He now made his general confession in the presence of the company of priests who then gave him the sacrament of the sick. The simple clerics went out; there remained only the dozen chosen priests,[90] who, in what they heard, found no mortal sin, nothing but the mark of a perfectly pure soul. Whilst the other brethren were coming back, Dominic made a sign to Friar Ventura. He was worried about his modesty. 'I have done wrong', he said, 'in speaking of my virginity before the brethren. I ought not to have said that.'[91] They gave him extreme unction. One of the brethren who had just come in again, however, took Ventura aside. The monk who served the chapel was saying to any who cared to listen that if Dominic died at the priory, he would not allow the body to be taken elsewhere and would bury it in the sanctuary. We can judge of the agitation of the Preachers. Ventura leant over Dominic and confided to him their keen anxiety. 'God forbid', he answered, 'that I should be buried elsewhere than under the feet of my brethren. Carry me outside. Let me die on the roadside and then you will be able to bury me in your church.'

A touching procession wound slowly down the hill to reach the city once more. The passers-by were surprised, stopped and suddenly fell silent. In the litter which the strong shoulders of his brethren were carrying, Dominic was scarcely breathing. At every moment they were afraid that he was going. St Nicholas at last. They carried him into the cell of Master Moneta, since he had none of his own.[92] A slight respite occurred. The brethren, one after the other, came up to him weeping. Each one recommended himself to him with his intentions. And he answered, with the same humility which had but lately made him tender his resignation because he deemed himself truly insufficient, 'Do not weep'. 'I shall be more use to you and bear more fruit for you after death than I ever did in life.'

At the end of a good hour, he sent for the prior—'Prepare', he said. The prior and the brethren vested for the solemn recommendation, then gathered round him. 'Wait yet.' He continued to command, master of himself and of his brethren in the final combat. The heavy silence and the waiting weighed upon the religious. Ventura bent over him—'Father, you know in what bitter sadness you are leaving us. Be mindful of us and pray to the Lord for us.' And the blessed Dominic raised his hands towards heaven. 'Holy Father, as you know, I have persevered with all my heart in following your will. And I have guarded and preserved those whom you have given me. I recommend them to you. Preserve them and keep them.'

Another moment of waiting. Each one tried to stifle his grief in order not to disturb the agony. Friar Rodolfo was on his knees near the dying man's head. He supported it with a piece of linen. With a fold of this linen he wiped the sweat of death from his face. 'Begin', murmured Dominic. Then, softly, the community of his brethren recited the *Credo*,[93] followed by the soul's recommendation. Dominic joined in with the prayers—this could be seen from the slight movement of his lips. The gesture became imperceptible. At one moment he raised his hands towards heaven. It was his last breath. Each one had noticed it—he surrendered his soul at the moment when the brethren were saying—'Come to his aid, saints of God. Hasten, angels of the Lord. Receive his soul and offer it before the face of the Most High'. It was the evening[94] of 6th August, 1221. He was not fifty years old.

While the brethren were singing the second part of the 'commendation' in the adjoining dormitory, Friar Rodolfo, whose function it was to perform this office, dressed his master's body for the funeral; he found on the bare flesh an iron chain, tightly girt around the loins, which he removed. It would one day be claimed by Master Jordan. They looked for a decent habit in which to vest the body. The master had only one tunic and the mud, dust and sweat of the road had soiled it. Again it was Master Moneta who gave him his habit.[95]

The customary life of the great convent of the Preachers was now suspended. The community had only one occupation—to surround the body of the dead man with the suffrage of its prayers. In procession it conducted the body to the church of St Nicholas. The great vigil began. The community divided itself into two watches, which would succeed one another in the choir. Each one must recite the seventy-five psalms which formed half the psalter. Thus the night would be spent. When the psalter was ended the hour of the obsequies would have sounded.

Dominic's body now reposed in the midst of his brethren, in his still open coffin, enshrined in prayer. Was he not still living among his Preachers? From time to time one of them cast a furtive glance interrupted by tears, at the profile of the prostrate form. Disease and death had accentuated the features, the aquiline nose slightly bent towards the right, the strong-willed chin, the prominence of the cheek-bones now heightened by the thinness of the cheeks, the fine brow.[96] When the friar then closed his eyes, he could see him, no longer pale and the features chiselled by death, but in that very living attitude so well described by Sister Cecilia.

> Average height, a thin body, a handsome and slightly fresh-coloured countenance, hair and beard slightly reddish, fine eyes. From his forehead and his lashes a kind of splendour radiated which attracted the respect and affection of all. He remained always smiling and joyful unless he was moved with compassion by some distress of his neighbour. He had long and beautiful hands; a voice that was deep, beautiful and resounding. He was never bald and his crown of hair was complete, shot through with occasional white hairs.[97]

The door of the church opened to admit the dean of the regular chapter of St Mark at Mantua and superior of the two priories at Bologna and Ronzano, Br. Albert Spinola.[98] He had benefited considerably from the Master's friendship in spiritual conversations full of warmth and fruit and had perhaps played a part in Diana's recent escapade.[99] He had just learnt of the death of his friend and came into the church with his heart full of grief. And yet, before this spectacle of peace and affection, joy gradually took the place of grief. He knelt by the body. Boldly he embraced it and placed a kiss on the brow. He stood completely still as if he were listening. Then, his face radiant, he got up. 'Good news, Father prior', he called to Friar Ventura, 'Master Dominic has given me the accolade and has told me that before the end of this year he will lead me with him to Christ.'

In the midst of the stream of visitors, who unceasingly succeeded each other in the church, arrived the Cardinal of Ostia himself and the numerous prelates who accompanied him.[100] He was not only suffering from losing the irreplaceable collaborator with whom he had just spent these two months. The wound touched the inmost centre of his religious feelings. This great churchman, daily more than fully occupied by the highest politico-religious business, was, to a greater extent than Innocent III, haunted by nostalgia for the interior life, by the appeal of the flight to the desert.[101] The meeting with St Dominic or St Francis overwhelmed him like a contact with the Gospel each time renewed. Twelve years later, when he had become Pope and was receiving some Dominicans who spoke to him of their patriarch, he defined his feelings in a word—'He is in heaven, joined to the apostles.'[102] At the root of the feeling of deep friendship of which Jordan of Saxony speaks, born of a long familiarity, lay a considerable share of Christian admiration for a saint, of pure attachment to the Gospel.

Thus the cardinal-legate insisted on celebrating all the ceremonies of the burial himself. He was assisted at the altar by the patriarch of Aquileia and numerous bishops and abbots. He sang the Mass, intoned the recommendation and, finally, performed the burial. So many high dignitaries celebrating the obsequies of the mendicant preacher! In the presence of the legate, which was in some sort that of the Pope, the brethren did not see so much the honour done to their founder as the magnificent praise by the Roman Church of the life of a mendicant preacher. The apostolic life of the Preachers under the form that Dominic had tenaciously defended received, in the presence of the highest prelates of North Italy and of a great crowd of Bolognese, a striking consecration.

The coffin was placed in the tomb. The pit was dug in the lower part of the church.[103] Friar Rodolfo had it lined on all sides with the hardest cement he could find, for the Preachers must not be robbed of their precious relic. A large slab was firmly cemented over the tomb. And, immediately, a large number of sick, of possessed, of poor or of simple faithful, began to invoke the intercession of the saint, around the tomb.[104]

CHAPTER XX

CANONIZATION

TWELVE years went by. So vigorous had been the impetus Dominic had given that his death had not retarded the forward movement of the order of Preachers. It was now commensurate with the vast framework outlined by the founder. There was no slackening either in the great mission in Lombardy; in other words it continued to move in the direction anticipated by the Preacher.

Jordan of Saxony, whom the Master had made a member of the chapter in Bologna two months after his entry into religion and whom the following year he nominated Provincial of Lombardy, thus entrusting to him the finest province and highest task in the order, became his successor at the head of the Preachers. Friar Stefano, the student of Bologna whom Dominic had acquired for the order in such an unusual fashion, three years later succeeded Friar Jordan at the head of the Province of Lombardy and actively directed that important mission. Eighteen houses of Preachers north of the Apennines formed and launched the apostolic troops who were operating in this field of the Master.[1] Convents of St Francis worked side by side with them on similar lines, and secular priests also took their part with success. From their episcopal thrones, bishops inspired by the same spirit lent the collaboration of their authority. Some of them were friends, sometimes sons of Dominic. At Brescia there was Friar Guala of Bergamo,[2] at Modena Gulielmo of Piedmont, the former Vice-Chancellor of the Roman Curia;[3] and in the very chair of St Peter reigned, under the name of Gregory IX, the former legate of Lombardy, the guide, counsellor and friend of St Dominic, formerly Cardinal of Ostia, Ugolino dei Conti.

Circumstances had for long been adverse. After the close of Cardinal Ugolino's legation, Lombardy, left to herself, had begun her fratricidal wars again. When Frederick II ventured to put order into the situation with overmuch severity, at one stroke the Lombard League re-formed. In the first two years of the reign of Gregory IX, from 1227, the situation became more tense than ever. The sharp struggle between the Church and the Empire had begun once more.

Dominicans and Friars Minor, however, had brought a new spirit which was too deeply longed for not to penetrate the Italian masses, even in these circumstances. The direct contact with the Gospel which the sons of Francis or Dominic brought with them broke the narrow horizon of immediate interests, the ground of old resentments, of inveterate greed and passions, the spirit of sect and of parochialism, and lifted men's minds to a unanimous and universal plane. The organizers of the mission of 1220–1221 had foreseen precisely what the evangelical preachers would bring—a response to the general aspirations of the Christian masses which the mentality of the élite and the practices of communal life strangely failed to recognize. The ideal of detachment, of mutual love and peace, which the new apostles proposed, while first practising it in their communities, did not consist only of negative precepts—to despise money and luxury, to renounce the conventicles of the sects, or lay aside the violence of wars. It was rather a positive gift to the Saviour, an entering upon the interior life and into mystical union with the poor and crucified Christ. Thus when, after the conclusion of the treaty of San Germano on 23rd July, 1230, a great easing of tension took place throughout Italy, the activities of the apostolic preachers experienced an unheard of expansion and publicity. Pope and emperor, leaving aside their reciprocal causes for complaint, preferred peace to war. The hour seemed to have come to imitate them, abandoning claims and perhaps genuine rights, in order not to continue ruinous and impious struggles. People were now going to begin to become Christians, that is, practise the overlooking of injuries and to forego revenge, to remit debts, to set prisoners free, to preserve conjugal chastity, to respect their neighbours and to be reconciled with their enemies, to profess the universal faith.

An extraordinary atmosphere of penance and devotion was established and in 1233 extended to the whole territory.[4] Men called it the 'alleluia', the 'great devotion'. Sometimes an unknown preacher with not much flesh on him and clad in rags, arrived in the main square of a town. He would blow on his horn. To the children and idlers who rushed up, he would cry out: *Alleluia! Alleluia!* answered the crowd. Then followed direct preaching, authoritative in tone, evangelical in form. More often than not, the mendicant preacher had no need to assemble the people. Scarcely had the news of his approach reached the town than they flocked to see the messenger of peace. They carried him along in procession with flags and music. Sometimes he was brought in triumph on the *carroccio* of the banner, symbol of the power of the city. The square was often too small to contain his audience and they would then erect a huge tribune for him outside the walls, sometimes half way between two towns. The two populations thus met, swelled by the inhabitants of the surrounding villages. A supernatural halo surrounded the new apostle. He was credited with a harvest of miracles, with prophecies, with raising people from the dead. While he was addressing the crowd, knights would form a hedge around his tribune. The people cut off pieces of his garments to have as relics. They gave him for a certain time unheard-of powers—making him arbitrator, legislator, duke and podestà of the cities.

The sermon finished, he took immediate action. His Gospel had nothing Platonic about it and could not remain merely a dead letter. People must change their lives. Banish luxury. Pray. Do good works. At Reggio the crowd helped to build the convent of the Preachers. Everywhere impressive scenes of reconciliation took place between hostile families and between representatives of enemy cities. The city statutes were revised and those articles which were against the Church corrected; all provisions calculated to protect peace, the weak and the faith were inserted. This could not be done without the active help of the élite. For a time they were subdued, carried away more or less sincerely by the intensity of the popular movement. Medieval man was always changeable, even at the height of prosperity and political excitement. After the preacher's visit, the town seemed a different place. Other cities followed the example, for the contagion was irresistible. In 1233, a number of towns of the Romagna, Lombardy and the Marches were simultaneously stirred and convulsed by the *alleluia*. The spiritual upheaval that that represented can be imagined.

Among these religious preachers there were Friars Minor—a Friar Leo of Perego who preached at Piacenza; in particular a Friar Gerard of Modena, who displayed exceptional skill in his correction of the statutes of Modena and Reggio. There were even seculars like the Brother Benedict who made his appearance in Parma. The principal preachers, however, were Dominic's sons. The movement was called 'the devotion of the Friars Preachers'.[5] There was Peter of Verona in Milan; Master Jacopino de Parma in Reggio and Parma; Bartolommeo de Vicenza in Padua; above all, John of Vicenza who, after rousing Bologna in April and May 1233, left for the Marches and produced upheavals no less considerable in Padua, Treviso, Feltre, Bellune, Conigliano, Vicenza, and finally and above all in Verona, until that day of 28th August, 1233 when, on the banks of the Adige to the south of Verona, in Paquara, he assembled the representatives and a part of the population of the Marches—400,000 persons, said a contemporary, who was clearly exaggerating—in a reconciliation scene on a gigantic scale. Here the fierce tyrant Ezzelino de Romano and his mortal enemy, the Marquis Azzo d'Este, were seen to meet face to face, to give each other the kiss of peace.

In July 1233, at the moment when the *alleluia* was nearing its apogee, the Provincial, Friar Esteban of Spain, in an official declaration, called to mind 'the graces granted at the present time to the Preachers of Lombardy and the other provinces'. The effects could be seen, he said, in the Lombard cities,

where more than a hundred thousand men who did not know whether they ought to adhere to the Roman Church or to heresy, were sincerely converted to the Catholic Faith of the Church of Rome, thanks to the sermons of the Friars Preachers. The sincerity was genuine, for these converts now pursued and held in abomination the heretics whom before they had defended. Moreover the majority of the cities of Lombardy and the Marches gave over into the hands of the brethren the management of their affairs and the reform of their statutes, with the power to suppress, add, retrench or modify, as they thought fit. They equally had recourse to them to stop wars actually in progress, to make peace and establish it once more among them, to arrange for the gains of usurers and ill-gotten wealth to be restored, to receive confessions, and, in short, for a number of other good offices which it would take too long to enumerate.[6]

It does not enter into our perspective to analyse the elements of this popular movement—the petty side of the impromptu tribunes; the deceptive character of the public reconciliations; the permanence, on the other hand, in the hearts of the people, of a Christian ideal of purity and brotherhood. On the other hand, it is essential to emphasize the link between this sensational manifestation and the more purely religious work which had preceded it since 1220 and which would survive it. Side by side with the tribune-preacher, whose personality alone appears in the limelight, worked numerous collaborators who are unknown to history. Their religious or legislative work had more depth, maturity and theological and canonical competence than the accounts of the chronicles permit us to envisage. Before the principal figure came on the scene, in case after case the purely evangelical action of mendicant preachers, operating from a convent of Dominicans or Friars Minor in almost every city of the plain of the Po, paved the way for the general religious fervour of 1233. John of Vicenza would not have stirred Padua to the extent he did if Guala had not already pacified it in 1229, and if, until his precious death in 1231, St Antony of Padua, by his virtues and his sermons, had not caused the Gospel to penetrate deeply into these people. The Preachers would not have succeeded in stirring up their 'general devotion' if Dominic had not himself given the impetus to the mission of Lombardy at the side of Cardinal Ugolino.

It was not mere chance, indeed, if the Provincial of the Preachers, in the declaration which has been cited earlier, expressly attributed to Dominic the supernatural success of the activity of his sons. Friar Stefano, it is true, was thinking of the heavenly intercession of the prayers and merits of the saint, whereas we think primarily of the drive and directives of the first Master of the Preachers which were at the root of the success. The great devotion of 1233 effected at least in part the programme assigned by the founder to his order and, even more precisely, to the mission of Lombardy.

There were naturally divergencies between the action of the founder and that of the preachers of the *alleluia*—deviations that were even rather important ones. In 1221 Dominic had left to the legate and his commissioners the diplomatic, political and legislative charge, the responsibility of bringing pressure to bear on the authorities to persuade them to fulfil their task as Christian magistrates. Dominic had never imagined that there would be attributed to him, like John of Vicenza, the exorbitant titles of political arbitrator, podestà and Duke of Verona—he who did not even want an administrative charge in the order to be assigned to anyone who was given the office of preaching. He had no less explicitly refused for his sons as for himself the episcopal authority that Guala was now exercising at Brescia. To set forth the truth by preaching, in the quality of a spiritual man without the authority of rank, to sit in no other tribunal than that of penance, private or public, such was his clear and resolute programme. To this programme the order continued to remain fundamentally faithful. It resisted the desire of the Sovereign Pontiffs to recruit bishops among the Preachers.[7] In 1232 and again in 1234, it confronted the would-be imitators of John of Vicenza with the legislation of the order, the prohibition against any other law-suits than those concerned with the faith,[8] above all, the prohibition of all political activity, even were it that of 'pacifier' or arbitrator.[9] In the face of a formal order from a Pope, however, or in the face of the unanimous wish of a population, it was really necessary to give way in certain particular instances.[10] It is undeniable that, in 1233, the ministry of a certain number of preachers was clearly orientated towards the politico-religious and inquisitorial functions desired by Gregory IX,[11] with all that they comprised, not excluding the stake for heresy.[12]

This fact, nevertheless, did not preclude a fundamental continuity between the origins and the outcome of the mission of Lombardy, between Dominic and the brethren of 1233. It will be understood in these conditions that the memory of Dominic was strictly present in the great *alleluia*—so much present even that the popular movement was to provide the framework and climate of the founder's canonization.

The canonization had not yet taken place, in fact, at this date—at which we have the right to be surprised. St Francis of Assisi had been canonized less than two years after his death (1228), St Antony of Padua a year afterwards (1232). Yet Gregory IX was not unaware of his friend's holiness. Nor had the Preachers forgotten their admiration for their Master. When it is reflected that the head of the order was Jordan of Saxony, the Provincial Friar Stefano, the prior and procurator of Bologna, Friar Ventura di Verona and Friar Rodolfo di Faenza, from whom evidence would soon be obtained, so true and at the same time so moving, on the holiness of their founder, we know this to be so. The reasons for the delay must be sought elsewhere.

For there to be a canonization, it is essential that the universal Church, or at least the main body of some particular Church, be interested. There is, in particular, no canonization without that popular emotion which is stirred up by the supernatural manifestation of miracles and which maintains such manifestation afterwards. In 1221, Dominic and his brethren had not, so far as the crowds were concerned, a notoriety similar to that of St Francis in 1226, or of St Antony in 1231. A cultus, however, had begun in Bologna.[13]

We are told of the numerous faithful who prayed day and night by the tomb, of sick persons who prayed for their cure and claimed to have received it, of wax votive gifts hung around the tomb. A donor offered to enclose the tomb and cover it with silk. Information coming from several sources at once showed that the brethren, far from encouraging this spontaneous cultus, considered it a duty to stifle it.[14] The trouble introduced into a conventual chapel already too small for their community seemed to them less dangerous than the accusation of boasting or love of gain which they feared to incur. Their humble condition as mendicants demanded that they should surely avoid all appearances of pious propaganda, from which less scrupulous religious would draw honour and profit, around their relics.

Gradually a silence about Dominic grew up. The population of a town of students very quickly changes. The holy man was forgotten. The brethren thus obtained peace and quietness thereby; each one of them could devote himself to his studies and his ministry in peace. Certain of them, however, felt in a vague way that this lofty disinterestedness was not far removed from negligence, and that there was some ingratitude towards God in keeping silence about the great example given by his servitor. The reconstruction of the church and the cloister, which were definitely too small, was undertaken after 1228 and completed about 1231.[15] After the original sanctuary of St Nicholas had been pulled down, the tomb, situated it would seem at the entrance to the now demolished choir,[16] would for the future be outside in the open. It remained there away from the eyes of the public, but exposed to the heat and the rain which streamed down upon it, for it was situated below the level of the new church.[17]

This was too much. The brethren who had known Dominic suffered in every fibre of their being. Was it for this that they had, not so long ago, carried their dying father back on their shoulders from Santa Maria dei Monti? It was at least essential to transfer the body to a more decent place. The Provincial of Lombardy and the authorities of the convent of Bologna took the matter in hand.[18] Master Jordan had been absent from Lombardy for some time.[19] This must have been about the end of 1232 or beginning of 1233. The idea of canonization then began to take shape. It probably came directly to the mind of the Preachers, stimulated by a desire to emulate the Minors which had become rather acute. We can imagine this to be the case. The lightning canonization of St Antony of Padua, following on that of St Francis, had recently unduly aroused their *esprit de corps*.[20] Jordan of Saxony, however, insinuates that the idea came from the Pope himself, when he was consulted as to the opportuneness of the translation.[21] The two explanations perhaps complete each other. The consultation at Rome was not necessary—the brethren could very well transfer the body of their father without authorization. Whoever thought then, not without shrewdness, of getting the Pope to intervene in order to disarm the final scruples of the Preachers, could easily guess what response he was going to elicit from Pope Gregory—precisely the one he desired.

Gregory IX, the former legate in Lombardy, reproached the brethren's representatives sternly for their negligence in the matter of the holiness of their founder. 'In him', he declared, 'I met a man who carried out in its fulness the rule of life of the apostles; I do not doubt that he is associated with their glory in heaven.'[22] Then and there, he decided that the translation would not be private, but canonical. This was formally to envisage canonization, the first step towards which he was thus authorizing. The ceremony had been planned for the general chapter at Pentecost (22nd May, 1233) which would gather round the Master of the order in Bologna all the provincials and a large number of the brethren. Gregory IX, who had himself celebrated Dominic's obsequies, could not leave Rome and the government of the Church to go in person to Lombardy. He appointed to replace him at this first great act, the Metropolitan of Bologna, the Archbishop of Ravenna with one or other of his fifteen suffragans.

The idea of the translation was scarcely broached when the brethren in Lombardy became enthusiastic. All opposition had vanished. On the contrary, all the more eagerness was shown, to compensate for the previous negligence. The needs of an absorbing ministry had up to this time prevented the Preachers from taking any trouble over their own history. The majority of them seemed to know nothing at all about the origins of their order. They turned 'in great numbers' to Master Jordan, who had just come back to North Italy, and begged him to relate to them the providential beginnings of the order of Preachers and, above all, to speak to them of Master Dominic, 'their founder and their leader at the same time as their brother'.[23] Jordan was only waiting for this opportunity. He set himself to write. The result of his work has come down to us—the 'Account of the origins of the Order of Preachers', which is still known as the *Libellus*, or 'little book'. The account is solid, sober, full of discretion and of delicate feeling. It makes the personality of Dominic stand out in his action as founder, in the midst of his brethren and of his friends. The marvellous, which so often filled accounts of this kind at the time, is, so to speak, absent; but each of the important stages in the life and work of Dominic appears there in its rightful place.

Jordan had been careful to obtain information from the original brethren whom he met in the course of his unceasing travels. It was time that he collected these facts together. None of the brethren in Lombardy, or scarcely any, had known Dominic for more than about twelve months. Jordan himself had only seen him on two occasions, each time for barely a few days. Now all the brethren would be able to get to know their Master, or discover him anew. They began to pray to him again and to get others to pray to him. Had he not promised to be even more useful to his brethren after his death that while he was alive?

Lombardy's great devotion was beginning to be demonstrated. The Dominican preachers spoke to the crowds of the sanctity of their Master.[24] More than them all, Friar John of Vicenza lent his sonorous voice to promote the cultus of the founder. At Bologna, after a long and painful interdict (1231–1232) which for some time drove the university from the city, the result of a sharp conflict between bishop and laity, the easing of tension had just begun. The religious preacher who was working to establish peace, made of the cultus of Dominic one of his levers with which to raise the minds of the mass and obtain complete conversion and reconciliation.[25] He related the life of the founder, his attitude, his miracles. Even better, he mentioned a revelation he claimed to have received about his Master.[26] In the supernatural aureole which surrounded the preacher like a halo, while the crowds listened to him with passionate attention, people thought they could perceive the mysterious effect of the saint's intercession. Popular piety was unleashed with that sudden violence which characterized the time of the *alleluia*. After 19th April, 1233 and the announcement of the submission to the arbitration of John of Vicenza of the conflict between the Church and the city, the population of Bologna not only discovered in the person of the preacher an envoy of heaven for its salvation and pacification; it began once more to suspect that it had a treasure in the relics of the father of Preachers. This increased its devotion. On 14th May an immense penitential procession gathered the whole city together. On the 16th, while John of Vicenza was preaching, the crowd saw a cross of light above his brow.

Such was the spiritual atmosphere which reigned in the city at the time when the solemn translation of the relics was being prepared.[27] The provincials and their companions arrived about 22nd May, the day of Pentecost, and swelled the community of St Nicholas with their complement. They represented the order in its entirety, from England to the Holy Land, from Spain to Poland and Dacia. The pontifical authorization had long since arrived. The sarcophagus of marble, which had been procured not without difficulty, was already in place.[28] Bologna was preparing for the event with intense excitement. The brethren, however, would have preferred to proceed with the opening of the original tomb more discreetly. The excitement of the population made them anxious to an extent we have difficulty in imagining, for religious ceremonies today no longer arouse comparable passions in the crowd. It was not that the brethren doubted the sanctity of their father, but they were uneasy about the state in which they were going to find the body in the cave which had for so long been exposed to the rain and the fierce heat. If an unbearable odour were to issue from this tomb, no more would be needed to produce a complete change of front in a superstitious crowd and turn the sentiments of the people into contempt, anger, perhaps into violent hatred even to the point of a riot against the Preachers. In the extreme tension of the feeling of the multitude, in the paroxysm of the passion for penance to which the crowd was abandoning itself, no one could measure the danger of such a situation. A disappointment, however unjustified for the crowd, might ruin the ministry of the brethren, perhaps for a long time to come.

It would be no less dangerous to act without the laity knowing. The civil authorities of Bologna suspected the intentions of the brethren, without wholly fathoming them. They feared a removal of the relics and firmly intended to prevent it. Thus they set an armed guard, night and day, around the tomb. In a situation such as this, there was no help left but from God. 'Anxious, pale, the brethren prayed, full of uneasiness.' On the preceding night, Friar Nicholas de Giovinazzo, Provincial of the Roman Province, had tossed and turned on his couch, begging the Lord to bring matters to a satisfactory issue. He need not have been afraid. . . . Friar Ventura had fixed the opening of the tomb for the night of 23rd–24th May, reserving the day of the 24th for the liturgical ceremonies. In this way they would be able to begin the chapter on 25th, the Wednesday after Pentecost, in conformity with the constitutions.[29]

In the middle of this night, then, a group of men assembled in the light of torches. The flame, from time to time, flashed on a breastplate or some weapon. Master Jordan, Friar Guala, Bishop of Bergamo, Stefano, the Provincial, Prior Ventura, John of Vicenza, Rodolfo, Guillaume de Montferrat and other brethren represented the Order of Preachers; the Bishop of Bologna Enrico di Fratta, and some of his clergy, the Church of the place; the podestà, Hubert Visconti di Milano, twenty-four nobles in arms, several of whom had been mounting guard at the tomb on the previous nights, numerous citizens from Bologna and the neighbouring towns, represented the laity, reconciled for the future with their clergy.[30] Friar Rodolfo, in his capacity as procurator, broke with the blow of an iron mallet the hard cement that he had placed there himself twelve years earlier. Nothing had been displaced since the day when, after having kept unceasing watch over the coffin, he had nailed it down with his own hands and sealed it in the grave. He exercised pressure on the slabs of stone with a strong lever. Eventually they moved. The coffin appeared right at the bottom under a few handfuls of earth which had been thrown on to it on the occasion of the burial; there was a small hole in the lid, from which an intense and marvellous fragrance emerged. It overflowed powerfully from the grave, and became of great intensity as soon as the nails were pulled out and the coffin opened. It overwhelmed those present. The brethren, bewildered for a moment, trembled in the whole of their being. A miracle! Heaven had spoken! They laughed and wept at the same time. Clergy and laity threw themselves on the ground and remained prostrate, crying out in praise and thanksgiving to God.

Rationalists as we are, we no longer experience either these terrors, these

surprises or these delirious joys. One must have measured the anguish of the
religious during those last few days to guess at the extent of their exultation.
There was no longer any question of danger. What they saw now was the
divine and therefore irrefutable proof of the sanctity of their Master. It was
the certainty of his speedy enrolment in the calendar of the saints. The
crowd, already moved, would not fail to react as a body and this voice of the
people which is the voice of God, would make itself heard in Rome forthwith. At seven centuries of distance we have to admit that the miracle of the
fragrance was the crucial event which made necessary the move from the
translation—a preparatory and quite hypothetical step—to the canonization.
Without this, neither the goodwill of the Pope, nor the hope of the
'primitive brethren' nor the oratorical successes of John of Vicenza would
have been sufficient to bring about the next step. This alone would transfer
to a whole people and then to the Church as a whole, the conviction of a few.

In our eyes, moreover, the fact is solidly established. This perfume,
different in its nature and its intensity from all known scents, would for long
persist in the grave, as on the hands and objects which had touched the relics
of the saint, and would frequently reappear in the church for more than a
year. It seemed truly supernatural. A fraud could not escape the vigilance of
the people of Bologna and of the brethren, especially of anyone like Friar
Rodolfo.[31]

Inside the wooden coffin, the body of Dominic was now a few bones.
Master Jordan gathered them up with reverence and transferred them to the
coffer which had been prepared. It was locked with a key that was handed
to the Podestà of Bologna. Meanwhile dawn had come. The pontifical legate,
Theodoric, Archbishop of Ravenna, arrived, accompanied by Gulielmo di
Piedmont, Bishop of Modena, and Gauthier of Marvis, Bishop of Tournai.[32]
A large number of clergy formed the prelates' suite. The news of the supernatural perfume had spread over the city like a spark on a powder train. The
crowd arrived, growing denser every minute. They came out from the
parishes in organized procession, bearing lighted tapers. The trumpets
sounded. *Benedictus Jesus Christus* was sung with fervour. The new sanctuary
and the cloister quickly filled and the throng overflowed on to the squares
and streets of the neighbourhood.

The archbishop reopened the coffer to identify the bones and inhale the
supernatural perfume in his turn. With the assistance of the other prelates,
he carried the relics in procession to the new church and placed them in the
marble sarcophagus. Then the Mass began with these words which put the
crowning touch to the Preachers' emotion: 'Receive the joy of your
glory. . . .' Meanwhile, a quiver once more ran through the crowd as they
heard the miracles that had just taken place related. Among others, a
paralytic student, Lawrence the Englishman, recovered the use of his limbs
at the invocation of the name of Dominic and leaped across the sanctuary for

joy.[33] The tide of marvels grew. Popular devotion multiplied the demonstrations of fervour around the new tomb.

A week later, at the close of the chapter, crowds of brethren who had come from the convents of Lombardy met at St Nicholas. Master Jordan asked for the coffin to be opened once more. In the presence of the podestà who brought the key, and of the citizens of Bologna, the Master of the order took the head of Dominic in his hands and showed it to all those present. The provincial at their head, three hundred brothers filed past and kissed the remains of their father with deep feeling.[34]

A few days later a delegation consisting of representatives of the bishop and the clergy, of the podestà and the townsmen, finally of the university of Bologna, arrived in Rome and demanded from the Sovereign Pontiff the opening of St Dominic's cause.[35] On 13th July a pontifical mandate nominated three commissioners for the inquiry in Bologna and indicated that the process of canonization had begun.[36]

The latter proceeded in accordance with the law of the time.[37] The inquiry was made successively in Bologna and in the Midi of France. It opened on the anniversary day of Dominic's death. At Bologna, a promoter, or 'procurator' of the cause had been appointed by the prior and the brethren of St Nicholas, the Preacher Philip of Vercelli.[38] From 6th to 15th August, he presented to the commissioners appointed by Gregory IX—Master Tancred, Archdeacon of Bologna; Friar Thomas, Prior of Santa Maria di Reno; and Friar Palmerio, Canon of Campagnola[39]—the witnesses he had chosen. They gave their evidence at length, sometimes taking an entire day. They are all known to us, for we have often met them at the side of their Master: the prior of St Nicholas, Ventura of Verona; Guillaume de Montferrat; the Prior of Padua, Amizo di Milano; Buonviso of Piacenza; John of Spain or of Navarre; the Procurator of Bologna, Rodolfo; and the Provincial of Lombardy, Stefano; Paul of Venice and Frogier di Penna. Directed to some extent by a questionnaire drawn up by the promoter on the eve of the first hearing, and then added to each day, these depositions have preserved a frank spontaneity which permeates the reports which the notaries have left us. Men connected with government or experienced preachers, the witnesses of Bologna had penetrated deeply into the spirit of the founder. Their informed and sober depositions are of incomparable value and history owes much to them.[40]

Having finished their task in Bologna by the Assumption, the Pope's commissioners, on 19th August, delegated their powers to subcommissioners in Toulouse.[41] The latter, through the intermediary of the prior and of a brother of Prouille, of the prior and a canon of St Antonin of Pamiers, in their turn interrogated a long series of witnesses in the last two centres. The investigation had been prepared from Bologna by the sending of a list of twenty-five questions, twenty-five virtues or traits which, according to the results of the Bologna inquiry, characterized Dominic's sanctity fairly clearly.[42] The witnesses of the Midi, to the number of twenty-five, confined themselves generally to confirming the terms of this list. This was clearly the case with the some three hundred supplementary witnesses who confirmed the depositions as a whole by adding their signature. Moreover, the memories that were evoked after twenty or twenty-five years were beginning to become blurred. This evidence, however, had its value—that of a witness like Guillaume II Peyronnet, Abbot of St Paul of Narbonne, from its grave and personal tone, or, more humble but none the less valuable, those of Guillaumette the wife of Elie Martin, and of Bécède, the nun of Sainte Croix.[43] They are known to us from the report which the sub-commissioners sent to their superiors in Bologna.

To all these documents, duly authenticated and transmitted to Rome, there was added a report of the miracles attributed to St Dominic, which was put together in Bologna in the second part of the year. Certain of these miracles went back to his lifetime; others dated from the translation.[44] The file thus constituted enabled judgements to be passed on the individual incidents. The process took place in the first half of 1234.

In July of that same year, Gregory IX gave his final verdict in a consistory held at Rieti. The account of the miracles which were considered as authentic was solemnly read, in the presence of the Pope and of his cardinals.[45] The Pope then proclaimed the sanctity of the founder, notified his insertion in the calendar of the saints, and fixed on 5th August, one day before the anniversary of his death, the date of celebration of the feast.[46] The Chancellery immediately issued an encyclical bull.[47] Copies of it were sent to the principal houses of the order.[48] Friar Raymond of Peñafort and Friar Godefroid, present at the Curia, respectively announced the news to Jordan of Saxony and to the convent of Strasbourg where Jordan happened to have just arrived. From St Agnes of Bologna, Diana in her turn let Jordan know. Clearly the news was circulating speedily on all sides. It arrived at the right time, for the feast of the new saint could be celebrated from its first year in the greater part of the order.[49] Shortly afterwards Jordan issued an encyclical to the order, in which he recounted the translation which was the source of the great event.[50]

The bull of Gregory IX is disappointing at a first reading. Drawn up in an oratorical style, with frequent Biblical allegories, it only takes on a personal and concrete turn in the final paragraphs in which the Pope recalls the deep intimacy which bound him to the Preacher while he himself was fulfilling a less exalted charge, the support and edification he had found in the charm of his friendship. However, when one takes up the text, one can discover in it, under the allegory drawn from Zachary,[51] a vast historical fresco. The Head of the Church, turning his eyes towards the vicissitudes of the evangelization of the world, saw it pass through four stages, under four successive teams of apostles who restored the Church's forward march as soon as it began to go astray or fail. First came the converting kings and martyrs; then St Benedict with his monks; St Bernard with the order of Cîteaux and of Flora; finally, at the eleventh hour, when the day was already declining towards evening, the more lightly-armed legions of the Preachers and the Minors, at the head of whom Dominic walked with St Francis. We are accustomed to this vision of the gradual growth of Christian development in which the advent of the mendicant orders constitutes one of the decisive turning-points. In 1206, in 1215, even in 1221 at the death of St Dominic,[52] no one then had a clear idea of it. The all-important event of the period still remained, in the eyes of the popes as in those of the simple faithful, the coming of the Cistercians. In 1234, on the other hand, the Church had become aware, at the top as also among the people, of the decisive importance of the apostolic orders, and of the historical dimensions of the Order of Preachers.

What constituted its importance was the 'rule of the apostles', which Dominic, on the evidence of Gregory IX, had succeeded in inscribing in his religious society in its entirety, after having written it in the book of his life. At the beginning of the century, in Osma, he had discovered no more than a part of it, that of the community of life and of canonical prayer. In 1206 he had conceived it in its entirety and, through it, had soon reached the heights of sanctity, that is, of love of God and his neighbour. 'A man of the Gospel, following the traces of his Saviour', of whom he spoke to all who were willing to listen, without interrupting the conversation he was holding with him in his heart, he truly pursued in the measure of his capacity the preaching of Jesus Christ upon earth. In his eyes, however, it was not enough to bring about this evangelical attitude in himself. He wanted to give it a permanent place in the institutions of the Church, under the form which it seemed to him the need of souls demanded at the time. There began the difficulty, since, for a long time now, this form of apostolic life, compromised by too many errors or schisms, seemed to be working against the supernatural community of life of Christians. Dominic needed greater foresight, energy and sanctity for carrying out the second part of his task. The bull of 3rd July, 1234 is the proof of his success. By this time the Church was aware of the privileged place he occupied in the course of her own history and this fact justified his canonization.

This indeed is the praise that should be freely given to Dominic. His work in the Church is not only the most extensive document we have on him, it is his 'letter of recommendation', his sanctity, his glory. For Dominic is a man of the Church and is defined by his work and place in the Church's history. It is remarkable that the first lines of his biography evoke the figure of a prelate, Diego, Bishop of Osma, in whose orbit he would reach maturity, and that his first steps as a scholar, while he was preparing himself for the clerical state, were made under the tutelage of an archdeacon uncle. In the future, everything in him was of the Church: his costume, his common life, his liturgical prayer, his preoccupations, his joys. He was the friend of priests and religious, and only completely expanded in their company. Thus he gave them the best of his heart, loved to preach to them or to tell them his secrets. If it was necessary to correct their faults, he wanted his brethren to do so with humility, taking good care not to 'speak against heaven', i.e. publicly to belittle the authorities of the Church, in order not to scandalize the clergy. He was completely at ease in canon law and knew how to make use of the system of papal bulls at the proper moment.

Thus the first glance he gave at the vast world was the true glance of a priest, that of a man who believes himself responsible for the salvation of others at the same time as for his own and feels like a wound in his own flesh all the blows that he sees falling on the body of the Church. This suffering made him clearsighted and enlarged his horizon to the utmost limits. By the time he had reached middle age, he had a complete vision of the Church, which went beyond the frontiers of Europe, the frontiers of Christendom. Similarly his gaze embraced in its tender concern the whole of Christian geography, in its depths it included the entire social edifice of the Church. In depth as in width he discerned the weaknesses and what was lacking, and sought the means to apply a remedy. He did this primarily by the gift of his own person and then by that of an institution which was to provide a solution for the greatest of these crises, that of the ministry of souls and preaching, whose position he permanently modified in Christian society and in the hierarchy.

Was it his evangelism which made him discover what was lacking in the Church and the remedy for it? Was it his love of the Church which made him appreciative of the renewal of life which apostolic evangelism could bring? It was both at the same time. St Francis looked at the Gospel as a layman, discovering in it an overwhelming emotion, the appeal that Jesus Christ addresses to every man who comes into this world. Dominic looked at it as a priest. In his eyes the programme was one and the same, the inspiration both clerical and evangelical. He knew that he was united in will with the apostles, with the primitive community of the Twelve, and sought by what means he could make response in this present reign of Pope Innocent or Pope Honorius to the watchword that he felt was addressed to himself as much as to all the clergy of his time—'Go, teach all nations. . . .' We should be gravely mistaken if in fact we thought that Dominic's love for the Church was only that of a man for the institution in which he was born, which had nourished and fashioned him and invested him with its joy. When he suffered from the spirit of sect and of schism, from the original anti-clericalism of the Waldenses or Catharists on every side, it was not only because he saw the hierarchic society to which he had given his life despised. It was because a slur was being cast on the unanimous community which, by the disposition of Christ, 'one should have as mother if one wants to have God as father', an extension down to his own time of the primitive community in which they had only one heart and one soul, and where all was in common among believers, in the radiance of the preaching and prayer of the apostles.

Thus the deepest source of his inspiration was not his love of the Church, or even his evangelism, but, as was the case for the apostles, his love of Christ Jesus. There are many forms of evangelism as there are many snares in it. Among his contemporaries many were satisfied with an evangelism in attitude, on the level of the imagination: bare feet, material mendicancy, an austere leanness of body, a negative separation which condemned en bloc the whole world, beginning with the clerical hierarchy. Dominic, passing over details which depended on an exegesis which is today partially out of date, discovered the permanent values of this evangelism, the abandonment to Providence, the attachment to revelation and above all the imitation of love for the Saviour.

This was the root of his sanctity. What did he do in fact along the road when he remained behind his companions 'to meditate on his Saviour;'[53] when he spent long nights in adoration, in contemplation, in intercession before the Crucified to whom he united himself by his cruel penances; when he offered with an ardour which he loved to excite also among his brethren the sacrifice of liturgical praise or the little office of the Blessed Virgin;[54] when, above all, he offered, frequently moved to tears, the sacrifice of the Redeemer, whose Body he then received as nourishment and whose Blood as drink? What did he do if it were not to turn towards God 'through Jesus Christ our Lord'? When day came and he went in quest of the sinners for whom he had prayed with such intensity in the night that he cried out, wounding his bare feet on the stones of the road, begging his bread as he went, and taking care to carry nothing with him but the Gospel of St Matthew or the Epistles of St Paul, what did he do in preaching the kingdom of God, abandonment to Providence, conversion and mutual love, but unite himself to God in accordance with the ways of the Gospel by identification with Christ, the first Preacher? Jesus fashioned St Dominic by giving him a particularly touching aspect of his features to reproduce that of the Master of Galilee saving men by enlightening them with the light of truth before redeeming them with his crucifixion.

Because it was divine action, it neither deformed nor limited the one whom it influenced, but on the contrary raised his personality to its highest point. The cult of truth sets free and purifies. The first trait of Dominic's sanctity is that he is very completely himself. Jordan has emphasized the simplicity of his bearing 'which made him dear to all'.[55] The great purity of his morals was the basis of this simplicity. He could give himself wholly to all, to the ministry of women as to that of men, because the delicacy of his chastity had set him completely free in such matters. His mortification, his poverty, his humility had similarly set him free. He could make himself all things to all men and, when he transmitted the revelation of the Master, be merely an organ of the Holy Spirit.

He had a natural liking for doctrine. As a priest, he benefited by the intellectual movement which for a century past had been developing in the Church. If he had not already been won to theological learning during his own studies, he would certainly have become so in the course of his interminable contests with the heterodox. The rigidity of the methods of interpreting the Bible which theology brought into focus at this time, seemed to him indispensable. He realized what they had to offer and very soon devoted himself to procuring the benefit of them for his sons, under their most effective form, that which could be acquired at the university of Paris; then he sought to procure this advantage for others through his sons. It is in this sense that his institution would renew not merely preaching in the Church, but the teaching of theology and its diffusion at all the stages of Christian society.

It is certain that he did not search for the truth solely to direct his life in a practical way or to learn to instruct others, but primarily to contemplate it in itself. The clear descriptions he gave of his interior life are indeed less eloquent than the extent of his meditation. The truth he learnt and contemplated was the privileged means of discovering God and uniting himself to him. His contemplation, however, could not remain shut up within itself. It had to find expression.

Undeniably, he was born to be a Preacher. He had the temperament for it. Simple, without inhibitions, generous, heroic, he naturally gave the best of himself. Moreover he had that liveliness of imagination that enabled him to see without difficulty the magnitude of what he was describing, whether deserving of praise or blame, and to give his words a spontaneous lyricism, a dramatic influence which made him a great orator. If he made his hearers weep, it was because he also was deeply moved, because he was convinced, and because he was speaking of that to which he had given his life. Then again it was because he loved the men to whom he was preaching.

With the love of his neighbour, we come to the deep springs of his temperament. It was a supernatural love, no doubt, but grafted on a spontaneous feeling, an inclination of the heart. There are spiritual people who yet remain self-centred and take others into their embrace only in a general love, a reflection of the love Christ bears them. Dominic loved them for themselves through natural impulse. He thought of them before he knew them, he sought them out, their wretchedness or their failures made him suffer too. His countenance, ordinarily serene, was troubled as soon as he discovered such wretchedness or imagined it. It was the sign of a sensitivity all the more easy to move, in that it retained its freshness, being in some sort kept in reserve by his silence, the austerity of his penance and the recollection arising from his contemplation.

This love, however, was not sentimental. How magnificent is Dominic's character—a man for whom love was primarily a matter of willing. He willed the salvation of those whom he loved, of all those whom he met. Their temporal salvation he willed too, independently of all religious perspective, as at times when he offered himself for sale to buy back a captive, when he obtained some cure or the removal of some great danger. But he could not forget that the principal peril of men on earth is that of their destiny, on the brink of eternity: the peril of error which makes the heart and practice of life go astray, far from true happiness; the peril of the will which fails and does not achieve what the spirit desires. To remove these perils from his neighbour, Dominic was ready for any sacrifice. If he could not convince by words, he would at least convince by deeds. If he could not move them by his acts, he would reach souls by the grace of God, the gift of which he sought by uniting himself to the Cross of Christ in extreme penance, practising mortification in drinking, eating and lying down to sleep, the flagellations of the night and the unending vigils of intercession. The Holy Spirit must surely speak more effectively through his lips when he had succeeded in purifying, by his reparation, what still formed an obstacle in him to the divine influence. Dominic, moreover, loved sufficiently to know how to be exacting. He set forth the truth which calls for and claims obedience. He gave the counsels which urge obedience. He commanded as soon as he had authority.

His strong-mindedness on this point was unparalleled. He never, or scarcely ever, went back on a decision taken after ripe reflection. Perhaps it was on that account that he took a long time to determine his plans, to take the decisions which seemed to be the right ones, to proceed to action. But what vigour, then, in the realization! Whether he was dealing with individuals or institutions, he drove them to the limits of their possibilities. No relaxation on this point. His love was too great to be satisfied with mediocrity. He lifted above themselves those who came to him and confided in him. This was not attachment to God, to the Church, or to his own ideas, but primarily a love of those whom he was urging in this way. His gentleness, which was very real, did not consist in his eyes in the watering down of an ideal which Christ had placed too high when he said, 'Be perfect as the heavenly Father is perfect'; it was no act of mercy to diminish or obscure that ideal. He demanded of others what he willed for himself, to go beyond the immediate task at every moment by our aspirations and our responsiveness, because God is calling us and urging us ever higher than the task of the moment. He manifested his compassion in 'consoling', that is, in renewing the strength of those whom he guided, through his preaching, his direction and the tender affection with which he infused his gestures and his words.

Thus he had a keen sense of the government of men. He reserved to himself the fulness of authority as soon as it was a question of execution: the right to give commands which claimed a total obedience, to dispense from a thing as he understood it, to confirm all subordinate authority, to receive personally the profession of all his religious. The community of life and, in a certain sense, the democratic inspiration of his order in no wise diminished the fulness of his authority in the realization of the common task. But for determining this task, fixing the principles and even its details, he relied on the community.

This instinctive trust was a complementary aspect of his love of men. One naturally judges others after one's own intimate experience. His fundamental goodwill, his purity, his generosity, were at the root of his kindliness. Very reserved in childhood and youth, he opened his heart more freely as his life advanced, to his brethren, to his friends, even to his adversaries. Detachment, which had become second nature, was no longer an obstacle to the spontaneity of his abandonment. His brethren preserved of him the memory of a countenance lighted up with kindness and 'with a great joy',[56] the echo of the serene poise of his interior self and his confident affection. Neither the overwork of the ministry, nor the weight of government and of disappointments, nor the general cares of the Church which he shared on his own plane, could efface this expression of joy, 'which easily won him the affection of all'.[57] He reserved for the night his tears of penance over the sinful world, but the day brought him back in the midst of his brethren, full of joy. Illness itself could not alter his smile.

His generosity, his devotedness, his sensitivity, that persistent joy which radiated over his face, producing the light over his eyes and brow that Sister Cecilia noticed, his fraternal gaiety, to use Jordan's expression, the fruit of a pure and loving soul, made him loved and greatly loved. He was loved from Osma days in the cloister; during the twelve years in the Narbonensis, by those who came in contact with him; then by his brethren, his familiars, the innumerable people who owed him debts of gratitude, in Rome and in Bologna. It was an affection mingled with trust, with gratitude, with tenderness, with veneration, finally with that something undefinably touching which the presence of a personality favoured by God, absolutely simple and sincere and wholly given, excites in the human heart. Of this tender veneration, the depositions of 1233 are not the only document. A prayer like the responsory *O spem miram* . . . which the Preachers still continue to sing is an effort to express this. No one, however, has better expressed it than the saint's successor, Jordan of Saxony, well fitted to understand him because he was himself a very great Preacher and a holy religious, in the prayer he composed after writing his *Libellus*, at the time of the canonization.[58] At the same time this composition recalls one after the other the great events of his life, which will throw upon his countenance a series of fleeting lights, and will awaken in our hearts the memory of what St Dominic was, and attract us to him.

Most holy priest of God, glorious confessor, eminent preacher, blessed Dominic, chosen man of the Lord, in your lifetime you were among all others the subject of God's kindness and chosen favour on account of your life, made glorious through its miracles and doctrine, and now we rejoice to have you as our special intercessor with the Lord God. It is to you, whom I venerate above all the saints, all the elect of God, it is to you that I cry from the depths of this vale of wretchedness. Come to the help, O best of fathers, come to the help, I beg of you, O merciful one, of my sinful soul, wholly lacking in graces and virtues, weighed down with wretchedness, wrapped in the bonds of vice and of sin. Help it in its distress and its misfortune. . . .

Through the power of your merits and the effectiveness of your good prayers, deign to give it life and health and to fill it to the brim with abundance of your blessings. I know, indeed I am certain, that you can do so. I have confidence that in your great charity you will do so. I hope from the deep familiar friendship that you have always had with Jesus Christ, your beloved chosen among a thousand, that he will not refuse you this and that you will obtain from your Lord and your friend all you please. Loved in such a way, could he refuse anything to him whom he loves ?

For it is you who, in the flower of your youth, vowed your virginity to the beauty of the spouse of virgins.

You who consecrated your soul, clad in the whiteness of holy baptism and enriched with the Holy Spirit, to the most chaste lover of virgins.

Who offered your body as a living sacrifice, holy and pleasing to God.

Who, fashioned by God's discipline and guidance, gave yourself wholly to him.

Who, early instructed in regular discipline, formed in your heart paths of ascent to God.

Who, rising from strength to strength, progressed unremittingly from what was good to what was better.

Who, once entered on the path of perfection, abandoned all and naked followed the naked Christ, preferring to amass treasures in heaven.

Who, with even greater effort, renounced yourself, and carrying your cross bravely, applied yourself to following the traces of the only true guide, our Redeemer.

You who, inflamed with the zeal of God and with a supernatural ardour, because of your boundless charity and the fervour of a vehement spirit, consecrated yourself wholly by the vow of perpetual poverty to apostolic observance and evangelical preaching and, for this great work, through a high inspiration of Providence, instituted the order of Friars Preachers.

You who, throughout the universe, made the glorious light of your merits and example shine upon God's holy Church.

Who, delivered from the prison of the flesh, rose up to the court of heaven.

Who, finally, in the vesture of your first garment of innocence, have won a place near to our Lord, there to be our advocate.

O come then to my help, I beg of you, come to the help of all those who are dear to me. You who so ardently desired the salvation of the human race, come to the help of clergy and people, of virgins and devout women. After the Blessed Virgin, our Queen, you are my dear hope, my comfort, my special refuge. Look kindly upon me and come to my help. It is with you alone that I take refuge; before you alone that I still dare to present myself; I prostrate myself at your feet and, a suppliant, I invoke you, my patron. I implore you, I recommend myself to you, wholly abandoned as I am. Deign to receive me with kindness, to guard me, to protect me, to help me, and to make me find again, through your intercession, that grace of God, the object of my desires. Through you may mercy be shown to me; may I deserve to obtain the remedy for the ills of the present life and the salvation of my soul for the life to come.

Yes, best of Masters, let it be thus I beg of you, illustrious guide, our foster-father, blessed Dominic. I pray you assist us in all our needs—be for us truly a Dominic, vigilant guardian of the Lord's flock. Guard us always and do not cease to govern those who have been entrusted to you. Make us pure and, when we are purified, recommend us to God. Then, after this exile, present us again with joy to the Lord of blessing, to your beloved, to the all-powerful Son of God, Jesus Christ, our Saviour, to whom alone belong honour, praise, glory, in company with the glorious Virgin Mary and of the whole court of the citizens of heaven, throughout the centuries to come and for all eternity.

APPENDICES

EXCAVATIONS, CONSTRUCTIONS AND RESTORATIONS

IN CALERUEGA (1952–1955)

THE excavations undertaken in 1952–1955 into the erection of buildings around four sides of the *torreon* went down to 4 and 5 yards in depth. Not many new facts were discovered. Doubtless the *torreón* was always a separate building (cf. *supra* ch. 1, n. 34) as was the custom for 'keeps' in the tenth and eleventh centuries (cf. *supra*, ch. 1, n. 41). It is possible, however, that earlier buildings have disappeared without leaving any trace because their foundations were shallow, as is the case for the *torreón* (Carro, *Caleruega* II, 47).

The demolitions carried out in 1952, on the other hand, have revealed several interesting facts about the sisters' building. The rough plaster on the façade of the building known as the vicariate along one side of the village square concealed a large gothic doorway towards the far left. This doorway is identical in its arched form and dimensions with the nuns' choir, a former church built by Alfonso the Wise in 1266 (Rodrigo, 331). A small gothic double window exists below the roof, slightly to the left of the gothic doorway. On the wall which terminates the building to the right of the façade, beneath the gable, two gothic double windows have been found, of which one has been retained. These windows prove by their position that the first storey of the vicariate went right up to the top of the house. There were no internal partition walls. Thus it formed a large room 46 yards long, covered by the roof itself, on which in 1952 remains of panelling could still be seen (Carro, *Caleruega*, I, 7 and also Pelaez, 81). No trace of any other windows besides the two large ones of the gable and the small one to the left of the door is left in the façade. It is possible windows might be found on the opposite façade which looks on to the sisters' cloister. This does not appear to have been investigated.

At right angles to the vicariate, and erected adjacent to it, the 'palace' likewise consists of a high gothic room of about 54 yards, lighted on the side which looks out on the *torreón* by seven fine gothic windows. An eighth window like the others, and also like that found at the extremity of the vicariate, provides daylight for the western end of the room. Some remains of doors between the vicariate and the palace, and between the vicariate and the sisters' cloister, have been found. To the left of the eighth window, a third room goes off at right angles to the palace. It is known as the novitiate. A large gothic doorway leads from the palace to this room, extending considerably above the storey which at present cuts the height of the novitiate into two. The division into two storeys is thus later than this thirteenth-century doorway. Again, it must have been a very lofty room.

The orientation of the vicariate is south-north; that of the palace, east-west; of the novitiate north-south. These three buildings form, with the sisters' choir, i.e.

the chapel of Alfonso the Wise, a perfect square. A cloister was built inside this square in the fourteenth and fifteenth centuries. The part which is continuous with the sisters' choir on the fourth side was reconstructed in the seventeenth century, the date at which a monumental portress's lodge was erected between the vicariate and the choir. To what date should any of the three large rooms or part of this be assigned? In view of the fine workmanship of the doors and gothic windows, they can only belong to the thirteenth century. As to the particular part or parts of that century, several dates are possible.

Carro (*Caleruega*, II, 52) would like to identify the vicariate with the hospice mentioned in two documents of 1237 and 1248—Martínez, nos. II and CCXVII. The hospice was explicitly called the hospice of the chapel of St Dominic; it was situated next to it. Now the chapel was constructed by the people of Caleruega shortly after the saint's canonization (July, 1234) on the site occupied by the high altar of the basilica, i.e. 50 yards from the vicariate. Identification of hospice and vicariate is thus possible from the point of view of site. It does not seem so from the point of view of the building itself, for the following reason. After 1234 the numbers of pilgrims necessitated the erection of the hospice, particularly for providing shelter for the poor and sick. It was obviously built through the generosity of the people of the neighbourhood and of the more wealthy pilgrims. The ownership and administration of the chapel and hospice belonged to the diocese, i.e. to the bishop and his chapter (Martínez, no. CCXVII). They took care to consolidate the foundation by purchasing land and property with the alms received. Thus in 1248 they purchased from Doña Urraca García (d'Aza) one of her Caleruega estates for the maintenance of the church, the hospice and those who served it (Martínez, no. CCXVII). It may be questioned whether the gifts made would have also allowed them to erect such a fine building as that of the vicariate, particularly if the palace and novitiate are added to the building, as Carro rightly suggests. The principal argument, however, against identification of the hospice with the vicariate is the close analogy of the latter's gothic doorway with that of the conventual church of 1266. These two buildings must be contemporary.

The name of 'palace' given to the second room suggests a feudal construction prior to 1266. Is this name, however, really old? It is only in the modern period that it is seen to appear in an account of the identification of the buildings made in 1735 by a local architect (Carro, *Caleruega*, II, 44; on this account see Pelaez 73, n. 1). The medieval documents do not mention it. It is perhaps an anachronism to imagine the construction of a 'palace' in Caleruega in the thirteenth century, *a fortiori* in the twelfth century. Along these lines anything might be imagined— for instance, that in the middle of the thirteenth century, Don Fernando García, who held the overlordship of Caleruega now become hereditary, had these gothic buildings constructed before pledging them to the Order of Santiago for 20,000 maravédis, as well as Caleruega and all his estates situated to the north of the Duero (Martínez, no. CCXIX). Sheer hypothesis. The following facts make such a supposition impossible.

In the course of the thirteenth century, if one relies on the documents, a single phase of construction in Caleruega is attested, prepared for by large transfers of property—the period inaugurated in 1266, when Alfonso the Wise had the sisters' convent built. One or other of the rooms was certainly built at this date and, in particular, the church. Now the relationship between the doors of the vicariate and the church and between the windows of the palace and those of the vicariate, the very perfection of the square which the three rooms form with the church, seem to prove that the whole set of buildings was constructed at the same time by the King of Castile. The disposition of the rooms itself confirms these indications. It will be noticed in fact that the room of the first storey of the vicariate, with the light entering at the end, is very suitable for the installation of a dormitory of regular form. A staircase starting from the left end could lead directly into the choir of the church, according to the customary arrangement of monastic houses in the West. This staircase would probably disappear in the seventeenth century when the monumental doorway was constructed. The palace and the room at right angles are in turn suited for a refectory and a chapter room. It thus seems probable to us that what are named vicariate, palace and novitiate were built at the same time as the choir to serve as buildings of regular life for the royal convent of Caleruega from 1266 onwards.

In conclusion, a few indications collected on the site and completed by the kindness of P. Carro, are given on the transformations which these venerable remains have undergone. The *torreón* has been topped with battlements—an unfortunate innovation. Battlements are not suitable for a keep of the first feudal age such as the *torreón* (cf. *supra* ch. 1, n. 41). The wooden gallery it possessed excluded battlements whose place it took. No trace of plaster or of any coat of paint was there to justify the supposition that the masonry on the inside of the *torreón* was hidden in Saint Dominic's time; it is therefore a pity that the virile and military character of these interior walls should have been weakened by covering them with plaster, a process which has been begun. The rather crude gothic window which stood over the entrance doorway has been removed and replaced by a semi-circular arch. The base of the *torreón*, uncovered to the extent of nearly 2 yards in depth by the levelling of the *patio*, has been surrounded by a flight of three steep stone steps which consolidates it and protects the foundations against damp. Finally the façade has been decorated with the arms of the Guzmán and the Aza, though under rather late forms. Although indeed there are in this way some regrets to express on these transformations from the point of view of history (the poets for their part will regret the storks of the *torreón*, permanently dislodged by the battlements), it must be added that the new keep is impressive and satisfactorily evokes the origins of Caleruega and of St Dominic.

Five or six yards to the north of the *torröen* the 'cave of the ancestress' was still in its primitive state in 1952. It was a subterranean cave 2 yards by 7 yards dug out of the earth at a depth of 5 yards. Castilian clay formed the floor, roof, the walls at either end, the stairway of about thirty steps by which one went down into it. Two semi-circular arches of stone, 28 inches in width, supported on small lateral walls, strengthened the roof (a third, median arch seems to have disappeared). To consolidate the roof which was now to be under the foundations of one of the new buildings, it has been covered with bricks. The two extremities have been walled up. The rest of the cave is intact at the moment but the cellar has been transformed into a chapel, unfortunately by covering the floor, walls, staircase and altar with marble, and furnishing it pretentiously. Scarcely anything now remains of this witness to the past, which it is, moreover, impossible to date.

The gothic room on the first floor of the vicariate, where some good cells have been established, has not been reconstructed. The rediscovered gothic doorway has, however, been given a place of honour and one of the two windows of the gable. In 1956 there was still a question of re-establishing the seven gothic windows of the palace. In this way one of the finest vestiges of the thirteenth century in Caleruega would be reconstructed.

By constructing three detached buildings, the torreón has been enclosed within a large courtyard and a convent built of more than a hundred cells. The buildings are not without distinction. So far they are not very Dominican for they do not possess a choir, only an oratory; this would be more suitable for Loyola than for Caleruega. It is possible that it is intended to install the choir in the handsome restored gothic room of the palace. If that proves to be so, St Dominic will not fail often to return among his brethren of Caleruega and to be moved to the shedding of tears, as formerly, on hearing their psalmody. There is no longer any question of restoring the room of the 'palace' with its seven gothic windows, which is, however, one of the finest survivals of the thirteenth century in Caleruega. A rectangular choir and three blocks of buildings, however, have been constructed opposite, enclosing the torreón in the centre of a square courtyard. The whole provides a convent of about a hundred rooms without any character, except perhaps a certain austerity.

THE FAMILY OF ST DOMINIC

THE Castilian preacher Rodrigo de Cerrato who visited Caleruega shortly after 1270 gave the following description of St Dominic's father—*vir venerabilis et dives in populo suo* (Rodrigo, no. 2), 'honourable and rich among the people of his village'. Taking into account the superlative which seems indicated by the expression 'among the people of his village', should the translation be 'the rich man of his village' or *ricohombre* of his village? The characteristic indicated by the first translation, which is a probable one, does not exclude that expressed by the other; on the contrary it implies it. At this period the lord of a place was the principal landowner in it. In any event the question of the *rica hombria* or nobility of St Dominic's father and of his relations with the noble families of Caleruega especially the Aza of Villamayor and, secondly, the Guzmán (cf. *supra*, p. 111), must be examined.

A Spanish tradition, however, affirms that Felix, St Dominic's father, was a Guzmán and his mother, Jane, a d'Aza. This tradition is not, as has often been said, an invention of the sixteenth century, a period of unparalleled greatness in Spain in which the historiography of the great institutions, churches, orders, royalty and nobility sought titles everywhere and to this end left no stone unturned without sufficient precautions. The tradition doubtless spread with printing from the sixteenth century onwards;[1] but it is found in the very middle of the fifteenth century,[2] and even in the first decades of that century, when Pedro de Guzmán, majordomo of Luis de Guzmán, Grand Master of the military order of Calatrava (1407–1414 to 1443), by order of his superior made a pilgrimage to Bologna to the tomb of St Dominic, a member of their family.[3] It is believed to go even further back still.[4] These first traces (first so far as our present information is concerned) do not give this information as a discovery, but as a fact already known. Nothing, indeed, justifies the supposition that it sprang from the documents of the archives of Caleruega, on which modern and contemporary historians base themselves.

For the deeds of foundation of the convent of the Sisters of Caleruega from 1266 to 1272 lend a third notable point of support to the Spanish tradition. The fact that more than twenty great lords abandoned their rights in honour of St Dominic is not in itself a proof of any relationship. They did so at the request of the king and under his obvious pressure.[5] The terms which some of them used should, however, be carefully considered. The majority use a succinct formula, completely stereotyped, which conceals the personal circumstances. They abandon only a limited advantage— their *divisa*, sign of the right of *behetria* or *naturaleza*. They give this to the king, for the monastery the king is founding, in conformity with the privilege established for the sisters.[6] Two of them, however, use a different formula, carefully circumstantial. It was doubtless composed by the first to use it in 1266, don Juan Pérez, son of don Pedro Nuñez de Guzmán and doña Urraca García de Villamayor;[7] shortly afterwards it served Diego García, son of don Garcí Fernández de Villamayor and doña Mayor Arrias, brother of doña Urraca García.[8] The same formula was perhaps found in one or other of the six charters of donation[9], now no longer extant, of don Juan García de Villamayor, brother of Diego García; then in the donation of 1271 of don Gil Gómez, lord of Roa, Aza, Iscar, etc., their cousin.[10] These four *ricos-hombres* gave much more than a right of *divisa*. They enumerate hereditary property, vassals and all the other rights they possess, in whatever manner they hold them or can hold them—in Caleruega for the first three, in Iscar for the fourth. Each one then sets forth the motive of his donation—'for the honour of God and of Saint Mary, and for the *naturaleza* and special devotion they Caleruega renounce their rights of *behetria* it is precisely this feudal meaning which is intended.

In itself the word designates a quality which derives from one's birth. In modern Spanish its meanings are manifold.[11] In the thirteenth century the most widespread meaning in legal documents is connected with *behetria*. *Naturaleza* is that quality of birth which gives to all the members of a certain lineage the right to be chosen as lord of a village. There is no doubt that in the charters by which the *diviseros* of Caleruega renounce their rights of *behetria* it is precisely this feudal meaning which is intended.

The feudal 'connaturality' that the *ricos-hombres* thus affirm with St Dominic can come from two sources: he is their 'co-natural' feudally either as member of the village or as member of the lineage of *behetria*. Several data seem to exclude the first term of the alternative. The charters do not mention the question of the village. Don Gil Gómez, lord of Roa, moreover, when he drew up his charter and spoke of *naturaleza* had no longer any rights in the village; he had abandoned them more than a year earlier.[12] Don Juan García, finally, drawing attention to his *gran naturaleza*,[13] could not refer to a quality connected with the village: such a quality has no potentiality for being either more or less great. Thus the other alternative is the only one possible. The natural quality which St Dominic shares with the lords of Caleruega is the community of lineage, the relationship of blood.[14]

If that is really the case, the evidence provided by the charters of the thirteenth century goes hand in hand with the Spanish tradition, the trace of which we have been able to follow, by working backwards, to the fourteenth century. Even if it could be established that the two series of documents are not independent and that the Spanish tradition has issued from a particular interpretation of the *naturaleza* of the charters, it would remain that at a time so close to their drawing up, when the technical terms of the overlordship of *behetria* were in current use, there was no hesitation in interpreting the term *naturaleza* by blood relationship. Nothing, however, as we have said, justifies us in supposing such an interdependence between the two series of sources. In these conditions the medieval tradition relative to St Dominic's family finds support in the documents of the archives of 1266, as in the *dives* of Rodrigo de Cerrato, and on this count is genuinely probable.

It details in turn the information given in the charters. If we had knowledge of these documents only, it would be impossible to know whether Dominic's father were of the lineage of Aza or not and whether the relationship that the Pérez de

Guzmán affirmed in regard to him in 1266 did not come to them solely from their mother, who was an Aza. The tradition, however, is formal: the relationship of the Guzmán was direct and through the paternal line. Thus the different branches of the Guzmán, who in 1266 appeared to be linked with Caleruega, had already been united about the end of the twelfth century with the Aza family, lords of *behetria* of Caleruega, through the marriage of St Dominic's parents.

Though probable, the Guzmán and Aza lineage of St Dominic, established by the finding of a tradition which cannot be followed beyond the fifteenth century, and by two words the interpretation of which is not categorical, is not however proved beyond question. Other explanations, though improbable, remain possible.[15] That put forward here raises certain difficulties. Neither Jane nor Felix appear in the contemporary Aza or Guzmán documents, either under the Christian name or in the full form. The fact is the more surprising in the case of Felix, for a considerable number of Guzmán signed the charters of Alfonso VIII, as the *ricos-hombres* of Castile had to do. Accordingly a certain genealogist would like to correct the name of Felix (which, he says, 'is unknown in his family and even in the entire kingdom'[16]) to that of Fernando—a suggestion which is completely arbitrary. Moreover in 1131, a 'cousin of St Dominic' signed a document at Caleruega bearing the quite simple name of Domingo Pérez.[17] People have likewise been astonished that the Spanish Dominicans of the thirteenth and fourteenth centuries should not have explicitly alluded to the illustrious parentage and relationships of St Dominic. In another order of ideas, if Felix de Guzmán was indeed lord of Caleruega, he must have lodged in the reconstructed keep, or at least in a residence for the lord adjoining. Now the saint's birthplace, quite clearly attested, is situated about a hundred yards or more away from there, as far as one can judge, at the other end of the little village of that time.[18]

This is a fact. The first argument in particular has some weight. At the end of the twelfth century, however, only the *ricos-hombres* who followed the king signed the royal charters.[19] If St Dominic's father had in point of fact agreed to establish himself on the domain of Caleruega in which he possessed important estates, he would no longer have any need to sign the royal privileges. It is possible, too, as will be seen, that he died rather early. Moreover, the fact that the name of Felix was rather unusual in Castile or at any rate in the Guzmán family (and, moreover, also in that of the Aza),[20] gives a singular significance to one of the statements in the charter of boundaries for Caleruega in 1272. The latter mentions in the territory, at the boundary of Baños, a 'land of don Felix', adjoining the valley of don García, an Aza.[21] This Felix was a *rico-hombre* since he was styled *don*. Now he disappeared from the scene in 1266, for none of the documents of 1266–1272 mentioned him. Was not he the father of St Dominic and an important landowner in the village? Moreover, the education of Dominic and his two brothers, who as has been seen were clerics, presupposes for the parents a social standing above the common.[22] The existence of the rural dean uncle points in the same direction— the dignitaries of the diocese, archdeacons and deans, in contradistinction to simple parish priests, were still recruited at this time from the ruling feudal class.

Finally, most of St Dominic's relations found burial, as a noble family, in a chapel of the neighbouring monastery of San Pedro de Gumiel. The fact is certain for one of his brothers;[23] it seems clear for his father and mother;[24] possible for the other brother.[25] Now this monastery chapel was also the necropolis of the Guzmán in the Middle Ages, and the patrimonial tower could be seen on the horizon only a short distance away.[26]

This converging of indications is impressive. It strengthens the probability of the Spanish tradition. The association of the immediate family of St Dominic with the lineages of Aza and Guzmán would provide the best explanation for the generosity of the members of these two lines, especially of the descendants of don Garci Fernández Aza de Villamayor, established in 1248, fourteen years before the interventions of King Alfonso X.[27] A contemporary historian moreover recalls that the Guzmán, though they were Castilian lords of long standing, were not well known until the end of the thirteenth century, and particularly the middle of the fourteenth century, when Enrique de Trastamare, son of Leonor of Guzmán, after having killed his half-brother, Pedro the Cruel,[28] mounted the throne of Castile. At the end of the twelfth century and for a long time afterwards, there could well be relatively simple people within this lineage, people who made no parade of the name of Guzmán. It is perhaps necessary to see in this fact, no less than in the discretion and care for impartiality of the first Dominican hagiographer, whom the others have simply copied, the reason for the relative uncertainty in which the identity of St Dominic's family has rested.

NOTES TO APPENDIX II

1. The first serious study of this tradition dates from 1586. It is to be found in Morales, IV, fos. 332 ro–351 vo. This valuable dissertation already makes use of the memoranda of Tafur and of the Caleruega charters. The later literature though extensive has added scarcely anything. After the somewhat superficial criticisms of the Bollandist Cuperus (*ASS*, Aug. I, 384–387), Brémond takes up the arguments of Morales with clarity and in an eirenic spirit; Mamachi, 11–31, summarizes Brémond before going over the whole ground again in a discourse full of bombast and abuse. Later historians, down to Getino, *Sermo ad Fratres*, *ASOP*, XX (1932), 790–796, confine themselves to pruning Mamachi's text. Getino has the merit of citing the witnesses for the tradition prior to Morales and of pressing the evidence of Rodrigo of Cerrato. In the interval the principal documents have been carefully edited. The name of Guzmán appears for the first time in the Dominican breviary of 1552. P. Juan de la Cruz is trying to prove its legitimacy in 1567 in his *Chronica de la Orden de Predicatores*.

2. *Andanzas e viajes de Pedro Tafur por diversas puntes del mundo avidos* (1435–1439) ed. Madrid, 1874, Ch. XVII relates the journey that Pedro de Guzmán, ambassador of Juan II (1406–1453), made to the tomb of St Dominic in Bologna, because, says Tafur, 'este bienaventurado padre fue natural de Castilla del linaje de Guzmán de la parte de padre, e de la madre, de los de Aza'. Pedro, acting in the name of Luis de Guzmán, had the chapel decorated with the family arms—Brémond, 168; Mamachi, 19 and 46. n. 8, after Morales, fo. 333, ro; repeated by Getino, *ASOP*, XX, 1932, 792. On Luis de Guzmán, cf. Rades y Andrada, I, 68, ch. 2.

3. Cf. preceding note.

4. In Italy, at the end of the fourteenth century people believed in St Dominic's nobility ('Lascio san Domenico il contado in Ispagna, dove era conte di Callagora [Calaroga]' ; *conte* is the translation of *ricohombre*—'ricohombre de Caleruega'—Giovanne Dominici, *Il libro d'amore di carità*', ed. A. Ceruti, Bologna, 1889, 89; (for the date, cf. xxx); similarly in Spain, from the end of the thirteenth century at least (Getino, *Sermo ad Fratres*, 792–793). In the latter case it was a question of Castilian translations which correct the Latin originals to mention this nobility (for the date of these translations ca. 1290, cf. the study of W. F. Manning, cited *supra*, ch. 1, n. 66). Getino, *Sermo ad Fratres*, 795, after Brémond, 103 and Mamachi, 13, cites ten lines discovered in the seventeenth century by the General of the Premonstratensians, Emanuel Garcías (*Chronica Ord. Praem.*, ch. 6, no. CXII) in a manuscript which may or may not be of the thirteenth century, where it is stated—'su padre fue Felix, de los de Guzmán'. This chronicle of Emanuel Garcías has never been published—Goovaerts, I, 291.

5. Cf. *supra*, ch. I and n. 47.

6. Martínez, charters CCXXXI, CCXXXIV, CCXXXV, etc.

7. Martínez, 305 (ch. CCXXXII, 22nd July, 1266).

8. Martínez, 304 (ch. CCXXX, without day or month; doubtless later than CCXXXIII of 25th July, 1266, which does not mention it).

9. Pellicer, fo. 48 vo had seen these charters; from them he gathered the motive for the donations

and cites it in italics: *por la gran naturaleza que tenia con el bienaventurado santo Domingo*. This formula, similar to that of the two charters, the text of which we have, seems well authenticated. Cf. Martínez, 305.

10. Salazar, *Historia*, III, 331 and Pruebas, 663; Martínez, 324.

11. 'Naturaleza se toma por la casta, y por la patria o nación'—Sebastian de Covarrubias, *Tesoro de la lengua Castellana o Española*, Madrid, 1611, sub. h.v. Cf. J. Corominas *Diccionario critico etimológica de la lengua castellana*, II, Berne, 1956, 490. When Cuperus, *ASS, Aug*. I, 387A explained the *naturaleza* of the charters of 1266–72 by community of soil, he was asserting what it was necessary to prove.

12. Martínez, 320 (ch. CCXLI, 25th July, 1270).

13. Cf. *supra*, n. 9.

14. *Naturaleza* thus here only signifies relationship indirectly through the system of *behetria* of which it is a technical term. Morales, fo. 340 ro had seen this clearly: 'Naturaleza siempre quiere dezir alli en el Bezerro parentesco, para que tuviessen derecho de poder tomar señor della la behetria entre parientes. Y fuera del Bezerro tambien significava parentesco el vocablo naturaleza.' The Bezerro in question is the catalogue of the *behetria* of Castile compiled in the fourteenth century. It is a pity that Brémond, 140, n. 1 and Mamachi, 16, n. 1 should have distorted this quotation by truncating it. They thus asserted, without proof, that *naturaleza* here directly signified blood relationship.

15. Here is a specious explanation. It is clear that the monastery of San Pedro de Gumiel, depending both on Cîteaux and on Calatrava, was the centre of the tradition relating to the cultus of the family of St Dominic (cf. *supra*, ch. I, II, III, III and *infra*, n. 23–26). It is natural that the monastery nearest to Caleruega should have taken over this cultus, with the burial places. The most ancient document about it which it has preserved, however, only gives to the parents of St Dominic, with the whole Dominican tradition, the names of Jane and Felix (cf. *infra*, n. 24). The first formal evidence of the Aza and Guzmán ancestries of Jane and of Felix, the only one prior to the sixteenth century, is that of Luis de Guzmán, related by Tafur (cf. *supra*, n. 2). Now Luis de Guzmán was from 1414 onwards, Grand Master of Caletrava, and thereby closely linked to San Pedro de Gumiel. Was it not probably he who, discovering in Gumiel the burial places of the parents and brothers of St Dominic, by the side of those of the Guzmán, imagined the relationship? The close connection which the charters have shown us of the Guzmán with Caleruega coming to the rescue, he no longer doubted the reality of his discovery and sent his majordomo to decorate the Bologna tomb with the Guzmán arms. The tradition was beginning its course.

The weakness of this explanation, however, is that it utilizes to the full the argument of silence and neglects the probable interpretation of the words *naturaleza* and *dives*. Above all it clashes with the fact that the tradition existed in Italy before the fifteenth century, thus before the intervention of Luis de Guzmán (cf. *supra*, n. 4).

16. Salazar, *Historia*, I, 89 and 348; III, 320; Mamachi, 6, no. 3 and 68, n. 3.

17. Martínez, 360 (ch. CCLXXI, 6th June, 1311). Pérez, however, was the patronymic of the Guzmán in the fourteenth century.

18. The charter of Alfonso X of 26th August, 1270, speaks of 'la Eglesia que es alli o santo Domingo nascio'—Martínez, 16 (ch. XIII) which confirms Rodrigo, 331. A gateway to the village existed quite close to it—Martínez, p. XIV; Carro, *Caleruega*, II, 65.

19. Only Alfonso X, after 1252, established that the charters should be confirmed by the *ricos-hombres* absent from the court—Brémond, 68; Mamachi, 68, n. 3.

20. Morales, fo. 341, ro, then Brémond, 67, have however, found a few noble Felixes in the archives of Spain: fifteen in six centuries! Cf. Mamachi, 7, n. 2. A single further example in the 328 charters of Caleruega; it is curious, moreover—a 'Dominicus Felicis' signs an appeal of the sisters at the convent on 12th September, 1283—Martínez, 348 (ch. CCLVIII).

21. Martínez, 23 (ch. XIX, 26th May, 1272). 'La tierra de don Felices.'

22. Children of peasants and artisans in the twelfth century had no easy access to schools and could not pursue lengthy courses of study; particularly not three children in the same family. Cf. Stelling—Michaud, *L'université de Bologna et la pénétration des droits romain et canonique en Suisse*, Geneva, 1955, 117 and n. 5.

23. Cf. *supra*, ch. 1, n. 102.

24. The inquiry of 1645 on the cultus of Jane of Aza (cf. *supra*, ch. 1, n. 81) mentions among other documents an inscription, now disappeared, of the former chapel of San Pedro in the monastery of Gumiel—*Hac in sacra capilla sancti Dominici/sanctus uterque parens sistunt./Illa Johanna in sancto Paulo Penafielensi;/ille Felix hic requiescit adhuc*—Brémond, 90. Manrique, III, 285, also publishes this inscription, which is likewise contained in the book of burials of the abbey, Pelaez, 125. The contradiction of vv. 2 and 3 (which Manrique liquidates by writing: *sepulta sunt*) would take the first 2 vv. back before the transfer of the body of Jane to Penafiel (shortly after 1318). Other indications will be found in Pelaez, 122–132.

25. Immemorial tradition of the monks of Gumiel, according to Morales, 340, vo (in 1586).

26. Morales, 340, ro and Brémond, 84–86, who moreover indicate, following various authors, the burial of some of the Guzmán family precisely in the chapel of San Pedro apostol—Fr Palacios. *El Monasterio de Gumiel de Hizán panteón de los Guzmanes*, in *Boletín Fernán González*, XXXI (1952).

27. Charter CCXVII of 23rd February, 1248—Martínez, 281. Although there is a sale, the cession is an act of generosity.

28. Getino, *ASOP*, XX 1932, 793.

CASTILE IN THE EUROPEAN POLITICAL SCENE AT THE BEGINNING OF THE THIRTEENTH CENTURY

THE wider relations between Castile and Europe in the time of Alfonso VI and Bernard de Sédirac[1] had not only brought about fruitful exchanges in the ecclesiastical order. The sovereigns had begun to turn their eyes to affairs beyond the Pyrenees. The dynasty itself had opened out more and the marriages of Alfonso VI with Constance de Bourgogne, then of his daughters with Henri de Châlons—whence came the first stock of the kings of Portugal, Raymond de Bourgogne, brother of Pope Callixtus II and father of Alfonso VII, the emperor, and Raymond de Saint Gilles, Count of Toulouse—had brought such preoccupations well within the orbit of his family interests.[2] In the course of the thirteenth century the European outlook of the Castilian dynasty had not disappeared, whatever was the preponderance in its preoccupations of the great work of the reconquest. Alfonso VIII, almost as soon as the disaster of Alarcos was over and he was momentarily at peace through a truce with the Almohades, was preoccupied with a matter which, if it had succeeded, would have secured for Castile a vast expansion beyond the Pyrenees, similar to that which Aragón then enjoyed. It was a matter of recovering the Gascon inheritance of Eleanor of Aquitaine, his mother-in-law, over which he possessed rights which his brother-in-law, John Lackland, would not recognize.[3]

The latter's cruel clumsiness since in 1199 he had succeeded his brother on the throne of Great Britain certainly justified the King of Castile in entertaining legitimate hopes of succeeding in his designs. He was already embarking on his enterprises. Around 1200 he obtained a coast and a fleet on the Atlantic, thanks to the spontaneous rallying of the Cantabrian Basques and the installation of populations from Castile between Santander and San Sebastian, which he occupied and fortified.[4] That same year he made a step forward. The betrothal of his daughter Blanche, niece of John Lackland, to Louis of France, son of Philip Augustus, at which ceremony, with a sensational gesture, the old Queen Eleanor had wished to be present despite her eighty years,[5] in appearance effected the union of the houses of Castile, France and Great Britain. In reality it strengthened the common front of those who coveted the possessions of the English king upon the Continent. The agreement thus arrived at was to show its effects from 1202 onwards. After that year Philip meddled in the quarrels of the barons of Poitou and their English overlord. To give himself an incontestable right to intervene, he had the feudal deposition of King John proclaimed in respect of all the lands he held from France. Then, between 1202 and 1206 he secured to himself by conquest, free alliance or negotiations, Normandy, Maine, Anjou, Touraine and even Brittany.[6] Eleanor having died in the meantime, on 31st March, 1204, Alfonso had moved in his turn. Little by little he achieved the conquest of Guyenne. When in 1206 he was finally forced to abandon his enterprise, it is said that he had gained possession of practically the whole of Aquitaine, with the exception of Bayonne, La Réole and Bordeaux.[7]

Since he was surrounded by enemies in Spain, beginning by his neighbours in Navarre and León, it is understandable that in 1202–1203, before embarking upon so dangerous an enterprise, Alfonso should have looked round for support from possible adversaries of John Lackland. There existed one, perhaps, right at the other end of Christian Europe, the new King of Denmark, Valdemar II (1202–1241).

At the time of Cnut the Great, in 1016, the Danes had conquered England. Though they had been forced to abandon it in 1041, they had none the less preserved their claims to this part of their kingdom.[8] Philip Augustus was well aware of this. In 1193 he deliberately married the sister of Cnut VI of Denmark, Ingeburgh, in order to acquire rights over Great Britain, whose crown he did not cease to covet throughout his entire reign.[9] In 1200, Blanche, the daughter of Alfonso VIII, thus became the niece by marriage of the King of Denmark. Denmark, in these particular years, was at an important turning point in her history. Towards the middle of the twelfth century she had gone through a rather critical period. It was the time when, thanks to the emperor Lothair, the enterprises of two powerful feudal lords, the Guelph, Henry the Lion, Duke of Saxony, and the Ascanian, Albert the Bear, Margrave of Brandenburg, had inaugurated the astonishing adventure of the *Drang nach Osten*, that drive eastwards which, in the following century, was to carry German expansion with Christianity to the furthest limits of Prussia and all along the Baltic.[10] Henry the Lion had proved himself a neighbour particularly venturesome and, finally, dangerous, so far as Danish independence was concerned. From 1152 to 1182 Denmark seemed reduced to the status of a Germanic fief. The dynasty, linked by marriage to that of Henry the Lion,[11] seemed to be inextricably bound to the Guelph policy. However the death of the Bear in 1170 and the defeat of the Lion in 1180, in the mighty duel which had set him against Frederick Barbarossa, had loosened the links and restored her liberty to Denmark.[12] The Germanic thrust had stopped for a time. The sons of Valdemar the Great (d. 1182), Cnut VI (d. 1202) and Valdemar II (d. 1241), brought Denmark to the height of her power and resumed the expansion towards the east for their own account.[13] In 1201 Cnut seized Holstein; in 1203 Valdemar had himself acclaimed at Lubeck, the city of Henry the Lion, as 'King of the Danes and the Slavs, lord of Nordalbingia'.

At this point the danger on the German-Danish frontiers reappeared. Otto of Brunswick, son of Henry the Lion, had been disputing the imperial crown with Philip of Suabia son of Barbarossa since 1197. Pope Innocent III, arbiter of the situation, had for long hesitated between the two competitors. In 1201, he came to a decision. He chose Otto of Brunswick. Installed in that part of ancient Saxony which bordered both on Denmark and on Brandenburg, strong in the new authority conferred on him both by the imperial crown and the leader of Christendom, it seemed probable that Otto of Brunswick would one day again take up his father's expansion movement, and break the new thrust of the Danes at a single stroke. Despite the relationship and alliances of the two kings the danger was no fictitious one.[14] Moreover Otto had for long been linked with England, being himself grandson of Henry Plantagenet and nephew of Richard the Lionheart,[15] who had recently conferred upon him the title of Duke of Aquitaine, entrusting to him the administration of Poitou.[16] In this way the alliance between the Guelph empire and England, which ten years later was to come to grief in the disaster at Bouvines, was strengthened. At the same time the advantage of a closer acquaintance between Castile and France on the one hand and Denmark and Brandenburg,[17] the two Marches in the north commonly opposed by their interests to Brunswick and England, on the other, became clear. In 1202 Valdemar II had just ascended the throne. This was the moment to suggest to him a matrimonial alliance similar to that which Philip Augustus had contracted with Ingeburg, his sister, ten years earlier. The King of France was well placed for suggesting such a step to the King of Castile. The latter however was surely capable of thinking of it himself. He was, through marriage, the uncle of Cnut VI of Denmark, of whom his own daughter, Blanche, had just become the niece.[18]

NOTES TO APPENDIX III

1. Cf. *supra*, ch. III, II II.
2. Desfourneaux, 140–141 with the genealogical table, 136–137.
3. Schirrmacher, 271; Cartellieri IV, 1, 234. Alfonso, and still more his wife, were reclaiming Gascony in the name of a donation of Henry II and Eleanor of Aquitaine, and of an enfeoffment by Richard, which John was said to have confirmed.
4. Schirrmacher, 268–269; Guinard, 338.
5. Schirrmacher, 270; Cartellieri, 37; Labande, 230.
6. Petit-Dutaillis, 139–149.
7. Schirrmacher, 272; Cartellieri, 233–236.
8. A Danish pretender was still trying to get his claim accepted in England in 1138, Gallén, 207.
9. In 1193 and in 1213, Philip Augustus asserted his rights—Gallén, *ibid.*
10. Jordan, 121–132 and 136–139; Calmette, 358–364.
11. Cnut VI married in 1177 Gertrude, daughter of Henry the Lion.
12. Jordan, 138.
13. Jordan, 187.
14. Cnut VI, brother of Waldemar, had married Gertrude, sister of Otto. In the year of Canute's death (1202) his sister Helena married William of Luneburg, Otto's half-brother—Gallén, 205–207 and genealogical table, I. This did not prevent Waldemar's enterprises on the Nordalbingia in 1203 nor Otto's counter attacks in 1209—Fliche, 86, n. 20.
15. His father had married as his second wife Matilda, eldest daughter of Henry II. Otto was of the first marriage.
16. Petit-Dutaillis, 148.
17. On the closer connection of Denmark with Brandenburg, or at least with the Ascanian dynasty, cf. *supra*, ch. IV, n. 21, and Gallén, 207–8.
18. Valdemar I of Denmark and Alfonso VII of Castile were cousins german through their wives (since 1157). Alfonso VIII was Uncle by marriage to Cnut VI, the wife of the one and the mother-in-law of the other being both two daughters of Henry II of England. Such liaisons brought with them no impediment to the eventual marriage between a daughter of the Danish house and the youthful Ferdinand, for they came from different beds—Gallén 204–205. For later alliances, see Mandonnet-Vicaire, I, 97.

ST DOMINIC'S APOSTOLATE IN TOULOUSE IN 1210

In the acts of St Dominic's canonization process in Toulouse, the three statements nos. 15, 16 and 17 form a small group. Guillelmine Martini, Noguière de Toulouse and Bécède, the nun of Sainte Croix, mention the way in which they gave the saint hospitality or rendered him service. Noguière refers to the statement of Guillelmine; Bécède gives evidence in parallel terms similar to those of Guillelmine. Both give a description of a long ministry of the saint in the locality where they were living. Where precisely was this?

It is clear in the first place that these three women gave their evidence before the Pamiers commissioners. The investigation of the Toulouse process was made in two centres only, Pamiers and Fanjeaux. The Fanjeaux statements are to be found in the acts of the process from no. 19 (to no. 26); those of Pamiers go as far as no. 17. In effect, between 3 and 17, all the witnesses whose place of origin is given except one (Noguière de Toulouse) are from the neighbourhood of Pamiers (nos. 3, 4, 5, 6, 7, 8, 11, 12, 13, 17). Bécède (no. 17) is a nun of Sainte Croix, a place in the Ariège, near St Girons, where a priory of the Order of Fontevrault is to be found. There is thus no doubt that Guillelmine Martini and Noguière de Toulouse (nos. 15 and 16) also made their statements before the Pamiers commission. Where were they, however, when they came to know Dominic?

Noguière was formerly in Toulouse, her native city. The close resemblance between the three statements thus leads us to think that the two others were there too. This hypothesis indeed is confirmed by the content of the statements of Guillelmine and Bécède. The latter gave evidence as to the opinion people had of St Dominic, not only in the diocese of Couserans, where her monastery was, but also in that of Toulouse. Had she then known Dominic there earlier? Moreover, both these women, as we have said, spoke of a prolonged ministry of the saint; the two of them alone had given him hospitality more than four hundred times. What place other than the one very large town of the region, Toulouse, could require so lasting a ministry? Now we know that Dominic was also given hospitality in Toulouse by Bishop Fulk himself, in whose house Aimery de Solignac, a Cistercian of Grandselve, often met him—Salagnac, II, 5. This fact further prolongs the duration of this ministry. At what date did it take place?

It cannot refer to Dominic's ministry in Toulouse after 1215. The saint was then lodging among his brethren in Peter Seila's house. Before April 1214, however, date of the reconciliation of the people of Toulouse (Cernai, no. 507) or rather, before February 1215, date at which the bishop was able to return to his city, occupying the castle of Narbonne, any Catholic ministry there was impossible, because of the interdict and of insecurity. This had been the case since the end of

May 1211, date of the solemn departure of the clergy at Fulk's order (Cernai, no. 234), or even since 2nd April, 1211, date of Fulk's voluntary exile (Cernai, no. 221). It is thus earlier than these latter dates that the greater part of Dominic's ministry in the city must be placed. If it is now realized that before March 1210 (Cernai, no. 162) the town was already under an interdict and had been since October 1209 (Cernai, no. 138 and Tudela, 97), and that, as has been said, the saint's apostolate before the crusade had principally been concerned with the region of Fanjeaux and Carcassonne, we shall be led to the conclusion that Dominic's principal apostolate in Toulouse, in the course of which he met Fulk and Aimery de Solignac, took place between March 1210 and May 1211.

This agrees exactly with what is known of the intensive ministry of Fulk among his flock during the year 1210 (Tudela, III). He was then turning to advantage the forced goodwill of Raymond VI and the people of Toulouse. It can thus be understood how on 15th May, 1211, Dominic was found in Lavaur at the side of Fulk, who had just abandoned Toulouse (Cernai, no. 221) and then made his principal donation to Prouille (Laurent, no. 8); how on 20th June, 1211, he found himself before Toulouse, near to Aimery de Solignac (Laurent, no. 9); why no sign of the saint's presence and activity in Prouille in 1210 and the first part of 1211 is found. Finally there are certain reasons for identifying one or other of the three female witnesses at the process of canonization with the hostesses mentioned by Ferrand, nos. 22–23, whom Dominic converted by the sight of his austerity during one particular Lent (that of 1211), 'somewhere near Toulouse'. It was doubtless at this time that he won over Sister Blanche and her husband, wealthy citizens of Toulouse, to religious life. Blanche became a nun of Prouille; her name appears in the list of sisters of 15th May, 1211 (Laurent, no. 9), but was not on the first list. Her wealth served to build half the great dormitory in dressed stone; she was sent to St Sixtus in 1221, at the head of seven nuns, and remained there henceforward (Percin, 22, no. 56; Echard I, 83, ch. 2 and Balme, II, 455, n. 1).

THE CUSTOMS OF 1216

1. In an earlier study, which so far as we are aware has not given rise to any serious criticism, the substantial identity of the *arctiores consuetudines* (Jordan, no. 42) taken over by the community of the Preachers of Toulouse in the summer of 1216, with the first distinction of the legislative document contained in the Rodez manuscript, to which must be added the first part of the prologue, the division and the *regula conversorum* which closes the document (Mandonnet-Vicaire, II, 211–218), has recently been established. In point of fact: 1. this collection of texts is expressly given the title of *consuetudines*; 2. the customs it contains belong to the category of *arctiores*, because they are borrowed textually and in great majority from the customs of Prémontré which shared with Springiersbach the right to this title; 3. lastly, these customs correspond point by point to the fairly detailed description of the content of the customs of 1216 that can be drawn from the accounts of Jordan of Saxony and the Bolognese witnesses at the canonization process: written customs as to liturgy and observance (meals, fasting, sleep, the wearing of wool, silence), with a detailed code of faults and penances.

It is not in itself impossible that in May 1220 the Bologna chapter abrogated the first *arctiores consuetudines*, which until that time Dominic as well as Reginald had observed with extreme severity, and replaced them by others very similar (which would be those of Rodez). It is, however, improbable. Such a supposition, which is not authorized by the findings of history, is guesswork. In particular, none of the information given by the Bologna witnesses on the legislative work of 1220 gives the slightest indication that such a change took place before their eyes; the declarations of these religious who, with one exception, all entered the order between 1217 and 1220, on the contrary suggest the continuity of the customs they have always known, and which they call 'the rule of St Dominic', with the rule they are observing in 1233 which is contained in the Rodez manuscript. Finally it must be pointed out that Dominic could not have allowed himself to disperse his brethren as early as 1217 and to send them to found convents, sometimes a few weeks after their clothing, if he had not been able to give them at this moment, to ensure their fidelity, regularity and uniformity, the text of the customs of observance in his order which after that time it would become useless and difficult to change.

Moreover, it has been possible to note in the prologue and first distinction of Rodez certain provisions of 1220 which are clearly presented as additions in an earlier text, i.e. that of 1216 (Mandonnet-Vicaire, II, 224–228). A further and significant instance of this will be seen in connection with the division and list which terminates the prologue.

Lastly, it can be noted that what we have called the 'charter of preaching' (cf.

supra, ch. XVI, p. 111), undeniably the work of the chapter of 1220, is completely different, in its drawing up, its literary presentation and absence of literary sources from the customs of the first distinction. It is, in particular, absolutely independent of the texts of Prémontré, of which it could, nevertheless, have taken advantage, especially for the legislation of the general chapter—as the first distinction did pre-eminently. This is the proof that the customs of observance of the order (1st distinction) and the charter of preaching (2nd distinction) were drawn up at two different periods, one in 1216, the other in 1220.

This having been said, it is certain that the prologue and first distinction of the Rodez manuscript contain elements which are not original. Is it possible to disentangle them and get back to the original text? The following are a few principles which, we think, enable the original text of the customs of St Dominic to be re-established with a considerable measure of accuracy.

2. The first investigation to be made is that of textual criticism. The only extant manuscript of the primitive legislation of the order is the Rodez text, i.e. a defective imitation of a copy in itself deficient. It so happens, however, that certain parts of this text, sometimes almost the whole, have been used: 1. in the rule of St Sixtus (= RS. Cf. Appendix VIII, no. 2, 8–11), in 1216–1218; 2. in the statutes of the Sisters of St Mary Magdalene (= SM. *Ibid.*, nos. 2 and 5) in 1228–1232; 3. in the 2nd constitutions of the Friars Preachers, known as the Constitutions of St Raymond, in 1239–1241; 4. in the institutions of the Sack friars (Ms British Museum, Nero A XII, Fo. 155r^0–174v^0). Moreover, these texts have as their source, often taken over literally, extensive passages of the customs of Prémontré (ed. Martène, *Rit.*, III). By comparing these different documents it is possible: 1. to correct the text of the manuscript of Rodez; 2. to discover the approximate date of certain additions between 1216, 1216–1218, 1228–1232, 1239–1241. Thus in ch. 17, §2, it is possible to reconstruct in accordance with RS, a sentence which had disappeared by 1236 which Denifle considered had been permanently deleted: *Prior in mensa loqui poterit, silenter et modeste, ita quod lector non impediatur.*

3. Certain additions or corrections can be discovered in this first distinction, either because they are indicated in the acts of the general chapters of 1236 or 1240 (6 in all: in ch. 6, 7 §2, 17 §2, 19 for 1236; ch. 21 §§34 and 39, for 1240); or because they contain terms of relatively recent date, such as those of Master of the order, prior provincial, prior conventual, etc. (*general chapter* (1220): prologue §3, ch. 14 §2, 23 §8 and 10, 24, §2; *Master of the order* (1221), ch. 16 §1; *prior provincial* (1221), ch. 23 §10; *prior conventual* (1221), ch. 14 §2; *provincial chapter* (1221–1225) prologue §3, ch. 14 §2, 23 §8 and 10, 24 §2); or again because they are introduced by the terms *Statuimus* and *Item* which indicate the complementary legislation of a general chapter (1220 and ff. Only examples to be found in the first distinction: ch. 15 §§1 and 3).

4. Other additions or modifications are finally indicated by the examination of the division and list of titles of the chapters which terminate the prologue in the Rodez manuscript. This division mentions two distinctions, describes them briefly

and adds—*Unicuique autem harum distinctionum propria capitula assignavimus et assignata scripsimus, ut cum aliquid a lector queritur sine difficultate inveniatur.* Then follows a list of chapters, all from the first distinction. There is no list for the second. This list will be examined later.

The mention of the two distinctions, the description of the first, the phrase that has just been quoted *in extenso*, finally the majority of the titles of chapters contained in the list, are borrowed from the Prémontré texts; they are primitive. This situation recently led Scheeben (*QF*, XXXVIII, 21) to admit, since the second distinction was only drawn up in 1220, that the whole Rodez document, prologue, 1st and 2nd distinctions, had been drawn up in 1220. In this case it would even have to be said, if one wanted to be logical, in 1221–1225, since the description of the 2nd distinction which forms part of this collection of texts is thus labelled: *De provinciali capitulo et generali, et studio et predicatione*, and the legislation of the provincial chapter dates from 1221–1225 (cf. *supra*, ch. XIX p. 111). No one will accept this conclusion. It must be admitted that in this phrase there is at least one addition. We believe it is the phrase in its entirety and that this addition was made in 1220 under the form: *De capitulo generali et studio et predicatione*, to which *provinciali* was added in 1221–1225. Before 1220, the description announced of the 2nd distinction remained blank, as did the 2nd distinction itself. The Prémontré text, which served as a basis for the whole of the document, in fact gave the example of reserving a blank distinction for later additions. Thus there is nothing to prevent the whole of these texts dating from 1216. The proof of this is to be found in the phrase which has been cited *in extenso*. This announces the list of the chapters of both distinctions; now the 2nd distinction, when it is drawn up, will not include any division into chapters, or *a fortiori* titles (Mandonnet-Vicaire, II, 275–276); that is why the Rodez text does not contain any other list than that of the chapters of the 1st distinction. The unfortunate promise was thus prior to the drawing up of the 2nd distinction, i.e. to 1220. The division, list of titles of the 1st distinction and this distinction itself are thus from 1216.

5. The titles of this list, however, do not correspond exactly to the actual titles of the Rodez document. The following is a parallel list, that of the prologue on the left, that of the actual chapter titles on the right.

De matutinis	*De matutinis*
De capitulo et prima	[De capitulo] (addition by a later hand)
	De mulieribus non intromittendis
[De] *Missa et horis aliis*	*De horis et de modo dicendi*
De refectione et cibo	*De refectione. De ieiunio. De prandio. De pulmentis*
De collatione et completorio	*De collatione et completorio. De lectis*
De infirmis et minutis	*De infirmis. De minutione*
De noviciis et silentio	*De magistro novitiorum. De recipiendis*
	De tempore probationis. De modo faciendi professionem
	De silencio. De scandalo fratrum
De vestitu	*De vestibus*
De rasura	*De rasura*

De culpis　　　　　　　　　　*De levioribus culpis. De gravi culpa. De graviori culpa. De fratre qui apostataverit. De gravissima culpa*

The first thing that will be noticed is the addition of three short chapters—*De mulieribus non intromittendis* (ch. 3), *De lectis* (ch. 10), *De scandalo fratrum* (ch. 18). The 2nd and 3rd, composed of phrases from Prémontré (D.I., ch. 14 and ch. 9 at end; this last source escaped Denifle and later historians), are original. At the beginning, however, they were not distinguished from ch. 9 (compline) and 17 (silence), which precede them; the phrase about the beds already occupied this place in the Prémontré text; the phrase about the scandal of the brethren was presented by the Prémontré text as 'What is to be done when one has offended a brother to whom one has not the right to speak'. Ch. 3 alone must be an addition to the primitive text (note—*loqui de Deo*; is this of 1220? Cf. D. II, ch. XXVII).

Ch. 4 about the Hours effectively mentions in its first phrase 'the Mass and all the canonical Hours'. It is principally a question, however, of the Hours, or rather of the manner of saying them. It was doubtless for this reason that the title of the chapter was subsequently changed.

The *De culpis* is replaced in the Rodez text by five chapters: *De levioribus culpis. De gravi culpa. De graviori culpa. De fratre qui apostataverit. De gravissima culpa.* (ch. 21 to 25). It will be noted that these subdivisions are inscribed at the head of each paragraph: *Hee sunt leviores culpe*, etc. Thus only a single general title was needed: *De culpis*. This was the case originally. It will be shown in Appendix 8, no. 9, that in the original text there was a special paragraph on faults of medium gravity, subsequently attached to the chapter on light faults and for the future included in this.

The *De refectione et cibo* is represented in the Rodez text by four chapters (5 to 8): *De refectione, De ieiunio. De prandio. De pulmentis.* These four chapters are based on Prémontré texts. At the end of ch. 6 and 7 are two additions from 1236 (*Acta*, I, 6, nos. 7 and 10). It is obvious that the *De ieiunio* and *De prandio* are only parts of the *De refectione*. Perhaps the original chapter has been cut, rather clumsily, moreover, (for 6 and 7 both refer to the fasts), after the additions of 1236 (and perhaps others which have escaped us) which made the chapter unduly long? The *De pulmentis* represents the original *De cibo*, the title of which is more accurate.

Up to this point the changes or additions of titles have not signified any considerable change of content. The division of *De noviciis et silencio*, on the other hand, corresponds to considerable additions. This chapter is actually represented by five chapters: *De magistro noviciorum. De recipiendis. De tempore probationis. De modo faciendi professionem. De silencio* (ch. 13 to 17). Only the first lines of ch. 13 and 14 go back to Prémontré and are definitely original. Moreover, the formula of profession of ch. 16 §1 is an addition of 1221 which does not coincide with that of ch. 14 §1. The second phrase of ch. 14 §2 (admission of a religious to another order), which mentions the provincial and general chapters is from 1220 (1221) at earliest; the third phrase, on the reception of the Cistercians, which contradicts a provision of the 1216 privilege, is from 1220 at earliest and alluding as it does to a provision of Honorius III (cf. *BOP*, I, 77, no. 135 and *supra* p. 111, n. 39), at latest from 1227. The manner of reception of a novice forms the subject of three divergent provisions, clearly of successive dates—ch. 14 §1, 2, 4; similarly for the fixing of the duration of the novitiate, ch. 14 §1, 15 §1, 16 §5. In both cases only the first prescription is clearly original.

Finally, it will be noted that the lengthy development of ch. 13, *humilitatem cordis*, etc. as far as *tempore opportuno*, attributes to the master of novices activities already mentioned, sometimes in accordance with the Prémontré texts, in the beginning of ch. 13 and end of ch. 16. It is possible that this development, so close in style to the 'charter of preaching', is an addition of 1220. Similarly the code of penalties for infractions of the silence, ch. 18, §4 which does not equate with the fault in ch. 22, no. 5.

It is thus certain that the original chapter *De noviciis et silencio* was considerably enriched between 1216 and 1227. It is for this reason that it has burst its boundaries and been distributed among five chapters. If the additions instanced are eliminated, the probable content of the original chapter will be found: ch. 13 §1, 14 §1, 1st phrase of §2, §3, 15 §2, 16 §2 to 4, 17 §1 and 2 (corrected in accordance with SM, cf. *supra*, no. 2), 18.

6. Certain additions, finally, are only revealed by internal analysis. One such can be discovered in §2 of the prologue which contains a general law of dispensation, thus making obsolete the particular indications as to dispensation to be read in ch. 1, 4, 6 and 11. This §2 can without difficulty be dated as 1220. On the grave fault, ch. 22, no. 13, cf. *supra*, p. 111, n. 69. Fault no. 15 in this same chapter is presented as an addition. Other faults interpolated or, at least, corrected, have already been pointed out in no. 3 of this Appendix.

7. At the close of this analysis it is thus found that the primitive customs of the Preachers were scarcely modified at all between 1216 and 1240. The only additions are ch. 3 and a notable part of ch. 14 to 16. Interpolations of phrases can be seen in other places. Several titles have been altered or added. The following is how the primitive document was constituted:

Prologue §1 and 3. *De Matutinis* (ch. 1). *De capitulo et prima* (end ch. 1 and ch. 2). *De Missa et horis aliis* (ch. 4). *De refectione et cibo* (ch. 5, 6 except last phrase, 7 §1, 8). *De collatione et completorio* (ch. 9 and 10). *De infirmis et minutis* (ch. 11 and 12). *De noviciis et silencio* (ch. 13 §1, 14 §1, 1st phrase of §2, §3, 15 §2, 16 §2 to 4, 17 §1 and 2 corrected, 18). *De vestitu* (ch. 19). *De rasura*, ch. 20. *De culpis* (ch. 21 divided into two paragraphs, 22 to 26). *Regula conversorum*.

THE BULLS OF RECOMMENDATION OF HONORIUS III

1. Between 11th February, 1218 and 28th May, 1221, thus in little more than three years, St Dominic obtained from Pope Honorius III a great number of bulls of recommendation for the brethren of his order. Of these only three were inscribed in the registers of the Curia. There is, however, a trace and sometimes the original, of thirty-one of these letters in the files of the various archives of Europe. Others will certainly be found as research continues among the collections of unpublished archives, especially among the collections of ancient bulls of the houses of Friars Preachers. Moreover these were far from being the only letters of Honorius relating to Dominic's brethren.

2. This abundance of bulls of recommendation in favour of an order which had scarcely come into being is all the more impressive since after the middle of 1221, Ie.e. after the death of St Dominic, it ceased altogether until the end of the pontificat of Honorius (1227), while the number of other letters also diminished considerably. it began again, however, on the morrow of his death. His successor, Gregory IX, formerly Cardinal Ugolino, gave his recommendation on 30th April, 1227, making use of a formula of 1221 which he frequently employed after that time. These two facts manifest sufficiently clearly the respective rôles of the Pope, of St Dominic and of Cardinal Ugolino in this stream of bulls.

3. The Pope did not hesitate to grant these documents and gave them the weight of his authority. He himself probably had inserted in the text which he was asked to sign such and such a significant adverb (*affectuose*, *liberaliter*) which it would indeed have been presumptuous on Dominic's part to put forward in his request. This emphasizes the Pope's sentiments in regard to the Preachers. The same sentiments are to be found in the wording of the bulls: the Pope's confidence in the providential character of the order becomes progressively more categorical: 1. *quorum utile ministerium et religionem credimus Deo gratam*; 2. *quorum et propositum sanctum et ministerium necessarium arbitramur*; 3. *Nos eorum sanctum propositum et necessarium ministerium favore benevolo prosequentes*. . . . Can we go further and think that the Pope composed a considerable part of the text himself? It is certain that the bulls of Honorius are quite different from those of Innocent III and in particular no longer present us with the overlong prologues, loaded with scriptural allegories, which his predecessor liked so much.

The actual wording of the bull, however, which was the work of notaries under the direction of the vice-chancellor, cannot be attributed to Honorius. The bulls were first of all prepared by secretaries under the form of minutes, in accordance with the request of the petitioners. Moreover, the Pope's decision was put into due form by the notaries and the vice-chancellor. After the end of 1219, it was an intimate friend and adviser of Dominic, Guglielmo di Piemonte, later bishop of Modena and Cardinal of Sabina, who held the latter office (Donner, 12–15). He certainly played a considerable part in introducing the shades of meaning of the Pope's sentiments, which he had perhaps himself suggested, into the clauses emanating from the Chancellery. Finally, the considerable diminution of the letters of Honorius and the total disappearance of his bulls of recommendation after Dominic's death show that the initiative in the matter was not the Pope's.

4. This initiative was in the hands of Dominic and Ugolino. The cardinal certainly intervened in the sense of suggesting that Dominic should ask for the bulls, of helping to draw them up and favouring the granting of them. He was in point of fact present at the Curia at the time when these bulls were granted—the first four months of 1218, the close of 1219 and the beginning of 1221 (Potthast, p. 678; Brem, 30 and 37). As to Dominic, he obtained these documents from the Curia by the steps he took, determined the essential points of their provisions in accordance with the needs of his convents or his brethren, directed their distribution in a masterly way as best suited the interests of the spread of his order. His strategy becomes even more clearly visible when we look closely at the list of the documents, their form, their content, their date, the place where they were eventually lodged.

5. These letters are of five different types, which are distinguished by their *Arenga*, i.e. by the first words of their prologue: I, *Si personas religiosas*; II, *Dilecti filii*; III, *Cum qui recipit*; IV, *Quoniam abundavit*. The fifth type, which is, moreover, quite secondary, has lost its prologue. It will be indicated by the number: V. Types I and III exist under two successive forms, type IV under three forms. Thus the sub-divisions I^1, I^2, III^1, III^2, IV^1, IV^2, IV^3 will be adopted. The following is the general table of the documents it has been possible to discover, with their date of issue by the Pontifical Chancellery, the place where their original is at present to be found or was to be found at the date of issue, the principal reference. A second table indicates their number in the collections of bulls or registers of Potthast, Pressutti, BOP, Ligiez, Laurent.

TABLE I

No.	Date	Situation	Principal Reference
		I^1 *Si personas religiosas*	
1	11.ii.1218	{Vatican / Poitiers	*Reg. Honorius*, II, n° 897 / Arch. of Vienna (France) corpus O. P. de Poitiers, bundle 78
		I^2 *Si personas religiosas*	
2	26.iv.1218	{Vatican / Toulouse?	*Reg. Hon.* II, n° 1069
3	26.iv.1218	Salamanca	BOP, 7, n° 8
4	11.xi.1218	Piacenza	Campi, II, 122 (fragment)
5	15.xi.1219	Zamora	BOP, 8, n° 9
6	28.xi.1219	Montpellier?	AFP, V, 1935, 77, n° 142
7	29.xi.1219	—	AFP, VI, 1936, 251, n° 148
8	13.xii.1219	Paris St. Jacques	Arch. Nat. Paris, L.240, n° 61

TABLE I–*continued*

No.	Date	Situation	Principal Reference
		II *Dilecti filii . . . prior et fratres*	
9	8.xii.1219	{ Vatican	*Reg. Hon.* IV, n⁰ 647
		{ Bologna	*BOP*, 8, n⁰ 10
10	13.xii.1219	Paris St Jacques	Arch. Nat. Paris L. 240, n⁰ 63
11	13.xii.1219	Montpellier?	*AFP*, V, 1935, 61, n⁰ 77
12	13.xii.1219	Würzburg	*AFP*, VI, 1936, 242, n⁰ 76, *ADD*, II, 160
13	13.iv.1220	Palencia	*ASOP*, I, 1894, 512, n. 1
		III¹ *Cum qui recipit prophetam*	
14	11.xi.1219	Sweden	*Diplomatarium Suecanum*, ed. J. G. Liljegren, I, Stockholm 1829, 198, n⁰ 178. Horoy, III, 336; Gallén, 4, n. 6
		III² *Cum qui recipit prophetam*	
15	4.ii.1221	Montpellier?	*AFP*, V, 1935, 61, n⁰ 78
16	4.ii.1221	Toulouse	*BOP*, 12, n⁰ 20
17	4.ii.1221	Magdebourg	*ADD*, II, 158
18	29.iii.1221	Fiesole	*BOP*, 13, n⁰ 22
19	31.iii.1221	Valladolid	Balme, III, 245–246
20	5.iv.1221	?	Rome, *Arch. gen. O.P.*, XI, n⁰ 158
21	6.v.1221	Schwerin	*Bullarium Danicum*, ed. A. Krarup, Copenhagen 1932, n⁰ 170
22	22.v.1221	?	Rome, *Arch. gen. O.P.*, XI, n⁰ 155
23	28.v.1221	Bologna	*BOP*, 14, n⁰ 26 (cf. Balme, III, 367, n. 1)
24	?	Bologna	*ADD*, II, 159
25	?	Minden	*ADD*, II, 159
		IV¹ *Quoniam abundavit*	
26	13.xii.1219	Würzburg	*ADD*, II, 170
27	6.v.1220	Barcelona St Catherina	*BOP*, 10, n⁰ 15
		IV² *Quoniam abundavit*	
28	18.i.1221	Vatican, Chancellery?	G. Erler, *Liber cancellariae apostolicae*, Leipzig 1880, 108
29	18.i.1221	Rome Sta Sabina	*BOP*, 11, n⁰ 18
		IV³ *Quoniam abundavit*	
	30.iv.1227	Olmütz	Rome, *Arch. gen. O.P.*, *Lib.* E., *BOP*, 18, n. 1; Ligier, n⁰ 144.
		V	
30	10.v.1221	Piacenza	*BOP*, 14, n⁰ 25
31	7.xii.1221	Barcelona St Catherina	*BOP*, 14, n⁰ 27

TABLE II

No.	Potthast	Pressutti	BOP	Ligiez	Laurent
	no	no	no	no	no
1	—	1,082	—	55	84
2	—	1,255	—	58	87
3	5,763	—	8	—	—
4	6,155	2,250	—	68	—
5	6,160	2,255	9	55, n. 3	97
6	—	—	—	55, n. 3	—
7	—	—	—	—	—
8	—	—	—	55, n. 3	—
9	{ —	2,288	—	71	103
	{ 6,177	2,288	10	71	103
10	—	—	—	—	103
11	—	—	—	—	—
12	—	—	—	—	—
13	—	—	—	—	—
14	6,155	2,250	—	68	—
15	—	—	—	—	—
16	6,542	3,062	20	68	129
17	—	—	—	—	—
18	6,600	—	22	68	132
19	—	—	—	—	133
20	—	—	—	—	129, n. 1
21	—	—	—	—	—
22	—	—	—	—	129, n. 1
23	6,669	—	26	68	146
24	—	—	—	—	—
25	—	—	—	—	—
26	—	—	—	—	—
27	6,246	2,423	15	80	112
28	—	—	—	—	127
29	6,508	3,009	18	88	—
30	6,660	3,371	25	96	143
31	6,730	3,604	27	104	—

6. The list is illuminating. Dominic had formula I registered in February (no. 1); he began again in April (no. 2). It will be seen that this second registration corresponded to an important addition in the text (I²). He likewise had formula II registered (no. 9). He did not do this for the others. The formality, which was costly, was not obligatory. It was principally necessary for a privilege of permanent value. The recommendation was only of provisional interest: in the initial period in which the order was little known. Formulae III, IV, V are thus not to be found in the registers of Honorius. After the end of 1220, at least, Dominic obtained the issue of the bulls free of charge—Laurent, no. 122.

7. If Dominic had to ask for an audience to obtain the new formulae, or to have some addition inserted in the text, it was sufficient for him to approach the chancellery to obtain the certified copies of the bulls previously granted. The variety of dates will be noted. They create a slight problem. Did Dominic go to the chancellery on each occasion? Or was it perhaps that the chancellery made out on different dates copies asked for *en bloc* some days earlier? The variety of the places where the

originals are to be found will also be noted. If these places are not necessarily those where Dominic had them sent, they are usually not without some connection with such places. From these dates and places important information may be drawn as to the activity of the founder in the spread of his order.

8. Dominic was clearly present at the Curia from 11th October to 26th April, 1218; in November and December, 1219; from 18th January to May, 1221. The almost complete calm of the year 1220 will be noted. It is true that Dominic obtained further letters from the Pope in the course of that year—but no recommendation. In the initial development of the order, the year 1220 represented a time of consolidation and organization. The first months of 1218, the last two of 1219 and the first part of 1221, on the other hand, were a time of redoubled initiative and creation—especially the end of 1219.

9. It may, perhaps, be thought surprising to see the pontifical chancellery issue between November 11th and December 13th of that year, almost simultaneously, the four principal formulae of recommendation (nos. 8, 9, 14, 26). It is true that the authenticity of no. 14 (formula III^1), preserved in a non-authenticated copy of the thirteenth century (Gallén, 4, n. 6), has been called in question. The argument from internal criticism which has elicited the doubt, however—the presence in the document of a phrase of formula II, which is no longer to be found in formula III^2—is not conclusive. This phrase, clause no. 5 (cf. *infra*, §15), is also found again in formulae IV^2 and IV^3. Moreover, the complementary clause no. 6, which is present in formulae II and IV, is also found in letter no. 14. There is thus no reason to doubt the authenticity of clause no. 5 in formula III^1, nor, consequently, that of the letter in question. The only argument that can be raised against it, or perhaps against its date, is its isolation. The second (fragmentary) example mentioned by Potthast (no. 6155), after Campi, is in reality of type no. I.

The issuing of deed no. 8 (formula I^2) on 13th December, 1219, is anachronistic. Formula I^2 had just been replaced on 8th December preceding, as will be seen, by formula II. This fact, however, can be easily explained. It was necessary to reconstitute the deed sent to the brethren in Paris on 11th February, 1218, which the founders of the house in Poitiers had taken away with them. It is possible that Dominic simultaneously claimed from the Chancellery in the middle of the previous month of November a series of copies of this deed and that he received them on November 15th, 28th and 29th and finally on 13th December.

10. The other three formulae of recommendation, II, III and IV, on the other hand, were issued simultaneously because they corresponded to three distinctly different interpretations. Formula II insisted, in terms that were altogether new, on the poverty of the Preachers, formula III on the preaching and pastoral activity of the brethren considered individually. Formula IV emphasized, in a formula that in 1219 was still rudimentary, their effectiveness against heresy. This latter document, however, gathering together in 1221 and above all in 1227 the clauses of the other two formulae, was to become the sole and universal formula of recommendation of the Preachers. An even moderately detailed analysis of these formulae and their clauses will give the proof of this.

11. Diplomatically, these letters of recommendation fall into the category of lesser bulls and in particular of mandates. They have all their characteristics—the mention

of the apostolic authority, the four words with spaces between in the last line, the hempen cord over which one or other of them is still sealed.

12. They are practically all addressed to the whole body of the prelates of the Church. The only exceptions are those of the two copies of formula V (to the bishop of Piacenza and his chapter; to the Bishop of Barcelona), nos. 3 (formula I², to all the prelates of Spain) and 27 (formula IV¹, to the Archbishop of Tarragona). The beneficiaries of the recommendation are as a general rule the brethren, taken collectively, especially for formulae I, II, IV, V: *fratres ordinis predicatorum* (I and II), *ordo fratrum predicatorum* (IV), *fratres predicatores* (V). Formula III, on the other hand, designates the brethren in their personal activities, *predicatores, de predicatorum fratrum ordine.* Accordingly it is issued several times to recommend isolated individuals (nos. 18, 19, 23). This is also the case for nos. 2 (I²) and 29 (IV²).

13. The preamble to the bulls, or their terms of enactment, contains a description of the ministry and religious life of the brethren. Formula I (1218–1219) thus describes their *utile ministerium et religionem Deo gratam*; *Verbum Domini gratis et fideliter proponentes, intendendo profestibus animarum, ipsum Dominum solum secuti, paupertatis titulum pretulerunt.* After 8th December, 1219, however, formula II completely modified the description of the *propositium sanctum et ministerium necessarium* of the brethren (cf. also IV): 1° *verbum predicationis . . . quod est pabulum animarum super . . . populos multos seminant incessanter*; 2° *sarcinis divitiarum mundanarum abiectis, quo expeditius currant per mundi huius agrum . . . in abiectione voluntarie paupertatis eunt.* This latter insertion is again found in formula IV. Formula III, which does not develop the programme of poverty of the brethren, sums up their preaching programme in a striking expression: *verbi Dei sunt evangelizationi totaliter deputati,* which is again found in formula IV under the form: *se dedicaverunt evangelizationi verbi Dei.*

14. The terms of enactment comprises a series of apostolic mandates. Their gradual elaboration can be seen in the successive formulae:

1. [eos] *habeatis commendatos* (I; II, IV² and IV³ add: *affectuose*; III, *propensius*; IV¹, *devotius*).

2. *in suis eis necessitatibus assistendo* (I, II, III, IV add: *liberaliter*).

3. *ad officium predicationis ad quod deputati sunt curetis benigne recipere* (I², II and IV; III: *caritative*; IV² adds: [*ad quod sunt*] *ex professione sui ordinis* [*deputati*], but this exactness of phrase does not occur again in IV³).

4. *ac populos vobis commissos, ut ex ore eorum ipsorum verbi Dei semen devote suscipiant, sedulo admonentes* (II, III, IV² and IV³).

5. *cuatinus ad illud suscipiendum vestris exhortationibus preparati, tanquam bona et fructifera terra, pro vitiorum tribulis, incipiant segetem germinare virtutum* (II, IV² and IV³).

6. *et dicti fratres, per cohoperationem vestram suscepti ministerii cursum felicius consummantes, optatum reportent sui laboris fructum et finem, salutem videlicet animarum* (II, III, IV).

7. *benigne permittentes presbiteris eorumdem, cum expedierit, penitentium confessiones audire et consilium eis inuingere salutera* (III, but missing in nos. 18 and 19, taken up again by IV³ under an abridged form).

8. *Quia vero vitia sepe sub specie virtutum occulte subintrant . . . presentium vobis auctoritate mandamus, quatinus, si qui de predicatorum fratrum ordine se dicentes in vestris partibus predicaverint ad questum se pecuniarum convertendo, per quod religionem eorum qui*

*paupertatem professi sunt contingeret infamari, vos tanquam falsarios capiatis et condemnetis
eosdem* (III, IV³).

15. At the close of this analysis we are able to bring a more circumstantial judgement to bear on the bulls of recommendation obtained by St Dominic and on his
policy in the matter. We have seen that it was largely inspired and sustained by
Cardinal Ugolino and the future cardinal of Sabina.

In February 1218, Dominic obtained, and had registered, the first of these bulls. It
recommended the groups of Preachers who were beginning to found their convents
to the prelates of the Church. In two words it described their religious life, their
ministry for souls, their poverty, and it covered them with the apostolic authority.
It asked that support should be given to them in their daily needs.

Two months later, Dominic had a further edition of this bull (I²) registered, in
which, as a result of the addition of a new clause, the first service demanded
of the prelates was to call upon the brethren to exercise the office of preaching, to
which they were assigned. In November 1219, Dominic was engaged in getting the
Chancellery to dispatch a series of copies of the bull thus completed, to recommend
his convents in course of foundation. The same bull was thus able to be used to
recommend the preaching of individual brethren. The final issue of this formula is
dated 13th December, 1219.

A few days earlier, however, the founder obtained from the Pope three different
bulls, numerous copies of which he at once had distributed (nos. 9 to 13; 14; 26).
The first of these new bulls (II) in its preamble described the activity of the Preachers
and above all their poverty, the extreme character of which it emphasized. The
terms of enactment took up again the clauses of the previous bull (I²), but stressed
each one of them by the addition of the significant words: *affectuose, liberaliter*.
Finally, it added new clauses to demand that the prelates should support the 'necessary' ministry of the brethren among their flocks, by their authority. This bull was
destined particularly for those convents that were in process of foundation. In fact
it would seem that it was only used to recommend communities.

The second of the new bulls (III) laid all the emphasis on the ministry of the
Preachers. In the prologue and the terms of enactment, unmistakable allusions to
the 10th canon of the Lateran Council (*viros predicatores ecclesie sancte pernecessarios,
pro eo quod ministrant pabulum verbi Dei; cum propter occasiones multiplices partiri expediat
interdum in alios sollicitudinem pastoralem; penitentium confessiones audire et consilium eis
inuingere salutare*) had as their obvious aim to present the Preachers to the bishops as
irreplaceable persons who will enable them to comply with the Council's canon.
It thus mobilized for the benefit of the Preachers both the considerable weight of the
requirements of the Council and also that of the authority of the Pope. A new
clause, however, was to protect the poverty of the mendicant preachers against
temptations and to reassure the prelates of the disinterestedness of these new apostles.
If it should happen that the so-called preacher should beg for money, the prelate was
to have him arrested and condemned as an imposter and slanderer of the order. This
bull, which also summed up the clauses of the first of the bulls of recommendation,
could doubtless be used for recommending a community. It was, however, specially
indicated for use as an individual testimonial. This was precisely the case of copies
nos. 18, 19, 23.

The third bull (IV¹), in December 1219, contained only a pressing mandate of recommendation in its terms of enactment. The emphasis was centred on the prologue or rather on the exposition. There the order of Preachers was seen in the perspective of the interventions of Providence against heretics and other 'mortal plagues' of the Church. *Quoniam abundavit iniquitas et refriguit caritas plurimorum, ordinem fratrum Predicatorum, sicut credimus, Dominus suscitavit, qui non que sua sunt sed que Christi querentes, tam contra profligandas hereses quam contra pestes alias mortiferas extirpandas se dedicaverunt evangelizationi verbi Dei, in abjectione voluntarie paupertatis.* This description was well calculated to draw to the Preachers the attention and support of, for example, the Archbishop of Tarragona, to whom this bull was addressed on May 6th, 1219 (no. 27).

In January 1221, this striking prologue was placed at the head of the terms of enactment of formula II. Thus formula IV² of which Dominic made but a limited use was constituted. He preferred to distribute formula III, which he had reproduced a considerable number of times during the first half of 1221, i.e. until his final departure from Rome and his death. The reason for this is clear and charged with meaning. Formula III presented the ministry of the Preachers along the lines of the 10th canon of the Lateran, that is, along the lines of a universal, ordinary and positive evangelization; formula IV² in the perspective of the struggle against heresy. We can understand why, in 1227, it was this latter formula that Gregory IX was to prefer. By inserting therein the appropriate clauses of the terms of enactment of formula III, he composed the definitive formula of recommendation of the order. There is room for regret that this bull contributed by its impressive prologue to placing the activity of the Preachers in a polemical perspective against the clear preferences of the founder.

GRANT OF HOUSES AT BRIHUEGA (1218)

THE deed re-edited below is contained in the first register or *Becerro* of the cathedral of Toledo, Fo. 39v., col. 2, preserved in the national historical archives of Madrid, section relating to the clergy. It was edited for the first time by Juan Catalina García, director of these Archives, in his book *El fuero de Brihuega*, Madrid, 1887, App. pp. 195–196. Since that time Fr L. Gonzáles Alonso Getino has reproduced it, after the earlier edition, in his *Vida de Santo Domingo de Guzmán, fundador de la Orden de Predicadores, por el Beato Jordan de Sajonia* . . . translated and annotated by Fr Getino, Vergara, 1916, 351–352 (cf. 179). It is here re-edited from the manuscript. The text has been seriously damaged by water (was this when the archbishop was drowned in the Rhône?). All the lacunae cannot be restored. The damage is particularly serious for the date. In the critical notes the data are given which enable the date of 1218 to be reconstructed with fair certainty. J. Gorosterrazu, in his biography of Don Rodrigo (Pamplona 1925, 229), led astray by faulty chronology which he took over without question from the early historians of Dominic, incorrectly assigns this deed to 1219. We here address our thanks to the director of the *Archivo histórico nacional*, Señor Luis Sánchez Belda, who procured for us the indications and texts of which we have made use.

DE DOMIBUS DE BRIOGA[1] CONCESSIS
ORDINI PREDICATORUM[a]

Notum sit omnibus *hominibus*[b] *hanc paginam* inspecturis *quod nos* R[udericus][2] dei gratia Toletane Sedis Archi*episcopus hispaniarum* primas nostre spontanee uoluntatis *dispositione* (?) fratri dominico ministro ordinis *fratrum* (?) *predicationis*[3] aliis fratribus eiusdem ordinis domos . . . *in brioga* que fuerunt de Johanne Caluo quas *uobis* (?) *Emilia*nus clericus sancti Michaelis de brioga *filius* (?) quondam eiusdem Johannis Calui titu*lo donationis* (?) reuocabilis[c] donavit. Ipso Emiliano *postulante* (?) autoriza-mus[d] et concedimus quiete *ac libere* (?) possidendas. Tali tamen apposita pactione[4]... *quod* (?) rato Emiliano viam uniuerse carnis *si* (?) forte (?) Archiepiscopo Toletano qui pro tempore fuerit . . . *illas* domos non placuerit amplius uos habere . . . detis[e], uel detis eas uassallis Archiepiscopi qui . . . facere suum forum, uel Archiepiscopo Toletano *abso*lute et libere sine cuiuslibet contradictionis obstaculo relinquatis. Et ut predicta concessio *quam* facimus firma et irreuocabilis ut annotatur *supra* perseueret presentem cartam de mandato nostro *scrip*tam et subscriptione manus proprie roboratam *sig*illi nostri patrocinio jussimus communiri. A*ctum* fuit hoc apud Tala-mancam. Era. M.CC[a] . . . [f] mense nouembris in presentia et sub testificati*one partium*[5] subscriptorum.

Nos. R. dei gratia Toletane Sedis Archiepiscopus hispaniarum primas. SS. et confirmo.

Ego. Bertrandus guadalphaiarensis archidiaconus confirmo.

Ego. J. guterrij canonicus Toletanus . . . .

Ego. P. sancti Dominici cappellanus Toletanus canonicus . . . SS.

Critical notes

(a) Title, in a different hand and ink, after the deterioration of the text; it completes a line where it is possible to read in the hand and ink of our charter: Era Mᵃ. CCᵃ. LVI (=1218). It is possible that this date forms the end of the preceding document which is in large part effaced.

(b) Damp has caused the right half of the charter to disappear, allowing a few letters to be seen. The restitutions are indicated in italics, purely hypothetical cases being indicated by (?). The length of the lacunae it has not been possible to fill in is indicated by . . . The punctuation and capitals of the original have been retained.

(c) The word begins a line after a lacuna, perhaps *irrevocabilis* should be read.

(d) Ms=*autoziramus*.

(e) Perhaps, *eas reddetis*, or *non possidetis*.

(f) There is exactly room for LVI, and no more; this gives, according to the Christian era, 1218.

Historical notes

(1) Brihuega.

(2) Rodrigo Jiménez de Rada, Bishop of Osma after the death of Diego de Acebo, from 1208 to 1210, date at which he was transferred to the see of Toledo. 1247.

(3) This title, the final letters of which are still visible, was used by the order in 1217, at the time of the dispersal of Toulouse, cf. Laurent, nos. 80 and 81 (where it is necessary to restore, after ms. *Toulouse* 490 fos. 100–101, *fratres predicationis*, wherever the editor has printed *predicatores*); the brethren took it with them to Spain in 1218–1219, Laurent, no. 95. Fulk of Toulouse was still using it, anachronistically, in 1221—Laurent, no. 134.

(4) The house of John the Bald having become Church property, the archbishop refused to bind his successor. In case of withdrawal, the property was to revert to Aemilian; if the latter should die, the archbishop would decide to whom it should go.

(5) The presence of the parties confirms the date of 1218, the only month of November when Dominic was in Spain. Cf. critical notes a and f.

THE RULE OF ST SIXTUS

1. On 23rd October, 1232 Pope Gregory IX gave a new legislation to the order of Penitents of St Mary Magdalene in Germany, founded since 1227 in accordance with the rule of St Benedict and the Cistercian constitutions (Simon, 202). What was now promulgated was the rule of St Augustine and the 'Institutions of the order of nuns of St Sixtus in Rome'. This concession was not an isolated gesture. Since the Order of Prémontré had abandoned its houses of women, at the beginning of the thirteenth century, the communities of nuns in the process of formation had scarcely any choice except among three approved institutions: that of Gregory IX himself, on which model the Poor Clares had been formed as well as other religious in Tuscany; that of Cîteaux, whose considerable expansion since the beginning of the century had just been bluntly frustrated by the general chapter; that of St Sixtus of Rome. Since about 1230, a good number of feminine communities, especially in Germany, took or received the latter (Grundmann, 220–235). It was from this source that the mention came of the 'Order of the nuns of St Sixtus' which was to be understood in the same sense as 'the Order of St Augustine'. This did not mean that there was then in existence a centralized society ruled by the 'Institutions of St Sixtus', but that a large number of houses in other respects independent followed the 'order' or the observance of these institutions (Grundmann 236–237; Creytens, *Montargis*, 52).

The Pope inscribed this legislative text in his bull. Unfortunately this bull was not registered and the original is now lost. On 1st January, 1291, Pope Nicholas IV renewed and confirmed the concession of his predecessor, in a bull which recopied in full that of 1232 (Simon, 258 and 142–153). This new bull, inscribed in the registers of Nicholas IV, is likewise known through a certified copy preserved in Breslau and by a *vidimus* of Mecklemberg. In view of the habits of the Pontifical Chancellery, it cannot be doubted that the text reproduced in 1291 is in every respect that of 1232. This can, moreover, be verified by comparing this text with that offered by two modern works which seem to offer a direct edition of the bull of Gregory IX no longer extant (Simon, 143).

2. Traditionally, however, the order of St Mary Magdalene added certain statutes to the 'Institutions of St Sixtus' (statutes edited in accordance with a manuscript of Vienna in *Raymundi Duellii miscellaneorum quae ex codicibus mss. collegit liber I*, Augsburg 1723, 182–198; German manuscript translation at the convent of Lauban, Romance translation ed. Discry, 84–145; re-edition Simon, 154–168, cf. 169–170). These statutes of St Mary Magdalene (=SM) gave to the 'Institutions' of St Sixtus, exclusively and on six different occasions, the name of rule of St Sixtus under which we shall designate them for the future (=RS). They are in actual fact directly extracted from the first Dominican constitutions, as these existed between 1228 and 1236. There in fact are to be found two of the legislative additions of 1228: IC (= first

constitutions OP), D.II ch. 14 and SM, ch. 19 (on these texts see Mandonnet-Vicaire
II, 282 and Vicaire, *Documents*, II, 117–118). On the other hand we find none of the
additions or corrections demanded by the chapter of 1236, which should normally
have come at the end of ch. 7 of SM and in the middle of ch. 15 where, on the
contrary, we find an insertion which was suppressed at this date (*Acta*, I, 6, nos. 7
and 12). It can even be stated with certainty that these statutes were extracted from
the Dominican constitutions at the latest in 1232. On the one hand, they are
organically linked to the rule of St Sixtus: five chapters of SM are limited to
references to the corresponding chapters of RS: SM, 5, 17, 18, 20, 23; RS (we
quote the Simon edition 143–153, pointing out that the division of the text into
chapters and the titles of these chapters are the work of the editor), 2, 10, 11 to 15,
24, 21; another chapter makes explicit, on the contrary, a chapter of RS, which in
some sort anticipates it: SM, 8 and RS, 7; seven chapters are a repetition of the
chapters of RS, which they specify; thirteen chapters complete RS adding certain
liturgical, personal and social data, indispensable to the life of the order. On the
other hand, the whole RS + SM was composed, as will be seen, for a convent of
Dominican nuns before it was assigned to the Penitents.

3. The interest of both these documents will be obvious. The statutes enable us to
go back to a text of the Dominican constitutions earlier than 1232. The rule of St
Sixtus can throw light on the history of St Dominic's foundations for women. The
name of 'Institutions of the order of nuns of St Sixtus' given to it by Gregory IX
was a reminder that in 1232 it was not the rule of the Roman community alone; in
fact, before spreading in Germany to communities which had nothing in common
with the Preachers, it had been put into practice in several of the houses founded or
prepared by St Dominic. Among the communities of Prouille, St Agnes of Bologna
and St Sixtus, a genuine similarity of observances is in fact found. After all, the community of St Sixtus was founded by the sisters asked for from Prouille at its
inception (Laurent, no. 104) and installed in the convent before the transfer of the
sisters of Sta Maria in Tempulo and St Bibiana, so that they might receive them and
instruct them *de ordinis observantiis*, and in particular to speak *per signum manuum*
(Montefiascone, 836). The rule they brought from Prouille had thus at least served
as a basis for that of St Sixtus. It is not impossible that at this time Dominic modified
this first rule, to bring it into line with the times and adapt it to the new house. It is
also possible that the four sisters of St Sixtus from the Midi who returned to Prouille
at the end of a certain time, brought back with them there these few changes
(Montefiascone, 836). They cannot have amounted to much. When Jordan of
Saxony in 1223 wished to inaugurate the monastery of St Agnes of Bologna he first
turned to Prouille to obtain foundresses who would be exemplary. Only when his
request could not be granted did he provide himself with foundresses from the
sisters of St Sixtus. At this period too, then, the tradition of Prouille must have
appeared as the fundamental tradition of the nuns of St Dominic. However this may
be, in 1236, the legislative unity between Prouille and St Sixtus was such that the
sisters from the Midi, in a petition to Gregory IX, did not hesitate to tell him that
at the 'moment of their conversion', that is when Prouille was begun as a house of
regular observance, they had all adopted as their rule (this is the meaning of *elegerunt
Domino famulari sub regula* . . .) 'the rule of the nuns of St Sixtus of Rome' (*BOP*, I, 86,

no. 149). This was apparently a stylistic formula to designate their own rule by the name under which the Curia, and Europe, knew and defined it—rule, or 'Institutions of the order of nuns of St Sixtus' (Gregory IX, 1232—Simon, 202; 1236, *BOP*, I, 86, no. 149. Cf. Innocent IV, 1248, *BOP*, I, 183, no. 200).

The external historical data are thus clear and almost categorical. They confirm an essential continuity between the rule of Prouille, the rule of St Sixtus and the 'Institutions' of the sisters of St Mary Magdalene in Germany which we still possess today. The internal investigation of this latter text does not confirm this assertion in every respect. Without weakening the assertion, it complicates the situation to a considerable extent (hence the doubts of Creytens—*Montargis*, 51).

4. The first statement that must be made is that in the text of the rule of St Sixtus edited in 1232 numerous technical terms or expressions have been found not referring to the 'Institutions' of Prouille or of St Sixtus but only to those of the German Penitents. With the terms *priorissa* and *prelata*, which fitted the three categories of sisters, are to be found fifteen times the term *prepositus* (*pr.*, four times; *pr. maior* twice; *pr. ordinis* once; *pr. generalis* eight times). The word *prepositus* was frequent in Germany to designate a superior of Augustinian religious, in the sense in which Italy used *prior*. Moreover under the form *prepositus maior*, or *ordinis* or *generalis*, it expressly designated the major superior of the Penitents (Simon, 45). The expression existed neither at Prouille nor at St Sixtus; it was not found in any of the numerous charters of these monasteries. Yet at Prouille since 1215, at St Sixtus in 1221, the authority of the saint was superimposed on that of the local 'priors'. It is possible that the term *prepositus maior* or *generalis* was only substituted in certain phrases, which would thus be original, for a term which designated St Dominic or his successors (*prelatus maior*, as in the 'Institutions' of 1220, or *magister*?) in the rule of the nuns after 1215. The expressions *prior provincialis, capitulum generale*, did not in any sense apply to Prouille or to St Sixtus before 1232, or afterwards. It is true that the saint's rôle in regard to St Sixtus was assumed by the provincial of Tuscany (Zucchi, 272–276; the provision was not clearly established until 1242— but the situation must have been older). The latter, however, only intervened among the sisters in the capacity of major superior and there was no point in mentioning his function in the order of the brethren in the rule; still less to name him at the side of the major superior or general provost, as if he were distinct from him (RS, ch. 17, no. 2). The first monasteries of Dominican nuns were not grouped either into provinces or general chapters. The Penitents, on the other hand, at the time when they received RS, already possessed ten convents which lent themselves, by their number and their geographical distribution, to the holding of general chapters as also to regrouping into provinces (Simon, 55; cf. 45).

5. The counter-test can be made by examining the statutes (SM). It will be found in fact that these texts contain no other technical terms than those adapted to an isolated feminine convent dependent on an order of men religious: *priorissa, prelata, capitulum, ordo noster* (for this latter term, cf. SM, ch. 13 and 19).

This condition of things leads to the following conclusions:

1. The statutes, extracted from the Dominican constitutions, were not composed for the order of Penitents, but for an isolated monastery, clearly of Dominican nuns, between 1228 and 1232.

2. They were borrowed unchanged by the Penitents (with the exception of the interpolation of the name of St Mary Magdalene in the formula of profession) at the time that they adopted the rule.

3. The rule of St Sixtus alone was changed to make it suitable for the order of Penitents.

We are at first surprised that it was the rule that was changed rather than the statutes (Creytens, *Montargis*, 53 should be corrected on this point); for it is the essence of a rule to be unchangeable, whereas the characteristic of statutes is that they can be periodically revised. The explanation is a simple one. It must be recalled that the statutes were not given to the Penitents officially by Cardinal Ugolino and could not be so given. They belonged to the monasteries of Dominican nuns attached to the order and there was no question of incorporating the German Penitents among the Preachers. The sisters adopted the statutes without the order's authorization to determine certain important points of their life which had been left in suspense. Moreover, Ugolino did not call the 'Rule' of St Sixtus a 'rule' when he granted it to the Penitents, but 'Institutions', which emphasized its flexible character. As a rule for the German sisters he had given them that of St Augustine.

6. The second discovery one makes on examining the rule of St Sixtus is that it makes considerable use of earlier rules as sources. It refers directly to the rule of St Benedict (ch. 4, 3 and RSB, ch. 37) and perhaps quotes it twice (ch. 8, 2 and 21, 1; RSB, ch. 48 and 55). It is true that these quotations may come from one or other of the innumerable customs inspired by the Benedictine rule. RS refers expressly to the customs of Cîteaux for the rule of the 'collation' (ch. 5, 1; Guignard, 185). It quotes the rule of St Augustine four times (prologue and ch. 4, 1; 8, 1; 14, 2) and moreover assigns this rule to the brethren who look after the nuns (ch. 25, 1). The conditions under which these quotations are made prove that the nuns to whom RS was addressed followed the rule of St Augustine, but had earlier known the rule of St Benedict and the customs of Cîteaux. This could apply to both the Penitents of St Mary Magdalene and to the sisters of Prouille, but not to those of St Sixtus.

7. No connection can be discovered between RS and the statutes relating to the sisters in the twelfth century statutes of the order of Prémontré (ed. Van Waefelghem, *Analectes de l'ordre de Premontre*, IX (1913), 63 to 67). On the other hand, the second part of the rule, in ch. 16, 17, 18, 19, 22, 23 is clearly related to the rule of the order of Sempringham (= SS, ed. Holstenius-Brockie, II, 467–536). The rule dates from the middle of the twelfth century, but the edited text refers to a decision of Innocent III. However, with the exception of a single passage where the dependence is in part literal (SS, 476 and RS, ch. 22. It is in error that Creytens, *Montargis*, 51, n. 3 cites a second literal borrowing), the parallelism is never complete. If RS like SS provides for a provost general (called by SS *prior omnium* or *magister ordinis*) who alone has the power to receive and send away religious of both sexes (SS 471; RS, ch. 19), three priests per house (SS 535 and RS, ch. 25), the four procurators (prior, procurator, cellarer and bailiff, SS, 476; RS, ch. 23), the religious in charge of the fenestra or turn (SS, 480, 518–519; RS, ch. 16), the entrance into the enclosure of persons of high rank (SS, 490 and RS, ch. 16), the entrance in case of Extreme Unction (SS, 535; RS, ch. 17), of fire or of theft (SS, 519; RS, ch. 17), it is no longer in agreement with SS on the total number of the

brethren (SS, 482: seven canons; RS, ch. 25: six brethren, three being priests) or of the turn sisters (SS, 518: 2; RS, ch. 16: 3), or the holders of office. RS has nothing to say of the curious system of triple nomination of the *preposita* and her collaborators, each one of the three officers exercising her office in turn (SS, 472, 520), by the superior general (SS, 472; SS, 520 seems, however, sometimes to make provision for an election, like RS, ch. 24), or the prohibition for the sisters of singing (SS, 523), or the entrusting of all the securities of the convent into the hands of the sisters (SS, 468, 516), or the numerous cases of entering the enclosure for sermons (SS, 490), for processions (SS, 525) and for elections (SS, 469); nor, finally, the cases of the sisters going out for election, canonical visitation and illness (SS, 468, 521). On the other hand, nothing can be found in SS comparable to RS, ch. 20 and 21 on manual work, reading and mental prayer (on this last point, however, cf. SS, 526).

It is doubtless possible to think that the necessity of summarizing a very diffuse rule may have led the editor of RS to deviate from the text of SS, at the same time taking the essence of its institutions, which he could, moreover, correct simultaneously. If this were the case, it would be possible to allow that this second part of the rule of St Sixtus was drawn up in Rome by St Dominic in the winter of 1220–1221 in view of the foundation of St Sixtus which he was engaged in preparing. The Papacy had indeed expressed the wish to regroup certain nuns in Rome under the rule of Sempringham. None of the parallelisms instanced, however, is really decisive. There were very considerable analogies between different sorts of feminine communities in Western Europe at the beginning of the thirteenth century. The resemblances of SS and RS can perhaps be explained by a common dependence on a source which is no longer extant. Even the paragraph of RS which corresponds literally, although partially, to a paragraph of SS, may come from this common source. Thus no categorical conclusion as to the source of the second part of RS can be made.

8. The first part, on the other hand, is indicative of an unquestionable source: the earliest 'Institutions of the Preachers' (= IC). Clearly the 'Rule of St Sixtus' and the 'Institutions of the Preachers' both present a close connection with the customs of Prémontré (= P) which, in these conditions, could be a common source and the origin of the reciprocal resemblance. This explanation, however, will not stand up to direct examination. It is sufficient to take one by one the analogous phrases of RS, IC and P, to note the divergences and resemblances of these elements pair by pair, as regards the terms and expressions of phrase, both in the words themselves and in their order, to realize: 1. that P is the primitive source; 2. that RS depends on P through the intermediary of IC and not vice versa. This analysis can already be made conclusively in regard to chapters 2, 3, 4, 7, 8, 9 of RS. The most fruitful conclusions, however, can be drawn from ch. 11 to 15, concerning the faults.

9. The first statement that can be made seems to contradict this assertion. Like P, RS has a chapter of medium faults which is not found in IC; moreover, the ends of its ch. 11 and 12, on light and medium faults, are analogous to those of the corresponding chapters of P (D. III, ch. 1 and 2), whereas the end of ch. 21 of IC, which has collected together the same material as ch. 11 and 12 of RS, is original. This, however, is only apparently so. It can, in effect, be proved that ch. 21 of IC

was originally divided into two paragraphs, dealing respectively with light and medium faults, directly inspired by the two corresponding chapters of P, and having the same final paragraphs. The following is the result of the analysis item by item of the faults of ch. 21 of IC. We find successively and in their original order: nos. 1 to 17, the series of light faults taken from P, D. III, ch. 1; no. 18, a fault transferred from P, D. III, ch. 2 (medium fault, reduced to the rank of light fault); no. 19, a fault transferred from P, D. III, ch. 3 (serious fault, reduced to the rank of light fault); nos. 20 to 25, a series of original light faults, concerning the preachers and the students. Then come nos. 26 to 37 (except no. 34, a fault originally serious, transferred in 1240 to chapter 21 of IC, *Acta*, I, 13, no. 9), the series of medium faults taken from P, D. III, ch. 2; nos. 38 and 40 (no. 39 is a fault originally serious, transferred in 1240 to ch. 21 of IC, *Acta*, I, 14, no. 14) two faults proper to the Preachers.

This description clearly shows the existence, at the beginnings of IC, of two distinct chapters: one on light faults, nos. 1 to 25, and the other for medium faults, nos. 26 to 40, composed in the same way: faults taken, in their original order, from the corresponding chapter of Prémontré, faults, the degree of seriousness of which has been reduced, coming from the later chapters of P, faults proper to the Preachers. If the two series had been welded together from the beginning, as was the case later, the faults coming from P and those proper to the Preachers would not have been arranged in two different series (1 to 17 and 26 to 37, on the one hand; 20 to 25 and 38 to 40, on the other). In particular, no. 18 would not have been taken from the P chapter of medium faults and attached to the light faults of P, when the rest of the P medium faults was to be added further on in the same series. At the end of each of these two chapters, as at the end of the following chapters, IC fixed the penalty for both types of fault in accordance with the corresponding final paragraph of P. When later (before 1240, cf. *Acta*, I, 14, no. 14) the two chapters were welded into one, doubtless because the distinctions of faults were found to be too subtle, the two final paragraphs were suppressed, to be replaced by a text expressing the average (IC, ch. 21, no. 41). It was then that the relationship of IC with P and RS on this point became obscure. It is clear, however, throughout the remainder of the chapter.

10. If the analysis is now extended to ch. 11 and 12 of RS on light and medium faults, it will be seen that the source, not only of their words, phrases and the order of the phrases, but sometimes even of their content is the two original chapters we have just distinguished in the present ch. 21 of IC, and not the corresponding chapters of P. In the first place we find at the head of RS, ch. 11, ch. 18 of IC (cf. P, D. I, ch. 9, end), transformed into a fault; then in the order of IC, ch. 21, faults nos. 1 to 9, 14, 16–18, 22, 23, 25—i.e. the majority of the faults coming from P, D. III, ch. 1 and 2, then several of the completely original faults of IC. The only omissions are the faults of IC which were not applicable to the sisters, in particular those concerning the sacred ministry, studies and preaching. It is nevertheless interesting to see how RS, ch. 11, nos. 14 and 15, has succeeded in modifying for the use of the sisters faults concerning the life of study or preaching of the Preachers (IC, ch. 21, nos. 22 and 23).

The analyses of ch. 12 and the following chapters, while they do not provide equally important elements of comparison, lead to the same conclusions. The first part of RS and more particularly ch. 2, 3, 4, 7, 8, 9, 11 to 15 of RS have been taken from the Dominican customs in their original form and depend through their intermediary on the customs of Prémontré.

11. This conclusion nevertheless requires a corrective. In a small number of cases, the text of RS is closer to P than to IC. In several of these cases it can be proved that the divergences of IC in relation to P and RS are not original and come from mistakes in the Rodez ms. by which we know IC. This can be verified by comparing the doubtful phrase of IC with the corresponding phrase of the constitutions of St Raymond, emanating from the authentic text of IC. The following are three examples: RS, ch. 12, no. 4 has a *cum* found in P and *II Const.* but missing in IC; ch. 12, no. 7, as P and *II Const.* has not the *suis* or the inversion *fuerit repertus* found in IC; RS, ch. 14, no. 2, as P and *II Const.* has *celaverit*, like the rule of St Augustine, against IC—*servaverit*. In two cases, however, it seems to us undeniable that RS has taken over elements from P, dropped by IC—at the beginning of RS, ch. 8 (*Ne sit notabilis habitus vester, etc., sufficiat moniali habere duas tunicas,* etc.; cf. P, D. IV, ch. 14. The phrases are quotations from the rules of St Augustine and St Benedict) and RS, ch. 14, no. 2 (*ut furtum, sacrilegium, vel aliud huiusmodi.* Cf. P, D. III, ch. 6). It must then be admitted that in inscribing the texts of the Preachers in the first chapters of the rule of St Sixtus, the legislator had at hand a text of IC closer to the customs of Prémontré than the Rodez manuscript.

Such are the data for internal criticism. How do they compare with the assertions of the external history of our documents?

12. The modifications introduced into RS in 1232 to make it suitable for the Penitents are revealed in certain terms, and divisions of phrases, or in certain provisions which are only applicable to these sisters and which were interpolated without difficulty in the earlier text. RS, ch. 1, must be one of such additions. From the literary point of view it is presented as a prelude before the beginning of the *norma vivendi*. Moreover it contains a formula of religious engagement with four vows prior to the profession (for the formula of profession is found in SM, ch. 14) which has never been Dominican; finally it mentions the transfer of a nun from one convent of 'the order' to another, a formula not applicable to the convents of Dominican nuns before 1232, since they did not form an order in the strict sense of the term. For the same reason ch. 19 must also be an addition of the same date. Other corrections, which reserve a right of dispensation or authorization to the provost, the provincial or the general chapter, presuppose nothing more than the change or interpolation of two or three words in the earlier text. They will be found in ch. 14, nos. 14, 19, 21; ch. 15, no. 4; ch. 17, nos. 2 and 3; ch. 18, nos. 1–3; ch. 20, no. 2; ch. 24, nos. 1–4. There is no reason to suppose that the changes have been much more considerable than these additions or obvious corrections, for in this case Cardinal Ugolino would not have been able to continue to give to this text the name of 'Institutions of St Sixtus'. By suppressing these limited additions, it is thus possible to reconstruct with sufficient probability the rule of St Sixtus properly so-called. From when did it date?

13. Clearly from a considerably earlier period. It is sufficient to compare the parallel chapters of the 'Rule of St Sixtus' with the Statutes of 1228–1232, to see at once

the archaic character of the former (RS, ch. 3, 4, 7, 8, 16–17, 20 and SM, ch. 7, 10, 15, 16, 3, 21). It went back at least to the foundation of St Sixtus in 1221. Did it come into being at this date? Clearly in the winter of 1220–1221, in Rome, Dominic could have composed it in full, or reconstructed an earlier text with a view to the foundation he was preparing to create. He then had at hand the customs of the Preachers of 1216, completed in May 1220. He had moreover to reinforce the rules of enclosure in the traditions of his sisters, to correspond with the intentions of the Pope and with the ideal he wanted to give his Roman nuns. The theory, however, of the composition in full of the rule of St Sixtus at this period must be excluded. Something has already been said, on the other hand, of the probability of a modification of the rule of Prouille during the winter 1220–1221, in the second part of the text. Finally the hypothesis of a modification of the first part of the rule of Prouille must be excluded and we must refuse to date from this time the massive introduction of the customs of the Preachers into this rule. For it is no longer possible to see how in this case the continuity of observance between Prouille and St Sixtus, which is affirmed by facts and texts whose evidence we have no right to ignore, could be maintained.

14. That is why we think finally that the 'Rule of Prouille-St Sixtus' was elaborated in its essentials (especially for chapters 2–15, 20, 21) by St Dominic for Prouille, between summer 1216 and winter 1220–1221, in the period following the adoption by the Preachers of their law of observance inscribed in the first distinction of the Rodez text. It is possible that this elaboration was made as early as the first date. It could equally have been made in Rome in the winter of 1218. The project, then envisaged by Dominic, of establishing an autonomous community of Preachers in Prouille by granting the masculine part of the convent the privilege of confirmation *Religiosam vitam*, the document of which Dominic procured in Rome on 30th March, 1218, probably led him to elaborate this new rule, to establish it in the feminine part of the community. In the course of the spring or summer of 1218, during those long months when Dominic's activity eludes us, between his departure from Rome and his arrival in New Castile, he was probably busy inaugurating the new legislation in Prouille. What had the rule of the sisters been up to that time? Was it a legislation special to them, already inspired by Prémontré, the first draft that Dominic modified to compose RS? It is probable. In the condition of the documents, however, it is very difficult to adopt this conclusion with certainty.

BIBLIOGRAPHY

and ABBREVIATIONS

Acta = Acta capitulorum generalium ordinis Praedicatorum, vol. I (1220–1303), ed. B. M. Reichert, *Moph*, III, Rome, 1898.

ADD = Archiv der deutschen Dominikaner, ed. L. Siemer, vols. I to IV, Vechta, 1937–1951.

AFH = Archivum Franciscanum historicum, Quaracchi 1908 ff.

AFP = Archivum Fratrum Praedicatorum, Rome, 1931 ff.

AHD = Archives d'histoire dominicaine, Paris, 1946.

AHDLMA = Archives d'histoire doctrinale et litteraire du moyen âge, ed. E. Gilson, Paris, 1926 ff.

ALKMA = Archiv für Literatur und Kirchengeschichte des Mittelalters, ed. H. Denifle and Fr Ehrle, Berlin and Fribourg-in-Br., 1885 ff.

ALTANER = B. —, *Der hl. Dominikus, Untersuchungen und Texte*, Breslau, 1922.

—, Armut = "Der Armutsgedanke beim hl. Dominikus", in *Theologie und Glaube*, 1919, 404–417.

—, Beziehungen = 'Die — des hl. Dominikus zum hl. Franziskus von Assisi', in *Franziskanische Studien*, IX (1922), 1–28.

—, Dominikanermissionen = *Die — des 13. Jahrhunderts. Forschungen zur Gesch. der kirchlichen Unionen u. der Mohammedaner-u. Heidenmissionen des MAs* (*Breslauer Studien zur historischen Theologie*, 3), Habelschwerdt, 1924.

AMATO = A. d' —, G.G. Palmieri, E. Graffi-Benassi, A. Branzi, O.M. Olivo, F. Frassetto, *Le reliquie di S. Domenico. Storia e Leggenda, ricèrche scientifiche. Ricostruzione fisica . . . .*, Bologna, 1946.

AMORT = Eusebius —, *Vetus Disciplina canonicorum regularium et saecularium . . .* , Venetiis, 1747.

ARGULETA, Apología = J. López —, — *por el Hábito canónico de Santo Domingo en la Orden de Santiago*, Madrid, 1725.

—, Continuación = — *de la Apología por el Hábito de Santo Domingo*, Madrid, 1731.

ARON = M. —, *Un animateur de la jeunesse au XIIIe siècle. Vie, voyages du Bx Jourdain de Saxe . . .* , Paris, 1930.

ASOP = Analecta sacri Ordinis Fr. Praedicatorum, Rome, 1893 ff.

ASS = Acta Sanctorum, Venice 1734 ff.

BALME = RR. PP. — & Lelaidier (vol. III and Collomb), *Cartulaire ou histoire diplomatique de S. Dominique*, with reproductions of documents, 3 vol., Paris, 1893, 1897 and 1901.

BARTHOLOMEW = — of Trent, *Legenda S. Dominici confessoris*, ed. in Altaner, 230–239.

BARTOLINI = Fr —, *Le antiche carte dell' Archivio del monastero dei SS. Domenico e Sisto* (*Miscellanea della Dep. rom. di Storia patria*), Rome, 1941.

BECQUET = J. —, 'Les premiers ecrivains de l'ordre de Grandmont', in *Revue Mabillon*, XLIII (1953), 121–137.

BERTHIER, Testament = J. J. —, *Le — de saint Dominique*, Fribourg 1892.

—, Tombeau = *Le — de saint Dominique*, Paris, 1895.

BOEHMER-WIEGAND = H. — and F. —, *Analekten zur Geschichte des Franciscus von Assisi*, Tübingen, 1930.

BOP = *Bullarium Ord. Fr Praed.*, ed. A. Bremond, vol. I, Rome, 1729.

BORST = A. —, *Die Katharer* (*Schriften der Monumenta Germaniae Historica*, 12), Stuttgart, 1953.

BOURBON = *Anecdotes historiques, légendes et apologues tirés du recueil inédit d'Étienne de Bourbon, dominicain du XIIIe siècle*, par A. Lecoy de la Marche, Paris 1877 (numbered according to the text).

BREM = E. —, *Papst Gregor IX bis zum Beginn seines Pontifikates* (*Heidelberger Abhandl. z. mittl. u. neueren Geschichte*, 32), Heidelberg, 1911.

BREMOND = A. —, *De guzmana stirpe S. Dominici demonstratio* . . . , Rome, 1740.

Bullarium Danicum = —, *Pavelige Aktstykker vedrorende Danmark* 1198–1316, ed. A. Krarup, Copenhagen, 1932.

CALMETTE = J. —, *Le Reich allemand au moyen âge*, Paris, 1951.

CAMPI = P.M. —, *Dell' historia ecclesiastica di Piacenza* (44–1435) *con mentione di famiglie, huomini illustri etc.* . . . , 3 vol., Piacenza, 1651–1662.

CANTIMPRÉ = Thomas de —, *Bonum universale de apibus*, Douai 1605.

CARRO, *Caleruega* = V.D. —, —, *cuna de Santo Domingo de Guzmán*, I and II, Madrid, 1952 and 1955.

—, *S. Domingo* = *Santo* — *de Guzmán, fundador de la primera orden universitaria, apostólica y misionera*, Salamanca, 1946.

CASTILLO = F. Del — y J. Lopez, *Historia general y vida de Santo Domingo y de su Orden de Predicadores*, 2 vol., Madrid and Valladolid, 1584–1592.

CATEL = G. de —, *Histoire des comtes de Tolose*, Toulouse 1623.

CAVAZZA = F. —, *Le scuole dell' antico studio bolognese*, Milan, 1896.

CECILIA = Die Miracula B. "Dominici der Schwester Cäcilia", ed. A. Walz, in *Miscellanea Pio Paschini*, vol. I, Rome, 1948, 293–326.

CELANO = Thomas of —, 'Legenda secunda S. Francisci', in *Analecta Franciscana*, vol. X, Quaracchi, 1926.

CERNAI = Pierre des Vaux de —, *Historia Albigensis*, ed. P. Guebin and E. Lyon, 3 vol., Paris 1926 to 1939 (numbered according to the text).

Chanson = *La* — *de la croisade contre les Albigeois*, ed. P. Meyer, vol. II, Paris, 1879.

CHAPOTIN = M.D. —, *Histoire des dominicains de la province de France. Le siècle des fondations*, Rouen, 1898.

Chronica Ia (IIa) = —, ed. B. Reichert, *MOPH*, I, 321–338.

COLMENARÉS = D. De —, *Historia de la insigne ciudad de Segovia y conpendio de las historias de Castilla*, Segovia 1637.

CONSTANTINO = — D'orvieto, Legenda S. Dominici, ed. Scheeben, *MOPH* XVI, Rome, 1935 (numbered according to the text).

I Const. = Constitutiones antique ordinis fratrum predicatorum, ed. H. Denifle, *ALKMA* I, 193–227 (enumeration of the paragraphs in accordance with the edition of *QF* XXXVIII and the translation of Vicaire, *Documents*).

II Const. = Les constitutions des Fr Prêcheurs dans la rédaction de saint Raymond de Peñafort, ed. R. Creytens, in *AFP* XVIII (1948), 5–68.

CONSTANT = M.D. —, *Sur les pas de saint Dominique en France*, Paris, 1926.

COTTINEAU = L. H. —, *Repertoire topo-bibliographique des abbayes et prieurés*, Mâcon, 1935–1937.

CREYTENS, Convers = R. —, 'Les — des moniales dominicaines au moyen age', in *AFP* XIX (1949), 5–48.

—, Montargis = 'Les constitutions primitives des soeurs dominicaines de —', in *AFP*, XVII (1947), 41–84.

Dania = Historia Ordinis Praedicatorum in —, 1216–1246, ed. J. Langebek and P. F. Suhm, *Scriptores rerum danicarum medii aevi*, vol. V, Copenhagen, 1783, 500–502.

15—S.D.

DEFOURNEAUX = M. —, *Les Français en Espagne aux XIe et XIIe siècles*, Paris, 1949.

DELHAYE = Ph. —, 'L'organisation scolaire au XIIe siècle', in *Traditio*, vol. V (1947), 211–268.

DENIFLE, Chartularium = H. — and E. Chatelain, — *universitatis parisiensis*, vol. I, Paris, 1889.

—, *Universitäten* = *Die Entstehung der* — *des Mittelalters bis* 1400, Berlin, 1885.

DEREINE, Chanoines = Ch. —, —, in *DHGE*, XII, 353–404.

—, Enquête = '— sur la règle de saint Augustin', in *Scriptorium*, II (1948), 27–36.

—, Prémontré = 'Les origines de —', in *RHE*, XLII (1947), 352–378.

—, Springiersbach = 'Les coutumiers de Saint-Quentin de Beauvais et de —', in *RHE*, XLIII (1948), 411–442.

—, Statut canonique = 'L'élaboration du — des chanoines réguliers, spécialement sous Urbain II', in *RHE*, XLVI (1954), 534–565.

DEWAILLY = L.M. —, 'Note sur l'histoire de l'adjectif "apostolique" ', in *Mélanges de science religieuse*, V (1948), 141–152.

DHGE = *Dictionnaire d'histoire et de géographie écclesiastiques*.

DICKINSON = J.C. —, *The origins of the Austin canons and their introduction into England*, London, 1950.

DICKSON = Ch. —, 'Le cardinal Robert de Courson, sa vie', in *AHDLMA*, IX (1934), 53–142.

D EZ PARDO = F. —, *S. Domingo de Guzmán*, Vergara, 1935.

DISCRY = M.F. —, 'La règle des Pénitentes de Sainte-Marie Madeleine d'après le ms. de Saint-Quirin de Huy', in *Bull. de la commission royale d'histoire*, CXXII (1956), 85–145.

DONDAINE, Actes = A. —, 'Les — du concile albigeois de Saint-Felix de Caraman', in *Miscellanea G. Mercati (Studi e Testi, 125)*, vol. V, Vatican City, 1946, 324–355.

—, Hiérarchie I (II) = La — cathare en Italie. I, "Le De heresi catharorum", in *AFP*, XIX (1949), 280–312 and II, "Le Tractatus de hereticis' d'Anselme d'Alexandrie O.P.", in *AFP* XX (1950), 234–324.

—, Origine = 'L' — de l'hérésie médiévale. A propos d'un livre récent', in *Rivista di Storia della Chiesa in Italia*, VI (1952), 47–78.

—, Valdès = "Aux origines du Valdeisme, une profession de foi de—", in *AFP*, XVI (1946), 191–235.

DONNER = G.A. —, Kardinal Wilhelm von Sabina, Bischof von Modena, 1222–1234. Päpstlicher Legat in den nordischen Landern, † 1251 (*Societas scientiarum Fennica. Commentationes humanarum litterarum*, II, 5), Helsingfors, 1929.

DOSSAT, Cathares et Vaudois = Y. —, '— à la veille de la croisade albigeoise', in *Revue historique et littéraire du Languedoc*, II (1945), 390–397 and III (1946), 70–83.

—, Clergé = 'Le — méridional à la veille de la croisade albigeoise', in *Revue hist. et litt. du Languedoc*, I (1944), 263–278.

—, Comté = 'Le — de Toulouse et la féodalité languedocienne à la veille de la croisade', in *Revue du Tarn*, IX (1943), 75–90.

DOUAIS = C. —, *Documents pour servir à l'histoire de l'inquisition dans le Languedoc*, 2 vol., Paris 1900.

DTC = *Dictionnaire de Théologie catholique*.

DU CANGE = —, *Glossarium mediae et infimae latinitatis*, ed. Paris, 1840 ff.

DUVAL = A. —, 'La dévotion mariale dans l'ordre des Frères Prêcheurs', in *Études sur la Sainte Vierge*, ed. H. du Manoir, vol. II, Paris, 1952, 739–782.

ÉCHARD = J. Quetif and J. Échard, *Scriptores Ordinis Praedicatorum*, 2 vol., Paris, 1719 and 1721.

Enciclopedia Universal = — *illustrada Europeo-Americana*, Barcelona 1908–1933.

ERENS = A. —, 'Les soeurs dans l'ordre de Premontre', in *Analecta Praemonstratensia*, V (1929), 5–26.

EUBEL = C. —, *Hierarchia catholica medii aevi*, vol. I, Münster, 1898.

EVERWIN DE STEINFELD = —, Epistola ad S. Bernardum, *PL*, 182, 676–680.

FÉROTIN, *Recueil* = M. —, — *des chartes de l'abbaye de Silos*, Paris, 1897.

—, *Silos* = *Histoire de l'abbaye de* —, Paris, 1897.

FERRANDO = Pedro —, *Legenda S. Dominici*, ed. Laurent, *MOPH*, XVI, Rome 1935 (numbered according to the text).

FLICHE = A. —, Chr. Thouzellier and Y. Azaïs, *La chrétienté romaine*, 1198–1274 (*Histoire de l'Église*, 10), Paris, 1950.

—, Enquête = 'Premiers résultats d'une — sur la réforme grégorienne dans les diocèses français', in *Comptes rendus de l'Académie des inscriptions et belles-lettres*, Paris, 1944, 162–180.

—, Montpellier = 'La vie religieuse à — sous le pontificat d'Innocent III (1198–1216)', in *Mélanges Halphen*, Paris, 1951, 217–224.

FLÓREZ = H. —, *España Sagrada*, 52 vol., Madrid, 1750 ff.

FOREVILLE = R. — and J. Rousset de Pina, *Du premier concile de Latran à l'avènement d'Innocent III* (*Histoire de l'Eglise*, 9, Pt. 2), Paris, 1953.

FRACHET = Gerard de —, *Vitae Fratrum ord. Praed. necnon chronica ordinis ab anno 1203 usque 1254*, ed. Reichert, *MOPH*, I, Louvain, 1896.

GALBRAITH = G. R. —, *The Constitution of the Dominican Order*, 1216 to 1360, Manchester, 1925.

GALLÉN = J. —, La province de Dacie de l'ordre des Frères Prêcheurs, vol. I, *Histoire générale jusqu'au Grand Schisme* (*Inst. hist. FFr. Praed. Romae ad S. Sabinam, dissertationes hist.*, 12), Helsingfors, 1946.

Gallia Christiana = —, new ed., Paris, 1870.

GALVAGNO, Major = — Della Fiamma, Chronica —, reproduction of the fragments extant in *AFP*, X (1940), 319–370, by G. ODETTO.

—, Minor = Chronica —, ab anno 1170 usque 1333, ed. Reichert, in *MOPH*, II, i, Rome, 1897.

GAMS = P.B. —, *Series episcoporum eccl. cath.*, Ratisbon 1873.

GANSHOF = Fr L. —, *Histoire des relations internationales*, I, *Le moyen âge*, Paris, 1953.

GEOFFROI D'AUXERRE = —, Epistola, *PL*, 185, 410–414.

GETINO = L. —, *Santo Domingo de Guzmán*, Madrid, 1939.

GIROU = J. —, *Simon de Montfort*, Paris, 1953.

GOOVAERTS = L. —, *Dictionnaire bio-bibliographique des écrivains, artistes et savants de l'ordre de Prémontré*, 3 vol., Brussels 1899–1909.

GLORIEUX = P. —, *Répertoire des maîtres en théologie de Paris au XIIIe s.* (*Études de philosophie médiévale*, 17–18), 2 vol., Paris, 1933.

GONNET = G. —, ''Waldensia'', in *Revue d'histoire et de philosophie religieuses*, XXXIII (1953), 202–254.

GRATIEN = P. —, *Histoire de la fondation et de l'évolution de l'Ordre des frères Mineurs au XIIIe siecle*, Paris-Gembloux, 1928.

GRAULE = H. —, *Histoire de Lescure*, Paris, 1885.

GRIFFE = E. —, 'Géographie ecclésiastique de la province de Narbonnaise au moyen âge', in *Annales du Midi*, XLVIII (1938), 363–382.

GRUNDMANN — = Herbert —, *Religiöse, Bewegungen im Mittelalter. Untersuchungen uber die geschichtlichen Zusammenhange zwischen der Ketzerei, den Bettelorden und der religiösen Frauenbewegung im 12. und 13. Jahrh. und uber die geschichtlichen Grundlagen der deutschen Mystik* (*Hist. Stud.*, 267), Berlin 1935.

—, Eresie = ''— e nuovi ordini religiosi nel secolo XII'', in *Relazioni. X. Congresso internazionale di Scienze storiche*, III, Florence, 1955, 357–402.

Gui = Bernard —, "Libellus de Magistris ordinis Praedicatorum and Historia fundationum conventuum ord. Praed.", in Martène, *Script.*, VI, 397–436 and 437–566.

Guignard = Ph. —, *Les monuments primitifs de la règle cistercienne*, Dijon, 1878.

Guinard = P. —, ' La péninsule ibérique. La reconquête chrétienne, de la dislocation du califat de Cordoue à la mort de saint Ferdinand', in *Histoire du moyen âge*, vol. IV, Paris, 1939.

Guiraud, Cartulaire = J. —, — de N.D. de Prouille, 2 vol., Paris, 1907.

—, Fondation = "Saint Dominique et la — du monastère de Prouille", in *Revue historique*, LXIV (1897), 224–257.

—, Inquisition = Histoire de l'— au moyen âge, vol. I, Paris, 1935.

Hauck = A. —, *Kirchengeschichte Deutschlands*, 5th ed., Leipzig 1925.

Hefele-Leclercq = Ch. Hefele, *Histoire des conciles*, translated and amplified by H. Leclercq, Paris 1907 ff.

Heimbücher = M. —, *Die Orden und Kongregationen der katholischen Kirche*, 2 vol., 2nd ed., Paderborn, 1933–34.

Heredia = V. Beltrán de —, 'La formación intelectual del Clero en España durante los siglos XII, XIII y XIV', in *Rev. esp. de Teologia*, VI (1946), 313–357.

Hessel = A. — *Geschichte der Stadt Bologna von 1116 bis 1280*, Berlin, 1910.

Hinnebusch = W.A. —, *The early English Friars Preachers (Dissertationes historicae, 14)*, Rome, 1951.

Hinschius = P. —, *System des katholischen Kirchenrechts, mit besonderer Rücksicht auf Deutschland*, 3 vol., Berlin, 1869.

Holstenius-Brockie = L. — and M. —, *Codex regularum monasticarum et canonicarum . . .* , vol. II, Augsbourg, 1759.

Horoy = C.A. —, *Honorii IIIi opera omnia (Bibliotheca patristica . . . series I)*, vol. II, Paris, 1879.

Humbert = Legenda S. Dominici, ed. WALZ, *MOPH*, XVI, Rome 1935 (numbered according to the text).

Humbert, Reg. = — de Romans, Opera de Vita Regulari, 2 vol., ed. J. J. Berthier, Rome, 1888 and 1889.

Huyghe = G. —, "La clôture des moniales, des origines à la fin du XIIIe siècle". *Etude historique et juridique*, Roubaix, 1944.

Irsay = St D' —, *Histoire des universités francaises et étrangères des origines à nos jours*, vol. I, Paris 1933.

Jolibois = —, *Revue . . . du département du Tarn*, II, Albi 1878–1879.

Jordan = E. —, *L'Allemagne et l'Italie aux XIIe et XIIIe siècles (Histoire du moyen âge, vol. IV Pt. I)* Paris, 1939.

Jordan = — of Saxony, Libellus de principiis ordinis praedicatorum, ed. H. Chr. Scheeben, *MOPH*, XVI, Rome, 1935. (numbered according to the text).

— Epistulae = Beati Jordani de Saxonia epistulae, ed. A. Walz, *MOPH* XXIII, Rome, 1951.

—, Oratio = — B. Jordani ad B. Dominicum, ed. H. Chr. Scheeben, in *ASOP*, XVIII (1928), 564–568.

Kirsch = B. — and S. Roman, *Pèlerinages dominicains*, Paris-Lille, 1920.

Koudelka = V.J. —, "Notes sur le cartulaire de S. Dominique", in *AFP*, XXVIII (1958), 92–114.

Labande = E.R. —, "Pour une image véridique d'Aliénor d'Aquitaine", in *Bull. de la Soc. des antiquaires de l'Ouest et des musées de Poitiers*, IV cent. vol. II (1952), 175–234.

Lagger, Albigeois = L. de —, 'L'— pendant la crise de l'albigéisme', in *RHE*, XXIX (1933), 272–315; 586–633; 849–904.

—, Réforme grégorienne = 'Aperçu de la — dans l'Albigeois', in *Studi Gregoriani*, vol. II, Rome, 1947, 211–234.

LADNER = R. —, 'L'ordo praedicatorum avant l'ordre des Prêcheurs', in Mandonnet-Vicaire, vol. II, 11–68.

LAMBERMOND = C.H. —, Der Armutsgedanke des Hl. Dominikus und seines Ordens, Zwolle, 1926.

LAURENT = M.H. —, Historia diplomatica S. Dominici, MOPH, XV, Paris 1933 (numbered according to the documents).

LESNE = E. —, Histoire de la propriété ecclésiastique en France, vol. V, Les écoles, de la fin du VIIIe siècle á la fin du XIIe, Lille, 1940.

LEVI, Documenti = G. —, '— ad illustrazione del Registro del card. Ugolino d'Ostia', in Archivio della R. Societá Romana di storia patria, XII (1889), 241–326.

—, Registro = Registri dei cardinali Ugolino d'Ostia e Ottaviano degli Ubaldini, Rome, 1890.

LIGIEZ = 'Epitome bullarii ordinis Praedicatorum . . . ', ed. M. Fr —, in ASOP, vol. II. (1897–1898), 184 ff.

LOENERTZ, Prouille = R.J. —, 'Archives de —', in AFP, XXIV (1954), 5–49.

—, S. Hyacinthe = 'La vie de — du lecteur Stanislas envisagée comme source historique', in AFP, XXVII (1957), 5–38.

LOPERRAÉZ = J. — Corvalan, Descripción histórica del obispado de Osma, 3 vol., Madrid, 1787–88.

LTK = Lexikon f. Theologie u. Kirche, ed. M. Buchberger, Fribourg-in-Br., 1930–1938.

LUCHAIRE = A. —, La croisade des Albigeois (Innocent III, vol. 11), Paris, 1905.

—, Registres = 'Les — d'Innocent III et les regesta de Potthast', in Troisiemes mélange, d'histoire du moyen age (Bibliothèque de la Faculté des Lettres, XVII), Paris, 1904, 1–83.

MAISONNEUVE = H. —, Etudes sur les origines de l'inquisition (L'Eglise et l'Etat au moyen age, 7), Paris, 1942.

MAMACHI = Th. M. —, Fr Pollidori, V.M. Badetti and H.D. Christianopoulo, Annalium Ordinis Praedicatorum, vol. I, Rome, 1756.

MANDONNET-VICAIRE = P. — and M.H. —, S. Dominique. L'idée, l'homme et l'oeuvre, 2 vol., Paris, 1938.

MANRIQUE = A. —, Cisterciensium . . . annalium, vol. III, Lyons, 1642–1649.

MANSELLI = R. —, Studi sulli heresie del secolo, XII, Rome 1953.

MANSI = J. —, Sacrorum conciliorum nova et amplissima collectio, Venetiis, 1759 ff.

MARTÈNE, Anecd. = E. — and U. Durand, Thesaurus novus anecdotorum, 5 vol., Paris, 1717.

—, Rit. = De antiquis Ecclesiae ritibus libri tres (ed. in Fo), Venetiis, 1783.

—, Script. = Veterum Scriptorum et monumentorum . . . amplissima collectio, 9 vol., Paris, 1724–1733.

MARTÍNEZ = E. —, Collección diplomática del real convento de S. Domingo de Caleruega . . . , Vergara 1931.

MARTYR RIZO = J.P. —, Historia . . . de Cuenca, Madrid, 1629.

MEDRANO = M.J. —, Historia de la provincia de España de la orden de Predicadores, Madrid, 1725.

MEERSSEMAN, Confréries I (II, III ou IV) = G.G. —, Études sur les anciennes — dominicaines, I, 'Les confréries de S. Dominique', in AFP, XX (1950), 5–113; II, 'Les confréries de S. Pierre martyr', in AFP, XXI (1951), 51–196; III, 'Les congrégations de la Viérge', in AFP, XXII (1952), 5–176; IV, 'Les milices de Jésus-Christ', in AFP, XXIII (1953), 275–308.

—, Loi pénale = 'La loi purement pénale d'après les statuts des confréries mediévales', in Mélanges J. de Ghellinck, Gembloux, 1951, 975–1002.

—, In libris gentilium = '—non studeant. L'étude des classiques interdite aux clercs au moyen âge ? in Italia mediovale e umanistica', I (1958), 1–13.

MEERSSEMAN-ADDA = G.G. — and E. —, 'Pénitents ruraux communautaires en Italie au XIIe siècle', in RHE, XLIX (1954), 343–390.

MENS = A. —, *Oorsprong en Betekenis van de Nederlandse begijnen en begardenbeweging*, Louvain, 1947.

MG SS = *Monumenta Germaniae historica*, Scriptores.

MIGUEL = S.T. —, *Historia de la vida de St. Domingo de Guzmán*, Valencia, 1705.

MIROT = A. —, *Manuel de géographie historique de la France*, 2 vol., 2nd ed., Paris, 1930–1950.

MOLINIER = A. —, 'Catalogue des actes de Simon et d'Amaury de Montfort', in *Biblioth. de l'École des chartes*, XXXIV (1873), 153–203 and 445–501.

MONTEFIASCONE = BENEDICT OF —, Chronique de Saint-Sixte, fragments in Echard, I, 83.

MOPH = *Monumenta ordinis fratrum Praedicatorum historica*, Louvain-Rome-Paris 1896 ff.

MORALES = A. —, 'Discurso del lignaje de S. Domingo', in *La crónica general de España*, vol. IV, Alcala 1586.

MOREL = M. —, *L'excommunication et le pouvoir civil en France, du droit canonique classique au commencement du XVe siècle*, Paris 1926.

MORTIER = E. —, *Histoire des maîtres généraux de l'ordre des frères Prêcheurs*, 8 vol., Paris 1903–1920.

MULHERN = Ph. —, *The early Dominican Laybrother*, Washington 1944.

NÚÑEZ-MARQUÉS = V. —, *Guia . . . y breve historia del obispado de Osma*, s. l. 1949.

PALACIOS = Fr —, "Gumiel de Izán, escuela primaria de Santo Domingo de Guzmán", in *Boletín de la institución Fernán Gonzáles*, XXXIV (1955), 872–896; XXXV (1956), 51–58.

PELAEZ = A. —, *Cuna y abolengo de S. Domingo de Guzmán*, Madrid 1917.

PELISSON = Guillaume —, Chronicon, ed. C. Molinier, in *De fratre Guillelmi Pelisso, veterrimo inquisitionis historico*, Le Puy 1880.

PELLICER = J. —, *Informe . . . de la . . . casa de Sarmiento de Villamayor*, Madrid 1663.

PERCIN = J. —, *Monumenta Conventus Tolosani Fr. Pr.*, Toulouse, 1693.

PÉREZ DE URBEL = J. —, *Los monjes españoles en la Edad media*, 2nd ed., Madrid, 1945.

PETIT-DUTAILLIS = Ch. —, *L'essor des États d'Occident* (Histoire du moyen âge, vol. IV, Pt. II), Paris, 1937.

PÉTREMENT = S. —, *Le dualisme dans l'histoire de la philosophie et des religions* (La montagne Sainte Geneviève, 5), Paris, 1946.

PFEIFFER = N. —, *Die ungarische Dominikanerordens-Provinz, von ihrer Grundung 1211 bis zur Tatarenverwüstung 1241–42*, Zürich, 1913.

PHILIPPEAU = H.R. —, 'La liturgie dominicaine des malades, des mourants et des morts', in *AHD*, 38–52.

PIERRON = J.B. —, *Die Katholischen Armen, ein Beitrag zur Entstehungsgeschichte der Bettelorden mit Berückssichtigung der Humiliaten und der wiedervereinigten Lombarden*, Freiburg-in-Br., 1911.

PISSARD = H. —, *La guerre sainte en pays chrétien*, Paris, 1912.

PL = *Patrologia latina*, ed. MIGNE.

POTTHAST = H. —, *Regesta Pontificum romanorum*, 2 vol. Berlin 1874–1875.

Proces. Bon. = Processus canonizationis S. Dominici apud Bononiam, ed. A. Walz, *MOPH*, XVI, Rome, 1935 (numbered according to the text).

Proces. Thol. = Processus canonizationis S. Dominici apud Tholosam, ed. A. Walz, *MOPH*, XVI, Rome, 1935.

PULGAR = P. DE —, *Historia secular y ecclesiástica de Palencia*, 3 vol., Madrid, 1679–1680.

PUYLAURENS = Guillaume de —, Historia albigensium, ed. Beyssier, in *Bibliothèque de la Faculté des Lettres*, vol. XVII, Paris, 1904 (according to the chapters).

QF = *Quellen und Forschungen zur Geschichte des Dominikanerordens in Deutschland*, ed. P. Von Loe, etc.

RÉCHAC = J. de — (known as de Sainte-Marie), *La vie du glorieux patriarche S. Dominique . . . avec la fondation de tous les monastères . . . de France et des Pays-bas*, Paris, 1647.

RHE = *Revue d'histoire ecclésiastique* (Louvain).

RHEIN = A. —, 'La seigneurie de Montfort. Catalogue des actes', in *Mémoires de la société archéologique de Rambouillet*, XXI (1910), 124–246.

RIVERA = J.F. —, 'Personajes hispanos asistentes en 1215 al IV concilio de Letran', in *Hispania sacra*, 4 (1951), 335–355.

ROBERT D'AUXERRE = —, Chronologia, ed. Holder-Egger, *MG SS*, XXVI, 226–276.

RODRIGO = — de Cerrato, Vita S. Dominici, in Mamachi, Appendix, 312–334.

ROISIN = S. —, 'L'efflorescence cistercienne et le courant de piété féminine au XIIe siècle', in *RHE*, XXXIX (1943), 342–378.

RUNCIMAN = St —, *The medieval manichee. A study of the christian dualist Heresy*, Cambridge, 1947.

SAKUR = E. —, *Die Cluniacenzer in ihrer kirchlichen u. allgemeingeschichtlichen Wirksamkeit*, 2 vol., Halle, 1894.

SALAGNAC = Etienne de —, *De quatuor in quibus Deus predicatorum ordinem insignivit*, ed. Th. Kaeppeli, *MOPH*, XXII, Rome, 1949.

SALAZAR, Historia = — y Castro, *Historia genealogica de la casa de Lara . . .* , 3 vol., Madrid, 1696–1697.

—, *Pruebas* = — *de la historia de la casa de Lara*, Madrid, 1694.

SAN MARTÍN = J. —, *La antigua universidad de Palencia*, Madrid, 1942.

SCHEEBEN = H. Chr. —, *Der heilige Dominikus*, Freiburg-in-Br., 1927.

—, Jordan = — *der Sachse*, Vechta, 1937.

SCHIRRMACHER — Fr W. —, *Geschichte Castiliens im 12. u. 13. Jahrhundert* (*Geschichte von Spanien*, vol. IV), Gotha, 1881.

SCHREIBER = G. —, *Kurie und Kloster im XII. Jahrh.*, 2 vol., Stuttgart, 1910.

SERRANO = *Cartulario de San Pedro de Arlanza*, ed. L. —, Madrid, 1925.

SIMON = A. —, *L'Ordre des Pénitentes de Ste-Marie-Madelaine en Allemagne au XIIIe s.*, Fribourg, Suisse, 1918.

SOEDERBERG = H. —, *La religion des cathares*, Uppsala, 1949.

SORBELLI = A. —, *Storia dell' Universita di Bologna*, vol. I, Il medio evo, Bologna, 1940.

SPAETLING = L. —, *De apostolis, pseudoapostolis, apostolinis. Dissertatio ad diversos vitae apostolicae conceptus saeculorum decursu elucidando*, Munich, 1947.

Studi Gregoriani = — *per la storia di Gregorio VII e della riforma gregoriana*, raccolti da G. Borino, 5 vol., Rome, 1947 ff.

TANGL = M. —, *Die päpstlichen Kanzleiordnungen von 1200–1500*, Innsbruck, 1894.

THEODORE = — of Apoldia, 'Vita S. Dominici', in *ASS*, August I, 558–628.

THOMASSIN = L. —, *Vetus et nova Ecclesiae disciplina circa beneficia et beneficiarios*, 3 vol. Lucca, 1728.

TIRABOSCHI = H. —, *Veterum Humiliatorum Monumenta*, 3 vol., Milan, 1766 to 1768.

TUDELA = Guillaume de —, 'La chanson de la croisade albigeoise', edited and translated from the Provençal by E. M. Chabot, vol. I, Paris, 1931.

TURK = J. —, 'Cistercii statuta antiquissima', in *Analecta s.o. cisterciensis*, IV (1948).

VAISSÈTE = Cl. Devic and J. —, *Histoire générale de Languedoc*, new ed., Toulouse, 1869 ff.

Vicaire, Bulle de confirmation = M. H. —, La — des prêcheurs, in *RHE*, XLVII (1952), 176–192.

—, *Documents* = *Saint Dominique de Caleruega d'après les* — *du XIIIe s.*, Paris, 1955.

—, 1207 = 'Saint Dominique en 1207', in *AFP*, XXIII (1953), 335–345.

—, *Fondation* = —, 'approbation, confirmation de l'ordre des Prêcheurs', in *RHE*, XLVII (1952), 123–141 and 586–603.

—, *Spiritualité* = Article Dominique (Saint) in *Dictionnaire de Spiritualité*, vol. III, 1519–1532.

VIELLIARD = J. —, *Le guide du pèlerin de Saint-Jacques de Compostelle*, XXIIth-century Latin text edited and translated into French . . . , 2nd ed., Mâcon, 1950.

VILLEMAGNE = A. —, *Bullaire du Bx Pierre de Castelnau*, Montpellier 1917.

VILLEY = M. —, *La croisade. Essai sur la formation d'une théorie juridique*, Caen, 1942.

VITRY = Jacques de —, . . . [*Liber*] . . . [*qui*] *occidentalis historiae nomine inscribitur*, Douai, 1597.

WERNER, E. = —, *Pauperes Christi. Studien zu sozial-religiösen Bewegung im Zeitalter des Reformspapstums*, Leipzig 1956.

WERNER, J. = J. —, 'Die Teilnehmerliste des Laterankonzils v. J. 1215', in *Neues Archiv der Gesellschaft f. ältere deutsche Geschichtskunde* . . . XXXI (1906), 577–593.

WESTENHOLZ = R. v. —, *Kardinal Rainier v. Viterbo (Heidelberger Abhandl. z. mittleren u. neueren Geschichte, 34)*, Heidelberg, 1912.

WINKELMANN = E. —, *Kaiser Friedrich II*, vol. I, 1218–1228, Leipzig, 1889.

ZARNCKE = L. — *Der Anteil des Kardinals Ugolino an der Ausbildung der drei Orden des heil. Franz (Beiträge zur Kulturgeschichte des Mittelalters u. Renaissance, 42)*, Leipzig, 1930.

ZIMMERMANN = H. —, *Die päpstliche Legation in der ersten Hälfte des 13. Jahrh*, Paderborn, 1913.

ZUCCHI = A. —, Roma Domenicana. *Note storiche*, vol. I, Florence, 1938.

NOTES TO TEXT

NOTES TO INTRODUCTION

1. I Const. 223 (dist. II, ch. 31); Jordan, no. 104; Constantino d'Orvieto, Matins hymn in the office of St Dominic, *Ordinarium juxta ritum SOFP*, Rome, 1921, 97; Robert d'Auxerre, 271.

NOTES TO CHAPTER I

1. *Nueve meses de invierno, tres de infierno.* cf. Kirsch, 9.
2. *Enciclopedia Universal*, 13, 992–995, art. *Clunia*, and Pelaez, 35–42. The latter work, which was pulped for want of purchasers, is outstanding both for wealth of information and for its critical sense. That of Martínez, a valuable collection of texts from archives, is less sure in its judgements. The interpretation of texts, moreover, is not always reliable. Cf. document CCXVII and its facsimile, 281–283.
3. D'Aremberg & Saglio, *Dictionnaire des antiquités grecques et romaines*, V, 804, art. *via*. The Roman road of Clunia has been studied between Olbega and Osma by Ed. Saavedra, *in Mèm. de la Academia de historia*, I, 1877–1879, 48.
4. Pelaez, 37. Cf. map in Loperraez, I, l, for what could still be traced of this Roman road in the eighteenth century. Serrano, 64, n. 3.
5. 'Calzada de Quinega', Martínez, 22–24 (ch. XIX, of 22. V. 1272). A little farther to the south there was also to be found a *Calçadiella*, which was perhaps the Roa-Simancas fork.
6. 'Clunia' in a bull of Pascal II in 1108, Pelaez, 52. 'Carrera de Crunna' (= Cluña) in 1272, Martínez, 23. The name is again found today in that of the village, Coruña del Conde.
7. Peñalba de Castro, Coruña del Conde, Hinojar and Quintanarraya.
8. Pelaez, 28–30.
9. For the history and character of this repopulation, cf. J. Pérez de Urbel, 'Reconquista y repoblación de Castilla y León durante los siglos IX and X', in *La Reconquista española, y la repoblación del país*, Saragossa 1951, 139–162. The author stresses the importance of Cantabrians and Basques in the east of Castile and the Douro. Aragonese and men of Navarre, numerous to the south of the Douro, were absent here as were the French.
10. Conquered by Ferdinand I (1037–1065), Pelaez, 45.
11. For all this, see Férotin, *Silos* 21–22; Pelaez, 44–50; Guinard, 301–343, Pérez de Urbel, II, 485–486.
12. Flórez, XXVI, 215–216; Loperraez, I, 71–72, 88–93, 112–114; Pelaez, 50–53.
13. The archdeaconries of Aranda, Roa and Aza, would thus have remained outside the diocese—Loperraez, I, 72.
14. Texts: Flórez, XXVI, Appendix XI to XIII, 466–469; Pelaez, 52, n. 1.
15. Text: Loperraez, III, 17; Pelaez 61, n. 1.
16. Loperraez, I, 165, 250–256; II, 189–202, 206–207, 210; Marques, 75–96; respective articles of the *Enciclopedia Universal*.
17. Rades y Andrada, I, fo. 11, ch. 1; Manrique, III, 283–5; Cottineau, I, 1364; Guinard, 339; Palacios, 881 and 51–53. The earlier abbey dated from 1073; Alfonso VI favoured it with a gift as late as 1110—Loperraez, I, 76 and II, 184–186. Suppressed in the nineteenth century, the abbey has fallen into ruins; in 1955 the final remains of the belfry were blown up with dynamite and sold (photo in Pelaez, 139); nothing is left but the great enclosure wall, a mile or so to the south-east of Gumiel, along the Gromejón.
18. Serrano, 130 and 166.
19. Pelaez, 57.
20. The bull of 1136 and a contemporary document noted by Arguleta, *Continuación*, quoted by Pelaez, 61, n. 1 and 63.
21. 'El val (de Fande) todo de revielas fastal monte es todo de Caleruega.' Martínez, 23 (ch. XIX of the 26.V.1272).
22. Serrano 130 and 166 (ch. LXIII and LXXXVIII of 10th May, 1062 and 26th February, 1117).
23. Férotin, *Recueil*, 121 (ch. LXXIX of 19th March, 1202).
24. Jordan, no. 5, then royal charter of 1237, Martínez, 2 (no. XI).
25. Becerro d'Arlanza's text, edited by Serrano, has modernized the spelling. The original version will be found in the copy by P. Sáez, given by Serrano, 131, n. 23.
26. 'Caleruega', Férotin, Recueil, 121 (ch. LXXIX, 19.III.1202). 'Chaleruega', Jordan, no. 5, variant of ms. O, first edition of the libellus of 1234. Royal charter of 1237—Martínez, 2 (no. XI). See also Serrano, 166 (ch. of 1117).

27. E.g. Martínez, 250, 252, 254 &c. (nos. CXCVII, CXCVIII, CXCIX).

28. Information for which warm thanks are due to Professor Paul Aebischer. The termination presupposes a diminutive suffix—*ocus, a, for the moment hypothetical. The explanation given by Palacios, 872, n. 1 (Caleruega = Calor longa) is fanciful.

29. An Arabic origin could equally well have been put forward, with the root cala (castle) as in Calatanazor, some thirty miles distant from Caleruega. The termination, however, is not Arabic. Prof. Aebischer therefore excludes this.

30. Martínez, 14 (no. X) and 250–252 (no. CXCVII).

31. Even in 1131 Bishop Bertrand reported in a document on the poverty of the villages which had difficulty in providing sufficient means for their own churches—Loperraez, I, 105.

32. The following statements have been made as a result of two direct examinations in 1950 and 1956. They sometimes correct but more often confirm the careful observations of Pelaez. Cf. Kirsch, 13–44.

33. Martínez, 324 (no. CCXLIV, 26.III.1272); Pelaez, 237–257.

34. The gothic doorway discovered in 1952 is of the same workmanship as that of the nuns' choir; the window at the end of the 'palace' is similar to that which has been discovered at the end of the vicariate—Carro, Caleruega, I, 6 and II, 51; cf. Appendix I. A direct investigation of the obvious resemblances was made in 1956.

35. Cf. Appendix I.

36. Pelaez, 257–263.

37. Marques, 70.

38. Cf. Pelaez, 258. This access has since been simplified by a new incision in the solid mass of the tower.

39. On the occasion of the deep excavations which had to be made in the ground between 1952 and 1955 for the foundations of the buildings around the torreón, all that was found was the slight remains of two walls, near the north-east and south-east corners of this tower towards which they pointed. The second fragment of wall is orientated north-south. No trace justifies the supposition that such walls were originally linked to the torreón. Cf. Carro, Caleruega, II, 46–47, completed by a letter.

40. Document CCXLIV, Martínez, 324, of 26.III.1272, assigns to the sisters houses 'que son cerca las vuestras torres'. This may, however, be a plural of majesty.

41. Cf. Pelaez, 71–75.

42. Don José Menéndez-Pidal, the architect, in 1952 dates this horseshoe arch to the eleventh century; it is of the same workmanship as those found in the Mozarabic constructions of that period. Other authorities would assign it to the beginning of the twelfth century. A careful comparative study would be needed to decide the question. This arch, however, whose yellow stone and careful workmanship form a striking contrast to the rest of the building, would seem to be a later addition. For the dating of the reconstruction of the tower it is necessary to take as a basis the cradled window recesses and the rough triangular arch of the door. This mixture of romanesque and primitive gothic elements found in the belfry takes us back to the middle of the twelfth century.

43. Martinez, xv, points this out. It was verified personally in 1950 before, through the recent building work, the triangular arch was replaced by a semi-circular one, the joinings of the stones covered over and the interior of the tower plastered.

44. Below the four openings of the gallery for defence (second storey), only the romanesque window and two small loop-holes are to be found; level with the ground is the evacuation point of a sewer; near the north-east corner, on the north front and thus towards the open country, is a curious safety device. Here the wall was reduced to a thin partition which could easily be pierced from within. The cavity was filled on the inside with earth or with debris. Thus in a desperate extremity a breach through which to escape could easily be opened. Carro, Caleruega, 46.

45. One final detail indicates the reconstruction of the tower: the floor-boards have been lowered. This was almost certainly at the time that the door and window were opened up, for the floor of the first storey corresponds to the latter. This floor was formerly higher to correspond to the loop-hole recesses, which are now about five feet above it. Similarly, the floor of the second storey was arranged to correspond with the doors of the defence gallery which are now a good six feet above it. Clearly, the archers did not have to perform an acrobatic feat each time they had to shoot an arrow or keep watch over the road.

46. An Arabic origin must be excluded. With its door facing south and its two loop-holes looking north it is true that the construction seems to favour the Moslems. In actual fact it simply overlooks the entrance to the valley of the Gromejón and is fitted for fighting on all sides because of its defence gallery. The orientation has thus no significance either Christian or Moorish. On the other hand, the square keep without a moat, and the gallery of wooden corbels which surmounted it, drew their inspiration from the traditions of the north in the tenth and eleventh centuries; the Moslem tradition was that of the rectangular castle of Byzantine type. Cf. H.W.M. von Caboga, Der Orient und sein Einfluss auf den mittelalterlichen Wehrbau des Abendlandes, Madrid, 1953, map, p. 33, and Étude concernant le problème d'une typologie, Rapperswil, 1952, 7 and 11. The tower of Caleruega on its spur of rock is of exactly the same type as the nordic mound shown on p. 11 (before A.D. 1000).

47. Cf. supra, p. 7 and nn. 3 and 4.

48. Martínez, charters XX, XXV, LXX, LXXVI &c.

49. Martínez, 81 (ch. LXX, 6.XII.1310). In 1390, the figures are 2,000, 200, 50 and 100, plus 500 goats. The diminution is considerable. Ibid., 138.

50. Martínez, 22–24 (charter XIX).

51. Especially in the domain of Bañuelos de la Calzada (the Roman road), Martínez, 24–25, 28, 48

(ch. XX, XXII, XLII). The final charter, of 21.IV.1287, especially forbade the cutting of timber in the nuns' woods in the territory of Caleruega.

52. For the resistance, lasting throughout eight years, of the Order of Santiago, cf. Arguleta, *Apologia* 74, quoted by Martínez, 328, n. 1. The order yielded only to force, Alfonso X having taken over its property after 1266.

53. For the definition of *Behetria* (=*benefactoria*) and the distinction between B. *de mar a mar* and B. *entre parientes*, see Morales, fo. 336.

54. On the *Behetria*, see *Enciclopedia Universal*, 7, 1467–1469, Guinard, 363–365.

55. Cf. *infra* 15 and n. 59.

56. On the right of *pressura* which allowed the occupation of such lands by immigrants who were freedmen, cf. J. de la Concha, 'Consecuencias jurídicas, sociales y económicas de la reconquista y repoblación', in *La Reconquista española y la repoblación del país*, Saragossa, 1951, 211–218.

57. Martínez 9 (ch. VIII), 304–24 (ch. CCXXX–CCXLIII) and 328–334 (ch. CCXLVII–CCXLIX). Pellicer, 46, handled 21 other charters which have not come back to the monastery and of which he has published only one; cf. Martínez, 305.

58. Martínez 9 (ch. VIII, 4.VI.1266). Register of another recapitulatory charter (25.VII.1266) in Pellicer 49–50; cf. Martínez 307; Pelaez 188, n. 1 and 199, n. 1.

59. On 19.III.1270 the Order of Santiago gave to the king the locality (*luegar*) of Caleruega, which it had acquired from don Fernán García on 15.IX.1258: Martínez, 328 and 285 (ch. CCXLVII and CCXIX). A domain which is sold is no longer purely de *behetria*.

60. Martínez, 281 (ch.CCXVII, 23.II.1248).

61. Cf. *supra*, n.59.

62. Martínez, 286 (ch.CCXX, 1259). But the order retained its right of overlordship, which it only surrendered in 1274, cf. *supra*, n.59.

63. Martínez, 307 (CCXXXIV, 23.X.1266); 305 (CCXXXI, 22.VII.1266).

64. *Ibid.*, 307, 320, 322.

65. *Enciclopedia Universal*, art. 'Behetria', 7, 1468, col.2.

66. Salazar, *Historia*, III, L. XVII, ch. 5 and Arguleta, *Apologia* 79, referred to by Martínez, 9, n. 1 and 307, n. 1, throw into relief the Villamayor ancestry of all the *diviseros* of Caleruega. Cf. Pelaez, 188. Don Pedro de Guzmán, whose genealogy is not known (cf. Pelaez, 168), doña Inés Pérez de Marañón, who was of Aza stock (cf. Salazar, *Historia*, I, 25), Ruy Perez de Arauzo de Salce, are outside this connection.

67. Morales, fo. 336, vº.

68. In this charter of 10th May, 1062, María Fortúniz surrenders to the abbey of Arlanza 'sua divisa cum sua hereditate' in Kalerueca as in numerous other places in the vicinity—Serrano, 131, n. 23.

69. Ferrando, no. 4.

70. 'Honestos et pios', Frachet, 67. The context indicates that *honestus* should be taken in the moral and not in the social sense.

71. 'Fuit autem pater ejus vir venerabilis et dives in populo suo. Mater vero honesta, pudica, prudens, miseris et afflictis valde compatiens et inter omnes mulieres terrae illius bonae famae praerogativa refulgens'. Rodríguez, 314.

72. The Castilian text of the thirteenth century, in which L. Getino thought he had found Ferrando's source is, in fact, a Castilian compilation of the legends of Humbert, of James of Voragine and other Dominican writers of the end of the thirteenth century. Cf. W. F. Manning, *An old Spanish life of St Dominic, Medieval studies in Honor of J. O. M. Ford*, Cambridge, Mass., 1948, 139–158. As to the ten lines quoted by P. Getino, cf. Appendix I, n. 4.

73. W. F. Manning, *The Life of St Dominic in Old French verse*, Cambridge, Mass., 1944, 13, favours 1235.

74. He signed a charter there on 26.III.1272, Martínez, 324 (ch. CCXLIV).

75. Cf. the *Libellus* of Jordan of Saxony, the source of all the legends. The latter have continued the work of depersonalization and effaced some of the details preserved by Jordan.

76. Martínez, xxi; Getino, S. Domingo, 21, after Mamachi, 24–25.

77. *Vir* . . . *dives* is a good rendering of *ricohombre*. It is clear that Rodríguez' Latin is modelled upon his Castilian: *populus* here has the twofold meaning of *pueblo*; *vicinus* that of *vecino* (inhabitant of the village); we should rather expect *dives homo* to express *ricohombre*. Thus at this time Ptolemy of Lucca translates: 'Apud hispanos omnes sub rege principes, divites homines appellantur, et praecipue in Castella'—*De regno* III, 22, S. *Thomae Opuscula*, ed. Perrier, I, Paris 1949, 359. On the other hand, the expression 'rico hombre of the village' is adequate in a village of *behetria*, rather than 'lord of the village'.

78. Pelaez, 68 and n. 1.

79. Rodríguez, 315.

80. Is it necessary to insist on the fact that the cellar was inside the house 'intravit illico cellarium'? This presupposes a large stone house: the peasants of Caleruega have their *bodegas* dug in the hill (cf. above p. 29). On the cellar of the ancestress, cf. Appendix I.

81. Altaner, 174, supports the dismissal of the matter by the Bollandists, ASS, *Aug.*, I, 384 and 387. Scheeben, 2 affirms that Felix was a farmer. Mandonnet does not mention the Spanish origins of St Dominic.

82. Appendix II.

83. The noblest at this period were the Aza, who were in possession of the *ricahombría* even for the younger branches of the family (Salazar, *Historia*, III, 334); originally the Guzmán only possessed the title for one particular individual among them (Morales, fo. 339, vº).

84. In 1206, don Fernán Gonzáles de Marañón, a cousin of the Aza family, was Grand Master of the

Order of Santiago. From 1212 to 1217 don Rodrigo Garces de Aza was Grand Master of Calatrava; he would be a first cousin of St Dominic; don Juan Gonzáles de Aza, Master a little later, would be of the generation of his nephews; as would also don Gómez Manrique, Master of the same order in his turn—Rades y Andrada I, fo. 3, ch. 2 and II, fo. 17. Salazar, *Historia*, III, 306 and 331.

85. Rodríguez, 314.

86. Rodríguez, 314–315. Altaner, 157, would have liked to think that this miracle was simply the one attributed by Frachet, 93, to a Sicilian lady, plagiarized and attributed to the mother of St Dominic. But, except for the bare fact of the multiplication of the wine, the two accounts have no connection with each other. Altaner did not know of the fact of the presence of Rodríguez at Caleruega.

87. Morales, fo. 340; Brémond, 86–92 and 286–289 (Appendix XIII); Mamachi, 29–31. The archives of the order preserved in the eighteenth century the copy of an informative inquiry made in April and May 1645, (3rd May in Caleruega), on the life and monuments of Bl. Jane. Pelaez, 122–132 criticizes and completes these details. However, the figures to be seen on the façade of the chapel at Caleruega are not lions, as he thought, but dogs bearing the torch. In 1955 the Passionist fathers who occupy the Peñafiel monastery and look after the tomb of the Beata did away with the monument and placed the relics and the statue on an altar.

88. Rodríguez, 314 (no. III).

89. 'Quam tuis Domine obsequiis mancipavi'—Rodríguez 315.

90. *ASS, Aug.* I, 566B.

91. Frachet, 67.

92. Jordan, no. 51.

93. It is true that Frachet, 67 and Rodríguez, 331, say 'germanus frater' and 'germanus ipsius'. But the unusual word of Jordan's *Libellus* must be retained. The manuscripts contain no variant. Moreover, the word is not called for by necessities of *cursus* or style. Jordan, who gives Mames his rightful name (and not the distorted name of Mannes) knew him very well, from 1218 onwards, in Paris. The brother had just arrived there to found the convent where Jordan was shortly to take the habit. In 1234 when the *Libellus* was put together, Mames was still living. If in the thirteenth century the word was sometimes taken in the broad sense (Frachet, 258, uses *uterinus* for a twin brother; Guillaume Le Breton, *Gesta Philippi Augusti*, I, Paris, 1882, no. 176, refers to three *fratres uterini*, sons of the late Gauthier, Chamberlain of France), Jordan has a taste for using words in their correct and even etymological sense.

94. Dominic died in 1221. Mames was still living when his brother was canonized (3.VII.1234), since he came to Caleruega when the news of it reached Spain, Rodríguez, 331. The date of 1230, at which certain authorities place his death without giving their source (cf. Altaner, 16. n. 5), comes from Manrique, *Cisterciencium . . . annalium*, IV. Lyons, 1649, 408. Cf. Mamachi, 373, n. 8. Rodríguez' information, directly derived from Caleruega, should be preferred to that of the modern Cistercian compiler.

95. Thierry shows great skill as a compiler. All he adds to his sources, which moreover are known, is his art of harmonization. That is sufficient indication of the value of the dates he inserts from time to time in his large biography, dates which are not given by his sources. They are not items of fresh information, but conclusions proper to Thierry, certain of which are clearly erroneous—Altaner, 187 and n. 1. The hypothesis, however, of a new piece of information, obtained, for instance, in the course of a general chapter through a conversation with a well-informed Spanish friar, cannot be excluded *a priori*.

96. *Infra*, ch. III, note 95–96.

97. Frachet, 67. That this hospice may have been that attached to the chapel of St Dominic in Caleruega, as Carro (*Caleruega*, I, 6 and II, 52) supposes, is not completely impossible, but is improbable. The hospice dates from after 1234. At that time, St Dominic's brother, if he were still living, would have been seventy-four according to Carro, at least more than sixty. In these circumstances all he would have brought the poor would have been what was left of his goodwill; he would not have been able 'to devote himself entirely to their service', as Frachet says.

98. This statement was then met with in Italy—Leandre Albert, *De Viris illustribus O.P.*, Bologna, 1519. A tradition, however, does exist at Silos—Férotin, *Silos*, 88.

99. Guinard, 338–340.

100. Rades y Andrada, I, fo. 10, c. 4.

101. Cf. *supra*, n. 17 and Appendix II, n. 2, 15, 23, 24, 25, 26, 28.

102. Affirmed by the best authorities—Jordan, no. 51; Rodríguez, 331. Sometimes erroneously latinized as Mamertus (St Mamert, Archbishop of Vienne).

103. Other saints of the same name exist, however, e.g. at St Flour. There is no guarantee that the Mames venerated in Castile is the Caesarean one.

104. Frachet, 67.

105. On the occasion of the dispersion in August 1217, he was sent to Paris to make a foundation there; he must already have been well-versed in the ways of the order—Jordan, No. 51.

106. Cf. *supra*, n. 94.

107. Erat autem ille frater Mames praedicator fervidus, honestus moribus, mitis humilis, hilaris et benignus'. Rodríguez, 332.

108. Mamachi, Appendix 365, n. 5, add. of a manuscript of Bernard Gui; *MOPH*, XXII, 153, apparat. Cf. Frachet, 67, n. 9. On the recognitions of relics in 1694 and 1827—Pelaez, 133–137.

109. Frachet, 67.

110. *Proces. Thol.* no. 21.

111. Text quoted by Taeggio, *Chronica brevis*, *ASOP*, V, 1901, 62.

112. Jordan, no. 5 (in the second edition of the *Libellus*). Borrowed from the story of St Bernard *Vita IIa auctore Alano*, PL, 185, col. 470, or perhaps from that of San Julian de Cuenca (†1208), *ASS januarii*, Paris 1863, 510 and Fr Escudero, *Vida y milagros del glorioso San Julian, obispo de Cuenca*, Cuenca, 1601, fo. 3, v°.

113. Barthelemy, 230. The same episode has already served for St Ambrose, St Isidore, St John Chrysostom etc.

114. Jordan, no. 9.

115. Jordan, no. 5.

116. 'Argent with sable scabbard'. They are already to be found in 1383, on the reliquary of St Dominic by Jacobo Roseto at Bologna. They are an attempt to represent the arms of Innocent V (1276). As far back as the sixteenth century they began to be crowded with unnecessary detail. The arms with the ornamented fleur-de-lis cross seem to be those of the Spanish Inquisition. Cf. *Archives heraldiques suisses*, LX, 1946, 43–44. Bibliography: *AFP*, XXI, 1951, 89, n. 54.

117. Jordan, no. 9.

118. Cecilia, no. 15.

119. Ferrando, no. 6.

120. Pelaez, 260–261.

121. Getino, 30, has collected the pious puns in which the Dominican hagiographers have indulged on the name of St Dominic, beginning with Jordan, no. 21.

122. Ferrando, no. 5.

123. *Proces. Bon.* nos. 20, 28, 31, 37, 42, 46; *Proces. Thol.* nos. 11, 15, 17, 18.

NOTES TO CHAPTER II

1. Bruno I of Cologne was separated from his parents and entrusted to an ecclesiastical school at the age of four, St Anschar and St Leo IX at five. Such a separation, however, usually took place about the age of six or seven—Lesne, 513, 456. Castillo, II, ch. 2 gives seven years old for St Dominic, which is at least an indication of the custom at the close of the Middle Ages.

2. Jordan, no. 5.

3. *Ibid.*

4. Lesne, 526–533 and *passim*.

5. Jordan, no. 5.

6. Castillo, II, ch. 2; Getino, 35. Palacios, 53–58 merely uses Castillo as his source.

7. Kirsch, 45–49; Palacios, 57.

8. Gumiel is not found among the fourteen traditional deaneries of Osma—Loperraez, II, 18. These divisions of the dioceses in the west were prior to the twelfth century. The large collection of diocesan charters published by Loperraez does not give the slightest hint of an eventual reorganization o. the diocese after its restoration. On the other hand a charter of 1148 mentions the Dean of Soria, another of 1152 the archdeacons (corresponding to rural deaneries) of Osma, San Esteban de Górmaz, Aza and Soria, another in 1270, of the rural deanery of Roa—Loperraez, III, 24, 29, 40. Since the nineteenth century the diocese has comprised twenty-eight such deaneries, and Gumiel figures amongst them. Possibly the legend of the saint's stay in Gumiel also grew up at the monastery of San Pedro de Gumiel. Cf. Appendix II, no. 15.

9. These three deaneries were lacking in the diocese as reconstituted in 1088—Loperraez, I, 72.

10. Jordan, no. 5.

11. Lesne, 453–8.

12. Férotin, *Silos*, 87. Based on a tradition that was already very ancient in the sixteenth century.

13. J. E. de Noriega, *Dissertatio historica de S. Domingo de Guzmán, Ord. Praed. Patriarcha, Canonico Regulari Praemonstratensi in observatissimo Monasterio de la Vid*, Salamanca, 1723. Cf. Martínez, XLI–XLII.

14. Arguleta, *Apologia* (1725) and *Continuación* (1731).

15. The expression is from Pelaez, 63, n.2, who criticizes it fully and sagaciously.

16. Férotin, *Silos*, 87, n. 3.

17. Lesne, 436–437, Delhaye, 229–232. Particularly those monasteries which, like Silos, were under the influence of Cluny.

18. Constitutions of Prémontré, 2nd edition (*ca.* 1174) D. IV, ch. III, ed. Martène, *De Antiquis Ecclesiae Ritibus*, III, Venice, 1783, 334; Bassano 1788, 328.

19. Lesne, 573.

20. 'Ut distincte et aperte sonans, audientium corda possit instruere', Rabanus Maurus, *De clericorum institutione*, PL, 107, 305.

21. *Proces. Bon.*, no. 21, 38, 46.

22. Lesne, 559, after PL 133, 49.

23. *De civitate Dei*, L. 21, ch. 14—*PL*. 41, 728. Cf. *Confess.*, L. 1 ch. 9—*PL*, 32, 667.

24. 'Continuo est virga super eos' *PL*, 149, 747A, B.

25. *De Vita sua*, I, 6, *PL*, 156, 847C.

26. *Proces. Bon.*, no. 25 and Constantin, no. 61.

27. At the beginning of the twelfth century, studies often terminated about the age of fifteen. One could go to the liberal schools as early as twelve or even ten. As the schools developed, however, the admission age was put later. John of Salisbury arrived in Paris at fourteen. If it is remembered that the custom existed at this time of conferring benefices on adolescents who went off to the schools and that in the three middle decades of the twelfth century Alexander III laid down that one might not receive

such benefices before the age of fourteen, it may be concluded that fourteen became the usual age for admission to the schools. In the thirteenth century it was at about fifteen that one's university studies began—Lesne, 445, 513; Delhaye 231 and n. 33, 261; Thomassin, I, 438, col. 1.

28. Jordan, no. 6.

29. Heredia, 318–319 and nos. 7 and 8, who, however, quotes instances of Castilian clerics for Compostela and Salamanca studying in France.

30. For Compostela, Heredia, 316–322. On the translators of Toledo see De Wulf, *Hist. de la philosophie médiévale*, I, 6th ed., Louvain-Paris, 1934, 67–68; J. M. Millás Vallicrosa, 'La escuela de traductores de Toledo' in *Homenaje a Avicenna en su milenario, Al Andalus*, XIV (1949), 291–319; Defourneaux, 43–45.

31. For Toledo, Beltrán de Heredia, 'Los orígenes de la Universidad de Salamanca' in *Ciencia Tomista*, 81 (1954) 70; for Salamanca, *ibid.*, 80–82; for Osma, cf. *infra*, ch. III, notes 72 to 77.

32. 'Postmodum autem missus est Palentiam, ut ibi liberalibus informaretur scientiis, quarum studium ea tempestate vigebat ibidem.' Jordan, no. 6. Moreover there was also a school of theology, since Dominic studied that science there too. (*Ibid.* no. 7). With a text relating to Pedro González Telmo O.P. (Florez, XXIII, 245), Jordan's text is the only mention we have of these schools prior to the institution of the university; but the institution itself clearly confirms the fact. Cf. Denifle, *Die Entstehung des Universtiaten des Mittelalters bis 1400*, Berlin 1885, 473–474. See Beltrán de Heredia, 'La Universidad de Palencia', 'Santo Domingo de Guzmán en Palencia', 'San Pedro González Telmo', in *Semana pro Ecclesia et Patria*, Palencia 1936. J. San Martín, *La antgiua Universidad de Palencia*, Palencia 1942, 6–12. The out-of-date study of Beltrán de Heredia, which he was kind enough to allow us to use, as J. San Martín very kindly allowed the use of his, still contains data of value; he himself has made an excellent restatement of it in the article cited above, n. 31, 70–77.

33. Denifle, *ibid.*, 474–476.

34. Between 1080 and 1085, at the time of Bishop or Archbishop Bernard—L. Serrano, 'Concilios nacionales de Palencia en la primera mitad del siglo XII', in *Semana pro Ecclesia et Patria*, Palencia, 1936, 5–6.

35. Serrano, 3–24.

36. Serrano, 20.

37. Cf. preceding note. As to the lists, Beltrán de Heredia, art. cited (*supra*, n. 31) 4–5, has indicated, at the end of the twelfth century and beginning of the thirteenth, certain names preceded by the title of master, which means that such persons were engaged in teaching (cf. Lesne, 461–462) Gerard, Lanfranc, perhaps also Tello, the future bishop.

38. This is what is certified by the text of Jordan quoted *supra*, n. 32. San Telmo only studied the liberal arts there.

39. Pare, Brunet, Tremblay, *La Renaissance du XIIe siècle, les écoles et l'enseignement*, Paris-Ottawa 1933, 138, 210.

40. For all that follows, cf. De Wulf, *Histoire de la Philosophie médiévale*, 6th ed., II, Louvain, 1936, 63–64. Pare, Brunet, Tremblay, 168–169. According to Señor Alonso Alonso, Gondisalvi, collaborator of Juan Avendauth, Bishop of Segovia, later Archbishop of Toledo († 1166) died in 1181 and not ca. 1150, as was said. 'Notas sobre los traductores toledanos Domingo Gondisalvi y Juan Hispano' in *Al Andalús*, VIII (1943), 115–188.

41. De Wulf, *Hist. de la philosophie médiévale*, I, 6th ed. Louvain-Paris 1934, 61–2, has shown that the philosophy (physics, psychology, metaphysics) which progressively developed in the schools of the twelfth century was not an extension of dialectics or of the arts faculty, but a fresh subject, mid-way between arts and theology.

42. Jordan, no. 6.

43. The statement comes from Hugh of St Victor, *Didascalicon*, III, 3—PL, 176, 768, who attributes this custom to Pythagoras (cf. Lesne, 569). Ferrando, no. 7, says that St Dominic abstained from wine during ten years (*decennium*), but that Diego made him give up the custom. The intervention must have corresponded to Dominic's entering the Osma chapter. The period of ten years would have to coincide with the length of his stay in Palencia. If the four years' theology are deducted, at least six years would remain for liberal studies. In view of Jordan's statement, this is a maximum.

44. If a clause of the first constitutions of 1220 is any criterion: 'In libris gentilium et philosophorum (fratres studentes) non studeant, etsi ad horam inspiciant', D. II, ch. 28 (1 *Const.*, 22).

45. Cf. as the antithesis of this, the remonstrances of Peter of Blois with two scholars, one of whom obstinately insisted, at an advanced age, on teaching the liberal arts, while the other hesitated to renounce legal studies in order to devote himself to theology: 'Duo sane sunt quae hominem ad legum scientiam vehementer impellunt, ambitio dignitatis et inanis gloriae appetitus', he wrote to the second—*Ep.* 140, PL, 207, 416. He called the first 'puer centum annorum et elementarius senex'. *Ep.* 6, PL, 207, 18. This is the 'puer-senex' reversed. Other indications in Delhaye, 264–5.

46. Jordan, no. 6.

47. On the significance of the title of master, given to him from 1216 onwards, cf. *infra*, ch. VII, n. 124.

48. Luke XI, 28; Jordan, no. 7.

49. *Ibid.*

50. 'Semper gestabat secum Matthei evangelium et epistolas Pauli, et multum studebat in eis, ita quod fere sciebat eas cordetenus.' Deposition of Fray Juan de España, *Proces. Bon.*, no. 29.

51. The *Libellus* states: 'gratiam ei deus scientiarum [I Reg. II, 3] adauxit, ut non solum ad lactis potum [I Cor. III, 2] redderetur idoneus sed et questionum difficilium humili cordis intelligentia

penetraret arcanum et solidioris cibi scrutinium sufficienti admodum facilitate glutiret'. Jordan, no. 7.

52. Mention of the 'libros manu sua glossatos' of St Dominic in Palencia, by Fray Esteban, *Proces. Bon.* no. 35.

53. In 1183 the canons of St Antolin found their private lives made freer by the authorization they received from their bishop, Raymond II, to make wills as they pleased—Gil González Dávila, *Teatro eclesiástico de las iglesias de los reinos de las dos Castillas*, II, Madrid, 1647, 152.

54. Lesne, 530–532.

55. Jordan, no. 10, mentions the 'libros, quos sibi oppido necessarios possidebat, cum omni suppellectili sua'. As to the 'house of St Dominic' which was shown in Palencia from the seventeenth century onwards and even at the beginning of the twentieth century and which has been demolished since, this could easily be the 'charity' he established. The pictures of it which are extant, however, scarcely give the appearance of a twelfth-century building. Moreover, how could this charity, which had to be poor and could scarcely be built of stone, have lasted through so many centuries! cf. Kirsch 56–57; Beltrán de Heredia, *La Universidad de Palencia*, 230.

56. Fray Esteban in his deposition at the Bologna Inquiry, claims that Dominic belonged to the Osma chapter even as early as the Palencia period, *Proces. Bon.*, no. 35. In that case he would have been able to live on his prebend. At the end of the twelfth century, this was the case with numerous *scolares canonici*—Lesne, 517–518. The Osma chapter, however, was not secularized and had not, it seems, taken any particular steps in favour of student canons. The maintenance of benefices during one's period at the schools was not yet a common rule. Some chapters practised it individually—Compostela, Gerona, Tortosa, etc., cf. Heredia, 321–324. It is, however, clear that Fray Esteban, who was speaking from hearsay, has confused the chronology. For instance, he places Dominic's preaching in Toulouse 'a few days' after the events of Palencia! Jordan, no. 11, on the other hand, situates the events of Palencia before Dominic's entry into the Osma chapter. So also does John of Navarre: at Palencia St Dominic was still 'in saeculo', *Proces. Bon.*, no. 29. Dominic was thus still living at the expense of his family.

57. Jordan, no. 7.

58. Ferrando, no. 7.

59. Jordan, no. 8; Bull of Canonization, *MOPH*, XVI, 192. It is the old theme of *puer-senex* taken up again by St Gregory in the first sentence of his well-known life of St Benedict (*PL*, 66, 126A) but which Jordan seems rather to have borrowed from the twelfth-century poets—E. R. Curtius, 'Zur literarästhetik des Mittelalters', II, 2. 'Puer-Senex' in *Zeitschrift für romanische Philologie* LVIII (1938), 143–151.

60. Lesne, 550–551.

61. Cf. his confidences at the moment of death. God has given him the grace to preserve his flesh uncorrupt, but he has not been able, he admits, to avoid finding more attraction in the conversation of young girls than in that of old ladies—Jordan, no. 93. Then he has a scruple at having dared to speak of his virginity, *Proces. Bon.*, no. 5.

62. Guinard, 319–21 and 337–40.

63. Jordan, no. 10—'Oborta est fames valida fere per universam Hispaniam.' Cf. *Proces. Bon.*, 100, and nos. 29 and 35.

64. Cf. *infra*, ch. III, nn. 70–71.

65. *ASS, januarii*, III (Paris, 1863), 510.

66. Du Cange, sub.h.v. no. 2. The *eleemosyna* is precisely the establishment depending on an abbey, a collegiate or other church, where the service of distribution to the poor is installed. For instance, when Alfonso VI of Castile, some years before these events, caused St Lesma to come to Spain, he gave him charge of a church near Burgos and of an *eleemosyna* for pilgrims—Flórez, XXVII, 450. On the word, which became general in the twelfth century for designating the *hospitium pauperum*, and on the institution, cf. E. Lesne, 'Les Eglises et les monastères centres d'accueil, d'exploitation et de peuplement', *Histoire de la propriété ecclésiastique en France*, VI, Lille 1943, 142–151.

67. *ASS, januarii*, III, 510. The text runs—'Antistes elesmum famulum jubet. . . .' It clearly refers to the 'famulus eleemosynarius'. The Latin text of Bollandus is a version of the Spanish text of Juan Marieta O.P. He summarizes Franciscus Scuderius, SJ, who must have used a Latin original: perhaps the now lost canonization process.

68. 'Multi moriebantur.' *Proces. Bon.*, nos. 29 and 35.

69. Jordan as well as the other witnesses points out that the men 'magnae auctoritatis' only intervened after Dominic had given them the example. There was, however, a hospice at the St Antolin chapter which had received a farm in 1162 from the bishop, Raymond II, to entertain the poor there—Loperraez, I, 137; Gil González Dávila, *loc. cit.*, *supra*, n. 53. Doubtless it was crowded out with hungry people.

70. Jordan, no. 10. 'Instituere eleemosynam' must be taken in the full sense of setting up an institution, a centre of charity, just as 'instituere scholam' can have the meaning of building a school—Lesne, 556. Juan de Navarra, *Proces. Bon.*, no. 29, for his part says definitely that Dominic sold his books and furniture 'pro cibu pauperum', which points to the daily distributions of food made in the charity centres.

71. Matt. XIX, 21.

72. Fray Esteban, *Proces. Bon.*, no. 35. The Councils of Paris and Rouen, in 1213–1214, forbade religious to bind themselves by oath or under threat of anathema not to sell the books of the community for the poor, for to sell in order to give is one of the principal works of mercy, Mansi, XXII, 832 and 900.

73. Ferrando, no. 21—cf. for a similar gesture made by Dominic in Languedoc, Jordan no. 35. The date is clearly indicated. It happened in Spain 'cum adhuc in suis partibus moraretur'. He was already of age. He had not yet joined the chapter of Osma, for he would then no longer have been free to dispose of himself. In short, he no longer had anything to sell except himself.

74. Fray Esteban indeed declared: 'Cuius exemplo quidam magne auctoritatis similia fecerunt, et ex tunc cum eo predicare ceperunt. Et sicut intellexi[t], post paucos dies venit idem frater Dominicus ad partes Tolosanas . . .', *Proces. Bon.*, no. 35. Clearly there is something wrong with the chronology here, but the facts are probably true.

75. Jordan, no. 4. The bishop in question in this paragraph is not Diego, as Jordan thought, but his predecessor, Martin Bazán († 1201). Diego was merely prior of the chapter. Jordan has rather confused the two figures. We attribute the search for new subjects for the chapter to Diego.

76. Fray Esteban, long before he knew St Dominic, had heard much good related of him and in particular the story of the charity centre 'a magnis viris'. *Proces. Bon.*, no. 35.

77. Jordan, no. 11. On the subject of the possibility of Dominic's later teaching in Palencia, for which there is no foundation in the sources, nor place in the chronology, cf. *infra*, ch. VII, n. 124.

NOTES TO CHAPTER III

1. The archives of the church of Osma were partially destroyed by a fire in 1505—M. H. Vicaire, 'St Dominque en 1207' in *AFP*, XXII (1953), 343 and n.48. Clearly they must have been reconstructed at once, for certain documents were of vital importance. Moreover, there were still extant in the middle of the sixteenth century many old documents of which an inventory has been preserved— Filiberto Díez Pardo, *Santo Domingo de Guzmán*, Vergara 1935, 50, n. 30; cf. *infra*, n. 83. In 1659 P. Argaiz, in order to compile, on the instructions of Bishop Palafox, the *Memorias ilustres de la santa Iglesia y obispado de Osma*, a manuscript preserved in the archives of the cathedral, had himself provided by the abbeys or churches of the neighbourhood with authentic copies of documents concerning Osma— Díez Pardo, no. 31. At the close of the eighteenth century, Loperraez-Corvalan used all these documents with intelligence and restraint, editing them in the third volume of his work, in order to compose a detailed history of the diocese of Osma. He did not, however, know the Dominican documents. It is of his book that use will chiefly be made. The *Teatro Eclesiástico de la Iglesia y cividad de Osma* (Madrid), 1648, a very cursory work, is of little value. Núñez Marqués may be considered a guide; his history is a compilation, but his descriptions are useful. Señor Alamo's article *Burgo de Osma* in DHGE, X, 1266– 1271, is excellent.

2. The charter of donation and confirmation of the property of the diocese dated 19th February, 1154 (Loperraez, III, 32–33) only mentions, so far as Osma itself is concerned, the property of the former monastery of San Miguel. That of 24th September, 1174 (Loperraez III, 36–38) adds, in the same phrase— *Burgum sancte Marie*, i.e. the locality which in the meantime had grown up around the cathedral of Santa María. Loperraez II, 38, assigns the date 1164 to the populating of this burgh or *villa*, which must be distinguished from the *castrum*, that is, from the reoccupied Roman town with its surrounding wall and its towers, where, moreover a fortress had been built. In actual fact the charter of 1170 (cf. following note) would seem to be the decisive charter dealing with the settlement of the place.

3. Charter of 22nd September, 1170 (Loperraez, III, 562), issued by Alfonso VIII, granted in response to 'tantis et lacrimosis petitionibus' of the bishop and canons. No authority and no council could claim to reap any advantage whatsoever on these lands which had been made over to the Church. Any man could establish himself there freely, except the inhabitants of the *castrum* of Osma.

4. For the renunciation of the right of spoliation, cf. *infra*, no. 82; on its significance see Lacger, 286. The manor and the fortress were made over to the Church in 1214 by Alfonso VIII as he lay dying. It was only very much later and never permanently that the bishop succeeded in taking possession of these rights and above all of the castle which was in the hands of lay occupiers—Loperraez, I, 144, 213 ff; II, 221; III, 49 ff.; Núñez-Marqués, 58–59.

5. Loperraez, I, 143.

6. For the time of the troubles, under Urraca, particularly in 1112, see Loperraez, I, 95. On Uxama, Núñez-Marqués, 52–59, in part based on Loperraez and Blas Taracena, *Carta arqueológica de Soria*; Alamo, 1267.

7. For a description of the place, its cathedral and cloister and the way they were furnished in the eighteenth Century, see Loperraez, II, 37 ff; for their present condition, Kirsch, 58–65; Núñez-Marqués, 1–43.

8. Ps. LXXX, III, 1 and 5.

9. The double windows of the chapter room of the twelfth century can be identified. The columns and romanesque capitals of this room (today the sacristy of the parish clergy), the vault of which is of more recent date, come from the former cathedral—Núñez-Marqués, 17–18. The cathedral now contains numerous images or statues of St Dominic, in particular a bas-relief in a stall which is always left empty and is lighted at the times of the offices. It is not so long since Mass was still celebrated thereon 4th August—Balme, I, 53. The custom has become obsolete. As to the saint's house which was still shown in 1920 in the lane behind the cloister (Kirsch, 64), and which is now destroyed, there was nothing authentic about it. Dominic, as a Canon Regular, certainly lived and slept in the claustral buildings.

10. The black cloak with the pointed hood of the canons of Osma in the time of St Dominic may be seen worn by the canon following St Peter of Osma on the latter's tomb in the cathedral (1258). The white habit was common to all Canons Regular of the twelfth century, and for this reason they were classed together under name of 'White Canons'—Jacques de Vitry, cited in Mandonnet-Vicaire I, 236, n. 18. The monastic reformers of the time, such as Cîteaux, also wore black and white. The origin of these colours would be the insistence of the new regulars on manual work; their garments, made with their own hands, could not be dyed—Dereine, Prémontré, 371, n. 3 and 373, n. 2; Echard I, 75a, rightly thinks that Dominic never altered his habit.

11. Erected in 1063 by the monks of Arlanza (Loperraez, III, 563), San Miguel had a certain renown in 1086 (Pérez de Urbel II, 476 and 482); by 1154 it had already been suppressed and incorporated in the diocese, as was the case with the monasteries of San Esteban de Górmaz, San Martín y Santa María de Górmaz, San Pedro de Aza, the origin of which is unknown—Loperraez, III, 32.

12. Cf. *supra*, ch. 1, n. 17. The monastery of San Miguel de Quintana del Pidio, given to Silos in 1190, might also be added—Núñez-Marqués, 81.

13. The first three in the diocese, the fourth in the Cistercians.

14. The popes themselves were from Cluny—Urban II (1058–1059), Pascal II (1099–1118), Callixtus II (1119–1124).

15. Pérez de Urbel, II, 426–432 and 483–4; Villey, 65–73; Defourneaux, 17–49, who (18, n. 1 and 27, n. 4) corrects the too narrowly nationalist judgements of the Spanish historians in the face of this 'foreign' influence (for example, Pérez de Urbel, II, 427). Men whose real country was the Church and who were working for the good of the countries where their order was established, cannot be called foreigners. On the other hand, in the reactions of their opponents, which were similar to those the reform elicited elsewhere, a solely national reaction should not be seen.

16. Pérez de Urbel, II, 431–432; Defourneaux, 35.

17. Loperraez, I, 76–94.

18. *Ibid.*, I, 95–101.

19. *Supra*, ch. II, n. 3.

20. Dom L. Serrano, 'Concilios nacionales de Palencia en la primera mitad del siglo XII', in *Semana pro Ecclesia et Patria*, Palencia, 1936, 3–24.

21. Easily effected in Catalonia and Aragon (1071) this change was carried out with some difficulty in Castile, through the will of Popes Alexander II and Gregory VII—Defourneaux, 28–32.

22. Despite what tradition has to say (cf. Pérez de Urbel, II, 433), it was not abolished by authority but gradually replaced—Defourneaux, 32, n. 4.

23. Pérez de Urbel II, 484–522; Defourneaux, 48–58. The intense movement of the Cistercian foundations was only interrupted during the minority of Alfonso VIII (1158–1168).

24. *Supra*, ch. I, p. 9.

25. Loperraez, I, 173–187.

26. *Ibid.*, I, 187–194.

27. He attributes to Bishop Diego the reform of the canons and the appointment of Dominic to the chapter. These, however, were the acts of Diego's predecessor, Martín Bazán, of whose very name Jordan seems unaware. Diego doubtless played a decisive rôle in these two matters, but the bishop alone had the authority to determine them.

28. It is remarked that Bishop Martin, like his predecessors very often followed the royal court far from Osma (from 1193–1195, for instance, he is found in the king's company in turn at Alarcos, Zorril, Fuentes, Toledo, Valladolid, Alarcos, Toledo, Palenzuela, Toledo, Valladolid, Alarcos . . . — Loperraez, I, 175–179), it can be concluded that he chiefly confirmed with his authority the spiritual initiatives of the prior of his chapter whose high apostolic value he was soon to learn to recognize.

29. Jordan, n. 4. At the same period St Julian of Cuenca was also looking round everywhere for good clergy, *ASS, januarii* III, Paris 1863, 510.

30. In 1225, the bishop of Palencia, whose schools had been flourishing in an exceptional manner for half a century, stressed the ignorance of the country clergy—Denifle, *Die Entstehung der Universitäten des Mittelalters bis 1400*, Berlin 1885, 476. What must have been the position then in dioceses with an even poorer teaching tradition?

31. Text in Loperraez III, 47 (bull of 11.V.1199). Immediate action if the misdemeanour was manifest. No action is possible on public rumour alone if there were no evidence: there must be witnesses. If there were public scandal, however one, had to apply to the accused the canonical measure of *purgatio*. Cf. *Ibid.*, I, 181.

32. Colmenares has discovered, without date or place of issue, the documents of a provincial council convened by Martin de Toledo (1194–1208), which ordered priests to turn out of their house and cease all contact with women under suspicion; this canon cannot be later than the bull, for it is highly improbable that it would have failed to quote it—Loperraez, I, 181.

33. Act of 31.V.1270, again confirmed in 1300—Loperraez, III, 201. It was granted, as requested: 'por si, e por todos los otros clerigos desde Archiprestago'. This does not mean that all the other clerics had children!

34. Jordan, n. 4.

35. The history of the canonical movement in the eleventh and twelfth centuries has been completely revised in the last twenty years, thanks in particular to the work of Charles Dereine. In Spain it has scarcely been studied except for Catalonia and Aragon. In addition to the fundamental studies of Dereine, Dickinson, Vincke, cf. L. de la Calzada, *La Proyeccion del pensamiento de Gregorio VII en los reynos de Castilla y Leon, Studi Gregoriani* III, Rome 1948, 1–87; ch. Dereine, 'L'élaboration du statut canonique des chanoines réguliers', spécialement sous Urbain II in *RHE*, XLVI (1951), 534–565; 'Coutumiers et ordinaires de chanoines réguliers', in *Scriptorium* V (1951) 107–113; 'Note sur l'influence de la règle de Grégoire VII', in *RHE*, XLIII (1948), 512–514, 'Les coutumiers de S. Quentin de Beauvais et de Springiersbach', in *RHE*, XLIII (1948), 411–442.

36. Loperraez, I, 102–116.

37. The buildings, begun by Pierre de Bourges (Loperraez, I, 93), made little progress under his successor because of the civil disturbances, Bishop Bertrand instituted a confraternity of prayer for the

dead on 4.IV.1130 (text *Ibid.*, III, 12; cf. I, 104–105) the alms from which helped. In 1136 the king assigned the church of La Vid to the construction of the canons' residence (*Ibid.*, I, 110).

38. On 4.V.1131, Innocent II referred to the 'fratres saeculares ejusdem loci'—Loperraez, III, 13. On 3.I.1136, on the other hand, Alfonso VII granted the church of Osma the tithes of San Esteban de Gormaz 'omnibus in eadem Ecclesia sub regula 5. Augustini servientibus, ad opus vestimentorum suorum'—Loperraez, III, 15.

39. See reports of the prior and the bishop—Loperraez, II, 77. In 1152 (charter of 10.VII—Loperraez, III, 27) the following dignitaries are mentioned—*prior, cantor, praepositus, camerarius, operarius* (? architect). The title *praepositus* was formerly traditional in Spain. The influence of Cluny substituted for it the title of *prior* (Pérez de Urbel II, 434). Here it designates the sub-prior. *Camerarius* is the bursar. Other lists mention a *sacrista, a preceptor* (cf. *infra*, n. 71). In 1270, the *personae* of the chapter were: *prior, tres archidiaconi, sacrista et cantor* (charter of 5.II.1270—Loperraez, III, 203).

40. Loperraez I, 130; cf. Vincke, 40. The Bishop of Osma was careful to make secure his authority over the Premonstratentians of La Vid, which was threatened by their dependence on the rest of the order. Any relationship at all between the cathedral chapter and Prémontré could not have failed to leave important traces in the documents because of this dependence, as well as on account of the observance. The latter made its appearance in the course of the twelfth century under the name of *ordo novus* or *arctior consuetudo*, as a complete disruption of the observance of the Canons Regular elaborated at the end of the eleventh century (*ordo antiquius*). It interpreted literally the observances of the *ordo monasterii* (cf. *infra*, n. 45), in particular, on manual labour. It was not made for cathedrals. On these expressions see Dereine, 386–389.

41. As Alamo does (*DHGE*, X, 1267), according to the Argaiz manuscript. A letter from the Osma archivist shows that Argaiz' opinion is only an hypothesis.

42. The canonical form of life had been considerably developed in the eleventh century in the north of Spain, in accordance with the Carolingian rule of Aix, to which the important chapters, like that of Barcelona, had remained persistently faithful. At the turn of the century under the stimulus of the kings of Aragon-Catalonia, great bishops who had been trained at St Sernin in Toulouse and St Rufus in Avignon, promoted the full regular life and promulgated in particular the observance of St Rufus—for instance, San Oldegaire, former Abbot of St Rufus, Archbishop of Barcelona and Tarragona († 1137). 350 monasteries of St Rufus in Spain are mentioned—A. Carrier de B., *op. cit., infra*, 20–21. The movement for the foundation of chapters of regular life in Spain was even more remarkable, from the point of view of numbers and rapidity, than that of the Cistercian foundations—Dereine, 367, 377, 379, 401–402. For the customs of St Rufus in Catalonia see A. Carrier de Belleuse, '*Coutumier du XIe.s.de l'Ordre de S. Ruf, en usage a la cathédrale de Maguelone*, Sherbrooke 1950 (critical edition); Ch. Dereine. 'S. Ruf et ses coutumes aux XIe et XIIs', in *Rev. Bénédictine* LIX (1949), 161–182 (in particular of Las Abadesas, near Ripoll); Vincke, 38–41.

43. The observance of St Rufus was only one of the various forms, which did not differ greatly among themselves, of the *ordo antiquus*. The charter of 26.VII.1148, a donation to the church of Soria, demonstrates the existence of these usual customs: 'addimus preterea ut Ecclesia B. Petri omnes illes bonas consuetudines habeat et manuteneat quam habent cetere ecclesie in quibus canonici regulariter vivunt'—Loperraez, III, 24. The letter to the brethren of Springiersbach also mentions this 'communis fratrum regularium consuetudo'—*PL*, 163, 497 and Mandonnet-Vicaire, II, 155 (on the subject of this letter cf. *infra*, n. 47). The customs of Soria, like those of Cuenca, must have been those of Osma; otherwise the Osma chapter would not have tried to obtain the submission of that of Soria in 1152—*ibid.* 29. They may possibly have been inspired by those of Jaca and Huesca (cf. *infra*, n. 66). Such connections will perhaps eventually enable the Osma statutes to be rediscovered, at least those that Bishop Martín had confirmed once more by the Pope in 1199: 'constitutiones . . . quas possemus restitutiones potius nominare, cum a longis retro temporibus hoc ipsum de oxomensis ecclesia fuerit, sicutarseris, a Romanis pontificibus ordinatum'—Loperraez III, 46 and Laurent, no. 1.

44. On the problem of the rule of St Augustine, considerable work has been accomplished since the study published in 1938, Mandonnet-Vicaire, II, 103–192; the prior date of the rule to letter 211, which we had defended at the instances of Mandonnet, has been more or less generally rejected by the critics (cf. in particular C. Lambot, *Rev. Bénédictine LIII* (1941) 41–58) and, likewise, the Augustinian authenticity of the rule. On the other hand, what was established as to the reappearance and misadventures of the text of the rule in the course of the Gregorian canonical reform, has been very appositely taken up again, confirmed and restated, particularly by Charles Dereine—cf. Dickinson,252–272; Dereine, *Chanoines* 387–390, and 'Vie commune, Règle de S. Augustin et chanoines réguliers', in *RHE*, XLI (1946), 365–406, 'Enquête sur la règle de S. Augustin', in *Scriptorium*, II (1948), 28–36.

45. We are adopting this position, which has the support of very competent patrologists, in connection with a problem which for us is secondary. For the opposite view see—Merlin, in *Analecta Praemonstratensia*, XXIV (1948), 5–19; Lope Cilleruelo, *El Monacato de S Agustin y su regla*, Madrid, 1949 and *Archivo Agustiniano*, XLIV (1950), 85–88; W. Humpfner *Augustinus Magister*, 1955, 241–254, Schuster, *S. Benôit et son temps*, translated by J. B. Gai, Paris, 1950, 248, thinks the *Ordo monasterii* and the *Regula* (in the masculine) can be attributed to Eugippa († 533).

46. For these texts see *PL*, 32, 1377–1384 and 1449–1452 (or again *PL*, 66, 995–998). Critical edition by De Bruyne, in *Revue Bénédictine*, XLII (1930), 316–342 and by A. C. Vega, 'El Escorial 1933' (off-print from *Archivo Agustiniano*, XXVII, 1933). Cf. Mandonnet-Vicaire, II, 129–130. The title of *ordo monasterii*, which has now become general among historians, will be used from now onwards instead of *disciplina monasterii*.

47. The letter to the brethren of Springiersbach of 2nd August, 1118, is the most important of these

documents—Mandonnet-Vicaire, II, 152–160. This community had assumed the leadership in Germany of a canonical movement, which Prémontré had developed, for the literal observance of the whole of the rule of St Augustine, including the *ordo monasterii*. Hence the *ordo novus* which had been substituted for the *ordo antiquus*—cf. Ch. Dereine, 'Le premier ordo de Prémontré', in *Revue Bénédictine*, LVIII (1948), 84–92; 'Les coutumiers de S. Quentin de Beauvais et de Springiersbach', in *RHE*, XLIII (1948), 411–442. For other indications in regard to the *Epistolae declarantes regulam S. Augustini*, see Dereine, 390.

48. For the significance of the rule of St Augustine, see the texts discovered by Jean Leclercq in Spain, 'Haec sunt quae debet scire et facere canonicus regularis' and 'De consortio malorum et bonorum,' edited in *RHE*, XLIV (1949), 566–568.

49. *PL*, 32, 1377–1379.

50. Spaetling, *Suppl.*, 1–8; J. Leclercq, *La vie parfaite*, ch. III, 'La vie apostolique', Paris-Turnhout, 1948, 82–108. Spaetling minimizes the rôle of *Actes*, IV, 32 in the primitive history of the apostolic life.

51. Mandonnet-Vicaire, II, 163–192. Dereine, 377 and articles mentioned *supra*, n. 35.

52. Synod of Rome 1059, under Nicolas II, inspired by Hildebrand, the future Pope Gregory VII; Mansi, XIX, 873, 898, 908.

53. Canon 120 of the famous *Regula canonicorum* of the Council of Aix-la-Chapelle, in 816, assigned to each canon: 'victus, vestitus et pars eleemosynarum' (cf. canon 122); it also allowed them a private house (canon 142)—Mansi, XIV, 231C, 232A, 243B.

54. The *De vita et moribus clericorum suorum*, in which this account is contained, was in fact to be found with the rule of St Augustine and his biography by Possidius, in the dossier of the Canons Regular at the end of the eleventh century—Dereine, 388.

55. Sermon No. II (356) *De vita et moribus clericorum suorum*, *PL*, XXXIX, 1574–1575. Lambot ed. S. *Aurelii Augustini, Sermones selecti duodeviginti . . .* , *Stromata patrist et mediaevalia I*, Utrecht-Brussels, 1950.

56. Luke X, 1.

57. Acts, IV, 32; cf. III, 44.

58. VI, 7–11.

59. Peter Damian, *Contra clericos regulares proprietarios*, Op. XXIV, *PL*, 145, 482D–490C. This minor work was addressed to Alexander II (1061–1073) then newly elected, and contains the clerical ideas characteristic of this Italian promoter of the Gregorian reform. The same ideas are to be found in other minor works on letters of St Peter Damian, Mandonnet-Vicaire, II, 168–172; Dereine, 386–390.

60. Vincke, 41.

61. The division of the episcopal and capitular menses had been decided upon for Castile at the Council of Palencia in 1100—L. Serrano, *Semana pro Ecclesia et Patria*, Palencia, 1936, II, after P. de Pulgar, *Historia secular y ecclesiástica de Palencia*, II, Madrid 1679, 130 and *Silva Palentina*, ed. Vielva Ramos, Palencia 1932, I, 154. It does not seem to have been put into effect in Osma in the twelfth century.

62. Loperraez, I, 110.

63. *Ibid.*, I, 100.

64. Charter of 26.VII.1148; *ibid.*, III, 24; cf. I, 126.

65. Charter of foundation of 10.VII.1152, *ibid.*, III, 27; cf. I, 127.

66. Account of an incident occurring on 1.VIII.1152, *ibid.*, III, 29–30; cf. I, 128–130.

67. Jaca, in Aragón, had become an episcopal see in 1063, through the occupation by the Moslems of the see of Huesca, which once more assumed its former function in 1096, when Jaca lost its bishop. Meanwhile a chapter of Augustinian regulars was set up in Jaca (1067). Another was constituted in Huesca. Despite the return of the bishop to Huesca, the two chapters remained on a footing of equality under the authority of the bishop—Vincke 37, 38, 42.

68. Charter of the repopulation of Roa, 22.XII.1143—Loperraez, III, 21.

69. Erection of the see, bull of 5.VII.1183; appointment of the bishop from 1182—Gams, 31.

70. J. P. Martyr Rizo, *Historia de la Ciudad de Cuenca*, Madrid, 1626, 36 and 136; Loperraez, I, 167–168.

71. Loperraez, I, 168.

72. Among the signatures of the canons of Osma, in a charter of 9.IV.1166—Loperraez, III, 558. For the significance of preceptor, see Lesne, 461–462.

73. Signature of a charter of 28.IV.1168. Bernier (Barnerius) had already signed the charter of 9.IV.1166, without the title of master. It is not known whether these two masters actually taught in the chapter, but the use of this title at least indicates that they had taught—cf. Lesne, 461–462.

74. Canon 18 of the Third Council of the Lateran (1179) did not order that a master should be set up in each diocese—this was a thing done fairly frequently—but that a benefice was to be reserved for the master so that he might do so gratuitously and give the poor the opportunity of studying—Hefele-Leclercq, V, 2, 1101.

75. *Quem sacrarum literarum notitia . . . decorabat*—Jordan, no. 4.

76. For Rodríguez, see Loperraez I, 195–207. A former student in Paris, he edited numerous works of history and exegesis, in the course of an extremely active life. For Master Melendo, see Loperraez I, 208–220; Rivera, 337.

77. Edited in Timoteo Rofo Orcajo, *Catalogo descriptivo de los los codices que se conservan en la Santa Iglesia catedral de Burgo de Osma*, Madrid, 1929, 9–13. This catalogue, dating from the end of the thirteenth century, lists very numerous commentaries on the Bible, especially of the New Testament, works of the Fathers of the Church (Irenaeus, Origen, Prosper, Gregory of Nazianzen, Denis, Isidore); sermons and homilies, liturgical works and computations; theological works by Honorius of Autun (*Elucidarius*), Hugh of St Victor (*De Sacramentis, Chronica*), a commentator on Peter Lombard (*Super IV Sent.*) Pierre

le Mangeur (*Historia scolastica*) and several anonymous *summae*; canonical works and the Digesta; finally a book each on physics, music, astrology, rhetoric, Priscian, etc.

78. Loperraez I, 180; Vincke, 42, whose study emphasizes the main responsibility of the sovereigns. The kings who, a century earlier, had been the great propagators of Augustinian regularity in the chapters afterwards changed their attitude and frequently urged secularization, which enabled them to dispose of prebends sometimes of considerable importance in favour of their own supporters. This policy led, at the close of the Middle Ages, to the universal disappearance of regular life among the canons.

79. Gil González Davila, *Teatro eclesiástico de las iglesias de los reinos de las dos Castillas*, II, Madrid, 1647, 152.

80. Charter of 28.IV.1168, Loperraez, III, 561; cf. I, 141–142.

81. This was the case, for instance, of the simonaical archdeacon and canon in 1174 (cf. *infra*, n. 83) and of Canon Pedro de Termes (before 1195) about whom the bishop censured the abbey of Arlanza for having 'received' him: 'ipsi episcopo invito et contradicente . . . cum bonis quae ab Ecclesia sua habuerat,' charter of 22.I.1195—Loperraez, III, 44.

82. Loperraez, I, 135 and 164. In 1180 (charter of 15th June), the king renounced a whole series of dues or taxes (among them the right of spoliation of the movable and immovable property of the deceased bishop) concerning the churches, giving them protection for the future against any exaction on the part of his functionaries, text *ibid.*, III, 38.

83. This decree, no longer extant, is mentioned in the bull of Innocent III (cf. *infra*, n. 85) and in an ancient inventory of Osma—Loperraez, I, 136.

84. 'De hoc autem quod rex et principes sui a Bernardo quondam oxomensi episcopo pecuniam recepisse dicuntur, ut eius electioni praestarent assensum, et quod idem episcopus Oxomensis archidiacono beneficia certi reditus et cuidam clerico ante electionem suam prioratum dicitur promisiosse ut uterque illorum, archidiaconus, videlicet et clericus, consentiret eidem . . .' Decretal of Alexander III at the Third Council of the Lateran (1179), L.V, III, ch. XI, *Convictus de simonia*, ed. Friedberg, 752—Loperraez, I, 146.

85. The dignitaries of the chapter who were candidates for some portion of the benefices, had tried to obtain exemption from Pope Lucius III from the common obligations. Instead, it was the bishop who obtained papal prohibition against receiving any canon, prebendary or dignitary who did not embrace regular life. The decree, no longer extant, is mentioned in the ancient inventory of Osma and in the bull of Innocent III (cf. *infra*, n. 86).

86. Bull of 11.V.1199, text in Loperraez III, 46; *PL*, 214, 604; Laurent, no. 1.

87. In oxomensi ecclesia sint de cetero canonci regulares, nec aliquis in portionarium vel secularem canonicum recipiatur deinceps in eadem.' *Ibid*. Cf. Jordan, no. 4 cited *infra*, n. 89.

88. Intelliximus . . . quod tu, de communi consensu totius capituli Oxomensis, auctoritate . . . archiepiscopi, consensu etian et consilio charissimi in Christo filii nostri A(lphonsi) regis illustris Castelle . . .'—Innocent III, bull quoted *supra*, n. 86.

89. 'Hinc accidit, ut daret operam suis id persuadere canonicis, crebris admonitione et exhortatione pervigili, quatenus sub regula beati Augustini ad observantiam canonice religionis consentirent, tantaque hoc ipsum egit sollicitudine, ut eorum animos, licet quosdam ex ipsis haberet contradictores, ad suum desiderium inclinaret'—Jordan, no. 4, who attributes the whole initiative to Diego and seems to be unaware that the chapter had already been living under the rule of St Augustine.

90. It is not only from Jordan's words that this conclusion is deduced ('licet quosdam ex ipsis haberet contradictores.' This interpolated clause forms a correction to Jordan's original text, which emphasizes its importance) and from Diego's efforts to procure recruits of value for the chapter. It is a fact that the lists of the members of the chapter who signed the charters of, respectively, 22.I.1195 and 13.I.1201 (Loperraez, III, 44 and 41) show only three identical names out of the twelve they comprise from one source or another: Diego, Juan and Pedro. Nine new canons out of twelve in six years is a large number. In actual fact, although Loperraez does not question that the signatures which follow that of the prior of Osma in the charter of 1195 are all those of canons of Osma (cf. Loperraez, I, 175), the fact is by no means certain. What does, however, make it probable is that the Osma text is only a copy of the charter of Arlanza. It is normal that the latter should have been specially signed by the canons of Osma. It should finally be noted that Loperraez reads the second signature on the Osma copy thus: *A. sacrista*; whereas A. Nunez de Castro, *Crónica de los . . . reyes de Castila*, Madrid 1665, 184, copied by numerous authors (among them Martínez, XLIII), has deciphered on the Arlanza original: *D. sacrista*, which people have been eager to read as Domingo. Only the discovery of the original document would enable the question to be solved, as to the D, but not as to the name it represented. Serrano, 236–237, only knew the text through Loperraez.

91. 'Volentes igitur quod a te videbitur pia deliberatione statutum debita firmitate gaudere, costitutiones ipsas (quas possemus restitutiones potius nominare, cum a longis retro temporibus hoc ipsum de Oxomensi ecclesia fuerit, sicut asseris, a romanis pontificibus ordinatum) sicut a te rationabiliter facte sunt, et a tuo recepte capitulo, auctoritate apostolica confirmamus'—Loperraez III, 46.

92. This is in effect the number of canons who signed the charter of 13.I.1201 in due order—Loperraez, III, 41. The bishop, who was really the superior of the chapter was the thirteenth. It is possible that this number was instituted at the time the chapter was originated and that it was maintained even in the time of the crisis—cf. the lists of signatures in 1166 (taking into consideration only those who explicitly describe themselves as canons) and 1195—Loperraez, III, 559 and 44. The number twelve is traditional in the history of the apostolic life. The monks had a liking for it and the Canons Regular of the Gregorian reform, even more so, for instance, in Spain, at Valencia and Majorca (Balearic Isles),

Vincke 49, n. 44. Cf. Mandonnet-Vicaire, I, 123, n. 34; II, 170, n. 11; 187, n. 58, 191, n. 68. Dereine 368, Meersserman in *Rev. d'Histoire ecclésiast. Suisse*, XLVI (1952), 24–25, n. 1 to 5.

93. Bull of secularization by Innocent VIII of 14.X.1488 (termination of the common refectory)—Núñez-Marqués, 128; Vincke 43. Final secularization by Paul III in 1536—Loperraez, I, 330.

94. Vincke, 43.

95. The compromise of 22.I.1195 between the communities of Osma and Arlanza, mentions Diego as a simple religious (the prior signs G.) and ignores Dominic—Loperraez, III, 44. This is the *terminus postquem* of the latter's entry into the chapter. The charter of 13.I.1201, the only absolutely certain chronological data for the first part of Dominic's life, presents him as sub-prior of the chapter (cf. *infra*, n. 113). This is the *terminus antequem*. It is possible to put it back considerably. Jordan no. 12, says that Dominic was elected by his brethren: 'suppriorem eum constituunt canonici sui'. At this date Diego was still prior (Bishop Martin only died on 27.VII.1201) and was in a position to nominate his sub-prior by himself alone, as was done in the case of the majority of religious. If he did not do so, it was because the constitutions recently put into force demanded a vote from the chapter, at any rate a consultative one. Loperraez (I, 186), considers that this provision which was still extant in the eighteenth century in several chapters in Spain, notably at Cuenca, the sister chapter to Osma, included the condition, which is to be found set out in detail in the other chapters, that the elected person should have at least four years seniority in the community. Dominic would thus have entered before January 1197—that is, in 1195 or 1196. 1196 is the more likely date, for sufficient time must be left for Diego to become prior and to search for new recruits. Since the ruling in the name of which Dominic was elected sub-prior around 1200, had just been put in force again, it would seem that there must necessarily have been hesitation in departing from the conditions it imposed. If in consideration of Dominic's remarkable qualities the regulation was never the less circumvented by dispensation, this cannot have been to any considerable extent. The dates 1196 or 1197 were finally adopted as probable. The office of sacristan assigned to him by a charter of 18.VIII.1199 (cf. *infra*, n. 112), according to a statement which is merely probable, equally presupposes in St Dominic a certain seniority. Among the canons the office of sacristan was important (those of St Rufus even ranked it immediately after the office of prior) and in a regularly constituted chapter could not be given to those who had only recently joined.

96. Coming to the Palencia schools at the age of fourteen or fifteen, he left them ten years later—cf. ch. II, n. 25, 43, 47. If he was thus twenty-four or twenty-five in 1196–1197, he was born between 1171 and 1173. This agrees with the data instanced *supra*, ch. I, n. 90 to 95, but does not throw any further light upon it.

97. II Cor. II, 16.

98. Eccl. L. 8.

99. Jordan, no. 12.

100. Dereine 370 and 394. He emphasizes that in Gregorian as in Carolingian times men did not enter a chapter of regular canons to exercise the ministry of souls, but primarily to devote themselves to canonical prayer in poverty. The apostolic ministry was not, however, excluded from the canon's horizon, as will be seen later. Manual work had not entirely disappeared either, cf. *infra*, ch. X, n. 100 and *supra*, n. 10.

101. Jordan, .n. 14, applies to the life of St Dominic in Osma the term of 'embraces of Rachael'—the object of the jealousy of Lia (Gen. XXIX, XXX), which technically signifies the contemplative life in the symbolical theology which was then the fashion of the day. Honorius III was to make the same application in regard to the life of the Preachers in their convent of studies at St Jacques, on 30.XII.1220 —Laurent, no. 122.

102. *Proces. Thol.*, no. 5.

103. Jordan, no. 13. The work is not mentioned in the thirteenth-century catalogue of the library of Osma (cf. *supra*, n. 76). Very much read in the cloisters, it must have deteriorated and could easily be lost. In the fifteenth century the Bishop of Osma had it recopied for the chapter in whose possession they still are, the *Collations* and *Institutions* of Cassian, cf. Rojo Orcajo, 125 and 255.

104. Acts II, 46.

105. *Proces. Bon.*, no. 7.

106. Jordan, no. 12.

107. 'While we devote ourselves to prayer and to the ministry of preaching'—Acts VI, 4.

108. Matt. VI, 6.

109. Jordan, nos. 12 and 13.

110. It was only in 1311 that the Council of Vienna restored the age for entering the priesthood to twenty-five—*Clem.*, I, tit. VI, ch. 3, *Generalem*, ed. Friedberg, 1140. As far back as 1179, however, the 3rd canon of the Council of the Lateran had authorized the age of twenty-five in case of necessity—Hefele—Leclercq, V, 2, 1090. No time was lost in making use of this tolerance, especially for holders of benefices. The bishop probably did the same in the case of Dominic, constrained by the dearth of subjects in the diocese. In any case he did not wait until the age of thirty, since St Dominic, arriving at Osma at the age of twenty-four, in 1195 at the earliest, could not in that case have been ordained before 1201 at the soonest. In such conditions he could not have been appointed sub-prior. Cf. Thomassin, I, 436; Hinschius, I, 18.

111. Before the organization of the seminaries, no ordination for the diocese as such existed. The Council of Trent made provision for ordination for a particular church.

112. *Proces. Bon.*, no. 27.

113. This was a charter of compromise between the chapter of Osma and the Cistercian abbey of Veruela. In modern times this charter has been studied by the Abbot of Veruela and the information

communicated to Fr Tomas Madaleno (*Manual de Dominicos. Informe de los blasones más gloriosos de la Religión de los Predicadores*, Blason I, cited by Martínez LIII). Despite the indirect character of the information, it seems reliable. It is certain that Bishop Martin throughout his episcopate took care to settle by compromises the contesting of rights which set it in opposition to other institutions as so often happened in the Middle Ages. On a so-called mention of Dominic as sacristan as early as 1195, cf. *supra*,n. 90.

114. Charter of 13.1.1201, Loperraez, III, 41; Laurent, no. 2. In 1270 the Bishop of Osma was to mention this sub-priorship—Martínez, 250 (ch. CXCVII, 13.VII.1270).

115. Cf. *supra*, n. 59.

116. The author of the *De vita vere apostolica* which is monastic in tendency, inveighs strongly against canons whose arguments are specious. 'Desinant ergo apostolorum vitam in solo baptismo, in sola praedicatione et miraculo accipere.' 'Sequi videretur . . . ut quemlibet immundissimorum clericorum quem constat utrumque facere, baptisare et praedicare, apostolicam vitam probatetur habere', *PL*, 170, 631D–632A. Dereine, 393–394 cites a series of authors who speak in this sense, especially in Germany. The principal theorists of the canonical life, however, have a more finely balanced thought. The reflections of Arno de Reichersberg and of Anselm of Havelberg on the reciprocal relations of action and contemplation prepare the way for the theory of the mixed life in St Thomas Aquinas.

117. 'Et sanctorum Patrum inexpugnabili sentencia sancitur, canonicorum ordinem omnibus ecclesie ordinibus preponendum merito. Nec mirum, cum Christo et apostolis eius succedat, in predicacionis, baptismatis ac reliquorum ecclesie sacramentorum officium subrogatus', *Coutumier du XIe siècle de l'ordre de S. Ruf en usage à la Cathédrale de Maguelone*, ed. A. Carrier, Sherbrooke, 1950, 97.

NOTES TO CHAPTER IV

1. Jordan, no. 14. On the classic theme of Lia-Rachel the texts of Innocent III, addressed to Cistercians engaged in the apostolate, should be added to those cited *supra*, ch. III, n. 100—Potthast, 785Q *PL*, 214, 675D (Fr Rainier); Potthast, 2391, *PL*, 215, 525A (Fr Peter of Castelnau). Cf. Altaner, 162; Mandonnet-Vicaire, II, 232 and n. 85.

2. Loperraez, I, 189.

3. Born 29th November, 1189 at Cuenca—Colmenares 158; Loperraez, 173. From 1195 onwards he is found associated with the king in various charters. He died prematurely 14th October, 1211, in Madrid and was buried in the royal abbey of Las Huelgas—Rades y Andrada, 20, col. 1; Schirrmacher, 286.

4. In 1199—Loperraez, 181. On the children of Alfonso VIII, many of whom died in infancy, cf. appendix no. 1, Schirrmacher, 681–689.

5. Doubtless nuns engaged in works of hospitality—Loperraez I, 189 and III, 47–48. The bishops of Segovia and Avila also signed, but after the lay signatures; it would seem certain that they were not present at San Esteban de Górmaz but signed later.

6. Loperraez, I, 189.

7. Loperraez, I, 188.

8. 23rd March at Burgos, 28th April at Palencia—Loperraez I, 188, which seems to indicate that at that time the bishop was following the court.

9. The earlier occasion was 25th May, 1202.

10. 'Accidit itaque tunc temporis Alphonsum, regem Castelle, inter filium suum Ferdinandum et quandam nobilem de Marchiis desiderare connunbium. Quam ob causam adiit prefatum episcopum exomensem, postulans fieri eum huius procuratorem negotii'—Jordan, no. 19. For the chronology of Diego's journeys, cf. study in Mandonnet-Vicaire, I, 83–88. Among the three possible dates—summer 1202, summer 1203, summer 1204, it is impossible to decide categorically. The reasons in favour of the second are: 1. It would seem that the visit Jordan mentions (*adiit*) must be identified with the coming of the king to San Esteban (but the king also went there on 25th May, 1202). 2. The date of 1203 is given by two chronicles published by Reichert (*MOPH*, I, 321) and the information given in *Chronica Ia* might well be the original statement (one ms. of this chronicle, however, says 1202). 3. The political data which are put forward to explain the project of the Danish marriage began with the disinheriting of John Lackland, 28th April, 1202. They were particularly important in 1203. In 1204, it was no longer the time for negotiation, but for action.

11. Cf. the study—*Une ambassade dans les marches*, Mandonnet-Vicaire, I, 89–98.

12. A native of Borgberge, near Dasel, to the east of the Weser H. Chr. Scheeben—*Jordan der Sachse*, Vechta 1937, 4.

13. Gallén, 204. Jarl Gallén in *excursus I* of his work on the Dominican province of Dacia (*Voyages de Saint Dominique au Danemark*) has confirmed, deepened and extended the conclusions of the Mandonnet-Vicaire study—Gallén, 196–216.

14. 'Multorum tamen laborum dispendio', 'laborosum iter rursus aggrediens'—Jordan, no. 16. On the value to be given to these expressions see Mandonnet-Vicaire, I, 97.

15. *Chronica, Ia. MOPH*, I, 321, the author of which might be Gérard de Frachet or even Pedro Ferrando, drawn up between 1263 and 1266. Cf. Mandonnet-Vicaire I, 96–97 and Gallén, 203–208. Berthold Altaner, on his side, after at first hesitating to identify the marches with Denmark (Altaner 141) finally accepted this theory Altaner, *Dominikanermissionen*, 4.

16. Cf. Appendix III.

17. Schirrmacher, 192–193.

18. One daughter only, Richisse, was not yet married; but she belonged to the previous generation— Gallén Genealogical Table I.

19. Gallén, 208 and n. 28.

20. Gallén, 209.

21. Orlamunde is situated on the Saale, on the western frontier of the ancient march of Misnia. The family, however, doubtless lived at the court of Denmark—Gallén, 209, n. 29. Valdemar, moreover, entrusted to Siegfried's son, Albert, who was very loyal to him, the Nordalbingia which he had won by conquest in 1203 from the inheritance of Henry the Lion—Gallén, 208.

22. Hefele—Leclerq, VB, 1091: L. III, tit. XXXIX, ch. 6.

23. There was a charter of confraternity between the chapter of Osma and the abbey of Silos: The subsistence to be given respectively in case of hospitality was determined—food for the men and fodder for the horses. Two animals per canon were envisaged, four for a dignitary of the chapter and for the bishop—Loperraez, III, 203.

24. Ganshof, 124.

25. Jordan, nos. 14 and 22, where the books for liturgical prayer are mentioned.

26. Jordan, no. 14.

27. Vieillard, plate VII; Ganshof, 152–153.

28. Maisonneuve, 78–82. Cf. *infra*, p. 73.

29. Cf. *infra*, ch. V, pp. 75ff.

30. The bibliography of Catharism is considerable and of unequal value. It has been completely brought up to date in the last fifteen years since the publications of A. Dondaine and of Hilarin of Milan. There is scarcely anything to be gleaned from the works of the Neo-catharists, such as Déodat Roché, which reconstitute an artificial Catharism in which gnostic apocrypha, neo-platonism and the theosophy of Rudolf Steitner have a larger share than authentic sources. In the following chapters Runciman and Soederberg will be used as general studies and above all Borst and the somewhat briefer study of Foreville, 330–343. For Languedoc, Dossat's latest findings have enabled us to correct Guiraud, *Cartulaire* and *Inquisition*, rich but sometimes erroneous.

31. Foreville, 332, 336; Borst, 90; Ch. Thouzellier, *Hérésie et croisade au XIIe s.*, in *RHE* XLIX, 1954, 855–872.

32. Outline statistics in Borst, 205, n. 11 and 208, n. 20. In 1250 the entire Catharist movement numbered some 4,000 Perfect, which possibly represents some hundreds of thousands of followers. The latter probably never reached the half-million. For the south of France, Dossat, *Cathares*, II, 79–80, considers that even in the localities where the heresy was most active, it never spread to the majority of the population. Moreover these Catharist 'believers' and 'listeners' ['auditeurs'] were very superficially attached to the sect.

33. Borst, 96, 121, 231–235.

34. Unlike the Catholics, they authorized loans with interest Dossat, *Cathares* II, 73 and Borst, 188.

35. Dondaine, *Actes*.

36. Jordan, no. 15.

37. Cernai, no. 53. This was the Cistercian bishop Guy de Carcassonne.

38. On hatred for the sign of the cross, because it recalls the victory of Satan over Christ, see Guiraud, *Inquisition*, 163–164, 362–363; Borst 219 and n. 24.

39. This was perhaps one of those deacons who kept Catharist houses of hospitality in the town—Borst, 211.

40. 'Fortiter et ferventer agens'—Jordan, no. 15. He spent only one night 'ipsa nocte qua . . . hospitati sunt', *ibid*.

41. S. Pertement, *Le dualisme dans l'histoire de la philosophie et des religions* (*La montagne Sainte-Geneviève*, no. 5), Paris 1946.

42. Cf. *infra*, ch. V, p. 75 and n. 98.

43. From the name of the priest who inspired it. Articles by Bardy, in *DHGE* and Vernet in *DTC*; Runciman 63–93; Borst, 66–71.

44. Article by Janin in DTC; Runciman, 46–62; gnostic background *ibid.*, 5–25.

45. Borst, 175–177, based on numerous texts. He shows, however, that as a result of the influence of the Catholic milieu the Catharists progressively reintroduced the notions of personal sin, penance, repentance. For the Albigensian Catharists in the time of Dominic, see Cernai no. 12, p. 13 and n. 5; Dossat, *Cathares* II, 71–72.

46. For Catharist docetism see Borst, 164, n. 6; for the Midi, Cernai, no. 11, p. 11 and no. 3; Dossat, *Cathares*, II, 71.

47. A Bogomil assertion, taken up again by the Catharists—Borst 165 and 219, n. 24; for the Midi, Cernai, no. 53, p. 47 and n. 3.

48. Jordan no. 15.

49. Jordan, no. 16 distinguishes two events: the reception of the embassy by the authorities (the king and his counsellors) and the (girl's) consent: 'exposita causa sui itineris, habitoque consensu' and, in the following phrase: 'consensus puelle'.

50. The word *consensus* in this connection signified at the beginning of the thirteenth century the marriage properly so-called according to the axiom, from then onwards commonly accepted, of Peter Lombard (Sentent. L. IV, dist. XXVII, ch. 2) 'consensus facit nuptias' independently of the consummation, *copulatio*. The proof that Jordan gives this meaning to 'consensus puelle' is in the following phrase: the bishop is to bring back the girl so that the marriage may be consummated 'copulandam'. Cf. G. Le Bras, article 'Marriage', *DTC*, IX, *ca.* 2151–2154 and 2159–2162.

51. The consent which makes the marriage, according to Peter Lombard's teaching, can be given independently of any form or usual ceremony; it can even be clandestine. It is effected as soon as there

are *verba de praesenti* (words constituting a consent to marriage) in contradistinction to *verba de futuro* (words constituting a promise of future marriage) which do not make a marriage even if they are accompanied with an oath. *Ibid.*, 2152–2153.

52. The case of the entry into religion of one of the parties between the exchange of consent by *verba de praesenti* and the *copulatio*. In this case the union is dissolved, which is not possible in a marriage properly so-called—*DTC*, IX, 2158–2159. At the end of the twelfth century Urban III still allowed the exception of the case in which one of the two parties should in the meantime become a leper. (Cf. *infra*, n. 69). At the beginning of the thirteenth century, however, Innocent III allowed only the entry into religion. *Ibid.*, 2159–2161.

53. On marriage by proxy see *Decretal.*, Lib. III, tit. XXXII, ch. 14; *DTC*, IX, 2161. Diego had been appointed procurator for the matter. Jordan, no. 14.

54. Jordan, no. 16.

55. The bishop's company would reach Montpellier in 1206 after a long return journey and, doubtless, a fairly prolonged stay in Cîteaux, Rome and Denmark. The departure should probably be assigned to 1205, most likely in summer. Cf. Mandonnet-Vicaire, I, 85–88.

56. Ganshof, 125.

57. Mentioned by Jordan, no. 17.

58. Jordan, no. 16.

59. Gallén, 213–216. Cf. *supra*, n. 20.

60. This is clear from a letter published by Loeber, *De Burggraviis Orlamundanis Commentatio*, Jenae 1741, 72; Von Reitzenstein, *Regesten der Grafen von Orlamunde*, Bayreuth, 1871, 67 ff. At the same time the letter mentions Siegfried of Orlamund who died in 1206, and his son Albert, under the title of Count of Holstein which he received in 1204; this dates the letter. The abbey of Heusdorf is situated near Apolda, not far from Orlamund. Cf. Gallén, 214 and n. 34.

61. Letter of Innocent III of 12th January, 1206, Potthast, no. 2651; *PL*, 215, 773–774; inserted in *Decretal* Lib. IV, tit. XXXII, ch. 14, where it is erroneously addressed to the Archbishop of Lyons (certain mss. however have corrected to Lund).

62. The Pope calls her *mulier*; Jordan referred to her as *puella*. Gallén, 214, hesitates. He thinks that Jordan was mistaken. It is not necessary to take this view—it is sufficient to note that the Pope is using the correct word, since the events he is speaking of took place after the girl's marriage. That she was of high rank is clear from the presence of two abbots at her taking the veil.

63. *Mediantibus internunciis.*

64. *Quidam nobilis.* He is not under the jurisdiction of the bishop and treats with his wife only through envoys, which presupposes that he lives at some distance.

65. *Misit ad eam, ut desponsationem factam carnalis copula sequeretur.* The two terms which mark the two stages—*consensus, copula*, as in Jordan of Saxony—should be noticed.

66. *Diocesana tua.* In actual fact neither Orlamund nor Heusdorf are in the archdiocese of Lund; they belong to the archbishopric of Mayence. Living at the court of Denmark, however, the niece of Valdemar belonged to the diocese of Lund.

67. The Pope replied on 12th January, 1206. The report must have been sent at latest at the beginning of December 1205.

68. The statement, the investigation, the summons and the appearance of the nun-bride before the Archbishop of Lund, in view of the remoteness of Heusdorf, if it was really Siegfried's daughter who was in question, must have occupied the first months of autumn.

69. A well-known decretal of Urban III (d. 1187) restored their liberty to a married couple when one of them became a leper before the consummation of the marriage—*Decretal.* Lib. IV, tit. VIII, ch. 3. Cf. *supra*, n. 52.

70. Innocent III still accepted this traditional exception, but unwillingly. He was to declare in his reply: *nos autem nolentes a praedecessorum nostrorum vestigiis in hoc articulo subito declinare . . . PL*, 215, 774A.

71. On the brutalities of Philip Augustus towards Ingeburg, see Hefele-Leclercq, V, 2, 1167–1168; 1226–1229; 1305–1308. As to the sentiments of Valdemar II who, after his brother Cnut VI had done everything possible to defend his sister against Philip Augustus, expressed them once more in a letter to the Pope in the autumn of 1205—speaking of the adversaries who threatened him, he said—'qualiter inter nos et regem Franciae res se habeat, vestrae magnificentiae non convenit revelari', *PL*, 215, 770D.

72. The only letter which has come down to us from all this packet of dispatches, a letter from the king to the Pope, speaks of a *nuntius* (*PL*, 215, 769C) and ends with these words 'Caetera nunciis nostris committimus enarranda', 771A.

73. Although the requests are no longer extant, Innocent III's replies were: 1. Request for liberation and transfer to Rome of the Bishop of Schleswig imprisoned by Valdemar. 2. Extraordinary powers granted to the archbishop for the visitation of his diocese. 3. Solution of the matrimonial case. 4. Support given to certain constitutions of the archbishop which the Pope, however, is careful not to confirm. 5. Power granted to the archbishop to appoint a bishop for the pagan lands which he proposes to conquer and evangelize. 6. Promise of confirmation, after a trial period of four years, of constitutions drawn up in a general chapter which the archbishop had decided to convene of the isolated houses of black monks. For these six letters see *PL*, 215, 771–776.

74. 'Remisso ad regem nuntio', Jordan, no. 17.

75. 'Ipsum cum clericis suis, nacta opportunitate, adire curiam festinavit', *ibid.*

76. He doubtless avoided crossing the Alps in mid-winter and stayed some time making his devotions in Rome. In any case he only crossed over to Provence to return to Spain in May or June 1206, cf. *infra*, ch. VI, beginning.

77. He asked him for the 'gratiam cessionis' and revealed to him 'sui cordis esse propositum conversioni Comanorum pro viribus operam adhibere', Jordan, no. 17. The intention to evangelize is sufficient to explain the desire for resignation (cf. note following). Jordan also insists on seeing in this the bishop's feeling of inferiority in the face of his episcopal responsibilities; this would scarcely be typical of Diego! For the Cumans, cf. *infra*.

78. Among others, from Cernai, 20: 'Anno Verbi incarnati MCCVI, Oxomensis episcopus . . . ad curiam romanam accessit, summo desiderio desiderans episcopatum suum resignare, quo posset liberius ad paganos causa praedicandi Christi evangelium se transferre.' According to the text, this occurred after 25th March, 1206. However, as happens with chroniclers, this date refers to the principal event which the text relates, that is to say to the Montpellier meeting. The visit to Rome, which is the preamble to that, could have been just before 25th March.

79. Jordan, no. 17 in two places. Cf. Scheeben's introduction, *ibid.*, 15–16.

80. Such corrections point to uncertainty. The mention of the Saracens is in conformity with probability since the Castilians are in question, that of the Cumans is no less so. Between 1219 and 1221 Dominic had hoped himself to evangelize these pagans of the east of Hungary, to whom he then sent some of his sons—*Proces. Bon.*, no. 43. Earlier, however, even in 1217, it was of the Prussians and other pagans of the north that he was thinking. He quickly sent his first missionaries to them. Cf. Mandonnet-Vicaire, I, 149–150; Gallén 3–9, 212 and n. 32.

81. Cf. *supra*, n. 78.

82. 'In P[ru]cia et aliis terris septentrionis', are the words of one of the mss. of the *Proces. Bon.* no. 12. The abbreviation *Pcia* poses a minor problem of palaeography. The most competent specialists, however, are categorical that Prussia is meant—Eubel, I, 370, n. 1; Altaner, *Dominikanermissionen*, 4; Von Walter-Wittenheim, *Die Dominikaner in Livland im Mittelalter* . . . Rome 1938, 5; Gallén, 202, n. 16, against Walz, *Proces. Bon.*, 134, n. 1 who would read Bruscia, the territory of the Don, which does not moreover correspond to the second part of the phrase.

83. For what follows, Hauck IV, 579–685; Gallén 209–216; Foreville, 265–269; 278–279; Fliche, 86–88.

84. *LTK*, sub. h.v.; Gallén, 210–211.

85. *LTK*, sub. h.v.

86. Kept informed of what was being done, Innocent III in the course of the autumn of 1205, thus characterized the expedition—'cum, de Christiani nominis injuria vindicanda juste ac pie cogitans, ex religioso mentis proposito contra paganos decreveris proficisci . . .'—letter to the Archbishop of Lund, Andrew Sunesen, 13th January, 1206—*PL*, 215, 775A. The Pope granted the archbishop power to establish a bishop in one of the cities he might have been able to christianize, after having cleansed it by expelling the pagans.

87. On the general character of the *Drang nach Osten*—Altaner, *Dominikanermissionen*, 186–188; Jordan, 121–123. Cf. previous note for the events of 1206.

88. On 10th October, 1204, the Bishop of Riga had obtained from Innocent III permission to make use for his mission, commuting their vows, of the priests and clergy of the neighbouring lands who had enlisted as crusaders for Jerusalem—*PL*, 215, 429 BC.

89. Cf. Honorius III's remarks on 25th January, 1217 (Potthast, no. 5432), Horoy II, 208–209.

90. On the brutality of the *Drang nach Osten* and the ferocity of the Slav reactions, cf. Jordan, 122 and n. 3, 124, 127, 129–132. As to St Dominic's desire for martyrdom and the detailed description he gave of it in similar terms to those recalled by Jordan, 122, cf. Jordan, no. 34 (length of the torture, limbs hacked one by one); *Proces. Bon.*, no. 29, but cf. *infra*, 156, n. [181].

91. Cf. *supra*, n. 73 and 86.

92. Rodríguez Jiménez de Rada, *Chronicon de rebus Hispaniae*, L. VI, ch. 27 (*Hispania illustrata*, II), Frankfurt 1603, 107–108. Defourneaux, no. 35. Bernard, like Diego, had gone to find the Pope who sent him back to his diocese.

93. 'Nex saltem ei, quamvis petenti, voluit indulgere, *vel in remissionem peccatorum iniungere*, ut manens episcopus, fines *Comanorum* ad praedicandum intraret. Jordan, no. 17. The insertion *in remissionem* etc., which must be of importance since the 2nd edition of the *Libellus* adds it, signifies an indulgence granted by Innocent III to all those who favoured the crusade and the apostolic mission, *PL*, 215, 1025B, 1470D, 1545B, 1545D, etc. Honorius III granted it in 1217 to the apostolic labours of all the Preachers—Laurent, no. 77.

94. The information this time comes from Cernai, 20: 'immo precepit ei ut ad sedem propriam remearet'. Expressed in these terms it almost looks like a reproach, which accords neither with the circumstances nor with the writer's intention. It must be understood in the sense that the Pope imposed his diocese on the bishop anew as a special mission. This does not mean that he forbade him to occupy himself on occasion with some other secondary apostolate. Thus the apparent contradiction between this order of the Pope and Diego's later conduct which formerly preoccupied us is lifted—Mandonnet-Vicaire, I, 148–149. As to the hypothesis of a previous understanding between Pope and bishop on the subject of the preaching in the Narbonensis which we had maintained *Ibid.* 141–156, after Mandonnet and which H. C. Scheeben severely criticized (*Dominikaner oder Innocenzianer*, AFP, IX (1939) 245), it is not impossible but remains hypothetical.

95. *PL*, 215, 774B. In precise terms: 1. If she wills to remain in her convent the marriage is dissolved, even against the will of the bridegroom; 2. although she appears to have taken the habit, by receiving the veil, she can return home there to preserve chastity within the marriage, which must be concluded; 3. if she has pronounced the vow of regular life, she must be constrained to enter religion.

96. Scheeben, 25, n. 15 and 16, displaces without any reason the journey which Jordan mentions in

no. 18. Such journey of prelates to Cîteaux, as formerly to Cluny, are frequent, cf. *infra*, n. 99, 100, 112 and Sakur, II, 101–113.

97. Cf. *supra*, ch. 1, n. 17.

98. Cf. *infra*, ch. V, 76 and 78; ch. VI, 80 and 82 and n. 5–6. On the rôle of the Cistercians in the apostolic work of Christendom, especially in the missions patronized by the Pope, cf. Ladner, in Mandonnet-Vicaire, II, 40–42.

99. Letters of the 29th January and 31st May, 1204, Potthast, 2103 and 2226. The journey to Cîteaux of Fulk of Neuilly to find preachers for the crusade there will be recalled—Mandonnet-Vicaire, II, 40 and n. 140; cf. I, 154.

100. Cernai, no. 71.

101. Cf. *infra*, ch. VI, 91 and n. 79 to 81.

102. To become a Cistercian in fact he would have to have resigned first (cf. *infra* n. 104 and 112). But the Pope had not allowed him to do this.

103. Jordan, no. 18.

104. In 1310 the bishop of Morocco, Peter, finding that all his priests were of the Order of Preachers, obtained from the Pope authorization to enter their Order. The vicar of the Friars Preachers received from the Pope power to accept the bishop's resignation. The latter made profession in the order and the vicar then gave him back his diocese in the Pope's name. *AFPX* (1940), 90.

105. Cf. *infra*, ch. VI, n. 17.

106. A Canon Regular of Maguelonne, he had tenaciously defended in Rome for three years (1196–1199) the office of archdeacon which the dean of the chapter wished to assign to someone else— Villemagne, 1 to 29.

107. On 26th January, 1205, Innocent III, reviving the courage of Peter of Castelnau, spoke of the 'otium contemplationis quod elegeras', Potthast, 2391—*PL*, 215, 525B.

108. The following, taken at random from one's reading, are a few examples of attachment and unity of spirit in regard to a religious order, which, without being identical with the symbolic reception of the habit, are analogous to it. The Cistercian Cardinal Conrad de Porto was received about 1220 in the priory of the Preachers of Bologna; he was enthusiastic for the life of the brethren and declared: 'Ego quidem, etsi alterius professionis habitum exterius preferam, vestrum tamen interius mentem gero. Nec dubuim vobis sit quin totus sim vester; vestrique ordinis sum; vobis me tota dilectione committo'— Ferrando, no. 43. At the same time Bishop William of Modena, the future Cardinal of Sabina, apostolic legate and great propagator in the Nordic countries: 'mores sancti Dominici explorans, se in fratrem ordinis ab eo petiit recipi. Cui sanctus annuens eidem tanquam patri ordinis negocia recommisit; quod idem episcopus ferventer observavit usque in hodiernum diem'—Barthélemy, no. 17. Cf. *infra*, n. 112.

109. Cf. *infra*, ch. VI, 91 and n. 79.

110. Jordan, nos. 18 and 20.

111. On the development of the order in Castile and the rôle of Alfonso VIII see Defourneaux, 50–58. In 1188 the king had obtained that the Abbess of Las Huelgas should play the same part in regard to the abbeys of Cistercian nuns of León and Castile as the Abbot of Cîteaux in regard to the order. This was already the point of departure of the particularist tendencies which were later to develop in Spain to a considerable extent.

112. The journey of St Malachy to Clairvaux under Innocent III, presented curious analogies with that of Diego to Cîteaux: visit to the monastery in the course of a journey to the Curia, enthusiasm for what he had seen of monastic life, an offer of resignation to the Pope, its refusal, monks brought back with him on his return to his see—St Bernard, *Vita Malachiae, PL*, 182, 1094–1095.

113. It will be noted that Diego's successor in Osma, Rodrígo Jiménez de Rada (1208–1210) was a former Cistercian. Did Diego effectively give his chapter a Cistercian orientation?

114. Jordan, no. 16.

NOTES TO CHAPTER V

1. Roger de Hoveden, *Chronicle*, ed. Stubbs, II, London, 1869, 167 and 178–180, sees in this danger one of the major causes of the Council of the Lateran in 1179. The whole of Canon 27 is taken up with it. In the Fourth Council of the Lateran in 1215, it occupies canon 3 and is the subject of a special decision. Mansi, XXII 210, 232, 986–990, 1069–1070.

2. See ecclesiastical and economic description by A. Molinier, *Sur la géographie de la province de Languedoc au moyen âge*, in Vaissète, XII, 130–135; also, ecclesiastical description of the province of Narbonne in Griffe, 363–382. Cf. Dossat, *Cathares*, 391–392; Ch. Higounet, *Le comte de Comminges de ses origines à son annexion à la couronne*, Toulouse 1949.

3. The seat of this bishopric which was in the first place at Maguelonne, was in the twelfth century at Substantion; since the fourteenth century it has been at Montpellier.

4. Vaissète, VI, 217–484; Luchaire; Guiraud, *Inquisition*, 375–419; Maisonneuve, 78–100, 136–154 and 158–202. Considerable use has here been made of Guiraud. Although his numerous facts are presented carelessly and in disorder (wrong dates, wrong references), they are irreplacable and valuable because they are directly taken from the archives of the Inquisition in Carcassonne and Toulouse (Doat documents).

5. From the opening of the *Sententia de terra albigensi* of the Fourth Council of the Lateran—Mansi, XXII, 1069D. The juxtaposition of the two terms is a commonplace in the documents relating to Provence and the Albigeois—cf. for instance, Puylaurens, ch. VI, VII, XVI.

6. Hefele-Leclerq, V, 1106–1107; Maisonneuve, 94–95.

7. On the expression *negotium fidei et pacis* and the two words *pax et fides*, see Cernai, nos. 57, 59, 61, 62, 67, 72, 74, etc. (the first four references relate to a letter of Innocent III), 138 (the legate Milon), 543–545 (Council of Montpellier), 571, 588, 594, 596 (in regard to Raymond VI, Raymond-Roger de Foix, Raymond VII), etc.; Puylaurens, ch. VII and XVII; *Proces. Thol.*, nos. 3, 7, 13, 18 (in regard to Dominic). General indications in Cernai, no. 27, n. 1 and III, XXXI, n. 14. As to the underlying reason for this connection from the point of view of the Church, cf. Council of Béziers, 1246; 'cum tempore pacis fides liberius valeat praedicari et inquisitio contra haereticos fieri et sacramenta ecclesiastica ministrari'—Mansi, XXIII, 695.

8. It was at Charroux (prov. of Bordeaux) in 989 and at Narbonne in 990 that the first effort of the bishops to impose peace on the feudal lords was made manifest; in 1031 Bourges inaugurated the system of diocesan militia; in 1054 it fixed and codified the system of the peace and truce of God; in 1095 it was spread from Clermont under the authority of the Pope. A. Luchaire, 'Les premiers capétiens' in *Histoire de France* by E. Lavisse, 2, pt. 2, Paris 1901, 133–138. More recently the peace had again been sworn at Béziers, in 1166; Rodez 1170, Albi, 1191, Montpellier, 1195 (cf. *infra*, n. 19). The high peak of this effort for peace which was continually growing was the series of oaths which the legate Milon made the Count of Toulouse, his Provençal barons, the city consuls, and finally, through the intermediary of the clergy, all the faithful whether nobles or commoners of the territory, take at Saint-Gilles in June 1209—namely, not to use mercenaries, to respect every peace and truce, to protect or restore the property of the Church, to do justice to all and not to levy new taxes, to turn the Jews aside from public offices, to punish heretics denounced by the clergy—*PL*, 216, 89–98. On 6th September following, the Council of Avignon again took up one by one all the elements of the *negotium fidei et pacis* beginning by preaching—Mansi, XXII, 783–794.

9. The question of unjust dues which the Church ordered to be withdrawn, played the principal part in the inevitable excommunication of Raymond VI in 1211—Villemagne, 249; Cernai no. 137 and n. 1, 138, 163, 394, n. 3.

10. Deposition of Arnaud de Crampagna, *Proc. Thol.*, no. 7.

11. 'Ad fidem nullus est cogendus invitus; sed per severitatem, imo et per misericordiam Dei, tribulationem flagellis solet perfidia castigari'—St Augustine, *Contra litteras Petiliani*, L. II, ch. 83, *PL*, 43, 315. 'Heretici propter heresim non sunt occidendi, sed propter characterem christianum quem habent ad caulam Ecclesie reducendi sunt'—Alain de Lille, *Contra hereticos*, L. II, ch. 22, *PL*, 210, 396D.

12. On the 'exposing as a prey' see Pissard, 37–39 and 61 and Morel, 42–50.

13. Cf. supra, n. 6. For the holy war, see Pissard et Villey, 217–226. The princes of the Midi did not protest against the principle of the holy war; they discussed the fact and the extent of their responsibility in the matter of heresy—Pissard, 41.

14. Fliche, *Enquête* and Lagger, *Réforme grégorienne*.

15. Molinier in Vaissète XII, 265–276; Luchaire; Dossat, *Comté*.

16. Cf. *infra*, n. 41.

17. Against the claim made that the troubadours were inspired by the Catharists, cf. Borst 107, n. 37 and particularly D. Zorzi, *Valori religiosi nella letteratura provenzale. La spiritualia trinitaria*, Milan 1954. This literature is no more Catharist than it is anticlerical and the repression of the Catharists by the Church is not responsible for the decadence of this literature—see L. H. Gere, 'The Troubadours, Heresy and the Albigensian Crusade' in *Dissert. Abstracts*, 16 (1956). As to a superiority of civilization of the Midi over the north at this time, its only existence is in the imagination of a few men of letters of today, historians do not recognize it; cf. M. Bloch, *La société féodale*, Paris, 1939, II, 43.

18. Vaissète, VI, 68, 110–111; VII, II, n. 8. The marriage of Raymond VI with the sister of Peter II finally brought peace in 1200. *Ibid.*, 190–191 and 213–214.

19. Peace of Albi 1191, re-affirmed by the Council of Montpellier in 1195—Vaissète 140 and 172; Mansi, XXII, 667–672; Lacger, *Albigeois*, 593–595.

20. Giraud, 'Les routiers au XIIe siècle', in *Biblioth. de l'Ecole des chartes*, III (1841–1842), 125–14 7; Maisonneuve, 89–98; Lacger, *Albigeois*, 587, 588.

21. Mansi, XXII, 231–232 and Hefele-Leclercq, V, 1106.

22. Letter of 29.V.1207, *PL*, 216, 1167B; Potthast, 3114; Villemagne, 243.

23. Cernai, 38, n. 3 and 39 n. 1, with the editor's notes. Both this editor and recent historians have emphasized the accuracy of Cernai's statements, despite that writer's tone of hatred for everything to do with the Catharists or their abettors.

24. Guiraud, *Inquisition*, 301–331; Dossat, *Clergé* 276–278.

25. Vaissète, VI, 172. His predecessor had been made prisoner and ransomed by the people of Capestang in 1195—Mansi XXII, 671.

26. Cernai, no. 99; Guiraud, *Inquisition*, 337.

27. Vaissète, 236; Guiraud, *Inquisition*, 339.

28. Fliche, *Enquête*, 177–179. For the wealth of the abbeys at the beginning of the thirteenth century, see Dossat, *Clergé*, 272–276.

29. R. Aubenas, 'La famille dans l'ancienne Provence', in *Annales d'hist. écon. et sociale*, VIII (1936), 523–541. This is principally concerned with the east of the Rhône, but the situation to the west of it was identical. Cf. A. Luchaire, *Manuel des institutions françaises. Période des Capétiens directs*, Paris 1893, 163–164; Fr Olivier Martin, *Histoire du droit français . . .* Paris, 1948, 111–112. On the co-lordship in the region of Toulouse, see Vaissète, VII, 151–152.

30. Guiraud, *Inquisition*, 325–327.

31. *Ibid.*, 279–299.

32. Cernai, no. 99.

33. *Ibid.*, nos. 99–100; Guiraud, *op. cit.*, 310–314.

34. Raymond-Roger, however, was not himself a Catharist—Tudela, 45, n. 6.

35. Guiraud, *op. cit.* 310–311, which corrects, in accordance with various items of evidence from the archives of the Inquisition, Cernai's affirmation, no. 48; Philippa was a Catharist, not one of the Waldenses.

36. Vaissète, VI, 227–228 and VIII, 1148–1151, where the text of the deposition of Bérenger d'Avelanet before the inquisitors in 1244 will be found.

37. The remark of Pons Adémar de Roudeille, quoted by Puylaurens, ch. VIII—'sumus enim nutriti cum eis (hereticis) et habemus de nostris consanguineis inter ipsos' is completely proved by the accounts collected by Guiraud, *op. cit.*, 261–331.

38. On this saying, see Borst, 74, n. 9.

39. Puylaurens, ch. VI and VII; Guiraud, *op. cit.*, 262–263.

40. See the chapter on the spread of the heresy, Guiraud, *op. cit.* 261–277. This chapter, with its accumulation of details, gives the impression that the feudal class, perhaps even the population generally, was affected by the heresy almost in its entirety. 'Affected', however, merely means that they listened to the discourses of the heretics. That was not tantamount to becoming 'believers', still less 'Perfect'. On the small number of the latter, cf. *infra*, n. 65. The 'believers' more often than not were influenced only very superficially. Dossat (*Cathares*, 79–80) noticing the small number of people made known to the inquisition as 'consoled', after a thorough investigation in the localities most affected, came to the very moderate conclusion—'the Albigenses were sufficiently numerous for the Church to consider that they constituted a danger'.

41. Gervase of Canterbury, *Chronica* ed. Stubbs, I, London 1879, 271.
Vaissète's translation, VI, 78, which is usually quoted, is as Dondaine observes (*Actes* 333), n. 15, considerably defective.

42. Cernai, no. 40.

43. Cernai, no. 39 and n. 1.

44. Cernai, no. 44.

45. Letter of Innocent III, 29.V.1207; Potthast no. 3114; *PL*, 215, 1167C.

46. Guiraud, *op. cit*, 109–110; Borst, 155, n. 18.

47. Especially, as far as respect for the conjugal bond was concerned, in the case of Guillaume VIII of Montpellier—Vaissète VI, 200–201, and in that of Pedro II of Aragon—Villemagne, 127–130, 144–147, 149–165. The Pope's firmness as to the validity of the marriage of Pedro II with Marie de Montpellier was a rude awakening for the king and contributed to his revolt in 1213; the uneasiness of Innocent when he communicated the final decision to the commissioners on 19.I.1213 should be noted—Villemagne, 151. His attitude was the same towards Alfonso IX of León, Philip Augustus etc. and was the obverse of what political opportunism might have counselled.

48. Cernai, no. 13; Puylaurens, ch. IV; Borst, 105–107.

49. *Jurata fornicatio*, Borst 180.

50. Cernai, no. 12 and 52; Borst 214, n. 6; 215, n. 8.

51. Guiraud, *op. cit.*, 333–363; Dossat, *Clergé*. Guiraud's judgement on the decadence of the clergy of the Narbonensis ('a dead Church') is exaggerated, as is his judgement on the success of the Catharists (cf. *supra*, n. 40). In both cases Dossat's opinion is more accurate.

52. Cernai, no. 20 and n. 4 by the editor.

53. The following prelates were involved. In 1198, Fréjus and Carcassone; in 1204–1205, Toulouse, Béziers, Viviers; in 1211–1213, Narbonne, Agde, Béziers, Carcassonne, Elne, Nîmes, Uzès; Auch, Rodez, Valencia. Mandonnet-Vicaire, I, 172, n. 43; Lacger, 628; Maisonneuve, 140–147. On the renewal of 1212, see Cernai, no. 307.

54. Dossat, *Clergé*, 268.

55. Puylaurens, ch. VII.

56. *Ibid.*, ch. VI and VII.

57. Mirot, II, 317–320. As far back as 1216, cf. *infra*, ch. XII and n. 45 and 54, Fulk had advocated this dismemberment in order to fight heresy.

58. Potthast, nos. 2103, 2224, 2226, 2229, 2774, etc.; *PL*, 215, 273, 355, 358, 361, 887, etc.; Villemagne, 54, 74–75, 78–79, 86, 98.

59. Lacger, *Albigeois*.

60. Vaissète, VI, 81; Lacger, 589.

61. Cernai, no. 42, n. 3 by the editor.

62. A year before his assassination he had been the subject of an attempt at deposition on the part of the legates, because under the influence of threats he had refused to act against the Béziers heretics—Potthast, no. 2129; *PL*, 215, 272; Villemagne, 189–191.

63. Lacger, *Albigeois*, 291 and 606 and Dossat, Clergé, 271, who corrects the unjustified generalizations of Luchaire, 21–22 and of Guiraud, *op. cit.*, 346–349. Elements of information in the letter to Bérenger of 28.V.1204, Potthast, no. 2224; *PL*, 215, 357; Villemagne, 82–83; Puylaurens, ch. V.

64. Puylaurens, prologue; Council of Montpellier, canon 4, Mansi, XXII, 941.

65. No figures, even approximate, are available. The Waldenses were small numerically in relation to the perfect. In 1250, Rainier Sacconi who was very well informed, estimated at 4,000 the total number of the latter in the world; 2,500 in Lombardy, 200 in the Albigeois—Borst, 205, n. 11; 208, n. 20. In the former place they had been hunted but not too severely for about twenty years past; in the Albigeois very violently after the terrible purge of the time of the crusade. If note be taken that about 1206, 600 Catharists (doubtless of the 'Perfect') met at Mirepoix; that in 1208 and the following years

60 of the Perfect were burnt at the château of Cassès, 140 at Minerva, 300 at Lavaur, a larger number at Béziers, etc., it will be realized that the number of 2,000 formal Catharists in the Albigeois at the beginning of the thirteenth century is not exaggerated.

66. The houses of the Catharists, at one and the same time places of worship and hospices or communities, were very numerous; sometimes ten or more of them could be counted in a locality—Guiraud, op. cit., 146–152.

67. Borst, 6–8. Their first books were borrowed from the Bogomils about 1190, Ibid., 8. First writings in the thirteenth century, ibid., 11–13. Against a co-called secret teaching see ibid., 8, n. 8 and 204, n. 5.

68. Borst, 205, n. 13 and 242, n. 11.

69. Supra, ch. III, p. 37 to 39 and nn. 50–60.

70. Cf. Mandonnet-Vicaire, II, 183–185. Study and general survey in Grundmann, Eresie 377–389.

71. Ibid., II, 186 and n. 55a (Germany); Meersseman-Adda (Italy). On the popular character of the theological disputes, see the anecdote recorded by Guiraud, op. cit., 267.

72. Mandonnet-Vicaire, II, 183–192.

73. For instance: rural life (Meersseman-Adda); hospitality (C. Dereine, 'Aspects de la vie hospitalière au XIIe siècle' in Bull. du cercle pédagogique, Louvain, 1947–1948, 17–23); eremitical life (A. Ceuneau, L'ermite saint Alleaume et la forêt de la grande Charnie, Rennes, 1948); pious women (A. Mens, Oorsprong en betekenis van de Nederlandse begijnen—begarden beweging. Louvain 1947); lay folk of every kind (M. D. Chenu, Moines, clercs, laics au carrefour de la vie évangélique (XIIe siècle), in RHE, XLIX (1954) 59–89). The variety of the social milieux affected by the movement would itself demonstrate its essentially religious origin. It is consequently impossible to see in it the religious projection of a social phenomenon. This remark is particularly important in regard to the Catharists. Cf. A. Dondaine: 'L'origine de l'hérésie médiévale' in Rivista di Storia della Chiesa in Italia VI (1952) 47–78; Ilarino da Milano, 'Le eresie popolari del sec. XI nell'Europa Occ.', in Studi Gregoriani, II, 43–89.

74. Founded in 1115 by Robert d'A, Cadouin, in Perigord, handed on its spirit to its foundations at Candeil and d'Ardorel which would ultimately become Cistercian.

75. Walter, I and II; Grundman, Bewegungen 38–49; Mandonnet-Vicaire-Ladner, II 33–40; Spaetling, 43–48; Mens, 16–22; R. Niderst, Robert d'Arbrissel et les origines de Fontevrault, P. 1952.

76. Canon 15 of Nicea; inscribed in the Decree, Causa VII, q. 1, c. 19. It was especially re-asserted at the time of the Gregorian reform.

77. Mandonnet-Vicaire, II, 187 and n. 58.

78. Ibid., 185 and n. 54. On the very rich meaning of the expression pauperes Christi which the Catharists also used, see Mens, 17 and 254; Dereine, RHE, XLIV (1949) 634; Borst, 91 and n. 6, Alverner, E. On the presence of women see Spaetling, 85 and n. 9.

79. Rom. X, 15.

80. Grundmann, Bewegungen 41–42; Mandonnet-Vicaire-Ladner, II, 33–40.

81. Manselli, 25–43; Borst 83 and n. 7–10. Its success is proved by the refutation, which caused it to be made known, of the Abbot of Cluny himself, Peter the Venerable, PL 189, 719–850.

82. The date of his death varied, according to historians, between 1124 and 1143. Manselli, 28, assigns it to 1132–1133.

83. Walter II, 130–140; Manselli, 45–67; R. de la Ruelle, art. Henri (l'hérétique) in Catholicisme, vol. V, Paris, 1958, 622 ff.

84. Puylaurens, ch. 1.

85. Mens, 38–40; Dondaine, Valdès, 191–235; G. Gonnet, 'Waldensia' in Revue d'hist. et de philosophie religieuse, XXXIII (1953) 202–252; Grundmann, Eresie 371 ff.; Manselli, 69–87.

86. W. Map, De nugis curialium ed. Th. Wright, London, 1850, 64. On the formula Nudus nudum Christum sequi, cf. Bull. de théol. anc. et méd. vol. VII, no. 977.

87. Dondaine, op. cit. 216–218.

88. Ibid., 232 (profession of faith). Cf. Gonnet, n. 45, 47, 48, 61, 88.

89. Puylaurens, prologue; Guiraud, op. cit., 259–260, 264–266, 270, 348; Liber antihaeresis, ed. Dondaine, Valdès 235; Grundmann, Eresie, 371 and n. 2; they were also to be found at Laurac, Avignonet, Carcassonne, Puylaurens, Pamiers-Puylaurens, ch. VIII; Lacger, Albigeois, 631.

90. At the beginning of the thirteenth century in the Narbonensis, they scarcely made profession of as many as four errors, according to Pierre des Vaux-de-Cernai: the wearing of open sandals after the manner of the apostles, the absolute prohibition of oaths and of the death penalty, the view that an imitator of the apostles, even if a lay-man, could consecrate the Eucharist—Cernai, no. 18.

91. Alain, 383.

92. Liber antihaeresis, ed. Dondaine, Valdès, 235.

93. Dondaine, Valdès, 224.

94. Alain, 385 and Cernai, no. 18.

95. Formal texts collected by Grundmann, 18 to 22 (the text of Raoul Ardent, 16, n. 4 antedated by a century should be added); Spaetling, 48–96; Mens, 23–26; Borst, 91 to 95.

96. Borst 102, n. 14.

97. Borst 66–71.

98. Everwin de Steinfeld, 679 D; Borst 91, n. 9.

99. In default of direct documents, several writers have put forward analogies to try to prove continuity. The dualist analogies with Manicheans, Messalians, Paulicians, presuppose nothing beyond the analogy of the fundamental opinion: radical opposition between the world and good. The analogies in worship and hierarchy with the primitive Church come up against the fact that the Bogomils in the

beginning had a rudimentary worship and no hierarchy. The archaic character of Catharist practices may come directly from the New Testament; it may equally come from the Eastern monastic practices on which Bogomilism gradually drew. Cf. discussions and conclusions of Borst, 68, n. 12–13.

100. Dondaine, *Origines*, has demonstrated the impossibility of denying the Bogomil origin of the apostolic character of the Catharist religion, especially in regard to the *consolamentum*, ibid., 64–74. With Guiraud, Runciman, Morghen, he believes in the ancient origin of the rite. Borst, 193–194 and n. 11, thinks that the texts of the New Testament (Acts, VIII, 17) were sufficient to inspire it; let us add—in the liturgical and monastic atmosphere of the Balkans in the eleventh century. Cf. preceding note.

101. Cf. the significant exposition of Borst, 27–58, on the modern interpretations of Catharist history.

102. Lacger, 293–294.

103. Mandonnet-Vicaire, II, 167–187.

104. Dereine, 379, 381.

105. Fliche, *Montpellier*, 221.

106. Cf. *supra*, n. 74.

107. Alain. Two other polemical expositions of value, likewise from the end of the twelfth century, are the work of southerners: Bernard, a Premonstratensian of Foncaude (near Montpellier), 'Foncaude et Ermengaud de Saint-Gilles', *Opusculum contra catharos*, PL, 204, 1235–1272. The part relating to the Waldenses, which was lost, has been rediscovered by Dondaine and edited by Gonnet, Waldensia' in *Rev. d'hist. et de philos. religieuses*, XXXIII (1953), 249–254). This Ermengaud was perhaps a Waldensian converted in 1208, at the same time as Durando de Huesca, Borst, 9. Cf. J. de Ghellinck, *L'essor de la littérature latine au XIIe siècle* I, Louvain, 1946, 160 and 168–171 and L. Veeres, in *Anal praem.*, 31 (1955), 5–35.

108. Borst, 13, 19, 21.

109. Lacger, *Albigeois* 630–632. Fliche, Montpellier.

110. Vaissète, VI, 216 and 221.

111. Canon 27, Hefele-Leclercq, V, 1106–1107; Maisonneuve, 94–95.

112. Mansi, XXII, 476–478; Maisonneuve, 108–114.

113. Potthast, no. 643; *PL*, 214, 537; Maisonneuve, 114–117 and 10–17. Note also this phrase in the confirmation of the deposition of the Bishop Guillaume de Béziers (18.II.1205): 'crimen hereseos, per quod blasphematur divina majestas'—Potthast, no. 2129; *PL*, 215, 272; Villemagne, 190.

114. On 21.IV.1198. He set out in detail the powers of the legates in his letters of 12.VIII.1199—Potthast, 95, 785 and 786, *PL*, 214, 82 and 675–677.

115. Geoffroi d'Auxerre, 412C.

116. See his letter of 12.IV.1199 to the legate Rainier. He exhorts him 'ut in Lia, Rachelis sterilitatem tua predicatione foecundes, dum quod in solitudine et claustri silentio didicisti, juxta mandatum evangelicum predicaveris super tecta, et talenta tibi credita erogaveris ad usuras'. He then gives him, in the name of him who sent his apostles to preach, the mission to preach and full powers: 1. to correct clerics and monks; 2. to judge and absolve violators of clerical immunity; 3. to confute heretics and bring them back to unity.

NOTES TO CHAPTER VI

1. Cernai, no. 20, placed the Montpellier meeting in 1206, i.e. after 25th March (style of the Incarnation). It can be dated more exactly. Arnaud left the meeting to make the preparations for the General Chapter at Cîteaux, which was to be held on 13th September. His departure was certainly before the Assumption. Moreover the discouragement of the legates, which brought about the Montpellier meeting, does seem to have been occasioned by Innocent III's letters of 9th and 11th May, relating to Bérenger de Narbonne (cf. *infra*, n. 9). Now it is necessary to allow a month for letters to travel from Rome to Montpellier. The meeting must therefore be placed after 11th June and before 15th August, certainly quite close to the former date—cf. Vicaire, 1207, 338, n. 21 (p. 345, May–August should be read).

2. Fliche, *Montpellier*.

3. Cernai, no. 20; Jordan, no. 20. The error in an edition by Cernai has led certain scholars to situate this meeting outside Montpellier contrary to the manuscripts; some even asserted, at Castelnau—whence the erroneous commemorative plaque that can be seen in the church of Castelnau on the outskirts of the town.

4. The sequel to this episode is based on the text of Cernai, nos. 20 to 26, all the details of which are valid. Though not an eye-witness, the writer knew several of those who took some part in the scene and had in his hands, when writing this part of his story, in 1213, the detailed archives of the mission—Cernai III, x to xxi. Jordan, nos. 20–21, whose account is parallel, shows serious inaccuracies. On the relations of the two sources and their value see Mandonnet-Vicaire, I, 141–150; Vicaire, 1207, 335–338.

5. The Bull of Institution for Peter and Raoul is lost. It must have been issued in October or November 1203. On 13th December the two legates had already treated with Bérenger at Narbonne and gone to Toulouse, where they proceeded with perhaps rather lengthy negotiations—Cernai, no. 6; Vaissète, VI, 229–230; Villemagne, 42–44. The Bull of Institution for Arnaud was dated 31st May, 1204, Potthast 2229; *PL*, 215, 358–360; Villemagne, 52–57.

6. There are still extant thirty or more letters of Innocent III on the subject of this legation for the period 1204–1207 alone. Cf. in particular the letters of 31st May and 7th December, 1204—Potthast, 2229 and 2337; *PL*, 215, 358–360 and 472–474; Villemagne, 52–57 and 60–63.

7. The legates were commissioned to make investigations about Bérenger as early as 1200. Further investigations in 1203, 1204, 1205, 1206, 1207, 1210 would have led up after many hesitations to his final deposition in 1211 or 1212 if death had not forestalled this measure—Villemagne, 73–106; Maisonneuve, 144–146. Bérenger, quite apart from his skill in legal procedure, enjoyed exalted protection—he was the natural uncle of King Pedro II of Aragon.

8. Potthast, 2224; PL, 215, 355–357; Villemagne, 78–84.

9. Potthast, 2774; PL, 215, 883–885; Villemagne, 96–99.

10. For a list of the complaints of the Church against the archbishop, especially as to the nomination and reform of the clergy, see the Pope's letters of November 1200 and 28th May, 1204—Potthast, 1177 and 2224; PL, 214, 903–906 and 215, 355–357.

11. Jordan, no. 20. A little more than a century earlier, Bernard of Toledo, returning from Rome where he had received the pallium, came across a council assembled at Toulouse. He was invited to participate—Defourneaux, 35.

12. Cf. ASS, March, I, 409 ff; E. Cauvet, Études sur Fontfroide, Paris 1875, 429–468; Villemagne.

13. Villemagne, 29–40.

14. The cathedral chapter of Maguelonne were of the Order of St Rufus. Peter had been canon there since 1182; he was elected archdeacon of the diocese in 1197—Villemagne, 3–4.

15. Letters of 6th August, 1202, 7th December, 1204, 11th May, 1206—Potthast, 1716, 2337, 2778. PL, 214, 1053B; Luchaire, Registres, 50; PL, 217, 159C. The title at this period signified that Peter had taught, doubtless in the capitular school—Lesne, 461–462. It was in canon law that he must have been master. Cernai, no. 57; 'in lege peritus'.

16. For a study of this long quarrel, terminated by Innocent III on 27th January, 1199, see Villemagne, 1–29.

17. On 6th August, 1202 Innocent III still gave Peter the title of archdeacon. He thus did not enter Fontfroide earlier than the end of 1202 or beginning of 1203. On 26th January, 1206, Innocent spoke to Peter of his vocation in these terms: 'cum igitur, exigente necessitate, te a contemplationis otio, quod elegeras, ad tempus duximus evocandum, ut in ministerium, missus, pro nobis, imo pro Christo, legatione fungaris . . .'—Potthast, 2391, PL, 215, 525C; Villemagne, 65.

18. This is also the interpretation of Vaissète, VI, 225 and Guiraud, op. cit. 376.

19. Cernai, no. 55 and n. 1. Villemagne, 302–304, puzzled by the comparatively long time elapsing between this death and the Pope's first reaction (10th March), adopted a date which is not based on any known source. It is not fair to say that Peter de Castelnau had no diplomatic talent (thus Scheeben, 29).

20. Cernai, nos. 24 and 58.

21. This title was given him by the Pope on 16th June, 1205—Potthast, 2540; PL, 215, 667A. It is specially stressed by Puylaurens, ch. VII and IX—'Magister Radulfus, persona litterata multum et honesta' and by the document of the Toulouse agreement 13th December, 1203—Catel, 236 and Villemagne, 42.

22. Cf. preceding note.

23. Cf. supra, n. 15 and 21.

24. Cernai, no. 50 and n. 3; Vicaire, 1207, 345 and n. 58.

25. Cf. Daunou, in Hist. litt. de la France, XVII (1832), 306–334. The article by A. Sabarthés in DHGE is more than sketchy. Cf. also Cernai, III, xiv—xv.

26. Cernai, no. 154.

27. Defourneaux, 182–193. The great majority of the Ultramontanes had gone back before the battle. Arnaud, however, with all his vigour, played an important personal rôle in it with a hundred knights—Puylaurens, ch. XIX.

28. Potthast, 2229; PL, 215, 358–360; Villemagne, 52–57; Maisonneuve, 175, 179–191.

29. See Molinier's note in Vaissète, VI, 289, n. 7 in regard to the expression: 'Kill them all, God will recognize his own.' The saying is completely unauthenticated. It is true, however, that Arnaud, like the French barons, wanted measures of bloodshed to terrorize the region—cf. Tudela, laisse 18, lines 25–30 and laisse 21, 1–8; Borst, 118, n. 32.

30. This was the general opinion—Luchaire, 46–61, 258–259; Borst, 119 and n. 34.

31. Maisonneuve, 114–117 and 154–166.

32. Innocent had borrowed from the canonists of the twelfth century the idea that Christendom should temper the prosecution which punishes the crime committed, by mercy which moderates or even suppresses the penalty as soon as the culprit is converted and repents—cf. Maisonneuve, 47, 116. The legates were of another opinion—ibid., 167.

33. Letter of 12th July, 1199; Potthast, 781; PL, 214, 699A.

34. Luchaire, 51–53; Maisonneuve, 123–125.

35. Zanoni; Grundmann, 72–91; Mandonnet-Vicaire-Ladner, II, 43–44; Mens, 45–58.

36. Pierron; Grundmann, 91–127; Mandonnet-Vicaire-Ladner, II, 44–45; Mens, 41–45 and 58–60.

37. Letters of 29th January and 31st May, 1204; Potthast, 2103 and 2229; PL, 215, 274B and 359C; Villemagne, 75 and 55.

38. Portalié, art. 'Augustin' in DTC, I, col. 2277–2280; Maisonneuve, 19–21.

39. In particular, the letters to Everwin de Steinfeld, Ep. 241 and 242, PL, 182, 434–437 and the three sermons on 'Capite nobis vulpes parvulas . . .' Cant. II, 15, sermons 64–66, PL, 183, 1084–1102.

40. PL, 183, 1086D, 1087A, 1101A.

41. For action against the heresies in the twelfth century, see Spaetling, 97–110. In the procedure of the Inquisition, these four stages can be noted: 1° preaching (and proclamation of the month of grace); 2° questioning and examination of the accused; 3° exhortation and instruction; 4° absolution or con-

demnation; 3° and 4° constitute the *sermo generalis*, L. Tanon, *Hist. des tribunaux de l'inquisition en France*, Paris, 1893, 329 and 427; C. Douais, *L'inquisition*, Paris, 1906, 165 and 259. The exhortation of the general sermon was moreover reduced to something quite short, the real exhortation having been made in the course of the trial.

42. On the formation of this power of coercion in regard to defaulting Christian temporal authorities in the time of Innocent III, see Maisonneuve, 154–196.

43. By trying to get the King of France, suzerain of the Count of Toulouse, to intervene in conformity with feudal law. To persuade him to undertake this campaign, he promised him the indulgence of Compostela and Rome, then the indulgence of the Holy Land—see letters of 31st May, 1204; 7th February, 1205; 17th November, 1207; 10th March, 1208; Potthast, 2225, 2404, 3223, 3353; *PL*, 215, 361, 526, 1246, 1358; Villemagne, 172, 177, 183, 321; Maisonneuve, 148–154.

44. Maisonneuve, 140–148.

45. In 1198 and 1199 the legate, Rainier, had obtained, among other powers, that of correction of the secular and regular clergy—Potthast, 785; *PL*, 214, 676A. The first embassy of Peter and Raoul only comprised powers against the heretics (cf. the complaint of Bérenger, Vaissète, VIII, 509). But, when Arnaud was appointed on 31st May, 1204, the Pope added special powers in regard to violators of clerical immunity and against those guilty of simony, and, finally, general powers to 'destroy, disperse, remove, construct and implant' all that should be necessary—Potthast, 2229; *PL*, 215, 360A; Villemagne, 56; at the same time he recommended the prelates to make no difficulties about the correction administered by his legates—Potthast, 2230; *PL*, 215, 360D; Villemagne, 59.

46. Potthast, 2129, 2224, 2337, 2380, 2441 (*PL*, 215, 569), 2516, 2540, 2557, 2561.

47. (Legatos quos) 'in sermone domini duximus destinandos'—Letter to Philip Augustus, 7th Feb., 1205—Potthast, 2404; *PL*, 215, 527A; Villemagne, 178.

48. Letter to Bérenger, 28th May, 1204; Potthast, 2103; *PL*, 215, 274B; Villemagne, 76.

49. Letter to Peter of Castelnau, 26th January, 1205, Potthast, 2391; *PL*, 215, 525D; Villemagne, 66. Same expression to characterize the legates for Philip Augustus, *loc. cit. supra*, n. 46. After II Tim. IV 2 and 5.

50. Letter of 6th December, 1204, Potthast, 2337; *PL*, 215, 474B; Villemagne, 63.

51. Letter of 31st May, 1204, Potthast, 2229; *PL*, 215, 360B; Villemagne, 57.

52. For details as to the sending of these letters, see Potthast 2103 and *PL*, 215, 274D–275A.

53. *Ibid.*

54. Cf. *infra*, ch. VII, 107 and nn. 73–79.

55. Villemagne, 42–44, after Catel, 236.

56. According to the letter of Innocent III, to confirm the penalty of suspension of the bishop pronounced by the legates—Potthast, 2129; *PL*, 215, 272; Villemagne, 189–191. This bull, of 18th February, gives no indication of its year in the Vatican records, but it is placed among the bulls of February 1204 (Luchaire, *Registres*, 48). There is no reason for displacing it to 1205, as historians do, following Vaissète, VI, 236.

57. Villemagne, 107–109; cf. Cernai, 46, n. 4. Lacger, 631. The text has been brought to light by Benoist, *Hist. des Albigeois et des Vaudois*, Paris 1691, I, 269.

58. It is, however, possible that Peter II had invited Raymond-Roger to carry out his own sentence—Tudela, 71 and n. 4.

59. Cernai, no. 20.

60. *Ibid.* For *si*, Scheeben has read *nisi*, an unauthenticated variant of certain editions. The meaning is thus distorted. Cf. Vicaire, 1207, n. 19.

61. 'Ut ceteris omissis, predicationi ardentius insisterent'. Cernai, no. 20.

62. 'Ut possent ora obstruere malignorum, in humilitate procedentes, exemplo pii magistri facerent et docerent, irent pedites absque auro et argento, per omnia formam apostolicam imitantes'—Cernai, no. 20.

63. 'Legati, hec omnia quasi quamdam novitatem per se arripere non volentes . . .'. Cernai, no. 21. As to the example of St Malachy, bishop and legate, here is what St Bernard said of him: 'A die primo conversionis suae usque ad extremum vitae, sine proprio vixit. . . . Nec enim vel domum propriam habuit. Erat autem pene incessanter circuiens parochias omnes; Evangelio serviens et de Evangelio vivens sicut constituit ei Dominus: *Dignus est*, inquiens, *operarius mercede sua* (Luke X, 7 . . .). Denique, cum exiret ad praedicandum, cum peditibus, pedes et ipse ibat, episcopus et legatus, forma apostolica hac, et inde magis mira in Malachia quo rara nimis in aliis', *Vita Malachiae*, *PL*, 182, 1097–1098. Note that it was at Clairvaux that Malachy had conceived this ideal.

64. Letter of 17th November, 1206, Potthast, 2912; *PL*, 215, 1024D; Villemagne, 69. On the contempt in which the clergy were held, cf. Innocent III, letter to the Cardinal of St Prisca, November 1200. Potthast, 1177; *PL*, 214, 905; Puylaurens, prologue.

65. See the opinion of Innocent himself on the mendicity of clerics. He took care to provide some revenue for a cleric whom he had just deposed: 'Ne cogatur in cleri opprobrium mendicare', letter of 7th May, 1199; Potthast, 693; *PL*, 214, 602A. Cf. another case, 5th July, 1205, Potthast, 2557; *PL*, 215, 682.

66. The opinion of the Cistercians is sufficiently indicated by the expression found in certain of their legislative measures to guarantee the subsistence of their religious 'absque rubore mendicandi', *Statuta capit. gen. O. cist.*, ed. D. J. Canivez, III, Louvain 1933, 155 (1276, no. 15)—Huyghe, 85. From the beginning of the century the constitutions had forbidden mendicity in the order—*Ibid.*, I, 340 (1207 no. 34) and 385 (1211, no. 32). As to the example of St Malachy's apostolic poverty, St Bernard eliminated mendicity from it in these terms: 'Evangelio serviens et de Evangelio vivens . . . Nisi quod frequentius, ipsum Evangelium sine sumptu ponens, de laboribus suis suorumque ferebat unde se et eos

qui secum laborabant in opere ministerii sustentaret', *PL*, 182, 1098A. It was similarly by working with his hands that the bishop, St Julian of Cuenca, Diego's colleague, supported his apostolic life. Cf. *supra*, 29 and nn. 64–67.

67. Cernai, no. 21.

68. *Ibidem* and Jordan, nos. 20–21.

69. 'Cum ordo noster specialiter ob predicationem et animarum salutem ab initio noscatur institutus fuisse, et studium nostrum ad hoc principaliter ardenterque, summo opere debeat intendere ut proximorum animabus possimus utiles esse', *I Const.* 194.

70. Bourbon, no. 83, cf. no. 251.

71. Puylaurens, ch. X.

72. On 29th January and 31st May, 1204, Potthast, 2103 and 2229; *PL*, 215, 275A and 309B; Villemagne, 54–55.

73. Cernai, no. 21.

74. Jordan, no. 22. St Norbert had acted similarly when he had decided upon apostolic life—'Juxta mandatum namque evangelii, neque peram, neque calciamenta, neque duas tunicas portabat, paucis solummodo libris et indumentis missae contentus . . . imitator apostolorum effectus', *Vita Norberti*, ch. 9 and 12, MG SS, XII, 675.

75. 'Habentes predictum episcopum super se maiorem et quasi caput totius negoti'—Jordan, no. 22; confirmed by Cernai, no. 67; Diego, Raoul and Peter had been 'predicationis . . . principes et magistri'. Cf. no. 51.

76. 'Nudis plantis et pedibus'—Puylaurens, ch. VIII. In fact Dominic, without imposing this penance on others, would love to practice it—*Proces. Bon.*, nos. 21 and 27.

77. 'Salutis monita seminantes, mendica(bant) hostiatim panem suum'. Cernai, no. 47.

78. Jordan, no. 21.

79. Luchaire, 91; Mandonnet, I, 39–40. An attempt was made to prove this point—Mandonnet-Vicaire, I, 141–156 (Étude V). Scheeben, *Dominikaner oder Innocenzianer* in *AFP*, IX (1939), 237–297, has emphatically rejected this. Certainly the chief sources (Cernai, Jordan) contradict Mandonnet's idea that the Pope had sent Diego to preach in the Midi (Tudela, however, *laisse* 2, V, 17–18 gives Diego the title of legate). They do not, however, prevent one supposing, with Luchaire, that he had perhaps charged Diego with a message or some advice for his legates. That is what is being suggested here, merely as a hypothesis.

80. Cf. *supra*, ch. IV, 57–60.

81. 'Mox, itaque, insiliente in eo spiritu Domini . . .'—Jordan, no. 20, after I Kings X, 10.

82. Cf. *supra*, n. 45.

83. It is worthy of note that the letter speaks of 'religious' and points out that they have not yet preached and dare not do so. All this fits in badly with the Bishop of Osma and quite well with the Cistercian abbots. If it is noted further that the chapter was held on 13th September and that Innocent's reply is dated 17th November, there will be no further hesitation in saying that the first occasion for the letter was a measure taken by the chapter of Cîteaux. This letter, however, at the same time regularized the position of the Castilians.

84. Potthast, 2912; *PL*, 215, 1024–1025; Villemagne, 68–71; Laurent, no. 3. The reply is addressed to Raoul alone.

85. Vaissète, XII, 310–325. Oath of fidelity of Etienne de Servian to the Viscount of Béziers and his guardian, 4th August, 1194—Vaissète, VIII, 430–431.

86. Cernai, no. 23. Servian was occupied by the crusaders on 21st July, 1209, Cernai, no. 83, n. 3. The lord, Etienne de Servian, a notorious heretic, made his abjuration in February 1210, which enabled him to recover his fief. The formula of his abjuration will be found in Vaissète, VIII, 584–587.

87. Vaissète VIII, 584. This Bernard de Simorre had been the adversary of the legates in February 1204 at Carcassonne, cf. *supra*, p. 70 and n. 57.

88. Cernai, nos. 24–25 and 46–47; Maisonneuve 126–131.

89. Cernai, no. 22.

90. In presupposing that the Montpellier meeting took place about 15th June, and taking into account the date of the Béziers dispute, cf. *infra*, n. 103.

91. Cernai, no. 23.

92. Cernai, no. 52.

93. Cernai, no. 23.

94. According to Luke I, 17, in their eyes St John Baptist was one of the greatest and most wicked devils—Cernai, nos. 10 and 25. Cf. Borst, 159–160.

95. In 1143 in Cologne; in 1144 at Liège (where the clergy succeeded in wrestling the majority of the heretics from the crowd), etc. *PL*, 182, 677C; 179; 938B. Cf. also the treatment inflicted on Pierre de Bruys at Saint-Gilles a few years earlier—*supra*, ch. V, 74 and n. 82.

96. Cernai, no. 86; Vaissète, VI, 28–29.

97. Cernai, no. 89, n. 3.

98. Cernai, no. 85.

99. An understanding to the Bishop of Béziers not to introduce Waldenses or heretics (= Catharists) into the city, and to expel from it as far as possible those who were found there. Text of the oath of 4th August, 1194—Vaissète, VIII, 429–430.

100. Letter of Innocent III to the Bishop of Agde and to the Abbot of Saint-Pons to confirm the penalty of suspension pronounced against the bishop by the legates—Potthast, 2129; *PL*, 215, 272; Villemagne, 189–191. For the date, cf. *supra*, n. 56.

101. Vaissète, VI, 236; *Gal. Christ.*, VI, 325A, where is to be found the epitaph, source of the information—'servorum deceptus fraude suorum'.

102. Cernai, no. 24.

103. On 17th June, 1206, the Pope charged his legates Peter and Raoul, with the Bishop of Pamplona, to examine the marriage of Pedro II de Aragón. The letter must have reached the Narbonensis about the middle of July. In September he entrusted them with a certain matter at the abbey of Saint-Gilles. In October Peter collaborated with the re-establishment of peace between the King of Aragón and the city of Montpellier. He signed the treaty on 27th October at Villeneuve-lès-Maguelonne. In November he had not yet returned to Raoul, since it was to the latter only that the Pope addressed his letter of 17th November about the preachers—Villemagne, 127, 227, 130, 68; Cernai, no. 24, n. 2.

104. Cernai, no. 24.

105. Report of the legates Arnaud and Milon to the Pope after the taking of Carcassonne—*PL*, 216, 139D. More than one hundred fortified localities were thus emptied; Cernai, no. 92, p. 93 and n. 2.

106. Cernai, no. 94. The fortifications of the city of Carcassonne assumed their present form in the fifteenth century but on the foundations of those of earlier times.

107. Cernai, no. 92 and n. 3, no. 93.

108. Bérenger, I, 1201–1207.

109. Cernai, no. 99.

110. Cernai, III, pp. xi to xv.

111. Cernai, no. 26.

112. Puylaurens, ch. VIII, said in effect: 'Fuitque una de primis congressionibus apud Viridefolium.' Verfeil is on the Girou, about twelve miles from Toulouse. In St Bernard's time it was the centre of heresy for Toulouse.

113. 'Viri apostolici, scilicet predicatores nostri, circuibant per castella, evangelizantes et disputante ubique'—Cernai, no. 26.

114. Jordan, no. 23.

115. Robert of Auxerre, 245; Vaissète, VI, 94–96; Maisonneuve, 96.

116. Cernai, 215–229.

117. Letter of Geoffroy d'Auxerre, 414B; Puylaurens, ch. 1; the beginning of the chronicle which relates the episode of 1145 was drawn up before 1273, perhaps about 1250.

118. He commented, among other passages, on John III, 13: 'Nemo ascendit in caelum, nisi qui descendit de caelo, Filius hominis, qui est in caelo.' The Text was very well chosen to combat the Docetism and subordinationism of the Catharists in the name of the Gospel. Puylaurens, ch. VIII.

119. They took in the material sense Is. LXVI, 1: 'Caelum mihi sedes est, terram autem scabellum pedum meorum', *ibid.* Puylaurens, ch. viii, who has given us the name of two of the heresiarchs, tells us no more about them. The first of the two was to find himself confronted by the legates at Montréal a few months later—*ibid.*, ch. IX.

NOTES TO CHAPTER VII

1. The slow-flowing Hers.

2. The Fresquel and its tributary the Tréboul.

3. Vaissète, XII, 200, 263; Guiraud, *Cartulaire*, CCXLI–CCLXII; *Inquisition*, 221, 266, 286–287.

4. Guiraud, *Cartulaire*, CCLVI–CCLVIII; *Inquisition*, 266, 285–286, 290, 324.

5. Cernai, no. 110 and n. 2; Guiraud, *Cartulaire*, CX–CXI, CCXXXII–CCXXXIII and CCXLIII–CCXLVII; *Inquisition*, 148–149, 288–291.

6. Guiraud, *Cartulaire*, CCXLVII and 58; *Inquisition*, 291.

7. Guiraud, *Cartulaire*, CCXLIII–CCXLVI; *Inquisition*, 288–291.

8. Balme, I, 139 and n. 2; Guiraud, *Cartulaire*, CCXLVII; *Inquisition*, 291, which corrects Balme, 116, who thought that Na-Cavaers, the mother, had no connection with heresy. A Cavaers was *bayle* of the king at Limoux about 1240, Vaissète, VII, notes 241 and 256.

9. Vaissète, VI, 1149–1151. Unlike the others present, the count did not 'adore' the Perfect. Cf. *supra*, ch. V, n. 36.

10. Balme, I, 108, n. 1; Guiraud, *Cartulaire*, CXXXIV–CXXXVI; *Inquisition*, 149, 204–205, 288.

11. Borst, 232 and n. 14. Perhaps he was associated with his predecessor while the latter was still alive, or perhaps he was merely his eldest son. *Ibid.*, 208, n. 23; Guiraud, *Cartulaire*, CXXXVIII–CXXXIX.

12. Guiraud, *Cartulaire*, CX–CXI.

13. *Ibid.*, CCLXX–CCLXXii, and *Inquisition*, 351–353.

14. Guiraud, *Cartulaire*, CCLXXIII–CCLXXV, and *Inquisition*, 354–355.

15. Cernai, no. 26, n. 4 and no. 110; Guiraud, *Cartulaire*, CXI and CCLI–CCLII; *Inquisition*, 269–270, 294–296.

16. Cernai, no. 135 and n. 3, 148, 167, 215–216, 227; Tudela, *laisse* 68, 5–15.

17. Puylaurens in ch. IX says in 1207. This should be understood, in the strict sense, after 22nd April, for the chronicler follows the Easter style. But it would suffice for a part of the episode to have taken place at the end of April to justify his assertion. To give the detail—after fifteen days of disputation and a few days' apostolate to follow it up (Cernai, no. 47), the missionaries were strengthened by an additional company which had left Cîteaux in March (Robert of Auxerre, 271) and which certainly arrived before the end of April. A *confirmatur* proving this exists. Peter of Castelnau, who left Montréal after the disputation, arranged a peace in Provence and had it signed also in April (Cernai, no. 27 and

n. 1). The disputation thus began at the end of March or beginning of April. It must have been concluded before 15th April in order to leave Holy Week free for the very heavy liturgical commitments.

18. 'Solemnior'—Puylaurens, ch. IX. This disputation was known to us through Cernai, nos. 26–27; Puylaurens, ch. IX; Jordan, no. 23. The value of the first mentioned text is incomparable, that of the second is considerable, the third is merely a brief mention. Several seventeenth-century writers have brought to light so-called official reports of the disputation which Scheeben, 41–49, utilized for his account of the events. He even announced, *ibid.*, 431, n. 57, the editing of a report reconstructed in accordance with these seventeenth-century texts. It has been shown (Vicaire, *1207*, 339–343) that these so-called reports are in no sense original and merely add improbable details to the Puylaurens text, ch. IX. Scheeben's account is, on this head, valueless; in particular, his chronology, woven out of the artificial combination of elements borrowed from seventeenth-century writers, is not to be trusted—cf. Vicaire, *1207*, 342, n. 43.

19. See the expressions applied to them by the sources—*athletae*, Cernai, no. 55; *pugiles nostri*, Puylaurens, ch. IX; *pugiles Dei, ibid.*, ch. X; *Christi milites*, Innocent III, in accordance with Cernai, no. 59.

20. See the expressions *vir apostolicus*, Cernai, no. 6 and 26 (cf. *à propos* of St Malachy, *PL*, 182, 1098D) of which the meaning, according to Dewailly 150, n. 3 (cf. 148, n. 1) should be interpreted as—the man who is striving to live the life of the apostles over again; *vir evangelicus*, Robert of Auxerre 271 and Jordan, no. 105.

21. This expression, taken from Ez. XIII, 5, frequently recurs in Innocent's letters to the legates—Potthast, 2103, 2229, 2912; Puylaurens, prologue.

22. After Matt. X, 27 commented by Innocent III—'per hoc manifeste denuntians quod evangelica predicatio non in occultis conventiculis, sicut haeretici faciunt, sed in ecclesiis juxta morem catholicum est publice proponenda'. Potthast, 780; *PL*, 214, 696A. Cf. *supra*, ch. V, n. 116.

23. The use of this expression from I Pet. III, 15, to designate the state of mind of the true apostle, was frequent—cf. Peter the Venerable, *PL*, 189, 726c. Innocent used it to characterize what he expected from his preachers on 31st May, 1204—Potthast, 2229, *PL*, 215, 359B; Cernai no. 47 and 56 and Robert of Auxerre, 271 apply it to them.

24. Scheeben, 42, affirms this categorically. He is, however, building on insecure foundations: 1. the fact of the Council of Mirepoix which he dates, without proof, during the summer of 1206 (cf. *infra*, n. 26); 2. a page of Perrin, 7. It is difficult to accord any sort of value to this page of Perrin which refers neither to a fact nor to a document. The author is far too imaginative.

25. Albigensian council of St Felix of Caraman in 1167—Dondaine, *Actes*, in particular 332–333.

26. Guiraud, *Inquisition*, 269; Dondaine, *Actes*, 332, n. 12. The date is not completely certain. The account, given in 1246, says: 'et sunt quadraginta anni, vel circa'.

27. Jordan, no. 22.

28. Cf. *supra*, 96–97.

29. Balme, I, 107 and n. 2. Guiraud, *Inquisition*, 207; Borst, 234.

30. Guiraud, *op. cit.*, 225 and n. 5.

31. Cernai, no. 26.

32. 'Et plures alii viri boni' . . . 'et multi alii nomina quorum non sunt scripta in libro vitae'—Puylaurens, ch. IX.

33. 'Disputaturi unanimiter', Cernai, no. 26.

34. Puylaurens, *ibid.*

34a. Cf. p. 140, n. 17.

35. Cernai, no. 26, n. 2.

36. Ch. IX.

37. *Manuel de l'inquisiteur*, ed. G. Mollat, Paris, 1926, I, 6.

38. Cf. Portalié, art. 'Augustin' in *DTC*, I, 2277–2280.

39. As, for instance, Cologne 1193. Certain Catharists were summoned to appear for judgement before a *conventus* of clergy and laymen in the presence of the archbishop and of the notables. The interrogation became a dispute with an appeal to Scripture. The Catharists, considerably shaken, asked for a further disputation in which their leaders could defend their belief. After this colloquy three days were spent in warning them of the penalties they were incurring and publicly beseeching them to be converted. The crowd eventually dragged them away from the clergy to burn them—Everwin de Steinfeld, 677B.

40. At Albi St Bernard changed his sermon into a dialogue, setting forth one after the other the Catharist and Catholic doctrines of the Eucharist. After this, he interrogated the crowd who swore as a body to return to the Catholic faith—Geoffroi d'Auxerre, 414D.

41. In 1165—account, Mansi, XXII 157–168; Lacger, Albigeois, 297.

42. In 1178—Vaissète VI, 82–84, after Roger of Hovenden, *Chronica*, ed. Stubbs, II, London 1869, 150–166.

43. Under Archbishop Bernard of Narbonne (1181–1191). This was the dispute related by Fontcaude, 793–795, the source of his own book—Vaissète, VI, 218–219.

44. Vaissète, VI, 231; Villemagne, 107–109.

45. Geoffroi d'Auxerre, 412C.

46. In his letter of 12th June, 1199, Innocent III, gave a remarkable exposition of the traditional thought of the Church on the public character of Christian preaching and the necessity of the Church's mission for it—Potthast, 780; *PL*, 214, 695–698; cf. *supra*, n. 22. The two petitions go back to the earliest Christian times. Abhorrence of the *conventicula* was shared by the Roman emperors—Maisonneuve 8 and n. 2.

47. This was the case at Lombers in 1165 and at Toulouse in 1178. When the heresiarchs solemnly asserted, in the presence of the crowd, that they had always held the articles of the Catholic faith, they were contradicted then and there by the Count of Toulouse and numerous witnesses who had heard them preach in quite another sense—Vaissète, VI, 83.

48. On the Catholic conformism of the Catharist believers, see Lacger, *Albigeois*, 295–298.

49. Geoffroi d'Auxerre, 412C.

50. I Pet. III, 15.

51. For the Catharists, for instance, Vaissète VI, 82. For the Waldenses, Bernard Gui, *Manuel de l'inquisiteur*, ed. G. Mollat, Paris 1926, I, 54. For the Catholics, *supra*, n. 23.

52. 'Fundamentum, a parte hereticorum, disputationis'—Puylaurens, ch. IX.

53. *Ibid.*

54. Cernai, no. 29; Puylaurens, ch. IX; Jordan, nos. 24–25.

55. On reading Puylaurens, it might be thought that the disputation consisted in supplying the judges with the contradictory *Libelli* without public discussions. Cernai is correct when he says that the *scripta* were drawn up after the oral debate. Puylaurens, too, draws attention to such a debate when he mentions the 150 persons who were converted *intellectis que dicta erant*.

56. Cernai, Puylaurens, Jordan, *ibid.*

57. Cernai, no. 54, relates the incident at the close of his story of the Preaching, after having mentioned the death of Diego. He had found no better place to insert it, he says. He thus does not seem to have thought that the incident occurred in the course of the April dispute. In fact he seems in his account to presuppose Diego's departure from the scene—'unus de nostris . . . qui socius fuerat episcopi oxomensis . . . ,' Jordan, nos. 24 and 25, relates the same incident, but places it at Fanjeaux. He fails to distinguish, however, two things which Cernai, nos. 29 and 54, separates—the sheet of paper, *schedula*, given by Dominic to his contradictor on the evening of a discussion and the general report, *redactum in scriptis* (*libellus*), transmitted to the judges for sentence. Cernai had the account directly from St Dominic's lips five years after the event. What Jordan indicates is in no sense comparable. That is why we are following Cernai, despite the existence at Fanjeaux of a local tradition no trace of which is discoverable before the fourteenth century and which was quite possibly elicited by Jordan's text—Percin, 3; Balme, I, 118 and 120, n. 1; Guiraud, *Cartulaire*, CCCXV–CCCXVI and 174; Kirsch, 114–117 and the editor of Cernai, no. 54, 48, n. 3.

58. Cf. Michel in *DTC*, XI, 1139–1152.

59. For the judgement by fire on the person of a repentant Catharist neophyte at Castres, see Cernai, no. 113.

60. Defourneaux, 29–30. The king would seem to have pushed the book back into the flames intact, saying: 'Ad libitum regum flectuntur cornua legum.' He had earlier caused a duel to be fought by champions.

61. No. 24.

62. Cernai, no. 26; Puylaurens, ch. IX.

63. For the report, see: La Popelinière, N. Vignier, J. Ussher, J. P. Perrin, cf. Vicaire, *1207*, 339. For what St Dominic wrote, Jean Bremer, quoted by *Antonianum XI* (1936), 448 and 483. The small pamphlet would be entitled *De corpore* (or *Ad decorem*) *Christi contra Albigenses*. Cf. Balme, I, n. at foot of p. 124. Cod. Reg. 584 of the Vatican, fo. 155, ro and vo contains a *schedula b. Dominici proiecta in ignem* which is merely an extract from Cernai.

64. Cernai, no. 27 and n. 1.

65. 'Tam per guerras, quas movebant ei nobiles Provinciae, mediante industria viri Dei, quam per excommunicationem', *ibid.*

66. Cernai, no. 47. Dominic, nevertheless, went to Carcassonne on 17th April—Laurent, no. 5.

67. Jordan, no. 26.

68. *Infra*, ch. VIII.

69. On the principal sources of the account, see Robert of Auxerre, Cernai, Jordan and cf. Vicaire, *1207*, 335–338. The first is contemporary with the events, the second dates from 1213 (to be corrected, p. 336, after Cernai, III, xviii), the third from 1235. If the two former provide information of first-hand value, the same cannot be said of the latter.

70. Cernai, no. 47. On the number 12 in the history of the apostolic life, cf *supra*, ch. III, n. 91.

71. They may even perhaps have been able to continue by water as far as the Aude, through the lagoons along the coast—Tudela, 39, n. 4.

72. Robert of Auxerre, 271.

73. The phrase quoted from Robert of Auxerre, composed of rearranged texts from I Pet. III, 15 and John XV, 13, which are to be found in part in Cernai, no. 47, equally in reference to the twelve abbots, comes word for word from the pontifical letter of 31st May, 1204—Potthast, 2229; *PL*, 215, 359B; Villemagne, 54. In this letter Innocent recalled the request for preachers he had made to the Abbot of Cîteaux on 29th January—Potthast, 2103.

74. Cernai, nos. 26, 47, 48, 51, 54.

75. Cernai, no. 3.

76. Bourbon, no. 251; Frachet, 8.

77. Cernai, no. 67; Puylaurens, ch. IX. Cf. the study, *La Sainte Prédication de Narbonnaise*, in Mandonnet—Vicaire, I, 115–139.

78. Letter of Innocent III 10th March, 1208—Potthast, 3324; *PL*, 215, 1356B; Cernai, no. 61.

79. Cf. *infra*, p. 109 and n. 110.

80. Cernai, III, p. xxxii, n. 21.

81. Vaissète, VI, 81.

82. G. G. Meersseman, *Études sur les anciennes confréries dominicaines*, IV, 'Les milices de Jesus-Christ', in *AFP*, 23 (1953), 275–308, in particular, 285–293.

83. Letter of Innocent III 18.11.1204, Potthast, 2129; *PL*, 215, 272B; Villemagne, 190.

84. Cernai, no. 70.

85. Cernai, no. 51.

86. Cernai, no. 300.

87. Cernai, no. 201.

88. A monk from Bonnevaux later recounted an incident which happened to one of the twelve abbots. This was probably his own abbot, or at least his abbot was probably then in the Albigeois. Frachet, 8; the Abbot of Bonnevaux was preaching in the Albigeois in 1212—Cernai, no. 298.

89. In the acts of the general chapter of Cîteaux in 1212 may be read: 'De monacho Prulliacensi nuncupato Petro heremita, praecipitur ut in instanti revocetur a praedicatione albigensium, nec ipse, nec alius aliquis sine licentia capituli generalis de cetero praedicationis officium audeat usurpare'—Canivez, I, 400, no. 50. This monk had perhaps come to the Albigeois with his abbot in 1207.

90. Balme, I, 471.

91. Westenholz, 24 and 170–171; Altaner 66. If Dominic's friendship for Rainier can be dated from their meeting in Italy in 1216, that between Rainier and Guy de Montfort is certainly prior to 1216 and could only have arisen in the Narbonensis.

92. See the description of the ideal preacher which is at the same time that of the Cistercians in the letter of 31st May, 1204—Potthast, 2229; *PL*, 215, 359; Villemagne, 54. On the formula, *verbo et exemplo*, cf. *infra*, ch. VIII, n. 216.

93. Cf. *supra*, ch. VI, n. 51.

94. Twelve apostles, Cernai, no. 47; two by two Robert of A., 271, Frachet 76 and Constantin, no. 55; on foot Cernai, no. 47 and Robert of A, *ibid.*; barefoot Puylaurens, ch. VIII, Frachet, 67 and *Proces. Bon.* no. 21; begging from door to door Cernai, no. 47.

95. Mandonnet-Vicaire-Ladner, II, 14 and 50–59. The ordinary monks do not form part of these categories—*ibid.*, 24–26 and *supra*, n. 89.

96. Bérenger of Narbonne and, clearly, Bérenger of Carcassonne seem to have followed the discussion from the latter's palace—cf. *supra*, 106, n. 68.

97. Cernai, no. 47.

98. Robert of Auxerre, 271.

99. Among the Cistercians *termini* were distant domains over which the abbot exercised jurisdiction. The conception was extended to every part of the territory where the jurisdiction of a prelate, in this instance of a delegated preacher, stretched. The Preachers adopted it to designate the diet or 'preaching' of a conventual house—later, even, a portion of this diet. Cf. Mortier, I, 501–502. Meersseman, *De domibus terminariis in antiquo comitatu Flandriae* in *AFP*, VIII (1938) 263–273.

100. Cernai, no. 27 and n. 3.

101. Cernai, no. 201 and n. 1 (correcting no. 47, n. 6).

102. He was to die close to Saint-Gilles just before 9th July, cf. *infra*, n. 139.

103. Cf. *infra*, ch. VIII.

104. Laurent, nos. 5 and 6. For William Claret, *Ibid.*, 24, n. 2.

105. P. 106, n. 68.

106. Balme, I, 471.

107. Bernard Gui found the original of this letter at the priory of Toulouse and transcribed it on 31st October, 1305. He has left a description of the seal—Balme, I, 188–189. He noted an identical seal at the foot of a second letter. *Ibid.*, 484. Since the first letter must date from 1208, and the second, about 1215, it will be seen that Dominic did not change his seal during this time.

108. J. Roman, *Manuel de sigillographie française*, Paris, 1912, 45 and *L'art et la vie au moyen âge à travers les blasons et les sceaux*, Paris 1950, 62.

109. Girou, 56.

110. The various mss. in which the description of the seal by Bernard Gui is found are not identical. One says the inscription could not be read easily. Another reads it—*Jhesu Christi et predicationis* (ms. Barcelone, Bibl. pub. Arm. I, III, 16; in ms. Dôle, Bibl. pub. 109, fo. 80 ro). Dondaine, *AFP*, XVII (1947), 136 reads S instead of J(hesu), Balme, I, 189. This inscription does not make sense. The *et* in particular is incomprehensible. It would seem that the paleographic sign has been confused with the S (= *Sigillum*), indispensable on a seal and that it is necessary to read this round inscription beginning by this S. This would give [*Sigillum*] *predicationis Jhesu Christi* Balme I, 189. Cf. Dondaine in *AFP*, XVII (1947), 135–136.

111. Laurent, no. 6. The expression *Sancta predicatio* is traditional—cf. letter from Innocent III of 10th March, 1208—Cernai, no. 61 and canon 10 of the Lateran Hefele-Leclercq, V, 1340. It refers to an expression of St Gregory, *sanctus predicator*, and indicates a ministry *verbo et exemplo*, Ladner, 55 and n. 204–5.

112. Balme, I, 484.

113. Laurent, no. 80. Loenertz 7, n. 6 has shown that charter 81, which contained an analogous expression, has been touched up at a later date. Similar ones were still found in 1230—Guiraud, *Cartulaire*, II, 4 and 5.

114. Laurent, no. 134.

115. Balme, I, 164, n. 1; cf. Guiraud, *Cartulaire*, II, 4, 5, 51–52; Percin 16, no. 32; Marteen, *Script.* VI, 453.

116. Laurent, nos. 95 and 134; cf. *infra*, II, Appendix VII.

117. Cernai, no. 51 and 67.

118. On this title cf. Mandonnet-Vicaire, I, 53, no. 48; 130, n. 89; II, 187, n. 58. For the very frequent use of this term by Cernai, note in particular nn. 101, 154, 286, 514, 525.

119. Used in the absolute sense, in the twelfth century the term designated a man who was teaching or had taught—Lesne, 461–3.

120. Mandonnet-Vicaire, I, 130, n. 89.

121. Catharist leaders—Eckbert de Schoenau, *PL*, 195, 17; *Annales de Margan, Rerum Britt. m. aevi Script.* London, 1864, XXXVI, I, 15; Cernai, no. 14 etc; Waldes: Bourbon, no. 342.

122. Jacques de Vitry, Ep. VI, ed. Boehmer-Wiegand, Analekten, Tübingen, 1930, 69 and *Historia orientalis*, bk. 2, ch. 32, *ibid.*, 71.

123. Mandonnet-Vicaire-Ladner, II, 51–59.

124. Laurent, no. 70. The title of *magister* was only given to Dominic from 1216–1217 both in the texts of the archives and in literary documents (Laurent, no. 70; Jordan, no. 49). There are two exceptions, a charter of 28th March, 1213 (Laurent, no. 41) where the term has the meaning of *prior monasterii monialium* from a previous phrase, and a conversation of 1214, related by Constantin, no. 55, where the title given to Dominic refers to his preaching. Thus there is no reason to give this somewhat late title its scholastic meaning as V. D. Carro would like to do in his *S. Domingo de Guzmán, fundador de la primera orden universitaria, apostolica y misionera*, Salamanca, 1946, 15, nn. 13 and 17. Gelabert, *S. Domingo de G. visto por sus contemporaneos*, Madrid 1947, 63–4 and n. 13. As to the interpretation: *magister sacri palatii*, anachronistic and without any foundation, cf. Altaner, 201–207.

125. Laurent, no. 134.

126. Cf. Mandonnet-Vicaire, I, 131.

127. He had even refused them a horse for travelling from Narbonne to Toulouse and only decided to give them one on their indignant protests—letter of Innocent III, 29th January, 1204, Potthast, 2103; *PL*, 215, 274C; Villemagne, 76.

128. P. 271.

129. Cernai, no. 48.

130. Jordan, no. 28.

131. The charter of 8th August, 1207 (Laurent, no. 6) mentions at the same time as Sans and Ermengarde, several other men of Villepinte 'qui ad sanctam predicationem donaverunt'.

132. Guiraud, *Cartulaire*, CV–CXIV; Borst, 211 and n. 31 (rôle of the deacons).

133. *Vita Malachiae, PL*, 182, 1098.

134. *Summa Aurea*, Paris 1500, L. II, tr. VII, ch. I, fo. L.II, C.I. It referred to the Lombardy Catharists.

135. Potthast, no. 2229; *PL*, 215, 359C; Villemagne 55.

136. Cernai, no. 20.

137. Jordan, no. 22.

138. Robert of Auxerre, 271.

139. His *depositio* is commemorated on 9th July. According to monastic custom, he must have been buried the day after his death—Henríquez, *Menologium cisterciense*, Antwerp 1630, 225.

140. R. of Auxerre, 271, does in fact mention returns three months after the arrival, thus at the end of July. The editor of Cernai, no. 51, n. 2, rightly notes that what was referred to were isolated returns. However, the general chapter of Cîteaux, 13th September, 1207 had to recall several abbots from mid-August onwards.

141. Cernai, no. 51; cf. no. 67.

142. *Laisse* II, 1.24–27; cf. *laisse* III, 1.12. The five years of preaching mentioned by Guillaume doubtless run from 1203–1208.

143. Cernai, no. 51 'post multum temporis' which indicates that this happened after Arnaud's departure for Marseille at the beginning of September, but well before the death of Peter de Castelnau, 14th January, 1208.

144. 'Animadvertentes etiam quod eadem praedicatio jam peregerit ex parte maxima cursum suum . . .'—Cernai, no. 67.

145. Cernai, no. 51.

146. Cernai, nos. 154–157 and 324 (preachings in 1210 and 1212).

147. Tudela, *laisse* XLVI, 1.9 (1210, in Toulouse).

148. Cernai, nos. 439 and 494.

149. Jordan, no. 28.

150. *Ibid.*

NOTES TO CHAPTER VIII

1. For the traditional 'route of St Dominic', cf. *infra* 257, n. 174.

2. Guiraud, *Cartulaire*, II, 104. In future this work will be referred to in this chapter as G, with an indication of the page and volume. Similarly, Laurent will be known as L, followed by the page.

3. These routes are vouched for in particular by the charters of delimitation of 1252 and 1316, G, II, 5–67 and 121–123.

4. Cf. *supra*, ch. I, II.

5. *Proc. Thol.*, no. 3 and no. 18. Cf. Frachet, II, 23.

6. For the early history of the monastery of Prouille, there are available, besides the general sources

for the life of St Dominic, the notice by Bernard Gui (Martène, VI, 437–456), the monastery charters (G; L, to be corrected by Loenertz), and finally extracts from an ancient ms. of Prouille which is quoted by Rechac, Percin, Echard. Examining the extracts in Percin, who makes considerable use of the ms., it appears to be a collection containing an ancient breviary (Percin, 4, no. 16), a cartulary (Percin 15, no. 24) and a chronicle (Percin, 16, no. 30). The breviary contained a legend of the saint, distributed among the lessons of the feast and its octave. The chronicle was a compilation certainly later than Bernard Gui (Percin 22, no. 54). It has no value in itself, but has perhaps collected some tradition peculiar to the sisters. The studies of Guiraud, *Fondation* and *Cartulaire* retain their value, although they need correction. See also: 'La naissance de Sainte-Marie de Prouille', in Mandonnet-Vicaire, I, 99–113, where will be found a criticism of Scheeben, 'Die Anfänge des zweiten Ordens des hl. Dominikus', in *AFP*, II (1932), 284–314, which none the less has its value.

7. Rechac, 119 and Percin, 4. The latter gives the source—the ancient ms. of Fanjeaux. This may be a *lapsus* and he may mean to refer to the ancient ms. of Prouille, which he is continually quoting. In any case, this text lacks authority and Mamachi, 159–160 and 163, n. 1, rightly neglects it: it distorts, and falsifies by combining them, several facts from the thirteenth-century sources as well as adding to them certain data which cannot be checked.

8. On a similar legend at the monastery of Törs—apparition of lights three nights in succession at the place where the foundation was to be—and elsewhere, cf. M.C. Daeniker-Gysin-*Gesch. des Dominikaner-innenklosters Törs*, Winterthür, 1957, 17.

9. Will of the parish priest of Fanjeaux, Jean Sésale, in 1423—Balme, I, 136, n. 1.

10. The cross and chapel (rebuilt in 1538—Percin, 4) and later destroyed, were replaced in 1860 and 1869—Balme, I, 136, n. 1 and Kirsch, 122–123.

11. Vaissète, V, 1033, 1047, 1062; XI, 205 (referring to Isarn and Guillaume de Prouille).

12. *Mota*: G, II, 44, 47, 55. The mound (*mota*) was the type of the tenth- and eleventh-century fortification in the West. In 1063 Rangarde de Carcassonne and his son Count Roger received half the castle of Prouille—Vaissète, V, 516.

13. *Sesonia, Sidonia*, from the charters—today Font-Saint-Martin, or stream of the Prouille.

14. *Castrum vetus*—G, II, 35, 40, 41, 43, 44, 60, 78, 84. The castle referred to is the mound. The *castrum vetus* is the locality, the old township.

15. G, II, 74.

16. G, II, 35, 39, 42, 50, 52. It must have been outside the monastery wall, for in 1294 work had to be done on it to bring in the water supply—G, I, 265.

17. G, I, 53; II, 77, 78 etc.

18. There is evidence for the existence of the cemetery G, II, 46 and 56. It could only belong to a conventual, which was not the case here, or parish church. For the authenticity of the charters see G, I, I and II, 73 (L. nos. 4 and 11) which mention the title of the parish cf. *infra*, n. 45.

19. G, II, 39, 62, 65–67, 84, 121–123, 169–171.

20. G, II, 37, 45, 58; Balme, I, 288, n. 1.

21. G, II, 65–67; 121–123; 169–171 (demarcation tithe between districts).

22. G, II, 47.

23. Whence the name of *Castrum vetus*: the locality is no longer fortified. It is possible that the ancient wall served as a foundation for the enclosure. The latter was only rebuilt in stone after 1294—G, I, 265.

24. Cf. decrees quoted *supra*, nn. 12 and 14.

25. There is no mention of a parish priest in the documents. The population has almost completely disappeared; the charters conferring almost the whole of the old township on the nuns (*supra*, n. 14) mention in all three houses. On the word *aliquando*, applied to the parish in a document, cf. *infra*, n. 45. The church had to be rebuilt in 1267—G, I. 28. It was still standing in the seventeenth century—Rechac, 197.

26. Because of the heresy or the anticlericalism of the authorities or of the impoverishment of the tithe district. The neighbouring chapel, St Sernin de la Ilhe, given to the sisters after the re-establishment of Catholicism, in 1265, with its tithes and all its dues, did not bring in a revenue of 20 francs of Tours, i.e. of 20 sous—G, II, 114–115.

27. This is surmised from the intervention of the bishop alone, to whose manse the church of Fanjeaux belonged (G, I, 6), for the concession of the church of Sainte Marie (*infra*, n. 45).

28. *Quasi destructa* in 1246—G, II, 58.

29. Signed various charters of the sisters in 1221, 1226—G, I, 56; II. 51. In 1212 he was given the title of *dominus*. He was no longer the lord, however. One property remained to him—G, II, 46. Later, there was a Bernard of Prouille—Balme, I, 272.

30. Signed or was mentioned in charters of 1226 and 1227—G, II, 51 and 54. He is mentioned in the former as brother of Isarn, in the latter as *miles de Proliano*.

31. 'Fuit vir catholicus et fidelis et bonus et non fuit faiditus et decessit in bono statu'—deposition of Arnaud de Laure on the occasion of the Carcassonne inquiry, *ca.* 1258—Vaissète, VII, 354; Delisle in *Recueil*, XXIV, 558j.

32. Balme, I, 169. Apparently he listened to and 'adored' Guilabert de Castres.

33. The information is unfortunately somewhat late, coming from Salagnac, 15 and de Frachet, 63–64. Is it possible to identify this Virgin of Prouille? There are various statues from the Prouille of ancient times now at Gramazié, Belvèze, Castelnaudary (church of St François). None is earlier than the end of the thirteenth century. Prouille has preserved several ancient statues of the Virgin. The only one which is of the twelfth century (a Virgin on a throne, in wood) did not originate from Prouille, but

came from the Dominican priory at Limoux. The Virgin of the basilica is a nineteenth-century reproduction after the thirteenth-century seal. There is no reason to think that it is a reproduction of a statue of the time. The only proof left of an ancient cultus of the Blessed Virgin is thus the title of the church of Prouille; this is, however, categorical. It should be noted that before 1240, the sisters of Prouille had deposited a small image of the Virgin at the abbey of St Hilaire—*Recueil*, XXIV, 299, no. 8.

34. Cf. Balme, I, 130–135; Guiraud, *Fondation*, 225–8, and *Saint Dominique*, Paris, 1899, 53–8.

35. On this movement—Grundmann, 170–438; Roisin, 342–378; Mens, 82–95; 273–322.

36. *Supra*, p. 99.

37. Guiraud, *Cartulaire*, CCLI.

38. Guiraud, *Cartulaire*, CCXLV–XXCLVI.

39. Cf. several instances cited in Balme, I, 131–132 and Guiraud, *Saint Dominique*, Paris, 1899, 54–55; *infra*, ch. IX, p. 111.

40. 'Femine nobiles, quas parentes earum ratione paupertatis erudiendas et nutriendas tradebant hereticis'—Jordan, no. 27.

41. Jordan, no. 27, confirmed by the charter of Bérenger Laurent, no. 5.

42. Cf. *infra*, n. 45.

43. Stronski, 3* to 113*.

44. Puylaurens, ch. VII.

45. There are three documents extant relating to the cession of Sainte-Marie de Prouille by Fulk of Toulouse: one dated 1206 (*Gallia Christ.*, XIII, 247, instr.; Laurent, no. 4), two of 1211 (Rechac, 198–199 and Loenertz, 38; Laurent, no. 11 and Loenertz, 39). The lack of authenticity of Mandonnet-Vicaire, I, 105, n. 39 had already been pointed out. Loenertz, 40–46, demonstrated that of the two others. He shows, however, that these spurious documents were established from a literary basis. 'D. Fulco . . . dedit et concessit ecclesiam beatae Mariae de Prulliano, ad preces domini dominici oxomensis, pro mulieribus conversis per praedicatores ad praedicandum contra haereticos et ad repellandam haeresim delegatos . . . absque decimis et primiciis.' This piece of information is valuable. It proves that the church of Prouille depended effectively on the bishop and on him alone.

It seems possible also to consider as valid other data of the Laurent document no. 11, under the critical form established by Leonertz, 39. The mention of the parochial title of Sainte Marie, of its disappearance (*aliquando*), and of the attachment of the church of Prouille to that of Fanjeaux; finally the date of 1211 and the literary formula 'et praecipue quia sibi visum fuit esse pietatis et misericordiae'. The first three indications are authentic (cf. *supra*, nn. 18, 25 and 27). As to the date of 1211 and the formula, a forger would have no reason for introducing these into his document unless he had found them with the others in some source of value.

46. G, II, 44 and 47; Laurent, no. 63.

47. The only mention extant of his intervention is in the 'manuscript of Fanjeaux' cited by Percin 4 (cf. *supra*, n. 6). It has no authority behind it. This lady had some leaning towards the Catharists, cf. *supra*, ch. VII, n. 8.

48. G, II, 47.

49. In 1243, she made an important gift to the sisters—G, II, 57; in 1246, she abandoned her rights to Raymond VII and entered at Prouille—G, I, 58; for other gifts about this time, see G, II, 7; *ca.* 1258, Arnaud de Laure said of her; 'fuit bona et catholica, et fuit monacha Pruliani ubi cum habitu moniaii decessit ut bona domina'—Vaissète, VII, 379; Delisle in *Recueil*, XXIV, 592G. Cf. *ibid.*, 670–671, declaration of the sisters.

50. Balme, 139 and n. 2 retraces her spiritual itinerary.

51. G, II 2, 35, 41, 42, 45, 46, 119. He had recently given to the Catharists his niece and ward Arnaude de Frémiac, whom Dominic reconciled, after she had spent six years as a Perfect, about 1211—Balme, I, 271.

52. G, II, 42, 45, 47, 52, 74, 75, 78; cf. Guiraud, *Fondation*, 244–245. Cf. Balme, I, 291 and n. 1.

53. G, I, 52; II, 36, 37, 38, 55, 75; for Bernard de Durfort, likewise a landowner at Prouille, see G, II, 41 and 120; and for Sicard de Durfort and his brother Pierre de la Ilhe, nephews of God Picarella—G, II, 52, 53, 55. On the Durforts, a powerful family of Fanjeaux allied to that of Foix, deeply involved in heresy—see Guiraud, *Fondation*, 244–246.

54. G, II, 44, 55, 57, 59; Balme, I, 542, n. 1.

55. G, II, 44.

56. The act calls them Papau—G, II, 56, Guiraud, *Cartulaire*, I, CCCXXIV, thinks that they also belonged to the Babon family.

57. William is already mentioned, side by side with St Dominic, in the first charter—G, II, 158 and L, 23. On his origins see Jordan, no. 29. His property belonged to Prouille, G, I, 2 and L, 70; G, I, 3 and L, 101. That the Raimunda Claret who appears in the list of foundresses was his sister is a likely conjecture.

58. Jordan, no. 29; G, II, 109, 120, 158, 159, 189 and L, 24, 26, 33, 38, 76, 77, 93. He must not be confused with another William Claret, who already in 1199 was a monk at Boulbonne—Balme, 263.

59. In 1217, he was a member of the Preaching of Toulouse. Laurent, no. 80. From the end of 1218, he was prior and procurator of Prouille—G, II, 160, 161, 46, 47, 163 (on 21st June, 1221, however, a charter gives the title of prior of Prouille to Fr Guiraud d'Esparros, who is not again mentioned elsewhere—L, 152); the last document he issued at Prouille is dated 4th September, 1224—G, II, 48. Bernard Gui claimed to have seen one dated 1229. The document may have disappeared; it may, however, be an error on the part of Gui, for no other mention of William is found in the numerous charters of Prouille after 1224. From then onwards the prior was Raimond Catalan—cf. charter of 9th

October, 1225, which enumerates the brethren of the Prouille preaching, without William— G, II, 51.

60. This word, derived from 'faide', private war, describes those men of the Midi, who, having refused to submit, took to flight and made war on the army of the Church; they were regarded as defenders of the heretics. Cf. Tudela, 232, n. 3.

61. Bernard Gui, in Martène, *Script.*, VI, 452 and in *MOPH*, XXII, 156 and n. 6. The motive given for his defection (that he could not accept the detachment involved in collective property in the order— Balme, 159, 526) does not hold water. Prouille, of which he was prior, had preserved all his property.

62. An echo of the 1224 crisis is found in Jordan, *Epistulae*, XVII and XXVIII. At the end of 1233, the Prouille sisters were expected at St Agnes of Bologna. In the summer of 1224, Jordan informed Bologna that they could no longer be expected, for reasons which he could not then explain.

63. *Supra*, n. 61.

64. *Proces. Thol.*, no. 4. Fr Guillaume, sacristan of Boulbonne. Perhaps he already had a brother in the monastery—the Fr B. Claret, who gave evidence immediately after him, no. 5. He was presented with a list of twenty-five paragraphs, a résumé of the saint's virtues, and asked if he was in agreement. He merely added a personal memory, very characteristic of a former procurator—Dominic distributed the tunics people gave him to the brethren.

65. G, II, 1; L, 25. The date of 8th August, 1207 has been corrected in accordance with the editor of Cernai, I, 43, n. 1. On the Gasc and the God, peasants of the place, G, II, 17, 44, 50, 51, 55, 79; 43, 46, 55; cf. Balme, I, 166–7.

66. G, II, 8. They 'entered the monastery' and made profession into the hands of St Dominic. The expression does not necessarily mean that they both became religious: they could quite well have lived as cultivators and *donati*. The former solution is, however, probable. In that case this Alazaïce should be identified with the one who appears in the first list at Prouille; Arnaud would have become a lay brother. He signs Prouille documents in 1212—G, II, 40, 76; Balme, I, 329 places his donation about this time.

67. He signed various Prouille charters in 1212, 1227, 1229, 1256—G, II, 39, 54, 56, 138. Cf. Balme, I, 326–329.

68. About 1227, G, II, 54 and 56.

69. He made a 'solemn vow' of obedience to the prior of Prouille, was to wear clerical dress, was to be 'lodged' by the community and would share in its spiritual benefits, but would not incur the obligation of its observances—G, II, 8–9.

70. G, II, 158; L, 23–24.

71. *Supra*, ch. VII, p. 106.

72. G, II, 159; L, 26–27.

73. G, II, 159–171. On these debates and the final victory of Prouille, see Guiraud, *Fondation*, 248–254.

74. This list has been preserved by the Prouille ms. (cf. *supra*, n. 6) and edited by Rechac, 197; Percin 6, no. 27 and Echard, I, 6, n. Q, who had a special copy sent to him. It is difficult to go back to the text of the ms.; the three editions mentioned do not agree (that of Rechac is the best). On the other hand the eleven (or twelve) names of list I are again found in list II of the nineteen nuns of 1211 given by a charter of Fulk (G, II, 109 and L, 29). It may well be wondered whether I has not been artificially composed from II. It should be noted that, in this case, the author of the ms. who identified the nine converted ladies of Fanjeaux with the Prouille foundresses, must have taken the first nine names of II. Now—firstly, there are 11 (or 12) names in I, which clearly presents a difficulty for the author of the ms; secondly, the order of I and II does not agree; thirdly, the form of the names is unmistakeably different in I and II it is better in II.

75. Canton of Capendu, on the Aude, a little before Carcassonne. The family of this nun was deeply involved with the party of the heretics—Vaissète, VII, 452 and cols. 339, 346, 347, 362, 365, 396.

76. Are Raimonde and Passerine two different names or a compound name? Since Passerine was a surname, the compound name is more probable.

77. We identify the Messande of the list (Manenta, Messana), with the Ermessenda of the 1211 charter.

78. No. 26. There is no reason to give a special meaning to the *dominae* found with *sorores* and *moniales* in the Prouille charters. It was a current term applied to nuns.

79. G, II, 158 and L, 24. The word *conversa* can have a meaning strictly concerned with religious life— e.g. lay-sister. Here in the expression *moniales conversae* it certainly signifies converted women in the literal meaning of the word—Mandonnet-Vicaire, I, 100.

80. *Proces. Thol.*, no. 23.

81. *Contra haereticos*, L, I, ch. 63. *PL*, 210, 366A—'Vel cathari dicuntur a cato, quia, ut dicitur, osculantur posteria catti, in cujus specie, ut dicunt, apparet eis Lucifer.' This was a popular belief among the Catholics. Alain de Lille was too intelligent to draw anything but a comic etymology from it.

82. Constantino, nos. 48–49; Bourbon, no. 27.

83. Prouille ms., cited by Percin 4, no. 17.

84. Constantino, *ibid.*, notes that they took the habit from the sisters of Prouille, who thus existed before they did.

85. The charter of 14th April, 1207, presupposes a recent, but already constituted monastery. Now in the preceding weeks, Dominic and his companions had been too much taken up with the Montréal disputation, to be able to occupy themselves with this. The foundation dates at least from March.

86. G, II, 158; l. 24. The charter of 19th March, 1209, used the same terms. It is, however, no longer significant, since this charter, for convenience, adopted the formulary of Bérenger's charter— G, II, 159; L, 26.

87. Prouille ms., cited by Percin, 4, no. 17.

88. This date, equally recorded by the Prouille ms., is given by Bernard Gui as an oral tradition of the monastery—Loenertz, 9.

89. In 1253, G, II, 60. In 1307, Prouille again received a piece of land situated near the old township—G, II, 84.

90. G, I, 265.

91. Huyghe, 72, 77, 81–82, 88.

92. Cf. *infra*, ch. XIII and n. 67; Appendix VIII, no. 3, 13, 14.

93. G, II, 58.

94. 18th August, 1248, G, I, 8. In 1256, 1257, 1258—G, I, 14, 16, 19.

95. *BOP*, I, 131, 134, 148, 150, 151, 153, 158, 159; Grundmann, 272–273, Bewegungen; Creytens, *Montargis*, 55.

96. Huyghe, 74–87.

97. Constitution *Periculoso*, *c. unic.*, *De Stat. Reg.*, III, 16 in VI.

98. G, II, 158; L, 24.

99. Jordan, no. 29.

100. On 2nd March, 1216, Noël is called prior—G, II, 189 and L, 76–77. Cf. L, 76, n. 1; similarly in 1218 (G, II, 44, 136 and L, 97, 99). From 26th November, 1218, however, William Claret bore the title of prior G, II, 160; L, 106. Meanwhile Fr Noël seems to have been drowned near Limoux—Bernard Gui, cited by Balme, I, 248.

101. Cf. preceding note. On 13th April, 1219 he styles himself prior and procurator—G, II, 161; L, III.

102. According to Gregory IX, who was himself informed by the sisters, in bull of 24th March, 1236—G, I, 7. Effect was given to this in a charter of 1230, G, II, 4. Before 1219, never more than two religious were mentioned (G, I, 136 and L, 107). In 1223, charters mention the prior, two or three canons and a number of brethren (G, II, 45, 46, 47); in 1225, six religious are mentioned, some of them brethren. The institution must date from 1218, on the occasion of the saint's last visit to Prouille.

103. Decree of 9th October, 1225—G, II, 51. On their rôle as advisers in 1258 see G, I, 256.

104. Cf. *supra*, n. 101. About 1225, there were three or four of them. In 1256, one can count 11—G, II, 9. These lay-brothers or sisters formed part of the order from its very institution—Mulhern, 89–93; Creytens, 'Les converses des moniales dominicaines au moyen âge', in *AFP*, XIX (1949), 7–16.

105. A late provision, dating from 1256—G, I, 256. On the lay-sisters of the Cistercian nuns, equally bound to stability, see Roisin, 367.

106. These lay persons, whom Mulhern, 90–92, incorrectly calls lay-brothers, are distinct from the lay brothers of the Preaching. Ten acts of donation at Prouille have been preserved, involving about twenty persons, prior to the final organization of the monastery under Humbert de Romans—G, II, 1, 2, 6, 8, 48, 53, 189. Several are no longer extant.

107. Serfs made a donation of themselves with their families in 1207 and 1224 (G, II, 1 and 48); clerks in 1241, 1247, 1256 (G, II, 6 and 8). The other donations are concerned with whole families.

108. In 1258 Humbert de Romans thus defined the *donati*: 'Donatos vero vocamus vel [1°] qui remanentes in seculo, sua dant domui in vita vel etiam post mortem, et domus obligat se eisdem ad aliquod subsidium temporale, vel [2] qui veniunt ad domum habitaturi in ea, obligant se ad castitatem vel ad fidelitatem servandam domui et serviendum eidem secundum quod eis injunctum fuerit, et domus obligat se ad providendum in necessariis, ita tamen quod si malae vitae fuerint notabiliter, domus eis amplius non teneatur et possit eos repellere, nec ipsi amplius, ex obligatione predicta, in aliquo teneantur', G, I, 256. The ten donations mentioned above fall into one or other of these categories.

109. Decrees of 1212 and 1230—G, II, 2 and 3–4. The words *hominium*, *commendare*, are used explicitly. It is a question of *donati* and nothing more, yet of *donati* who foresee the case in which eventually they might become a friar or nun of their convent.

110. In 1220, one lay-brother at Prouille, Pierre-Roger, was found to be secretly attending the Catharist meetings—Guiraud, *Inquisition*, 348.

111. The position of the peasants in Languedoc became worse between the eleventh and the thirteenth centuries. Free men in increasing numbers bound themselves to lords or to institutions in servile homage—Paul Ourliac, 'Les villages de la région toulousaine au XIIe siècle', in *Annales*, IV (1949), 268–277, especially 272–275.

112. Jordan, no. 35.

113. Cf. V. Berlière, *Les monastères doubles aux XIIe et XIIIe siècles* (*Mém. Lettres, Acad. Royale de Belgique, II, XVIII*) Brussels, 1924—St Hilpisch, *Die Doppelklöster*, Munster, 1928.

114. O. Decker, *Die Stellung des Predigerordens zu den Dominikanerinnen* (1207–1267), QF, 31, Vechta 1935; Grundmann, 208–252 and 274–303; Creytens, 41–43.

115. 'Proponens . . . aliquam inde pecuniam ad consummationem prefati monasterii feminarum secum assumere et reverti'—Jordan, no. 28.

116. Cf. *infra*, ch. IX, 151 and Appendix IV.

117. In February, he came to baptize de Montfort's infant daughter, probably at Montréal. Cf. *infra*, ch. IX, 289.

118. G, I, 52–53 and II, 109; Laurent, nos. 8 and 9 (15th May, 1211); Cernai, nos. 222–226 and 231, n. 5.

119. Despite the spurious character of the charter of concession of the sanctuary as such, we give documentary value to the facts of its narrative. Cf. *supra*, n. 45.

120. On 25th May, 1214, Fulk renounced the tithes and first-fruits of certain lands of Prouille situated in the tithe area of Fanjeaux—G, II, 76; L, 62. If he had not conferred upon the sisters the

tithes of the church of Prouille he would have had to multiply deeds of this sort in regard to the many properties of the sisters situated within the tithe district of Prouille. No trace of any is found.

121. Cf. the insistance of St Dominic, in the course of his negotiations.

122. G, I, 53; Laurent, no. 8. On this very fine demesne cf. Balme, I, 220–222.

123. G, II, 109; Laurent, no. 9. Bram had been conquered the previous year with much cruelty—Cernai, no. 142.

124. Cernai, no. 214.

125. G, II, 109; Laurent, no. 12. The deed seems to have been drawn up at Pamiers. One should clearly distinguish this person, doubtless originating from Villasavary (called *Vilarium* at the time—cf. Laurent, no. 63. It is useless to instance, as Laurent does, Villar-en-val, near Limoux, or a hypothetical Villar in the Ariège, as Balme does), from the cleric of Fanjeaux of the same name, later parish priest and notary, who finally donated himself to Prouille in 1247; he was one of the richest landowners of the township (Balme, II, 330). Cf. G, II, 6; Guiraud, *Fondation*, 238.

126. *Proces. Thol.*, no. 2.

127. G, II, 2–3, 35 and 74; Laurent, nos. 13–16, 19–20, 25.

128. G, II, 119; Laurent, no. 21. The confirmation to be read in G, I, 53 f. and II, 120; L, 24 and 41 are not authentic—e.g. Koudelka, 100 ff. On the two brothers and their lineage, see Vaisséte, 83–86.

129. G, I, 53; L, 48–49. Cf. also L, 65 and Jordan, no. 37.

130. Cf. *infra*, ch. IX.

131. G, II, 54, 75–6, 154, 110; L, 36–37, 40–43, 49, 57–58, 63–65. On these various persons, see Guiraud, *Fondation*, 243–248 and the erudite notes of the editor of Cernai, based on the tables.

132. The charters of these three persons are no longer extant, but their gifts were confirmed by the Pope on 8th October, 1215—L, 62. On Pierre de Vic, lord of Quercorbes see Laurent, nos. 68 and 86 and Balme, II, 32 n. a and 35–36; on Guy de Lévis, Maréchal of Montfort, ancestor of the Lévis-Mirepoix, see St Olive, *Archives du château de Léran*, I, 21–42.

133. 'Cuilibet, sive militi, sive rustico, licitum erit delegare in ellemosinam de hereditate propria usque ad quintam partem, ad consuetudinem et usum Francie circa Parisius', *Statuts de Pamiers*, ch. X—Mansi, XXII, 857.

134. Loenertz, *AFP*, 24 (1954), 37–47, has shown the lack of authenticity of Laurent, no. 58, which would despoil of its tithes, without compensation, the church of Fanjeaux in favour of Prouille. These tithes were only granted, with the church, in 1221—Laurent, no. 134. At the same time, Fulk certainly gave to Prouille tithes on Fanjeaux in 1214, for they are confirmed by the Pope in 1215—Laurent, no. 62; Jordan, no. 37.

135. Cf. *supra*, n. 128.

136. On 9th October, 1212 and 4th May, 1213—Laurent, nos. 30–33 and 42–45.

137. Laurent, nos. 23, 25, 29, 30, 32, 33, 35, 42, 43, 44, 45.

138. Nos. 8, 27, 28, 47, 48.

139. Nos. 23, 35.

140. Nos. 8, 31, 33, 34, 52, 53, according to the custom which encloses the house of regular life within the church; cf. *ecclesia = abbatia*, no. 33; *ecclesia = domus*, nos. 8, 52, 69.

141. Charter of Bérènger, G, II, 158; L, 24, Jordan, no. 27.

142. 'Nunc et in perpetuum'.

143. The rule of St Sixtus, cf. *infra*, Appendix VIII.

144. Balme, II, 431; Simon, 145.

145. Cf. Balme, II, 431, n. 3 and 4.

146. G, II, 109; L, 29.

147. Another Bérengère, Blanche, another Guillelmine, Françoise, Arnaude, Arsende, Experte. On Blanche, cf. Appendix IV.

148. Taeggio, *Chronica brevis*, anno 1206 in *ASOP*, V (1901–1902), 85; Mamachi, 158, no. 30. Cf. Rechac, 197.

149. Grundmann, 203–208; Huyghe, 65–67 and 74–87.

150. In 1213, Dominic was vicar-general of the Cistercian bishop, Guy de Carcassonne. At this period he was seen to preach in the company of Cistercian abbots or lay brothers (Balme, I, 471; Frachet, 76; Constantin, no. 55). Cf. Mandonnet-Vicaire, I, 107, n. 46.

151. The Cistercian nuns had no special rule; they followed the rule and customs of the men's order, completed by the statutes of the general chapters. They had their own general chapter at the nuns' abbey of Tart.

152. Canives, I, 405; Grundmann, 204; Mandonnet-Vicaire, I, 107, n. 46. The formal interdictions of 1228 did not, however, prevent these incorporations from multiplying—Roisin, 342–361.

153. *Infra*, Appendix VIII, no. 8–11 and 14.

154. Benoit de Montefiascone, quoted by Richard, I, 83.

155. This rule, contained in a bull of Gregory IX of 1232, is edited by Balme, II, 425–453 and Simon, 142–153. It will be studied in Appendix VIII.

156. Appendix VIII, nos. 3 and 13.

157. G, I, 7.

158. Appendix VIII, no. 14.

159. If this rule actually existed, it would not be impossible for Dominic to have used texts of Prémontré to compose it. The *consuetudines arctiores* of Prémontré suited these converted Catharist ladies. Copied in part, moreover, from the Cistericon customs, they preserved the earlier observance of the sisters of Prouille. Thus composed, in short, they were later able to be adapted without difficulty,

to the customs of the Friars Preachers, in turn composed with the help of the Prémontré texts. Cf. Appendix VIII, nos. 11 and 14. One would also like to bring in the fact that Prémontré from the beginning had double convents similar to what Prouille would be after the institution of the Preachers. The feminine communities, however, had been separated since 1140, and then condemned to extinction in 1198—Erens, 6–10. Thus the rule of St Sixtus borrowed nothing from the rule of the sisters of the first statutes of Prémontré (ed. Van Waelfelghem, in *Analectes de Prémontré*, Louvain, 1913, 63–67).

160. Balme, II, 450, n. 1. The information refers in its final phrase to a provision of the rule of St Sixtus, which itself came from St Benedict.

161. G, I, 2; L, 70–71. It will be noted that gifts made by the native inhabitants are not as a rule mentioned in this document.

162. G, I, 3–5; L, 100–104.

163. G, I, 7.

164. Jordan, no. 27. The test is of 1234.

165. G, I, 8.

166. G, I, 13.

167. G, I, 8.

168. G, I, 19.

169. Creytens, 58–64. Humbert de Romans received the order from the Pope to elaborate these new constitutions in August 1257. They were brought to completion the following year—*ibid.*, 59, n. 68.

170. No. 27.

171. Humbert, no. 19; but already certain manuscripts of Ferrand, no. 16. It was Humbert who gave the order in 1257 to substitute the name of Dominic for that of Diego in the legends—*Acta*, I, 98.

172. 'Quod a nobis aedificatum fuit et constructum', December 1230, G, II, 78; cf. I, 6 and 15.

173. Jordan, no. 28.

174. *Proces. Thol.*, no. 3.

175. Jordan, no. 37.

176. Kirsch, 123–124.

177. Ferrand, nos. 22–23.

178. *Proces. Thol.*, nos. 15, 16, 17.

179. Ferrand, no. 21; Cecilia, ch. I.

180. Laurent, no. 67.

181. Jordan, no. 92: '*quoniam hoc genus illecebrosum est nimis et efficax illaqueandis animabus . . .*'

182. *Ibid.*

183. Jordan, no. 28. Jordan's chronology is too long. He mentions two full years spent by Diego in the Narbonensis; it was scarcely more than a year—Cernai, nos. 48–50 enables the dates to be corrected.

184. Cf. *supra*, ch. VII p. 114.

185. That Dominic accompanied Diego is a supposition. The fact that a large number of preachers had come together for this disputation makes his presence probable. His future friendship for Arnaud de Crampagna confirms it.

186. Cernai states clearly—'Dum igitur recederet, tendens in Hispaniam, venit apud Apamiam', no. 48.

187. Jordan, no. 23, mentions frequent disputes, in particular at Pamiers. It was on the occasion of one of these encounters that Dominic must have found William Claret.

188. 1200–1212. He had received a mandate, in May 1207, for the correction of Bérenger de Narbonne—Potthast, no. 3113; Villemagne, 103–104. After 1208, associated with Fulk, he acted energetically for the crusade against the heretics. He had doubtless wholly succeeded Raoul from the summer of 1207 onwards.

189. Cernai, no. 48.

190. The abbot of the canons on whom Pamiers depended—Cernai, no. 116 and n. 1; Vaissète, IV, 430.

191. To whom Pamiers had been entrusted in April, cf. *supra*, 108 and n. 101.

192. Cernai, no. 198 and n. 3.

193. In 1198, Vaissète, V, 1616; Guiraud, *Inquisition*, 311. On the 'paréage', i.e. association and sharing of revenues between an ecclesiastic and a lord in the Toulouse region, see Vaissète VII, 152 and 212.

194. Cernai, no. 48 and n. 3 and 4; no. 198.

195. Cf. J. Lahondès, cited by Cernai's editor, no. 199, n. 4. It was the mother of Sicard and of Pierre de la Ilhe, knights of Fanjeaux, and 'faidits', who is mentioned in several charters of Prouille, in 1226—G, II, 52, and in 1227—G, II, 55. Sicard was most probably the author of the massacre to which we refer Cernai, no. 199, n. 5.

196. Cernai, no. 48.

197. Cernai, no. 48 mentions only them; Puylaurens, however, ch. VIII, who insists that the Waldenses were also concerned, likewise mentions 'the other heretics', the Catharists.

198. Cernai, no. 48.

199. Puylaurens, ch. VIII.

200. I Cor. XV, 34.

201. On Arnaud de C, cf. Cernai, no. 48 and n. 1; Puylaurens, ch. VIII; Vaissète, VIII, 578, 798, 876, 1142 (he figures in several documents relating to Pamiers from 1209).

202. Cernai, no. 48.

203. He later acted as a collaborator of the Inquisition—Douais, *Documents*, I, CXXXVI and CLII.

204. He signed an agreement between Fulk and Dominic on 17th April, 1221—Laurent no. 134.
205. *Proces. Thol.*, no. 7. He was then sacristan of St Antonin.
206. As Cernai notes, no. 4—'praecipue pauperes'.
207. Puylaurens, ch. VIII.
208. Cf. *supra*, 84 and n. 33–36.
209. Pierron, 22–117; Grundmann, 100–117.
210. Grundmann, 118–127, correcting Pierron 117–160. It is a question of the poor men of Lyons, not of Lombardy. The Pope only approved a *propositum conversationis*, not an order.
211. Bernard Prim held a disputation about 1208 against Isarn de Castres at Laurac-le-Grand—Pierron, 172.
212. 'Fuerunt et alii heretici convicti etiam inimicorum judicio evidenter'—Puylaurens, ch. VIII.
213. Cernai, no. 116, n. 2.
214. Puylaurens, ch. VIII who cites this trait as a proof of the weakening of the Catharist believers.
215. Laurent, nos. 5, 7, 24.
216. On the formula in the High Middle Ages, cf. Mandonnet-Vicaire-Ladner, II, 57; as used by Innocent III, *ibid.*, I, 119–121; it will be found again on the occasion of the foundation of the Preachers in Toulouse—Laurent, no. 60 and in the canon of the Lateran on preaching (X)—Hefele-Leclercq, V, 1340; Frachet, 102. Cf. *supra*, ch. VII, n. 92.
217. The departure from Prouille occurring about August (time of the first Cistercian defections, cf. *supra*, 127, n. 140 and 143), the departure from Pamiers must be placed about September 1207—cf. Cernai, no. 48, n. 2; Loperraez, I, 193, places Diego's arrival in Osma in October.
218. 'In senectuta bona', says Cernai, no. 49.
219. 'Dum redire disponeret', *ibid*.
220. Cf. Vicaire, 1207, 343–345, where this date is carefully authenticated. Indications about the tomb and relics of Diego will also be found there.
221. On 14th January, 1208—Cernai, no. 55, n. 1, based on Cassan's necrology. Cf. Vaissète, V, 36.
222. 'Vir mitissimus ac disertus'—Robert d'Auxerre, *MG*, *SS*, XXVI, 271. 'Vir magnus et magnifice extollendus'; 'vir Deo plenus'—Cernai, nos. 20, 21. 'Vir venerabilis vitae . . . quem sacrarum litterarum notitia et secundum saeculum natalis ingenii, magis autem morum insignis decorabat honestas' —Jordan, no. 4. 'Electus pugil'—Puylaurens, ch. VIII.

NOTES TO CHAPTER IX

1. Sources for the history of the Albigensian crusade in Cernai, Tudela and Puylaurens, the first two of whom have formed the subject of remarkable editions. The history will be found in Vaissète, VI, 261–518 (fundamental), Luchaire (classic, but brief), Villey, 217–226, Belperron (*La croisade contre les Albigeois et l'union du Languedoc à la France*, Paris, 1942) shows a reaction against the errors propagated by a certain popular literature, Girou (a popular account). The following pages, directly based on the sources mentioned, recall facts commonly admitted; no critical justification is given except for facts which are disputed or less well known.
2. Cernai, no. 67.
3. Cernai, no. 72, 103 and 128.
4. Cernai, no. 313 and Vaissète, VI, 285.
5. Tudela, 77 and 83.
6. By water, along the Rhône and the coastal lagoons of the Mediterranean and perhaps of the lower Aude—Tudela, 39 and n. 4.
7. Cernai, nos. 89–90, Tudela, 55–62 and the official report of the Pope's legates—*PL*, 216, 139c, are in agreement in their explanation of the taking and destruction of the town in this way. (A similar case was to occur at the siege of Saint Antonin—Cernai, no. 315). The barons, clergy and laity, however, were clearly determined to make an example by giving no quarter to the towns which resisted them—Tudela, 57.
8. He had taken the cross in February 1213 and was to set out on 21st April, 1213. He was, however, hindered from so doing and arrived only in April 1215, to return again in June, after having peacefully journeyed across the country—Cernai, no. 417, 421, 550, 563–565.
9. From the beginning of his reign, Innocent III had prescribed this rule for the temporal authorities of the Midi: 'ut . . . bona hereticorum confiscent et de terra sua proscribant', Letter to the prelates of the Midi of 21st April, 1198—Potthast, no. 95; *PL*, 214, 82D.
10. The crusaders judged and burnt in accordance with a custom of the north (Brayna = Braine or Brienne?), Tudela, 79 and n. 5.
11. First stakes at Castres—Cernai, no. 113; 140 Perfect burnt at Minerva, no. 156; 300 (Puylaurens, ch. XVII) at Lavaur, no. 227; 60 at Cassès, no. 233, etc.
12. As they did at Moissac, 'avidissime'—Cernai, no. 353, where 300 had their throats cut—Tudela, 277.
13. Tudela, 27.
14. Cernai, nos. 77–78. Acts in *PL*, 216, 89 to 98.
15. Diplomatic documents in Molinier and Rhein; portraits in Cernai, nos. 101–107, 180, 253, 258, 357, etc; Tudela 86 and nn. 1 to 88. Life in Girou.
16. He had heretics burnt, traitors dragged at the tail of a horse and hanged, once he even had prisoners mutilated (Cernai, nos. 135, 142, 227, 337); but it was a question of customary penalties or atrocious reprisals (nos. 125–127). These military brutalities had not the sadistic character of the

cruelties of his adversaries, Raymond-Roger de Foix, Raymond de Termes, Bernard de Cazenac and his wife Elise de Turenne, not to mention the others, nos. 173, 361, 530, 582, 606—Puylaurens, ch. XIX.

17. This word derived from 'faide', private war, indicates those men of the Midi who, having refused to submit, took to flight and made war on the army of the Church; they were considered as defenders of the heretics. Cf. Tudela, 232, n. 3.

18. The Count of Nevers, the Duke of Burgundy and the Count of St Paul . . .—Cernai, no. 101; Tudela, 85.

19. At the beginning of 1213, he tried to stop the conquest. In 1214, he reserved the attribution of the conquered territory to the council. In 1215 he reserved a part of the inheritance to the descendants of Raymond VI, Cf. Luchaire, 193 to 260.

20. E.g. Cernai, no. 253, 270, 450, 462, etc.

21. Cernai, no. 458.

22. Cernai, nos. 226, 351, 526 and Tudela, 254, n. 1.

23. Cernai, no. 462.

24. Texts collected in Cernai, III, xxxiii and n. 1 and 2; Tudela, 115, 129, 141, 163, etc.

25. Alice de Montmorency (appreciation in Cernai, no. 107), Guy de Montfort, Matthieu II de Montmorency, Bouchard de Marly, and the young Amaury de Montfort and Guy de Bigorre, the two eldest of a large family, among whom was the famous Simon of Leicester, born at the very beginning of the crusade.

26. Cf. *infra*, 149.

27. At Mirepoix. The Montfort established themselves at Castres.

28. Cernai, nos. 125, 264, 305, 488 and nn. 1, 544.

29. Jordan, nos. 31 and 34; Cernai, no. 51; Puylaurens, ch. X.

30. Jordan, no. 29.

31. Laurent, no. 7. Did he afterwards remain at Limoux, to administer the property and act as parish priest (Scheeben, 98)? It is certain that his name crops up chiefly in connection with the Limoux charters—Laurent, no. 5, 7, 80, 89. None of the estates that Claret administered, however, caused the trouble that the Limoux property did. Moreover charters nos. 12 and 66 show that he was at Pamiers and Prouille in 1211 and 1216.

32. Laurent, no. 5.

33. Raymond VI having demanded a new legate from the Pope, Innocent granted him for his reconciliation, his notary, Maître Milon, to whom he gave instructions on 1st March, 1209—Potthast, no. 3683; Cernai, no. 69.

34. Cernai, no. 110 and Tudela, 85, assert that Fanjeaux was emptied of its knights and inhabitants—'neither grown person nor little child had remained there'. The township belonged concurrently to the Count of Foix and to Dame Cavaers. The former was never able to recover Fanjeaux, despite his attempts, cf. *infra*, n. 43. Dame Cavaers, whose name does not appear in the later Fanjeaux documents, had to take refuge in the county of Foix, most probably with her relatives in Castelverdun. Her daughter, Cavaers the younger, did not appear again in Fanjeaux until February 1224, on the morrow of the final departure of the French. She was then closely linked with the Catharists—Guiraud, *Cartulaire*, II, 47; Balme, I, 139–141, n. 2.

35. They were damaged, since it was necessary to put them into a state of defence again, cf. following note. There was, however, no burning of Fanjeaux, whatever a deposition of 1246 may state—Balme, I, 173 and 183, n. 2.

36. Cernai, no. 110 and Tudela, 85. This vassal was still with de Montfort on 30th July, 1210; he signed one of his donations at Béziers on that day—Vaissète, VIII, 601; date corrected by Rhein, no. 90.

37. The deed is lost, but the donation is confirmed by the Pope in the bull of 8th October, 1215—Laurent, no. 62. It was made simultaneously in the name of Peter and of his brother.

38. Cernai, no. 110. It was the Duke of Burgundy who advised de Montfort to go and occupy the township without delay and not to leave it in the hands of the Aragonese. Fanjeaux must not be confused (as Girou does, following others) with the castle of Fanjau in Largentière (Ardèche) which Raymond VI gave back to the Church as a pledge at Valencia in June—Cernai, no. 75; Tudela, 32, n. 2; Mansi, XXII, 770C.

39. At Alzonne (cf. the donation at Prouille), which Montfort had occupied the day before—Cernai, no. 110.

40. Numerous deeds make us acquainted with the crusaders to whom Simon enfeoffed the townships and the neighbouring castles; there is nothing similar in connection with Fanjeaux. This is clearly because he had reserved it for himself.

41. In the direction of Castres, Cabaret, Mirepoix and Pamiers, Lombers and Albi, Limoux-Cernai, nos. 112, 114–119.

42. He kept Castres, the key of the Albigeois, which he was to entrust to his brother Guy; he installed Lambert de Thury close to Limoux; he gave Mirepoix to Guy de Lévis and, later, Saissac to his cousin, Bouchard de Marly; Laurac and Castelnaudary to Hugues de Lascy; Montréal and Bram to Alain de Roucy. He reinstalled the abbot of Saint Antonin in Pamiers.

43. Cernai, no. 134.

44. Cernai, nos. 135–136.

45. Cernai, no. 136.

46. 5 miles to the north-east—Cernai, no. 142.

47. 5 miles to the south of Fanjeaux—Cernai, nos. 148–150.

48. Cernai, no. 252; Tudela, 209–215.

49. Cernai, no. 258.

50. Cernai, nos. 266, 269–270; Tudela, 127; Puylaurens, ch. XVIII.

51. At Saint-Martin-la-lande, between Bram and Castelnaudary, Cernai, nos. 264–276; Tudela, 217–227.

52. Cernai, no. 284. The people in question were Simon and Geoffroy de Neauphle. The latter was killed and Simon de Montfort made a foundation at Prouille for his soul on 1st December, 1212—Laurent, no. 34.

53. Cernai, no. 423, n. 1; Rhein, nos. 113–114; Laurent, nos. 47 and 49.

54. Cernai, no. 449. No document justifies the supposition that Dominic was then at Muret or accompanied Montfort, for a text of Bernard Gui, which is merely a text of Cernai in which Dominic's name has been interpolated, cannot be called a document. Cf. Meersseman, 'Les milices de Jésus-Christ' in *AFP*, 33 (1953), 306, n. 57.

55. Jordan, no. 37. The 'nostre car frayre Domenge' of the Laurent charter, no. 82, is perhaps only a stylistic formula.

56. *Chronica IIa, MOPH*, I, 322. Cf. Bourbon, no. 288. On Pétronille, see *infra*, n. 58. Other relations with the Montfort are indicated in Balme, I, 444–447, and II, 42–43; Salagnac, I, no. 9.

57. Laurent, nos. 8, 27, 34, 41, 47, 49, 59 (taken from Jordan, no. 37), 69, 82, 144. On the Casseneuil gift, mentioned by Jordan (no. 37), cf. *infra*, n. 247.

58. *Chronica IIa, MOPH*, I, 322. It was Pétronille the younger, later religious and prioress in the monastery of the Cistercian nuns of Saint Antoine in Paris, who was born in February 1211—Balme, I, 239–240, and Cernai, 257, n. 4. Her godfather was Guillaume Cat, knight of Montréal—Cernai, no. 266. This and the fact that three months later she was put out to nurse at Montréal, seems to indicate that she was baptized there.

59. *Chronica IIa, MOPH*, I, 322; Cernai, no. 511 and n. 1. Fulk was also there—Rhein, no. 122. It should be noted, however, that at this time Dominic held the place of the Bishop of Carcassonne—Constantin, no. 55. It was most probably on this occasion that the crusaders Hugues de Lascy, sire of Laurac and Castelnaudary, and Alain de Roucy, sire of Montréal and Bram, made gifts of importance to Prouille.

60. *Proces. Bon.*, no. 26.

61. During the Lent of 1213, Dominic discussed with Fr Stephen of Metz and a Cistercian lay-brother, in the bishop's palace at Carcassonne, Montfort's very critical situation. Dominic roused the courage of the others—Constantin, no. 55.

62. Jordan, no. 46.

63. *Ibid*.

64. By suppressing, for instance, the egalitarianism of succession which was ruining the feudal power. The sworn peace of Provence, thanks to him, was continuously kept from 1209 to 1215—Cernai, nos. 27 and 487, and n. 4.

65. Puylaurens, ch. XXVIII.

66. Cf. *supra*, 144 ff. Puylaurens, however, whose judgement is balanced, does not extend to Montfort the reproach of cupidity which he makes against the French—ch. XXV and XXVIII.

67. Constantin, no. 51 and Salagnac, II, 3. The first belongs to a series of tales which the author received from Toulouse before 1247, several of which perceptibly embellish various statements in the Toulouse process. An historical basis can, however, be found in them—the conversion in 1236, after twenty-two years, of the Perfect Raymond de Gros. Guillaume Pelisson who relates this in detail in his *chronicon* (ed. by C. Molinier, *De fratre Guillelmo Pelisso*, Annecy, 1880, 42–43) seems curiously unaware of certain details in Constantin. Altaner, 67, thinks they are embellishments. Scheeben, 95–96, is even more severe. It was on this anecdote that reliance was placed for classing Dominic as the first inquisitor until the time of Echard (I, 11, n. Y). In this connection, on the quarrel between Manrique and the Preachers, see *ASS, Aug.* I, 414–418. Cf. also Mortier, I, 665–666.

68. This was a summary action against the heretics, such as the crusaders embarked upon when they installed themselves in conquered localities. This can be seen from the fact that Dominic was able to save an unrepentant condemned person, which would have been impossible in the course of regular procedure. Certain laymen did not even want the converted to be spared *in extremis* (Cernai, nos. 113 and 154). According to law, a guilty party, even if repentant, must suffer his penalty. The setting free of a repentant party was a favour (cf. Cernai, no. 156). Dominic here played the rôle of Guy des Vaux-Cernai after the taking of Minerva, or of Robert de Courson at Morlhon—Cernai, nos. 155–156 and 513.

69. There is a great distance between actions such as these and the future Inquisition, for there is in them neither the systematic seeking out of heretics, which properly constitutes the *inquisitio*, nor its continuity. Puylaurens, ch. XXV and XXVIII, reproaches the French for quickly losing their interest in repression. Finally, Dominic, in addition, had no jurisdiction. Not having, and not wishing to have, any spiritual authority of his own, as will be seen, he could not be a judge of the faith, except by delegation from a legate or a bishop, cf. *infra*, nn. 206 and 219.

70. The two stages, conviction and exhortation to conversion, formed part of the procedure *contra haereticos* (cf. *supra*, ch. VI, 85 ff, nn. 38 to 41). Dominic practised it in 1206–1207. At that time it lacked the sanction of the secular arm.

71. He is thought to have joined the Preachers. Perhaps this is an erroneous interpretation of Constantin, from the fact that Raymond was received at the convent after his conversion; cf. Pelisson, *loc. cit.* 43, who would not have failed, it would seem, to mention his entering the order. On the heretical activity of this personage, cf. Balme, I, 492–496.

72. Salagnac, II, 3. Cf. Foncaude, 755C: 'Nec voce predicationis, nec baculo discipline, seu

severitatis'. The Castilian proverb (expressed, moreover, in the speech of Languedoc) authenticates the speech (cf. Altaner, 246), the date of which, on the other hand, is anachronistic. Salignac, in fact, situates it on 15th August, 1217. It was in 1209, not in 1217, that one could use the future tense of the coming of the crusaders. Accordingly Scheeben, 439, n. 236, emphatically rejects the anecdote. It is possible, indeed, that Salagnac, who wrote after 1278, attributed to Dominic the speech of Bérenger de Carcassonne in 1206 or 1207; cf. *supra*, ch. VI, 93–97 and n. 109. This is not the only error in this text, which states that Simon de Montfort was then dead and Louis de France a crusader, both of which statements are incorrect.

73. *Supra*, ch. VI, 93–96 and n. 109.

74. *Supra*, ch. VI, 91–96 and n. 117.

75. Jordan, no. 33. He had just convicted his Catharist opponents of manifest error. The nobles then set themselves to defend them in their own fashion. Scheeben, 439, n. 236, places this sermon in Toulouse, but through a mistaken interpretation of Barthélémy, no. 5.

76. *Supra*, ch. VI, 85 and n. 38 to 41. Among the finest apostrophes of this kind, may be instanced the letter of Innocent III to Raymond VI, on 29th May, 1207—'Your flesh is not of bronze and you are not of a different nature from those who are suddenly stricken with fever, struck down by leprosy, made stiff by paralysis, thrown to the ground by demons or scourged by incurable diseases, to say nothing of the other misfortunes which fall unexpectedly upon men, etc. . . .', *PL*, 215, 1166C.

77. Account in Cernai, no. 175, n. 3.

78. The archdeacon, Guillaume of Paris, Guy des Vaux-de-Cernai, Fulk of Toulouse, Jacques de Vitry, the canon, Guy of Prémontré, preached the crusade in turn in France and in Teutonia. On their preaching mission and the way in which they received it, see Cernai, no. 285 and 439. Much preaching was also done in the army itself—for examples, see Cernai, no. 298, 324, 342; Tudela, 201, etc. In regard to this last example, the editor, *ibid.*, n. 2, thinks that Dominic was among those preachers who encouraged detestation of heresy among the crusaders on the occasion of the first siege of Toulouse; it is true that he was there (Laurent, no. 10), but that is all that can be said.

79. Echard, I, 56B; Scheeben, 96–98 have rightly emphasized this position.

80. Four local witnesses emphasize his indefatigable attachment to the *negotium fidei et pacis*—*Proces. Thol.* no. 3, 7, 13, 18.

81. Bull of 10th March, 1208—Potthast, 3323; Cernai, no. 61; *PL*, 215, 1356B. For Avignon, Mansi XXII, 785BC.

82. Cf. *supra*, ch. VI, 91-end; VII, 99 ff; VIII, 115–119.

83. For these three places, Balme, I, 173 and 187.

84. *Supra*, ch. VI, n. 114; Laurent, nos. 8–9.

85. *Supra*, ch. VI, n. 118–119.

86. Cf. Appendix IV.

87. *Supra*, ch. VIII, 132 ff. Laurent, no. 12 and the depositions of the canons of St Antonin de Pamiers, *Proces. Thol.*, nos. 6–8.

88. Cf. *Proces. Thol.*, nos. 3–5. The abbey of Boulbonne was then on its original site, 2 miles south of Mazères (canton of Saverdun, Ariège), Cernai, no. 284, n. 2.

89. Frachet, II, 4.

90. *Proces. Thol.*, no. 17.

91. Balme, I, 173.

92. Salagnac, I, 9. Constant, 86–312, has endeavoured to gather together even down to the smallest details the local traditions of the Midi of France relating to the presence and ministry of Dominic. There is little for history to retain from this medley.

93. Threads of the woof. Cf. 'La Curne de Sainte Palaye', *Dictionnaire hist. de l'ancien langage françois*, Niort, n.d., III, 208, n. 6.

94. Balme, I, 171–173, 186–188, 271–272, 468–469, 470–471.

95. Reconciliations in the Lauragais are instanced forty years later before the Inquisition—Balme, I, 170–173; Act of reconciliation at Tréville, to the north of Castelnaudary, *ibid.*, 186–189. It seems that Dominic continued his 1207 apostolate around Prouille in 1208 and the beginning of 1209. The remark quoted by Constantin, no. 62, must in fact be referred back before the crusade—that Dominic stayed for a longer time in the diocese and city of Carcassonne than in the diocese and city of Toulouse, because 'in the diocese of Toulouse he found many people to honour him, whereas at Carcassonne everyone opposed him'. After 15th August, 1209, the population of Carcassonne was radically renewed and the heretics clearly did not return.

96. Cf. Appendix IV.

97. Cernai, no. 162.

98. Tudela, 109, after March.

99. Cf. *supra*, n. 81.

100. Tudela, 111 and n. 3. The Abbot of Cîteaux collaborated: he even went into Agen and its surrounding region.

101. Puylaurens, ch. XV and XVIIa and Tudela, 112, n. 2 and 113. Meersseman, 'Les milices de Jésus-Christ', *AFP*, 23 (1953), 289–293. This confraternity had no connection with the Militia of the faith of Jesus Christ, a military order founded at Carcassonne after Simon's death. No document relates it in any way with St Dominic.

102. Balme, 171–172. There can well have been a certain time between the two acts in one or other of the texts mentioned.

103. *Proces. Thol.*, no. 17.

104. *Proces. Thol.*, no. 15 and 16.

105. Tudela, 144, n. 3.

106. Cernai, no. 221 and n. 3.

107. Cernai, no. 234.

108. Cf. *supra*, n. 58.

109. Laurent, nos. 8–10. Charters 8 and 9 do not expressly indicate Dominic's presence at Lavaur. The way, however, in which these donations are presented at Prouille leaves no doubt as to the fact.

110. Frachet, II, 3. The episode could doubtless be assigned to the occasion of the second siege of Toulouse, in October, 1217. Dominic, however, was in the process of preparing to leave the country and almost certainly Toulouse. We know, on the other hand, that he was present at the first siege in June, 1211. The chapel of St Antoine was outside the walls near the castle of Narbonne—Balme, I, 255, n. 1.

111. He had doubtless realized this on the occasion of the baptism of Pétronille de Montfort.

112. Laurent, charters 13–54, end of 1211–25th May, 1214. Charters 23, 25, 30, 42, 54, indicate his certain presence in Prouille or in Fanjeaux, the remaining ones a very probable presence, especially during the whole of the year 1212, the months of April and May 1213 and the first six months of 1214—with, however, a probable presence at Pamiers (December 1211) in the Agen district (17th July or 5th July, 1212), Pamiers (1st December, 1212), Carcassonne (first six months of 1213, cf. *infra*), finally Toulouse, after 25th March, 1215.

113. Cf. Laurent, nos. 41, 47 and 49 and Constantin, no. 55. The Lent referred to in the latter text, after that of 1212 (when Guy was not yet bishop) and prior to 12th September, 1213 (date of the death of Pedro II), can only be that of 1213.

114. In February 1213, Cernai, no. 418. He was in Paris on 3rd March.

115. 'Vices episcopi . . . in spiritualibus exercebat'—Constantin, no. 55. At this time, when the institution of the vicar-general was still quite recent, the office was that of a temporary and limited substitution for the bishop, without judiciary power—E. Fournier, *Les origines du vicaire général*, Paris, 1922. Since Guy only returned in 1214, there is no reason to suppose that he relieved Dominic of his functions before that date. The text sets out in detail the emphasis on preaching, on Lent, on observance, lodging in the bishop's residence. On the site of the bishop's palace, see Cernai, no. 563, n. 3.

116. Laurent, no. 54. Cf. du Cange, sub. h. v.; *Proces. Thol.*, no. 19; Laurent, no. 134.

117. 'Habebat . . . ecclesiam Fani Jovis'—Jordan, no. 37.

118. Percin 4, no. 18; Kirsch, 117–118; Constant, 143–145; Bonhomme, *Montréal, Fanjeaux, Prouille, guide du pèlerin*, Toulouse 1934, 31–32.

119. Laurent, no. 2.

120. Jordan, no. 21. Scheeben, 93 has misread the text otherwise he would not have had to refute it.

121. Laurent, nos. 6, 12, 23, 25, etc. Others omit the *Dominus*, nos. 22, 29, etc.

122. Balme, I, 172, 173, 271, 272, 468—statements before the Inquisition of converted persons.

123. Laurent, no. 5, 7, 10, 24.

124. Laurent, no. 10. Whence the complete title he gives himself in the letter of penance of Pons Roger—*frater Dominicus, oxomensis canonicus, predicatorum minimus*, Balme, I, 187.

125. *Proces. Bon.*, no. 28; *Proces. Thol.*, nos. 3 and 18; Constantin, 62. Three witnesses, of whom one was at the time archdeacon of Toulouse, speak with accuracy and detail of the election to the bishopric of Couserans. John of Spain speaks of two or three elections and gives details: in Béziers and Comminges. For the second name, however, it is probable that he confuses *Convenarum* with *Conseranum*—cf. also note following.

126. *Proces. Thol.*, no. 3. It was thus the former bishop of Comminges, a see vacant at this time, who was offering Couserans. The confusion of Juan de Navarra is not difficult to understand. The exact date of the death or retirement of Navarre de Couserans, the bishop and legate whom it was a question of replacing, is not known.

127. After the death of the bishops Pierre d'Aigrefeuille (6th July, 1212), Bertrand de S. Gervais (13th January, 1215), or Raimond Niger (20th April, 1215). On the occasion of the first vacancy (it is noted that it lasted six months!), Guillaume, archdeacon of Paris, had been elected; he, too, however, had obstinately refused—Cernai, no. 366 and n. 3.

128. *Proces. Thol.*, no. 18.

129. No. 3.

130. No. 5; Constantin, no. 62.

131. Cf. *supra*, ch. VI, 88 and n. 60.

132. Prologue to the 10 canon on the institution of diocesan preachers—'Cum saepe contigat quod episcopi propter occupationes multiplices, vel invaletudines corporales, aut hostiles incursus, seu occasiones alias (ne dicamus defectum scientiae, quod in eis est reprobandum omnino, nec de cetero tolerandum), per se ipsos non sufficiunt ministrare populo verbum Dei, maxime per amplas dioeceses et diffusas . . .'—Hefele-Leclercq, V, 1340.

133. 'Erant autem tunc temporis in exercitu Uticensis et Tolosanus episcopi et etiam episcopus Carcassonne, Guido, qui nunquam ab exercitu recedebat'.—Cernai, no. 317. This was somewhat the case with the bishops of Osma, Diego's predecessors.

134. Vaissète, VI, 458–459 and 477–481; Luchaire, 259–260.

135. *Supra*, ch. VI, n. 61.

136. Fr Rodolfo, Procurator of the convent of Bologna—*Proces. Bon.*, no. 32.

137. *I. Const.*, II, 31, § 3.

138. This paragraph of the institutions of 1220 is explicitly attributed to the saint. It is possible that

the final words were added to the text about 1233, to permit the judicial activity of the inquisitors which was taking shape at the time. Dominic, however, was not averse to this.

139. It is remarkable that all those who instance Dominic's zeal in proceeding against heretics explicitly attribute to him as sole weapons preaching and controversy or disputation—*Proces. Bon.*, no. 27; *Thol.*, nos. 7, 13, 18, to quote only witnesses of his activity in the Midi.

140. *Matth.* V, 15. Ferrand, nos. 22–23.

141. *Proces. Thol.*, no. 4; Frachet II, 13. His apostolate with Guy des Vaux-de-Cernai, Fulk the Abbot of Villelongue, Aimery de Grandselve, all four of them Cistercians, should also be recalled. To the end of 1207, he continued to be Diego's *socius*—Cernai, no. 21.

142. Luke X, 1.

143. *Proces. Thol.*, no. 25, seal of 1215, Balme, II, 115; Frachet, 34, 36, 120–121. The staff which has been preserved at Bologna as a relic of the saint is of this kind—Balme, III, 455–456. He is seen with one of this type in a miniature of the pamphlet *Quomodo S. Patriarcha Dominicus orabat*, Cod. Rossianus, 3, fo. 13, ro. *ASOP*, XV (1922), 95*. Mark VI, 8 authorizes the staff which Matt. X, 10 forbids.

144. Frachet, II, 25, states that it was a knife of no value (vilis)—a ms. corrects: 'Quem raro portavit'. The saint himself, however, spoke of 'his' knife—Humbert, *Reg.*, II, 46. The Discalced Carmelites of the Via Palazzuolo of Florence show pilgrims a knife of St Dominic, with a handle of yellow boxwood, and a blunted blade.

145. According to John of Spain—*Proces. Bon.*, no. 29, cf. Frachet, IV, 1. Frachet, II, 4. It will be recalled that the Catharist preachers carried the Gospel about with them in a little bag—*supra*, p. 111. Frachet's latter account clearly indicates that Dominic had neither bag nor satchel for his books.

146. *Proces. Thol.*, no. 18; cf. no. 4. Matt. X, 10 and parallels.

147. *Proces. Thol.*, no. 18.

148. *Proces. Thol.*, no. 14. Constantin, no. 32, details of which account are embellished.

149. *Proces. Bon.*, no. 28.

150. Puylaurens, ch. VIII; Frachet, II, 2.

151. Because of Matt. X, 10; Luke, X, 4; Ex., III, 5; after the middle of the century, however, Acts, XII, 8; Mark, VI, 9 would be brought forward in the opposite sense, in a lasting controversy which set calced Dominicans against discalced Franciscans, over the real content of the *vita apostolica*. Cf. among others, the pamphlet of Thomas Sutton in *AFP*, III (1933), 74–80, *Contra aemulos fratrum O.P.*, with the conclusion: 'ambulare sine calceamentis est bona penitentia, sed non est de necessitate perfectionis evangelice sive apostolice'.

152. Cf. *supra*, ch. VI and n. 85. Council of Montpellier—Mansi, XXII, 945B.

153. *Proces. Bon.*, no. 27; cf. no. 21 and 42. These texts are later than 1215.

154. *Ibid.*, no. 27.

155. *Ibid.*, no. 21 (the incident occurred a little later).

156. Frachet, II, 2.

157. Percin, 22, no. 54; Balme, II, 248. On the floods of the Aude at the time—Cernai, no. 122 and n. 1; on those of the Hers—Balme, II, 33, n. a; on those of the Garonne—Cernai, no. 356 and n. 4; 605 and n. 2.

158. *Proces. Bon.*, no. 21. Ford on the Hers—Tudela, 189. Ford on the Garonne—Puylaurens, ch. XVIIa.

159. Frachet, II, 4.

160. *Proces. Thol.*, no. 10.

161. The three summers of 1209, 1210, 1212 were particularly oppressive—Cernai, no. 153, 322; Tudela, 77 and 259.

162. Frachet II, 24.

163. On the road to Carcassonne shortly after leaving Montréal, to the right—Balme, I, 408; Kirsch, 108–109; Constantino, 184.

164. Constantino, no. 42.

165. *Proces. Thol.*, no. 17.

166. *Ibid.*, no. 15.

167. *Ibid.*, nos. 15–17; Ferrand, no. 22.

168. *Proces. Bon.*, no. 31.

169. *Ibid.*, no. 25; Constantino, no. 61.

170. *Proces. Thol.*, nos. 15 and 17.

171. Ferrando, no. 22; Constantino, no. 56. There, two different Lents are referred to, which shows his custom.

172. It was this idea that Jordan put in the mouth of Diego at the Montpellier discussion—*clavum clavo retundite*. According to Ferrand no. 22, Dominic practised it; he thus converted, through the edification he gave them, some of the Catharist women believers.

173. Frachet, II, 2.

174. Ferrando, no. 20.

175. *Proces. Thol.*, no. 18.

176. Constantino, no. 62. Cf. *supra*, n. 94.

177. Ferrando, no. 20.

178. Jordan, no. 34.

179. The present cross replaces one of the seventeenth century which was itself a replacement of a very ancient cross—Percin, 6, no. 29; Balme, I, 199 in the place called *Sicari* (stabbers). This name is the only unfavourable element to be found in tradition. It presupposes in fact that the ambushed men

sought to assassinate Dominic. Jordan, no. 34, merely says that they were to seize him to hand him over to their leaders who would clearly have ill-treated him.

180. *Proces. Thol.*, no. 3.

181. Jordan, no. 34; cf. *Proces. Bon.*, no. 29. Dismemberment was one of the favourite tortures of the lords of the Midi—Cernai, no. 582. Cf. *supra*, 57, n. 90.

182. Cernai, no. 130. At this date, however, the abbot was entrusted with a mission by the Count of Foix. Guillaume de Roquefort was the brother of the Bishop of Carcassonne. The Cistercians, however, were hated by the lords of the Midi—Cernai, no. 277, 395 and n. 6.

183. Cernai, no. 361.

184. 'Negotium Jhesu Christi in partibus istis', he said, 'nunquam prosperum sortietur effectum, donec aliquis de nobis predicatoribus pro defensione fidei moriatur. Et utinam ego prior persecutoris exciperem gladium!'—Cernai, no. 360.

185. On the occasion when, braving the Count of Toulouse who had given him the order to leave the town forthwith if he wanted to preserve his life, he remained there, expecting death from day to day—Cernai, no. 22.

186. 'Nec apostolorum fraudatus est gloria', Ferrand, no. 20, quoting Acts V, 41.

187. *Proces. Bon.*, no. 3 and 41.

188. *Proces. Bon.*, no. 28.

189. *Proces. Thol.*, no. 10.

190. *Proces. Bon.*, nos. 3, 41, 42. Cf. the provision in the future constitutions, I Const. II, XXXIV.

191. Salagnac, I, 9. Cf. Constantin, no. 25; Frachet, 74 and 84.

192. *Proces. Bon.*, no. 3, 42; Constantin, no. 42.

193. Ferrand, no. 22. On the night rising during a journey, see Echard, I, 412; *ASOP*, I, 325, n. 3.

194. *Proces. Thol.*, no. 3.

195. No. 6.

196. No. 18.

197. No. 17.

198. No. 18.

199. No. 18.

200. *Proces. Bon.*, no. 37.

201. No. 26.

202. *Proces. Thol.*, no. 18.

203. *Proces. Bon.*, no. 27.

204. Jordan, no. 35.

205. No. 34.

206. E. Amann, 'L'epoque carolingienne' in *Histoire de l'Eglise* (Fliche et Martin), VI, Paris 1937, 346–350.

207. Alain de Lille, *Liber penitentialis*, PL, 210, 295D. This confessor's directory, drawn up by a theologian who became a Cistercian and composed a large treatise against the Albigensians at the end of the twelfth century, cf. *supra* p. 77 is particularly interesting here. Cf. also Yves de Chartres, *Décret*, P. XV, ch. 76, *PL*, 161, 880, and ch. 80, c. 881.

208. Yves de Chartres, *Décret*, ch. 185, *PL*, 161, 897.

209. This was imposed on Henry II and in the Midi, on Raymond VI, Cernai, no. 77.

210. Alain de Lille, *Liber penitentialis*, PL, 210, 293D.

211. This decretal constitutes practically the only text on the penance of heretics in the vast literature of the penitentials, a clear sign of the practical non-existence of heresy in the West from the eighth century to the beginning of the eleventh century. Reginon de Prum makes no mention of the subject at all. The decretal will be found in the penitential *Corrector*, Lib. XIX of the *Décret* of Burchard, ch. 105, *PL*, 140, 1004–1005; in the *Décret* of Yves de Chartres, L. XV, ch. 117, *PL*, 161, 886–887. Again it is the only text of this type in the Decretal of Gratian, ch. 41, C. XXIV, q. 1. The lists of penances elaborated by the Councils of the Midi of the thirteenth century, especially that of Narbonne (1235), are precisely intended to palliate the paucity of the canonical collections.

212. Pseudo-Roman Penitential, L. VI of Halitgaire—*PL*, 105, 726, 727; Burchard, *PL*, 140, 980–981; Yves de Chartres, *PL*, 161, 897–898. Summarized and transformed by Alain de Lille—*PL*, 210, 297, where important details will be found on the practice of the *Carena* (= quarantine, forty days), identified with the public penance of lay people—295–296.

213. Alain de Lille, *PL*, 210, 298A.

214. Balme, I, 186–197. The letter is undated. It clearly indicates a lengthy absence on the part of Arnaud de Cîteaux, from whom Dominic held his powers. It thus cannot be earlier than 1208. After June, 1209, Arnaud was back. Later Dominic would rather seek his powers from Fulk or from other legates. Accordingly this document is commonly dated ca. 1208.

215. On the crosses of penance, cf. Balme, I, 176, n. 2; L. Tanon, *Histoire des tribunaux de l'inquisition en France*, Paris, 1893, 490–498.

216. The Council of Béziers had to draw up a canon to demand that those who wore them should not be derided—C. VI, Mansi, XXIII, 693.

217. Cf. *supra*, ch. IV, 50–52 and n. 37, 38 and 47.

218. 'Qui hoc nobis injunxit officium'—Balme, I, 187.

219. Dispensation from the fast in the case of illness and during the hard outdoor work in the summer.

220. Borst, 180–185, on continence, the three Lents, abstinence from all that proceeds from animal semen; 190, 191, on the prayers to be said seven times a day. Dominic prescribed the interruption

three times a year of the Catharist abstinences, in order to make plain the complete distinction between Catholic observances and those of the dualists.

221. Jordan, no. 36; *Proces. Thol.*, nos. 17, 19, 26; Constantin, no. 62.

222. *Proces. Thol.*, no. 17.

223. No. 19.

224. No. 23.

225. No. 19.

226. Nos. 19 and 8.

227. No. 9.

228. No. 24.

229. Salagnac, I, 9.

230. Jordan, no. 101; according to Barthélémy, no. 11, it was on the occasion of a journey to Rome. A tradition, however, places the marvellous occurrence on the road between Carcassonne and Montréal; first a chapel and then a plinth were erected there, on the right-hand side of the road, about a mile or so from the township—Balme, I, 431–433 and n. 1; Kirsch, 108; Constant, 182–184. Cf. Frachet, 162.

231. Frachet II, 4.

232. Constantin, 32. On the greed for gain of ferrymen on the rivers at the foot of the Pyrenees, cf. J. Vieillard, *Le guide du pèlerin de Saint Jacques de Compostela*, Paris, 1950, 20—'Cum enim flumina illa admodum stricta sint, tamen de unoquoque homine tam de paupere quam de divite quem ultra navigant, unum nummum more accipiunt . . . vi etiam indigne capuint'. A tradition sets the incident on the Tarn—Balme, I, 211, n. 1.

233. Frachet, II, 13. Later, in Rome, a similar prodigy would be recounted—Cecilia, no. 6.

234. Jordan, no. 46; Constantin, no. 55.

235. Jordan, no. 103.

236. Jordan, no. 105; *Proces. Bon.*, nos. 3, 21, 38.

237. Jordan, no. 107; *Proces. Bon.*, no. 27.

238. It is remarkable that each time that the witnesses mention Dominic's joy at this period of his life, it is always joy in trials, 'overflowing joy', *Proces. Thol.*, no. 18; *Proces. Bon.*, no. 7, 21, 22, 39, 41, 48; Frachet II, 2; Cecilia, no. 3.

239. In this paragraph a simple paraphrase has been made of the portrait of the preacher which Dominic had inserted in 1220 in the institutions of the Preachers. We shall return to it later.

240. *In medio Ecclesiae*: these are the first words of the Introit of the Mass of St Dominic.

241. A play on words falling from the pen of Innocent III, Pierre des Vaux—Cernai, Guillermo of Tudela, clearly after he had become famous in the crusade—Cernai, no. 105 and n. 2; Tudela, no. 118 and n. 1, 139, 161.

242. Constantino, no. 56.

243. Jordan, no. 31.

244. Constantino, nos. 55–56. He doubtless arrived in Carcassonne in October 1212, with the German crusaders—Cernai, no. 354: a local tradition made him one of the founders of the convent of Metz—Mamachi, 371; Balme, however (II, 335, n. 1) following a text of Pelisson now impossible to discover, mentions that Stephen was in the Midi, in Toulouse, in 1223. It would seem justified, in this case, to allow that he had remained there since 1212, had been following Dominic since 1214, had participated in the choice of the rule of St Augustine in 1216 (Salagnac-Gui, 155–156), and perhaps had acted as Dominic's *socius* on his journey to Rome in 1217—Echard, I, 16, n. K. If this were not so, nothing says that he did become a Dominican only after his return to Metz—Altaner, 68.

245. Laurent, nos. 66, 83, 85, 91. According to Bernard Gui, he was at Prouille as far back as 1214; Laurent, 76, n. 1.

246. Laurent, no. 66; Balme, 8.

247. Jordan, no. 37. The charter—Laurent, no. 58 (1214) which grants the tithes without imposing the responsibilities of the church is not authentic; cf. Loenertz, 37–47. The concession of the church with its tithes and responsibilities dates from 1221—Laurent, no. 134. There was, however, a concession of tithes from Fanjeaux by Fulk before 1215, for it is mentioned in the bull of 8th October, 1215— Laurent, no. 62. Moreover, Dominic, who in 1214 was parish priest of Fanjeaux had a personal right to them.

248. 'Comes etiam Montisfortis, qui speciali ipsum devotione fovebat cum assensu suorum, castrum insigne, quod dicitur Cassanuel, dedit ei et suis sequacibus, quicumque ei in officio inchoate salutis assisterent'—Jordan, no. 37. The date is fixed as 1214 by Dominic's presence in Prouille and the possession of the church of Fanjeaux instanced by Jordan, *ibid.* There is no doubt that what is here referred to is the famous township of Casseneuil (*Cassanolium*), conquered in August, 1214 (Cernai, nos. 519–527) by Montfort, who immediately received it as his possession by a deed of the legate Robert de Courson (Cernai, no. 523, n. 1 and Dickson, 101), before having it in trust from the Pope on 2nd April, 1215 (Cernai, no. 556). This township does not appear among the property of the sisters of Prouille confirmed in 1215 (Laurent, no. 62), but in that of the Preachers, confirmed in 1216 (no. 74: *villa de Cassenolio*, which, phonetically, cannot be Caussanel as Laurent, *ibid.*, n. 2 and Constant, 104– 107 would have it. The word *villa*, which at the time meant a place without walls (Du Cange), exactly corresponds to the situation of Casseneuil at that moment). Dominic had expressly asked the Pope for confirmation of this gift of de Montfort's (Jordan, no. 40). Several of the witnesses for these years instance the presence of *castra* among the Dominican property in the Midi (*Proces. Bon.*, no. 26; *Thol.*, no. 18). On 13th December, 1217, Dominic obtained from Montfort a safeguard for his property

in the Agen region which could only concern Casseneuil (Laurent, no. 82). This township was after-wards given to the sisters of Prouille who, we are told, exchanged it for other rights—Percin, 14, no. 18; one is rather led to think that the sisters lost it very soon after the death of Montfort (1218), when the inhabitants of Toulouse took it back. Jordan, no. 40, characterizes this donation by calling it revenues. It was a question of the count's revenues in the locality, the 'alberge' (dues for procuration and lodging), 'acapte' (dues payable on the death of a tenant by his heir for the right of investiture) and 'aides' (dues payable on the marriage of the lord's heir, for his ransom or his crusade)—commercial dues doubtless to the exclusion of the rights of justice.

249. 'De ordinis institutione fuerat tractatum'—Jordan, no. 37.

250. 'Que vero de iisdem redditibus sibi possent substrahere, impartiebantur sororibus monasterii de Prulano'—Jordan, no. 37. This phrase forms part of the additions to the second edition of the *Libellus*, which carried special authorization.

NOTES TO CHAPTER X

1. Cernai, no. 503 and n. 2; 506. On Pietro de Beneventum, see 503, n. 4; Zimmermann, 44–45.
2. Cernai, no. 507, n. 5; Puylaurens, ch. XXIII.
3. Cernai. no. 359.
4. Mansi, XXII, 935–954; Hefele-Leclercq V, 1298–1303; Cernai, nos. 543–549.
5. Mansi, XXII, 783–798; Hefele-Leclercq, V, 1283–1287; Cernai, no. 138.
6. Cardinal Robert de Courson, instructed to prepare the way for the Lateran Council in France. This legislation (Mansi, XXII, 817–854 and 897–924) seems also to have been promulgated at Bordeaux, Clermont and perhaps Rheims. The legate wanted to promulgate it at Bourges—Dickson 90, 100, 103, 112. It was in virtue of his office as legate that Robert de Courson legitimately convened the Council of Montpellier (Mansi, XXII, 950–951) held by Pietro de Beneventum—Dickson, 109–110, against Luchaire, 236. On this legislation see Dickson, 124–127.
7. The guardianship of the castle of Foix entrusted to the abbot of St Thierry—Puylaurens, ch. XXIII, cf. Cernai, no. 503, n. 1; guardianship of the castle of Narbonne given to Fulk—Cernai, no. 549; delegation in legal matters conferred on the archbishop of Aix, for Avignon—V. Chevalier, *Gallia christiana novissima*, VII, no. 381.
8. Vaissète, VI, 453.
9. Cernai, no. 549 and Puylaurens, ch. XXIII.
10. Laurent, no. 61.
11. There is no trace of him after 25th May, 1214 when he was parish priest of Fanjeaux—Laurent, no. 54. He did, however, receive various properties outside Toulouse in June and September—Laurent, no. 56, 57; Jordan, no. 37 (cf. Cernai, no. 527).
12. Balme I, 484.
13. Pietro de Beneventum, after a brief stay in Narbonne, moved on to Castelnaudary in April 1214 and then left for Aragon. He only returned to the neighbourhood for the Council of Montpellier on 8th January, 1215—Cernai nos. 503 and 542. Dominic had clearly received no special mission in April, 1214; a month later, he was still *capellanus* (parish priest) in Fanjeaux.
14. Cernai, no. 545, mentions innumerable abbots and other superiors with the bishops in Montpellier.
15. Balme, I, 187 and Laurent, no. 10.
16. Constantin, no. 55.
17. Jordan, nos. 31 and 37.
18. Appendix IV.
19. Vaissète, VI, 482; J. de Malafosse, 'Le château Narbonnais', in *Revue des Pyrénées*, 1896, 345–374 and J. Chalande, 'Les fortifications romaines et du moyen âge dans le quartier Saint Michel, Toulouse', in *Bulletin de la soc. archéol. du Midi de la France*, XVIII (1914), 76–82 and 217–230, particularly, 222–227. It was defended by at least five towers and separated from the wall by a substantial moat.
20. The usual provision in regard to *receptores*, again repeated at Montpellier—Mansi, XXII, 952.
21. Balme, I, 484.
22. *Ibid.*, n. a.
23. The deed is merely dated with the year of the Incarnation 1215 (thus it must have been drawn up between 25th March, 1215 and the same date in 1216). It bears the mention—*comite Montisfortis principatum Tolose tenente*. It was thus earlier than the installation of Simon as count of Toulouse and at any rate before 7th March, 1216 (Vaissète, VI, 482). Before this date, however, Fulk had not yet returned to Toulouse (Cernai, no. 573, n. 2) and Dominic, hardly back from Rome, had not had the time to produce new results from his apostolate. The deed was thus prior to the departure of the two men for the Lateran Council, in September, 1215. It was after the cession of Toulouse in trust to the Count de Montfort at the end of May, 1215 (Cernai, no. 565 and 564, n. 1). It must date from the beginning of the summer. Balme II, 9, n. a, followed by Laurent, no. 67, n. 1, allowed himself to be influenced by the omission of any mention of this possession in the charter of confirmation of the Prouille properties dated 8th October, 1215 (Laurent, no. 62). He is wrong, however, in thinking that Dominic received this donation for Prouille. This charter is probably of the same date as Laurent, no. 60, cf. *infra*, n. 44.
24. Laurent, no. 67. On this hospice, see Catel, II, 151 and Salvan, *Histoire générale de l'Eglise de Toulouse* . . . II, Toulouse 1859, 513; Percin, 15, no. 24 and Balme, II, 10–11 and notes.
25. Laurent, no. 78, of 28th January, 1217.
26. Scheeben, 164–165, has the merit of having discovered the true character of this foundation.

Koudelka, 99, n. 18 points out that the Pope said 'become' and not 'become again'. The idea of return to their former voluptuous life, however, is clearly indicated by the regret for the 'delights of Egypt'.

27. Simon, 1–10.

28. 'Presentium auctoritate statuimus ut omnibus qui publicas mulieres de lupanari extraxerint et duxerint in uxores, quod agunt in remissionem proficiat peccatorum', letter of 29th April, 1198, Potthast, no. 114—*PL*, 214, 102.

29. A. Charasson, *Un curé plébéien au XIIe.s., Foulques, curé de Neuilly-sur-Marne*, Paris 1905, 49–62.

30. Borst, 85.

31. *Gallia Christiana*, XII, 121. For other indications on Languedoc, see Simon, 7.

32. Jordan, no. 38.

33. Vicaire, *Fondation*, 125–127.

34. Jordan, no. 38.

35. Text rediscovered by Balme in the national archives in Paris and dated by him 1215 in error—Balme, I, 504–506. Cf. Koudelka, 100, n. 1.

36. Balme, I, 504. On the office of provost, see Vaissète, XII, 320–321.

37. Laurent, no. 61. For the commentary on this deed, see Balme, I, 504–507.

38. Vicaire, *Fondation*, 127–128. Mid-January, because Dominic had not arrived at Toulouse earlier than this. The charter granting the community his house, plate and linen can scarcely be later than the community's inception.

39. During the restoration of the façade in 1957 by MM. Fort et Rouquet, it was found that a restoration was carried out in the sixteenth century. It was then that the Renaissance doorway with the triangular pediment was erected.

40. No. 38.

41. The inquisitors lodged there until 1585, when they went to install themselves in the convent of the Jacobins; they held their tribunal there, however—Percin, 14, no. 21.

42. The 1957 restoration has confirmed this hypothesis. The Gallo-Roman wall, the section of which has now been left uncovered on the left of the façade rises to about 39 inches above the floor of the first storey.

43. Balme, II, 54–55; Chalande, *Histoire des rues de Toulouse*, Toulouse 1927, 33. The present church was built on the site of the audience chamber of the tribunal in 1648. The chapel of St Dominic's room must have been restored at that time, but it already existed earlier. There was on the altar a picture representing the flagellations of the saint and later a picture of the rosary. There too was to be seen the crucifix said to be St Dominic's—Balme, I, 423, n. 3; Percin, 14, n. 20. See in Balme, I, 505, a picture representing the chapel in 1893. The frontispiece of the house shown in Balme, II, 55, has also disappeared. The chapel was still in existence in 1926—Constant, 291–295.

44. Laurent, no. 60. The charter bears the same chronological indications as that of the Arnaud-Bernard hospice. Its date should thus be placed between the end of May and beginning of September 1215. It was probably drawn up at the moment when Pietro de Beneventum had just left Toulouse, thus in the middle of June—Cernai, no. 567. For the events—Cernai, nos. 550–567.

45. All the religious decisions of any importance in the affairs of the Albigeois formed the subject of a council during these years, according to the customs of the Church and of the feudal world. In particular, de Montfort's decision in 1214 to endow Dominic's group of preachers—Jordan, no. 37. John of Navarre tells us that this was equally the case two years later in regard to Dominic's decision to disperse his Toulouse preachers—*Proces. Bon.*, no. 26. De Montfort, Arnaud de Cîteaux, Fulk of Toulouse and other prelates gave their opinion. This is an indication that they had already intervened in the foundation, cf. Jordan, no. 37, 39, 47.

46. Vicaire, *Fondation*, 129–130, where an attempt is made to dissipate the mistakes and anachronisms which have traditionally obtained on the question of the approval and confirmation of the order.

47. 'Religiose proposuerunt incedere.' The *propositum* was the rule of life. The word *religiose* signified the community life. On the expression '*religiose* (viventes)' used by the charters for religious not of the classical type, see Dereine, *Prémontré*, 371, n. 4.

48. Matt. X, 10; Luke, X, 7.

49. I Cor. IX, 9, cf. Deut. XXV, 4; I Tim, V, 17–18.

50. I Cor. IX, 14.

51. I Cor. IX, 11.

52. *Supra*, ch. IX, 148 and n. 81.

53. Mansi, XXII, 785.

54. *Supra*, ch. VII, 113 and n. 138.

55. Ladner, 20–21.

56. Ladner, 26–28.

57. Cf. the phrase *et aliis* . . . Laurent, no. 60.

58. The advantages are granted *in perpetuum*, a proof that the mission was so also.

59. No. 42. The phrase concerns a decision of 1216, already put into practice in 1215.

60. Although Fulk's charter does not say so, that of the Brothers Seila justifies the conclusion. Otherwise, of what use would the crockery and linen have been?

61. Cf. Fulk's charter.

62. Jordan, no. 28, cf. *supra*, ch. VII, n. 128–130.

63. Jordan, nos. 40 and 42; cf. no. 37.

64. It marks the revenue as of a provisional character, by the interpolation—'(*tantum reditus*), eis adhuc habere complacuit', no. 42.

65. Jordan, no. 37.

66. C. 26–30, *Causa*, XIII, qu. 2 ed. Friedberg, 696–697. Other indications in Mandonnet-Vicaire, I, 134, n. 106 and G. Lepointe, art. *Dîme* in *Dict. de Droit canonique*, Paris, 1949.

67. On the expression, *pauperes Christi* or *Dei* applied to religious, cf. Lacger, *Albigeois*, 611; Mens, 17 and 254; Borst, 91.

68. Letter of Honorius III, 30th October, 1220, no. 2742 of Pressutti, *Regesta Honorii papae III*, I, Rome 1888, 455, who read *tararum* for *terciarum*, cf. Denifle, *Die Entstehung der Universitäten des MAs bis 1400*, I, Berlin 1885, 475 and n. 1038; Beltrán de Heredia, 336.

69. Cf., for instance, Alain de Lille, *Distinctiones dicionum theologicalium*, art. Bos, *PL*, 210, 721C–D.

70. Matt. X, 9–10.

71. 'Must I and Barnabas, alone among them, be forbidden to do as much? Why, what soldier ever fought at his own expense? Who would plant a vineyard and not live on its fruits, or tend a flock and not live on the milk which the flock yields? This is not a plea of man's invention; the law declares it. When we read in the law of Moses, Thou shalt not muzzle the ox that treads out the corn, must we suppose that God is making provision for oxen? Is it not clear that he says it for our sakes? For our sakes it was laid down that the ploughman has a right to plough and the thrasher to thrash, with the expectation of sharing in the crop. Here are we, who have sown in you a spiritual harvest; is it much to ask, that we should reap from you a temporal harvest in return? If others claim a share of such rights over you, have we not a better claim still? And yet we have never availed ourselves of those rights; we bear every hardship, sooner than hinder the preaching of Christ's gospel. You know, surely, that those who do the temple's work live on the temple's revenues; that those who preside at the altar share the altar's offerings. And so it is that the Lord has bidden the heralds of the gospel live by preaching the gospel.' I Cor. IX, 6–14.

72. Both property and tithes appear among the sisters' possessions in the bull of 8th October, 1215— Laurent, no. 62. Casseneuil, on the other hand is expressly attributed to the Preachers by Jordan, nos. 37 and 40 and Laurent, no. 74. Simon de Montfort, however, who had received the right to dispose of it from the legate, Robert de Courson (who was exceeding the limits of his competence) in September 1214—Cernai, no. 523, n. 1—had had this right withdrawn from him by a decision of the Pope in April 1215; all he retained was the custody of it—Cernai, no. 555 and Pissard, 58–60.

73. Potthast, no. 4833—*PL*, 216, 919.

74. Matt. X, 10.

75. Pierron, 173, 176, 179–180.

76. For instance, B. Altaner, *Der Armutsgedanke beim hl. Dominikus*, in *Theologie und Glaube*, 1919, 416. Cf. Lambermond, 10–15.

77. The proposals made by the Poor Catholics which the Pope confirmed were not the rule of an order; they were proposals for itinerant preachers, not for conventual religious. Only their lay converts could be formed into communities (as at Elne, for example), who lived by the work of their hands as the first Franciscans did. Special treatment has been given to this question in Mandonnet-Vicaire, I, 162, n. 19 and II, 193, n. 73; cf. also Grundmann, 106 and n. 70; 117, n. 92; 130, n. 115; 133 and n. 117–118; 140–141.

78. *Supra*, ch. VI, 89 and n. 63–66.

79. Mansi, XXII, 828 and 908. The word *ordo*, here, should not be rendered by (religious) order, but by class, social category—cf. Innocent III's letter of 5th July, 1205 to Raimond de Rabastens—*PL*, 215, 682.

80. Letter of 17th November, 1206—Laurent, no. 3 and letters in favour of the Poor Catholics— Pierron, 23–29, 33–38, 40–41, 44–46.

81. I Cor. IX, 14.

82. Luke X, 7; cf. Matt. X, 10.

83. Vita Malachiae, *PL*, 182, 1097–1098.

84. This is the origin of the errors of Scheeben in ch. 2 and 3 of the 3rd part, the least satisfactory of his fine work. He erects his so-called reconstructions on gaps in the documentation.

85. No. 38.

86. 'Ceperunt magis ac magis ad humilitatem descendere'; cf. *Rule of St Benedict*, ch. 7 on the 12 degrees of humility, a veritable Jacob's ladder.

87. Scheeben, 141 and 148, denies it without proof. His assertions are as peremptory as they are gratuitous. Cf. Mandonnet-Vicaire, I, 167, n. 27.

88. Cf. *supra*, ch. III, 41 ff.

89. Cf. *supra*, ch. IX, 157 ff.

90. Acts II, 46 and VI, 4. Thus the Catharists recited their common prayers 7 or 14 times a day— Borst, 190–191.

91. Until 6th May, 1221, the Preachers, when they had no proper church, were obliged to go to various churches in the town (*discurrere per loca*) to hear Mass; now they were often lodged outside inhabited centres. At this date the Pope granted them the privilege of the portable altar—Laurent, no. 142. Cf. Vicaire, *Fondation*, 131. n. 4, on the subject of the unfortunate correction of the editor of the text. This clumsy correction, moreover, goes back a long way—Balme, III, 343, n.a. and 345.

92. Cf. preceding note.

93. Laurent—no. 70.

94. *Proces. Bon.*, no. 27. It was perfectly natural that Dominic and his brethren should have been permitted to celebrate in this chapel from 1215 onwards. The concession of ownership was not necessary for that. It became necessary the following year, when the Preachers installed their monastery on the land where the chapel was. This disposes of one difficulty in the deposition of John of Navarre which has embarrassed many historians—Vicaire, *Fondation*, 132, n. 1.

95. Vicaire, *Fondation*, 126 and n. 2, 127. It is the gesture by which, in 1265, Niccolo-Pisano represented Reginald's profession on St Dominic's tomb in Bologna.

96. Scheeben, 161 and 204, denies it however—gratuitously. At this time not only was it inconceivable to think of Catholic religious without their habits and proper emblems on which the Councils of Paris, Rouen and Montpellier had recently legislated, but the apostolic Christians, Catharists, Waldenses and Poor Catholics too (Pierron, 174 and 181).

97. Cf. *supra*, ch. III, n. 10.

98. Mansi, XXII, 941 and 945.

99. *Ibid.*, 945.

100. Rechac, 205; Echard, I, 85; Mamachi, I, Appendix 5 (frontispiece); Balme, II, 115. Mamachi reproduces Echard's design; Balme transforms it freely and modifies the inscription. The design discovered by Echard in Quetif's papers was perhaps approximative. Thus we prefer to rely on the direct reading of the inscription by Rechac—*minister predicationis*, and not, *predicationum* (Echard), which has no meaning. The formula *minister predicationis* dates from 1215, *supra*, p. 355 and Balme, I, 484. After 1216, Dominic bore the title of *prior S. Romani*, *prior* or *magister predicationis* (*S. Romani*) as Fulk put, not without a certain archaic flavour, in the charter of 1221, to the base of which is appended the seal (Laurent, no. 134), *magister ordinis predicatorum* (cf. *supra*, ch. VII, 111). The shuttle shape was classical for seals of ecclesiastical superiors at this time.

101. *Supra*, 166.

102. Charter of 21st April, 1221—Laurent, no. 134.

103. Humbert, no. 40. The information clearly states that the master taught the brethren *multo tempore*; since their departure took place in the middle of the year 1217, the beginning of the teaching must be placed when the community began to exist as such, in 1215.

104. This figure cannot be guaranteed; it seems called for by symbolic reasons—cf. note following.

105. The symbolism of the seven stars is again found in connection with St Edmund of Canterbury and St Bruno—W. Wallace, *Life of St Edmund of Canterbury*, London, 1893, 563; *ASS*, Oct. III, 602–603.

106. B. Jarrett, *The English Dominicans*, London 1921, 2–3; W. A. Hinnebusch, *The Early English Friars Preachers*, Rome, 1951, 443–445, who establishes the reliability of this information and gives details on this master who went on to Bologna, where he found the order once more (Frachet, 20), then in 1224 became Bishop of Coventry, where he specially favoured the Preachers.

107. No. 39.

108. The monastic tradition, taught by the *De opere monachorum* of St Augustine, also reached the Canons Regular, through the *Ordo Monasterii*, cf. Dereine, *Chanoines*, 389–390, 399 and Springiersbach, 427–430; they saw in it a necessity for imitating the apostles. This was equally the case with San Julián, Bishop of Cuenca, according to the *Martyrologuim romanum*: (28th January) 'opere manuum more apostolico sibi victum quaerens'. Some of those following an apostolic way of life such as the Humiliati and the Catharists (Borst, 188), accepted it also. The Waldenses, however, prohibited it strictly, on account of John VI, 27: 'Labour not for the meat which perisheth, but for that which endureth unto life everlasting'—Gonnet, 219, 223–224, 229–230. Thus the Poor Catholics, to distinguish themselves from the Waldenses, accepted manual work for those who were not occupied in disputing or exhorting—Pierron, 174, 178.

109. 'Totum hoc fuit factum consilio et voluntate domini fratris Dominici et fratris Willelmi Raimundi'—Laurent, no. 61.

110. Laurent, no. 66.

111. No. 38.

112. Laurent, no. 70 and Jordan, no. 44.

113. Cf. *supra*, ch. IX, 150–151 and 162f.

114. No. 28.

115. No. 39.

116. This is the fifteenth-century prose translation of the second part of the *Chanson de la Croisade*. This translation, widely utilized by Vaissète in place of the song which disappeared until the end of the nineteenth century, is unfaithful to the original and systematically belittles Fulk, showing him as a wicked and cruel traitor—Stronski, 96*–99*. On the only unfavourable account in the actual song, see 95*. We shall return to this episode later (1216).

117. Stronski, 95*, 99*–104*. To the narrative and anecdotes collected by the author must be added the evidence of apostolate drawn from the Inquisition documents by Balme, I, 171–172, and n. 180 and Douais, *Documents*, I, LXXV and nn. 1 to 3; Cernai, 464; Bourbon, no. 15, n. 3.

118. The letter of convocation of the council published by Mansi, XXII, 950–951, where this phrase is found, is in the name of the legate Robert de Courson. Pietro di Beneventum, however, himself convened the council he was to preside over—Cernai, no. 542.

119. Balme, I, 187. The delegation to Dominic of the powers of preacher against the heretics by Arnault de Cîteaux must have been sufficiently permanent—perhaps until the arrival of Pietro di Beneventum?

120. Peter of Castelnau, Raoul de Fontfroide, Arnault de Cîteaux, Navarre d'Acqs, Garsie de l'Orte,

Pietro di Beneventum. Guy de Carcassonne, the leader and St Dominic's friend, was likewise a vicar of Arnault the legate.

121. In the Albigeois, in Constantinople, in East Prussia, Pomerania, Poland, Tuxany—Ladner, 40–42.
122. Cf. supra, ch. VI, 84 and n. 30 to 36.
123. Supra, ch. VIII and n. 205 to 210.
124. Luchaire, 104–113; Pierron, 22–51; Ladner, 43–48.
125. PL, 215, 1514B. Cf. Pierron, 29–30.
126. Pierron, 172.
127. It is the word used by Luchaire, 113. It must be corrected by what is said supra, n. 74. An initial stage of the Preaching, but not of the order.
128. Mandonnet. Cf. Mandonnet-Vicaire, I, 44. On the probability of a liaison between Innocent III, Pietro di Beneventum and Dominic, see ibid., I, 172–176.
129. Jordan, no. 40. On the formula 'qui diceret et esset', taken from Apoc. II, 9, see Mandonnet-Vicaire, I, 159, n. 10; cf. also MG, SS, V, 351; Annales regni francorum, ed. Kurze, 1895, ad annum 749.

NOTES TO CHAPTER XI

1. 'Ordo predicatorum per quem horum temporum novissimorum periculis dispensatio divina providit'—Jordan, no. 2. These words give a particular zest to the title of Guillaume de St Amour's pamphlet De periculis novissimorum temporum. The theme had been launched by the Pope himself at the close of 1219 in the bull of recommendation of the order which would henceforward be classic: 'Quoniam abundavit iniquitas et refriguit charitas plurimorum, ordinem fratrum Predicatorum, sicut credimus Dominus suscitavit'. Type IV¹ and IV²—Appendix VI.
2. Cf. L. Oliger: Ein pseudo prophetischer Text aus Spanien uber die heiligen Franziskus u. Dominikus (XIII Jahrh), in Kirchen geschichtl. Studien P. Michael Bihl OFM. dargeboten—Colmar, 1941, pp. 13–28.
3. The following pages comment on the prophecies or visions collected by Frachet, I ch. 1 to 3; study by Ladner, 49–64.
4. Ladner, 50–57.
5. Ladner, 59–60; M. Reeves, 'Joachimist Expectations in the Order of Augustinian Hermits' in RTAM, XXV (1958) 111–114.
6. Ladner, 60–64, after the Expositio magnae prophetae Abbatis Joachim in Apocalypsim, Venice, 1527.
7. Schott, 'Joachim, der Abt von Floris', in Zeitschr. f. Kirchengeschichte, XXII (1901), 356–388.
8. Hefele-Leclerc, V, 1329.
9. Ladner, 13–14 and 50–55.
10. Ladner, 50–59 and n. 229.
11. Ladner, 24–26; Dereine, Chanoines, 391–392, 395, 403.
12. In primum Regum expositiones, PL, 79, 100D, 153A, 154A, 158B; In Ezechiel, PL, 76, 1004C. Cf. Ladner 53–54, 67. On the authenticity of the former work, see P. Verbreken, 'Le commentaire de S. Gregoire sur le premier b. des Rois', in Revue Bénédictine, LXVI (1956), 159–217.
13. PL, 196, 776C, 778C, 786C, 794B, etc.
14. Ladner, 61–64; Foberti, Gioacchino da Fiore e il Gioacchinismo antico et moderno (Padua 1942) 147, protests against those who seek to recognise in an order, the ordo or class of men described by Joachim. The text, however, lent itself to this interpretation since more than one of Joachim's contemporaries took it in this way.
15. Ladner, 64, n. 254.
16. Epist. Ia ed. Boehmer-Wiegandin Analekten zur Geschichte des Franciscus von Assisi, Tübingen 1930, 65.
17. 'Hec est vere religio pauperum Crucifixi et ordo predicatorum, quos fratres Minores appellamus'—Historia Occidentalis, bk. II, ch. 32, Douai 1597, 349. Cf. Epist. Ia, ed. cited, 67. Cf. Frachet, 183 for another example of the use of ordo predicatorum as a common noun.
18. Historia Occidentalis, Douai 1597, 349. On this text and on the date at which Jacques de Vitry became aware of the Preachers (1222?) see Mandonnet-Vicaire, I, 231–247.
19. Jordan, no. 40. Dominic received a bull from the chancellery on October 8th (Laurent, no. 62). As a week or two usually elapsed between the Pope's concession and delivery of the text by the chancellery, it may be concluded that Dominic was in Rome and visiting the Pope at the end of September or beginning of October. This places his departure from Toulouse at latest at the beginning of September.
20. For description of the Cottian Alps route, probably used by the travellers, see Balme, I, 352.
21. The only absentee was the Bishop of Uzès, who was looking after the province in accordance with Innocent's prescriptions. Cf. list of participants from the Midi in Cernai, no. 572, n. 2 and Werner, 587–589.
22. Cernai, no. 571 and notes.
23. Cernai, no. 570, note 1.
24. Chanson, 171–193 (lines 3162 to 3593). The writer was not present at these debates, but he was informed about them where they took place; his impassioned and dramatic account is open to criticism but is not without value—cf. A. Meyer's introduction LXXI–LXXV.
25. Cf. supra, n. 19.
26. Jordan, no. 40. Already in 1211 Dominic for preference used the title of preacher—Laurent, no. 10. The brethren, who received this function from their bishop in 1215, used the title from the time of the following charter of Fulk, in July, 1216—Laurent, no. 70. They obtained it from the Pope six months later—Laurent, no. 77. This confirms Jordan's statement.
27. For what follows, see Vicaire, Fondation, 132–136.

28. Mandonnet-Vicaire, II, 267–268 and n. 62.

29. *Ibid.*, 244, n. 5 and 267, n. 62.

30. *Ibid.*, II, 244, n. 5.

31. Not all, however—from 1207 to 1212 Prouille received gifts from the local people exclusively.

32. Scheeben, 146, 148, 161, 172; cf. account by A. Lemonnyer in *AFP*, I (1931), 472–477.

33. Mandonnet-Vicaire I, 161–164, in particular n. 20.

34. No. 40.

35. Bernard Gui does not fail to emphasize this audacity—'pro eo quod praedicationis officium majorum esset Dei in ecclesia praelatorum'—Gui, 400C.

36. Potthast, no. 2912; *PL*, 215, 1024–1025.

37. The canons of Val-des-Écoliers near Paris had just taken the decision to accept only revenues and alms, refusing lands and other property that could bring in money. Cf. letter of approval of the bishop in September 1215, in d'Achery, *Spicilegium* . . . , III, Paris, 1723, 584.

38. Laurent, no. 62.

39. Mandonnet-Vicaire, I, 163 and n. 20 and II, 242–243, n. 3–4.

40. *Proces. Bon.*, no. 12, deposition of Guillaume de Montferrat. Cf. Brem, 102–103.

41. This remains an hypothesis. If it be noted that the coming of St Francis to the Lateran Council (cf. *infra*, n. 64) and his visits to Ugolino at this date are even more hypothetical (the majority of the critics do not date the cardinal's friendship for the saint earlier than 1217—Brem, 111–118; Altaner, *Beziehungen*, 9; on the other hand Zarncke, 103–106, shows that it was possible as early as 1210), it will be seen to what extent a meeting of Dominic and Francis at Cardinal Ugolino's is conjectural in 1215. This meeting, the only one sufficiently attested by the documents (Thomas of Celano, *Legenda secunda*, ch. 109), would take place in the first weeks of 1221; a meeting of the two saints in Rome, which could form the basis of the legend recounted by Frachet, I.P., ch. I §3, is just possible, but no more—Altaner, *Beziehungen*, 22.

42. If it be supposed, as is natural, that the canons were recorded in the order in which they were promulgated.

43. Matt. IV, 4.

44. Hefele-Leclercq, V, 1340; c. 15, X, *De officio judicis ord.*, I, tit. 31.

45. Canon 18—Hefele-Leclercq, V, 1101.

46. Hefele-Leclercq, V, 1341; c. 4, X, *De magistris*, V, tit. 5.

47. Note also the presence in the St Etienne chapter in July 1216 of a certain G, described as *capiscol*, e.g. professor of theology and sacristan—Laurent, no. 70.

48. A reflection, of which it is impossible to say whether it comes from Dominic or from Pedro Ferrando inspired by the decisions of St Dominic—Ferrando, no. 31. An identical reflection of Honorius III to the Parisian students on 19th January, 1217 will be found in Laurent, no. 76.

49. Hefele-Leclercq, V, 1342; c. 7, X, *De statu monachorum* III, tit. 35.

50. Hefele-Leclercq, V, 1344; c. 9, X, *De religiosis*, III, tit. 36.

51. In order to avoid the vague or even inaccurate interpretations of several historians, we have determined the significance of the terms of the 13th canon by examining its later applications— Mandonnet-Vicaire, I, 178, n. 58. The expression 'canonical statute' by which we sum up our conclusions will make it possible to understand the mandate given by Innocent IV in 1243 to the hermits of Tuscany— '[mandamus] quantinus . . . vos . . . regulam beati Augustini et ordinem assumatis . . . salvis observantiis seu constitutionibus faciendis a vobis, dummodo ejusdem ordinis non obvient institutis', L. Empoli, *Bullarium ord. Eremitarum S. Augustini*, Romae, 628, 164.

52. On this movement, cf. the recent studies of Mens, Meersseman-Adda and Meersseman, *Confréries*.

53. L. Le Grand, *Statuts d'Hôtels-Dieu*, Paris, 1901.

54. Meersseman, *Loi pénale* 997, has particularly insisted on the extraordinary novelty of the orders of knights such as that of Santiago de la Espada, which from certain of their members exacted neither a vow of chastity nor of common life, but only of obedience.

55. This is the theory of Grundmann, solidly established although over-systematized—cf. Dereine, 'Les origines de Prémontré', in *RHE*, XLII (1947), 354–357.

56. Gratian, ch. XIX; Dereine, *Statut canonique*, 548–561, in particular 556–557, where he emphasizes how the formula, established at the end of the eleventh century to prevent people passing from canonical to monastic life, *vel arctioris vitae obtentu*, developed into *nisi arctioris vitae obtentu* under Alexander IV— cf. *DHGE*, XII, 395–398; K. Fina, 'Quem suam requirere. Eine Studie zur Geschichte des Orden-swechsels im XII Jahrh' in *Augustiniana VII* (1957), 33–56.

57. At the close of 1091 Urban II composed a history of the perfect life, the flow of which was in his eyes divided between the monks and the canons. This history met with tremendous success—cf. Dereine, *Statut canonique*, 545–551.

58. H. Tiraboschi, *Vetera humiliatorum Monumenta*, II, Milan, 1767, 134. Cf. Mandonnet-Vicaire, II, 304, n. 26.

59. Mandonnet-Vicaire, I, 162, n. 19 and II, 193, n. 73.

60. *Ibid.*, II, 303–306.

61. Grundmann, 139–156 has shown in particular that the Pope's position had undergone no modification in regard to the apostolic penitents. Cf. Mandonnet-Vicaire, I, 170 and n. 38. Scheeben, 176, thinks that Innocent had changed and that in canon 13, the real responsibility for which was his, he was giving expression to his new position, for he was not the type of man to yield to the prelates. That, however, was what he did in the Albigensian affair.

62. In 1210 the Pope had allowed Raymond VI to defend himself against the accusation of murder and

heresy, but the legates ordered by the Pope to hear his defence in September 1210 at Saint-Gilles would not allow him to make it, alleging his failure to keep his earlier promises. Having lied as to the details, why should he not lie as to the substance of the debate? It is true that in the case of a Raymond VI, the procedure of the oath of liberation scarcely provided a guarantee!—Luchaire, 168–172; cf. Pissard, 31, 40 ff.

63. Mansi, XXII, 1069–1070. Cernai, no. 572 and 263, n. 1.

64. This is the opinion of Grundmann, 142–148, after a meticulous investigation. The expression of Jacques de Vitry, who in regard to the Franciscans in 1216 drew attention to their 'institutiones sanctas a domino papa approbatas' should be added—Epist. Ia, ed. Boehmer-Wigand, Tübingen 1930, 67.

65. Mandonnet-Vicaire, II, 305; Grundmann, 134.

66. Jordan, no. 41.

67. Mandonnet-Vicaire, I, 166 and n. 25.

68. Proces. Bon., no. 25.

69. The documents which show that the sentiments of John of Navarre were those of all the brethren, although no indication justifies the supposition that there was any sort of disappointment in the order, either in 1216 or later, on the subject of the Sovereign Pontiff's reply, will be found in Mandonnet-Vicaire, I, 181–183 and n. 66, and in Vicaire, Fondation, 137–141. The reply even seemed to them so favourable that to explain it their thoughts turned to a miraculous intervention of Providence—Constantino, no. 21.

70. Jordan, no. 45.

71. Jordan, no. 41. The insertion belongs to the second edition of the Libellus.

72. Canon 15 of Nicea (325)—Hefele-Leclercq, I, 597–601.

73. The travellers were in Narbonne in the middle of February.

74. As Raymond VI and his son did—Chanson, V, 3733–3739; Vaissète, VI, 476–477.

75. Vaissète, VI, 477–481.

76. Laurent, no. 66. Cf. the 'vobis domino Dominico' which shows that Dominic was present. On the other hand, an impersonal reference to him in a charter of Prouille of 21st April, 1216 does not necessarily signify his presence but merely the superior authority he always had over Prouille—Laurent, no. 68.

77. On 28th February, 1216, Simon was still in Narbonne—Rhein, no. 141; on March 5th he was at Carcassonne—Rhein, no. 142; on March 7th he was already in Toulouse—Vaissète, VI, 482—as also on 8th when he took the oaths, in the presence of Fulk and other prelates—Rhein, no. 143 and Cernai, no. 573 and n. 2. By March 11th Simon was at Rodez. This rapidity of movement is typical of the man.

78. Vaissète, VI, 482.

79. Jordan, no. 41.

80. Proces. Bon., no. 2, 33; Jordan, no. 42, 48, 87, 88.

81. In March 1217, in a charter, William Claret is called 'brother of the preaching of St Romain'—Laurent, no. 80.

82. A late tradition which is represented only by Etienne de Salagnac (MOPH, XXII, 150, 1.9) and Bernard Gui (Gui, 400). Jordan, no. 41, seems to indicate Toulouse.

83. This was the opinion of Echard, I, 12, n. E, who does not give his reasons.

84. I Const., II, ch. XVII (in regard to the general chapter) and Jordan, no. 109—cf. Rom. VIII, 14.

85. Supra, ch. III, I, 36–37 and nn. 43–47.

86. Jordan, no. 42. The meaning of Eligere regulam is 'adopt a rule in common', not 'choose' one among a number. In actual fact, there was never a question of choosing anything else.

87. Dominican breviary, August 28th, office of St Augustine, 5th lesson of Matins and 3rd antiphon of Lauds.

88. Humbert, Reg., I, 45. Scheeben, 192, is mistaken when he declares that the inspiration of the rule of St Augustine was not 'apostolic'. The document mentioned by Humbert is nothing more or less than the ordo monasterii—Mandonnet-Vicaire, II, 129.

89. Salagnac, IV, 2 (MOPH, XXII, 171–172).

90. Humbert, Reg., I, 51.

91. Ibid.

92. Mandonnet-Vicaire, II, 196, n. 88; cf. I, 163, n. 20.

93. Cf. Jordan, no. 76; Ferrando, no. 43; Constantino, no. 36. On the reception the Preachers met with in Germany, see Grundmann, 155.

94. Origins of this statute in the 1059 canon—Mansi, XIX, 873; Mandonnet-Vicaire, II, 176–182; Dereine, Statut canonique.

95. Canons 12 to 31—Mansi, XXII, 945–946.

96. Canon XXI; already indicated by canon 14 of Avignon—Mansi, XXII, 792.

97. Canon 25.

98. Canon 27.

99. Canons 30–31.

100. Canons 16, 17, 24, 26. The Mansi edition is very defective; the sentences are incomplete, the titles, disjointed, do not correspond to the content. The 'districte praecipimus' refers to the wearing of the surplice. As to the motive which dissuaded the canons from wearing the surplice, this was not poverty but relaxation—cf. ch. 20 of Historia Compostellana, referred to by Heredia, 317, n. 6.

101. Supra, ch. V, I, 70f and n. 64.

102. No. 42.

103. 'Consuetudo est jus scriptum, more statutum', Evrard de Béthune, cited by Du Cange, sub h.v. This was already more or less the definition of Gratien, c. 5, Dist. I, ed. Friedberg, 2.

104. Dereine, *Chanoines*, 386–390; cf. *supra*, ch. III, I, 36 and nn. 40–41.

105. Dereine, *Springiersbach*.

106. Humbert, *Reg.*, II, 2–3.

107. Vaissète, IV, 380, no. 21; V. Leclercq, *Hist. littér. de la France*, XXI (1847), 597–598; Balme, 478–479 and n. 2. Salvan, *Histoire générale de l'Eglise de Toulouse*, II, Toulouse 1859, 510, mentions Dominic's close relations with Jean Ier, Premonstratensian abbot of La Capelle, near Toulouse, where, he says, Dominic liked to rest. He gives no other reference except 'our chronicles'.

108. Cf. *supra*, ch. VIII, n. 150 and Appendix VIII, nos. 11 and 14. Among the saint's relations with the Premonstratensians should be mentioned the miracle he wrought in the presence of one of them— *Proces. Thol.*, no. 9.

109. The presence of the *regula conversorum* (*I Const.*, II, ch. 37, § 1 and 3, 226–227) at the end of the second distinction would seem to date it from 1220 (Vicaire, *Documents*, 115 and 183). It must, however, be noted that it is placed after the end of this distinction, even after the 'extraordinary' statutes. Moreover, it is related to the first distinction which it completes by serving as a substitute for certain prescriptions of the first text inapplicable to lay brothers or sisters. There is no reason against assigning to it the date of 1216—Mandonnet-Vicaire, II, 223 and n. 55. Laurent, no. 70, mentions the lay brothers together with the canons in 1216.

110. The following pages are based on the critical study—'La legislation des Prêcheurs', in Mandonnet-Vicaire, II, 203–239 and on Appendix V, *The Consuetudines of 1216*.

111. Ed. Martène, *Rit.*, III, Bassano 1788, 323–348; Antwerp, 1737 (in fo.) 893 ff. The oldest text edited by R. Van Waefelghem, 'Les premiers statuts de l'Ordre de Prémontré', in *Analectes de l'O. de Pr.*, IX (1913), published separately, does not enter into the question. F. Lefebvre, *Les statuts de Prémontré réformés sur les ordres de Grégoire IX . . .*, Louvain 1946, X–XIV dates the text with which we are concerned from about 1174.

112. 'Sicut scriptum est in regula canonicorum', in the 'regula conversorum', dist. II, ch. 37 (*I Const.*, 227).

113. Prologue: dist. I, ch. 14 and 25; *regula conversorum* (*I Const.*, 194, 202, 211, 226–227). On the use, and disappearance, of the term *canonicus* in the legislation of the Preachers, see Mandonnet-Vicaire, I, 237–239, correcting in accordance with *AFP*, XVIII (1948), 22, nn. 52 and 28, what is said as to the disappearance of the term *canonicus*.

114. Ch. 14, *I Const.*, 202.

115. Ch. 5–7; 8, 10; 19. The list indicated by Jordan, no. 42, will be recognized, even to their order.

116. The graded system of penances of Prémontré, inherited by the Dominican order, was much more developed than that of the other canons. It placed at the disposal of the Preachers, who were to be directors of souls, a remarkable means of formation and of refinement of conscience.

117. Honorius III confirmed the contemplative character of Dominican life in his bull of December 30th, 1220—Laurent, no. 122. The reversal of the situation effected by the genius of St Dominic will be emphasized by comparing this letter with that of Innocent III to Peter of Castelnau, of 26th January, 1205—*PL*, 215, 525. In 1205 the life of a preacher meant renunciation of the contemplative life. In 1220 it signified that life. Cf. Mandonnet-Vicaire, II, 232–233 and n. 85.

118. The possibility cannot be excluded that this text may have been interpolated in 1220 in the original chapter *De noviciis* indicated in the original list of the chapter titles of the prologue (*I Const.*, 195). This chapter was the one most modified in the Customs of 1216; cf. Appendix V, no. 5.

119. Ch. 13 (*I Const.*, 201).

120. Mandonnet-Vicaire, II, 181. The Customs most orientated towards study and the ministry are those of St Rufus; cf. ch. 17, 41, 42, 69, ed. Carrier, *Coutumier . . . de l'Ordre de St Ruf, en usage à la cathédrale de Maguelonne*, Sherbrooke, 1950, 64, 75, 76, 97.

121. Ch. 17 (*I Const.*, 203–204). This text, such as it has come down to us, was modified in 1236. For the restitution of the original text, cf. Appendix V, no. 2. It is possible that the list of penalties is not primitive.

122. Ch. 21, no. 20 to 25 and 37, 38; ch. 22, nos. 12 and 15 (*I Const.*, 206 and 208). On the existence of a chapter on faults of medium gravity in the original text of the Preachers, as in that of Prémontré, see Appendix VIII, no. 9.

123. Mandonnet-Vicaire, II, 225–226.

124. Ch. 1, 4, 6, 7, 11 (*I Const.*, 196, 197, 198, 200). On the subject of the canonical office, it is said that it must be recited *breviter et succincte*. Cf. the commentary on this rule by Humbert—*Reg.* II, 85–86.

125. Ch. 8 (*I Const.*, 199). Cf. Luke X, 7–8.

126. Ch. 22 (*I Const.*, 208). Cf. *infra*, ch. XVI, n. 69.

127. 'Proposuerunt et instituerunt', no. 42. The second edition adds 'tantum reditus eis adhuc habere complacuit'. This gives a provisional character to the formula.

128. There has been no change in the authority of the charter. Its application gave rise in 1217 to a conflict between collectors of tithes, settled on September 11th, 1217—Laurent, no. 81.

129. 'Frater Dominicus rigide et perfecte servabat regulam que ad se et hortabatur fratres, et precipiebat eis quod regulam plene observarent, et delinquentes rigide puniebat' *Proces. Bon.*, no. 43. Numerous reports of this type will be found collected in Mandonnet-Vicaire, II, 215–218. In such reports it is primarily the observances of 1216 that are in question.

130. The Bolognese witnesses of the canonization process mention the saint's legislation about thirty times under the terms of *ordo, constitutio, regula*—this latter term is repeated sixteen times—*Proces. Bon.*, no. 6, 12, 22, 25, 28, 31, 38, 41, 43, 47, 48.

131. Cf. *supra*, n. 112.

132. Ch. 14 (*I Const.*, 202). This was again the formula used in 1219 in Bologna—Frachet, 153.

133. Mandonnet-Vicaire, II, 226 and n. 65, 66.

134. 'Ego frater N. offerens trado meipsum Ecclesiae sanctae Genitricis Dei Mariae, sanctique illius'.

135. 'Et promitto conversionem morum meorum et stabilitatem in loco, etc.' On the equivalence: *conversatio* (or *conversio*) *morum* and *communio* (or *communitas*), cf. *loc. cit.*, n. 65.

136. *Ibid.*, n. 67. On the evolution of the idea of stability in the twelfth century (from stability *in loco* to stability *in ordine*)—*ibid.*, 231 and n. 79, 80.

137. De Valous, *Le monachisme clunysien des origines au XVe siècle*, Paris—Ligugé 1935, 76–77, who quotes the expression of Peter the Venerable, Ep. II, 22—*PL*, 189, 237—'the monk is the serf of his abbot'. Cf. Vicaire, *Fondation*, 126–127.

138. Meersseman, *Loi pénale*, 997.

139. Cernai, no. 48.

140. Mandonnet-Vicaire, II, 244, n. 5.

141. Titles given by Fulk in the charter of July, 1216—Laurent, no. 70.

142. Laurent, no. 6, 23, 25, 66. On the power of Dominic as a result of these professions made into his hands, see Vicaire, *Fondation*, 598–602.

143. Prologue (*I Const.*, 194).

144. Cernai, 573 and n. 2. On April 30th he was in Paris with de Montfort—Cernai 574, n. 1.

145. The first fortnight of July—the deed is dated July; Fulk, moreover, was already in Nîmes on 19th July—Vaissète, VIII, 694.

146. 'Ammoniti et adducti precibus venerabilis patris nostri'—Laurent, no. 70.

147. Was this a pure coincidence? In Toulouse St Dominic thus received the Arnaud-Bernard hospice and the chapel of St Romain. The two leaders among the burghers of the white confraternity, that is the orthodox party in Toulouse, were named respectively Arnaud Bernard and Pierre de St Romain—Puylaurens, ch. XV.

148. Laurent, no. 70.

149. In October 1216—*Gallia Christiana*, XIII, 77, cf. *infra*, n. 171–172.

150. Cf. *supra*, ch. X, 176-7 and nn. 93–94.

151. 'Domina Raimunda quae fuit uxor Thomae de Inter ambabus Aquis', Guiraud, *Cartulaire*, II, 4.

152. Deeds of 23rd and 28th October, 1216—Laurent, no. 71–73; Balme, II, 63–65.

153. 'Edificatum est claustrum cellas habens ad studendum et dormiendum desuper satis aptas'. No. 44.

154. Cf. *supra*, n. 56.

155. Salagnac, II, 9; *MOPH*, XXII, 12–13; Jordan, nos. 48 and 51.

156. Jordan, no. 51.

157. Jordan, no. 49.

158. Jordan, nos. 49 and 51.

159. Jordan, no. 51. Likewise before the summer of 1217.

160. *Ibid.* 'Oderius' corresponds to the name Odier and not Oderic. Likewise before the summer of 1217.

161. Already present among the brethren on 23rd October, 1216, when he bore the title of prior of St Romain—Laurent, no. 71.

162. Gui, 459 and ms. Toulouse 273, First series, f. 112A, cited in Pélisson, 7, n. 2.

163. No. 44. The word *circiter* was introduced as a correction in the second edition. Bernard Gui made every effort to discover the names of 15 brethren of Dominic in 1216; he had no other source than that at our disposal—*Fratres qui cum beato Dominico regulam elegerunt*,—Salagnac 149–157. Scheeben, 189, enumerates 14 brethren, but in the all round figure of 20 or 22, without saying on what his statement is based—perhaps on Echard, I, 16, n. K, which adds to the brethren mentioned by Gui, 3 brethren from the Midi, who were founders of convents from 1219–1221: Arnaud, Raymond du Fauga, Ponce de Samatan.

164. Clearly omitting the vow of obedience to a superior.

165. He had loyally kept it until April 21st, 1216—Laurent, no. 68.

166. Explicitly affirmed for the clerics from 1216, as was the white colour, by the *regula conversorum*, Dist. II, ch. 37 (*I Const.*, 227). At this time the scapular included an inseparable hood, came down to the knees and covered a little of the top part of the arms. Thus the lay-brethren, who wore no cappa, could have in addition to a grey scapular of the same shape and size as that of the canons, a long, wide coloured scapular, which formed a real cloak (like a chasuble of ample shape). On the dress of the brethren, cf. the decisive dissertations of Echard, I, 71–77. The scapular-hood said to be St Dominic's, formerly preserved at Prouille, was of the type indicated for clerics—Percin, 25, no. 6.

167. Canon 26 of the Council of Montpellier—Mansi, XXII, 945. It is attested by John of Navarre, no. 26. The rule, however, made no mention of it. Dominic and the Italian brethren did not wear it. Thus it was the habit without surplice that Reginald saw in his vision of the Virgin Mary—Jordan, no. 57. Dominic succeeded in eliminating it from the order, which was a considerable economy and accentuated the poverty of the habit.

168. In accordance with the canons of Montpellier.

169. Simon had spent only two or three days in Toulouse since he had been awarded the county, in March, 1216. He came back there, dramatically, in September, to leave again in the middle of the month—Cernai, 585–587 and n. 1. He had just imposed a heavy fine on the inhabitants of Toulouse. It was then that he must have restored the considerable number of churches, that Raymond VI or his vassals were retaining, to the detriment of the ruined see. The trace of the operation by which de Montfort restored to Fulk the churches which the latter handed over to Dominic has been preserved—see Constant, 312.

170. On December 1st, 1212, statute II; Mansi, XXII, 856.

171. *Gallia Christiana* XIII, 77.

172. See at the same period the identical attitude of Guillaume Peyré of Albi. He incorporated a large number of his churches in communities of monks and canons, the better to ensure the parochial ministry, at the risk of greatly enfeebling his authority—Lacger, *Albigeois*, 600.

173. His letter is known by the Pope's reply on January 28th, 1217—Horoy, *Honorii III opera omnia*, II, no. 219, p. 179; *regesta*—Pressutti, no. 287, 51. Since it was not the Pope's custom to reply immediately, Fulk's letter must be dated October or November.

174. Jordan, no. 43.

175. Canons XXX and XXXI of Montpellier had just fixed this minimum number for the priories of incorporated churches—Mansi, XXII, 946.

176. Church of the Holy Trinity of Loubens, which appears in the privilege of confirmation of 22nd December, 1216—Laurent, 74. The localization of Jordan, no. 43, 'in villa Apamiensi' (i.e. in the town of Pamiers) is approximative. Loubens is about eight miles south of Pamiers.

177. This church is called by Jordan, no. 43, Ste Marie de Lescure. This name is found in the privilege of confirmation of 1216—Laurent, no. 74. No church of this title, however, is known between Sorèze and Puylaurens. In the French edition of this book it has been suggested that this may be N.D. de la Drèche, a church partially situated on the territory of Lescure, a pontifical fief, which since 1214 the Pope had been concerned to bring back to orthodoxy. Lescure d'Albi, however, is 35 miles or so from Sorèze. It may thus be supposed that Dominic in turn received in 1215 a church situated between Sorèze and Puylaurens, in 1216, N.D. de Lescure, of Albi. Jordan probably mistakenly combined the two items of information. Canon Becamel, of Albi, in a letter has brought forward the objection that no document gives to N. Dame de la Drèche the name of N.D. de Lescure; that the name of Lescure is, moreover, fairly common in the Midi and that there is no reason to think *a priori* of Lescure of Albi; that Bernard Gui, who lived at Albi and there collected all the Dominican souvenirs of the early days makes no comparison of this kind; that Gui copies exactly Jordan's localization and that there is therefore no reason for holding it in suspicion. As a hypothesis Canon Becamel indicates a N.D. de Lescout between Sorèze and Puylaurens, the only N.D. of that neighbourhood. Balme, II, 47, n. 1 and 77, n. 2, had already thought of this. The convergence of Gui, Jordan and the bull of confirmation as to the wording *Lescura* is perhaps less impressive than would appear at first sight—Gui reproducing Jordan, who was certainly not unaware of the bull of confirmation of the order. Is it not probable that the pontifical copyist, who was the real party responsible for the wording *Lescura*, slightly distorted the name of Lescout (L'escolt) into a form of Lescure which was familiar to him?

NOTES TO CHAPTER XII

1. Definitely before the end of November, since he obtained a bull in Rome on 22nd December; it is necessary to allow a full month for the journey. A Toulouse charter of October 23rd mentions Dominic, but it specifies that it was not he who received the gift but Bertrand, described as prior of the house and church of St Romain. Dominic had already left—Laurent, no. 71.

2. The only *socii* of Dominic mentioned during these years are Bertrand of Garrigue and John of Navarre—Jordan, no. 51 and *Proces. Bon.*, no. 25. The former, however, remained in Toulouse; the second (of whom Balme was thinking—II, 123) would not have shown the weakness which will be recounted later, if he had had experience of itinerant mendicity at Dominic's side.

3. Whence the title of 'prior of the house and of the church St Romain' given to him in three charters of 23rd and 28th October—Laurent, no. 71–73. There had been no election. Dominic had simply appointed a vicar during his absence.

4. Cf. *supra*, n. 1 and 3.

5. *Proces. Bon.*, no. 38.

6. Born at Garrigo near Alès; first provincial of Provence (1221); died at the Del Bosquet abbey of Cistercian nuns, near Orange; subject of a cultus (6th September): Cf. Jordan, no. 51–52, 55; Frachet, 74, 80, 287; Laurent, no. 71–73; *Chronica Ia, MOPH*, I, 338; Gui, 418; *MOPH*, XXII, 151 and n. 3.

7. Jordan, no. 51.

8. Jordan, no. 44.

9. Cernai, no. 574–585; Puylaurens, ch. XXV–XXVIII; *Chanson*, vv. 3732–5651; Vaissète VI, 485–497.

10. Cf. the remarks of Meyer, *Chanson II*, lxxvi to lxxx on the duplicity with which the song credits Fulk on this occasion, and Stronski, 94*–95*. The bishop must have been over-bold in promising the inhabitants Simon's mercy. Puylaurens, ch. XXVII attributes only pacific and kindly intentions to the bishop.

11. Cernai, no. 585; *Chanson*, vv. 5554–5651.

12. Puylaurens, ch. XXVII.

13. *Epistula*, I, ed. Boehmer—Wiegand, 66.

14. The Pope was at the Vatican from 21st November to the end of December—Potthast, no. 5361 to 5404.

15. Tangl, 229, 233, 306. On the establishment of the Dominican privilege on the basis of the twelfth century privileges, especially those of Cîteaux, see Schreiber, II, 367–368.

16. Even though we are in possession of the original and this text has been edited over and over again (Laurent, no. 74, cf. p. 87), even in facsimile, the only satisfactory edition is that of *ASOP*, XII (1915–1916), 262–264; cf. Loenertz, *Prouille* 489.

17. Vicaire, *La bulle de confirmation*, 177 to 179. The so-called bull *Nos attendentes* (Laurent, no. 75), to which the name of confirmation has often been given since the sixteenth century, is a fanciful composition of the fourteenth century—cf. *Ibid.*, 176–192.

18. Pietro di Beneventum could not have been in Rome at this time but was perhaps in Aragón—Zimmermann, 85, 86.

19. Pressutti, I, no. 53, 60, 70, 72, 130, 143.

20. The formula concerns the newly cleared lands which the brethren cultivated with their own hands —Schreiber, I, 259 and II, 373 and n. 1. This only applied to the gardens of the Preachers.

21. The privilege granted the right of burial which the donation of St Romain had refused (Laurent, no. 70).

22. Laurent, no. 86.

23. In February, 1219—Laurent, no. 92.

24. Mandonnet-Vicaire, II, 231–232 and nn. 78 and 84.

25. Bull of June 16th, 1201—Tiraboschi, *Vet. Humiliatorum Monumenta*, II, Milan 1767, 141.

26. Bull of April 6th, 1210 (Potthast, no. 3968)—*PL*, 216, 242.

27. Cf. *supra*, ch. XI, 193.

28. *Villa de Cassenolio. Villa* at this period signified a town without ramparts, which was the case of dismantled Casseneuil.

29. Jordan, no. 40.

30. *Ibidem*, no. 42.

31. From December 22nd, 1216 to January 21st, 1217.

32. After January 2nd, 1217—Potthast, no. 5408.

33. Bulls of January 17th, 19th, 20th—Potthast, nos. 5414, 5417–5419, 5426, 5427.

34. Bulls of December 5th, 1216, January 23rd and 27th, 1217—Potthast, no. 5380–5381, 5430, 5435.

35. Bulls of January 18th—Potthast, nos. 5421–5423.

36. Cernai, 468 and n. 2.

37. The letter is known by the Pope's reply—Horoy, 219; Pressuti, I, no. 287.

38. Potthast, no. 5425; Pressutti, I, no. 265.

39. Potthast, no. 5424. Denifle, *Chartularium*, 83–84; Laurent, no. 76.

40. 'Qui . . . iam diu secus frumenta doctrine sedentes melius amodo fructificare valeant transplantati . . .' cf. *supra*, 197, n. 48.

41. Potthast, no. 5428 and 5434; Laurent, no. 77 (21.1.1217).

42. Thomas de Cantimpré, *Bonum universale de apibus*, Douai, 1627, 31. Salagnac, II, 1 (*MOPH*, XXII, 13–14) relates the same thing with slightly different details. Neither explicitly refers to the letter of 21st January, 1217 (Salagnac's words could be interpreted in this sense; according to him the incident occurred after the Council of 1215—the Pope, concerned with regulating several points of the *negotium fidei* of the Albigeois, decided to write to Dominic and his brethren; but Dominic was in Rome, quite near him) but it can only be this letter that is in question. The substance of the anecdote is authentic—cf. Vicaire, *Fondation*, 594, n. 1. It can be noted indeed in the original, that in the address of this letter, the word *Predicatoribus* has been substituted by the Curia for the word *predicantibus*, scratched out—Koudelka, 94–100. Echard, I, 14, G has clearly grasped the importance of the insertion of the name of preacher in the address.

43. *I Const.* II, ch. XXXII § 1.

44. *Ibid.*, § 2.

45. 'Officium predicationis ad quod deputati sunt . . .'—bull of April 26th, 1217; 'officium predicationis ad quod sunt ex professione sui ordinis deputati . . .'—bull of 18th January, 1221—Laurent, no. 87 and 127.

46. Phil. IV, 13; Acts VIII, 4; II Tim. IV, 2–5.

47. On the significance of the formula *in remissi onem peccatorum iniungens*, equally utilized by the bulls of the crusade, cf. *supra*, ch. V, n. 109. Salagnac, I, no. 5, regards this provision as a benefit comparable to that of confirmation.

48. Decretal of Alexander III, c.x.V, tit. 33 (Jaffé), no. 14037. Cf. Schreiber I, 47–55.

49. Decretal of Innocent IV, c.I.VI, *De verborum significatione* V, tit. 12 (Potthast, no. 15127).

50. Laurent, no. 81. Loenertz, 7, n. 6 has shown that it is in error that the Laurent edition has *Fr. Predicatores* where the basic copy of the text, in ms. Toulouse 490, everywhere has *Fr. Predicationis*. Percin, 21, no. 50 is more correct, but not wholly so.

51. Cf. *supra*, ch. VII, 107, 109 and 111.

52. *Ibid.*, nn. 111 to 115.

53. Laurent, no. 95; Appendix VII.

54. Laurent, no. 134.

55. Bull of February 11th, 1218—Laurent, no. 84. Charter of the 14th March, 1219, in Bologna—Laurent, no. 93.

56. Horoy, 219; *regesta*, Pressutti, I, no. 287.

57. Potthast, no. 5436; Laurent, no. 78.

58. Werner, 585, nos. 65 and 66.

59. Letter of January 21st, 1214—Potthast, no. 4900—*PL*, 216, 965.

60. Werner, 586, no. 113: *De Datia episcopus*. This is the only reference to Scandinavia. In these conditions, it is impossible to doubt, whatever has been said (e.g. Metzler, in *LTK*, I, 419), that Andrew of Lund was absent in 1215.

61. It would seen that the archbishop eventually recovered himself and came to see Innocent III in the spring of 1216. In a bull of January 25th, 1217 (Potthast, no. 5432) Honorius referred to a visit of the Archbishop to Rome and to a favour he received on this occasion, shortly before the Pope's death—Horoy II, 209–210; *Bullarium Danicum*, no. 113. Moreover in 1215 at Riba, Andrew Sunesen confirmed privileges of the local church which Innocent in turn confirmed on June 3rd, 1216, in Rome. Now Riba is the port from which the Danes embarked for Rome (passing Bruges or Dunkirk, then across France), *Samling af Adkomster for Ribe Domkapitel*, ed. O. Nielsen, Copenhagen, 1869, 35–36. (Here thanks are due to Dr Jarl Gallén, who has communicated these facts.) If Andrew Sunesen had really come to Rome in the spring of 1216, he did not return there in person at the beginning of the following year. Otherwise his presence at this latter date could almost be affirmed, so much does the number, nature, tone and gradation of the bulls over the lapse of a considerable time seem to manifest it. First of all, personal privileges; then powers or favours for persons of the kingdom or institutions of the archbishopric; to crown the whole, general powers as primate and visitor; lastly, a final personal privilege—Potthast, nos. 5431, 5432, 5438, 5439, 5441, 5444, 5445 (Pressutti, no. 312 should be added), 5455 between January 25th and February 11th. The bull of February 28th, no. 5478, which forms part of a collection of identical letters, no longer presupposes the presence of Andrew of Lund or the ambassadors.

62. One of the motives put forward by the archbishop for not coming to the Council was the excessively small number of horses imposed on him by the letter of convocation—according to the 4th canon of the Third Council of the Lateran, to which the letter of convocation referred (Hefele-Leclercq, V, 1092) there could not be more than from 40 to 50! Doubtless the Pope had limited them still more, for the archbishop demanded at least 30 'ad crucis negotium promovendum' *PL*, 216, 966. He wanted to be accompanied by numerous important laymen whom he would engage in the crusade. In 1217, there was no longer any obstacle to the embassy being accompanied by important people, with the precise object of preparing the crusade in the East and the expedition to Esthonia (1219).

63. Potthast, nos. 5450 to 5452, 5459, 5460, etc.

64. Nos. 5440, 5456, 5471, 5479.

65. Nos. 5430.

66. See beginning of Honorius' first bull of January 25th—'Ille charitativae dilectionis affectus et sincera devotio charitatis quam ad personam nostram, dum essemus in minori officio constituti habuisse dignosceris, nos invitant ut te prosequimur praerogativa gratiae specialis et hisquae secundum Deum a nobis duxeris expetenda benignum impertiamur assensum'—Horoy, II, 209 (Potthast, no. 5432).

67. Potthast, no. 5431, 5432.

68. No. 5445 of February 1st, 1217.

69. Nos. 5459 and 5481.

70. Nos. 5459.

71. Final privilege to Andrew of Lund, on February 11th—Potthast, no. 5455. Cf. 4820 and also 5432.

72. Bourbon, no. 158. The anecdote is not dated but it presupposes a stay in Rome before Dominic was wholly occupied with his brethren and sisters—1215 or 1216. His preoccupations as to recruitment are more natural at the second date.

73. The deposition of Guillaume de Montferrat (*Proces. Bon.*, no. 12) is here followed step by step. For the interpretation of the text, cf. Altaner, *Dominikaner-missionem*, 4 and nn. 17 and 18.

74. Ferrando, no. 32. On this custom and its reasons, cf. Honorius III, bull of March 17th, 1226, *BOP*, I, 16, no. 34 (to the brethren in Morocco).

75. Bourbon, no. 158.

76. Cecilia, no. 12 (a recluse near the Lateran gate) but not no. 13 (recluse of St Anastasia) whom he did not meet until later.

77. Constantino, no. 50 to 58, has collected several accounts on this subject—particularly no. 55, the conviction of the Cistercian lay-brother—'non ignorans quod ei multa dominus revelaret'. Cf. no. 25; Jordan, no. 46–47; Ferrando, no. 40; *Proces. Bon.*, no. 26 and 36; *Proces. Thol.*, no. 20; Frachet, 72, 83, 84; Cecilia, no. 9; Bourbon, no. 158.

78. Jordan, no. 46–47, 62.

79. For instance, the apparition of the Blessed Virgin, the presentation and meeting with St Francis in Rome for which Frachet alone is responsible (*MOPH*, I, 9–11). This vision which Dominic is said to have kept silence about, and which is supposed to have been handed on by some unknown Friar Minor to an unknown master of the Preachers, of which Franciscan and Dominican hagiographers (before Frachet) know nothing, has no historical foundation. Altaner, *Beziehungen*, 12–18. The account is of no more value than that of the vision of Innocent III of the collapse of the Lateran—Constantino, no. 21; cf. Mandonnet-Vicaire, I, 159, n. 9.

80. Jordan, no. 46. Jordan is a witness of substance. It is certain, moreover, that the brethren of the Midi thought that Dominic's mind had been made up by a revelation, *Proces. Thol.*, no. 20. Dominic, however, was in no need of this prodigy. What he had learnt in Rome and Toulouse, both on the human and on the supernatural plane, was certainly sufficient to prompt his gesture. Cf. 285, n. 62.

81. Cf. the scruple he felt at the time of his death over what was a very natural confidence—*Proces. Bon.*, no. 5; Frachet, 75. He hardly ever spoke much of himself—Mandonnet-Vicaire, I, 144, n. 19; B. Jarrett, *St Dominic*, London, 1957, p. 176.

82. Constantino, no. 25.

83. The Byzantine artists have transmitted to the Latins the staff as symbol of a messenger, in particular of an angel-messenger; whence Gabriel's staff in the Annunciation, which soon acquired its cross and fleur-de-lis and eventually became the stem of a lily. Here the staff signified the mission of the Roman Church, the well-head of the Dominican preaching. It was a power—whence the interpretation of staff and book by Salagnac, I, 2 (*MOPH*, XXII, 8): 'quasi geminas claves scientie scilicet et potentie'. Cf. the remarks of Humbert, *Reg.*, I, 48 on the 'status nuntii' of the preacher. For further indications see Vicaire, *Fondation*, 595, n. 4.

84. Humbert, *Reg.*, II, 38, notes the widening of Dominic's horizon on the morrow of the confirmation.

85. *Proces. Bon.*, no. 12.   86. Constantino, no. 26—after John XII, 24.

86a. A letter from the Pope would therefore be needed before any of its provisions could be set aside. Cf. an example of April or May 1219, Frachet, 25–27.

87. *Supra*, n. 40.   88. Laurent, no. 79: *Justis petentium.*

89. Thus a letter from the Pope was necessary, to be able to deviate from these provisions. For an example in fact, dating from April or May, 1219, see Frachet, 25–27.

90. Laurent, no. 86.

91. Humbert, *Reg.*, II, 39.

92. There was no reason for staying on in Rome after February 7th. He could have been in Toulouse by the beginning of March, 1217. There he got the chapter of the convent to adopt an agreement which was afterwards concluded with the monks of St Hilaire in March, 1217—Laurent, no. 80. Balme, II, 119, n.a. would have liked to change the month (May instead of March) because he believed in the legend of the saint's teaching in the Curia on the epistles of St Paul during Lent 1217. Altaner, *Dominikus*, 201–207, has destroyed this legend.

93. The charter of March, 1217 (Laurent, no. 80) mentions this common chapter of the brethren of Toulouse and Prouille.

94. Laurent, no. 80. The date of the month is not given. It could be the 3rd, 10th, 17th or 31st—the 24th would create a difficulty, for it was Good Friday. Since, however, the style of the Incarnation was followed, it could only be the 31st—Koudelka, 113.

95. *Ibidem*, Cf. Balme's commentary, II, 123–125.

96. Cernai, no. 587–612; Puylaurens, ch. XXVIII: *Chanson*, vv. 5653–8491, Vaissète, VI, 497–517.

97. *Chanson*, v. 5832.

98. *Ibid.*, v. 8455.

99. 'Et invocato sancto spiritu, convocatisque fratribus . . .'—Jordan, no. 47. There was no more suitable day for this gesture than this feast. Moreover, it was only at the beginning of May that he was able to join de Montfort in the course of the latter's move from Agen (April 18th) to Carcassonne (May 7th), then into eastern Provence (Cernai, no. 591, n. 4 and Rhein, 155). It is known that he actually consulted Simon.

100. Jordan, no. 47.

101. Cf. *supra*, n. 106.

102. *Proces. Bon.*, no. 26. Cf. Jordan, no. 62.

103. *Proces. Bon.*, no. 26.

104. Traditional date, retained by Salagnac, V, 3 (*MOPH*, XXII, 15) in an anecdote which contains anachronisms (cf. *supra*, ch. IX, n. 72). It is confirmed by the chronology of the journey of the brethren of Paris: one of the groups, travelling fast, arrived in Paris on September 12th, which implies departure in the middle of August—Jordan, no. 52.

105. Jordan, nos. 47–48, indicates no other chapter of the brethren but that of Toulouse, in which Dominic made known his plan. This, however, does not exclude the possibility of a supreme assembly at Prouille.

106. Salagnac, II, 3 (*MOPH*, XXII, 15). The indication is linked with that of the date of August 15th, the value of which has been seen (*supra*, n. 104). Etienne de Salagnac perhaps took this detail, as he did many others, from Peter Seila; or else from a tradition of Prouille.

107. Jordan, no. 48.

108. Laurent, no. 92 (February 1219); no. 111 (March 31st, 1220); but no longer in charter no. 121 (December 27th, 1220).

109. Jordan, no. 48.

110. Schreiber, II, 324, n. 4 and 331, n. 3.

111. Laurent, no. 74, p. 86.

112. Ferrando, no. 32. St Dominic probably wanted to be free to go away on a mission.

113. It will be noted that when Dominic in 1219 sent Reginald to Paris to represent him, the latter found himself higher than Matthew in authority, and gave the habit—Jordan, nos. 61 and 66.

114. Laurent, no. 92.

115. Jordan, nos. 54, 62; Frachet, 150; Salagnac, 10; *Proces. Bon.*, nos. 24 and 26.

116. *Proces. Bon.*, no. 26.

117. Salagnac, I, 8 (*MOPH*, XXII, 11).

118. Jordan, no. 51. On the earliest brethren as a whole, cf. Bernard Gui—Salagnac, 149–157, with the learned notes of Käppeli.

17—S.D.

119. Jordan, no. 51; *Proces. Bon.*, no. 26.

120. Laurent, nos. 92, 111, 122, 139, 149; Jordan, nos. 48, 51, 64; Frachet, 248; Salagnac, 12, 150, 151; Bourbon, nos. 8, 268; *MOPH*, XVIII, 17, 79–82; Echard I, 92; Chapotin: *Histoire des Dominicains de la province de France*, Rouen, 1898, 114s. † after 1225.

121. Jordan, no. 51.

122. *Ibid.*; Cecilia, no. 3 (Altaner, 169, too easily excludes the presence of Fr Lawrence the Englishman in Rome in 1221, asserted by Sister Cecilia). On the other hand, there is nothing to say that the Fr Lawrence of Frachet, 225, was the Englishman. The Fr Lawrence, master in theology, mentioned by Pelisson, 37 and 39, was Lawrence of Fougères—Echard, I, 100.

123. Jordan, nos. 51–52; *Proces. Bon.*, nos. 25–29; Salagnac, 155. † after 1236—Balme, I, 128, n. 1.

124. Cf. *supra*, 253 and n. 6, where the references to the sources will be found.

125. Cf. *supra*, ch. I, 18; Balme, III, 80.

126. Jordan, nos. 51–52; *Raymundiana (MOPH,* VI), 2nd series, 14, 55, 102; Diago, *Historia de la Provincia de Aragón*, Barcelona, 1599, 157B; Echard, I, 16, n.K; other indications in Balme, II, 379 and n. 1; *MOPH*, XXII, 153, n. 8. † after 1241.

127. Cf. *supra*, ch. XI, n. 160.

128. Jordan, no. 49.

129. Jordan, no. 49. For some unknown reason (cf. Echard I, 15, n. 1), to *Guomicius* (or *Gnomicicus*, which is translated as Gómez) the name of Suero has been added, which enables us to attribute to him what is known of Fr Suero (*Suggerius*), the first provincial of Spain: *Raymundiana (MOPH,* VI) 1st series, 21; Getino, 'capítulos provinciales y priores provinciales de la orden de S. Domingo en España', in *Ciencia Tomista*, XIII (1916), 91–96; Martínez, lii. Bernard Gui, however, knows nothing at all of Fr *Guomicius* except the name (*MOPH*, XXII, 156).

130. Jordan, no. 59.

131. Jordan, nos. 31, 49, 50; Frachet, 159 (same account as Jordan no. 50 and Thomas de Cantimpré, *Bonum universale de apibus*, Douai 1627, 349–351, with supplementary details); Bourbon, no. 288.

132. Jordan, no. 49. The Ucero is the river that runs through Osma.

133. Jordan nos. 49–50; Frachet, 159. The anecdote was not new; it was recounted of other persons, cf. Cesarius of Heisterbach, *Dial. miraculorum*, Dis. 10, ch. 34, Cologne, 1851, 241; Humbert, *Reg.*, I, 282.

134. Bourbon, no. 288. Etienne de Bourbon had himself met Brother Dominic.

135. Jordan, no. 49.

136. It seems clear that the canons of Osma who had informed several witnesses at the process of canonization about Dominic's life in Spain (*Proces. Bon.*, nos. 14, 29; *Proces. Thol.*, no. 5) had joined the order. He is thought to be recognizable in the Fr Domingo, perhaps sent by the chapter of Osma to act as *socius* to St Dominic after Diego's death, and Fr Miguel de Ucero, a native of the region of Osma (cf. *supra*, n. 132).

137. The phrase does not come from Peter himself, as has been said following Balme, I, 506, but from Gui, 464–465. On Peter Seila, see Laurent, no. 61; Jordan, no. 38; Ferrando, no. 26; *Chronica Ia*, 324; Puylaurens, ch. LXI; Salagnac, II and 151–152; Pelisson, 13, 17, 20, 27, 42; Gui, 402, 456, 463–465, 470; Percin, 47 and 56. Of an important family in Toulouse, he was sent in 1219 to make a foundation in Limoges, then at Cahors in 1226; he was inquisitor in Toulouse in 1233, prior in 1235 and died on 22nd February, 1257.

138. Jordan, no. 38. He is said to have died in 1220—Percin, 24, no. 4.

139. Gui, 459, was moved to exclaim: 'praefatam ecclesiam patri nostro gratis collatam et confirmatam, filii improvidi penitus deserentes'. The public roads which surrounded the convent prevented it being enlarged. The brethren left it about Christmas 1230 and moved to the 'garden of the Garrigues'. St Romain reverted to the chapter of St Etienne, became the Collège de Comminges, belonged to Prouille (fourteenth century), to St Etienne once more, to the Benedictine nuns of the suburb of St Cyprian (fifteenth century), to the Fathers of Christian Doctrine (1604). The church, rebuilt by the latter, was destroyed at the Revolution. In the middle of the nineteenth century there remained only the former library of the Doctrine Fathers which had become a printing press. Today it is still possible to see a gothic window (? fourteenth-century) in the back room of a *pâtisserie* at the corner of the rue St Rome. All trace of the original Dominican cloister has disappeared—Laurent, no. 70 and n. 1; Gui, 458–459; Percin, 42–43; Balme, II, 69–70; Constant, 297–300.

140. *Proces. Bon.*, no. 26.

141. Salagnac, 155.

142. Canon 11 (12) of the synods of Paris and Rouen (1213–1214)—Mansi, XXII, 828 and 908. Mansi's text is not absolutely reliable; the insertion 'in opprobrium Domini et ordinis' of the Parisian canon becomes at Rouen 'in opprobrium domus et ordinis'. The text should be identical in the two collections. The Paris text is the right one; the word 'order', indeed, should not be interpreted, as is the case with the Rouen version, in the sense of (religious) but in that of (clerical) class. Cf. Innocent III's letter to Raymond de Rabastens, July 5th, 1205. *PL*, 215, 682. To allow a cleric to beg was to humiliate the clergy as a whole and to do wrong to the Lord.

143. *Proces. Bon.*, no. 26 and Laurent, nos. 111 and 114.

144. Prologue of 1228, *I Const.*, 193–194. Cf. Mandonnet-Vicaire, II, 267–268 and n. 62.

145. Laurent, no. 81.

146. Laurent, no. 82.

147. Puylaurens, ch. XXVIII.

NOTES TO CHAPTER XIII

1. Laurent, no. 82.
2. Laurent, no. 84.
3. Galvagno della Fiamma, *AFP*, X (1940), 344; quoted by Taeggio, *Chronicae ampliores*, ed. *ASOP*, V, 1901, 120; on the poor reliability of this author, cf. Vicaire, *Bulle de confirmation*, 186. Borselli, *ASOP*, III, 599.
4. On the city of Bologna at this period, cf. Hessel; for the schools and university—Cavazza and Sorbelli. A recent bibliography will be found in S. Stelling—Michaud, *L'université de Bologne et la pénétration des droits romain et canonique en Suisse aux XIIIe et XIVe siècles*, Geneva, 1955.
5. Denifle, *Universitäten*, I, 38.
6. Balme, II, 185, n. 2 and 3.
7. Frachet, 191, where he is described as *senex* and as *prior fratrum*.
8. Laurent, no. 84.
9. For what follows, see Appendix VI, the bulls of recommendation of Honorius III.
10. Brem., 30.
11. Brem., 70–107.
12. Vatican, Honorius III, lib. II, ep. 897, fo. 221; Pressutti, n° 1082.
13. Jordan, no. 49.
14. *Ibid.*
15. *Ibid.*, no. 55.
16. The critical edition of Jordan by Scheeben which reads, *et quidem frater Bertrandus*, has been followed. The early editions had *quidam*, which indicated a different Bertrand from the one Jordan had already mentioned (no. 51). It is surprising that Scheeben's critical apparatus does not indicate this important variant, since he makes use of two of these editions (to replace lost mss) to establish his text (E and O).
17. Jordan, no. 51.
18. Jordan, nos. 51–52.
19. 'Conduxerunt', *ibidem*.
20. This was the name still given to them in 1219.
21. Synod of Paris, P. II, canon II—Mansi, XXII, 823. Cf. 908.
22. On the tremendous throng of students from the twelfth century onwards, see Denifle, *Chartularium*, I, 50; on the crowding together of student lodgings, schools and houses of ill-fame, see Jacques de Vitry, *Histoire Occidentale*, Douai 1597, 277–278; on the taxation of lodgings by the University, see Denifle, *Chartularium*, I, 79, 98 etc.
23. Cf. *infra*, ch. XIV for the attitude of the chapter of Notre Dame and of the numerous parishes dependent on it. On the self-importance of the Parisian clergy, see Cernai, no. 22.
24. Jordan, no. 64. Obviously Matthew of France knew Reginald when the latter was teaching in Paris.
25. *Gallia Christ.*, VII, 87–90; final act before his departure in August 1218; on 7th December, 1219 the Pope had already received the news of his death in the crusade—Pressutti, no. 2286; he had joined the Albigensian crusade in Carcassonne in the Lent of 1211—Cernai, nos. 213, 230.
26. *Gallia Christ.*, VII, Instr., 89–91.
27. Laurent, nos. 83 and 85.
28. Vaissète, VI, 511, note by Molinier and VIII, 706 and 736–738.
29. Complaint of Raymond VII after Peter's return to Toulouse—Pelisson 27–28. The complaint was very much after the event, but Peter's attitude was already the same in 1218.
30. Laurent, no. 86.
31. There was also the addition of the insertion—*salvis statutis concilii generalis* (after mentioning the immunities and customs).
32. Laurent, no. 79, cf. the corresponding clause of no. 74. The word *monasterium* designated either the cloister or the community for which the later term of *conventus* was not yet fixed.
33. Laurent, no. 80.
34. Name given to the group of the Preachers of Prouille, on 4th March, 1226; Guiraud, *Cartulaire*, II, 31. It was a genuine convent of Preachers. If it had no place in the province of Toulouse, it was because it was abandoned shortly before 1236, when the brethren left Prouille. For a clothing there, see *Cartulaire*, II, 4 (1230). Cf. Creytens, 'Les convers des moniales dominicaines au Moyen Age', in *AFP*, XIX (1949), 8, n. 21. Cf. also the declaration of the General Chapter of 1644, *MOPH*, XII, 198.
35. Vatican, Honorius III, lib. II, ep. 1069, fos. 251–252; Pressutti, no. 1255.
36. Appendix VI.
37. These are the initials given by Ligiez, no. 58 and Laurent, no. 87, which are both recorded in the original register. The early editions which all derive from Réchac, who in turn has used copies of the register by Bzovius. (Loenertz, 32, n. 34), have sometimes F . . . sometimes I . . . in the place of T . . ..
38. Echard, I, 16, n. K. According to a ms. by Bernard Gui, he was only the second prior of Montpellier; Gui, however, says elsewhere that he had been a companion of Dominic's in Languedoc, thus in 1217 at latest—Balme, III, 83 and n. 2.
39. No. 49.
40. *BOP*, I, 7, no. 8.
41. Where the Pope was from 27th April to 25th June. Potthast 5764–5844.

42. Jordan, no. 53; *Proces. Bon.*, no. 26.

43. 'In the beginning of the year of the Lord 1218'—Jordan, no. 55, i.e. shortly after Easter which fell on April 15th.

44. According to Cesarius of Heisterbach—*Homiliae festivae*, Cologne, 1615, 23, whose account—somewhat obscure and contradictory—has formed the subject of a careful criticism by Christianopoulo, ed. *ASOP*, I, 1893, 370–372. The name of Peter of Spain sometimes given to the lay-brother is an invention of Galvagno, *AFP*, X (1940), 344.

45. Dist. I, ch. 14 (I *Const*, 202). Cf. *infra*, ch. XVIII, pp. 342–3.

46. Jordan, no. 55.

47. 'In hac romana urbe, predicationis insistens officio, iam moratur'—Ferrando, no. 33.

48. Present in Rome at least from March 6th to May 16th, 1218—Pressutti, nos. 1137–1139, 1142, 1157, 1164, 1201, 1259, 1268, 1337. The letter of June 18th, no. 1447, shows that the bishop had already left Rome at this date.

49. The expressions *peregrinatio, transitus* used in the documents are equivocal and can equally well indicate the crusade which was preparing to leave from Genoa for the east or the pilgrimage to Jerusalem. There is, however, no mention of the Bishop of Orléans in the history of the Fifth Crusade—J. Greven, 'Frankreich und deu fünfte Kreuzzug', in *Historisches Jahrbuch*, 43 (1923), 15–52. For the conditions of the Jerusalem pilgrimage at the time of the crusade, see Balme, II, 200–202.

50. Jordan, nos. 56–58, 60–66, 69–70; *Proces. Bon.*, nos. 41 and 46; Ferrando, nos. 33–36; Frachet, 25–27, 102, 152–153, 248, 249. Doinel, *Notice sur le décanat du Bx. Réginald d'Orléans, Mém. de la Soc. archéol. et hist. de l'Orléanais*, XVIII, 1884, 47–69. Biographies of Bayonne (1871) and Constant (1897). Cf. also Echard, I, 89–90 and Altaner, 46–47 and 104.

51. Jordan, no. 64.

52. Cernai, nos. 422–436. Reginald, however, did not accompany him—no. 422, n. 1 (against Balme, I, 401).

53. He was in Cahors in October 1214, with Simon de Montfort—Cernai, no. 536, n. 1. On November 7th, he was still with him in Rodez—no. 537, n. 5. There is nothing to indicate whether Dominic was there too.

54. Ferrando, no. 33. Ferrando's information, nos. 33–36, sometimes contradicts Jordan, nos. 56–58, certainly wrongly (in particular F.36 against J.57); it does, however, contain important data not found elsewhere that can be accepted. Cf. Altaner, 46–47.

55. Ferrando, no. 33; Echard, I, 30; Brem, 104.

56. Jordan, no. 57, who heard the account from St Dominic's own lips. This account, later repeated by all the biographers and progressively distorted, has finally come to signify, in accordance with a hagiographical theme to be met with in other orders, the showing by the Blessed Virgin of a new habit of the order (the scapular); Barthélémy, 233, was the first witness of this distortion, which Echard (I, 71–75) has rectified; see Duval, 741, n. 11.

57. Cernai, no. 423.

58. Ferrando, no. 36.

59. Frachet, 25. Not for the whole order, but for Bologna.

60. The last indication of Manassé's presence in Rome, May 16th, 1218. Cf. *supra*, no. 48.

61. Pressutti, no. 1380; Balme, II, 200 and n. 3 who incorrectly presumed that the bishop was still in Rome on June 18th; cf. *supra*, n. 48.

62. At the beginning of May—Brem, 30.

63. Laurent, no. 88.

64. There is one indication, however. It must have been in Bologna, where he was studying, that Esteban de España made Dominic's acquaintance in 1218—*Proces. Bon.*, no. 35.

65. 'Magnam perpessi sunt ibidem paupertatis angustiam', no. 55.

66. On August 6th, 1218, the former had certainly been in Paris some time—*Proces. Bon.*, no. 26 and Jordan, no. 53. It is to be supposed that Bertrand accompanied him, because they had to be two, and a 'combination'—*combinatio*—to use the expression of the time, was not usually split up and separated.

67. 'Qui postmodum in Hispania prior extitit de Manino [*al.* Manionio]'—Jordan, no. 31. This incomprehensible place indication should, we think, read 'Maiorico', Madrid, as will be seen later. As to the Friar Minor Albert de Mathelica, who also accompanied Dominic according to a fourteenth-century chronicler Peter Calo (Mamachi, Appendix 344–345), his accounts are neither reliable nor interesting.

68. Laurent, no. 86 and Appendix VIII, at end.

69. Vaissète, VI, 519.

70. Where he would find him again in 1219, *Chron. Ia*, 324.

71. Bourbon, 17; Echard, I, 6 (following Gui) and 161.

72. Even if it could be proved that the bas-relief of the north porch of Burgos cathedral represented St Dominic and St Francis presented by the bishop to St Ferdinand and Berengaria (Christianopoulo, *ASOP*, IV, 41–43; Balme, II, 232–233 and n. 1), it would still have to be proved that the sculptor's purpose was to represent a contemporary historical scene (which one, moreover?) if it was wished to draw from this an indication of the coming of the Preacher to Burgos. Such a purpose would seem to have been quite foreign to the sculptors of the first half of the thirteenth century. Moreover it is sufficient to consider that the whole tympan represents the classic scene of the Last Judgement to realize that these personages constitute the cortège of the elect at the right hand of Christ, symmetrical with the cortège of the demons and the damned to be seen on his left hand. The sculptor has given to these elect the characteristics of a king, a queen, a priest and, it would seem, of a Friar Preacher and a Friar Minor (not

of their founders, for the statues have no halo). This merely proves, beyond question, the esteem in which the two new orders were held in Burgos.

73. For what has been made of them, cf. Getino, 130–152.

74. No. 59.

75. Interrogated through the intermediary of St Raymond of Peñafort who instituted an official inquiry, the sisters declared and proved that they had been received into the order by St Dominic. They did not claim to have been founded or given the habit by him—Martinez, 291–302. As to an earlier monastic existence of the sisters under the invocation of Santa María de Castro, this is a clear mistake. The sisters' first charters show that they belonged to the order of Preachers from the beginning. When they had permission to construct a chapel, in 1233, they put it under the invocation of Santa María. From that time on, as can be read in their charters they styled themselves: Moniales de Santa Maria de castro (or castri or in vico) Santi Stephani de Górmaz. Cf. Christianopoulo, ASOP, I, 1894, 514–518.

76. The scene of discouragement in question is not dated. It is usually placed before the gift of Brihuega, from which may be dated the stable position of the Preachers in Spain, thus before November.

77. Ferrando, no. 40.

78. According to a deed found in 1888 in the National Historical Archives of Madrid—reproduced in Appendix VII. This text is incomplete and sometimes unreliable. It remains clear, however, that by this deed the Archbishop of Toledo made authoritative an earlier, revocable concession, which can only be that of the cleric Aemilian of Brihuega. It was to this priest that the house was to revert in case of revocation, except in the event of his death, when the house would revert to the archiepiscopal see. This proves that it was Church property; the archbishop thus possessed at least a third-party right over it; that is why he completed his authorization by a concession.

79. Appendix VII. The text explicitly says that Dominic was one of the parties present; this enables us to fix the date of the year, which is illegible, as 1218.

80. Loperraez, I, 195–207. Biography by Gorosterratzu, 1925.

81. Werner, 588 (no. 32); Hefele-Leclercq, V, 1320.

82. Brihuega, Guadalajara, Talamanca, Madrid and Segovia; the latter place was the seat of a suffragan diocese.

83. Cf. supra, n. 77.

84. Jordan, no. 49.

85. Instauratis, no. 59.

86. Frachet, 224, who mentions the taking of the habit.

87. Laurent, 95. The place of the deed is not noted, but it is specified by the mention of the lord of Madrid.

88. Laurent, no. 108.

89. The explanation given here agrees in the main with that of Christianopoulo, ed. ASOP, I, 512–514.

90. The letter is not dated. It will, however, be noted that: 1. it was prior to the general chapter of 30th May, 1221 when the title of magister ordinis was adopted: Dominic here uses the title then not fixed of magister praedicatorum which he had been using conjointly with that of minister praed. since 1216 (Laurent, no. 70); 2. it was later than the summer of 1219, date at which Mames was assigned to Madrid. He had already been there a certain time; 3. that two facts refer to the general chapter of 1220: (a) the general law of dispensation there set down; (b) the brethren's renunciation of all property which certainly contributed to the abandonment to the sisters of the monastery of Madrid and its property. It may be concluded that the letter is slightly later than May 17th, 1220, when the general chapter was held. Its purpose was in fact to comment on the installation of the sisters in the building that had just been assigned to them.

91. The letter was written in Latin. The original, still preserved in Madrid in the 16th century is no longer extant. A fourteenth-century copy was edited by Balme, III, 79–80 (ms. Paris, BN. lat., 4348, fos. 155 v—156 r); another copy, also no longer extant, has been preserved in an eighteenth-century copy, in the general archives of the Dominican order, ms. LII, fo. 87, I (Rossell collection of 1357). Two sixteenth-century Spanish translations exist. Cf. Balme, III, 78, n. a. As to the fact that Dominic used Latin in writing to nuns, a parallel is given by the numerous Latin letters of Jordan of Saxony to his spiritual daughters.

92. Balme, III, 80, n. 6.

93. Thus we interpret Jordan, no. 31.

94. He was there, in fact, shortly before Christmas—Frachet, 71.

95. Frachet, 73–74.

96. Colmenares 184. This relic which we were able to examine at close quarters in 1956, is a fragment of rather fine woollen cloth.

97. Frachet, 71–73.

98. Colmenares, 183; Kirsch, 76.

99. Frachet, 71 and 73.

100. Jordan, no. 59.

101. Medrano, no. 426.

102. Castillo, 82; Colmenares, 182; Medrano, no. 414.

103. Nos. 104–105.

104. Ps. XXIX, 6.

105. Ps. XLI, 9.

106. ASS, October VII, 682.

107. 'The witness has heard certain brethren say that he had himself scourged and scourged himself

with a triple iron chain . . . he has heard this related by those who gave him the discipline'. *Proces. Bon* , no. 25. 'Each night with his own hand he gave himself the discipline with an iron chain—once for himself, once more for the sinners in the world, a third time for those in purgatory.' Constantino, no. 61. The report of Constantino di Orvieto, which is the basis of the Segovia tradition, has a systematic and abstract character, very different from the lively account of John of Navarre. On the iron chain which Dominic wore round the loins until his death, see *Proces. Bon.*, no. 31. On the hair-shirt—*Proces. Thol.*, nos. 15, 16, 17; Frachet, 73.

108. Friendship: Jordan, 36, 37, 39, 104, 107; *Proces. Bon.*, nos. 8, 12, 18, 27, 33; Barthélémy, 235. Gentleness: Jordan, 36; *Proces. Bon.*, nos. 7, 22, 32, 48. Joy: Jordan, 34, 36, 103–104; *Proces. Bon.*, nos. 7, 21, 22, 39, 41, 48; *Thol.*, no. 18; Frachet, 68; Cecilia, no. 3.

109. Jordan, nos. 10, 11, 15, 35, 100, 103, 107; Ferrando, no. 40; Constantino, no. 39; *Proces. Bon.*, nos. 29 and 35; *Thol.*, nos. 3 and 18.

110. Between 1208 and 1214—San Martín, 31.

111. San Martín, 29–31.

112. On October 30th, 1220—Pressutti, no. 2742. Text: San Martín, 77–78.

113. The first document in the archives of Palencia is a bull of recommendation of the order (type II, *Dilecti filii*) obtained by Dominic on April 13th, 1220 (*ASOP*, I, 1894, 511–512). There is no reason to suppose, as Christianopoulo does (*ibid.*), that this bull was obtained to cover a foundation already made and not, as was the case everywhere else, to prepare for one. The recommendation was in fact destined to facilitate the first initial contact with the bishop. It had no longer any point once the foundation was made, i.e. authorized by the bishop. In these conditions it is clear that the foundation, envisaged by Dominic in April, was decided upon at the first chapter of Bologna. The only reason which induced Christianopoulo to situate it in 1219, against all probability, is that this date was assigned to the certainly later chapter of Barcelona. A criticism of this statement will be found *infra*, ch. XVI, n. 123.

114. Jordan, no. 59, mentions his departure from Spain in 1219, thus after Easter, 7th April, 1219. As he had not travelled during Lent, he could not have reached the Narbonensis before mid-April at earliest. He left Toulouse to go to France (Frachet, 74) before the fresh siege of the town on June 16th, 1219 (Vaissète, VI, 531). It is thus between April 7th, 1219 and June 6th, 1219 that his stay in the Narbonensis must be placed, not too close to either date and in the main in May. On his presence in Prouille in 1219, cf. ch. VIII, n. 100.

115. Resignation of Bernard-Raymond of Rochefort in 1211—Potthast, nos. 4223 and 4224. Eubel does not mention his return to Carcassonne which is referred to in the Prouille charters.

116. On November 26th, 1218—Laurent, no. 89.

117. April 13th, 1219—Laurent, no. 94.

118. Balme, II, 280–282 and n. 2. Prouille did not recover their property until 1224; and the alarm only ceased in 1262.

119. Gui, cited by Balme, II, 248 and n. 3; Percin, 22, no. 54 places this death in 1219. The charters show that he was no longer alive on November 26th, 1218—Laurent, no. 89; the fatal flood no doubt came from the autumn rains.

120. Laurent, nos. 91 and 96.

121. This Friar Noël was not the former prior, who died in 1218, but a Preacher referred to in a deed of 1223—Balme, II, 348 and I, 397, n. 1.

122. Vaissète, VI, 531.

123. Echard, I, p. 11. According to Percin, 22, n° 56, Dominic received into the order at St Romain in the course of his visit, Fray John de Johannis de Gargas.

124. Frachet, 74. This could not be before April 16th and was at the latest at the end of May. It can, in fact, be calculated that the journey did not last three weeks (*ibid.*), that Dominic remained 'only a short time' in Paris (Jordan, no. 60) and that at the end of the journey to Bologna, which did not take a month, he found himself 'in the course of the summer' in this latter town (*Proces. Bon.*, nos. 41 and 46). Why does Scheeben state that the convent of St Romain was empty or abandoned?

125. The usual route followed by the pilgrims to Santiago, particularly Parisians and Germans, Cernai, no. 247; cf. Tudela, 205, n. 4.

126. Frachet, 74.

127. *Ibid.*

128. Cf. *supra*, n. 124.

129. Jordan, no. 59. There is no reason to call this figure in question with Scheeben, 270; Jordan, who was beginning to frequent the Preachers, was in a good position to know it.

NOTES TO CHAPTER XIV

1. Jordan, no. 53; *Proces. Bon.*, no. 26.

2. Laurent, no. 139. M. Poëte, *Une vie de cité, Paris* . . . , I, Paris, 1924, 177–180.

3. Jordan, no. 53.

4. On Jean de Barastre, see Balme, II, 253, n. 1 and Glorieux, I, 274. Jean had been teaching at least since 1209, cf. deed of Simon de Poissy, *infra*, n. 5.

5. Donation of Simon, in 1209, in Echard I, 17, n. L.

6. Vaissète VIII, 578. Balme, II, 253, n. 3. Was it to this circumstance that the brethren owed their welcome in the hospice, or to the fact that they came from the Midi?

7. Laurent, no. 139.

8. Balme, II, 253, thought that the University intervened because this territory originally depended

on it. The donation of Simon de Poissy shows that this was not the case. The seignorial rights which belonged to Simon had been ceded to Jean de Barastre in 1209—Echard, I, 17, n. L. According to the Laurent charter, no. 149, the University intervened 'tanquam domina et patrona': evidently then Jean de Barastre had given it a share in these two titles which belonged to him, clearly so that the Corporation of the University should succeed him after his death.

9. 'De mandato nostro', said the Pope, 'docet fratres de ordine predicatorum in theologica facultate', Bull of May 4th, 1221, Laurent, no. 140. The Pope's order was later than the constitution of December 11th, 1219 to which it refers. Earlier it seems that Michael de Fabra had been his brethren's professor, if his epitaph is reliable—Balme, II, 379, n. 1.

10. Laurent, no. 139. Note that he himself was living near to St Jacques—Denifle, *Chartularium*, I, 420.

11. Clause of the letters of recommendation of types II and IV—cf. Appendix VI.

12. Laurent, no. 139. On the difficulties later caused to St Jacques by the canons of St Quentin, see Chapotin, *France*, 23.

13. Laurent, no. 149. This was the first grant of the fraternity of the order.

14. E. Bernard, *Les dominicains dans l'université de Paris ou le grand couvent des Jacobins de la rue Saint-Jacques*, Paris, 1883; C. Douais, *Essai sur l'organisation des études dans l'Ordre des Frères Prêcheurs au XIIIe et au XIVe siècles* (1216–1342), Paris—Toulouse, 1884; F. Ehrle, 'San Domenico, le origini del primo studio generale del suo ordine a Parigi . . .,' in *Miscellanea Dominicana*, Rome, 1923, 85–134.

15. Frachet, 138.

16. Bull of February 27th, 1220—Laurent, no. 107.

17. Dominic arrived in Bologna during the second half of August (cf. *infra*, n. 115); if the duration of the journey (three weeks or a month) and that of his stay in Paris ('paubulum demoratus'—Jordan, no. 60) be taken into account, his arrival should be placed in June 1219.

18. On December 11th, 1219, the Pope noted that the divine office had never yet been celebrated in the chapel of St Jacques, on account of the prohibitions mentioned—Laurent, no. 101.

19. Cf. illust. no. 3.

20. Balme, II, 390, n. 4.

21. This was precisely what was in question in the final agreement concluded in December 1220 between Saint Jacques and the canons of Paris: complete handing over of the offerings of the faithful at St Jacques on certain days, and of the legacies for the dead whose obsequies took place at Saint Jacques, indemnity for loss of earnings—Laurent, no. 120. Right of burial granted by the Pope on July 29th, 1220—Laurent, no. 117.

22. In the name of this principle: *quia non potest esse quin multa proveniant capelle sancti Jacobi que provenirent ecclesie sancti Benedicti si non esset fundata in eorum parochia capella sancti Jacobi*—Laurent, no. 120. As if the preaching of the brethren, in renewing the devotion of the faithful, did not multiply their generosity!

23. Cf. *supra*, ch. XIII, n. 25.

24. On February 27th and December 27th, 1220—Laurent, nos. 107 bis and 121.

25. On the *collatio*, a homely conference in contrast to the official sermon, see *Chron. IIa*, 329.

26. Jordan, no. 57.

27. Jordan, no. 3.

28. No. 54. On the date of this foundation, cf. *infra*, n. 59.

29. On the youth of the novices in the early days, see Frachet, 141.

30. Jordan, nos. 66–78. Cf. Frachet, 116, 175.

31. Luke I, 48.

32. Jud. XI, 30.

33. Frachet, 30, 56, 183, 224; Cantimpré, 14, 56, 150–151, 341–342, 435; Echard, I, 148–149.

34. Bourbon, 346; Echard, I, 18, n. Mand 115, col. 2.

35. Bourbon, 398–399; Echard, I, 18, n. M. cf. *infra*, n. 63.

36. First prior of Poitiers—Balme, II, 308. Cf. *infra*, ch. XVI, n. 128.

37. Echard, I, 21 (n. T), 92, 115–117; Salagnac, 31, 60, 188; *MOPH*, XVIII, 79–80, 83; Mamachi, 641; Chapotin, *France*, 6, 43, 67. For long Provincial of France and Prior of St Jacques, he became Bishop of Agen in 1245 and died before April 1247.

38. Bourbon, ii to xi.

39. *Proces. Bon.*, nos. 12–13.

40. Bourbon, no. 395 and n. 1.

41. Jordan, no. 73.

42. Frachet, 183. For other analogous motives, see Bourbon, nos. 21, 63, 94; 219; 399. Frachet, 168, 175.

43. Bourbon, no. 74.

44. Jordan, no. 69; *Proces. Bon.*, no. 12.

45. Frachet, 183; Jordan, nos. 70–73. Cf. the Burgundian friar—Frachet, 194.

46. Jordan, no. 70. Cf. no. 96.

47. Laurent, no. 92. On the donors see Balme, II, 256, n. 2 and 253, n. 3.

48. Laurent, no. 114.

49. Laurent, no. 60.

50. Information of John of Spain—*Proces. Bon.*, no. 26. One of the prescriptions of the new diocesan statutes of Paris in 1213–1214, it will be recalled, obliged superiors to allow their religious to travel on horseback and to carry money for the journey (cf. *supra*, ch. XII, n. 149). Even if Fulk's charter still

imposed the contrary practice on the Paris brethren, Matthew of France had the power to dispense them from it. In 1229, after the order had adopted the apostolic rule *de non equitando* and *de expensis non portandis* (in 1220) and the obligation had been strengthened (in 1228), Jordan of Saxony expressly declared his right to dispense from it if he thought fit—Jordan, *Epistulae*, Ep. XLIX.

51. *Proces. Bon.*, nos. 5, 6, 12, 22, 28, 31, 48.

52. *Proces. Bon.*, no. 31. Nos. 4 and 12 detail the régime of fasts observed by the saint, no. 13 the régime of silence.

53. *Proces. Bon.*, nos. 25 and 48.

54. *Proces. Bon.*, no. 32.

55. *Proces. Bon.*, nos. 12, 32, 43, 47; Ferrando, no. 32.

56. *Proces. Bon.*, no. 26.

57. Chapotin, *France*, 10. Cf. Echard, I, 18, n. M; Balme II, 290–312.

58. Having confused the sending of the brethren to Orléans (Jordan, no. 54; he read 1219 instead of 1218) with the foundation of the convent, which was the sixth in order of precedence in the chronological list, he concluded from this that the oldest convents on the list also dated from 1219, cf. Echard, I, vi.

59. The chronology of the first foundations of convents presents considerable difficulties. The documents are missing. The only reliable document is the list in order of precedence at the provincial chapter, determined by the order of seniority of the houses, edited by Echard, I, iv–xv, in accordance with a document of 1303 (Bernard Gui). This text, however, gives relative, not absolute dates. The charters making the grant of the convent church, when they are dated, are sometimes very much later than the installation of the religious in the sanctuary (five and even 10 years according to Dereine. *Statut canonique*, 557; cf. Loenertz, *Prouille*, 43), *a fortiori* than their arrival in the town, and still more so than their mission. Moreover, in these early years what was meant by a foundation? There was not yet any general chapter to erect a convent canonically. No trace has come down to us of an erection of this kind by St Dominic. Was it then the mission of the founders, their arrival in the town, their provisional or permanent installation which indicated the foundation? To take an example where all is known in detail: was the Paris convent founded on 15th August, 1217 (mission), on 12th September, 1217 (provisional installation in Paris), on 6th August, 1218 (installation at Saint Jacques) or on 3rd May, 1221 (permanent gift of Saint Jacques to the brethren)? If we are to judge by the case of Orléans, it was not the mission or the installation in a hospice which counted for the foundation, but the installation of the founding group in a house of their own. The church was not indispensable—cf. Barcelona, *infra*, ch. XVI, n. 123 and Laurent, no. 142.

60. Jordan, no. 54. He says *in ipso etiam anno*, thus in the year of our Lord 1218 (no. 53); which signifies—before 7th April, 1219; thus before Dominic's arrival. Echard, I, 18, n. M, interprets: *intro spatium anni*, thus between 6th August, 1218 and the same date in 1219. He bases his statement on Gui (ed. Echard, I, vi), who gives 1219. The mission would then date back to Dominic and his stay in Paris. The interpretation seems forced. Perhaps, however, Echard was right in correcting Jordan. Dominic had just passed through Orléans—did he not pave the way for the foundation there by a visit to his old acquaintance Bishop Manassé de Seignelay? Cf. also *Chronica Ia*, 324.

61. Cf. *supra*, ch. XIII, n. 90.

62. Gui, 463 (beginning of Lent: 11th February, 1220). On the foundation of Limoges, see Jordan, no. 38; Frachet, 85, *Chronica Ia*, 324; Salagnac, II; Gui, 463–464; Douais, *Les frères Prêcheurs de Limoges*, Toulouse, 1892, 4–6.

63. The first prior of Rheims was a Fr Philippe—Bourbon, no. 462. He received a commission from the archbishop in 1224—Balme, II, 305. The convent was clearly earlier. Did the preaching of Fr Henry of Cologne in Rheims in 1221 indicate the installation—Bourbon, no. 453 and Scheeben, 349? *Chronica Ia*, 324, places the *mission* of the Rheims convent between those of Limoges and Orléans, thus from as far back as 1219. The order of precedence at the provincial chapter places Rheims after Lyons (substituted for Limoges) and before Metz—Echard, I, vi; this dates the foundation at latest in 1221. Nothing more can be said on the matter. Balme, II, 300–306, makes a few conjectures of unequal value.

64. Cf. the entry shortly afterwards of Frs. Jordan, Henry and Leo—Jordan, nos. 74–75.

65. The sending of Fr Reginald to Paris, perhaps suggested by Matthew of France.

66. He remained in Paris only a short time—Jordan, no. 60. He would be in Bologna in the second half of August.

67. Frachet, 72.

68. *Proces. Bon.*, no. 12.

69. Description in Balme, II, 336–338.

70. Frachet, 76; Echard, I, 40, n. K.

71. Frachet, 72.

72. Galvagno, *Major*, 320 and 345, affirms this. On Amizo de Solario, the former pontifical notary, see Echard, I, 48, n. A; Tiraboschi, II, 241; *AFP*, X (1940) 320, n. 3. Galvagno, whose evidence is of some value when facts concerning Milan are in question, instances *ibid*. the acquisition of two other religious: Guido de Capitaneis and Rogier de Merate.

73. Constantino, no. 59.

74. Jordan, no. 60.

75. Jordan, no. 58.

76. Jordan, no. 63 and Ferrando, no. 33.

77. Jordan, no. 64.

78. Frachet, 169, dates the anecdotes from a certain feast of St Stephen. Reginald, arriving on 21st December, 1218, and leaving at latest in November 1219, spent only two feasts of this saint in Bologna—

26th December, 1218 and 3rd August, 1219 (The Finding of St Stephen). It would seem impossible to situate the development of the psychological crisis indicated by the beginning of the account between 21st December and 26th, 1218. There remains the date of 3rd August, 1219. The texts of the two Masses are identical. This date of course fell in the vacation period.

79. Frachet, 169–170; Salagnac, 33 and 158; Echard, I, 122–123; Denifle, ALKMA, II, 232.

80. *Major ecclesia.* One might perhaps translate: the nave, in contradistinction to the choir or to the chapels. In this case the church referred to would be St Nicholas, which would explain the fact that Moneta had heard Mass in St Proclus, a neighbouring church.

81. *Acts* VII, 56.

82. Frachet, 169–170.

83. Frachet, 25.

84. 'Chronique de Sainte-Agnès', ASOP, I, 181, n. 10; Frachet, 20. The step the brethren took in approaching the chaplain was prior to Reginald's arrival.

85. Having passed through Bologna on his way from Florence on 9th October, 1218, he was at Vicenza in January 1219, in February in Venice, on 10th April at Modena, then in Bologna where he remained at least until 18th—See Levi, *Documenti*, 8.

86. *Proces. Bon.*, no. 30.

87. *Ibid.*

88. *Proces. Bon.*, nos. 30–34; Frachet, 27, 275. He died at the same time as Roland of Cremona, ca. 1250.

89. On this family, cf. *infra*, n. 125.

90. For this description, cf. Laurent, no. 93; Frachet, 198. The 'piece of enclosed land' (*clusum*) mentioned by the charter was a surface unit. Cf. Laurent, no. 126. The deeds of acquisition of five of these houses by the brethren have been preserved: from Petronio Triclo (11th July, 1220), from Gilbert the donkey-driver (22nd July), from Ghibellino of Ferrara (10th October, 1221), from Rainaldo, university courier (17th February, 1223), from Piccolo Ricardo (8th April, 1224)—Laurent, no. 115, 116; Mamachi, Appendix 375–376; ASOP, IV, 169, n. 1 and 170, n. 3. It was after 1208 that this suburban district was included within the walls—Hessel, 439.

91. 'Chronique de Sainte-Agnès', ASOP, I, 181, n. 10.

92. Laurent, no. 93.

93. The last clothing mentioned at the Mascarella took place in Lent 1219—*Proces. Bon.*, no. 46. The gift of St Nicholas dated from 14th March. Easter was 7th April. Roland of Cremona took the habit at the end of April or beginning of May—cf. *infra*, n. 109.

94. Frachet, 190–191, placed his meeting with Fr Richard the elder, prior of the brethren, and his entry into the order, at St Nicholas, *ubi de novo venerant fratres*. Echard, I, 91, insists on the authority attributed to Richard and thinks that Reginald was not yet there: he thus corrects Frachet and places this meeting at Santa Maria della Mascarella, as early as 1218. The correction may be considered arbitrary, with Mamachi, 508, n. 3, for Reginald's arrival did not take away from Richard his office as prior. The entry would date from about April 1219. On Fr Tancred, cf. also Jordan, no. 100; Constantino, no. 35 and 65 (cf. Barthélémy, 237; for criticism of this information—Altaner, 71); Echard, I, 90–91.

95. He entered at la Mascarella and was clothed by Reginald in Lent 1219, which we interpret as Ash Wednesday, February 20th—*Proces. Bon.*, no. 46. On his place of origin (the Penna of the Ancona Marches rather than that of the Abruzzi) see Echard, I, 55, n. A and Balme, II, 262. A Frogier appeared again in 1254 in the acts of the Roman province—Altaner, 35, n. 3.

96. *Proces. Bon.*, no. 41 (on the exact date see Echard, I, 54, n. A). In 1233 he was in the Venice house where he died later. Frachet 40 and 270.

97. According to the 2nd edition of the *Vitae Fratrum*, Guala was sacristan when Roland of Cremona took the habit. Frachet, 26, n. 22. He had thus entered before Easter, 1219. He founded Brescia, where he became bishop in 1229, carried out various missions and died on 3rd September, 1244, at the abbey of Astino (near Bergamo). Cf. Balme, II, 357–364 and Kuczynski, *Le Bx Guala de Bergame . . .* Estavayer, 1916.

98. Already in the order when Roland took the habit, according to Frachet, 26, who notes his titles of master and professor in arts and canon law, his competence in civil law, his later titles of prior of the Roman province and penitentiary and chaplain to the Pope. The mss. of Brussels and St Antonin thus complete his name: *Clarus de Sexto dioecesis Florentine*. If, however, this Fr Clare is to be identified with the one mentioned by Frachet, 21, he was a native of Bologna. Cf. Echard, I, 92–93.

99. Cf. *infra*, n. 109.

100. Entered under Reginald, before St Dominic's arrival (August 1219), *Proces. Bon.*, no. 20. Founder of Piacenza, he gave evidence in 1233 at the canonization process—*Proces. Bon.*, nos. 20–24. Further details in Echard, I, 49, n. A.

101. *Dania*, 500. These are the first known Swedish students in the west of Europe—Gallén, 3. It is not said that they received the habit at Dominic's hands—this would certainly have been mentioned if it were the case.

102. Frachet, 19. It was Alexander Stavensby, for long professor of theology in Bologna who told this story. For Fr Henry, the convent is 'Bethany'—Jordan, no. 75. On the entry of Fr Giacomo de Ariboldis de Modoetia and Robaldo di Albinga, see Galvagno, *Major*, 320, and nn. 5 and 346, where a few other names will be found, among them that of Philip Carisi de Vercelli, procurator of the brethren during the canonization process.

103. 81, 152, 153, 166, 194, 196, 198.

104. Jordan, nos. 110–120. Cf. dissertation of Christianopoulo on this institution, ASOP, I, 116–121,

in which he corrects where necessary the statements of Frachet, no. 58; Bourbon, no. 189; Cantimpré, 309; Galvagno, etc . . .

105. Frachet, 153.

106. Frachet, 198.

107. Frachet, 152. This was the penance for a grave fault. A similar fault, assigned in 1236 to the chapter on light faults (*I. Const.* D. I, ch. 21, no. 39; *Acta*, I, 14, no. 14) was previously in point of fact among the grave faults. Thus Reginald was here applying the rule strictly.

108. Frachet, 169.

109. At the end of April or beginning of May, 1219, if account be taken of the fact that Ugolino was in Bologna (cf. foll. note) and that Fr Rudolfo was in the community (Frachet, 27).

110. After 10th May when he was in Modena, Ugolino came to Bologna and remained there at least until 18th May—Levi, *Documenti*, 8 [244]; Brem, 36.

111. Frachet, 25–27, 168, 275; Salagnac, 32–33 and 124; Pelisson, 8, 10, 11, 12; Echard, I, 125–127; Glorieux, I, 42; E. Filthaut, *Roland von Cremona OP* . . . Vechta, 1936; *AFP*, X (1940), 282–288 and XI (1941), 109–137.

112. On the origin of his trouble see Frachet 168.

113. According to two mss., Fr Guala is here referred to. The little bell was not worth 20 imperial sous.

114. Frachet, 25–27.

115. Dominic was already at St Nicholas on September 1st, 1219—*Proces. Bon.*, no. 46. He was not yet there on 3rd August when Moneta entered—Frachet, 169–170; and probably on 15th August—cf. *supra*, no. 101. Cf. *Proces. Bon.*, no. 41.

116. A. Dondaine, 'La hiérarchie cathare en Italie', in *AFP*, XIX (1949) 208–312; XX (1950) 234–324. For catalogue of the Catharist bishops, see pp. 267–306.

117. Jordan, no. 60.

118. *Proces. Bon.*, no. 30.

119. *Proces. Bon.*, nos. 12, 32, 43, 47; Ferrando, no. 32.

120. Jordan, no. 60.

121. *Proces. Bon.*, no. 32. Cf. no. 38, 42.

122. Jordan, no. 42.

123. *Proces. Bon.*, no. 32.

124. On Diana, see H. Cormier, *La Bse Diane et les Bses Cécile et Aimée*, Rome, 1892; M. Aron, *Un animateur de la jeunesse au XIIIe s: Jourdain de Saxe*, Paris—Bruges 1930, 138–152. For the whole of this paragraph see 'Chronique de Sainte-Agnès', in Cormier, 149–150 and *ASOP*, I, 181, n. 10.

125. Cf. Melloni, *Atti e memorie degli uomini illustri in santità o morti in Bologna*, I, pt. 2, Bologna 1779, 195–209; Cormier, *op. cit.*, Appendix B (genealogy); *ASOP*, I, 181. As many as fourteen important towns were governed at this time by members of the family.

126. Frachet, 82–83; *Proces. Bon.*, nos. 35–36. Pierre Calo, no. 18 ed. Mamachi, Appendix 344.

127. *Proces. Bon.*, no. 36. The account would seem to date Dominic's first coming to St Nicholas. The 'fere per annum' of no. 37 must thus be understood of the total duration of the saint's presences in Bologna after the entry of Fr Stephen.

128. Noted by Bernard Gui as the oldest of all the Lombardy convents (after Bologna)—Echard, I, XIV; cf. also the list in order of seniority about 1280, given by Christianopoulo (*ASOP*, I, 187 and n. 3; 52, n. 3)—Bologna, Bergamo, Milan, Verona, Piacenza, Brescia, Faenza, Parma, Genoa. Since Milan dates from March 1220, Bergamo was earlier.

129. Frogier de Penna had lived with Dominic in the 'convent' of Florence at the beginning of September, 1219 (the decision in favour of this date with Echard, I, 55, n. C against Scheeben, 322, is because it is the only one compatible with Frogier's '4 months and more'; Scheeben's chronology would presuppose 10 months of contact between Frogier and Dominic), *Proces. Bon.*, no. 46. At this time the brethren were still living in a hospice (St Pancras—Mamachi, 605, n. 2); it was not yet the religious house in the strict sense. The list in order of seniority for the Roman province places Florence after Rome (Echard, I, 32, n. A) which dates from December, 1219. In 1220, on the other hand, the brethren had acquired a church (St Paul—*ASOP*, I, 189, n. 5), one of the former priests or canons of which caused them difficulties—Constantino, no. 52. After having changed their establishment several times (for further details, not all equally reliable, see Mamachi, 603–606), and after the influential intervention of Ugolino on 14th June, 1221 (Laurent, no. 151), the prior John of Salerno, and the brethren received the church of Santa Maria Novella on 9th November, 1221—Mamachi, Appendix 77. Cf. Balme, II, 365, n. I.

130. A convent was already in existence at Easter, 1220; Fr Solomon, the founder of Lund, was received into the order there at that date—*Dania*, 500. Borselli took the date of 1220 from the foundation inscription of the Dominican church of Verona—text in Balme, III, 133, n. 1.

131. The church of St Eustorga of Milan was given to the Preachers by a charter of 24th November, 1220 (Laurent, no. 118), by Ugo Settala, treasurer of the church of Milan and vicar of the archbishop, Henry Settala then in the East, the canons who served this particular church having surrendered it. The supporting evidence of an old Dominican lectionary of Milan and of Bernard Gui established the fact that the brethren were already installed by 15th March, 1220 (Echard, I, XIV and 20, n. R). There is nothing surprising in the delay before the charter was issued (cf. *supra*, n. 59). It presupposed the intervention of several earlier documents, to one of which, dated 10th August, 1220, it refers. The prior who was founder was a Fr Giacomo. This gives a certain credit to the statements of Galvagno della Fiamma, but not to all of them. His short chronicle also gives the date of 15th March, 1220 for the

provisional installation of the brethren at St Eustorga—*Minor*, 23; but the longer version has: 15th February, 1220—*Major*, 322 (is this a simple *lapsus?*). He calls the two founders Giacomo de Ariboldis de Modoetia and Robaldo de Albinga (anecdote on this friar in Frachet, 225-227). Dominic is said to have received them in Bologna, where they were studying, in 1219. In this case they could not have arrived in Milan for a foundation in March 1219, as Galvagno says—*Minor*, 23 and *Major*, 320 and 346. The intervention of Cardinal Ugolino in 1220, in Milan, which Galvagno imagines, for the cession of St Eustorga is in contradiction with the legate's itinerary—Levi, *Documenti*, 9 [245]. Dominic's visits to Milan in December 1217, August 1219 and June 1220 certainly contributed to the foundation—Echard, I, 20, n. R; Balme, III, 115-127.

132. *Proces. Bon.*, no. 24.
133. *Proces. Bon.*, no. 20.
134. After Verona and before Brescia (cf. *supra*, n. 128). A recommendation from the Pope of the type I² (cf. Appendix VI), issued 11th November, 1219, resulted in Piacenza (Potthast, no. 6155). It was almost certainly brought by Fr Buonviso, who was at the Curia in November 1219. In any event it signifies the continuation of the ministry in the town. On 20th April, 1221, six Preachers were there and served as witnesses in the swearing of the oath by the city authorities before the Legate Ugolino— Laurent, no. 135. On 10th May, the Pope sent a special recommendation of the order, of type V, to the bishop and chapter of Piacenza—Laurent, no. 143. The foundation came shortly afterwards—Balme, III, 346-348, following Campi, *Storia eccl. di Piacenza*, II, Piacenza 1651, 120-123, whose date of 1218, however, for the first arrival of Fr Buonviso in Piacenza cannot be accepted!
135. Jordan, no. 61.
136. Jordan, no. 62.
137. Dominic was in Viterbo before 11th November, 1219—Potthast, no. 6155, but he remained some time in Florence—*Proces. Bon.*, no. 46 and Constantino, no. 46. Moreover the duration of his stay in Bologna cannot be reduced—Jordan, no. 60; note the opposition between the expressions: *mansionem faciens* and *paululum demoratus*.

NOTES TO CHAPTER XV

1. *Proces. Bon.*, no. 12.
2. *Proces. Bon.*, nos. 20-22.
3. *Proces. Bon.*, no. 46. Scheeben, 323 places the journey from Bologna to Rome through Florence, mentioned by Frogier, in 1221; but the natural sense of the words and the duration of four months and more mentioned by the brother contradict this interpretation—according to which he would have remained with Dominic for about ten months at least. The other historians accept the normal interpretation.
4. According to an indication of the necrology of Santa María Novella—Mamachi, 605, n. 3.
5. *Ibidem*.
6. Constantino, nos. 46 and 52. Cf. Echard, I, 33, n. A; Altaner, 66 and n. 5. Christianopoulo, in a careful note, corrects Echard's chronology and places Béné's conversion in May 1220. At this period, in fact, the brethren were already in possession of the church of St Paul, of which Hugh of Sixtus was canon—*ASOP*, I, 189, n. 5.
7. He obtained two bulls on 11th November—Appendix VI, § 6, nos. 4 and 14 and [5] 10.
8. Gregorovius, *Geschichte der Stadt Rom in MA*, V, Berlin 1908, 120-121.
9. Potthast, no. 6131 ff; on 17th December, he was at Civita Castellana—no. 6184—and again in Viterbo until 2nd June, 1220; he did not return to Rome until 26th October, for the coronation of Frederick II.
10. Levi, *Documenti*, 9; Brem, 36; Potthast, no. 6124.
11. In July 1219, there were about thirty of them in Paris; there must have been about fifty of them in Bologna, if we note the difference of the terms used by Jordan—nos. 59 and 60. To these two houses must be added Prouille (the house of Preaching), Toulouse, Lyons, Madrid, Segovia, Limoges.
12. Brem, 74-101 and Zarncke, 56 and 103-106.
13. Laurent, no. 77.
14. Cernai, nos. 393 and 509.
15. Laurent, no. 84. Cf. Appendix VI, § 3, 14, 15.
16. Type II, *Dilecti filii*, from 8th December, 1219.
17. Type III, *Cum qui recipit* from 11th November, 1219.
18. Type IV, *Quoniam abundavit*, from 13th December, 1219—cf. Matt. XXIV, 12.
19. Laurent, no. 117—dated 29th July, 1220; cf. *Rom.* I, 1.
20. Laurent, no. 103.
21. Laurent, nos. 107 and 107 bis.
22. Laurent, no. 117.
23. Laurent, nos. 121 and 124. On 7th March, 1222, he used even stronger terms: 'Cum nos, quibus incumbit specialius exaltare ac fovere religionem, in suavi sancti vestre institutionis odore plurimum delectemur, conceptum devotionis vestre fervorum singulari quodam affectu prosequimur, et aliquid vobis libenter amplioris dilectionis et gratie impertimur', *BOP*, I, 15, no. 28.
24. 'Qui fuit amicissimus ordinis et beati Dominici ab initio, familiaritate cum eo in curia pape contracta', *Chron. IIa*, 334; Donner, 9-17. Koudelka, 98 ff, thinks this friendship dated from 1216.
25. Barthélemy, no. 17. Was it on account of this spiritual fraternity that *Chron. Ia*, 335, counted Guillaume among the cardinals of the order? He was buried in the Dominican convent at Lyons.

26. Donner, 13. On the functions of the vice-chancellor, see P. Fabre, *Le liber censuum de l'Eglise romaine*, II, Paris 1910, 73.

27. He again obtained a bull from the curia on 17th December—Laurent, no. 104; he obtained a further one on 17th February, no. 105. It is difficult to say whether his stay in Viterbo was then continuous and if he did not return to Rome in between, for instance at the beginning of March 1220. Perhaps the *redeundo Roman* of Buonviso (*Proces. Bon.*, no. 20) is in favour of the second hypothesis.

28. Type I^2, Appendix VI, § 6, no. 2.

29. Type I^2, Appendix VI, § 6, no. 5.

30. Type I^2, Appendix VI, § 6, no. 6. The bullarium which forms the basis of the collection of Rodez ms. comes from a convent in the south of France which is not that of Toulouse. Only the convent of Montpellier could have bulls such as nos. 6 and 11 in their archives. That is why we consider as certain what Planzer, *AFP*, V (1935) 19, suggests as an hypothesis.

31. Gui, 529. It should be noted that in Narbonne the brethren had made a foundation earlier but it could not be maintained in the face of the hostility of certain people—cf. Balme, III, 83–85.

32. Laurent, no. 99.

33. Laurent, no. 101.

34. Laurent, no. 102.

35. Laurent, no. 77.

36. Appendix VI, § 14.

37. Appendix VI, § 15 and 16.

38. Cf. *infra*, the death of Reginald. It was not until 29th July that the Pope could thank the canons for the grant of the cemetery—Laurent, no. 117.

39. Jordan, no. 75.

40. Laurent, no. 120.

41. Pressutti, nos. 2279, 2410, 2412, 2509, 2518. Balme, III, 109–110 and 144–146.

42. Laurent, no. 117.

43. Charter of confirmation of the surrender of the tithes in Balme, III, 32–33. This document, dated 1225, sets out the reasons for the gesture of 1220. Another trait of generosity—according to Laurent, no. 120, the brethren continued the hospitality of St Jacques and received strangers.

44. *Chron. IIa*, 322; Bourbon, no. 288. Numerous links between the benefactors of St Jacques and the feudal milieu of the south-west of Paris which had fought in the Albigeois can be found—Balme, II, 253, n. 3 and 255 and III, 34–37.

45. Laurent, no. 111.

46. Laurent, no. 114; the deed is not dated, but it is attached to a deed of May 1220—Balme, III, 37, n. 1. See Koudelka, 114 for the end part of this deed, and date.

47. Cf. *supra*, n. 43.

48. According to the bullarium of the Rodez ms.—*AFP*, V (1935), 48, no. 18.

49. Type II, Appendix VI, § 6, no. 11.

50. Laurent, no. 134.

51. Appendix VI, § 10–16.

52. Mandonnet-Vicaire, I, 163, n. 20. Cf. a contemporary document which compares the establishment of the hospital of the Holy Spirit and the reconstruction of St Sixtus—Zucchi, 333.

53. Benedict of Montefiascone, ed. Echard, I, 83.

54. Heimbucher, I, 417.

55. Laurent, no. 88.

56. Bull of 4th December, 1219. Laurent, no. 100, mentions this visit; it took place in November 1219, since on the 12th of that month the religious obtained an important bull—Pressutti, no. 2252.

57. Laurent, no. 100.

58. Gesture mentioned by Laurent, no. 104.

59. Laurent, no. 104.

60. Prior of St Sixtus from 1311 to 1318, during which time he composed an original chronicle, based on direct information, of which only extracts are left to us—see Echard, I, 83 (cf. 536). He places the foundation in 1220 (cf. 'ab initio erectionis, an. 1220'). He thought that the saint had received the house for his brethren and only transformed it, as a matter of conscience, into a convent of sisters when he later learned of its original destination. This latter assertion is contradicted by the Pope's letters.

61. Laurent, no. 136.

62. The fact, which Potthast does not mention, is clear in Pressutti, nos. 2303 to 2309.

63. For the description which follows, see Zucchi, 323–328; 333–337.

64. Laurent, no. 88.

65. Scheeben, 291–292 invokes the Pope's letters to Sempringham. Zucchi, 260, rightly considers that the argument is not conclusive. A different argument is given here.

66. Zucchi, 337–344.

67. Constantino, no. 36 and 39. The accounts of Constantino cannot be taken as wholly trustworthy—he embellishes his information to the extent of distorting it. Cf. Altaner, 58–74. The miracle of the raising to life of the workman, however, seems also referred to by Jordan, no. 126.

68. IV Kings IV, 34.

69. Altaner, 63.

70. Today, Via Valle delle Camene. This identification, following Père Koudelka, who bases himself on the monastery charters, rejects that of Zucchi, 267.

71. He brought back to Lombardy Buonviso who at this time seems to have been his accredited *socius*—*Proces. Bon.*, no. 22. Guillaume de Montferrat would seem to have remained in Viterbo—*ibid.*, no. 12. Frogier was now separated from Dominic after a daily contact of 'four months and more'. As he had been with him since 1st September, 1219, it was thus some time in January 1220 that Dominic left him, leaving him behind in Rome—*ibid.*, 46.

72. *Proces. Bon.*, no. 12.

73. Jordan, no. 94; *Proces. Bon.*, nos. 6, 8, 12, 22, 23; *Proces. Thol.*, no. 15.

74. *Proces. Thol.*, no. 15.

75. The calculation is easily made. He took eight days to go from Rocamadour to Orléans—Frachet, 74. The medieval traveller, on foot, normally accomplished stages of 15 to 25 miles.

76. See *Proces. Bon.*, nos. 21 and 42, for this period of his life. This was already his habit in the Narbonensis.

77. No. 42. On the discomforts of this kind of hospice, its dirt, its overcrowding, see Frachet, 36, 39, 40. On the rising at night even while travelling, for Matins, see *ASOP*, I, 325, n. 3 and Echard, I, 412.

78. No. 4.

79. Nos. 6, 13, 20, 31, 42, 43.

80. Nos. 6, 31.

81. Cecilia, 6.

82. *Proces. Bon.*, no. 12.

83. *Proces. Bon.*, no. 13.

84. Jordan, no. 106; *Proces. Bon.*, nos. 7, 13, 18, 20, 28, 31, 37, 42, 46, 52.

85. Laurent, no. 105.

86. The expression *prior et fratres O.P.* which, in the context, should be taken in the conventual sense, is found in Laurent, nos. 102 and 103—cf. Balme, II, 396, n. a. After 17th February, 1220 (no. 105), the expression *prior OP* will be found (no. 119), and *prior et fratres OP* in the sense of prior of the order (nos. 128 and 130). On 28th April, 1221, no. 138, the expression is replaced by *magister et fr. OP.*

87. *Proces. Bon.*, no. 2.

88. Nos. 2 and 33.

89. Jordan, no. 86. The letter must have reached the religious about Easter for the necessary arrangements to be made and the delegates to be in Bologna on 17th May.

90. Jordan, no. 63.

91. No. 64.

92. Frachet, 248–249.

93. Jordan, no. 64. On the Benedictine convent of Notre Dame des Vignes or des Champs and the later history of Reginald's tomb, looked after from the 17th century to the time of the Revolution by a community of Carmelite nuns, see Balme, III, 15–16. The cultus of Blessed Reginald, continuous from the origin, was recognized in 1875.

94. Laurent, no. 107 bis.

95. No. 107.

96. Nos. 108, 109, 110.

97. Math. X, 41 and recommendation III, Appendix VI, § 6, no. 13 ff.

98. Matt. XXV, 40 and bull of 29th July, 1220—Laurent, no. 117.

99. Appendix VI, § 6, no. 13.

100. Villanueva, XIX, 178 and 310 (donation to the Carthusians on 21st December, 1219, to recognize their merits).

101. Appendix VI, § 6, no. 27. The letter which remained in the hands of the brethren, finally reached Barcelona.

102. Laurent, no. 113.

103. Names rectified by the critical apparatus of *BOP*, I, 11, no. 16. The text of the charter, in the 18th century edition which is the only one which has come down to us, reads Mansu, Aquilari. Fr Russo, *L'eredità di Giocchino da Fiore. La congregazione Florense*, in *Archivio storico per la Calabria e la Lucania*, XXI (1952), 139, gives—Sillia, or rather Mesa, the region in Calabria in which the monasteries of St Martin de Mesa, San Salvatore de Mesa, San Pancracio de Mesa or de Stella, are to be found.

104. Donner, 17, n. 2.

105. *Dania*, 500.

106. Gallén, 4–5, corrects *Dania* 500 here.

107. *Dania*, 500.

108. Appendix VI, § 6, no. 14.

109. Laurent, no. 125.

110. On account of the opposition of the archbishop of Uppsala—Gallén, 5–6.

111. That of the convent of Lund, by Fr Solomon.

112. Altaner, *Dominikanermissionen*, 141–142; Rassovsky, *Les Comans, Annales de l' Institut Kondakov à Prague*, X (1938), 155–178.

113. Potthast, nos. 5598, 6863, 6864.

114. *Proces. Bon.*, nos. 32 and 34. Only those indications referring to the end of his life are certain. Jordan's mention of the Cumans in 1206 (no. 17) corrected to Saracens in the second edition of the *Libellus*, is valueless.

115. Scheeben, 358–361, after *Dania* 500 and Frachet, 305, thought it even possible to establish the existence of a convent in Hungary before May 1220, founded at Stuhlweissenburg (*Alba Regalis* or

Székesfehérvár) by a certain Fr Paul. A criticism of this interpretation will be found in ch. XIX, n. 41.

116. *Dania*, 500—cf. Scheeben, 360; *AFP*, XIX (1949), 83, n. 9.

117. Scheeben, 360; *AFP*, XIX (1949), 83, n. 9.

NOTES TO CHAPTER XVI

1. He must also have received at Viterbo the bull of 6th May, 1220 for the Archbishop of Tarragona—Laurent, no. 112. As he had to be in Bologna on the 16th, he had ten days in which to travel some 215 miles; this was normal. As to the date of the general chapter, over which there is no hesitation among historians, cf. Balme, III, 56, n. a.

2. *Proces. Bon.*, nos. 20 and 22.

3. Cf. *supra*, ch. 15, nn. 5 and 6.

4. At this time some fifteen foundations had been made—Madrid, Segovia, Toulouse, Montpellier (?), Lyons, Limoges, Paris, Bologna, Brescia, Verona, Florence, St Sixtus, Friesach, Stuhlweissenburg (?). Madrid and St Sixtus were still houses for men, Prouille housed the two communities, one of men, one of women. Paris sent four brethren, the other houses at least two, which made, apart from Bologna, at least thirty.

5. *Dania*, 500.

6. Jordan, no. 86.

7. As to his age when he entered the order, Scheeben, *Jordan*, 8, and *QF*, XXXV, 35 give about thirty-five. With better foundation, Aron, 45, says—scarcely less than 43.

8. On Jordan, see Aron; Scheeben, *Jordan* and *Beiträge zur Geschichte Jordans von Sachsen*, *QF*, XXXV, 1938.

9. *Proces. Bon.*, no. 2. We interpret 'eodem anno' according to the obvious meaning (in 1220). If we were to translate: in the year which followed the brother's clothing, it would be possible to conclude from this that he had already entered in the autumn of 1219—which would provide a better explanation of the details of the account.

10. On Paul of Hungary who entered before the 1220 chapter, was prior of Bologna from 1220–1221 and was then sent to Hungary by the second chapter, see 'Chronique de Sainte-Agnès', *ASOP*, I, 181, n. 10; Laurent, no. 126; Frachet, 305; Pfeiffer, 18–21; Mandonnet-Vicaire, I, 249–269.

11. *I Const.* 218 (II D, ch. 17).

12. *Proces. Bon.*, no. 43.

13. This description is based on the chapter ceremonial that the Bologna assembly in point of fact adopted—*I Const.*, 218–219 (D. II, ch. 17). The reasons which allow us to identify the texts of 1220 in the primitive constitutions will be given later.

14. *Proces. Bon.*, no. 2.

15. *Proces. Bon.*, no. 33. The word *inutilis* is technical in this case; it designates the superior who can no longer render service—Guignard, 83 and 84 (charter of charity of Cîteaux); *I Const.*, 215 (D.II, ch. 9). Cf. also Luke XVII, 10; Jordan, no. 1.

16. *Proces. Bon.*, no. 2.

17. *Proces. Bon.*, no. 33.

18. Each time that the assembly was too numerous or insufficiently competent—Customs of Cîteaux XXX,—Guignard, 258; 12th canon of the Lateran—Hefele-Leclercq, V, 1342 (where the four elected persons preside and confirm; *I Const.*, 212–213 (D.II, ch. 1–3, provincial chapter).

19. He declared in fact in 1229 in letter XLIX 'that he knew fully all the acts, institutions and intentions of all the general chapters'—Jordan, *Epistulae*, 55. He missed the chapter of 1221, however. He would not have been able to speak in this way had he not been closely concerned in the definitions of 1220.

20. *I Const.* 219 (D.II, ch. 18). This work is likewise found in the profession formula—*I Const.*, 202–203 (D.I, ch. 16), (but this formula dates from 1221); and in the paragraph on the daily chapter *I Const.*, 196 (D.I, ch. 2); we are still dealing with a later correction. The original text mentioned, as did the text of Prémontré which is its source, the reading of the *regula* (of St Augustine) at the chapter: the order in fact borrowed this custom. The word *institutiones* which occurs in the Rodez text shows that the order tried, later and without result, rather to have the constitutions read. For the significance of the alternation *regula, institutiones, constitutiones*, cf. Meersseman, *Loi pénale*, 979, n. 9.

21. Preamble of 1228, *I Const.*, 194.

22. Cf. *supra*, ch. XI, n. 124.

23. *I Const.*, 194 (Prologue).

24. Appendix VI, § 14 and 15.

25. *I Const.*, 194 (Prologue). Cf. Frachet, 150.

26. Meersseman, *Loi pénale*.

27. Humbert II, 46. Meersseman, *Loi pénale*, 978.

28. *Acta*, 8.

29. Meersseman, *Loi pénale*, 975–988. On the private origins of this innovation see *ibidem*, 988–1002.

30. Later chapters gave no definition of him either. In the medieval Dominican constitutions, there is nothing about the head of the order. Jordan's conception in 1229 should, however, be noted.—Ep. XLIX, Jordan, *Epistulae*, 56—one who had the power of dispensing from even the most binding laws, apart from three exceptions. This was indeed the plenitude of executive power.

31. *I Const.*, 220 (D.II, ch. 20 and 21).

32. Laurent, nos. 105, 113, 119, 128, 130, 132.

33. Laurent, nos. 134, 138, 145 of the 17th and 28th April and 24th May, 1221. Letter to the sisters of Madrid—Balme, III, 79. Foundation inscription of Dominican church in Verona, *supra*, ch. XIV, n. 130.

34. The picture of the Preacher fighting against the devil, or against the enemies of the Church in the whole universe, goes back to Dominic—*Proces. Bon.*, no. 36; cf. Vitry, 349 and Mandonnet-Vicaire, I, 236, n. 18; Jordan, no. 114; Frachet, 18, n. 1; Bull of Canonization—*MOPH*, XVI, 192. Honorius III gave the Preachers the name of 'lightly-armed soldiers' *expeditus*—recommendation type II (*Dilecti filii*), Laurent, no. 103; cf. Jacques de Vitry, *loc. cit. supra*. Cf. St Thomas—'officium predicatorum et doctorum est officium militum', *In II ad Tim.*, ch. 2, lesson 1.

35. *I Const.*, 202 (D.I, ch. 14). This vow disappeared from the constitutions in 1255—Creytens, 'Les constitutions des Fr. Pr. dans la rédaction de S Raymond de Peñafort', in *AFP*, XVIII (1948), 19 and n. 40.

36. Seeing no possibility of finding a Dominican monastery, Diana entered the house of the Benedictines of Ronzano, *ASOP*, I, 182, n. 10.

37. For examples of these different professions—Jordan, nos. 56, 74, 75; *Proces. Bon.*, nos. 25, 41, 46; Frachet, 170, 183, 192; *Chronica IIa*, 327.

38. *ASOP*, II, 639 (*I Const.*, D. II, ch. 13, a phrase forgotten by Denifle). Jordan, no. 87.

39. This was the explanation given by Bernard Gui, *Acta*, I; Chapotin, 20. In point of fact Bologna, then in full process of construction, is sufficiently large. At this time Paris was too small.

40. On the origins and development of this institution at Monte Cassino, then at Cîteaux, etc.— Schreiber, II, 296, n. 2 and 324–334; J. Hourlier, *Le chapitre général jusqu'au moment du Grand Schisme, origines, développement, étude juridique*, Paris 1936. Cîteaux texts—Guignard, 79–84; for Prémontré—Martène, *Rit.*, III, 334 (D. III, ch. I and II), to which must be added the formulary *Pour la célébration du chapitre général en usage en 1217*, ed. Pl. F. Lefèvre—*Les Statuts de Prémontré* . . . Louvain 1946, 144–145 (for the date, 12˙ʃ and not 1227, cf. xxix).

41. Hefele-Leclercq, V, 1342–1343.

42. It is not known whether in 1220 a document had been drawn up on the recruitment of the members of the chapter. What is to be found on this point in the primitive constitutions dates from after Dominic's death. Perhaps the same system was envisaged as in 1220—the election of representatives by the various houses?

43. *I Const.*, 214 (D. II, ch. 6); cf. 194 (Preamble of 1228).

44. *I Const.*, 219–220 (D. II, ch. 20). Before the intervention of the chapter, the prior could, however, give a limited mission.

45. *I Const.*, 220 (D. II, ch. 21).

46. *Proces. Bon.*, no. 33. *I Const.*, 214–215 (D. II, ch. 8 and 9); cf. for Cîteaux, Guignard, 83–84. For an example of correction of the Master in chapter (Jordan of Saxony), see Frachet, 117.

47. *I Const.*, 219 (D. II, ch. 18 and 19).

48. Jordan, nos. 86–87; *Proces. Bon.*, nos. 2 and 33; Humbert, II, 46.

49. Bernard Gui in what is known as the Rodez ms., ed. *ASOP*, II, 1895–1896, 621–647. Cf. Mamachi, 592.

50. Denifle in *ALKMA*, I (1885), 165.

51. Mandonnet-Vicaire, II, 203–230, where every endeavour was made to treat the question thoroughly, in 1938. The explanation there given has never been contradicted. In an independent critical study, indeed—H. Ch. Scheeben, *QF*, 38 (1939), 20, correcting his earlier position, in turn recognized the 1220 legislation in the Rodez manuscript. We have summarized our earlier study under a more synthetic form in Vicaire, *Documents* 113–121, clearing up certain divergencies between Scheeben and ourselves.

52. Cf. 'Les institutions des Prêcheurs (1220 and 1221–1227)', in Mandonnet-Vicaire, II, 287–292. The principles of this restitution will be found *ibid.*, 273–283. Since it is possible that certain elements of the original text have disappeared or been modified without leaving any trace, the restitution is doubtless incomplete. It is however trustworthy for the great majority of the texts. Since 1938 no objection has been put forward against this attempt at restitution. H. Ch. Scheeben, *QF*, 35 (1939), 25 in his independent study has assigned the date of 1220 to precisely the same texts—cf. Vicaire, *Documents*, 114–116.

53. *I Const.*, 195 (prologue), from which we have withdrawn the word 'provinciali', which corresponds to the complementary text (1221–1225), edited in Mandonnet-Vicaire, II, 284–287.

54. Mandonnet-Vicaire, II, 287–289. The procedure of the chapter according to this text is parallel to that indicated in the *ordo* of Prémontré of 1217 (*supra*, n. 41). In actual fact, analogous arrangements were already in existence for the chapters of Cîteaux—cf. Guignard, 258, 263, 270, 271. No literary dependence, however, can be noted between the various texts referring to this.

55. In 1212, the general chapter of Cîteaux reserved to itself the right to allow its religious to preach— Canivez, I, 400, no. 50. It was the same at Prémontré, according to the statutes of 1234, ed. Lefèvre, *Les St de Prémontré* . . . Louvain 1942, 90. This, however, was not the canonical mission.

56. *I Const.*, 222 (D. II, ch. 26). Cf. *Proces. Bon.*, nos. 38, 42 and 47.

57. Hefele-Leclercq, VI, 201.

58. Although many historians continue to speak, not without thoughtlessness it must be admitted, of the supposed influence of the poverty of St Francis on St Dominic, nothing is said of this. The meeting of the two saints remains hypothetical. The only plausible hypothesis places this meeting after the Bologna chapter, at the beginning of 1221, in Rome (cf. *supra*, ch. XI, n. 4 and ch. XII, n. 87). Moreover,

and this is the most important point, the type of Franciscan mendicancy at this time had nothing to give Dominic and his brethren. Dominic was seeking a model of conventual mendicity for religious to whom he forbade all other work but their spiritual labour of prayer, study and preaching. Now at this time St Francis had no real conventual organization and did not wish to have, but envisaged making his brethren live primarily by their manual work—*Regula bullata*, no. 7 and *Testament*, no. 5—Boehmer-Wiegand, 5 and 25.

59. From the so-called 'Règle de St Etienne', ch. IX and XIII, ed. *Rit.*, IV, 310 and 311. Actually the rule is that of the 4th prior of Grandmont, Etienne de Liciac (1139–1163)—Becquet, 134. The text edited by Martène and that in *PL*, 204, 1135–1162, is that corrected and published by Clement III in 1188. It is that existing at the time of the Bologna chapter, but with the complementary statutes given by Honorius III on 1st March, 1219, edited by Martène, *Rit.*, IV, 322–325. For the Dominican mendicant practices, see *Proces. Bon.*, nos. 32, 42; Frachet, 29, 127; Cecilia, no. 3.

60. *Règle*, ch. IV–VI, IX, XIII—Martène, *Rit.*, 309–311.

61. *Règle*, ch. LIV–LV, *loc. cit.*, 315–316. Corrected by the institution of a prior taken from among the clerics, set over the clerics and the lay brethren—statutes of 1219, I and II, *loc. cit.*, 322.

62. The order of Grandmont did not extend beyond the boundaries of France. It had numerous houses in the Midi.

63. *Proces. Bon.*, no. 26.

64. Several crises, of which two, in 1185–1188 and in 1219, were very serious, had occurred, the lay brethren using their authority to persecute the priests by half starving them. The order had fallen 'in derisum et fabulam'—to use the words of Innocent III—*PL*, 214, 1107. Cf. Martène, *Thesaurus*, I, 845; *Rit.*, IV, 322 (ch. VI); Vitry, 313–315.

65. *I Const.*, 224 (D. II, ch. 31). Cf. *Proces. Bon.*, no. 32.

66. The beggar for money was looked upon as an imposter and had to be arrested by the authorities by orders of the Pope—bull type III, cf. Appendix VI, § 15, no. 8. Anecdote referring to Dominic in Frachet, 153. Later prescription in *I Const.*, 225 (D. II, ch. 34).

67. The bond between a preacher and his usual *socius* was known as the *combinatio*; to break it was a fault—*Acta*, 251–252.

68. The fault for the use of a horse without grave necessity will be found in *I Const.*, 208 (D. I, ch. 22). It was not earlier than 1220. 1. It did not come from Prémontré. 2. When Dominic in 1219 was concerned with stopping the use of a horse in Paris it would seem that he did not base himself on the rule, but relied on the brethren's goodwill—*Proces. Bon.*, no. 26. 3. It is not inserted at precisely the same place, in the chapter on grave faults, in the Rodez ms. as in the Sack friars' Constitutions (ms. British Museum, Nero A XII fo. 161v.) which came from *I Const.*, a proof that it was added later in the margin of the ms. The fault of carrying money is not found in the Rodez ms. Is this an accidental omission in this ms. which is written with some carelessness (cf. *AFP*, XVIII (1948), 19, n. 38 and 39; 20, n. 41; 22, n. 55)? It is found in fact in *II Const.*, 43. Moreover the three prohibitions as to the horse, the carrying of money and meat, always go together—*I Const.*, 194 (Preamble of 1228); Letter XLIX of Jordan, *Epistulae*, 55 (1229); *II Const.*, 43. The fact that *I Const.*, 208 sets down faults for the horse and meat only must be a mistake of the legislator rather than of the ms., for the Sack friars' constitutions (*loc. cit.*) do not give the money fault either. It is true that they do not give the fault for meat.

69. *I Const.*, 225 (D. II, ch. 35).

70. On the canon of Marbach who supervised the studies of the brethren with a view to the priesthood, see Amort, I, 391; Denifle, *ALKMA*, I (1885), 185, n. 2.

71. *I Const.*, 222–223 (D. II, ch. 28–29).

72. *I Const.*, 223–224 (D. II, ch. 31–34).

73. *I Const.*, 195 (Prologue).

74. What are referred to are pieces of parchment folded into four, six or eight divisions on which the students recopied the scholastic texts which afterwards composed their personal theological equipment.

75. In this prescription, which, through Gratian's *Decretal*, goes back in part to Cesarius of Arles, by pagans must be understood the poets of ancient times. The philosophers are principally Aristotle and Avicenna.

76. By 'secular branches of learning' must be understood not the liberal arts in the strict sense of the term—grammar, arithmetic, music, etc., but the subjects which had been added to them in the course of the 12th century—physics, medicine, natural sciences, etc.; cf. canon 8 of the Council of Tours (1163)—Mansi XXI, 1179—reiterated by the constitution of Honorius III, 22nd November, 1219—Laurent, no. 98. On this point Dickson in *AHDLMA*, IX (1934), 119 should be corrected. The statutes of 1213 in Paris forbade the secular sciences to parish priests, allowing them only theology, *sacra pagina*—Mansi, XXII, 845.

77. Allusion to Matt. VI, 34. A Preacher should have no care for the morrow.

78. An ancient law of the Church forbade priests to act as lawyers in secular cases, cf. Paris, 1213; Montpellier, 1214—Mansi, XXII, 831 and 944. The Preachers were even more radical.

79. *Ponere os in coelum* (Ps. LXXII, 9) meant at the time to allow oneself to pass public judgment on one's superiors, and to decide things which were within the superior's province. Cf. Pierre le Chantre—*PL*, 205, 133 BC, 139D; Cernai, no. 593, n. 4 (critical apparatus). Van den Eynde—*Antonianum*, 26 (1951), 244.

80. Cf. Dominic's attitude—*Proces. Bon.*, no. 41; Frachet, 74.

81. The Rodez text has been corrected here and the earlier version restored, preserved, it seems to us, in the institutions of St Sixtus—Simon, 166. Cf. Mandonnet-Vicaire, II, 292 and n. 28.

82. To carry no money on their journey—*Proces. Bon.*, no. 38; to have no property and to live on alms, nos. 42, 47; to speak only of God or with God, nos. 37, 41, 47.

83. *Proces. Bon.*, nos. 38, 41, 47.

84. On Jordan's commentary on Priscian, see M. Grabmann, 'Der Kommentar des sel. Jordanus von Sachsen († 1237) zum Priscianus Minor', in *AFP*, X (1940), 5–19. On his literary heritage—Scheeben in *Hist. Jahrbuch des Görres—Gesellschaft*, 52 (1932), 56–71. The commentary, clear and succinct, gives an impression of living simplicity. At that time there was no work in Paris comparable in the matter of style.

85. Cf. *I Const.*, 223 (D. II, ch. 31, 3) and Jordan, nos. 104–105.

86. Cf. *I Const.*, 219–220 (D. II, ch. 18 and 20); Encyclical in *AFP*, XXII (1952), 182–185; Jordan, no. 78.

87. Cf. *I Const.*, 218–219 (D. II, ch. 17) and Jordan, nos. 16, 79, 109.

88. I.e. his vow of religion.

89. I.e. the canonical rule.

90. Luke X, 35.

91. Salagnac, 8.

92. The gift of oratory was considered as supernatural. 'Non minoris sublimitatis est in clericis evangelizandi gratia, quam in monachis miraculorum potentia'—Anselm de Havelberg—*PL*, 188, 1091. On the current expression *gratia predicationis*, see Jordan, nos. 38, 39, 69, 77. 'Propter eorum [Fr Pred.] gratiam predicationis etalia miranda que faciebant, totus mundus exauditu stupebat'—Luis de Valladolid, *De conventu parisiensi*, ed. Martène—Durand, VI, 551E.

93. Frachet, 146.

94. This is the special function of bishops, preachers, and doctors, to be able to act through an overflow of contemplation, 'ita majus est contemplate aliis tradere, quam solum contemplari'—*Summa theologica*, IIa, IIae, q. 188, a. 6; cf. q. 182, a. 1 ad 1um; III, q. 40, a. 1, ad 2um.

95. Acts, IV, 32.

96. Acts, VI, 4. Cf. Acts, II, 46; III, 1 and 12.

97. Matt. XXVIII, 18–20.

98. Luke IX, 1–4; X, 1–11.

99. This must have been the case with the Ste Trinité in Loubens, with the church between Sorèze and Puylaurens and perhaps with other churches which the Dominican documents do not mention, among them the former chapel of the village of Villenouvelle, St Sernin. This latter church and three others, restored in point of fact to the chapter of St Etienne, served to found 4 prebends known as the prebends of St Dominic, lasting till the end of the *ancien régime*—Constant, 312.

100. This would be the case with Casseneuil—Percin 14, no. 18; but the people of Toulouse must have quickly recovered the place.

101. The sixth part of the tithes, exchanged for the permanent possession of the church of Fanjeaux, in turn transmitted to Prouille, on 17th and 28th April, 1221—Laurent, nos. 134 and 138.

102. Canon 11—Hefele-Leclercq, V, 1341.

103. On 22nd November, 1219—Denifle, *Chartularium*, I, 90–93; Laurent, no. 98.

104. Cf. *supra*, ch. XI, § 7 ff.

105. 'Thus knowing that if their order had a dwelling-place in the city of Metz their presence would greatly profit not only the layfolk by their sermons, but also the clergy by their courses in sacred learning, after the example of the Lord Pope who had given them a house in Rome and of many archbishops and bishops . . .' Conradin advised the inhabitants of Metz to help them to get a convent—Laurent, no. 136 (22nd April, 1221).

106. Otherwise he would not have contemplated convening a chapter there in 1222!

107. The prescriptions of 1220 on the formation of the preachers encourage this. The provisions found in *I Const.*, 226 (D. II, ch. 36), are later.

108. Jordan of Saxony there commented on St Luke to the brethren.

109. Laurent, nos. 139 and 140.

110. Laurent, no. 140.

111. The Paris diocesan statute III, 20, established in 1213 by Robert de Courson, forbade religious to leave their cloister to go to the schools. Those who had done so had two months in which to return. They had to study within the confines of the cloister—Mansi, XXII, 838. On becoming a formal conventual and no longer a simple hospice, St Jacques fell under the prohibition of this statute.

112. Vitry, 349. Cf. Mandonnet-Vicaire, I, 233–234 and n. 15 and II, 97, n. 45.

113. Mandonnet, 'La crise scolaire au début du XIIIe siècle et la fondation de l'ordre des Frères Prêcheurs', in *RHE*, XV (1914), 34–39, summarized in Mandonnet-Vicaire, II, 83–100. The study is rather too systematic in character. The two parts of the doctrinal inheritance of the bishop, *ordo doctorum* and *ordo predicatorum*, were clearly distinct at the beginning of the thirteenth century, thanks to the scholastic movement (cf. *supra*, ch. XI, 111 and 111). In 1220 the order of Preachers had no consciousness of being *ipso facto* an order of theological doctors and, moreover, Honorius III sincerely hoped to obtain the masters and schools which the Council demanded, from the dioceses. He did not think of asking for them from the Preachers. The university orientation of the doctrinal ministry of the latter, however, was inaugurated from this time onwards, and for the future was to be affirmed in the Church in accordance with the scheme correctly described by Mandonnet.

114. Laurent, nos. 74 and 86.

115. Laurent, no. 111 (30th April, 1220).

116. Laurent, no. 92 (February 1219)

18—S.D.

117. Laurent, nos. 122, 124, 139 (30th December, 1220; 2nd January and 3rd March, 1221).

118. Laurent, no. 126 (13th January, 1221).

119. Laurent, no. 118 (24th October, 1220).

120. Jordan, no. 100.

121. This is what is related in the first part of a notice of the *Liber anniversariorum* of the convent of St Catharine in Barcelona, it would seem from the thirteenth century. The second part of the notice places the fact in 1219, i.e. before Easter 1220 (19, III). Hence the date of 1219 traditionally assigned to the foundation—L. Alcade, 'El Liber Anniversariorum del antiguo convento de Santa Catalina de Barcelona' in *Homenatge a A. Rubió i Lluch*, II, Barcelona 1936, 535; cf. 'Chronique de Jacques Domenech [1357]', in *AFP*, XIV (1944), 9. However, the first part of the notice, which is all that merits attention, reproduces in large characters an item from the epitaph of Berenger de Palou, with this difference that the latter does not mention Bologna or St Dominic, but Paris—San Raimundo de Penyafort, *Diplomatario*, ed. J. Ruis Serra, Barcelona 1954, 8 (no. IV). Cf. E. Valls Taberner, *San Ramón de Penyafort*, Barcelona 1936, 15–16.

122. Laurent, no. 112.

123. *BOP*, I, 14, no. 27.

124. Balme, II, 369–386.

125. On the demand of the brethren the bull of 31st December, 1220 (Laurent, no. 123), sought to persuade the bishop and canons of Amiens to grant a church to the Preachers, whom they had earlier welcomed and appreciated in their ministry, thus at latest in the summer. The foundation came to nothing.

126. Cf. *supra*, ch. XIV, n. 63.

127. The charter (Balme, II, 308) which granted the brethren the church of St Christopher is dated 1224 (or 1225) shortly after the death of the bishop Guillaume Prévost; but the gift itself was earlier since it was made with the approval of the deceased bishop. The founders, however, whose prior was Fr Guillaume (*ibid.*), brought from Paris the bull of recommendation of 11th February, 1218 (Laurent, no. 84), replaced by several documents in December 1219 (Laurent, no. 99, 103 (n. 1); Ligiez 55 (n. 3)). This seems to place the mission in 1219, or at the beginning of 1220. Poitiers was founded before Orléans (Echard, I, vi).

NOTES TO CHAPTER XVII

1. Laurent, no. 113.

2. Cf. *supra*, ch. VI.

3. Bull of St Dominic's canonization—*MOPH*, XVI, 191. On the order of Flora which sprang from Cîteaux in 1189 through a reform and which had about 40 monasteries on the death of Gregory IX, see Fr Russo, 'L'eredità di Giocchino da Fiore. La congregazione Florense', in *Archivio storico per la Calabria e la Lucania*, XXI (1952), 131–144.

4. On 25th March, 1221, Honorius III, in order to obtain missionaries, demanded from the archbishops religious 'of any order, but particularly those of Cîteaux'—Potthast, no. 6599. Cf. Altaner, *Dominikanermissionen*, 1.

5. *Proces. Bon.*, nos. 2, 6, 20, 30.

6. *Proces. Bon.*, nos. 30, 41, 42.

7. This was the case with Fr Ventura de Verona, who was soon to be prior of Bologna (1221), and who was called *senex* even in Dominic's time—*Proces. Bon.*, no. 7 and Frachet, 27, n. 27.

8. 'Fovea hereticorum'—Boehmer-Wiegand, 65. Cf. the energetic terms of Innocent III—*PL*, 216, 711.

9. Cernai, nos. 6, 8, 9, etc.

10. Luchaire, *Innocent III*, I, 84–91 and 91–97.

11. The table which follows is taken from the studies of A. Dondaine, 'La hiérarchie cathare en Italie' I and II, in *AFP*, XIX (1949), 280–312 and XX (1950), 234–324. Note in particular the table in II, 306.

12. These figures taken from the *Summa* of Raynier Sacconi, a former Catharist bishop who became a Friar Preacher, seem reliable, since they are in some sense official in the sect—cf. Dondaine, *Hiérarchie* II, 285, n. 14.

13. If Fr Stefano is to be believed, about 1233 they lost more than 100,000 believers, i.e. as many as remained to them in 1250—*Proces. Bon.*, no. 39.

14. Cf. *infra*, no. 56.

15. Winkelmann, 76–95.

16. Thomas de Spalato, *Historia pontificum salonitanorum et spalatinorum*, MG, SS, II, XXIX, 580.

17. *Ibidem*. This portrait of St Francis preaching is very impressive. Did he too receive a commission from Ugolino within the framework of the general enterprise?

18. *Proces. Thol.*, nos. 3, 7, 13, 18.

19. Winkelmann, 76–177; Jordan, 198–215.

20. Winkelmann, 76–84; Brem, 26–38.

21. Levi, *Registro*, 3–6 and *Documenti*, 59 (295)—80 (316).

22. Cf. *supra*, ch. V (beginning).

23. Appointed imperial legate on 17th April, 1220, he was in Verona on 22nd July, in Mantua on the 31st, on 18th August at Borgo-San-Donnino, on the 25th at Reggio, on 1st September and 14th in Bologna, then from Milan he moved into Tuscany—Winkelmann, 90–95.

24. Winkelmann, 106 and 112–117.

25. Meersseman, *Confreries*, II, 55–70; IV 293–295. The writer, who attributes the idea and first development of this strategy to Dominic, fails to make the necessary distinction between Dominic's own practice and that of his sons ten years later. In 1220–1221 Dominic was concerned with preaching and with that alone; Ugolino directed and reserved to himself the politico-religious action; the later legates (among whom Preachers will be found) and the bishops (among whom was a single Preacher after 1230) succeeded him in this action. After 1233 and despite the resistance of the order, partly through the wish of Gregory IX, partly through the initiatives of certain religious, some Preachers took over the whole of the operations.

26. II Celano, ch. 109. Cf. Altaner, *Beziehungen* 4–8, 22.

27. Laurent, no. 113.

28. *Proces. Bon.*, nos. 2–6, 20–22, 41–42.

29. *Proces. Bon.*, no. 22.

30. The renunciation of the provost and canons was on 10th August, 1220; this deed is recalled by the grant of the church to the Preachers by the bishop's vicar-general on 24th October, 1220—Laurent, n. 118. Cf. *supra*, ch. XIV, n. 130.

31. *Proces. Bon.*, no. 6.

32. G. F. Rossi, 'La fondazione della prima abbazia di S. Bernardo in Italia, Chiaravalle della Colomba', in *Divus Thomas* (Piacenza), LVII (1954), 53–89.

33. Buonviso remained with Dominic 10 months which must be calculated at latest from October 1219—*Proces. Bon.*, no. 20. On the Piacenza convent see *supra*, ch. XIV, n. 133.

34. Constantino, no. 59.

35. Constantino, no. 58. The year is not indicated. Only in 1220, however, could Dominic have been in Bologna on 15th August.

36. One cannot refrain from connecting this *Alatrinus* with the Roman subdeacon whom the Pope sent to Frederick as far back as the summer of 1219 and about whom he wrote numerous letters in the summer of 1220—Potthast, nos. 6270, 6352, 6395; Zimmermann, 90–92. The categorical statements of Constantino, however, make this impossible as to person and date. For the various people possible, see Altaner, 69, n. 2.

37. Scheeben, 322, against Echard, I, 34, n. G; *QF*, I, 13; for another anecdote on this Master Conrad, who was a lector, see Frachet, 249; not, however, 211.

38. *OTC*, IX, 1048–1052.

39. *Proces. Bon.*, no. 42.

40. *Ibidem*.

41. Paul of Venice, in fact, spreads this ministry over two years, i.e. over 1220 and 1221—*Proces. Bon.*, no. 41.

42. The careful study of Dominic's journeys between Rome and Bologna (*Proces. Bon.*, nos. 30 and 46 and Constantino, no. 46 and 52) led Christianopoulo to this conclusion—*ASOP*, I, 187–192, in particular, 189, n. 5. It would be unchallengeable if absolute reliance could be placed on the smallest details of Constantino's text. After 27th December, 1220 the Pope dispatched a series of letters which presupposed Dominic's presence in Rome, at least from Christmas, perhaps from a fairly long time.

43. *Proces. Bon.*, no. 37. Cf. 6, 33, 47.

44. Nos. 6, 8, 37, 47.

45. No. 6.

46. No. 4.

47. No. 6.

48. Nos. 3, 32, 41, 43, 47; cf. *Proces. Thol.*, no. 18.

49. Modena—Constantino, no. 59; Rome—Cecilia, nos. 1 and 5; Bologna—Peter Calo, no. 18 in Mamachi, Appendix 343–344, who gives very interesting details on this popular preaching; the tradition which he relates, after 1330 (Altaner, 116, n. 1) is perhaps sound; that related by Borselli about Faenza (*ASOP*, I, 188) is more doubtful.

50. Cf. *supra*, no. 47 and *I Const.*, 223 (D. II, ch. 31); Jordan, no. 104.

51. Frachet, 74–75; Constantino, no. 44.

52. Cf. *supra*, no. 48.

53. Laurent, no. 60. Recommendation type III—Appendix VI, § 6 and 16.

54. *I Const.* 223 (D. II, ch. 31); *Proces. Bon.*, nos. 13, 29, 32, 37, 41, 47.

55. *Proces. Bon.*, no. 6, 37, 47.

56. Cf. prayer to ask for the gift of tears in the Dominican Missal.

57. Mark I, 15; *Proces. Bon.*, no. 43.

58. Bourbon, no. 421; Frachet, 80.

59. *Proces. Bon.*, nos. 17, 27, 32, 38, 42, 47; Jordan, no. 108.

60. No. 38. Cecilia, no. 1, claims that the smallness of his scapular was because people cut it to obtain relics.

61. Nos. 17, 32, 38, 47.

62. Nos. 17, 32.

63. No. 47.

64. No. 31.

65. *Ibidem*.

66. *Ibidem*.

67. No. 31. According to Fr Reginald, later Archbishop of Armagh (1247) who was present at the scene, the small pieces of bread were multiplied—Frachet, 80.

68. No. 22; Bourbon, no. 209. This is a different event from those reported by Fr Rudolfo, no. 31 . The two brothers were eye-witnesses.

69. Constantino, no. 28, combines the two events related by *Proces. Bon.*, nos. 22 and 31, and localizes the whole at St Sixtus; Cecilia, no. 3. Criticism of these texts in Altaner, 65, n. 1.

70. *Proces. Bon.*, no. 4.

71. No. 42.

72. Frachet, 29. For another description of conventual mendicancy, see Constantino, no. 28; Cecilia, no. 3.

73. Frachet, 127.

74. Frachet, 163.

75. Laurent, nos. 118 and 145.

76. Cf. the phrase of the first prior of Lyons, Fr Arnaud—Bourbon, no. 7: 'He preaches doctrine boldly despite certain people, for, thanks to his poverty, he has no fear that they will cut short his supplies'. Or the phrase of Eudes de Châteauroux, which alludes to the feudal mentality—'If the first preachers (i.e. the apostles) had been rich, men would have demanded money of them to believe in them, as they do today in the case of kings'—Berthier, *Testament*, 17.

77. Frachet, 139–140.

78. Laurent, nos. 115 and 116.

79. *Proces. Bon.*, no. 38.

80. Cuthbert, 323–325 and Gratian, 128 and n. 1.

81. For what follows see 'Chronique de Sainte-Agnès', *ASOP*, I, note at foot of p. 182.

82. Reminiscent of Jordan, no. 40 which in turn is a biblical reminiscence—Apoc., II, 9 and III, 9.

83. Laurent, no. 121 (27th December, 1220) and ff.

NOTES TO CHAPTER XVIII

1. Winkelmann 104, 106; Potthast, no. 6395.

2. The bull of 8th December, edited by Laurent, no. 119, under the date 1220, in actual fact is dated 1221. This is a plain copy of Laurent, no. 105, which it reproduces anachronistically after Dominic's death.

3. As can be seen from Potthast.

4. Before writing the bull of 31st December, the Pope had direct information from Dominic (*Prior ordinis predicatorum*); before writing the bulls of 27th December and 30th and 2nd January, 1221, to recommend Fr Guillaume who was going away to continue his studies in Paris, the Pope obviously made certain of the consent of the head of the order—Laurent, no. 123 and 121, 122, 124.

5. Laurent, no. 120.

6. No. 121. The convent was situated in the rue St Denis; remains of it may be seen at no. 166— Balme, III, 153, n. 1.

7. No. 124.

8. No. 122.

9. No. 124; cf. 'preces per dilectum fratrem Wuillelmum, familiarem nostrum eiusdem ordinis, eo affectuosius et fiducialius iterantes, quo placida et placita conversatione sua nobis meruit complacere'— nos. 122 and 124.

10. *Proces. Bon.*, no. 12. Balme, III, 151–152 and Altaner, 26, n. 3 accept this identity which Laurent, p. 142, n. 1, questions without giving his reason. Perhaps because in 1219 Guillaume had completed the years of theology envisaged by Dominic. This was a fact. Thus it was not Dominic who took the initiative of sending Guillaume back to Paris, but Guillaume himself, by calling upon the Pope to intervene. The end of the bull of 30th December, 1220—Laurent, no. 122—clearly shows that the Pope was aware that he was somewhat forcing the hand of the authorities of the order.

11. Winkelmann, 119, n. 1 and 151–152; Zimmermann 76, 96.

12. *Proces. Bon.*, no. 13.

13. Laurent, no. 140.

14. No. 139.

15. No. 123.

16. No. 136 (22nd April, 1221). Perhaps the brethren were already in the town. This is all that can be learnt of the origins of the Metz house. The traditional data (cf. Balme, II, 307 and III, 289–291) lack reliability. On the first prior, Fr Guerric, cf. *supra*, ch. XIV, n. 34.

17. No. 125 (11th January, 1221).

18. Gallén, 5–6.

19. Appendix VI, § 16.

20. Laurent, no. 123.

21. Appendix VI, § 6.

22. *Bullarium Danicum*, no. 170; Gallén, 7–8.

23. Laurent, no. 131.

24. Balme, III, 231.

25. Scheeben, 357, sees in the prior Dominic mentioned in the charter, a friar distinct from the founder and the beneficiary of the testimonial *Cum qui recipit* of 18th January, 1221 (cf. *infra*, [111]). Perhaps he is basing himself on the phrase to be read at the end of the charter: 'nostro nomine et nostri

prioris et conventus totius' (Laurent, no. 131). There, however, it is a question of the community of the entire order and of its prior, which the two brethren are effectively engaging. Cf. following note.

26. As can be seen in the majority of the Prouille charters and, elsewhere, in Laurent, nos. 71, 72, 145, 148 (cf. *AFP*, XX (1950), 328–329), 150, 151.

27. On 28th December, 1227, the order gave up the church, which reverted to the hospice—cf. Mamachi, Appendix 93.

28. Laurent, no. 143.

29. No. 142. The copy edited dates from 6th May; others however, date from the 5th—cf. following note.

30. Examples of this bull of 5th May, 1221, will be found in Montpellier (*AFP*, V (1935), 52, no. 39), in Friesach, Würzburg, Petau, Trèves (*AFP*, VI (1936), 234, nos. 27, 28, 29, 200; *ADD*, II, 169). The copy of the archives of the order edited in Laurent, no. 142, bears no indication of which archives it comes from.

31. Appendix VI, § 6, nos. 18, 19, 23, 29, to which can be added no. 2, a personal, but not individual testimonial (fr. P.T.R.).

32. This latter, preserved by the Roman sisters of Sts Dominic and Sixtus (today Monte-Mario) came from Bologna—Balme, III, 367, n. 1.

33. *ASOP*, III, 169, n. 1 and Frachet, 304. It is not impossible that this Dominic of Segovia should be identified with the Dominic of Spain mentioned by Jordan, nos. 31, 49, 50 and Bourbon, no. 288. Jordan, no. 49, says that he remained at Bologna after he was sent there at the beginning of 1218; but how are we to interpret the incomprehensible *Manino, Manionio* of no. 31, of which he was prior in Spain, otherwise than by—*Maiorico?* The principal reason against the identification is not this, in our opinion, but the obvious mediocrity of Fr Dominic of Spain and the disappointments he caused the founder.

34. Laurent, no. 128. Cf. *BOP*, I, 12, no. 19 which mentions these two archive depositories.

35. No. 130. Cf. *BOP*, I, 12, no. 21. In relation to the preceding deed, only the prologue is different.

36. Laurent, no. 74.

37. No. 79.

38. The *vel arctioris vitae obtentu* clause instituted by Urban II at the end of the 11th century to defend the profession of the canons against the monks, was changed after Alexander III into *nisi arctioris vitae obtentu*, to the advantage of the Cistercians. Cf. Dereine, *Statut canonique*, 548–557; article 'Chamousey', in *DHGE*, XII, 599. In allowing this restriction to lapse in 1221 in regard to the Preachers, the Papacy attacked the privilege of the Cistercians and soon turned it to the benefit of the Preachers—see following note.

39. Dist. I, ch. 14, *I Const.*, 202. This prescription, which mentions the provincial chapter must have been slightly later than 1221. It follows from a bull of Gregory IX of 21st June, 1235 (*BOP*, I, 77, no. 135) that Pope Honorius had forbidden both Preachers and Cistercians to receive religious of each other's order, without authorization from the Pope and from the head of the order of the religious in question.

40. Acts I, 14.

41. e.g. Laurent, no. 123.

42. *Proces. Bon.*, no. 29.

43. Jordan, no. 86.

44. 'Chronique de Sainte-Agnès', *ASOP*, I (1893), note p. 182.

45. Balme, III, 79–80.

46. *Dania*, 500.

47. Laurent, no. 122.

48. In January 1221, according to Celano—*Vita secunda*, ch. 109. According to the very searching investigation by Altaner, *Beziehungen* 22, this is the only information based on a reliable foundation.

49. On Conrad see *Revue Bénéd.*, XXII (1905), 232–243; XXIII (1906), 62–81; 373 391; D. Willi, *Päpste, Kardinäle u. Bishöfe aus dem Cistercienserorden*, Bregenz 1912, 21–22.

50. He was present on 3rd November, 1217 at the 2nd siege of Toulouse (document quoted, Cernai, vol. II, no. 602, n. 1). Cf. Cernai, vol. III, p. xciii.

51. Zimmermann 46, n. 1, 73 and n. 2, 76.

52. Ferrando, 43.

53. Gallén, 9–10; Loenertz, *AFP*, XXI (1951), 14.

54. Westenholz, 32–36. On his burial and the Preachers see *Chronica IIa*, 335.

55. Mamachi, Appendix published a certain number of charters of Santa María in Tempulo (no. I, V–VIII, X, XII, XV, XXVII, XXX, XLII, XLV) re-edited in Bartolini. Certain charters of St Bibiana are edited in G. Ferri, 'Le carte dell'Archivio Liberiano dal secolo X al XV', in *Archivio della v. società rom. di storia patria*, XXVII (1904), 147–202. On the subject of the two monasteries, cf. Zucchi, 261–269 and 316.

56. Laurent, no. 137, 141, 147.

57. *AFP*, XX (1950), 328–329 (replacing the defective edition of Laurent, no. 148, document of 15th May, 1221).

58. Partial version of this no longer extant text in Echard, I, 83. On Benedict of M., *ibidem*, 536–537.

59. Ed. Walz, cited under the reference Cecilia.

60. Cecilia, no. 4, 10, 12.

61. Cf. Cecilia, no. 2 and 3 with Jordan, no. 100 and *Proces. Bon.*, no. 22 already transformed by Constantino, no. 28.

62. As Zucchi, 255–256.

63. E.g. what is said about Cardinal Stefano de Fossanova, Friar Tancred, the canals of St Sixtus, the Nomentana bridge, etc. Sister Cecilia is not responsible for the gross errors in dates of the modern historical tradition. Her accounts easily lend themselves to arrangement in chronological order (nos. 3, 4, 11, 12, 13, 1, 2, 5, 14, 8, 9, 10, 6, 7, 15—cf. Vicaire, *Documents*, 199) over a period of time which does not exceed a Lent and Paschaltime. The most questionable accounts seem those in which the things remembered by Sister Cecilia, or even more so in the case of Sister Angelica alone, are interspersed with a written legendary tradition (the repast of the angels, the resurrection of the boy Napoleon). This written tradition, because of its enormous bulk, seriously distorted in the Middle Ages the account of eye-witnesses—when it was not substituted entirely for personal memories. This is particularly the case when an account comes across an episode similar to something in the Gospel—cf. M. Fr Lanzoni, 'Il miracolo di Napoleone Orsini . . .', *Miscellanea Dominicana*, Rome 1923, 10–20.

64. Laurent, no. 137; Montefiascone, 83b.

65. *Ibidem*. Cecilia, 2 and 14, speaks of all the nuns in the city whom the Pope wished to gather into one community, which is a clear exaggeration.

66. Montefiascone, 83a (*sub arcta clausura et diligenti custodia*).

67. For what follows, see Huyghe, in particular 24–30, 74–87, 89, 91–95. Cf. *supra*, ch. VIII, n. 96.

68. Holstenius-Brockie, *Codex regularum*, II, Augsburg 1759, 467–536. The rule was approved by Eugenius III (1145–1153) Huyghe, 89.

69. Cecilia, no. 2.

70. *Ibidem*. Scheeben, 329 and Zucchi, 263, n. 1, firmly reject this information—the cardinals could not serve as mere supernumeraries. There was no question of that. The affairs of the Roman convents were family affairs for the Pope and the cardinals (Laurent, no. 137). Their personal influence on nuns and their families was indispensable at certain times for the success of the enterprise. In 1223 when there was a question of persuading four sisters from St Sixtus to go back to St Agnes of Bologna, Honorius himself went to St Sixtus, accompanied by Cardinal Ugolino, the Provincial of Tuscany and several other of the Preachers. The Pope addressed them himself—'Chronique de Sainte-Agnès', *ASOP*, I, 182, n.

71. Laurent, no. 137, 141, 147; *AFP*, XX (1950), 328–329; Jordan, no. 100; Cecilia, nos. 2 and 14.

72. He only appears in two accounts by Cecilia—nos. 2 and 14.

73. Simon, 21–33 and Zarncke, 26–77.

74. He was still in Rome on 3rd March, 1221, when he signed a major privilege—Potthast, no. 6576 and p. 678. He was in Siena on 25th March—Winkelmann, 168, n. 1. It will be noted that Cecilia, no. 2, mentions his presence on 24th February, but not at the procession for their final entry into St Sixtus, which was in April—Cecilia, no. 14.

75. Laurent, no. 137.

76. Already a nun in 1194 and abbess since the end of 1204 or beginning of 1205—Bartoloni, 18, 27, 31, 33–47.

77. On 26th November, 1219, the whole proceeds of one property were devoted to sending a procurator to the Pope for the affairs of the convent—Mamachi, Appendix 59.

78. On 25th November, 1220, she set aside 6 pounds [livres provins] from the Senate to restore the convent premises—Mamachi, Appendix 65. At this date she was still at the head of the abbey and striving to preserve the ancient installation.

79. He appears in the sisters' affairs after 26th November, 1206—Bartoloni, 35, 39, 42, 46, 54. In 1221, he possessed a part of the abbey property as security for five large debts outstanding—*AFP*, XX (1950), 328.

80. Cf. charter of 26th November, 1219 and the sending of a messenger to the Pope—Mamachi, Appendix 59 and bulls of 4th and 17th December, 1219, 25th April, 1221, and the Pope's replies (Laurent, nos. 100, 104 and 137).

81. Cecilia, no. 2. The account is not very clear. It is supposed that the nuns and the abbess had made profession and given the property of the monastery to Dominic in a preparatory ceremony at Santa María. Later, the ceding of rights to St Sixtus by the abbess is again mentioned. Perhaps this is merely an imperfection in the account. It would seem normal that the essential gesture, the profession, should have been made at St Sixtus, for according to the mentality of the time, such an act bound not only to the person but to the place. The three cardinals, it is said, agreed to take part in the ceremony. This was by no means pointless—to prevent any failure to take the step on the part of the sisters or any violent intervention on that of their families. Despite modern historiography which places the event in 1220 (with the exception of Scheeben and N. Maurice Denis—R. Boulet, *Romée*, 2nd ed. Rome, 1948, 516, n. I), the date of 1221 is firmly fixed, not only by the secondary synchronisms but also by the charters of 25th November, 1220 and 15th April, 1221—Mamachi, Appendix 64–66 and *AFP*, XX (1950), 328. In November 1220, abbess Eugenia was still in enjoyment of her full rights. In April, 1221, she was described as 'formerly abbess' and Dominic alone completed the deed.

82. Lectionary of St Sixtus (thirteenth century)—Mamachi, Appendix, 9–14; Cecilia, no. 14, which served as a basis for Thierry whose account was repeated by Martinelli, *Imago B. Mariae V. quae apud . . .* SS. Sixti et Dominici moniales . . . asservatar, Rome, 1635. This was translated and used by Fr M. Torrigio in his *Historia della veneranda Immagine . . .*' Rome, 1641; G. G. Meersseman, *Der Hymnos akathistos im Abendland*, I, Fribourg, 1958, 53 ff. and n. 4. The Virgin is the type of the *Hagiosoritissa*.

83. Frachet, 75–76.

84. Frachet, 81; cf. 111, 134.

85. 'Chronique de Sainte-Agnès', *ASOP*, I (1893), 182, n.

86. Frachet, 178.

87. Cecilia, no. 11.

88. No. 14.

89. Cecilia, no. 14 (cf. no. 5), places this second stage between 24th and 28th February, 1221 (1st and 3rd stages). This is not impossible but is unlikely. If as early as the 28th St Sixtus was ready to receive the sisters on a permanent basis, why these three stages? They are inevitable, on the other hand if, as the text, moreover, suggests, the gift of Santa Sabina and the removal of the brethren had occupied a certain time. It is thought that the sister has confused the dates of the 2nd and 3rd stages.

90. Cecilia, no. 14; cf. nos. 3 and 4.

91. Article 'Sabine (Sainte–)' by M. D. Darsy in *Dict. d'archéol. et de liturgie*, XV, 218–238, where plans and a bibliography will be found.

92. *Cum multa sollicitudine multo que labore*—Montefiascone, 836.

93. Darsy, *Dict. d'archéol. et de liturgie*, XV, 232; cf. 222. Also 'La chambre de saint Dominique', in *Vie dominicaine*, V (1939), 43–44.

94. *BOP*, I, 15, no. 2. Numerous cases have already been met in which the gift of the church was considerably later than its occupation.

95. On 15th April Dominic was called in a charter prior of the venerable monastery of St Sixtus— *AFP*, XX (1950); 328; this can only refer to the convent of sisters. The same document, however, mentions the existence even at this date of the monastery *in Tempulo* with its servants in whose name Dominic liquidated a debt of the said monastery. Thus the translation had not yet taken place. It was an accomplished fact by the 25th—Laurent, no. 137; it doubtless took place several days earlier, since the pontifical chancellery had had time to deliver the charter. If account be taken of Cecilia, no. 14, it could have taken place on a Sunday, the first Sunday after Lent, 18th April, 1221.

96. Montefiascone, 836.

97. After the arrival of these isolated persons, there would have been 44 religious, according to Cecilia, no. 14. It will be noted that the figure is not exaggerated. This gives a certain weight to the figure of 104 given by Cecilia, no. 6. Was this the maximum attained shortly before the saint's departure? The nuns of Santa María, Santa Bibiana and Prouille formed a community of 60 according to Montefiascone. He again mentions, however, isolated persons 'multas et alias dominas saeculares', afterwards received by Dominic, who also joined the sisters.

98. According to Montefiascone, the nuns of Santa Bibiana and other convents numbered 21. Honorius indicates the same proportions, without giving any figure—Laurent, no. 137.

99. Cecilia, no. 14.

100. The charter of 15th April shows that St Sixtus already had its community before the transfer of the Roman sisters; this cannot be other than the community of the sisters of Prouille. The latter had not been there long for the transfer had certainly been made without delay. The *post haec* of Montefiascone, 836, should be ignored.

101. He was in fact in Rome with his clergy on 17th April—Laurent, no. 134.

102. Laurent, no. 134.

103. Laurent, no. 138.

104. He speaks of the parish priest who had to be instituted by the master (of the order), *vel prior in dicta ecclesia a dieto magistre instituto.*

105. Guiraud, *Cartulaire*, II, no. 332.

106. Montefiascone, 836; Percin, 22, no. 56.

107. The minimum, according to the rule which will be discussed shortly.

108. *AFP*, XX (1950), 328–329.

109. Mamachi, Appendix 5–9.

110. Laurent, no. 137.

111. No. 141. Cf. no. 147.

112. No. 1, 3, 6.

113. Nos. 3, 6. She also makes him appear as procurator of the brethren of St Sixtus before the transfer, which does not agree with Constantino, nos. 28 and 39.

114. Montefiascone, 836.

115. Mentioned in the charters of Santa Maria at least after 1214, conventual prioress after 1215 (Mamachi, Appendix 42, 44), she was in charge of the turn at St Sixtus—Cecilia, no. 9.

116. Cecilia, nos. 6, 9, 10.

117. Montefiascone, 836.

118. Critical edition in Simon, 142–153. Cf. on these texts, *infra*, Appendix VIII.

119. Montefiascone, 836.

120. Jordan, no. 100; Frachet, 190; Cecilia, no. 1, 2, 3, 6, 12. According to Cecilia, no. 3, from the time of Lent the brethren were about a hundred in number. This information, however, intended to stress the importance of a miracle, has no sure foundation and no great probability.

121. Cecilia, nos. 3 and 6. The reference in no. 3 is a mistake on the sister's part if it is true that he entered the order after the foundation of the monastery of St Sixtus—no. 6. He was at Siena in 1227— Mamachi, Appendix 93.

122. Jordan, no. 51.

123. Cecilia, nos. 1, 3, 11.

124. No. 6.

125. M. D. Darsy, 'La chambre de saint Dominique', in *Vie dominicaine*, V (1939), 43–44.

126. Cecilia, nos. 5, 6 (end), 8.

127. This comes, moreover from an anecdote without authority, cf. *supra*, I, 19f.

128. *Cum maxima mansuetudine et verborum dulcedine*—*Proces. Bon.*, no. 48.

129. No. 5.

130. No. 32.

131. Nos. 4, 5, 6, 17, 22, 32, 37, 43, 48.

132. Jordan, no. 107; Cecilia, no. 15.

133. No. 107.

134. No. 103.

135. Nos. 6, 17, 22, 37.

136. *Proces. Bon.*, no. 37.

137. Cecilia, no. 6 *ad finem*.

138. Cecilia, no. 6.

139. *Proces. Bon.*, nos. 4, 6, 37, 43, 48.

140. Cf. Appendix VIII, no. 9.

141. Frachet, 75–76.

142. Frachet, 79. Cf. 35, 53.

143. Cecilia, no. 7.

144. *Proces. Bon.*, no. 36; cf. 211, n. 35.

145. Cecilia, no. 6. The linking together of the *potus* and the *collatio* or spiritual conference is a custom peculiar to the Preachers (*I Const.*, 199–200, D. I, ch. 9) who to gain time have fused two distinct practices of the Cistercians, the *bibere* and the *collatio* (*Us de Cîteaux*, ch. 80 and 81—Guignard, 185–186). The rule of St Sixtus expressly preserved the Cistercian use (ch. 5, ed. Simon, 145).

146. Jordan, no. 104.

147. Jordan, no. 107.

148. The prior of the brethren, Fr Tancred, witness to and actor in the scene. Thus Jordan is very well informed. He does not expressly say it was a resurrection, he even rather excludes this. Later biographers, however—Constantino, no. 35; Barthélemy, no. 15; Cecilia, no. 2—do so. On this development see Altaner, 63–64.

149. Jordan, no. 100. For a criticism of the legendary tradition, cf. Lanzoni, cited *supra*, no. 63.

NOTES TO CHAPTER XIX

1. Constantino, no. 52; Mamachi, 605, n. 3 and 635, n. 2.

2. Jordan, no. 88.

3. *I Const.*, 217–218 (D. II, ch. 15, § 1, and 16, 1 and 3). This expression, which we meet with five times in these texts, does not come up again in the later legislation. It belongs to the first provincial legislation. The latter is prior to 1224, date when the election of the provincial by his chapter was decided upon (cf. *infra*, n. 16). In view of the fact that all the elements of this legislation (provincial territorial limits, chapter and prior) are contemporary (*infra*, n. 14), there is no reason for not dating this legislation from 1221, date at which the prior provincial certainly made his appearance—Jordan, no. 88.

4. In the new profession formula—*I Const.*, 202–203 (D. I, ch. 16). On the earlier formula, *supra* ch. XI, 11–11. In 1220, the head of the order was still called *prelatus maior*—*I Const.*, 220 (D. II, ch. 20 and 21).

5. Cf. in particular the change of title in the two acts of Ugolino—Laurent, no. 145 and 151. On 24th May, 1221, *magister Dominicus, prior ipsius ordinis* is spoken of; on 13th June, *frater Dominicus, magister totius ordinis*.

6. *I Const.*, 221–222 (D. II, ch. 24 and 25).

7. *I Const.*, 217–218 (D. II, ch. 16, § 1; 17, § 1, 3, 4). The second sentence of ch. 16, § 1 is a later addition: in 1221 the provincials were appointed by the general chapter, not elected. This § 1 in 1221 merely signified the control of the provincials by the general chapter. § 2 is a later addition, as is clear from the *statuimus* and is, moreover, divergent from § 1. § 3 forms part of the 'provincial bloc'— Mandonnet-Vicaire, II, 276–277 and 280–281). § 4 and 5 date from 1236 (*Acta*, I, 7 and 8). Ch. 17, § 2 also dates from 1236 (*Acta*, I, 6). It is not impossible for § 5 to date from 1221, though we are inclined to think that it is from 1228. § 6 dates from 1225, and serves as a transition between the legislation of 1220 and that of 1225. The other phrases in these two chapters, between which there is a literary connection, are the only ones which refer to the province under the original name of *provincia vel regnum*. For their date of 1221, cf. *supra*, n. 3 and *infra*, n. 14.

8. Paris, Bologna, Montpellier, Palencia or Oxford.

9. This provision is clearly prior to that in D. II, ch. 4, § 2, which dates from 1225.

10. Hefele-Leclercq, V, 1342–1343.

11. The anomaly of the expression in the Dominican constitutions proves its dependence. One fact emphasizes this. The expression does correspond to reality in the case of the chapters for which provision was made by the councils: in point of fact the houses of canons were organized into ecclesiastical provinces. In the thirteenth century none of the Dominican provinces, as will be seen, corresponded to an ecclesiastical province, or to a kingdom.

12. This canon inspired the Dominican provisions concerning: 1. the cutting up into sub-divisions, in accordance with the ruling idea *provincia vel regnum*; 2. the designation of the four presidents; 3. the nomination of visitors; 4. the choice of the place for the next chapter.

13. The idea of the assembly by provinces of the isolated Benedictine abbeys goes back to 1131, to the Council of Rheims. After that a provincial chapter was held in each metropolis. From 1135 onwards,

the customs of Springiersbach made provision for provincial chapters for its houses of canons. In 1202 Innocent III extended this institution to the isolated houses in Italy and then in Denmark, England, Normandy, certain provinces of France, etc. In 1215 it was made general for canons as for monks—cf. Ph. Schmitz, *Histoire de l'ordre de Saint Benoît*, III, 42–50; G. G. Meersseman, 'Die Reform der Salzburger Augustinerstifte (1218), eine Folge des IV Laterankonzils (1215)', in *Zeitschr. f. Schweizer Kirchengeschichte*, XLVIII (1954), 81–95.

14. It could be thought that the institution of the provincial prior was earlier than that of the provincial chapter. This was Scheeben's idea—*QF*, XXXIX (1939), 32. One has only, however, to note his original title—*prior provinciarum vel regnorum*—to see at once the dependence of the institution of the prior in relation to Canon XII and thus in relation to the institution of the provincial chapter.

15. Laurent, nos. 145 and 151.

16. This prescription will be found in D. II, ch. 15, and of § 1. It was prior to the 'provincial bloc' which will be referred to later. We assign it to 1224. In that year, in fact, a second wave of provincials was seen to emerge, succeeding the provincials nominated by the general chapter, in France (Pierre de Reims)—Chapotin, 67, n. 1; Lombardy (Fr Stefano), *AFP*, X (1940), 372–373; Roman province (Fr Clair), *AFP*, IV (1934), 126; Teutonia (Conrad de Höxter), *QF*, XX, 88, n. 3 and XXXV, 154–156.

17. No. 88.

18. Cf. *infra*, n. 55.

19. Except Scheeben, 370–373.

20. *Acta*, I, 2. Gui, 403. He does not indicate his sources.

21. 'Cum fratre Giliberto priore scilicet provinciali'—*Acta*, I, 2. The phrase is that of Jordan, no. 88, with the exception of the gloss—*scilicet provinciali*, Gui, 403B.

22. 'De Theutonica, Hungarica et Romana provincia, nondum potui certitudinem invenire'—Gui, 403D.

23. Echard, I, 1.

24. *I Const.*, 212 (D. II, ch. 1).

25. For detailed study of the question by Christianopoulo, see *ASOP*, I (1893), 49–53.

26. Jordan, no. 88 and Frachet, 305.

27. The recommendation bull of 15th November, 1219—Laurent, no. 97—has remained in the Zamora archives. The house was not founded until after Barcelona (1222) and Santaren—*ASOP*, I, 511.

28. *ASOP*, I, 518–521 for a critical study by Christianopoulo.

29. Nominated by the chapter of 1221, since as early as 18th January, 1222, he received a letter from the King of Castile, St Ferdinand—Castillo, I.P., L. II, ch. 1, 157. Cf. P. L. G. Alonso-Getino 'Capitulos provinciales y priores prov. de la Orden de Sto Domingo en España', in *La Ciencia Tomista*, 13 (1916), 91–94.

30. Chapotin, 61 and n. 2.

31. Echard I, ii; Gui, 469. It was earlier than the following one (Puy), which was again in 1221.

32. Charter of donation of the church of St Laurent to the provincial Bertrand de Garrigues by the elected bishop Stephen of Chalancon, in October 1221—Percin, 23, no. 68; *Gallia Christiana*, II, 711.

33. Cf. preceding note and *Chronica Ia*, 338, which states 'positus a beato Dominico'.

34. Gui 403 affirms this; Echard I, 21, 92, 116, queries it on account of the silence of Salagnac and Bourbon in their information on Matthew of France. Gui's testimony, however, is formal. Cf. Meersseman in *MOPH*, XVIII, 82.

35. All that is known is that it was earlier than the convent of Parma—*ASOP*, I, 187.

36. Taeggio, cited by Mamachi, 650, n. 3, dates the foundation from 1221.

37. Charter of Bologna of 17th February, 1223—*ASOP*, III, 169; *MOPH*, I, 304.

38. Scheeben in *AFP*, IV (1934), 125.

39. Frachet, 305, from a report of 1259; Pfeiffer, 15 to 26.

40. Mandonnet-Vicaire, I, 249–269.

41. Altaner, *Dominikanermissionen*, 142 ff. Basing himself on the date in *Dania*, 500, Scheeben (361) whom we followed in the French edition of this story admits the foundation of a convent at Alba Royale (Székesfehérvár) before May 1220, by a Fr Paul, prior in Hungary, distinct from the Master Paul who was at this time prior of Bologna. Bela Iványi, however, in *Mélanges Mandonnet*, II, Paris 1930, 439–440, and above all Loenertz, *S. Hyacinthe*, 22–25, have shown the improbability of this duality of persons and the incompatibility of the Hungarian data in *Dania* with those of the reliable report of 1259—Frachet, 305.

42. Pfeiffer, 185.

43. According to *Dania*, 500, the Fr Solomon who entered at Verona at Easter 1220 was left as priest at Friesach by Fr Paul, on his way to Hungary after Pentecost 1220. The latter detail is incorrect and how much can be retained of the anecdote is now clear—the first mention of the convent of Friesach and of the presence of Dominicans in Germany.

44. *Bullarium Danicum*, no. 170.

45. Jordan, no. 55. Cf. Scheeben, 362.

46. Rano or Ranoldus, according to *Dania*, 501, dean of Roskilde, bishop elect of that diocese, had entered the order in Paris in the course of the journey which he was making to Rome for confirmation of his bishopric. He is said to have become provincial the following year. This could only have taken place when the see was vacant in May, 1225—Gallén, 13 and n. 7.

47. *Dania*, 500, cf. *supra*, n. 41 and 43.

48. *Dania*, 500; Scheeben, 361–363.

49. *Homiliae festivae*, ed. Coppenstein, Cologne, 1615, 14—*ASOP*, I, 370–372.

50. Except with authorization from the Pope—*I Const.*, 202 (D. I, ch. 14); Fr Christian, however, must have kept silence about his Cistercian origin.

51. For preaching at Rheims see Bourbon, 391. He undoubtedly bore the title of first prior of Cologne —*ibidem* and Jordan, no. 66, 70, 79, 82.

52. Scheeben, in *QF*, XXXV, 154–156.

53. Jordan, no. 88; *Chronica IIa*, 325; *Acta*, I, 2; Gui, 403; Nicholas Trivet, *Annales sex regum Angliae*, ed. T. Hog. London, 1845, 209. Despite Trivet, it is difficult to attribute 12 religious to the founding community. This detail, which Jordan does not give, seems a conclusion drawn from D. II, ch. 23 of the institutions (*I Const.*, 222). This prescription indeed, which presupposes that the order was highly developed, is probably later than 1221. In fact only four brethren were sent at this date with Paul of Hungary—Frachet, 305.

54. Cf. *supra*, 361 and n. 21 as to why it is not possible to give him this title from 1221, despite Bernard Gui.

55. R. J. Loenertz, *Une ancienne chronique des provinciaux dominicains de Pologne* in *AFP*, XXI (1951), 13 and n. 1; 14, n. 1. On St Hyacinth and his biographer, see Altaner, *Dominikanermissionen*, 196–214; O. J. Woroniecki, *Sw. Jacek Odrowaz*, Katowice, 1947.

56. Loenertz, *AFP*, XXI (1951), 14–15.

57. Frachet, 194–195. On the beginnings of this province see Altaner, *Dominikanermissionen*, 9–15; R. Loenertz, 'Documents pour servir á l'histoire de la province dominicaine de Grèce', *AFP*, XIV (1944), 72–115.

58. It is this collection of prescriptions that is called 'provincial document'—Mandonnet-Vicaire II, 276–277 and 279–282; Vicaire, *Documents*, 120–121. This collection includes the following paragraphs: D. II, ch. I, § 1; 2; 3; 4 § 1a and 2; 5, § 1; 7; 8 § 1; 9 § 1 and 2; 10, § 1; 11, § 2; 13; 15, § 3; 16 § 6 (list in Vicaire, *Documents*, 120, slightly amended). This collection, later than 1221, cannot be later in date than 1227, since the provinces which it organized prepared the meeting of the chapter of 1228—*I Const.*, 193. It is possible to be more definite than this. It was later than 1224 since in that year the first provincial legislation as given in ch. 15 and 16 of the Rodez ms. was being completed (cf. *supra*, n. 16). Moreover, the alteration which it established in the composition of the general chapters created numerous difficulties before 1228, since that year it was necessary to convene a special general chapter to remedy them—*I Const.*, 193 and 214 (Preamble of 1228 and D. II, ch. 6); Humbert, *Reg.*, II, 58. This presupposes that the alternation provided for by the provincial text had come into use at least twice—thus 1226 and 1227. The provincial document is at latest of 1225. It will be noted that that year the chapter was held in Bologna, among the lawyers. It is indeed in that year that the date of composition, which in 1938 we could not take the risk of determining, must be set. The bringing into being of elective provincial chapters in 1224 (first definite mention for France—Chapotin 48 and 67) supplied the general chapter of 1225 with the first elected provincials.

59. D. II, ch. I, *I Const.*, 212.

60. D. II, ch. 5 and 10, *I Const.*, 213 and 215. In the edition of the text of Rodez, the institution of the minor provinces appears as contemporary with that of the major. Actually the first provincial of Poland was nominated in 1225 (cf. *supra*, n. 55). The juridical provisions relating to the minor provinces, however, may very well have been interpolated, with slight alterations in the provincial document in 1226 or at latest 1227. The name given to them of *provinciae superadditae*, the additional character of the paragraph in which they are mentioned, with a significant *statuimus*, make it essential to posit this question. The date of the first provincial of Dacia would seem to be 1226 (cf. *supra*, n. 46). The order of enumeration of the minor provinces, which has varied, provides a *confirmatur* of this. We have taken the historical order of the foundations to be that of the order of precedence (Echard, I, 1)—Poland, Dacia, Greece and the Holy Land (already the Acts of the chapters of 1239–1240–1241 mention—Poland, Dacia, Syria, Holy Land, Greece—*Acta*, I, 11, 13, 18), which seems to prove—1. that Greece and the Holy Land were contemporary; 2. that they came into being after Dacia, thus in 1227. In this case the addition relating to the four minor provinces would date from 1227. These particulars are welcome. Up to this date no document had revealed the date of creation of the minor provinces and one had to be satisfied with the date of 1228, clearly erroneous, given by Bernard Gui.

61. On the spirit of this legislation, see the celebrated commentary by Denifle—*I Const.*, 165–193; G. R. Galbraith, *The Constitution of the Dominican Order, 1216 to 1360*, Manchester, 1925; Mandonnet-Vicaire II, 230–239; David Knowles, *The Religious Orders in England*, Cambridge, 1948, 146–162; L. Moulin in *Rev. intern. des sciences administratives*, 1951, 42–67 and 1955, 1–104 (all relevant).

62. *Proces. Bon.*, no. 7. The text does not say he was elected. The election of the prior by the community, however, was legislated from 1216—Laurent, no. 74, *I Const.*, 221 (D. II, ch. 24). Only founders were nominated by the chapter.

63. Laurent, no. 126.

64. No. 150.

65. Mamachi—Appendix 375–376.

66. On 17th February, 1223 and 8th April, 1224—*ASOP*, IV, 169, n. 1 and 170, n. 3.

67. *ASOP*, IV, 165, n. 3.

68. Laurent, no. 126.

69. *ASOP*, I, 181–182 and 'Chronique de Sainte-Agnès', *ibidem*, no. 10.

70. 'Fere per totam Marchiam trevisinam'—*Proces. Bon.*, no. 41. On his companions see no. 42.

71. Bull to the prelates for the purpose of accrediting Ugolino—14th March, 1221—Potthast, no. 6589; Horoy, 740–741; complementary mandate of 25th March—Potthast, no. 6598, Horoy III, 752.

72. Winkelmann, I, 167–177; Brem, 42–52; Chr. Touzellier, 'La légation en Lombardie du cardinal Ugolino (1221). Un épisode de la 5e croisade', in *RHE*, XLV (1950), 508–542.

73. For the cardinal's itinerary, see Winkelmann, I, 168, n. 1.

74. *Proces. Bon.*, nos. 7, 30, 41.

75. Laurent, no. 145.

76. Laurent, no. 151.

77. Mamachi, Appendix 76–79, acts of 8th, 9th and 12th November, 1221.

78. This was Maître G[uillaume] Gasco—Laurent, nos. 150 and 151.

79. Winkelmann, I, 168, n. 1.

80. 'Chronique de Sainte-Agnès', *ASOP*, I, 182, n.

81. 'Circa finem mensis iulii', *Proces. Bon.*, no. 7. He preceded Ugolino who was in Bologna on 28th.

82. He was not present at Dominic's death.

83. What follows reproduces almost word for word the account of Prior Ventura of Verona and the Procurator Rodolfo, both witnesses of first importance—*Proces. Bon.*, nos. 7–10, 31, 33, 34. To this have been added some details related by Guillaume de Montferrat, Buonviso, Fr Stephen—*ibidem*, nos. 12, 15, 20, 22, 37; Jordan, nos. 92–98; Frachet, 84, 85, 88; Salagnac, III, 2, no. 5 (*MOPH*, XXII, 33).

84. This double visit, mentioned by the 'Chronique de Sainte-Agnès', *ASOP*, I, 182, n., can only be placed at this particular time.

85. Frachet, 83.

86. According to Buonviso, in connection with an illness of Dominic in Milan in 1220—*Proces. Bon.*, no. 22.

87. By Jordan, no. 93, who was not a direct witness.

88. Ferrando, no. 50, adds: 'Have charity, keep humility, possess voluntary poverty.' It is surprising that neither Ventura, Rodolfo nor Jordan cite this phrase presented by Ferrando as a solemn testament, accompanied by a malediction against those in the order who should be defaulters in respect of posessions. Does not the expression come rather from Jordan of Saxony who gives it and comments on it to Diana in Letter XVII in 1223?—J. J. Berthier, *Le testament de saint Dominique, avec les commentaires du card. Eudes de Châteiauroux et du Bx. Jourdain de Saxe*, Fribourg, 1892.

89. Description of the primitive liturgy of the dead among the preachers by Philippeau, after the prototype of 1254. It is this again that will be found, almost intact, distributed among the present Dominican processional and breviary. The account we are going to read already agrees with this as to the essential points—viaticum, extreme unction (here according to the collegiate rite—see Philippeau, 44), prayers at the agony, great commendation, funeral toilet, vigil. There is nothing unexpected. Philippeau points out the preponderant influence of the university customs of Paris and Bologna on the Dominican rite, which he thus characterizes—a canonical version of the post-Carolingian recensions of the Roman sacramentary, 40–41.

90. *Proces. Bon.*, no. 5 and Jordan, nos. 92 and 125.

91. Ventura, no. 5, links this up with the confession; but it is clear that that is connected with the preceding allocution.

92. Salagnac, 33.

93. Bourbon, no. 334.

94. The sleep in the course of which Fr Guala had the vision of Dominic at the very time when the latter was dying—Jordan, no. 95, could be the siesta. This, however, is not certain for we are told that at that time Guala was ill. The numerous events, however, which took place since the morning, oblige us to fix this death in the course or at the end of the afternoon.

95. Salagnac, 33.

96. This has been based on the anatomical reconstitution made in 1945, on the occasion of the scientific analysis of the relics, by Prof. C. Pini of Bologna (why has an affected attitude, so little worthy of the saint, been given to this otherwise satisfactory reconstitution?), Amato, etc. *Le reliquie di S. Domenico. Storia e Leggenda*; *ricerche scientifiche*; *ricostruzione fisica* . . . Bologna, 1946. The pages of Prof. F. Frassetto are particularly important here.

97. Cecilia, no. 15. This portrait which one might have feared would be somewhat conventional has received remarkable confirmation from the learned study of the relics (cf. prec. note) especially the study of the hair (white with a few traces of red), the teeth (which, with the palate and partially calcified large pharynx found in the tomb are proof of a strong sonorous voice), and the skeleton (5 feet 5 inches), slenderness of the body, long, fine hands). He must have been agile and quick of movement; the skin somewhat pale and white, with freckles. The type is Mediterranean, ibero-insular. The absence of baldness is confirmed by the presence of hairs among the relics, which invalidates the contrary evidence of Frachet, 121.

98. Frachet, 84; Aron, 143–144, where details will be found on this religious, founder of St Mark of Mantua and of its daughter houses, St Catherine of Bologna and the Holy Trinity of Ronzano.

99. The convent of the Augustinian nuns of Ronzano, which Diana tried to escape to, also depended on Albert Spinola—Aron, 144.

100. On these numerous and distinguished prelates see Scheeben, 390.

101. Brem, 99–102.

102. Jordan, no. 125.

103. *Proces. Bon.*, nos. 9 and 15. In the choir of the religious, before the altar which is at the entrance, it would seem—Berthier, *Tombeau*, 12.

104. *Proces. Bon.*, no. 9; Jordan, nos. 97, 98; Frachet, 84, 85, 88.

NOTES TO CHAPTER XX

1. Bologna, Bergamo, Verona, Milan, Brescia, Piacenza, Faenza, Parma, Asti, Genoa, Venice, Padua, Pavia, Treviso, Cremona, Jesi, Cuma, Reggio.

2. After 1230—Kuczynski, 79–128.

3. Donner, 18–72.

4. Sulter; Winkelmann, II, 435–484; Kuczynski, 58–60 and 121–128; Meersseman, *Confréries*, II, 57–59 and IV, 293–296 and Th. Kaeppeli, *Mélanges Auguste Pelzer*, Louvain 1947, 276–277.

5. Winkelmann, II, 347, n. 2.

6. *Proces. Bon.*, no. 39. On the subject of heretics at the stake which Fr Stefano also mentions, cf. *infra*, n. 12.

7. Cf. the formal precept given by Jordan to the chapter general of 1233 against any attempts among the brethren to obtain a bishopric—*Acta*, I, 4; Frachet, 141–142 and 209–210. If we accept two missionary bishops, Fr Guala was the first Friar Preacher to be promoted to the episcopate.

8. *I Const.*, 224 (D. II, ch. 31).

9. For ordinance of a provincial chapter in Lombardy instanced against a 'pacificatory' friar in 1232, see G. Caro in *Neues Archiv.*, XXII (1897), 429 and 433. For admonition of the general chapter of 1234, see *Acta*, I, 4.

10. There is no justification for thinking that John of Vicenza was called to Bologna by Jordan— Scheeben in *QF*, XXXV, 71–72; on 20th June, however, John of Vicenza gave his judgement as arbitrator—*de mandato et licentia magistri ordinis*—Sulter, 107.

11. It was not until 1233 in Provence, 1234 in Lombardy and France, 1235 in Tuscany that the Dominican provincials received from Gregory IX the power to appoint permanent pontifical inquisitors, whose function the Pope had instituted in 1233—Meersseman, *Confréries*, II, 55–60 and n. 16.

12. The proscriptions against the heretics inscribed in the urban statutes under the influence of Ugolino in 1221 comprised only the penalty of banishment. The penalty of death by burning was decreed and imposed in Lombardy by the constitution of Frederick II in 1224. It did not spread at that time but only in 1231 through the action of Gregory IX. In fact, Fr Etienne, in the deposition we have quoted, also mentions that in 1233 a number of heretics were burnt in the Lombard cities. Cf. Kuczynski, 94–108, who corrects the serious errors of Ficker on the history of the penalty of burning in northern Italy.

13. For the history of the translation, see Sulter, 77–79; Winkelmann, II, 450–451; Altaner, 210– 228; Scheeben, 389–407. The latter study, a careful work, corrects the others in considerable degree.

14. Jordan, nos. 97–98 and 122–124; *Proces. Bon.*, no. 9 (Ventura). Against Altaner (227–228), who practically taxes Jordan and Ventura with officious lies, Scheeben, 392, reacts very successfully.

15. On 6th November, 1228, Guiffred, Cardinal-Legate of Lombard, granted an indulgence to anyone helping in the building of the new church—*ASOP*, IV, 174, n. 2; in 1230, people spoke of the church of St Nicholas *noviter facta*—I Supino, *L'arte nelle chiese di Bologna nei secoli VIII–XIV*, Bologna 1932, 164; on 8th August, 1231, the Preachers again purchased a portion of land from the Lovello, clearly in order to complete the constructions—Balme, III, 409, n. 2.

16. Berthier, *Tombeau*, 11 and n. 2.

17. *Proces. Bon.*, no. 15.

18. Scheeben, *QF*, XXXV, 70, justly remarks against Altaner, 214, that the project of translation was still attributed to Fr Stefano and the brethren in Lombardy, never to Jordan—*Proces. Bon.*, nos. 39 and 40; Jordan, nos. 124 and 125.

19. In autumn and winter 1232–1233, Jordan seems to have been in Germany, then in the neighbourhood of Rome and Naples—Scheeben, *QF*, XXXV, 67.

20. Salimbene, *MG SS*, XXXII, 72, maliciously insinuates this. The Bishop of Modena was, however, too much attached to the order and to Dominic, for the expression attributed to him by Salimbene to have any probability.

21. Jordan, no. 125.

22. Jordan, no. 125; Salagnac, 18–19.

23. Jordan, no. 1. Cf. Altaner, 11 and 213; Vicaire, *Documents*, 17–18.

24. *Proces. Bon.*, no. 39.

25. Altaner, 212–218, supposes that Jordan himself had called John of Vicenza to Bologna: 1. to preach the peace there; 2. to elicit in the population a fervour capable of forcing the canonization. This is to credit him with much calculation! Neither point is established or even probable. Against the first see Scheeben, *QF*, XXXV, 71. Against the second, cf. *supra*, n. 18. Moreover, although the contemporaries, beginning with Fr Stefano (*Proces. Bon.*, no. 39) have stressed the rôle played by John of Vicenza, which is easily understandable, it is clear that the friar's preaching came after the idea of translation. Jordan, nos. 124–125 not only mentions slow-moving negotiations, but indicates quite different reasons for the intention to transfer the relics. John of Vicenza did not take the initiative in promoting the cultus of Dominic, but he did seize on this theme at the right moment and provide it with powerful orchestration.

26. *Proces. Bon.*, no. 39. This perhaps refers to the vision related by Thierry, no. 302 (Dominic 'presents' the deceased brethren to the Lord as St Francis does for his). Setting the founders in parallel is typical of the emulation of the two orders. John may have participated in the previous year in the canonization of St Antony of Padua?—Sulter, 56. As to the authenticity of his visions, the mockeries of Salimbene—*MG, SS*, XXXII, 76, 79, 83, throw a rather disturbing light on them.

27. According to the evidence this follows Jordan, nos. 127–129; *Proces. Bon.*, nos. 10, 11, 15, 34, 40, 44; Constantino, no. 67.

28. In front of the choir of the religious, in the nave, near the altar of the faithful, on the women's side, as far as can be judged in view of the transformations which the church has undergone. As to the sarcophagus, it was raised, in marble, without historiated carvings—Berthier, *Tombeau*, 13 to 19

29. *I Const.*, 218 (D. II, ch. 17).

30. On 19th April, 1233, city and bishop came to an agreement to defer to the arbitration of John of Vicenza. This was given on 31st May, then corrected on 20th June—Sutter, 71, 92, 107–108.

31. According to all the witnesses. This fragrance had already been manifest in the church after the saint's burial—*Proces. Bon.*, no. 9; already during his lifetime—Frachet, 82–83; for a similar fragrance near the bodies or on the tomb of ff. Jordan, Conrad, Pelagius, see Frachet, 130, 250, 295 (*id.*, Peter of Castelnau, see Cernai, no. 79); during Jordan's lifetime, under the form of diabolical temptation—Jordan, nos. 115–119. On this odour of sanctity, see E. Lohmeyer, 'Vom göttlichen Wohlgeruch', in *Sitzungsber der Heidelberger Akad. philos. hist. Klasse*, 1919, 49, n. 2 and other quotations—Altaner, 220, n. 2. Scheeben, 399–400, particularly insists on its historical character.

32. A great friend of the order, founder and protector of the convent of Lille, legate in the Albigeois from 1232 to the beginning of 1233, when he received the mission, on 22nd January, to look after the bishop of Saint-Paul Trois-Châteaux, who was retiring to the Dominican convent of Puy—Chapotin, 67 and 70; *ASOP*, IV, 54; Zimmermann, 137; Meersseman, *AFP*, XVII (1947), 7–10 and 18–19.

33. Jordan, no. 126; Ferrando, no. 52. For other miracles on this day see Ferrando, nos. 54, 56.

34. A further translation would take place in 1267, to the present tomb carved by Nicolo Pisano—Berthier, *Tombeau*, 20–25. In 1943 yet another was carried out in order to put the relics in safety and the cenotaph in security. It was then that the radiography and mensuration published in Amato were carried out. The cenotaph was put back in position and the body brought back on the occasion of the important celebrations from 8th to 15th September, 1946.

35. According to the letter from the commissioners of Bologna to the sub-commissioners of Toulouse—*MOPH*, XVI, 169.

36. *MOPH*, XVI, 115–117.

37. For the history of the canonization see Walz, *MOPH*, XVI, 92–113; Vicaire, *Documents*, 195–199.

38. On Philip Carisi of Vercelli, see *ASOP*, III, 696; he was three times provincial of Lombardy (Galvagno, *Minor*, 94; 95–97; 99) and died after 1266 (*ibidem*, 99). There is no reason to identify him as Echard does (I, 103–106), with the provincial of the Holy Land in 1237, who must have been the first prior of Rheims—Balme, II, 306, n. 1.

39. On these three personages see Altaner, 221. The first was known as a master in canon law. The second soon afterwards became Bishop of Imola. All three received at this time several commissions from the Pope.

40. Ed. Walz, *MOPH*, XVI, 123–167 (= *Proces. Bon.*).

41. *MOPH*, XVI, 169–172.

42. For list of the 25 articles see Vicaire, *Documents*, 197. Scheeben, 402 and Walz, *MOPH*, XVI, 109, thought—it is not known why—the reconstitution of this list impossible.

43. Ed. Walz, *MOPH*, XVI, 176–187 (= *Proces. Thol.*).

44. When he composed his *Libellus*, Jordan only acquainted with in writing and only related a small number (six) of the saint's miracles—Jordan, nos. 99–102; cf. Altaner, 21–23. In the account of the translation, on the other hand, he was acquainted with a catalogue of miracles read before the Pope and cardinals on the canonization day, and he summarizes this—Jordan, no. 126. With two exceptions, all these miracles will be found in the collection terminating the ms. of the *Libellus* transmitted by the Bollandists (*ASS, Augusti*, I, nos. 89–95) and Ferrando, nos. 52–62 (miracles contemporary with the translation or later) and in the later collections of legends—Frachet, 75; Constantino, nos. 36, 54, 65; Barthélemy, no. 15 and Thierry, no. 230. On the value of this collection, see Altaner, 21–23; Scheeben, 405 and *MOPH*, XVI, 14 and 16–18.

45. Jordan, no. 126.

46. At this time 6th August was occupied by the feast of St Sixtus, Pope and Martyr—*Proces. Bon.*, no. 8. The introduction of the feast of Our Lady of the Snow on 5th August by St Pius V necessitated the transfer of the feast of St Dominic to 4th August—Altaner, 226.

47. Ed. Walz, *MOPH*, XVI, 190–194.

48. *BOP*, I, 68, n. 2 shows knowledge of certified copies of the bull in the archives of the convents of Paris, Toulouse, etc. Ligiez, *ASOP*, IV, 255–256, mentions a certain number of others—Bordeaux, Montpellier, Spalato . . . .

49. Jordan, *Epistulae*, no. 43 (Scheeben, *QF*, XXXV, 78), where we see also that the provincial of Lombardy had invited Jordan to the celebrations in Bologna. For those in Toulouse, see Salagnac, 16–18; Pelisson, 22–25. For the history of the liturgical text of the feast of St Dominic, see Scheeben, *AFP*, II (1932), 338 ff.

50. Although today there are no manuscripts in which Jordan's text, nos. 121–130, which contains the account of the translation, is in the form of an encyclical, such texts have existed. Moreover, the style of this piece, so different from that of the *Libellus*, is indeed that of an encyclical. Cf. Vicaire, *Documents*, 16–17; against Scheeben, *MOPH*, XVI, 16–18.

51. VI, 1–8.

52. Altaner, *Dominikanermissionen*, 1.

53. *Proces. Bon.*, nos. 3 and 45.

54. On the unquestionable Marian devotion of Dominic and his first brethren, cf. Duval, 739–754.

This devotion assumed very varied forms, among which were those recitations of the *Ave Maria* in series which form the basis of the rosary. In Dominic's particular case, the best focal points in the sources remain the legislative attitude he took up as to the office of the Blessed Virgin and over the profession formula (*I Const.*, 195 and 202, D. I, ch. 1 and 16)—Duval, nos. 8, 11, 20.

55. Jordan, no. 107.
56. Jordan, no. 103.
57. Jordan, nos. 103 and 104.
58. On this prayer, cf. Vicaire, *Documents*, 200–201. It will be remarked that this prayer: 1. sums up Dominic's life such as Jordan of Saxony could see it after the drawing up of the *Libellus*; 2. dates at the earliest from the time of the canonization since it invokes Dominic as special intercessor for the order; 3. seems to make allusion to the vision of John of Vicenza (Dominic 'presents' all his brethren to God, *supra*, n. 26) which had so much influence on the cultus of the saint in Bologna in 1233–1234. The Prayer, which dates from 1234–1237, could well have been composed by Jordan at the time of the canonization celebrations, as in the case of the encyclical on the translation.

INDEX

OF THE PRINCIPAL REFERENCES TO PERSONS AND PLACES

Names of persons, places, collectives in small Roman type. Names of writers forming the subject of critical remarks in capitals. Technical terms or titles of institutions explained in the text, in italics. Where a reference occurs in the text as well as in the notes, the page number is followed by a + sign and the note number in italics, which is in turn followed by the note page number in brackets. Where the reference only occurs in the notes, the relevant chapter number is given in Roman numerals, followed by the note number in italics and the note page in brackets. a.=abbey; arch.(or abp)=archbishop; bp=bishop; C.=count; c.=convent; Cal=cardinal; ch.=chapter; d.=diocese; fam.=family; fr=friar; m.=monastery; pr.=province; St=saint; sr=sister; r.=river; t.=town; w.=wife.

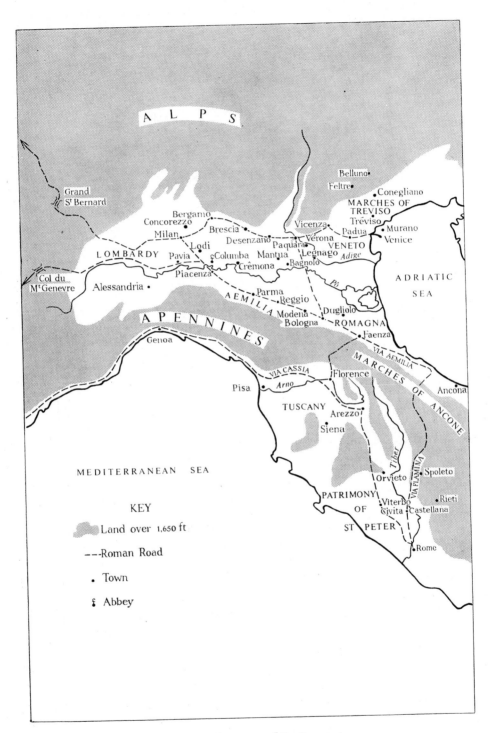

Italy at the time of St Dominic

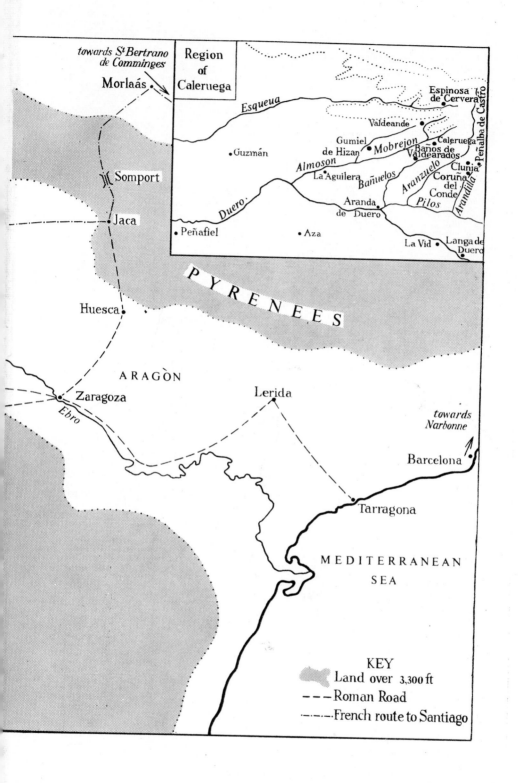

towards St Bertrano
de Comminges

Morlaás

Region
of
Caleruega

Somport

Jaca

PYRENEES

Huesca

ARAGON

Lerida

Zaragoza

Ebro

towards
Narbonne

Barcelona

Tarragona

MEDITERRANEAN
SEA

Esqueua

Espinosa
de Cervera

Valdeande

Gumiel
de Hizan   Mobrejon   Caleruega
              Baños de
              Valdearados
Almoson
       La Aguilera   Bañuelos   Clunia
                              Coruña
Guzmán   Aranzuelo   del
              Aranda   Conde
              de Duero   Pilos

Duero

Peñafiel   Aza

Peñalba de Castro

Arandilla

La Vid   Langa de
          Duero

KEY
Land over 3,300 ft
--- Roman Road
-·-·- French route to Santiago

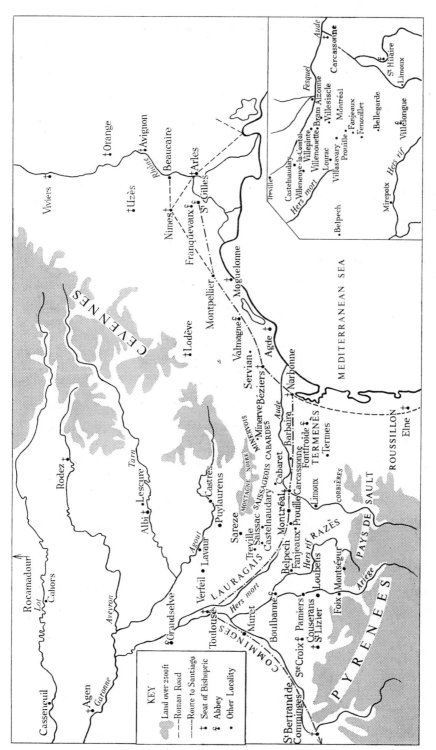

The land of the Albigenses

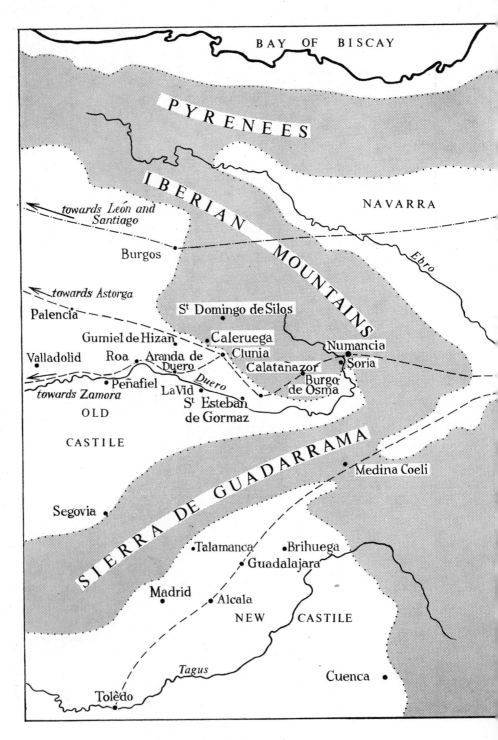

Spain at the time of St Dominic